BTEC Level 2

edexcel
advancing learning, changing lives

BUSINESS LEVEL 2

BTEC First

Carol Carysforth | Mike Neild
with Catherine Richards
Consultant editor: Nicola Mortimer-Stokes

A PEARSON COMPANY

Published by Pearson Education Limited, a company incorporated in England and Wales, having its registered office at Edinburgh Gate, Harlow, Essex, CM20 2JE. Registered company number: 872828

www.pearsonschoolsandfecolleges.co.uk

Edexcel is a registered trademark of Edexcel Limited

Text © Pearson Education Limited 2010

First published 2010

13 12 11 10
10 9 8 7 6 5 4 3 2

British Library Cataloguing in Publication Data
A catalogue record for this book is available from the British Library.

ISBN 9781846906206

Edited by Rachael Williams
Designed by Wooden Ark
Typeset by Phoenix Photosetting
Original illustrations © Pearson Education Limited
Illustrated by KJA-artists.com
Cover design by Visual Philosophy, created by CMC Design
Picture Research by Emma Whyte
Cover images: *Front*: Image Source Ltd; *Back*: Pearson Education Ltd: Jules Selmes c; Shutterstock: Andresr tl, Monkey Business Images tr
(Key: b-bottom; c-centre; l-left; r-right; t-top)
Printed in Spain by Graficas Estella.

About the websites

You can find links to the websites mentioned in this book. In order to ensure that the links are up to date, that the links work, and that the sites are not inadvertently linked to sites that could be considered offensive, we have made the links available on the Pearson website at www.pearsonschoolsandfecolleges.co.uk/hotlinks. When you access the site, search for either the express code 6206V, title BTEC Level 2 First Business or ISBN 9781846906206.

Disclaimer

This material has been published on behalf of Edexcel and offers high-quality support for the delivery of Edexcel qualifications.
This does not mean that the material is essential to achieve any Edexcel qualification, nor does it mean that it is the only suitable material available to support any Edexcel qualification. Edexcel material will not be used verbatim in setting any Edexcel examination or assessment. Any resource lists produced by Edexcel shall include this and other appropriate resources.

Copies of official specifications for all Edexcel qualifications may be found on the Edexcel website: www.edexcel.com

Contents

Credits

The publishers would like to thank the following for their kind permission to reproduce their photographs:
360° Solutions: p.378; **Alamy Images:** Aardvark p.261, AfriPics.com p.57, Ashley Cooper p.33, dynamitestockimages p.327, Krys Bailey - Editorial p.411, p.428, John Foxx p.325, David J Green p.309, Jeff Greenberg p.123, Bob Handelman p.361, Nick Hanna p.371, Asia Images p.113, p.211, PSL Images p.37, p.51, Huntstock Inc p.259, Frantzesco Kangaris p.455, Roy Lawe p.1, p.15, ACE STOCK LIMITED p.78, OJO Images Ltd p.129, p.144, MBI p.269, p.364, Gary Moseley p.12, David Pearson p.299, Martin Phelps p.424, AKP Photos p.60, TRISTAR PHOTOS p.74, Simple Signs p.250, Lourens Smak p.367, p.384; **Amaze:** H. Robinson p.330; **Athertons Estate Agents:** p.170; **Corbis:** Bettmann p.214, Rachel Frank p.150, Mirko Iannace p.160, Jose Luis Peleaz, Inc / Blend Images p.349, p.439, Inspirestock p.409, Brooks Kraft p.231, Leonard Lenz p.204, Sigrid Olsson / PhotoAlto p.167, Leah Warkentin / Design Pics p.372, Danny Moloshok / Reuters p.324, Mike Segar / Reuters p.292, p.339, Reuters p.376, Image Source p.288, p.47, Buero Monaco / zefa p.103; **Courtesy of Asda:** p.278; **Digital Vision:** p.375; **DK Images:** p.343; **Getty Images:** AFP p.65, p.100, p.290, p.335, p.388, AFP p.65, p.100, p.290, p.335, p.388, Hulton Archive p.43, Colorblind p.342, Jon Feingersh p.27, p.157, Paul Gilham p.229, Andrew Holt p.68, Iconica p.239, p.258, p.301, Wire Image p.345, Alberto Incrocci p.320, Ghislain & Marie David de Lossy p.272, White Packert p.383, PhotoDisc p.32, p.395, Alan Thornton p.235, Craig Wetherby p.29; **Image Source Ltd:** p.426cr; **Imagestate Media:** John Foxx Collection p.351, p.354; **iStockphoto:** Murat Baysan p.90; **JCB:** p.59; **Julian Lobb:** p.252; **moneysupermarket.com:** p.461; **Pearson Education Ltd:** p.435, Martin Beddall p.63, Gareth Boden p.39, p.369, p.413, Rob Judges p.185, p.271, Lord and Leverett p.132, Citrus Media p.117, Peter Morris p.449, Tudor Photography p.341, Jules Selmes p.3, p.95, p.183, p.196, Ian Wedgewood p.180; **Peninsula Business Services Ltd:** p.224; **Photo used with kind permission of the British Red Cross:** p.40; **Photos.com:** p.159; **Plain English Campaign:** p.209; **Rex Features:** Gregory Pace / BEI p.11, Jonathan Player p.7, Chris Ratcliffe p.454, Brian J. Ritchie p.393; **Rights Reserved to Ruth Amos:** p.401; **Shutterstock:** Andresr p.242, Yuri Arcurs p.67, Marcin Balcerzak p.218, Stephen Coburn p.186, Mikael Damkler p.426tl, Sideways Design p.276, Jamie Duplas p.247, Janos Gehring p.93, p.166, Monkey Business Images p.234, Hugo Maes p.241, Carlos E Santa Maria p.207, Matt p.84, Catalin Petolea p.353, Tony Ramos Photography p.441, Photosani p.124, Nice Pictures p.357, Dmitriy Shironosov p.169, Scott O Smith p.219, Sofia p.452, Ssakarya p.295, Szefei p.303, Tracy Whiteside p.213, Dani Vincek p.121; **St Ann's Hospice:** p.434; **Sue Semple:** p.356; **Thank you to St Helens Council Sports Development Team:** p.154
All other images © Pearson Education

The authors and publishers would also like to thank the following individuals and organisations for their approval and permission to reproduce material:
p.12 My Travel Group plc; p.40 The British Red Cross; p.40 Tesco Stores Limited; p.44 ITV; p.59 JCB; p.63 Chester Zoo; p.74 Virgin Atlantic; p.90 Ashford Colour Press; p.117 Sarah Duncalf and South Cheshire College; p.154 Thank you to St. Helens Council Sports Development Team; p.170 Kerry Hamer and Athertons Estate Agents; p.190 Sandra Crowe and Halifax/Lloyds Banking Group; p.209 The Plain English Campaign for permission to use the Crystal Mark logo; p.224 Joanna McGowan MA, GIPD, BA (Hons) and Peninsula Business Services; p.252 Julian Lobb; p.277 Alison Yaldren, PR Advisor, and B&Q plc; p.299 Carphone Warehouse plc; p.330 Helen Robinson and Rick Curtis of Amaze; p.251 Gibbs' Reflective Cycle (source: Gibbs G (1988) *Learning by Doing, A guide to teaching and learning methods*, Further Education Unit, Oxford Polytechnic: Oxford); p.356 Sue Semple and Heinz plc; p.378 Sam and Oliver Marsden of 360° Solutions; p.401 Ruth Amos of Steady Stairs; p.299 Divine Chocolate; p.426 Glasses on Spec; p.434 St Ann's Manchester Midnight Walk: St Ann's Hospice provides both terminal care and care for people following hospital treatment such as radiotherapy and chemotherapy; p.456 Debenhams; p.461 Simon Nixon, Ian Williams and Moneysupermarket.com.

Every effort has been made to trace the copyright holders and we apologise in advance for any unintentional omissions. We would be pleased to insert the appropriate acknowledgement in subsequent printings of this publication.

Acknowledgements

Dedication

Carol Carysforth and Mike Neild would like to dedicate this book, with love, to their ever-expanding family and especially to the two latest arrivals: Daisy Mia Carysforth and Thomas Jack Neild, 'with our wish that you both enjoy health, good fortune and happiness throughout your lives'.

Authors' acknowledgements

The assistance of a great number of people has been invaluable in helping us to write a book that accurately reflects current business practices and meets the needs of today's BTEC First learners. We are therefore indebted to the following people and organisations for their help:

For advice about content and help with learner voices: Rhonda Lobb at Blackburn College, Eileen Jepson at Runshaw College, BTEC First business students at Blackburn College plus Sam Knight who bravely told us how he copes with his finances for unit 20.

For agreeing to be featured in WorkSpace case studies and for cheerfully answering our many questions: Sam and Oliver Marsden of 360° Solutions; Gemma Harkness and St Helens Council Sports Development Team; Sandra Crowe and Halifax/Lloyds Banking Group; employment law guru Joanna McGowan MA, GIPD, BA(Hons) and Peninsula Business Services; Sue Semple and Heinz plc; Simon Nixon, Ian Williams and Moneysupermarket.com; Julian Lobb; Kerry Hamer and Athertons Estate Agents; Helen Robinson and Rick Curtis of Amaze. Thanks are also due to Carphone Warehouse plc; Divine Chocolate; Bob Ward at Glasses on Spec; Chester Zoo, South Cheshire College and Ashford Colour Press.

For help with individual units and case studies: Susan Holden LLB (Hons), LLM and Peter Gold LLB (Hons) for sharing with us their consumer law expertise; Antony and Paul Carysforth for their professional contributions on website construction and e-marketing; Alison Yaldren at B&Q for her helpful input on consumer relations.

We are also grateful to Nicola Mortimer-Stokes, one of Edexcel's most experienced external verifiers, for scrutinising every assessment activity in this book to ensure it meets the stated criteria and is fit for purpose.

Our thanks are also due to everyone in the Pearson team who worked so hard on this book. Lewis Birchon, our publisher, for his help, support and vision and for providing some imaginative ideas just when they were needed; Céline Clavel, the crème de la crème of editors, for her calm, competent efficiency; Rachael Williams, our copy editor, for her scrupulous attention to detail and disarming way of pointing out our mistakes; Juliet Mozley and Elizabeth Evans, our proofreaders, for their expert and friendly assistance.

Finally, we would like to thank all the teachers and tutors who bought or recommended the previous version of this book to their students. We simply hope that you will find this edition to be even better.

Carol Carysforth and Mike Neild
January 2010

About your BTEC Level 2 First Business

Choosing to study for a BTEC Level 2 First Business qualification is a great decision to make for lots of reasons. This qualification will equip you for a career in a wide range of industries as business underpins more or less any job you might have in the future – from starting your own enterprise to working for a charitable organisation.

Your BTEC Level 2 First in Business is a **vocational** or **work-related** qualification. This doesn't mean that it will give you *all* the skills you need to do a job, but it does mean that you'll have the opportunity to gain specific knowledge, understanding and skills that are relevant to your future career.

What will you be doing?

The qualification is structured into **mandatory units (M)** (ones you must do) and **optional units (O)** (ones you can choose to do). This book contains 15 units – giving you a broad choice no matter what size your qualification.

- BTEC Level 2 First **Certificate** in Business: 2 mandatory units and optional units that provide a combined total of 15 credits

- BTEC Level 2 First **Extended Certificate** in Business: 2 mandatory units and optional units that provide a combined total of 30 credits

- BTEC Level 2 First **Diploma** in Business: 4 mandatory units and optional units that provide a combined total of 60 credits

Unit number	Credit value	Unit name	Cert	Ex. Cert	Diploma
1	5	Business purposes	M	M	M
2	5	Business organisations	M	M	M
3	5	Financial forecasting for business	O	O	M
4	5	People in organisations	O	O	M
6	5	Providing business support	O	O	O
7	5	Verbal and non-verbal communication in business contexts	O	O	O
8	5	Business communication through documentation	O	O	O
9	5	Training and employment in business	O	O	O
10	5	Personal selling in business	O	O	O
11	10	Customer relations in business		O	O
12	10	Business online		O	O
13	5	Consumer rights		O	O
16	10	Business enterprise*		O	O
19	5	The marketing plan	O	O	O
20	5	Managing personal finances	O	O	O

* If you are taking Unit 17: Starting a small business, you may be interested in *BTEC Level 3 National Business Student Book 2* (ISBN 9781846906350), which includes coverage of the unit.

How to use this book

This book is designed to help you through your BTEC Level 2 First Business course. It contains many features that will help you use your skills and knowledge in work-related situations and assist you in getting the most from your course.

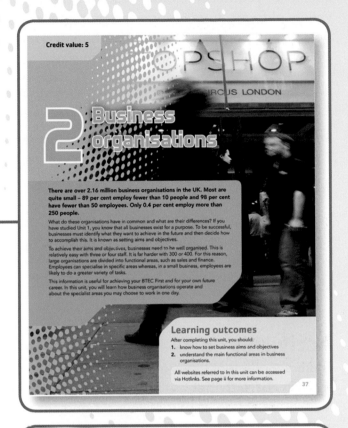

Introduction

These introductions give you a snapshot of what to expect from each unit – and what you should be aiming for by the time you finish it!

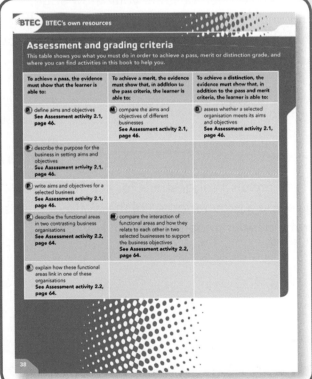

Assessment and grading criteria

This table explains what you must do in order to achieve the assessment criteria for each unit. For each assessment criterion, shown by grade buttons such as **P1**, **M1** or **D1**, there is an assessment activity.

Assessment

Your tutor will set **assignments** throughout your course for you to complete. These may take a variety of forms, from reports and presentations to posters and podcasts The important thing is that you evidence your skills and knowledge to date.

Stuck for ideas? Daunted by your first assignment? These students have all been through it before...

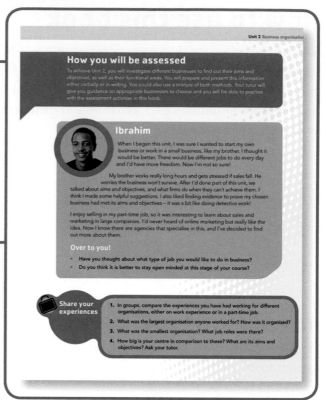

Activities

There are different types of activities for you to do: **assessment activities** are suggestions for tasks that you might do as part of your assignment and will help you demonstrate your knowledge, skills and understanding. Each of these has **grading tips** that clearly explain what you need to do in order to achieve a pass, merit or distinction grade.

There are also suggestions for activities that will give you a broader grasp of the world of business and a deeper understanding of key topics.

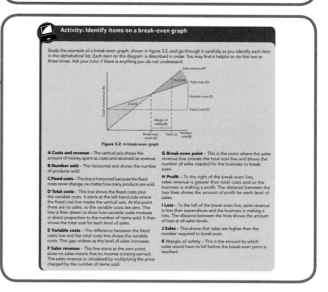

Personal, learning and thinking skills

Throughout your BTEC Level 2 First Business course, there are lots of opportunities to develop your personal, learning and thinking skills. Look out for these as you progress.

PLTS

Develop your independent enquirer skills. Plan questions that will enable you to learn most about the job.

Functional skills

It's important that you have good English, maths and ICT skills – you never know when you'll need them, and employers will be looking for evidence that you've got these skills too.

Functional skills

Find out what the CBI does and then assess whether its argument could be biased in any way.

Key terms

Technical words and phrases are easy to spot, and definitions are included. The terms and definitions are also in the glossary at the back of the book.

Key term

Team briefing – staff meeting to discuss information relevant to the team and its work.

WorkSpace

Case studies provide snapshots of real workplace issues, and show how the skills and knowledge you develop during your course can help you in your career.

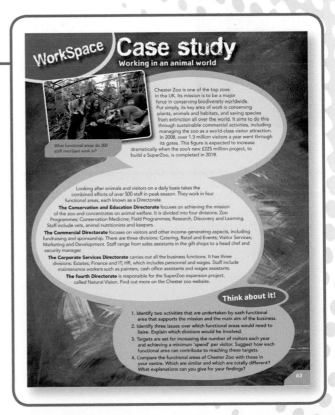

Just checking

When you see this sort of activity, take stock! These quick activities and questions are there to check your knowledge. You can use them to see how much progress you've made.

Edexcel's assignment tips

At the end of each chapter, you'll find hints and tips to help you get the best mark you can, such as the best websites to go to, checklists to help you remember processes and really useful facts and figures.

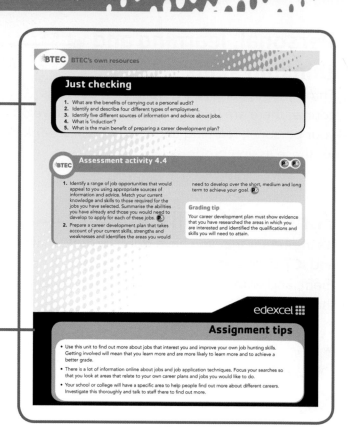

Have you read your BTEC Level 2 First Study Skills Guide? It's full of advice on study skills, putting your assignments together and making the most of being a BTEC Business learner.

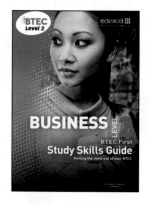

Your book is just part of the exciting resources from Edexcel to help you succeed in your BTEC course. Visit www.edexcel.com/BTEC or www.pearsonschoolsandfecolleges.co.uk/BTEC for more details.

1 Business purposes

In 2008, the UK was ranked 22nd out of 192 nations based on the average earnings of each population. This gives people living in the UK many benefits, from free health care and education, to the ability to buy the products they want, such as televisions, computers and cars.

How do countries and their citizens become wealthy? The only way is to earn money and this is done every day by businesses in the UK and their employees. Not just large businesses like Coca-Cola and Tesco, but tiny ones around the corner from you. Newsagents, taxi drivers, childminders, plumbers – they all play a part in this process. So, too, do hospital staff, charity workers and your tutors.

Learning about business purposes means you will find out about the wide range of business organisations that exist and how they contribute to the well-being of the nation. You will learn how businesses are organised, owned and classified in the UK.

To create wealth, countries need a stable government that encourages industries to succeed. The UK government wants Britain to thrive and aims to provide a business environment in which this can happen. You will learn about the role of government, as well as the businesses that are thriving or declining locally and nationally, and the reasons for this.

Learning outcomes

After completing this unit, you should:

1. understand the purpose and ownership of business
2. understand the business context in which organisations operate.

All websites referred to in this unit can be accessed via Hotlinks. See page ii for more information.

Assessment and grading criteria

This table shows you what you must do in order to achieve a pass, merit or distinction grade and where you can find activities in this book to help you.

To achieve a **pass**, the evidence must show that the learner is able to:	To achieve a **merit**, the evidence must show that, in addition to the pass criteria, the learner is able to:	To achieve a **distinction** grade, the evidence must show that, in addition to the pass and merit criteria, the learner is able to:
P1 identify the purpose of four different business organisations **See Assessment activity 1.1, page 9**	**M1** contrast the ownership and purposes of two different business organisations **See Assessment activity 1.1, page 9**	**D1** evaluate how an organisation has responded to changes in the business environment **See Assessment activity 1.6, page 36**
P2 describe the different types of business ownership, linking this to the size and scale of four different organisations **See Assessment activity 1.2, page 13**		
P3 explain how businesses are classified using local and national examples **See Assessment activity 1.3, page 17**	**M2** compare areas of growth or decline in the primary, secondary and tertiary classifications of business activities **See Assessment activity 1.6, page 36**	
P4 outline the role of government in creating the business climate **See Assessment activity 1.4, page 28**		
P5 explain the characteristics of the local business environment **See Assessment activity 1.5, page 35**		

How you will be assessed

To achieve Unit 1, you will investigate businesses that operate in your local area and nationally, and find out how changes in the business environment can affect them. Your assessment could include both practical and written tasks, as well as presentations. The Assessment activities in this book will help you prepare for this.

Emily

I wanted to learn about business because my parents run a car hire firm and like working for themselves. They often talk about the business, like when they changed their partnership into a limited company, and I wanted to know what this means and to understand why they did it.

My brother did a BTEC First Diploma two years ago and really enjoyed it, and this tempted me to do the same course. He is now completing a BTEC National Diploma at college and likes that too.

When I found out that the first unit would include information about the government's role, I was worried I would not understand it. But when we prepared our presentation to summarise this as a news broadcast I really enjoyed it. I can now discuss some business stories in the newspaper with my dad, which has really impressed him!

The unit also included researching businesses where I live, which has helped me to understand our family business better and where it fits in. I now know how much our area has changed since my grandparents were young and why.

Over to you!

- Do you ignore anything you hear about the government or the economy?
- Is this because you find it boring or because you do not understand it?
- How important do you think it is for people who work in business to understand it?

Rankings revisited

1. Suggest three countries that came above and three that came below the UK in the 2008 rankings of average earnings per population. Give reasons for your choices.
2. Zimbabwe came at the very bottom of the list. Can you suggest why?
3. What could the UK do to move up the rankings? Compare the ideas you have now with those you have when you have completed this unit.

   Check all the rankings at the Nations Online website.

1. Understand the purpose and ownership of business

1.1 The purpose of business

All businesses exist for a specific reason, or purpose. The purpose of many businesses is to:

- produce goods
- sell goods made by someone else, and/or
- offer a service to customers.

Some organisations, such as charities, exist for social or environmental reasons. They aim to help others or promote environmental causes.

- BMW produces cars (including the Mini in Britain) and Cadbury makes chocolate. River Island sells clothes, whereas Clinton Cards sells greetings cards. First Choice and Thomas Cook provide travel services; Sheilas' Wheels and esure provide insurance services.

- Asda and Tesco supply a wide range of goods in their stores, through their Direct catalogues and online, and offer financial services, including insurance, as well as their own credit cards. They also provide home delivery services.

- Garages may service cars and sell them as well. Computer shops may sell laptops and software and also do repairs. Most hairdressers sell hair products, as well as cutting and styling hair.

- Greenpeace and Friends of the Earth both promote environmental causes, whereas the NSPCC and Barnado's focus on child welfare.

Activity: Goods or services?

Investigate the following businesses. Check their websites. Say whether they provide goods, services or both: a) Boots the Chemist; b) Apple; c) Halfords.

Key term

Profit – the amount left from sales revenue after deducting the cost of producing or supplying the goods or service.

Activity: Can you swim for free yet?

The government aims to get at least two million more people active by 2012. Free swimming is the first step – available in 2009 to under 16s and over 60s. Find out what is available now in your area.

1.2 What price to charge?

Businesses providing goods or services must decide how much to charge. This depends upon whether they aim to make a **profit** or not.

At a profit

Most businesses aim to be profitable, where the amount of money earned from selling goods or services is greater than the amount spent on running the business. It costs money to run a business and to buy stock or provide a service (see Unit 3). The price is set above this level to make a profit.

Free

The government provides some essential goods and services free of charge, such as health care, refuse collection, road maintenance, social services, education and the emergency services. Many

voluntary organisations provide free services, such as Oxfam and Save the Children, which provide medical assistance and essential supplies when there is a major disaster.

At cost

This means that the amount charged is enough to recover the cost of providing the goods or service without making a profit. For example, tutors who buy specialist materials for adult learners, such as cake-decorating materials, sell them on for the same price they paid. A local drama group may only aim to recover the cost of hiring a hall and other production costs to ensure that tickets are cheap enough to be attractive.

Below cost

This means that the price charged is less than the cost of making or supplying the item. Examples include NHS prescriptions for expensive drugs, bus passes for school children, NHS dental care and extra refuse bins. The difference between the amount charged and the full cost is subsidised by the government or local council because it is socially desirable that everyone can afford to buy them.

Discussion point

Samaritans and Relate are both charities. Neither aims to make a profit. Samaritans provides free counselling to people in distress or despair at any time, day or night. Relate provides relationship counselling and normally charges for this. The fee is set to cover the cost of the session or, in some circumstances, may be subsidised. Relate also offers free counselling for young people.

As a class, decide why all Samaritans counselling is free of charge, whereas Relate counselling is not. Then suggest why Relate varies its charges for different groups of people. Visit the Samaritans and Relate websites to find out more.

1.3 Business ownership

Most businesses in the UK are under **private ownership**. Many of these are small enterprises, like the newsagents and hairdressers in your area. Others are much larger operations. The Arcadia Group Ltd is the largest privately owned retailing empire in the UK and includes Topshop, Dorothy Perkins, Burton, Evans, Bhs and Miss Selfridge. Its billionaire owner is Sir Philip Green. Many small businesses are owned and run by one person, others by two or more people working in partnership with each other. Some enterprises are family businesses, sometimes employing several family members doing different jobs. Famous examples include Baxters (soups), Patak's (sauces) and Warburtons (bread).

Key term

Voluntary organisations (also charities) – not-for-profit organisations that provide a service and are run by professional staff and volunteers.

Did you know?

- Freecycle is a popular scheme that enables people to give away items they no longer need. Find out more on its website.
- Retailers often sell some goods at cost or below cost. The term for these goods is **loss leaders**. The idea is to tempt people into the store in the hope they will buy other goods as well.

Functional skills

Practise your speaking and listening skills by listening to other people and contributing relevant and useful suggestions to the discussion.

Key term

Private ownership – relates to businesses owned by individuals who aim to make a profit.

Key term

Public ownership – relates to businesses owned by the government.

Discussion point

The Institute of Family Business is a not-for-profit organisation that supports the estimated three million family businesses in the UK. It estimates that fewer than one in ten survive beyond the third generation. As a group, what reasons can you suggest for this?

In most businesses there is someone in charge, such as Sir Philip Green at Arcadia, but not always. Some people set up in business as a cooperative where there is no single boss or leader (see page 8).

A business may be under **public ownership** and controlled by the state, on behalf of the people. A business can also be controlled by trustees, who oversee the business' affairs. This is the case with charities. They operate in the voluntary sector, so called because in addition to paid staff, volunteers are often employed.

Activity: Investigate a family business

Warburtons is now run by the fifth generation of the family. Check out the family tree at the Warburtons website.

Types of privately owned businesses

- **Sole trader** – the smallest type of business. It is owned by just one person even though there may be several employees. The sole trader is personally responsible for every aspect of the business, from keeping the premises clean to doing the accounts and paying tax on the profits. Examples include builders, decorators, florists and many local retailers. The sole trader can keep all the profit each year, after paying tax.

- **Partnership** – owned and run by two or more people. The partners are jointly responsible for running the business. Most partnerships are small, such as local accountants, solicitors, doctors and vets. However, a few larger organisations operate on the basis that the employees become partners when they join the company.

- **Private limited company** – easy to identify because its name always ends with 'Ltd'. Each owner has a share of the business and is therefore known as a 'shareholder'. If the company is successful, then the shareholders receive a financial reward in the form of dividends. In many private companies, the owners have two roles. As well as being shareholders, they are also directors and run the company. This is the case with many family businesses in the UK.

- **Public limited company** – the largest type of private business. These companies end their name with the letters 'plc'. The shares are usually traded on the stock exchange and can be owned by members of the public and institutional investors, such as large banks or insurance companies. The directors are paid a salary to run the company and can choose whether to own shares or not. This type of business can raise a large amount of money by selling shares, and use this to expand or develop the enterprise. All the shareholders have limited liability.

Did you know?

- There are over 4.6 million private enterprises in the UK, employing over 20 million people.

- John Lewis operates a special type of partnership. All the group's 69,000 staff who work in John Lewis and Waitrose stores are partners and receive a share of the profits as a bonus each year (see also Unit 3, page 86). Find out more about the business by visiting the John Lewis Partnership website.

Remember

Private businesses normally need to make a profit to survive so will charge a price for their goods and services that enables them to do this.

Limited and unlimited liability

Sole traders have **unlimited liability**. This means they are personally responsible for all the debts of the business and risk having to sell their own personal possessions if they owe money to banks or suppliers. The benefit of forming a private or public limited company is to gain **limited liability**. As such, shareholders' personal possessions remain safe if the company has to close as they are only liable for the amount they have invested in the business. A partnership may be unlimited or the partners may choose to set up a limited liability partnership (LLP).

Charities and voluntary organisations

Unlike privately owned organisations, these businesses do not exist to make a profit. Instead, their main purpose is to provide benefits for various groups in society. They are also called 'not-for-profit' organisations because they reinvest any **surplus** they make into the operation to improve their services and further their aims.

- **Voluntary organisations** – mainly staffed by volunteers. They range from specialist groups like Snail Wood Conservation Group to large, nationally recognised groups like Girlguiding UK and the Youth Action Network, which operate all over the country. Visit their websites to find out more.

- **Charities** – may also be small and employ only a few staff. Others are massive national or international operations such as Cancer Research or the British Red Cross.

- **Social enterprises** – businesses formed with a social purpose. An example is Jamie Oliver's restaurants Fifteen, which he has opened to enable disadvantaged young people to train professionally for a catering career.

Key terms

Surplus – the amount remaining from donations, fund-raising and commercial activities after essential expenses have been paid.

Social enterprises – businesses that use any profit, or surplus, to fulfil their social objectives.

What is the purpose of charities, voluntary organisations and social enterprises such as Jamie Oliver's restaurants?

Discussion point

Visit the Co-operatives UK website. Find out how cooperatives work and read case studies on worker cooperatives. In groups, debate the benefits and drawbacks of working together with no overall boss.

Activity: Government departments

The work of some government departments affects business activities more than others. Divide into groups. Each group should investigate two or three of the ten departments shown in Figure 1.1. Find out what work they carry out and suggest two ways their work could affect business organisations. Present your findings to the rest of your class. Use the government's own website Directgov to help you.

PLTS

Practise your creative thinking skills to think of all the connections you can between your chosen department(s) and UK businesses.

Activity: Find three voluntary sector enterprises

NHS health trusts now use social enterprises to help provide cheaper health care services, such as affordable dentistry for everyone. Investigate this further at the NHS Networks website. Find one that operates in your region or works in an area that interests you. Then search the Internet to find two examples of voluntary organisations in your own area.

Cooperatives

The main difference between a cooperative and other private organisations is that there is no overall 'boss' who is in charge. In a workers' cooperative, the business is jointly owned and run by everyone who works there. They share the profits and make joint decisions about how the business should be run. Most workers' cooperatives in the UK are quite small, unlike the CRS (the Cooperative Retail Society) which is owned by its customers and operates all over the country.

The government

Some enterprises in the UK are owned or controlled by the state, such as government departments, and organisations funded by the government.

- **Government departments, agencies and other public bodies** – deal with various matters and carry out specific functions at national level, such as education, health, defence, environmental issues, policing, national transport and tax collection. All departments of state are overseen by a government minister and each has its own budget. Ministers bid for money each year from the Treasury (the government department that manages the government's money).

- **Local authorities** – provide services for the local community, such as social services, road maintenance, environmental health, refuse collection and recycling, and public libraries. The services vary, depending upon the size and type of area, so that those in a rural community are different from those offered in a city.

- **Health trusts** – receive money from the government to deliver health care without making a profit.

- **Public corporations** – government-owned businesses, such as the BBC and the Royal Mail service. These businesses are expected to operate profitably, just like private organisations.

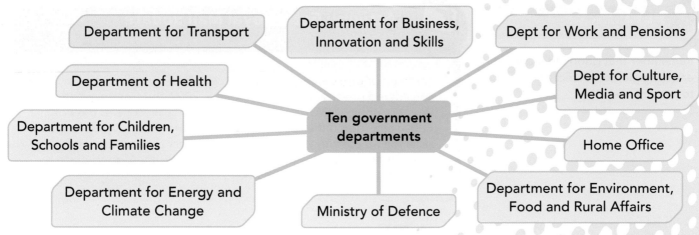

Figure 1.1: Examples of government departments

The government also owns four banks: Northern Rock, most of RBS (the Royal Bank of Scotland) and Lloyds Banking Group, and part of Bradford and Bingley. The government took over these banks to rescue the UK banking system when the banks lost huge amounts of money on bad loans made to the US housing **market**. You will learn more about how this affected British businesses in section 1.2.

Key term

Market – all the possible consumers who might buy a product or service.

BTEC Assessment activity 1.1

The government can sell businesses it owns to the private sector to raise money. This is known as **privatisation**. In 2009 it considered selling off the Met Office, which employs 1,250 people at its main centre in Exeter.

Met Office weather forecasts help businesses in both the private and the public sector to plan ahead. In the middle of winter, knowing when snow is expected is very important for all transport companies including airlines, such as EasyJet, and train operators – as well as haulage companies and delivery firms. Local councils, too, may need to buy more grit and salt for the roads. Many charitable organisations, such as Help the Aged and Shelter, are also concerned about the effect of very cold weather on vulnerable people, such as the elderly and homeless, and take action to try to help them.

Prepare a factsheet on business purposes by answering the following questions.

1. Identify and describe the purpose of each of the following organisations mentioned in this activity: The Met Office, EasyJet, your own local council, Shelter. Use their websites to help you. **P1**

2. Explain how the ownership of the Met Office will change if government privatisation plans go ahead.

3. Contrast the ownership and purposes of **one** of the business organisations described above with **either** a retailer in your own area **or** with another charity of your own choice. **M1**

Grading tip

Contrast two or more organisations by identifying their similarities and differences. If you explain these fully and correctly in your assessment, you will gain a merit grade.

Did you know?

Nearly six million people work in the public sector. They include health workers, teachers, the Civil Service and staff in town halls.

Activity: Get a Royal Mail update

Trade unions represent the work force. When the government considered privatising the Royal Mail in 2009, the Communication Workers Union (CWU) launched a campaign called *Keep the Post Public* and toured the country to get support. Practise your research skills to find out why the CWU was so against privatisation and whether the Royal Mail is still in public ownership. A good place to start is the Communication Workers Union website.

1.4 The size of businesses

Some businesses are very small and consist of only one person or a few staff, such as a taxi firm, takeaway or hairdressers' salon. Others are very large and may employ thousands of staff, such as the NHS, retailers Marks & Spencer and Sainsbury's, and manufacturing companies like BAE Systems and Rolls-Royce.

You can assess the size of a business if you know any of the following factors.

The number of employees

This is the easiest method to use, but be careful if there are many part-time employees, as this may give you a misleading result.

Did you know?

Small- or medium-sized enterprises are businesses with fewer than 250 employees.

Activity: Turnover versus profit

Some new **entrepreneurs** have confused turnover with profit – to their cost. It is quite possible to have a high **sales turnover** yet make a loss! In groups, discuss how this could happen.

Table 1.1: The size of an organisation, assessed by the number of employees

Number of employees and size of organisation	
Small	1–99
Medium	100–249
Large	250+

The sales turnover

This is the value of goods sold or the income from services. A small business may sell between £1 million and £5 million of goods each year, while a medium-sized business would aim for sales of £20 million or more.

The scale of its operations

There is usually a link between size and scale, but not always, as you will see below.

1.5 The scale of a business

The **scale of a business** relates to the size of its operations, rather than its physical size. An independent local chemist may sell 20 packs of

Key terms

Entrepreneur – a person who risks their own money to build up a successful business.

Sales turnover – the amount of money the business obtains by selling its goods and services.

Scale of a business – relates to the size of its operations and whether it sells on a large scale, globally, or on a small scale, to just a local area.

disposable nappies a week, whereas Boots or Superdrug sell thousands. These businesses therefore operate on a far larger scale and need more workers, more equipment, more outlets and greater investment.

Businesses that operate on a small scale usually supply only a local area, such as an independent chemist. Others may trade on a wider basis, perhaps across a region, or nationally, like Boots and Superdrug. Some organisations expand into Europe or provide goods or services globally.

Operating on a large scale gives businesses certain advantages, known as **economies of scale**. So, although the overall costs of running a large business are higher than a small firm, they can produce or sell each item, or unit, more cheaply (at a lower **unit cost**). For example, Amazon buys huge quantities of books, DVDs and other items from suppliers. It can therefore negotiate lower prices and pass the savings to customers. This makes it difficult for smaller firms to compete with it.

The links between business ownership, size and scale

You would normally expect there to be a link between size, scale and ownership. Sole traders are usually small in size and scale, whereas public limited companies have the money and resources to be far larger and operate on a wider scale. However, there are exceptions. Some private limited companies are huge, such as the Arcadia Group (see page 5), which went global by opening a Topshop in New York in 2009.

In addition, many small businesses sell over the Internet, which means that a sole trader may be receiving orders from all over the world.

The ability to operate on a large scale depends upon several factors including:

- **The type of goods or service offered** – Providers of perishable goods often operate locally, such as small outlets that sell sandwiches and hot snacks. Some items are specific to a region or country. You would not have much use for skunk repellent in the UK, for example. Other goods have global appeal, such as computers, clothes, cars and jewellery, so can be sold in many countries.

  Some services, too, are limited to an area. Most solicitors and accountants focus on UK laws and regulations and only the largest firms employ international experts. In contrast, banking and hotel services are required worldwide, so many of these businesses operate on an international basis.

- **The cost of expansion** – Operating on a large scale requires more investment in equipment, staff and other resources. A product may have to be adapted for a different market and global advertising costs money. Spending large sums on expansion can endanger the whole business if the scheme is unsuccessful.

- **The ambitions of the owner** – Some entrepreneurs prefer operating on a small scale if the profit is enough to meet their needs, while others want their business to grow as large as possible.

Did you know?

A business that wants to expand may transfer from being a sole trader, partnership or private limited company to plc status. This is often referred to as 'going public' or **floating** the business. As a plc it can now raise more money by selling shares on the stock exchange.

Key terms

Economies of scale – savings made by large businesses that can produce or sell items with lower unit costs than small businesses.

Unit cost – price of making or selling each item.

In what way is the Arcadia Group different from many other private limited companies?

Remember

- The scale of operations will depend upon the market for the goods and services offered by the business and whether this is global, national, regional or local. You will learn more about markets in section 2.3.

- There are risks involved for a business when it grows in size or starts to operate on a larger scale because additional investment (money) will be needed, which may, or may not, pay off. There is usually a link between the **size of a business** and its scale, but not always.

Key term

Size of a business – relates to its physical size, number of employees and value of its sales turnover.

- **The skills in the business and knowledge of the market** – It is risky to expand, especially abroad, without researching the foreign market first. There may be many regulations and laws to consider as well as ethnic and cultural differences to take into account.

- **The size of the potential market/level of competition** – It is unwise to expand without checking there are enough potential customers and that all sources of competition have been identified.

There are always risks for businesses that expand or try to operate on a large scale, and timing can be crucial. Even large, successful companies may encounter difficulties if unexpected events mean that demand suddenly falls.

 Did you know?

- Tesco, one of the world's most successful companies, launched Fresh & Easy stores in the US after meticulous research to check how American consumers ate and shopped. The stores opened in late 2007 – just as the recession hit the US – and lost £204 million in the first 17 months. Expansion plans were postponed. Tesco may lose up to £1 billion if it has to pull out of the US.

- eBay enables many small traders to operate on a larger scale by selling goods over the Internet without even having their own website. A feedback system operates that enables reliable traders and buyers to identify each other, and the PayPal system helps safeguard payments.

Case study: A bumpy ride!

MyTravel Group plc, the holiday business, began life as Pendle Travel Services. In 1972, this small Lancashire firm was bought by an ambitious entrepreneur, David Crossland. He then purchased another company, AIR Tours. He renamed it Airtours and under this name built up and expanded his business, developing and offering package holidays. Airtours was floated on the London stock exchange in 1987 and rapidly became the world's largest holiday business, worth £2 billion.

By 2003, things were very different. A downturn in the travel business after 9/11 coupled with unsuccessful expansions in the US and Europe resulted in debts of over £600 million. The company did not become profitable again until 2007, after it had sold off its loss-making European businesses and Florida timeshare resort. It changed its name to MyTravel, then merged with Thomas Cook and now trades under the name Thomas Cook Group plc. The aim of the merger was to reduce costs in order to compete more successfully with Internet companies such as Expedia and Travelocity.

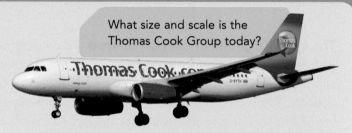

What size and scale is the Thomas Cook Group today?

1. David Crossland started out as a sole trader and ended up running a plc. Explain how the change of ownership can be linked to the changing scale of his operations.

2. What size and scale is the Thomas Cook Group today? Find out on the Thomas Cook Group website.

3. Merging two companies is a quick way of expanding a business and enables many duplicated costs to be cut. Suggest three types of possible savings if two travel agents merge into one.

4. Another way of expanding quickly is to buy out a competitor. Boots Alliance, which own Boots Opticians, did this when it bought Dolland and Aitchison, another optician, in 2009. Suggest two benefits Boots gained by taking this action.

Assessment activity 1.2

Prepare a poster on business ownership, which includes information on size and scale. Do this by carrying out the following activities.

1. As a group, select four businesses, each with a different type of ownership and identify the size and scale of each one.

2. On your own, write a description of each one. Link the type of ownership to the size and scale of each business. Then show how they differ in size and scale on your poster using either graphics of your choice or a brief explanation. **P2**

Grading tip

Make your links by listing the main facts, then see if these fit a known pattern or whether one example is different from normal. Then explain clearly what you have found, providing facts to support what you are saying.

1.6 The classification of businesses

All businesses are classified into **industrial sectors** based on what they do.

- The **primary sector** obtains or produces raw goods.
- The **secondary sector** manufactures or constructs goods.
- The **tertiary sector** provides services to businesses and/or individuals.

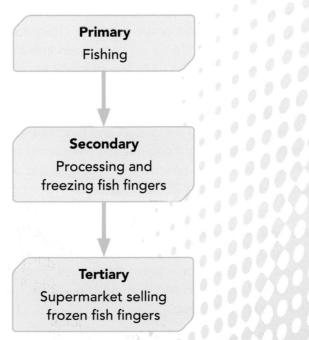

Figure 1.2: The names of the sectors show they are linked in a sequence, often referred to as the chain of production.

Key terms

Industrial sectors – primary, secondary and tertiary sectors by which all business activities in the UK are classified.

Primary sector – involves growing, extracting or converting natural resources into raw materials.

Secondary sector – manufactures goods. It converts raw materials into products for sale to businesses and private individuals.

Tertiary sector – provides services to businesses and individuals.

Key term

Industry – relates to a group of businesses undertaking the same activity and offering the same or similar products, for example, the advertising or catering industries.

Activity: Find ten manufacturers

Using Table 1.3, find examples of ten UK manufacturing businesses. Ideally, at least four should be in your own area. Use reference books in your library to help you as well as the Internet.

Activity: Wind power and more

If you are concerned about climate change then you may support the activities of the British Wind Energy Association and its members, who are involved not only in onshore and offshore wind farms, but also in harnessing tidal and wave power. Find out more about operations of BWEA and its members by visiting the BWEA website.

The primary sector

The activities of businesses in this sector are all involved with producing or obtaining raw materials or natural products from the land or sea. The main categories are shown in Table 1.2.

Table 1.2: Categories and activities in the primary sector

Category	Activities
Agriculture, hunting and forestry	The production of crops, such as vegetables and cereals, animal farming, landscape gardening and horticultural businesses
Forestry and logging	Planting, conserving and felling timber, including Christmas trees
Fishing	Fishing fleets, fish farms, for example, trout hatcheries, salmon farms and freshwater mussel growers
Mining and quarrying	Coal mining, oil and natural gas extraction, quarrying all types of stone, slate, gravel, sand and clay, salt production

The secondary sector

The secondary sector includes all those businesses that manufacture, process or assemble products. This sector also covers energy production and the construction industry.

- **Manufacturing** – all businesses that make or produce goods in the UK, regardless of size or product. The Office for National Statistics (ONS) divides manufacturing companies into different product groups, which enables us to see which types of manufacturer are thriving and which are not.

- **Engineering** – a key feature of many manufacturing industries, mainly in relation to the design and functioning of machinery and equipment. Light engineering companies make small items where precision is important, such as scientific equipment. Heavy engineering companies make goods comprising large sections of metals, such as ships or cranes.

- **Energy production** – the production and distribution of electricity, gas and water. It therefore includes businesses like E.ON and British Gas as well as regional water companies, such as Severn Trent and water collection and bottling companies. Wind farms are also included in this group.

- **Construction** – includes house builders such as Bryant Homes and civil engineering companies such as John Laing and Carillion and Sir Alfred McAlpine. Between them they construct all types of buildings in addition to motorways, bridges, roads and railways. Also included are electricians, plumbers, plasterers, joiners, painters and glaziers who work on building sites.

Table 1.3: Product groups in the secondary sector

Product group	Examples
Food products, beverages and tobacco	Meat and poultry, fish freezing, fruit and vegetable processing, dairy products and ice cream, breakfast cereals, pet food, bread, sweets and chocolate, wine, mineral water, soft drinks, beer and tobacco
Textiles and textile products	Cotton and woollen goods, soft furnishings, carpets, knitted and leather clothes
Leather goods	Handbags, luggage and footwear
Wood products (not furniture)	Sawmilling, wood containers, plywood and veneers
Pulp, paper products, publishing and printing	Paper, cartons, boxes, wallpaper, book and newspaper publishing, reproducing sound/video recordings and computer media
Coke (carbon fuel), refined petroleum products, nuclear fuel processing	Petrol, diesel, nuclear energy
Chemicals, chemical products and man-made fibres	Chemicals, industrial gases, dyes, plastic, synthetic rubber, paint, printing ink, pharmaceuticals, soap, detergents, perfume, glue, man-made fibres, unrecorded media (for example, blank DVDs)
Rubber and plastic products	Rubber tyres, plastic tubes and packaging, plastic floor coverings
Non-metallic mineral products	Glass, ceramic goods (for example, sinks, baths and tiles), bricks and cement manufacture, finishing of ornamental and building stone
Basic metals and fabricated metal products	Iron, steel, aluminium, lead, zinc, tin and copper goods, central heating radiators and boilers, cutlery, tools, locks, wire, screws
Other machinery and equipment*	Pumps, compressors, furnaces, ventilation equipment, agricultural machinery, power tools, earth-moving machinery, domestic appliances
Electrical and optical equipment*	Office machinery, computers, electric motors, batteries, electric lamps, televisions and radios, medical and surgical equipment, cameras, watches and clocks
Transport equipment	Motor vehicles, trailers, caravans, motor vehicle parts and accessories, ships, boats, trains, aircraft and spacecraft, motorcycles and bicycles
Other manufacturing	Furniture, mattresses, jewellery, musical instruments, sports goods, games and toys, brooms and brushes, recycling of scrap metal

* Engineering industries

What types of business does the secondary sector include?

The tertiary sector

This is the largest sector. It includes every type of business offering a service and is also known as the service sector.

- **Private services** – purchased by businesses and individuals. They are offered by privately owned businesses such as retailers, accountants, banks, private clinics and private hospitals, publishers, transport and distribution firms, travel agencies and many others.

- **Local and national public services** – provided by the government and local authorities, for example, education, emergency services, housing, law and order, defence and military activity, social services, local planning and recreational facilities.

- **Voluntary and not-for-profit services** – provided by charities and voluntary groups in areas such as social care, community health care, global development, environmental and wildlife protection.

The Office for National Statistics groups the service sector into different categories by activity, because private, public and voluntary providers may offer the same service. For example, health care may be provided by private care homes, clinics and hospitals, as well as NHS hospitals and by voluntary organisations, such as WellChild and Help the Aged.

Table 1.4: Service groupings in the tertiary sector

Service group	Examples
Wholesale and retail trade	All wholesalers and retailers including market stalls and dispensing chemists, plus repair/ maintenance businesses such as garages, watch repairers, cobblers
Hotels and restaurants (including camp sites)	Hotels, restaurants, youth hotels, holiday centres, takeaway food shops and stands, pubs and bars
Transport, storage and communication	Taxis, furniture removals, freight transport by road, rail, sea, canals and air, all passenger transport, pipelines, cargo handling and storage, travel agencies and tour operators, post and courier services, telecommunications
Financial services	Banks, building societies, finance houses, insurance companies, pension funds
Property, renting and business activities	Estate agents, car hire firms, all rental firms, computer consultants, software developers, office equipment repairers, solicitors, accountants, market research companies, quantity surveyors, architects, advertising agencies, recruitment companies, security firms, industrial cleaners, photographers, secretarial agencies, call centres, debt collectors, exhibition organisers
Public administration and defence	Government agencies which oversee health care, education, defence activities, the justice system, the police and fire service
Education	All pre-schools, nurseries, schools, colleges, universities, driving schools and private training firms
Health and social work	Hospitals and nursing homes, doctors, dentists, vets, social workers
Other community, social and personal service activities	Sewage and refuse disposal, professional organisations and trade unions, religious and political organisations, film and video production and distribution, radio and television, theatres, fair and amusement parks, news agencies, libraries, museums, sports centres, dry cleaners, funeral directors, hairdressers, beauty therapists, nail bars, gyms and fitness centres, nature reserves

Just checking

1. Why are some goods sold below their cost price?
2. Why do privately owned businesses need to make a profit?
3. Why do some sole traders feel safer if they form a limited company?
4. What is the difference between the size of a business and its scale?
5. What is the difference between the primary sector, the secondary sector and the tertiary sector?

 Assessment activity 1.3

Work in an even number of small groups to start this activity. In your group, identify ten different local businesses as well as ten national businesses. Your aim is to find one business for every category in **each** industrial sector, i.e. primary, secondary and tertiary. Try to be as imaginative as possible! The Yellow Pages (book or website) or your local newspaper may be useful. List your businesses' names and decide on your own group code to identify the sector to which each business belongs. Give your list to your tutor or teacher, who will score each correctly identified and categorised business. See if your group can achieve 20 out of 20!

After you have made any amendments suggested by your tutor, exchange your list with another group. It is now your task to help to classify each of the businesses on the list you have been given, again into primary, secondary and tertiary industries. Your tutor will observe your group during this activity and note the contribution of each person on an observation record.

Use your completed lists as the basis for preparing a short talk, on your own, to give to your tutor to explain how businesses in the UK are classified, using local and national examples. You can illustrate your talk with visual aids where you think these are appropriate. Your visual aids plus the notes you have prepared for your talk, and your tutor's observation record, will provide evidence that you have successfully completed this activity. **P3**

Keep this information safely. You may find it useful when you do Assessment activity 1.5.

Grading tip

A good explanation should include reasons or examples to support the statements you are making.

 PLTS

Practise your team-working skills by taking responsibility for your own work and being fair and considerate to other people in your group.

2. Understand the business context in which organisations operate

All business organisations exist in an environment that includes other people and organisations. Some aspects of this environment are out of the control of individual businesses, but can affect them in many ways. For example, on page 12 you learned that Tesco's expansion into the US was badly affected by the economic downturn in that country. So, what is an 'economic downturn' and does this affect all businesses in the same way?

The government tries to help UK businesses to succeed, even when there are economic problems. It also sets the legal framework for businesses. All businesses must obey laws and regulations, such as paying the minimum wage and working safely. They also need to know the market for their goods or services and be alert to any changes. In some cases they may need to adapt or change their activities to stay in business, as you will see.

2.1 The role of government

All governments in the Western world want to create an environment in which businesses thrive. This is because businesses create wealth for the nation as a whole and the people who live there. You will learn more about this later in this section.

The activities of three different governments affect UK businesses.

The European government

The European government makes policies and laws that affect all member states of the European Union (EU). It is concerned with social and environmental issues as well as other areas including agriculture, immigration, justice and security.

- The EU protects the **internal market** by allowing businesses within the EU to trade across borders without any controls or restrictions.

- The EU tries to ensure that all businesses compete fairly with each other and promotes **competition laws** to keep prices low for consumers within the EU.

- Businesses in the EU also benefit from **product standardisation**, which means that most products can be sold all over Europe without needing to be adapted or changed.

You can find out more about the activities of the EU, and the names of all the member countries, on the EUROPA website.

Did you know?

EU members benefit from the free movement of goods and people throughout Europe. This means British businesses have access to 500 million consumers without worrying about import or export regulations. It also means individuals can live and work anywhere in Europe.

Activity: EU members and activities

1. How many members of the EU can you name? See how many your group can suggest before you need to research the rest.

2. Pet passports, parental leave, Blue Flag beaches, bans on cosmetic testing on animals and reduced/abolished roaming charges on mobile phones are just a few of the changes brought about by the EU. For each of these changes, suggest the type of businesses in the UK that might have been affected and in what way.

The UK national government

The UK government makes laws that apply to everyone in the UK but also has to abide by EU directives on agreed areas, such as employment rights, product safety and competition. The government tries to attract foreign businesses to locate in the UK to increase employment prospects. Examples of foreign companies operating in the UK include Microsoft, Fujitsu and Nissan.

The government aims to create a sound and stable **economy** in the UK with continued growth to guarantee future employment and to help businesses to flourish. It also encourages new entrepreneurs to start and grow businesses in the UK.

Activity: Devolved government

The UK has a devolved government. This means that it has given certain powers to national parliaments or assemblies in Northern Ireland, Scotland and Wales. If you live in one of these areas, find out more by visiting the government websites.

Local government

Every area in the UK has a local council, but their titles vary. City or county councils cover a large area whereas district or borough councils operate in smaller communities. All councils want their area to prosper and so have economic development plans to tempt businesses to relocate or start up in their area. They promote their own area and give advice about grants and other incentives to attract new businesses. They also have legal powers to take certain actions for the benefit of the local community.

Did you know?

In 2007, the UK was the sixth best place to do business in the world according to the Institute of Economic Research in Munich, based on its fair tax policy and sound trade and labour market policies.

Key term

Economy – the financial situation of a country as a result of all the items that are produced and consumed there.

Did you know?

Local governments get money in grants from the government, from home owners in the area who pay council tax and also from businesses that pay business rates on the properties they have.

Activity: Local council

Find out the name of your local council, then check its website and see what it does to attract businesses to your area.

Activity: Check out help and advice

The UK has a network of organisations to help British businesses. **UK Trade and Investment** (UKTI) focuses on attracting businesses to the UK. It provides information about different sectors in the UK. You can sign in to the UKTI website (it is free), create a 'My UK' page and customise this to obtain information on your region and sectors in which you are interested.

The site also links to the **Regional Development Agency** (RDA) websites, where you can find information on sectors in your region. RDAs help new and existing businesses in an area. They are also responsible for the **Business Link** service. This provides free information on starting or expanding a business, marketing, finance, technology and exporting.

Local Enterprise Agencies provide help locally, often using the expertise of successful business people in the area to assist new entrepreneurs.

In small groups, carry out the following activities.

1. Investigate the UKTI website. Choose a sector that interests you (for example, IT, food and drink, aerospace) and find case studies of businesses that have located to the UK.

2. Check the Investment Regions section to find your own Regional Development Agency and identify the main industries in your own area.

3. Find out about Business Link and the help it offers new businesses by visiting the website.

4. Find the name of your local Enterprise Agency on the NFEA (National Federation of Enterprise Agents) website. These agencies give free information and advice to local businesses, often in conjunction with local government. Find out what your nearest agency does to help businesses in your area. Present your findings, in groups, to the rest of the class.

Keep this information safely. It will help you when you do Assessment activity 1.5 and 1.6.

2.2 The government and the economy

The UKTI website claims the UK is a good place to set up a business because it is a leading global trading nation with a strong, stable economy. Having a strong and stable economy is a key aim of all UK governments. To achieve this they have four economic objectives:

1. **steady economic growth** – so the economy grows each year

2. **full employment** – so everyone who wants a job can find one

3. **sustained low inflation** – so prices and wages increase a small amount each year

4. **a surplus on the balance of payments** – which means that the UK exports more than it imports.

Key term

Inflation – where the prices of goods are increasing.

A quick guide to Britain's economy

The economy might sound complicated, but how it works is quite simple. When consumers buy goods they spend money. Firms use this to hire labour and pay wages. These workers then buy more goods and so on. The more this happens, the greater the number of people employed and the richer everyone becomes.

The government gains because it receives taxes from people in work and pays out less in benefits because unemployment is low. The government can then spend more on public services such as health care and education to improve the life of everyone.

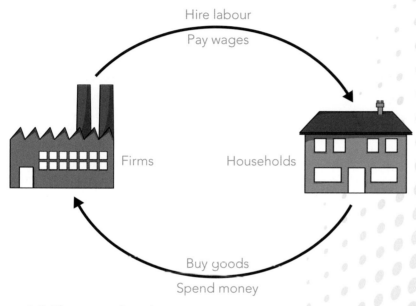

Hire labour
Pay wages

Firms   Households

Buy goods
Spend money

Figure 1.3: The economic cycle

The job of the government is therefore to:

- encourage consumers to spend by setting low tax rates and paying state benefits to those below a certain minimum income level

- encourage businesses to increase **investment** in new machinery, equipment and staff by keeping **interest rates** low and promoting **business confidence**

- encourage exports of goods and discourage imports

- spend money on new projects for the future, such as road-building and schools.

Did you know?

The government gets its money through taxation and by borrowing money. Individuals pay income tax, companies pay corporation tax and both employers and employees pay National Insurance. VAT (value added tax) is added to goods and services. The government uses this money to provide public services in Britain.

Remember

Investment means using profits or borrowing money to buy more or better machinery, equipment or buildings. Companies that invest in the business stay up to date and are more competitive.

Key term

Interest rates – the cost of borrowing money. If interest rates are at 5 per cent per year and you borrow £100 for a year, this costs you £5. If interest rates increase, you will be less likely to borrow. Lenders will want to lend more, however, as their reward for lending has increased.

Case study: Where did the money go?

Business and consumer confidence fell sharply in 2008 as a result of the credit crunch. This was caused by a banking crisis when the banks lost billions of pounds in bad loans to the US housing market. This meant they had no money left to lend to UK businesses or individuals. House buyers could no longer get mortgages, so houses stopped selling and prices fell. Jobs were lost in many areas, including banking and construction. Fears about widespread unemployment meant people spent less so other businesses suffered. Thousands of new cars remained unsold so workers in the car industry were laid off or worked fewer hours. Some retailers closed down, including Woolworths and MFI.

The government tried to get the money flowing again. It put billions of pounds of new money into the banking system and reduced interest rates to stimulate spending. The government's role was to protect British businesses and jobs, and to get the economy out of recession.

1. **Business confidence is the degree to which businesses believe levels of future consumer demand will be sustained and increased. What do you think businesses do when they lose confidence and why?**

2. **What factors do you think boost consumer confidence and make people willing to spend money?**

3. **Why do low interest rates tempt some people to spend? Discuss your ideas as a group.**

4. **As a group, list all the ways in which your own household would change its spending habits if it was seriously short of money. Then identify the businesses that would be affected, both positively and negatively, as a result.**

5. **Many businesses depend upon other businesses to buy their goods or services – for example, the brick industry needs builders and the steel industry needs cars to be made. Bearing this in mind, add any other businesses that might also be affected by your decisions to the list you made in Question 4.**

Key terms

Gross Domestic Product (GDP) – total amount earned or produced by the nation as a whole.

Productivity – amount of output a person produces. If this increases, the cost of producing each item is less.

Economic growth

When the economy grows, the nation is earning more money each year. Economic growth is measured by putting a monetary value on all the goods and services produced in the country. This is called **Gross Domestic Product (GDP)**.

It can be calculated in three ways (all add up to the same figure):

- **by expenditure** – how much everyone spends each year
- **by income** – how much everyone earns each year
- **by output** – calculating the value of all the goods and services produced in a year.

To see how this works, think of a farmer. The more they produce the more they earn and the more they can spend. If they want to increase their income they must produce more, either by working harder or by investing in machinery that will increase their **productivity**.

The more we produce and the more we earn as a nation, the more money we have to spend. This means our **standard of living** improves, too, which is one of the main benefits of economic growth.

How is economic growth measured?

Discussion point

The more people earn, the more tax they pay. This helps to redistribute wealth from the rich to the poor. In 2009, the government announced reduced allowances and higher taxes for high earners. Do you think this is a good idea or not? Discuss your views as a group.

Some people argue that quality of life is more important than economic growth and wealth, especially as the downsides include pollution and working long hours. Which would make you happier? Discuss your ideas and take a vote as a group.

Functional skills

Use your maths skills to find out more. If you earn £160,000 you have no allowances and pay tax at 20 per cent on the first £37,400, 40 per cent on the next £112,600 and 50 per cent on the rest of your salary. How much do you now take home?

Activity: Update on the economy

In 2009, the British economy was in **recession** as GDP had fallen by 6 per cent in 18 months. The government predicted the economy would start growing again in 2010 or 2011. Have they been proved right yet? Search the Internet or check the National Statistics website to find out.

Key term

Recession – when GDP falls continuously for more than six months.

Remember

Over the long term, the UK GDP usually grows by about 3 per cent a year. In the short term it fluctuates – it has ups and downs. This is called the **economic cycle**. The government tries to moderate major fluctuations, so when demand falls it tries to boost this. If demand is high this can trigger inflation, which needs a different response.

Full employment

This means that everyone who is able to work and wants a job can have one. This benefits everyone. Workers have more money and greater self-esteem. Businesses can hire the staff needed to expand their operations. The local community flourishes as everyone has more money to spend. The government gains more in tax and pays out less in benefits.

Discussion point

Some people say that if benefits are too generous, many people simply cannot be bothered going to work. Do you agree? Discuss your ideas as a class.

Did you know?

In the 2008/09 recession, the government allocated an additional £1.7 billion to help people find work and £260 million to help young people get access to training and education.

Remember

When demand is high and supply is low, prices rise. If demand is low and supply is high, then prices fall. This is why greengrocers lower their prices to sell unwanted goods at the end of the day, but charge more when popular items are in short supply. Another term for this is **market forces**.

Activity: Footballers' wages

Use the forces of supply and demand to explain why top footballers earn so much money.

Key term

Deflation – when the prices of goods are falling.

Unfortunately this does not always happen. People might lose their jobs for several reasons.

- **Seasonal unemployment** – when people are in jobs for only a short time each year, such as ride attendants at Alton Towers.
- **Technological unemployment** – when people do not have the skills needed by employers.
- **Cyclical unemployment** – happens during a recession when businesses lay off workers because there is no demand for their goods or services.
- **Structural unemployment** – when whole industries change so people have skills that are no longer needed in the areas where they live, for example, coal mining.

Sustained low inflation

Inflation occurs when prices are rising. This means the cost of living is increasing. In the UK, inflation is assessed in two ways.

- **The Retail Prices Index (RPI)** calculates the cost of a typical 'basket of goods'. The difference in price for these goods, from one year to the next, gives the rate of inflation. Many firms use the RPI as the basis for agreeing pay rises.
- **The Consumer Prices Index (CPI)** is the UK government's preferred measure. This does not include mortgage payments and council tax, which are included in the RPI.

If inflation is more than 4 or 5 per cent, this causes problems for both businesses and individuals. It makes British goods more expensive so they cannot compete with cheap imports. People on fixed incomes (for example, learners and pensioners) struggle with increasing costs. Savings lose their value because these buy less each year. If you had £10,000 saved in 1950, it would have bought you more than it would now.

To try to control inflation, the government tries to reduce levels of consumer demand, because this can cause prices to rise. One way is to increase interest rates, to tempt people to save money rather than borrow money to buy expensive items.

The government's inflation target is a CPI of 2 per cent. At this level, prices are stable. Monitoring inflation is the responsibility of the Monetary Policy Committee (MPC) at the Bank of England. This group meets each month to decide whether interest rates should be lowered or increased.

The opposite of inflation is **deflation**. This means that prices of goods are falling. This may seem good news, but what really happens is that many people stop spending, hoping that goods will become cheaper still. This reduces demand for goods and services, sales fall and employees are laid off.

A surplus on the balance of payments

The UK earns money for every export it sells abroad and it spends money on every import it buys from abroad. If it sells and buys the same amount of exports and imports, the balance of payments is equal. If it imports more than it exports, the UK is paying out more than it earns. If it does the opposite it makes a surplus, which is better for the nation as a whole.

Activity: Inflation and interest rates

Find out the current rate of inflation (or deflation) and the rate of interest. Then decide, as a class, whether these are favourable for businesses or not.

Did you know?

- In September 2009, the CPI was 1.1 per cent but RPI was down to -1.4 per cent, one of the lowest figures ever. This meant deflation was more of a worry than inflation.

- The UK balance of payments would be in surplus more often if UK consumers bought British goods, not imports. However, the government cannot limit imports as this is against the principles of the EU and the World Trade Organization (WTO), which promotes free trade around the world.

Why does the UK normally import more goods than it exports?

Remember

Low interest rates encourage businesses to borrow money to expand or invest in new technology.

Activity: Could you do the government's job?

You are the government. You have to cope with economic problems. In groups, decide what you would do to sustain economic growth, keep unemployment low, manage inflation (or prevent deflation) and obtain a balance of payments surplus. Then check your ideas with the table on page 26.

Table 1.5: The government's role in the economy

Aim	Actions
Economic growth	Keep interest rates low so businesses will invest in new equipment and technology, and consumers will borrow to buy expensive items Provide incentives for workers to train to improve their skill levels Keep tax rates low to encourage entrepreneurs to start businesses and so that consumers have more **disposable income** to spend Spend government money on new projects, for example, roads and hospitals
Full employment	Keep benefits low and make it difficult to claim benefits for long periods Insist anyone who is unemployed goes on a training course Provide incentives for industries to take on new workers during a recession
Keeping inflation low	Reduce consumer demand and spending by: • increasing interest rates to tempt people to save more • increasing taxes to reduce people's disposable income Award public sector workers only small pay rises
Preventing deflation	Encourage consumer demand and spending by: • reducing taxes so people spend more. In 2008, the government reduced VAT to 15 per cent until 1 January 2010 to boost spending • reducing interest rates so people get less reward for saving money and are tempted to borrow to buy expensive items Increase government spending, for example, by building new roads and hospitals
Balance of payments surplus	Give information and advice to exporters Encourage banks to lend money to exporters Persuade foreign businesses to locate in Britain and produce goods here Promote British goods and services to foreign governments and other major buyers Keep inflation rates low so that UK goods remain competitive against foreign goods

Key term

Disposable income – amount left from wages after paying taxes and essential bills.

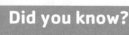

Did you know?

In 2009, the weak pound attracted foreign tourists to Britain, which helped the British economy. However, imported goods were more expensive. Argos warned it was spending 10 per cent more on imports from China and increased its catalogue prices by 5 per cent. Some British businesses gained, though. Tesco switched the source of its own-label chocolate and chicken nuggets from France and South Africa to UK suppliers to save money.

The competitiveness of British industry

To sell abroad, British industry must be able to offer goods and services at competitive prices. Britain is mainly successful selling goods and services that require technical knowledge and expertise. It cannot compete with countries like China and India, which make mass-produced goods cheaply, because wages and taxes in the UK are so much higher.

To compete successfully, businesses in the UK need:

- to invest in new equipment and technology to stay ahead of their rivals

- low taxes and business rates so that the cost of running the business is low and prices can be kept down

- low inflation to keep other business costs and prices down

- a competitive exchange rate. This means the value of the pound is low so that British goods and services are cheap to foreign buyers.

Activity: How many euros?

Work out how the value of the pound would affect you as a tourist. In 2005 it cost only £60 to buy €100. In 2009 it cost £90 to buy the same amount of euros. Check out today's rate online to see whether or not the pound is stronger. Then, as a group, suggest how the value of the pound affects UK businesses that specialise in European travel.

Equality

The motto of the EU is 'United in diversity'. Equal rights in the workplace are a legal requirement throughout the EU. This means that everyone must be treated the same, fairly and with respect, irrespective of their race, nationality, ethnic origins, gender or disability. You will learn more about this if you study Unit 9.

Treating people equally makes good business sense because businesses need a variety of talented and skilled workers to fulfil their goals. They want people who can bring different ideas and views to a problem and who can relate to the variety of customers they may deal with. Businesses also need to retain good workers and develop a reputation for being fair and honest in the marketplace if they are to be competitive in the modern world.

Remember

- The value of the pound is also based on the law of demand and supply. The more pounds people want, the higher the price and vice versa. The pound is stronger when interest rates are high because foreign investors buy pounds to invest money in the UK to get high returns. If interest rates fall, investors sell pounds to invest in other currencies so the value of the pound falls too.

- The EU does not just want equality among people, but also among regions. To achieve this it provides Structural Funds to help certain regions. Between 2007 and 2013 the UK will receive €9.6 million. Find out if your area will benefit at the BERR website.

How does a business benefit if it has a diverse workforce?

Functional skills

Find out what the CBI does and then assess whether its argument could be biased in any way.

Discussion point

The Equality Bill makes companies with over 250 employees publish the average pay of male and female staff. This is because women still earn only 87p for every £1 earned by men despite the Equal Pay Act. The CBI (Confederation of British Industry) argues the pay gap is because fewer women have high-paid jobs and that the cost of complying with the new law – about £211 million – would be better spent providing more childcare and careers advice. Do you agree? Discuss your views as a group.

 ## Assessment activity 1.4

Westleigh College media centre has asked for your help. They are preparing a short film that features your local MP and includes interviews with local entrepreneurs.

They want to add a section that says what assistance and economic conditions UK businesses need to be able to flourish and have asked you to read out a five-minute bulletin to this effect. To help, your tutor has listed the following areas as important: support from European, national and local government; economic growth; full employment; low inflation; surplus on the balance of payments; competitiveness; equality.

1. Using these areas as headings, prepare a short statement under each one that outlines the government's role.

2. Read out your prepared statement to your tutor, taking the part of a regional newsreader. **P4**

Grading tip

Outline means you simply have to give a brief summary about what can happen and why, not a detailed description.

2.3 Business environment characteristics

Remember

The business environment is constantly changing. All businesses need to keep up to date with events that affect them, and adapt or change their activities if necessary.

The business environment is the world in which businesses operate. Changes to this, both minor and major, can have a major effect on what they do and how successful they are, as you will see in this section.

Figure 1.4: Business environment characteristics

Markets

All businesses need a market for their products. This does not mean a physical marketplace, but certain groups of people who want to buy their goods or services.

There are several different types of market.

- **The mass market** – refers to products virtually everyone uses, such as washing powder and baked beans.

- **Product markets** – relate to the demand and supply of all types of goods and services, such as food, clothing, travel, cars and houses.

- **Financial markets** – relate to the buying and selling of stocks and shares, currency exchanges and borrowing or investing money.

Businesses undertake market research to identify the market for their product or service. But markets do not stand still. They change over time for several reasons.

- **Fashions and lifestyles** – affect the goods and services people buy. Today we download music rather than buy CDs, which has affected many businesses from music producers to record shops. Vinyl record shops now serve a niche market whereas they once served the mass market.

- **Cheap foreign imports** – can force the closure of some British companies, such as those making shoes, motorbikes and paper.

- **New opportunities to make profits** – attract businesses away from unprofitable activities. This is why many farmers **diversified** into running holiday homes, caravan parks, farm shops and animal attractions after crises such as the Foot and Mouth epidemic of 2001.

- **Technological developments** – affect the product market, such as digital cameras, 3G mobile phones, HD televisions and wireless printers, as fewer people want to buy earlier generation versions.

Did you know?

Some markets are known as **niche markets**. These are small markets for specialist products, such as snowboards or greenhouses. They are often ignored by large businesses, which find it more cost-effective to produce items for the mass market.

Key term

Diversify – to carry out a different business activity, instead of (or as well as) the original one.

What other products have been affected by fashion and lifestyle changes?

Activity: Down on the farm

Check out the Farmer Giles Farmstead website for an example of a farm that has diversified. Then find some in your own area.

Did you know?

- In the 2008/09 recession, a survey by the British Chambers of Commerce found that 12 per cent of businesses planned to cut wages and 58 per cent were introducing a wage freeze, which meant staff received no annual pay rise.

- Even if a sector is declining, some industries within it may be doing well. Many manufacturers cut jobs in 2008/09 but the UK canning industry benefited because people ate in to save money, so demand for canned food and drinks increased. You can find out more about this industry by visiting the Crown Holdings website. Crown Holdings is the owner of Crown Food Europe, the UK's biggest can maker.

Economic trends

As you have seen, economic trends affect business and consumer confidence.

- **Employment** – When employment rates are high, people feel confident about their future and are more likely to spend money. If unemployment is increasing, people are more wary. If they lose their jobs, they have less disposable income and may have to rein in their spending dramatically.

- **Income** – This is affected by employment and by tax rates, as this impacts on disposable income. If income tax rates increase, people have less to spend. If VAT increases, many items are more expensive. Inflation also affects what people can buy because prices are increasing.

- **Growth** – Economic growth (see page 22) means the UK is producing and earning more each year and people have more money to spend. However, growth may not apply to all industries and all businesses. Some may be declining even when others are thriving.

Relative growth and decline by sector

Over time, whole sectors can grow or decline.

- **Absolute growth or decline** means that, on its own, a sector is getting bigger or smaller. If this type of decline happened continuously, one day a sector would disappear.

- **Relative growth or decline** means a sector is doing better or worse compared with other sectors. It may be growing relative to other sectors but still not doing very well. Or it may be declining relative to other sectors, but doing quite well on its own.

Employment by sector

One way to find out which sectors are growing or declining is to check the number of people employed in each one. An increase usually means that a sector is growing, although some factors can be misleading. Industries that employ many part-time staff can seem larger than they really are. Retailers, caterers and care homes, for example, all hire more part-time staff than manufacturers.

Technology can have the opposite effect. Today fewer staff are needed in retail stores, banks, offices and many factories because computers, automated processes and robots do much of the routine work instead, from printing invoices or counting out cash to building fridges or cars. This means fewer employees are required by many large businesses.

Table 1.6: Share of UK employment by sector

Year	Primary (%)	Secondary (%)	Tertiary (%)
1998	2.0	23.0	75.0
2000	1.7	21.8	76.5
2003	1.4	19.9	78.7
2005	1.4	17.0	81.6
2008	1.6	17.6	80.8

Output by sector

All sectors produce output, from the fisherman who catches a small number of fish to the fast food outlet that sells dozens of pizzas every day. Output figures are also affected by automation as well as greater efficiency. In the UK, both farming and manufacturing have become more efficient so output can increase even if employment is falling. The key fact is the share between sectors. This shows that the share of output of the tertiary sector is rising relative to the primary and secondary sectors.

Table 1.7: Share of UK output by sector

Year	Primary (%)	Secondary (%)	Tertiary (%)
1998	4.0	28.7	67.3
2000	3.5	26.5	70
2003	3.1	22.5	74.4
2005	3	22	75
2008	1.2	23	75.8

Both tables 1.6 and 1.7 give us the same result. They show that overall:

- the primary and secondary sectors have declined
- the tertiary sector has increased.

Decline of primary and secondary industries

- **The primary sector** – Although there has been a slight increase in the number of people employed in the primary sector, its *share* of UK output has fallen steadily. However, within the sector itself, output has risen. Areas that have declined include traditional fishing fleets as well as coal mining and quarrying. Areas that have increased have included organic food production, wind farming, fish farming and oil and natural gas extraction.

Activity: What's unemployment now?

By September 2009, the recession had increased unemployment to 2.46 million. Employment fell most in construction and manufacturing, but also in the service sector. It was forecast to reach three million by 2010. Was this forecast correct? Check the National Statistics website to find out more.

Did you know?

Since 1973, productivity in British agriculture has grown by 55 per cent and total output by 25 per cent.

Activity: Primary sector update

Statistics about the primary sector are available at the Defra Economics and Statistics website. If you live in a rural area, use these to find out more about your region. Check, too, if your area is benefiting from the Rural Development Programme, jointly funded by the EU and the government.

• **The secondary sector** – Between 2005 and 2008, employment in manufacturing increased slightly, as did output. Areas that flourished included food and drink, drugs and pharmaceuticals, weapons and ammunitions, energy (electricity, gas and water), electrical and optical equipment, paper and publishing.

Did you know?

• Demand for organic food fell in the recession of 2008/09. As a result, some organic food producers asked for permission to produce food non-organically to stay in business.

• Total production output fell dramatically by 6.5 per cent at the start of 2009. The worst hit were industries involved in transport equipment, basic metals and metal products and machinery and equipment. Later in the year, the decline slowed down.

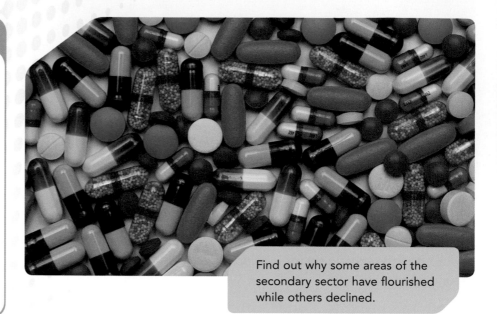

Find out why some areas of the secondary sector have flourished while others declined.

Areas that declined include heavy engineering, textiles, leather and clothing, fur products, knitwear, wood products, iron and steel, machinery and equipment. This sector was hard-hit by the 2008/09 recession. The most vulnerable areas were metal products, engineering and construction. Over 140,000 jobs were lost in the motor industry. BAE Systems, Britain's biggest defence firm, cut 500 jobs. The closure of the Sanyo UK factory in Lowestoft was a defining moment. For the first time since that invention, no factory in Britain made televisions.

Growth of tertiary service industries

Until 2008 the service sector showed continuous growth, particularly in computer services, other business services, wholesale and retail, travel and recreation, security, education, health and social work, hotels and restaurants. The financial services industry and estate agents were also doing well.

Activity: Services sector update

By 2010 the service sector was showing tentative signs of recovery. Search for 'services sector' on the Internet to find out what is happening now.

Then, in 2008 and 2009, employment fell. This was caused by job cuts in the financial services industry following the banking crisis. The falling property market affected jobs in the service sector, especially estate agents, architects, quantity surveyors and solicitors. Travel and leisure firms lost business and as more people cut back on meals out, hotels, bars and restaurants suffered. Accountants, legal firms and marketing firms also had problems. Advertising firms cut staff as their clients reduced spending and Sage, the software giant, also reduced its staff. Some retailers were badly affected but others did well, such as Lidl and Aldi, as people searched for bargains.

Case study

Put your foot in it!

Working in the footwear industry today is a far cry from its origins. From Ugg boots and Birkenstocks to Nike Air Max and Manolo Blahnik, never has the choice been so great – both online and in-store.

It was not always like this. Although footwear has been made in Britain for over 700 years, there have been many changes in that time. In the 19th century, hand-crafted shoes gave way to those made by machines and many workers feared they would lose their jobs, as the machines worked so quickly. Soon, mass-produced shoes were on sale to everyone.

In the mid-20th century, the industry was booming. High street shoe shops such as Clarks and Timpsons were a feature of most towns, selling British shoes. But nothing lasts forever. Branded trainers replaced canvas pumps and sandals, and chain stores started selling cheap imported fashion shoes. By 1990 the old mass market was dead. So, too, were some famous names such as Dolcis and Stylo.

The new wave of shoes ranged from designer names like Jimmy Choo to niche market businesses like Start-rite and Alt-berg. Retail outlets included new concepts like Office and updated ones, like Jones the Bootmaker. A few old names survived, such as Clarks, but other firms changed direction completely. Timpsons went from selling shoes to repairing them to key cutting. The British Shoe Corporation, which resisted change, disappeared.

Shoe buying also moved from specialist shops to include fashion chain stores, department stores, sports shops, online stores and eBay. The UK footwear industry, though, lives on and is now worth over £5 billion. Twenty per cent is exported all around the world. Not the load of old cobblers you might first suppose!

Think about it!

1. Identify the sector to which each of these shoe-related industries belongs:
   a) sheep shearing; b) leather tanning; c) shoe makers; d) shoe repairers; e) shoe shops.
2. What are 'niche market businesses'? Can you think of another example from the shoe industry?
3. How has the market for shoes and people's shopping habits changed over the past 30 years? Discuss your ideas and own buying habits as a group.
4. What are the risks for businesses that resist change?
5. In the 19th and early 20th centuries most regions of Britain had a core industry that provided employment for most of the population, like shoemaking. Find out which one(s) were prominent in your area and what happened to make them close down.

Keep your work for this case study safely. You will find it useful when you do Assessment activity 1.6.

The legal framework

The legal framework relates to all the laws and regulations that are passed by the EU and by the government. Some affect all businesses, such as health and safety. Others only relate to certain types of businesses, such as food handling regulations.

Health and safety, e.g. fire regulations, protective clothing

Environment, e.g. packaging and pollution

Employment, e.g. minimum wage, working hours, discrimination

Company laws, e.g. setting up or running a business

The business organisation and its legal framework

Information, e.g. data protection, copyright

Advertising, e.g. accurate claims, adverts to children

Planning, e.g. building or altering premises

Competition, e.g. no price fixing or collusion

Consumer protection, e.g. sale of goods, food and product safety

Figure 1.5: The business organisation and its legal framework

Businesses need to know which laws affect them and keep up to date with any changes. Complying with legislation increases costs for the business and can divert attention away from the main business activity. The problem for the government is finding the right balance between protecting the interests of workers, consumers and others affected by the business while not making it harder for businesses to operate profitably and successfully.

Activity: Business regulations

Find out which regulations affect different types of business at the Business Link website. Click on 'My Business' then 'Regulations and Compliance'. Then create a regulations checklist for the business idea of your choice by completing a short questionnaire. The result is a list of all the regulations that would affect you. Compare your list with examples produced by other members of your class for other business ideas.

Discussion point

Pink Ladies was set up by women to provide safe transport for other women, but was taken to court by Warrington Council for discriminating against men. The business set up as a private club to avoid operating as a licensed private hire firm when it would have to pick up men. In July, the directors were fined by Warrington Magistrates' Court for breaking the law, but vowed to fight on. Was the council right to take this action? Debate the issue as a class. Then search for 'Pink Ladies' on the Internet to see if it still survives or not.

Assessment activity 1.5

Maria Bencini is 30, lives in Malta and speaks fluent English. She runs a thriving restaurant and three years ago she married an Englishman, Tom. Tom's parents are not well so he wants to return to the UK. His family live in your region, but Maria will need tempting to move there.

Working in groups, carry out the first three tasks.

1. Use the UKTI website to find out six reasons why the UK is a good place in which to do business.

2. Investigate the characteristics of the business environment of your own area. This means identifying the range and types of businesses that operate there, the type of markets they serve, important trends in those markets and which sectors or industries are growing and declining.

3. Carry out a regulations checklist on the Business Link website to identify examples of the laws or regulations Maria must comply with as a restaurant owner. Provide your own answers to supplementary questions you will be asked by the website, such as whether the business will play music or provide outside seating areas.

4. On your own prepare a convincing argument why Maria should relocate to your region, including an explanation of the characteristics of your local business environment. Then email her. You can either include your arguments in your email or send them as a separate attachment. **P5**

Present your ideas to your group. You can then vote on which group would be most likely to persuade Maria to leave Malta.

Just checking

1. How do businesses benefit from UK membership of the EU?
2. What are the government's economic objectives?
3. How can the government try to stimulate consumer demand?
4. Why does the government try to keep inflation low?
5. What factors cause the markets for goods and services to change?
6. Which sectors are growing and which are declining in the UK?
7. What is meant by the 'legal framework' in which businesses operate?

BTEC Assessment activity 1.6

1. Working in groups, contribute to a class display about your region. Show how it has changed over the last 100 years. Include examples from all three sectors (primary, secondary and tertiary). Assess if they reflect the changes that were taking place nationally in the UK or not. Start by using the information you have already obtained on industries in your area (see pages 17 and 20). Then talk to relatives and family friends about how the region has changed since they were young. Visit your community library for more information. Include a short section that summarises any effects of the 2008/09 recession on your area.

2. On your own, compare areas of growth or decline for each sector. Decide why these changes have occurred and which local trends reflected national ones and which trends did not. Decide which of your findings are the most important and summarise these in a short report on your region. **M2**

3. On page 33, you learned about the shoe industry. All the following shoe companies responded differently to the threats they faced from operating in a changing market: a) Start-rite; b) Clarks; c) Timpsons; d) Jones the Bootmaker. Read about their history on their websites.

4. Use your information to prepare an information sheet on the 'The importance of responding to change in the business world'. Do this by choosing **one** of the companies listed in Question 3 and evaluate how well it has responded to changes in its business environment by taking account of how successful it is today. Present your findings to your tutor and provide a copy of your information sheet. **D1**

Grading tip

Evaluate means obtaining and reviewing information based on the facts, then explaining what you have found out, making sure that you provide the evidence to support your conclusions.

 edexcel

Assignment tips

- Ask yourself the following questions when you are investigating your business.

  - What factors affected it?

  - How did it respond?

  - Could it have done anything else?

  - What has been the result and how successful is the business now?

- Always check the 'About Us' section of a business website for useful information. The link may be shown at the bottom of the screen, not in a main menu, especially on a retail site.

- Create a separate file for any research you carry out, such as investigating industries in your area or finding out how a business responded to changes in its business environment. Label each file clearly and put all your information in the right file as you go. That way you will not lose anything important or waste time trying to find information you need.

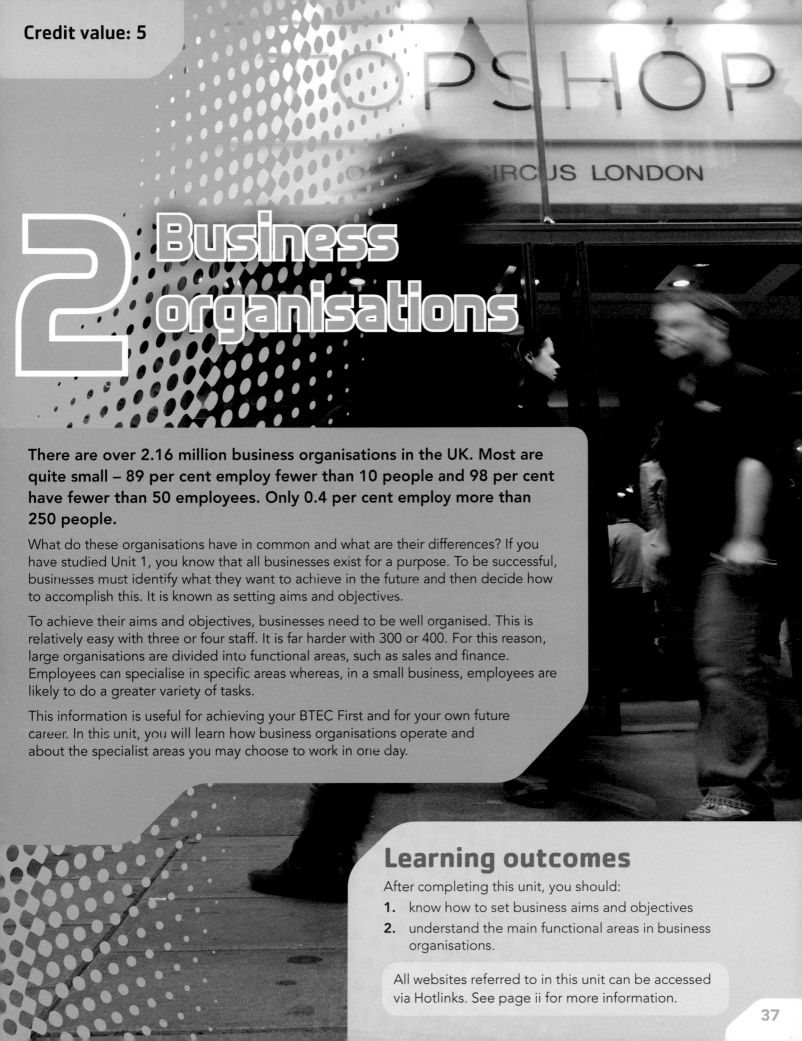

2 Business organisations

There are over 2.16 million business organisations in the UK. Most are quite small – 89 per cent employ fewer than 10 people and 98 per cent have fewer than 50 employees. Only 0.4 per cent employ more than 250 people.

What do these organisations have in common and what are their differences? If you have studied Unit 1, you know that all businesses exist for a purpose. To be successful, businesses must identify what they want to achieve in the future and then decide how to accomplish this. It is known as setting aims and objectives.

To achieve their aims and objectives, businesses need to be well organised. This is relatively easy with three or four staff. It is far harder with 300 or 400. For this reason, large organisations are divided into functional areas, such as sales and finance. Employees can specialise in specific areas whereas, in a small business, employees are likely to do a greater variety of tasks.

This information is useful for achieving your BTEC First and for your own future career. In this unit, you will learn how business organisations operate and about the specialist areas you may choose to work in one day.

Learning outcomes

After completing this unit, you should:

1. know how to set business aims and objectives
2. understand the main functional areas in business organisations.

All websites referred to in this unit can be accessed via Hotlinks. See page ii for more information.

Assessment and grading criteria

This table shows you what you must do in order to achieve a pass, merit or distinction grade, and where you can find activities in this book to help you.

To achieve a **pass**, the evidence must show that the learner is able to:	To achieve a **merit**, the evidence must show that, in addition to the pass criteria, the learner is able to:	To achieve a **distinction**, the evidence must show that, in addition to the pass and merit criteria, the learner is able to:
P1 define aims and objectives **See Assessment activity 2.1, page 46**	**M1** compare the aims and objectives of different businesses **See Assessment activity 2.1, page 46**	**D1** assess whether a selected organisation meets its aims and objectives **See Assessment activity 2.1, page 46**
P2 describe the purpose for the business in setting aims and objectives **See Assessment activity 2.1, page 46**		
P3 write aims and objectives for a selected business **See Assessment activity 2.1, page 46**		
P4 describe the functional areas in two contrasting business organisations **See Assessment activity 2.2, page 64**	**M2** compare the interaction of functional areas and how they relate to each other in two selected businesses to support the business objectives **See Assessment activity 2.2, page 64**	
P5 explain how these functional areas link in one of these organisations **See Assessment activity 2.2, page 64**		

How you will be assessed

To achieve Unit 2, you will investigate different businesses to find out their aims and objectives, as well as their functional areas. You will prepare and present this information either verbally or in writing. You could also use a mixture of both methods. Your tutor will give you guidance on appropriate businesses to choose and you will be able to practise with the assessment activities in this book.

Ibrahim

When I began this unit, I was sure I wanted to start my own business or work in a small business, like my brother. I thought it would be better. There would be different jobs to do every day and I'd have more freedom. Now I'm not so sure!

My brother works really long hours and gets stressed if sales fall. He worries the business won't survive. After I'd done part of this unit, we talked about aims and objectives, and what firms do when they can't achieve them. I think I made some helpful suggestions. I also liked finding evidence to prove my chosen business had met its aims and objectives – it was a bit like doing detective work!

I enjoy selling in my part-time job, so it was interesting to learn about sales and marketing in large companies. I'd never heard of online marketing but really like the idea. Now I know there are agencies that specialise in this, and I've decided to find out more about them.

Over to you!

- Have you thought about what type of job you would like to do in business?
- Do you think it is better to stay open minded at this stage of your course?

Share your experiences

1. In groups, compare the experiences you have had working for different organisations, either on work experience or in a part-time job.

2. What was the largest organisation anyone worked for? How was it organised?

3. What was the smallest organisation? What job roles were there?

4. How big is your centre in comparison to these? What are its aims and objectives? Ask your tutor.

1. Know how to set business aims and objectives

1.1 Mission statements

Many large organisations have a **mission statement** that briefly identifies the main purpose of the business and how it sees itself. Some businesses have a **vision statement**. Others have both a mission statement and a vision statement.

The wording may be different depending upon the sector and its ownership.

- **Privately owned businesses** focus on customers, employees, the cost of their products or how they give value for money. Tesco's mission statement is: 'We create value for customers to earn their lifetime loyalty.'

- **Publicly owned organisations** may mention the service they provide, the work they do and include statements about quality, efficiency and customer service. The Department for Transport's mission statement is: 'Working to deliver a transport system which balances the needs of the economy, the environment and society.'

- **Not-for-profit and voluntary organisations** focus on the services they provide, the causes they support or their aims in helping those in need. The mission of the British Red Cross is as follows.

> 'The British Red Cross helps people in crisis, whoever and wherever they are. We are part of a global voluntary network, responding to conflicts, natural disasters and individual emergencies. We enable vulnerable people in the UK and abroad to prepare for and withstand emergencies in their own communities. And when the crisis is over, we help them to recover and move on with their lives.'

Many mission statements are quite short. Others are longer. They include the aims and objectives of the business, in other words, what the business is going to do and how it is going to achieve the mission.

What does the British Red Cross aim to do?

Activity: Mission statements

You can read the mission statements of dozens of companies on the sampleshelp website.

Check the mission statement of Adidas. It includes information about the aims of the business over the long and medium term.

1.2 Business aims

All businesses have **aims** they want to achieve. These are long-term plans, probably over the next three to five years. Businesses will probably want to focus on one or more of the following areas:

- **Profit and profit maximisation** – privately owned businesses aim to make a profit, as do those in public ownership (see Unit 1, page 4). Most aim to increase profits every year. Some want to achieve profit maximisation, which means making as much profit as possible.

- **Survival** – when trading is difficult, some businesses may make little or no profit, and focus on trying to stay in business until times improve.

- **Break-even** – one method of surviving is to focus on breaking even over a certain period. This means making enough money to cover the total costs involved in producing and selling the goods or services, and running the business. Although there is no profit, no money is lost. You will learn about break-even in Unit 3 (page 76).

- **Growth** – many businesses want to sell more every year and focus on expanding the business. They may plan to open more branches, start trading abroad or buy out a competitor.

Figure 2.1: The focus of business aims and objectives

Key terms

Aims – the longer-term visions or goals of the business.

Profit maximisation – making as much profit as possible.

Break-even – covering the costs of making the product and running the business, but no more.

Market share – the share of customers that buy from a certain supplier, or purchase a specific product or service.

- **Market share** – many companies aim to increase their market share each year by winning customers away from their rivals.

- **Service provision** – relates to offering a new service or improving current services to attract more customers. For example, some supermarkets enable customers to shop online and have groceries delivered at the time of their choice.

- **Develop their relationship with other businesses** – may involve joint initiatives to help achieve other aims.

Remember

Aims are set to provide a focus for the business. The aims and objectives always link to the main purpose of the organisation.

Key term

Objectives – specific, measurable targets to help achieve an aim.

Activity: Nectar programme

Loyalty Management UK Limited is the company behind the Nectar programme. Visit the Nectar website to find out more.

How many other businesses does this company work with? Can you tell why?

Remember

Objectives are **targets** that managers and their staff must achieve. They will vary, depending upon the work done in each department of the business, but all will contribute to achieving the aims of the business.

Activity: Be SMART

Decide on one personal aim for this year, for example, saving more or getting fitter. Then write two SMART objectives to help you achieve your aim. Compare your ideas with others in your group.

PLTS

As a self-manager, what checks would you carry out to ensure you keep on track to achieve your objectives?

1.3 Business objectives

Objectives are more specific than aims. They are set over the short to medium term. Objectives are necessary because aims, in themselves, are too general and may be quite overwhelming. Your aim may be to go to university, run your own business or be an accountant one day. However, unless you are very focused, it is difficult to keep this in mind all the time. It is far more sensible – and achievable – to break down this major ambition into a series of smaller steps. This is the role of objectives.

SMART objectives

An obvious objective on your current career path is to achieve your BTEC First. Precise, measurable targets will help you do this. You will have to concentrate on doing your best as you achieve one unit at a time. You should set these goals using SMART objectives.

- **Specific** – you need a clear statement about what you will do. Usually, it is quantified, which means it has a number in it. For example: 'Complete Unit 2 in eight weeks.'

- **Measurable** – achievement can be checked. Recording your progress and keeping a record of your completed assessments will enable you to measure your achievements.

- **Achievable** – you can attain your target if you work hard. You can do really well if you stretch yourself.

- **Realistic** – your target should be sensible so that you stand a chance of achieving it. For example, it would be unrealistic to aim to complete Unit 2 in a week.

- **Time-constrained** – every objective should include a date for achievement or review. This acts as a warning, as well as a spur, if you are falling behind.

You either achieve a SMART objective or need a good reason for not doing so. This type of objective is useful for learners in schools and colleges. It is also important for managers and employees in business.

I know which direction to take, but does anyone know how far it is?

What is the difference between aims and objectives?

1.4 Failing to meet aims and objectives

It is not always possible to meet aims and objectives. Businesses will want to know why they have failed and then take action to correct this as soon as possible.

A business may not meet its aims and objectives for several reasons. Many of them relate to the type of external changes mentioned in Unit 1. Businesses often try to forecast these changes in advance by doing a PEST analysis.

- **Political** – a change of laws or regulations may affect the business, such as the introduction of drink driving laws or the smoking ban, which adversely affected the pub trade in Britain.

- **Economic** – the economy may go into recession, as it did in 2008/09. As a result, consumer demand for the goods and services of many businesses fell dramatically.

- **Social** – people's buying habits and lifestyles might change. The demand for carpets fell when wooden floors became popular.

- **Technological** – the launch of a new, technologically superior product or service by a competitor can have a serious effect.

1.5 Consequences

Unfortunately, it is impossible to foresee every possible event that can occur, such as a major customer or supplier going out of business or an unexpected fall in demand that sharply reduces forecast sales income.

Did you know?

- Successful businesses regularly monitor their achievement of aims and objectives. They also research changes in their markets, so that unplanned events rarely take them by surprise. Sometimes, this may force them to change their aims.

- TomTom, the Sat Nav manufacturer, saw sales fall and losses mount when mobile phones started having Sat Nav and more new cars were launched with inbuilt Sat Nav.

- Business failures in Britain were forecast to peak at 32,400 in 2010 as a result of the 2008/09 recession. A key survival strategy is to focus on **cash flow**. You will learn about this in Unit 3 (page 83).

Discussion point

In 2009, AEG Live – the company behind Michael Jackson's planned concerts at the O2 arena – was faced with a major problem when the star died. They had to refund about £51 million to ticket holders. They reportedly lost about £300 million because of the cancelled shows.

Many businesses can have serious problems if a major customer or key supplier goes out of business. In the case of AEG Live, their major supplier was a famous singer who died, but the problem was similar.

In groups, identify the possible outcomes of this type of problem. Discuss ways in which firms can prevent or minimise the consequences. Then compare your ideas.

AEG Live had to refund ticket holders when Michael Jackson died. What are the possible consequences of such an incident?

Remember

Businesses that do not meet their aims and objectives must analyse why and take corrective action. Then they must revise their aims and objectives.

Key terms

Diversify – to broaden the range of products made or activities undertaken.

Dividend – the reward paid to shareholders for investing in the business, similar to interest on a bank account.

If a business suspects that it will not achieve its aims and objectives, it must take immediate action. Its choices include:

- **reducing costs**, often by closing some branches, freezing or cutting salaries or laying off staff
- **reducing prices** to boost sales, although giving discounts will lower overall profits
- **diversifying** into new products or services, or doing the opposite, focusing just on the **core business activity** (all major supermarkets promoted or extended their 'basic' brands to improve sales during the 2008/09 recession)
- **scrapping** expansion plans
- **finding new or better ways** of meeting customer needs
- **cutting the dividend** paid to shareholders
- **revising** the current aims and objectives to ensure they are realistic in the current business climate.

If nothing works and the business runs out of money, it will have to stop trading. A sole trader will go **bankrupt**. For a company, the term used is **insolvent**.

Case study: Towards the final countdown?

In a recession, one firm's solution can create another firm's nightmare. When many organisations reduced advertising spending to cut their costs, the knock-on effect caused major problems for local newspapers, and also for broadcasters like ITV. Both newspapers and broadcasters depend upon advertising for much of their revenue (the income received by a business from sales and other sources).

ITV already had to cope with competition for advertising from a larger number of competitors, as a result of multi-channel TV and the Internet. The recession saw its advertising revenues fall by 12 per cent in the first six months of 2009 to £909 million.

In response, ITV's executive chairman, Michael Grade, abandoned the 2012 revenue targets. He said the company was focusing on reducing costs and concentrating on its core business as a producer/broadcaster. It intended to boost online revenues at itv.com as well as overseas programme sales, and sell off non-core operations such as the website Friends Reunited. About 600 jobs were cut. Programme budgets were also cut but not on very successful shows, like *The X Factor*.

1. Why did Michael Grade decide to abandon ITV's existing revenue targets for 2012?

2. As a class, decide what the expression 'core business' means.

3. In 2005, ITV bought the Friends Reunited website for £175 million and lost £150 million when they sold it in 2009. Suggest reasons why its value fell so much.

4. What actions was the company taking to save money? Check recent press reports online to see what else ITV has done and how successful it has been.

5. Critics say the problems are not because of the recession, but because of unpopular programmes. They argue ITV is past its sell-by date in a digital age. Do you agree? Discuss this issue as a class and take a vote.

1.6 Aims and objectives in different sectors

Aims and objectives vary between organisations in different sectors. These businesses have different purposes.

- **Private sector businesses** provide goods and/or services, and must make a profit to survive. They can only break even or make a loss for a very short time, or they will have to close.

- **Public sector businesses** are owned by the state. Many provide essential services free of charge or below cost price, such as the NHS. Remember that the government also owns businesses that aim to be profitable, like the Royal Mail.

- **Voluntary sector organisations** raise money that is used to support a particular cause. They aim to make a surplus, after the costs of the business have been deducted, and reinvest this into the business.

These purposes affect their aims and objectives, as you can see in Table 2.1.

Did you know?

- The ability of many public sector organisations to meet their targets is often highlighted in performance tables, such as school league tables. This is because they are financed by public money, raised by taxation.

- You can tell the ownership of a business from its website suffix: **.co.uk** and **.com** are for the private sector, **.gov** for the public sector and **.org** for the voluntary sector.

Table 2.1: Business purposes and their aims and objectives

	Private sector	Government-owned businesses	Public sector	Not-for-profit/ Voluntary sector
Business examples	Manufacturers, retailers, banks, architects, builders, private hospitals	BBC, Met Office, Royal Mint, Royal Mail	Government departments, local councils, NHS hospitals, state schools	Community groups, charities, for example, Help the Aged Social enterprises, for example, *Big Issue*
Purpose	To provide goods and/or services To make a profit		To provide a quality service to the community	To provide a free service to the needy To promote a particular cause
Examples of aims	Maximise profits by increasing sales and reducing costs Increase market share Expand the business		Improve service provision Operate within budget, that is, break even	Increase surplus Increase range of services
Examples of objectives	Increase sales Increase number of customers Reduce costs Improve product quality		Meet customer targets, for example, patient waiting times Keep costs low	Increase revenue from donations Reduce costs

Just checking

1. Describe six possible business aims.
2. What factors affect the type of aims businesses have?
3. Explain the role of objectives in supporting business aims.
4. What does 'SMART' stand for?
5. Convert 'sell more' into a SMART objective.
6. For a business, what could be the consequences of failing to achieve its aims and objectives? What types of action could it take?

Assessment activity 2.1

Two years ago, your friend's parents opened a sandwich shop near a local sixth form college. Their business has done quite well, but recently another shop opened in competition. A travelling snack van has also started parking near the college. As a result, trade has fallen.

Your friend thinks there is a lot of potential for his parents' business if they appealed to a wider market, such as firms on the nearby industrial area. He looked at other types of food they could offer to entice learners away from the competition. He reckons his parents have no focus and the best way to improve the business would be to set some aims and objectives.

1. Help your friend by preparing an explanation about aims and objectives for his parents that describes what these are. You need to relate these to different sectors to show how they are appropriate for all types of businesses, regardless of their size, activities or ownership. **P1**

2. Add a second section that identifies the purpose or reason for setting aims and objectives. This should include an explanation of the benefits for the business owners, particularly if they set SMART objectives. **P2**

3. Carefully consider aims that would be appropriate for the sandwich shop. Choose two or three, then write appropriate objectives for each one. **P3**

   Present your ideas to the rest of the class. When each person has completed their presentation, take a vote on which aims and objectives would be the best to adopt. Your presentation materials and your tutor's observation record will provide evidence that you have successfully carried out these tasks.

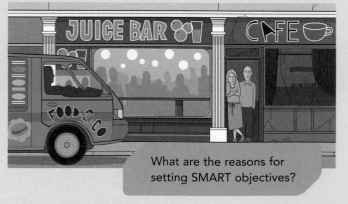

What are the reasons for setting SMART objectives?

4. a) As a class, identify three different organisations from each sector: private, public and not-for-profit/voluntary. Try to choose organisations that have a completely different purpose as well as different types of ownership. Then divide into small groups to investigate the aims and objectives of each one on their websites. Summarise these on flip chart paper and pin them up around the room.

   b) On your own, compare these aims and objectives by identifying the differences and similarities. Then see how they relate to their sector, the size of the business, the purpose of the business and its ownership. Write a summary of what you have found. **M1**

5. a) Choose one organisation and check its performance over the last 12 months. This could be one of the businesses you investigated in Task 4 or one of your own choice. It should be large enough so that you can find information about its aims and objectives on the website (often in the company report) as well as its current performance. You will also find press reports with useful information online if you use a good search engine like Google. Sometimes finding what you need may take a bit of detective work!

   b) Use the information you found to assess the extent to which the business is meeting its aims and objectives. Identify any problems it is experiencing and the action it is taking to try to remedy these. Write your findings in a report for your tutor headed 'Meeting aims and objectives at (*followed by the name of your chosen business*)'. **D1**

Keep your work safely as you may be able to use this same organisation for Assessment activity 2.2 (see page 64).

Grading tip

Making an assessment means making a judgement by looking at the evidence for and against something.

2. Understand the main functional areas in business organisations

All businesses must carry out a number of functions to ensure the business runs smoothly. These functions also link to the aims and objectives of the business and what it wants to achieve. In a small business, all these jobs may be done by a few people. In a large organisation, people specialise in different tasks.

2.1 Functional areas in business

In a large organisation, the functional areas in which people work are divided into different departments. Each carries out the tasks that relate to its own area.

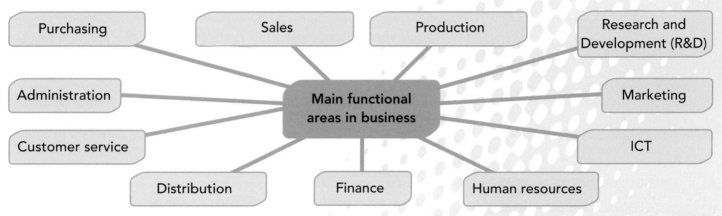

Figure 2.2: Main functional areas in business

The purpose of functional areas

The purpose of functional areas is to ensure that the vital business activities are carried out promptly and efficiently. This is essential if the business is to achieve its aims and objectives. In addition, specific areas will support certain types of aims and objectives.

- Sales and marketing will be involved in achieving targets linked to **developing new markets** or increasing sales.

- R&D as well as production will be involved in **developing new products**. Some ideas and improvements may come from customer feedback received by sales or customer services, or from market research done by marketing.

- ICT will be responsible for the organisation's internal and external electronic communications including email, the organisation's website and the **intranet**. Good communications are vital so that **functional areas can work together effectively**.

- Finance will be expected to monitor and support aims and objectives linked to **keeping costs low** or reducing them, in order to improve or maximise profitability.

Remember

All large organisations have functional areas, but they vary depending upon the work carried out.

Key term

Intranet – a private area on the network where information can be accessed only by authorised users.

The sales function

Sales is a vital function in every business. Most businesses have sales targets as part of their aims and objectives. Meeting these targets is the responsibility of the sales staff or sales team.

The job of the sales staff varies depending upon the industry. Shops selling basic products, such as sweets or magazines, do not need to do much. Most customers just choose the goods they want, pay and leave.

Customers expect more assistance if they are buying a complex or expensive item, such as a laptop computer or a car. Stores that sell these products need knowledgeable sales staff, who are able to present their products and link them to the customer's specific needs.

Business buyers expect a high-quality service as well as in-depth advice and information. They may be buying highly complex and expensive industrial equipment, and may need to negotiate special finance arrangements – particularly if they are overseas buyers. Business buyers will also expect discounts for bulk purchases. Sales representatives often travel to meet potential customers, as well as routinely visit existing customers.

Employing a skilled sales force is expensive, especially if they are paid bonuses or commission. However, there are many benefits. An effective salesperson can convert many enquiries into firm sales and build strong links with customers to encourage repeat business.

All sales staff should know there are a number of laws that protect customers, and understand which type of sales activities are legal and which are not. Find out more about selling in Option Unit 10 and about consumer rights in Option Unit 13.

Sales functions

- organising sales promotions
- responding to customer enquiries
- selling the product or service to customers, either over the telephone or face to face
- preparing quotations or estimates for customers
- negotiating discounts or financial terms for business customers
- providing technical advice
- keeping customer records up to date.

The production function

Production refers to the manufacture or assembly of goods. Production staff must ensure that goods are produced on time and are of the right quality. Today, quality is 'built in' at every stage of the process, starting with the raw materials.

Stocks of raw materials are stored near to production. Storage can be expensive, particularly if a manufacturer uses a large number of parts,

Why do shops selling complex items need knowledgeable sales staff?

Remember

There are strong links between sales and marketing. In many businesses, this may be a joint department. Sales can pass on important customer feedback to help marketing colleagues.

Discussion point

Many firms employ sales representatives to visit customers, such as hairdressing suppliers GHD, Matrix and Paul Mitchell, who call on salons regularly. Identify the benefits and drawbacks of this method of selling, both for the supplier and the customer.

such as a car producer. Therefore, many operate a **just-in-time** (JIT) system. This involves having an agreement with specific suppliers to provide small quantities, quickly and when they are needed. This benefits both parties. The suppliers know that they have a regular buyer, and the manufacturer no longer needs to store large quantities of goods or worry about having sufficient stocks on the premises all the time.

Today, many production processes are automated. Machines or robots do all the routine or dangerous jobs. Many products are made in a continuous process by machines, from cling film to meat pies. Operators check that the 'line' is functioning correctly by checking consoles and computer screens, as well as by watching the work as it progresses. Some industries use Computer Integrated Manufacturing (CIM), where the control of the process is done by computer.

When a process cannot be automated, teams of operators may work together and take responsibility for a sequence of operations. This makes the job more interesting. It is easier to ensure high quality and to introduce changes quickly. This method is used by many car manufacturers who often want to vary certain models.

The production function also includes all the following aspects.

- **Production planning** involves deciding what will be made, when, and which machines and operators will be used. A realistic timescale must be predicted, bearing in mind other jobs in progress.

- **Production control** means constantly checking progress, to ensure production plans are met, and taking remedial action if problems occur. This could be because of machinery breakdown, substandard raw materials or labour shortages.

- **Machine utilisation control** aims to minimise problems by keeping all equipment and machinery in good working order. It involves checking to ensure none is overloaded or overused, without being routinely checked and maintained. If a machine malfunctions, it may produce damaged goods. If it breaks down, production will cease. Many organisations have a maintenance plan showing when machines will be out of operation for inspection and servicing. These dates are then taken into consideration when production plans are made.

- **Staff utilisation control** concentrates on making sure all staff are working effectively and efficiently, and are concentrating their efforts on key production areas and targets. This is very important in industries that are labour-intensive and use more people than machines, such as assembling circuit boards or sewing jeans.

- **Final quality checks** ensure the product is of the correct standard. This can be done by examining each item by hand, or passing each one through a machine, checking that the size and tolerance is correct. Alternatively, items may be selected for inspection on a random sampling basis. This is the case when producing a large number of identical items.

Did you know?

- Freshcook makes ready meals for Marks & Spencer. M&S sets down precise standards for all its suppliers. Freshcook has to balance the twin requirements of both quality and productivity to keep M&S satisfied.

- The term 'line' refers to the production line. Keeping the production line moving is so vital that if it stops, warning lights may flash or sirens may sound.

During final quality checks, items may be selected on a random sampling basis. Can you explain why?

Activity: Investigate production

In groups, investigate manufacturing processes on YouTube. Find clips that show automated production, CIM, **lean production** and continuous production. Try to find interesting products, such as Porsche cars or the Nintendo Wii. Identify the best one(s) you think everyone should watch.

Functional skills

Practise your speaking skills. Justify your choice to your group and explain your reasons as concisely and persuasively as you can.

Key terms

Lean production – a method of manufacturing aiming for minimum waste, high-quality products and continuous improvement. It originated at the Toyota car plant in Japan.

Quotation – in business, a quotation states the price a job would cost. It is issued by a potential supplier. It is usually itemised and more precise than an estimate.

Did you know?

The difference between the cost of an item and its selling price is the **gross margin**.

Production also prepares items for dispatch. This may involve simply packing the finished items and transporting them to the dispatch section. It may also involve various finishing processes. For example, paper is produced in huge rolls. These may be transported intact but usually the paper is cut, boxed and packaged.

Production functions

- storing and checking raw material stocks
- planning production schedules to maximise equipment use
- producing or assembling the finished product
- checking the quality of the product throughout the production process
- checking production is on schedule, and resolving delays or problems
- checking, packing and storing the final products before distribution
- scheduling routine machinery inspections and maintenance
- carrying out repairs to machinery and equipment as required.

The purchasing function

All businesses need to buy a wide variety of items on a routine basis.

In a large organisation, buying consumable items like paper is undertaken by specialist buyers. Bulk purchasing normally saves money, therefore this is usually cheaper than each department buying its own paper. Purchasing staff may take out contracts with regular suppliers and ensure that the terms of the contract are met in relation to delivery, cost, quantity and quality. Major purchasing decisions, such as a new building or computer system, are only made after a thorough and rigorous process. It involves obtaining and comparing several **quotations** and requires the approval of the senior managers or directors.

Purchasing staff are responsible for ensuring that the company pays a competitive price for its supplies. This is not necessarily the cheapest price but takes account of other factors, such as the reliability of the supplier, the quality required and the delivery date.

Retail buyers must also take account of customer needs, alternative sources of supply, current fashions and trends, as well as the proposed selling price to the customer. Many businesses both purchase and pay for goods online. This speeds up the buying process and reduces the need to hold large stocks on the premises.

Purchasing functions

- ordering raw materials, stock and consumable items from suppliers
- solving supply problems, for example, changing supplier
- evaluating alternative sources of supply in relation to price, reliability, quality, payment terms, terms of delivery, and so on.

- agreeing stock levels with managers and stock controllers, and reordering as necessary

- finding suppliers to meet new requirements or changes in demand

- monitoring new sources to achieve cost savings or other benefits

- dealing with problems on delivery, for example, quality or quantity

- maintaining good relationships with suppliers

- (in a retail business) deciding the best lines to stock for the new season, bearing in mind current sales levels and future trends.

Activity: Fashion shops

Top fashion stores such as Topshop or Zara aim to turn over stock quickly in order to take advantage of new fashion trends, but buyers do not always get it right. As a group, identify the implications for a retailer if stock fails to sell. What actions can the retailer take?

Fashion shops take advantage of new trends to turn over stock quickly, but what if stock does not sell?

The administration function

All businesses need administrators to carry out a variety of support activities in order to help business operations run smoothly. Routine administrative tasks include opening the post, preparing documents and sending emails. Others require more creativity and flexibility, such as arranging travel or important events. Senior administrators may also monitor budgets and interview new staff for their departments.

Most administrators also deal with external customers, who judge the business on the service they receive. Poor or sloppy administration can be disastrous for a company's image and reputation. A lost order, badly typed letter, important message not passed on or wrong date scheduled for a meeting can cause problems and the company may lose customers. Efficient administration means that everything runs smoothly and managers can concentrate on the task of running the business.

In a small organisation, an administrator is often a 'jack-of-all-trades' who can turn a hand to anything, from checking and paying invoices to keeping the firm's website up to date. In a larger firm, administration may be carried out in every department, rather than just one. A sales administrator may make overseas travel arrangements whereas an administrator in human resources would arrange job interviews. You will learn more about administration if you study Option Unit 6.

Did you know?

In many organisations, the purchasing and administration functions are done within other departments. They are not separate departments on their own.

Activity: Interview

Arrange to interview an administrator at your centre to find out about their job.

PLTS

Develop your independent enquirer skills. Plan questions that will enable you to learn most about the job.

Did you know?

Technicians, engineers and consultants often undertake customer service functions when specialist knowledge is required.

Activity: Rolls-Royce

Rolls-Royce has four business areas – civil aerospace, defence aerospace, marine and energy – and customises its customer services for each area. Divide into four groups, each researching one area. Find out about the products and the range of services provided to customers at the Rolls-Royce website.

Share your findings with the rest of the class.

Administration functions

- distributing and dispatching post
- organising, storing and retrieving paper and electronic records
- organising meetings and preparing meetings documents
- responding to customer enquiries and dealing with callers
- preparing documents using word processing, spreadsheet and presentation packages, such as PowerPoint®
- researching information
- sending and receiving messages by telephone, fax and email
- making arrangements for visitors
- making travel arrangements
- purchasing office stationery and equipment supplies
- making arrangements for events, such as interviews or conferences.

The customer service function

All businesses must look after customers who have an enquiry, concern or complaint. Today, customer expectations are high. When people contact a business they expect a prompt, polite and knowledgeable response. For this reason, many businesses have customer service staff who handle enquiries and complaints positively and professionally. Organisations that manufacture and sell complex industrial products usually employ technical specialists to give detailed advice and information to customers. The company BAE Systems, for example, sells planes like the Eurofighter and Hawk jets. Replying to the queries of their customers requires specialist knowledge.

Customer service staff also deal with complaints and problems. To ensure customer complaints are dealt with quickly and consistently, most businesses have a special procedure. In some cases, action is needed to ensure the problem does not occur again. Customer service staff must also be aware of the customers' legal rights. You can learn more about customer relations in Unit 11 and about consumer rights in Unit 13.

Customer service functions

- answering customer enquiries about products and services
- providing specialist information to meet the needs of customers
- solving customer problems
- providing after-sales service, including replacing damaged goods, arranging for repairs or for spare parts to be obtained and fitted
- dealing with customer complaints according to company procedures
- analysing records of customer complaints to resolve problem areas
- using feedback from customers to improve customer service.

The distribution function

Distribution means ensuring that goods are delivered to the right place, on time and in the right condition. Some companies, such as Amazon and John Lewis, deliver direct to the customer, particularly when goods are bought online. Other businesses hold stocks in giant regional warehouses for delivery to stores around the area. Superstores may use special vehicles that can also carry chilled or frozen items. Other businesses have to move more difficult loads or hazardous substances, such as large engineering parts, cars or chemicals.

Why is planning vehicle routes important?

Distribution involves more than just arranging for goods to be collected. For distribution to be cost-effective, costs must be kept as low as possible. This means, for example:

- planning vehicle routes to avoid back-tracking – this keeps fuel costs down and saves time.

- making sure vehicles do not return empty, which is only possible if goods are both delivered and collected. Vehicles that only deliver goods operate on a local basis to minimise 'empty journey' time.

Working out the routes of many vehicles, with different loads – some urgent and some not – can be very complicated. Computer programmes are used by staff skilled in **logistics** to work out the best routes.

Many organisations **outsource** both storage and distribution to external contractors. This means paying a specialist firm to do the work. This is often cheaper than employing experts in the business.

Distribution functions

- ensuring all goods are appropriately stored, packed and labelled before dispatch

- checking vehicle loads are safe and secure

- ensuring goods are dispatched at the right time

- checking that all deliveries match orders precisely and notifying sales if there is a discrepancy

- completing the delivery documents

- planning and scheduling vehicle routes

- notifying staff of delivery schedules so they can inform customers

- dealing with distribution problems, for example, vehicle breakdown.

Key terms

Logistics – planning and controlling the movement of goods.

Outsource – to hire an outside firm to do a specific job, such as distribution, security, payroll, cleaning, marketing or PR (public relations).

 Did you know?

The term **supply chain** is sometimes used to describe each stage of the process from the goods leaving a factory to their arrival in a store.

 Activity: Potter Group

Investigate a national warehouse, distribution and logistics business online. Visit the Potter Group website to find out more.

The finance function

Most entrepreneurs consider this the most important function in the business. All businesses need a regular stream of income to pay the bills. Finance staff record all the money earned and spent.

Large businesses often employ different types of financial experts.

- **Management accountants** monitor departmental budgets and current income from sales, prepare cash flow forecasts and specialise in analysing day-to-day financial information.

- **Financial accountants** prepare the **statutory accounts**. These relate to the balance sheet and profit and loss account that all companies must produce each year for tax purposes. Most produce a cash flow statement as well. You will learn more about cash flow in Unit 3.

- **Credit controllers** monitor overdue payments and take action to recover bad debts. You will find out about credit control in Unit 3.

Finance staff support the accountants by keeping financial records, chasing up late payments and paying for items purchased. All businesses use computer accounting packages to record financial transactions and prepare their accounts, as well as spreadsheets to analyse financial data. Some finance departments prepare the payroll and pay staff salaries, but other businesses outsource this to a specialist bureau.

Finally, businesses often need money to fulfil specific aims and objectives linked to growth, expansion or simply updating their equipment or machinery. These items may be bought with money held back (called **reserves**) from past profits, but usually additional money will be needed. If the business needs to borrow money, it will want the lowest interest rates possible and good repayment terms. The senior financial manager often decides where to obtain these funds.

Finance functions

- producing invoices, checking payments are received and chasing up overdue payments
- recording money received
- checking and paying invoices received
- preparing the payroll and paying staff salaries
- monitoring departmental budgets to avoid overspending
- issuing regular budget reports to all departmental managers
- producing cash flow forecasts and regular financial reports
- advising senior managers on sources of finance for capital expenditure
- producing the statutory accounts each year.

Key terms

Statutory accounts – the accounts every company must prepare each year to comply with the law.

Reserves – profits kept back for later reinvestment in the business.

Activity: Financial systems

What financial systems are in place in your centre to monitor spending against the budget? Arrange to interview someone who can tell you about this.

Remember

An efficient finance function is crucial for businesses to achieve aims and objectives linked to improving profits and lowering costs.

The human resources function

The human resources (HR) of a business are its employees. If staff are well trained and committed to the aims of the business, the organisation is more likely to be successful.

HR is responsible for recruiting new employees and ensuring that each vacancy is filled by the best person for the job. Hiring the wrong person can be costly and cause problems both for the individual and the firm.

Normally, new employees attend an **induction programme**. They are told about the business, their rights and responsibilities as employees, the company rules and the requirements of their new job. Arranging appropriate training and assisting with the continuing professional development (CPD) of staff is another aspect of HR.

HR aims to help the business retain good, experienced staff. Analysing staff turnover figures shows the rate at which people leave the organisation. If these are high, it is important to identify and remedy any problem areas. Some reasons for leaving are justifiable, such as moving to another area or for promotion elsewhere, but dissatisfaction with the job or the company should be investigated.

Employees normally expect to be treated and paid fairly, to have appropriate working conditions, to have training opportunities and support if they are ill. They also want a varied and interesting job, and praise when they have worked particularly hard or well. These factors help **motivation**. HR can help this process by monitoring working conditions, having staff welfare policies and ensuring that company pay rates are fair and competitive.

Many organisations have staff associations that monitor the views and conditions of staff. In other businesses, trade unions may represent the workers, especially on pay and conditions. Senior HR staff liaise with these organisations, keep them informed of changes and developments, and are also involved in any negotiations with senior management.

All employees and employers have legal rights and responsibilities in relation to health and safety, employment and **data protection**. HR staff must make sure that the business complies with current laws and stays up to date with legal changes and developments. You will find out more about this if you study Option Unit 9.

HR functions

- advertising vacancies and notifying staff of promotion opportunities
- receiving and recording all job applications, arranging interviews and notifying candidates of the result
- sending a contract of employment and other information to new staff
- arranging staff training and encouraging continuing professional development
- monitoring the working conditions of staff
- checking health and safety, and keeping accident records

Did you know?

In some companies, HR is called **personnel**.

What do new employees learn during an induction programme?

Key terms

Motivation – making staff members keen to work hard, which benefits everyone.

Data protection – laws restricting the type of information that may be held on employees and customers, and how it is used.

Activity: Investigate HR

In your centre, talk to someone responsible for recruiting new staff, arranging staff development and monitoring health and safety. Find out more about what tasks are involved.

Key terms

Network – a system of linked computers that can communicate and share information.

Server – a computer that allows access to files and programmes stored as shared resources on a computer network.

Activity: Security measures

Identify the security measures at your centre to safeguard the IT system. Then decide what type of data is critical in order in order for a business to operate again quickly. Discuss your ideas with your tutor.

- recording sick leave and reasons for absence
- carrying out company welfare policies, for example, long-service awards and company loans
- advising managers on the legal rights and responsibilities of the company and its employees
- recording grievances and disciplinary actions, and their outcomes
- monitoring the terms and conditions of employment
- maintaining staff records
- liaising with staff associations or trade unions representing staff.

The ICT function

The number of crucial business tasks carried out on computers and the importance of the data stored in the system mean that any system failure can be catastrophic.

Most organisations have a computer **network** where staff computers are linked through **servers**. Maintaining the servers, installing new (communal) software and additional hardware, such as printers and scanners, is all part of the ICT function. ICT staff may also be involved in the purchase or issue of computer supplies and consumables to ensure that they are compatible with the system. ICT specialists will be expected to update senior managers on technological developments that would benefit the company. In addition, current equipment will need replacing and software upgrading at regular intervals.

Above all, ICT specialists are responsible for system security. They must ensure that only authorised users have access to the system, protect the system against viruses and hackers, and make sure there is a full back-up system to restore critical data in an emergency.

Finally, ICT specialists help and assist other users, from solving problems to advising on the use of new software or updating the company's intranet. The website is likely to be maintained by the ICT staff, but the content will normally be devised by marketing staff, as you will see on the following page. You will learn more about this if you study Option Unit 12.

ICT functions

- recommending new/updated systems and software to keep abreast of technological developments and of the needs of the business
- buying and installing new hardware and software, and providing information or training as appropriate
- assisting users who have computer problems
- repairing the computer system when required
- advising on/obtaining/issuing computer supplies and consumables
- connecting new or additional equipment to the system
- installing a security system that limits access to authorised users and protects against hackers and viruses

- maintaining the company's website
- monitoring computer use for compliance with the company IT policy
- operating a back-up system for critical data so this can be recovered quickly in an emergency.

The marketing function

Marketing is all about identifying and meeting customer needs. Many businesses consider this so important that they are said to be **marketing-led** so everyone puts the customer first.

Another way to understand marketing is through the **marketing mix**. This involves choosing the best options to market the service or product successfully. A well-known method consists in asking questions relating to the four Ps: product (or service), price, promotion and place.

Marketing staff start by identifying future customer needs. Products are then developed or services offered to meet these needs, using the four Ps (see Table 2.2 on the following page). If this is done well, it gives the company an edge over its competitors. This is what happened when Apple introduced the iPhone and when Nintendo brought out the Wii and DSi.

It is no use developing new products or services if no one knows about them. Marketing is therefore responsible for the promotional activities that tell the customer what is available, by advertising, doing sales promotions or **publicity campaigns**.

The company's website is a major way of communicating with actual and prospective customers. Marketing staff usually look after the style and content of the website, ensuring it is kept up to date. They may also send regular newsletters by email to registered users. Monitoring the popularity of the website and obtaining information on the customers who use it may be undertaken by the company or outsourced to a specialist agency. Using electronic methods of marketing is known as **e-marketing**.

Marketing functions

- carrying out market research to obtain feedback on existing and potential products and/or services
- analysing market research responses, and advising senior managers of the results and implications
- promoting products and services through a variety of advertising and promotional methods, for example, press, TV, online, direct mail, sponsorship and trade shows or exhibitions
- obtaining and updating profiles of existing customers to target advertising and promotions appropriately
- producing and distributing publicity materials, such as catalogues
- designing, updating and promoting the company's website.

Why was the iPhone marketing campaign so successful?

Key terms

Publicity campaign – a linked combination of marketing activities, often used for a new product launch.

E-marketing – relates to electronic and online promotions, such as email newsletters, website competitions or advertising on search engines like Google (often on a pay-per-click basis).

Did you know?

Marketing is another activity that can be outsourced to a specialist agency. Some specialise in certain aspects of marketing, such as direct marketing and online marketing.

Activity: New media

Many businesses now spend more on online marketing than on traditional methods. This is called **new media** because it uses SMS messages and podcasts, as well as the Internet. Check the Top 100 interactive agencies on the New Media Age's website.

Table 2.2: The marketing mix

The 4 Ps	Questions to ask
Product	Who are our customers? What do they want to buy? Are their needs changing? What products are we offering and how many are we selling? What new products are we planning? In which areas are sales growing and how can we sustain this? For which products are sales static and how can we renew interest? Which sales are falling and what, if anything, can we do?
Price	How much should we charge? Should we reduce the price at the start, to attract more customers, or charge as much as we can, when we can? Can we charge different prices to different types of customers? What discounts can we give? What services or products should we give away or sell very cheaply, and what benefits would this bring?
Promotion	How can we tell people about our products? Should we have specialist sales staff? Where should we advertise to attract the attention of our key customers? How else can we promote the product – should we give free samples or run a competition? Where and how can we obtain free publicity? Should we send direct mail shots and, if so, what information should we include?
Place	How can we distribute our product(s)? Should we sell direct to the customer or through retailers? Do we need specialist wholesalers or overseas agents to sell for us? What can we sell over the telephone? How can the Internet help us to sell more?

Did you know?

- **Viral marketing** happens when people spread a message, forwarding emails or website links. It is very cost-effective. Success depends largely on the message being funny, appealing or controversial. One award winner is BlendTec's *Will it Blend?* YouTube campaign. Watch some of their videos and check the number of other viewers they have had.

- At Google, about 36 per cent of staff work in R&D. In 2008, Google's budget for R&D was a massive $2.79 billion.

The research and development (R&D) function

This function involves new product developments as well as improvements to existing products. In many industries, it also includes product design. Improvements to existing products are often ongoing as a result of market research or customer feedback.

New products, such as smartphones, new drugs, WiFi and high-definition televisions, may be developed thanks to scientific or technological scientific advances. Others, such as Google or the Nintendo Wii or DSi, may occur simply because someone had a good idea.

Research can be divided into two types. **Pure research** aims to help us learn and understand more about a lot of things, from outer space to DNA. It is mainly carried out by universities and scientific establishments. **Applied research** focuses on investigating how new discoveries could be used to improve products. For example, non-stick pans were developed from space research. This is the type of research done in business organisations.

R&D staff work with designers to develop a usable product that can be manufactured at a reasonable cost, can be sold at a competitive price and is safe to use. The activities undertaken, however, vary considerably, depending upon the industry. R&D attracts staff very experienced in their own industry and their own field, from software developers to food technologists.

Many organisations aim to improve both product design and performance continually.

- **Industrial design** relates to the appearance of a product – from a computer to a car – or to the packaging of a standard product – from perfume to soap. Designers want their product to stand out from its competitors and to look attractive. The Apple MacBook Air stands out because it is ultra thin. Today, most products are designed using computer-aided design (CAD) packages, which enable designers to sketch a basic shape and then vary the dimensions and sizes of certain parts.

- **Engineering design** relates to product performance. For a computer, this means more memory and greater operating speed.

Technological advances through R&D not only affect our lives but also the ways in which businesses operate. New developments in computer software and hardware have changed the way all departments create, store and share data, and communicate with their customers. New types of machinery and equipment have revolutionised production processes.

R&D functions

- (in the pharmaceutical industry) scientists researching and developing new medicines and drugs

- (in the food industry) technologists working with chefs to prepare new products such as ready meals, sauces or flavourings

- electronic and IT companies concentrating on new technology products and software, such as HD televisions, the Xbox 360 and iPod accessories

- (in the aerospace and car industries) engineers focusing on improving performance and safety while reducing emissions or noise, and designers concentrating on the shape and look, internally and externally.

Did you know?

Apple encourages and supports independent software developers who want to design and submit new apps (applications) for the iPhone. They can put them in the App Store and get 70 per cent of the selling price for each one sold. Visit the Apple website to find out more.

Remember

Functional areas support business aims and objectives by achieving targets appropriate to their own area of work. The exact activities will depend upon the industry.

Case study: Digging the dirt!

In 1945, Joseph Cyril Bamford built a tipping trailer in his garage. He sold it for £45. Today, his business – JCB – is a global giant with over 7,000 employees. The world headquarters is located in the Midlands. A helicopter and a jet plane fly in customers. JCB has manufacturing facilities in several countries.

The strategy of JCB is: 'to deliver the best customer support in our industry – putting the customer at the very heart of our business'.

Work in pairs and find out more about JCB on their website, available via Hotlinks (see page ii). Support all your answers to the following with information from the website.

Joseph Cyril Bamford, founder of JCB. Visit JCB's website.

1. **What is the company's mission statement?**

2. **The company says it practises 'lean manufacturing'. What does this mean?**

3. **How important are the following for JCB?**
   a) quality
   b) R&D.
   Explain why.

4. **You work in purchasing. You have been asked to find out the benefits of buying from JCB. List at least six customer support features or activities that would impress you.**

5. **Find the qualities that JCB requires from its employees. Identify how many you currently have and how many you need to work on.**

6. **On JCB's website, identify three different features that you think are marketing-led to promote the JCB brand.**

2.2 Internal and external links
Relationships and interactions with other functional areas

No functional area in a business organisation can work in isolation. In a small firm, people responsible for different functions usually interact informally and on a continuous basis. Salespeople know which customers pay their bills promptly and which ones still owe money. Managers know without being told which members of staff are hard-working. A customer query can quickly be solved by asking everyone in the office for advice. In a larger organisation, people may work in separate departments and rarely meet each other. However, they still need information and support for the business to operate effectively. Good communication between departmental managers and staff is essential.

External links

Most functional areas deal with external people or organisations.

- **Suppliers** will be contacted by purchasing (or by production if there is not a separate purchasing function) when orders are placed, amended or chased up. R&D may also be in touch with specialist suppliers. Finance will check suppliers' invoices before paying them to ensure there are no mistakes.

- **Customers** will be contacted by sales staff, customer service and finance for queries relating to payments.

- **The bank**, or banks, used by the business may be contacted by finance about issues relating to the company's bank accounts, its business loans or overdraft facilities, and the company payroll.

- **Government agencies** may be contacted by several functional areas. HR may be in touch with Job Centre Plus about job vacancies. If their staff frequently travel abroad, sales may contact the Identity and Passport Service. Finance and payroll staff will communicate with HMRC (HM Revenue & Customs – the tax office).

Activity: Functional activities

A business aims to maximise its profits. Identify how this would affect the activities of the purchasing, HR, finance, sales and marketing functions. Compare your ideas as a group.

Look online to find out what this government department does.

Information flows

The table below shows some of the reasons why internal links and communication between departments are essential.

Table 2.3: Information flows between functional areas

Functional areas	Information flows
Sales and production	Sales must know production schedules and agree delivery dates of orders with production so that customers are not expecting dates that cannot be met. Production must tell sales about production problems that will affect customers.
Sales, purchasing and production	Sales will tell purchasing what needs to be created and in what quantities. The raw materials should then be available when production needs them.
Sales and finance	Finance must know about customer enquiries in order to check their credit rating before sales are made. Finance will be involved when discounts are agreed, or when problems occur with customer payments.
Purchasing and finance	Orders produced by purchasing are matched against deliveries received and copied to finance. Finance matches these against the invoice before making any payments.
Distribution and finance	Finance must know when goods have been dispatched so that they can send out invoices.
Distribution and sales	Sales must be able to inform customers when deliveries are due and must be aware of any problems.
Sales and marketing	Sales and marketing must liaise over sales promotions and adverts so that sales staff can expect/handle enquiries.
Finance and all other departments	Finance monitors departmental spending and the achievement of financial targets, which will include controlling costs.
HR and finance	HR and finance will liaise over salary increases and bonuses.
Customer service, sales and marketing	Customer service must pass on feedback from customer that could affect future product developments or future sales.
R&D and production	R&D and production liaise over new product developments and methods of production.
HR and other functional areas	HR handle job vacancies, promotion opportunities, training courses and CPD for all areas/staff.
ICT and other functional areas	Any changes, maintenance or security issues must be negotiated with and communicated to all staff.
Administration and all departments	Administrators are involved whenever information is required and organise meetings between departments.

Flows of goods and services

The flow of information matches the flow of goods and services through the business.

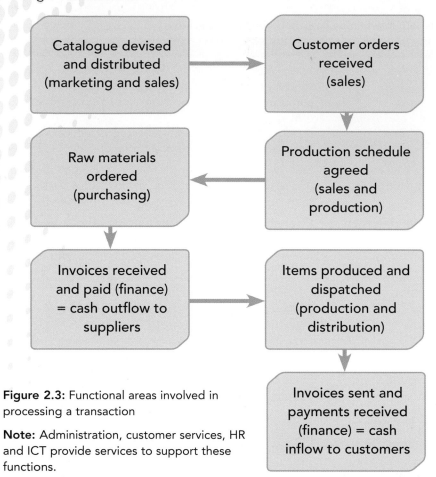

Figure 2.3: Functional areas involved in processing a transaction

Note: Administration, customer services, HR and ICT provide services to support these functions.

PLTS

Practise your creative thinking by being imaginative with your ideas and suggestions.

Activity: Launch a product

You work for a company that is developing and launching a new product. In small groups, decide which functional areas would be involved, what they would do and how they must link for the launch to be successful. Present your ideas to the rest of the class.

Just checking

1. Explain why large businesses need functional areas.
2. Identify six functional areas or departments found in many businesses.
3. Identify the difference between the sales and the marketing functions.
4. What is the role of R&D?
5. What does outsourcing mean? Why is it done? Give three examples of functions or tasks that might be outsourced.
6. Why is it important that information flows between functional areas?

Case study
Working in an animal world

What functional areas do zoo staff members work in?

Chester Zoo is one of the top zoos in the UK. Its mission is to be a major force in conserving biodiversity worldwide. Put simply, its key area of work is conserving plants, animals and habitats, and saving species from extinction all over the world. It aims to do this through sustainable commercial activities, including managing the zoo as a world-class visitor attraction. In 2008, over 1.3 million visitors a year went through its gates. This figure is expected to increase dramatically when the zoo's new £225 million project, to build a SuperZoo, is completed in 2018.

Looking after animals and visitors on a daily basis takes the combined efforts of over 500 staff in peak season. They work in four functional areas, each known as a Directorate.

The Conservation and Education Directorate focuses on achieving the mission of the zoo and concentrates on animal welfare. It is divided into four divisions: Zoo Programmes; Conservation Medicine; Field Programmes; Research, Discovery and Learning. Staff include vets, animal nutritionists and keepers.

The Commercial Directorate focuses on visitors and other income generating aspects, including fundraising and sponsorship. There are three divisions: Catering, Retail and Events; Visitor Services; Marketing and Development. Staff range from sales assistants in the gift shops to a head chef and security manager.

The Corporate Services Directorate carries out all the business functions. It has three divisions: Estates; Finance and IT; HR, which includes personnel and wages. Staff include maintenance workers such as painters, cash office assistants and wages assistants.

The fourth Directorate is responsible for the SuperZoo expansion project, called Natural Vision. Find out more on the Chester zoo website.

Think about it!

1. Identify two activities that are undertaken by each functional area that supports the mission and the main aim of the business.

2. Identify three issues over which functional areas would need to liaise. Explain which divisions would be involved.

3. Targets are set for increasing the number of visitors each year and achieving a minimum 'spend' per visitor. Suggest how each functional area can contribute to reaching these targets.

4. Compare the functional areas of Chester Zoo with those in your centre. Which are similar and which are totally different? What explanations can you give for your findings?

BTEC Assessment activity 2.2 (P4) (P5) (M2)

1. You have been asked to contribute to a careers event at your centre by preparing an information leaflet on different functional areas in business. Do this by working in small groups to investigate the functional areas of at least two completely different organisations. Find out the titles of the functional areas, the work they do and identify how they link together.

   You can visit the websites (available via Hotlinks, see page ii) of any of the four businesses listed below. They provide useful information. You can also use the business you investigated for Assessment activity 2.1 or one your group has visited.

   - Barnado's, children's charity
   - innocent, fresh fruit smoothie producer
   - Marks & Spencer, retailer
   - Google, online search engine provider.

   a) On your own, describe the functional areas in one chosen business to start your leaflet, then explain how they link together. **P4** part, **P5**

   b) Complete your leaflet with a written description of the functional areas in a **contrasting** business organisation of your choice. This could be one of the businesses above, Chester Zoo (see WorkSpace case study, page 63), your centre or a business you know well yourself. **P4** part

2. Again working in your small group, identify how the functional areas of the business organisations you have investigated relate to each other to support the business objectives. Identify how the functional areas work together to contribute to achieving the objectives.

If you know the objectives of the business or if these are given on the website, choose two or three and, in each case, identify how the functional areas will contribute to their achievement.

If you cannot find the objectives for a business you have investigated online, decide how the functional areas would need to work together in order to achieve the following objectives:

   a) increase revenue by 10 per cent in the next year
   b) improve customer satisfaction
   c) reduce costs by 5 per cent.

On your own, decide which of the conclusions you have reached are the most important for your own businesses. Then write a report to your tutor in which you summarise your findings. **M2** (part)

3. Identify the similarities and differences between the two organisations you have investigated. Look at the functional areas and the links between the organisations, and the way they support the business objectives. Add your conclusions to the report you started in your answer to question 2. **M2**

Grading tip

To identify links between functional areas, look for the flows of information between them. You can use Table 2.3 (page 61) to help.

 edexcel

Assignment tips

- Choosing the right businesses to investigate is vital for this unit. Talk to your tutor before you make a decision. If you work part-time, you may want to use your employer as one organisation, but only if you work for a relatively large company.

- Ideally, you will use the same businesses for both sections of the unit so you can relate the information you learn about their aims and objectives to their functional areas. This saves you work. It also enables you to link and develop your information more easily.

- Functional areas in organisations you investigate rarely match exactly those mentioned in textbooks and often have different titles. Some functions may be combined, such as sales and customer service.

- Remember that contrasting businesses should always be as different as possible.

- You can find information about functional areas in the careers section of many websites.

3 Financial forecasting for business

All businesses need money to survive in order to buy materials and pay wages and other types of expenses or costs, like utility bills (gas, electricity and water), business rates and advertising. Money coming into a business is called income or revenue and usually comes from customers who pay for the goods and/or services that the business provides.

If a business' income is greater than its expenditure, it is said to be making a **profit** since more money is entering the business than leaving it. If the reverse is true – expenditure is greater than income – then the business is making a **loss**. If this situation continues, the business could have to close.

In this unit you will learn about costs, revenue and profit. Then you will learn about two ways in which businesses can keep track of their finances: break-even analysis and cash-flow forecasting.

When you have completed this unit, you will know how business finance works. This means that when you work in a business you will understand what is happening around you. Alternatively, if you want to start your own business, you will know the importance of controlling the finances.

Learning outcomes

After completing this unit, you should:

1. know about costs, revenue and profit in a business organisation
2. be able to prepare a break-even analysis
3. be able to create a cash-flow forecast.

All websites referred to in this unit can be accessed via Hotlinks. See page ii for more information.

Assessment and grading criteria

This table shows you what you must do in order to achieve a pass, merit or distinction grade and where you can find activities in this book to help you.

To achieve a **pass**, the evidence must show that the learner is able to:	To achieve a **merit**, the evidence must show that, in addition to the pass criteria, the learner is able to:	To achieve a **distinction** grade, the evidence must show that, in addition to the pass and merit criteria, the learner is able to:
P1 identify the difference between start-up and operating costs, variable and fixed costs **See Assessment activity 3.1, page 75**	**M1** explain the importance of costs, revenue and profit for a business organisation **See Assessment activity 3.1, page 75**	**D1** evaluate the importance of cash flow and break-even for the effective management of business finance **See Assessment activity 3.5, page 92**
P2 identify the different types of revenue **See Assessment activity 3.1, page 75**		
P3 outline the differences between gross and net profit **See Assessment activity 3.1, page 75**		
P4 calculate break-even using given data to show the level at which income equals expenditure **See Assessment activity 3.2, page 81**		
P5 present the break-even as an annotated graph showing break-even **See Assessment activity 3.2, page 81**	**M2** demonstrate the impact of changing cost and revenue data on the break-even point of the business **See Assessment activity 3.3, page 82**	
P6 prepare an annual cash-flow forecast using monthly data **See Assessment activity 3.4 page 91**	**M3** analyse the implications of regular and irregular cash inflows and outflows for a business organisation **See Assessment activity 3.4, page 91**	

How you will be assessed

To achieve this unit you will use a variety of different methods, such as researching information, using case study materials and carrying out business calculations. You will also make presentations to demonstrate that you can meet the learning outcomes for the unit, as set out in the grading criteria (see table on page 66). The Assessment activities in this book will help you prepare for this.

Gareth

I chose to do this BTEC First because I've always been interested in business. This is mainly because my uncle runs a courier service. He employs 11 drivers who deliver urgent packages for customers who are happy to pay high rates for good service. He drives a Mercedes and I want to do the same one day! I also know that I will learn a lot about different aspects of business which will help if I want to work in an area like finance later.

When I started this unit, I knew it was important because my uncle is always going on about cash flow and profit. Even so, I was a bit worried because maths isn't one of my strong points. However, I soon realised that the numbers I was expected to work with really mean something. They are essential to run a successful business and realising this has made it much easier.

I have talked to my uncle about things I have done on the course and he agrees that unless he handles the money side of his business well, he will go out of business. He spends half a day a week checking his cash flow and bank balances, and identifying people who have not paid bills on time.

Over to you!

- What have you heard or read about already that links to business finance? Bankruptcy? Profit? Closing down sale – 50 per cent off? Bank loans? Anything else?

- Are you confident working with numbers, especially when you know what they mean? Quick test: you have a part-time job and earn £40 a week. Your boss says you are getting a 5 per cent pay increase. Would you quickly know how much more you will earn?

 **It's all about money**

1. Suggest two possible sources of income and two types of expenditure for a typical fitness centre.

2. The chief executive of a charity states that he has to make sure that, overall, his organisation must 'break even'. What do you think he means?

3. You have sources of income and expenditure, just like a business. How often do you 'break even' in a normal week? Do you often have money left over or do you normally run out part-way through the week? What does this tell you about the difficulties of running a profitable business?

1. Know about costs, revenue and profit in a business organisation

1.1 Types of business costs

There are three main types of business costs:

- **Start-up costs** – These are incurred before a business can start to operate, such as the deposit on rented property, and the purchase of equipment and initial stock.

- **Fixed costs** – This is money spent once a business is up and running. It is spent on items that are needed no matter how many items the business sells to its customers. For example, a newsagent has to pay the shop rent and heating bills whether they sell lots of papers and magazines or only a few. Fixed costs are called **indirect costs** since they are not directly linked to the amount of money coming from customers.

- **Variable costs** – These are also incurred once a business is operating. This time the amount spent is directly linked to the number of items sold or the amount of services supplied. For example, the number of tyres bought by a car manufacturer is directly linked to the number of cars made and sold.

1.2 Costs incurred at start-up

Plans for the new Wembley Stadium were produced in 2000. It was finally completed in 2007 and cost £798 million to build. All of this money had to be found before a single ticket could be sold.

Remember

The term '**start-up costs**' refers to all the money that needs to be spent on setting up a business before it can start trading.

Key terms

Fixed (or indirect) costs – arise no matter how many items are produced.

Variable (or direct) costs – money paid out in direct proportion to the number of items produced and sold.

Activity: List expenditure

In a group, under two headings 'Fixed expenditure' and 'Variable expenditure', list as many items you can think of for a person who runs an ice-cream van.

Did you know?

Quite often business people underestimate how much they will need to get a business started. The total cost for the Wembley Stadium was £798 million but the original estimate was only £326 million. The increase was a massive 244 per cent. Fortunately most businesses do not get things so badly wrong.

Why were the start-up costs for the new Wembley Stadium so high?

Not many businesses need that much money to get started. However, it is almost impossible to imagine any business that would not need to spend any money before it started to operate.

There are two main types of start-up cost. First of all, money needs to be spent on capital items such as machinery, furniture and rental deposit. This is called '**capital expenditure**' and is a term used to describe items purchased that are expected to last for some time before they need to be replaced. The other type of start-up cost is when money is spent on building up manufacturing or retail stock. You would hardly expect to go to a new store to be told, 'Sorry, we have got nothing to sell you – we've only just opened!'

The idea of start-up costs can also be applied to situations where businesses plan a large expansion or to produce a new type of product.

1.3 Operating costs

Operating costs, sometimes called **expenses**, refers to the money spent on a regular basis, once a business is up and running. They are divided into fixed and variable costs.

Some businesses have mostly fixed costs. For example, a nail bar has several fixed costs such as property rental, business rates and staff wages. The main variable cost would be the products used on the clients, such as nail polish, but these would be a small fraction of the total costs. On the other hand, some businesses have relatively high variable costs, compared with the fixed costs. High-volume producers of consumer goods, such as washing machines, buy in large quantities of steel and other components. In this case, variable costs would account for most of the expenditure.

Remember

Businesses spend money on **capital items** when they buy something that should last for a long time, often years.

Activity: List costs

List as many start-up costs as you can think of for someone opening a large pet store. Compare your list with others in your group.

Remember

All successful businesses constantly monitor their business costs and aim to keep these as low as possible.

Activity: Identify different costs

1. In small groups, identify two types of fixed cost and two types of variable cost for each type of business listed below. Compare your ideas with other members of your group.

   a) cinema; b) a combined petrol station and convenience store; c) newsagent; d) car manufacturer; e) pizzeria; f) mobile hairdresser; g) a hairdresser who has a salon; h) an airline.

2. You sell hot dogs. The costs for one hot dog are as follows: sausage = 8p; onions = 3p; bread roll = 7p. If you sell 150 at a fair, what are your total variable costs?

Total costs

All businesses need to know the total amount of money they have spent on operating costs over a certain period of time, such as a month. This is found by adding the fixed costs and variable costs together, which gives the **total costs**.

Key term

Total costs – all the fixed and variable costs added together.

1.4 Revenue

Sources of revenue

Revenue refers to the money flowing into a business. It is also called income and it is the opposite of costs. This money can come from several sources.

- **Sales** – This is the main source of revenue for most firms. It comes from customers who pay for goods or services.

- **Leasing** – This income can come from a person or another business using part of the business's property – say the upstairs area of a two-storey property. Other businesses specialise in leasing expensive items or equipment, such as cars or photocopiers.

- **Interest** – This is earned when a business has kept back some of its profits in a bank account that pays interest.

Calculating total revenue

You need two items of information to calculate the total revenue for goods sold to customers:

- the selling price of the item/unit

- the number of units sold.

Once this information is available, use the following formula to calculate total revenue.

> **Total income = unit sales price × number of units sold**
>
> For example, if a car manufacturer produces 1,000 cars a week and sells them for £12,000 each, the total income would be:
>
> **£12,000 × 1,000 = £12,000,000**

1.5 Calculating gross and net profit

The profit made by a business is the amount of revenue left after all the costs have been paid. It is a key measure of how well the business is being run. Normally, profit is measured in two stages: **gross profit** and **net profit**. The first is largely out of the owner's control, but the second shows how well the business is being managed. The activity on the following page shows the difference.

Key term

Revenue – the total amount of money going into a business.

Did you know?

It is possible to earn a small amount of interest even when money is only deposited overnight. This normally occurs when banks lend large amounts of money to each other.

Activity: Calculate income

A sandwich shop sells the following items in a particular day: 100 sandwiches at £1.75 each, 85 cans of drink at 60p each and 45 pies at £1.10 each. Calculate the income from each item separately and then add them to get the total for the three items combined.

Key terms

Gross profit – the amount left over from revenue when the **cost of sales** is deducted.

Net profit – the amount left when the operating expenses are deducted from the gross profit figure. It is sometimes called 'profit before tax'.

Sales income → minus cost of sales → equals gross profit → minus operating costs → equals net profit

Figure 3.1: Calculating gross and net profit

Activity: Improve Tom's profits

Greenbank News is a newsagent's shop owned by Tom Greenbank. The following figures show the income and expenditure for a typical week:

- Sales income: £4,000
- Cost of newspapers, magazines, sweets and other items for sale: £2,500
- Other expenses such as staff, rent, heating, cleaning: £1,000.

Despite working hard, Tom seems to have little money left each week for his own use. He therefore wants to increase the profit he makes. As a first step, he decides to calculate his gross and net profit. He must then think of ideas to improve these.

Read through the sections below and then, in groups, identify the actions Tom could take to improve his profits.

PLTS

Practise your creative thinking skills by being imaginative in the ways Tom can improve his business.

Gross profit

Gross profit is the amount of money left after Tom has paid for all of the goods (newspapers and so on) which he has bought to sell in his shop. This is known as **cost of sales**. The calculation is:

> **Gross profit = sales revenue - cost of sales**
>
> In the case of Greenbank News, this is:
> ### £4,000 - £2,500 = £1,500

The cost of sales figure is mainly outside Tom's control since the price he pays for the goods he purchases is fixed by the suppliers. This means that the real test of how well Tom is running his business is how he spends the rest of the business' income.

Key term

Cost of sales – the money spent by a business on materials for manufacturing or resale.

Did you know?

Businesses have to pay tax on their net profit.

Net profit

Net profit is calculated by subtracting Tom's expenses, or operating costs, such as staff wages, heating, rent and business rates, from the gross profit. The calculation is:

> **Net profit = gross profit - operating costs**
>
> For Tom's business, this would be:
> ### £1,500 - £1,000 = £500

This is the real measure of how the business is being run. If Tom wants to improve the profitability of the business, he could try to reduce his operating costs.

Discussion point

Tom is thinking of increasing his selling prices so he will make more gross profit. Would this work? As a group, discuss the advantages and disadvantages of increasing or lowering the prices he charges. Would it make any difference if he sold a specialist product?

Maximising profits

The 'health' of a business is measured by how much profit it makes. When a business makes a large profit, it means that the owners receive a good income and have money to reinvest in the business. This should ensure that the business makes a good profit in years to come. The process of constantly looking to improve profits to make as much as possible is called **profit maximisation**.

There are two basic ways of maximising profit:

- increasing sales income
- reducing costs.

Key term

Profit maximisation – making as much profit as possible.

Increasing sales income

There are several ways this might be achieved, as shown in Table 3.1. None can guarantee success as each has risks attached.

Table 3.1: Methods of improving sales income

Method	Risk
Increase prices of product(s)	Sales could fall
Reduce prices	Not enough extra sales would be made to compensate
Increase advertising	Extra cost may not be covered by increased sales
Sell a new kind of product	Product may not be popular
Increase the scale of the business by operating over a wider area, for example, nationally or internationally	This sort of expansion costs money, which may not be recouped by additional sales, particularly if there is stiff competition

Businesses will look at these options and make decisions as to which have the least risk involved.

Reducing operating costs

Even small businesses have many types of operating cost. Table 3.2 lists some of the more obvious examples. The methods of reducing costs fall into two main categories:

- minimise usage
- find a better purchasing deal.

Table 3.2: Examples of reducing operating costs

Item of expenditure	Use less (minimise usage)	Reduce purchase price (find a better purchasing deal)
Labour	Reduce staffing levels	Increase productivity Sub-contract service activities such as computer maintenance. This is also known as outsourcing
Raw materials	Use less material in each product Reduce scrap/wastage	Look for cheaper suppliers Purchase large quantities at discounted prices Look for alternative, cheaper materials (for example, plastic instead of wood)
Utilities (gas, water, electricity)	Use energy-efficient items (for example, heating boilers, light bulbs) Have lights which switch off automatically when not in use	Regularly compare utility prices, looking for the best tariff to suit the business' particular needs
Consumable items such as stationery	Send documents by email rather than by post Minimise opportunities for staff to steal items	Look for cheaper suppliers (investigate online sources)

One approach is to write a list of all items of expenditure for one year and then rank them in order, starting with the highest first and then concentrating on those where the most money is being spent. For example:

Staff wages	£200,000
Raw materials	£150,000
Property rental	£50,000
....	
Ball pens	£20
Paper clips	£4.50

Activity: Check out premises prices

One way of reducing costs is to move to cheaper premises, and websites can help. Check out the EG PropertyLink website. Find the price of different commercial properties in your own area.

Remember

Businesses will always try to keep costs as low as they can because costs always reduce profit.

Obviously, there is more potential saving by attempting to reduce staff wages and raw material expenditure than having a massive investigation into the use of paper clips, where the most that can be saved is £4.50!

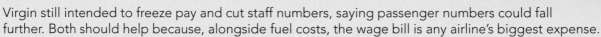

Case study: Flying high or bumping along?

In 2009, Virgin Atlantic reported a profits increase to £68.4 million. Only days earlier, BA, its main competitor on transatlantic flights, had announced a loss of £401 million. Why the difference?

> Why did Virgin report profits in 2009?

Virgin Atlantic had gained for a number of reasons including the success of its premium products, winning market share and cutting costs. It pushed its Premium Economy seats, where passengers pay about £200 more for extra legroom and better food. It also offered cheaper tickets to boost passenger numbers. BA lost money when its high-end clients, who travel First Class or Business, reduced their spending in the recession. They provide more than 50 per cent of BA's revenue, despite representing only 11 per cent of passenger numbers. The airline was losing £3 million a day and to save money, the chief executive, Willie Walsh, and his finance director said they would work for no pay during July. Although Willie Walsh got pilots to agree to a pay cut and longer hours, the idea of a pay freeze or cut was less popular with cabin crew and ground crews. Most also took a dim view of working for nothing for a month to save £10 million. Other BA plans included taking 16 planes out of service and offering cut-price tickets.

Virgin still intended to freeze pay and cut staff numbers, saying passenger numbers could fall further. Both should help because, alongside fuel costs, the wage bill is any airline's biggest expense.

1. **Identify the two major costs for all airlines.**
2. **Virgin Atlantic Airline's pay rates are lower than BA's. Explain the significance of this related to potential profits or losses.**
3. **How effective do you think two top staff working for no pay for a month will be in helping BA? Give a reason for your answer.**
4. **Why do you think cabin crew and ground staff are more reluctant to accept a pay cut than airline pilots?**
5. **Is it better for an airline to fill a plane at any price or not? Identify the advantages and disadvantages of selling cheap tickets.**
6. **What would you do if you ran BA? List four actions you think should be taken to improve profits. Compare your ideas with other members of your group.**

1.6 Why is profit important?

You learned in Unit 1 that the aim of most businesses is to make a profit in order to survive. The more profit a business makes, the 'safer' it is. It also has more options about what it does in the future.

- The owner(s) will be more motivated to work hard because they are being rewarded for the risks they are taking running the business.

- Profits can be used to expand the business.

- The money can be used as additional investment in new equipment or machinery to increase productivity, as you saw in Unit 1.

- A **loan** could be repaid, which would reduce the interest payments (another cost).

Key term

Loan – amount of money lent to a business to help it to grow or to improve cash flow. The money borrowed has to be repaid as well as regular interest payments.

- Profit that is not spent can be kept in the bank in a high interest account. This is known as **reserves** and is very useful in an emergency.

Did you know?

Businesses produce a profit and loss account each year, showing their income, expenditure, gross profit and net profit.

Just checking

1. Can you think of two start-up costs for a florist's business?
2. Name the two main categories of operating costs.
3. Explain the difference between gross and net profit.
4. Name two ways in which a business could try to increase its profit.

BTEC Assessment activity 3.1   P1 P2 P3 M1

Hannah has worked in catering but now wants to start her own business making a range of high-quality biscuits to an old family recipe. Hannah realises that running the business successfully will involve more than just her catering skills.

She has seen a unit for rent in an industrial park. Each unit has all main services provided (gas, electricity, water and telephone landline) and tenants pay the bills based on usage. Hannah also needs to buy a small second-hand van to make deliveries. Her father has agreed to help her, providing she repays him in monthly instalments over the next two years. This will enable her to use the £10,000 that she has saved up in her bank account to put towards other start-up costs.

The unit next door is rented by a printer with six staff. The owner has asked if he could hire Hannah's van on days when she does not need it, as he could then deliver orders more quickly when he is busy. Hannah likes this idea.

She has now asked for your advice about the financial side of starting and running her business.

1. Hannah is confused about the difference between start-up and operating costs. She is also not sure about the difference between variable and fixed costs. Identify three examples of each of these types of cost that would apply to her business. Then write a brief explanation about each cost type to help Hannah understand exactly what each term means. **P1**

2. Identify all Hannah's possible sources of revenue. Calculate her total revenue if in a week she sold 200 packets of biscuits at £1 each, received £50 from the printer for the use of her van and £20 in interest from the bank. **P2**

3. You tell Hannah that she must make a profit if her business is to succeed. Explain exactly what this means and then outline the difference between gross and net profit for her, using figures to illustrate your answer. Include information about where the different amounts come from, for example, cost of sales. **P3**

4. You tell Hannah that costs, revenue and profit are all important to running a business. Explain in turn what each means and also how they are linked together. Emphasise the importance of each of these for her business and discuss what could happen if she does not control her costs, bring in enough revenue or make a profit. **M1**

Grading tip

To achieve the pass criteria, you must be able to explain clearly what different terms mean, such as variable costs. To achieve **M1**, you must be able to apply your knowledge of costs, revenue and profit to a business organisation.

2. Be able to prepare a break-even analysis

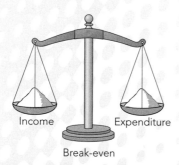

Profit, loss and break-even

Key terms

Break-even – businesses break even when income and expenditure are equal.

What if? – refers to the need for business managers to look at the options open to them, and to assess the potential outcomes.

In the last section, you learned it is important for revenue to be greater than costs because this means the business makes a profit. When income is less than the total expenditure, the business is making a loss.

In between these two situations, when income equals expenditure, the business is said to be **breaking even**.

2.1 Balancing costs or expenditure with revenues or income

Businesses constantly need to change and adapt to survive. When they are deciding what to do, they need to decide the possible effect on costs and revenue of taking different actions. For example, they may want to:

- invest in more efficient machinery to improve efficiency
- launch a major advertising campaign to try to boost sales
- upgrade an existing product or introduce a new one
- run their own distribution network rather than rely on specialist firms
- relocate to bigger premises.

For each investment decision the key question is, 'Will it be worthwhile?' In other words, will the additional income received cover the extra costs? Break-even analysis can help to answer this question and is therefore an aid to business decision making. Business managers constantly need to ask, **'What if?'** They look at possible actions they can take and then try to estimate the consequences in each case.

2.2 Presenting break-even graphically

Break-even is often shown using a graph, because this can be used to illustrate and analyse all the main aspects of break-even. It can also be calculated using a formula, as you will see on page 81.

Did you know?

The weekly cost of running a black taxi cab in London can be £200 (for fuel, insurance, maintenance and so on). Most of these are fixed costs. Cab drivers estimate that it can take the first two days of a week for fares (income) to cover these costs. This is a special form of break-even.

Activity: Identify items on a break–even graph

Study the example of a break-even graph, shown in figure 3.2, and go through it carefully as you identify each item in the alphabetical list. Each item on the diagram is described in order. You may find it helpful to do this two or three times. Ask your tutor if there is anything you do not understand.

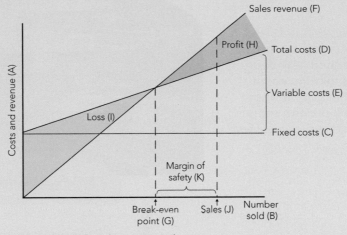

Figure 3.2: A break-even graph

A Costs and revenue – The vertical axis shows the amount of money spent as costs and received as revenue.

B Number sold – The horizontal axis shows the number of products sold.

C Fixed costs – This line is horizontal because the fixed costs never change, no matter how many products are sold.

D Total costs – This line shows the fixed costs plus the variable costs. It starts at the left-hand side where the fixed cost line meets the vertical axis. At this point there are no sales, so the variable costs are zero. The line is then drawn to show how variable costs increase in direct proportion to the number of items sold. It then shows the total cost for each level of sales.

E Variable costs – The difference between the fixed costs line and the total costs line shows the variable costs. This gap widens as the level of sales increases.

F Sales revenue – This line starts at the zero point, since no sales means that no income is being earned. The sales revenue is calculated by multiplying the price charged by the number of items sold.

G Break-even point – This is the point where the sales revenue line crosses the total cost line and shows the number of sales needed for the business to break even.

H Profit – To the right of the break-even line, sales revenue is greater than total costs and so the business is making a profit. The distance between the two lines shows the amount of profit for each level of sales.

I Loss – To the left of the break-even line, sales revenue is less than expenditure and the business is making a loss. The distance between the lines shows the amount of loss at all sales levels.

J Sales – This shows that sales are higher than the number required to break even.

K Margin of safety – This is the amount by which sales would have to fall before the break-even point is reached.

Did you know?

'Tax freedom day' is the day in the year when the average Briton has earned enough to cover all of the government taxes they will pay that year. Estimates vary, but it generally falls in the third or fourth week in May. Ask your tutor and family members how they feel about this.

Key term

Margin of safety – amount by which sales would have to fall before the break-even point is reached.

Case study: Ewan's Electricals – Part 1

The information below will help you to construct a break-even graph. Read it carefully and then follow the instructions in the activity that follows to complete the graph.

Ewan Jones has a shop that sells hi-fis and other domestic electronic sound equipment. He has found out that the shop next door is becoming vacant and is thinking about using it to expand his business by selling flat-screen televisions. He jots down some figures that he thinks would apply to the first year of trading.

Will Ewan be able to expand his business?

Fixed costs (rent, wages, insurance, etc.): £20,000

Average cost of a television: £400

Average selling price of a television: £600

Ewan wants to know whether the expansion of his business would be viable. He has asked you to draw up a break-even graph so that he can have a clearer picture of the issues involved in his ideas. You will need a sheet of graph paper and a sharp pencil to do this. The following stages (see below) will help you to construct the diagram step by step. Then use your graph to do the second part of this case study on page 80.

Functional skills

If you are good at ICT, then you may prefer to use a spreadsheet package to create a break-even graph.

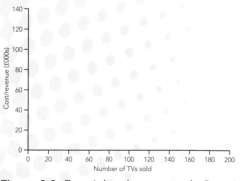

Figure 3.3: Ewan's break-even graph, Step 1

Step 1: Completing the axes

You ask Ewan what is the maximum number of TV sets he could sell in one year. When he tells you 200, you make the horizontal scale go from 0 to 200.

You now need to calculate the maximum possible sales revenue to decide the scale of your vertical axis. From the figures Ewan has given you, you can work this out.

£600 × 200 = £120,000

Because this figure has a lot of zeros, you decide it would be simpler to make the vertical scale go from 0 to 120 and put '£000s' on the axis label to show that your numbers represent thousands. You then label both axes.

Step 2: Adding the fixed cost line

Ewan has calculated that his fixed costs will amount to £20,000 a year. So this line must start at the £20,000 point on the vertical axis and continue horizontally to the right-hand side of the graph.

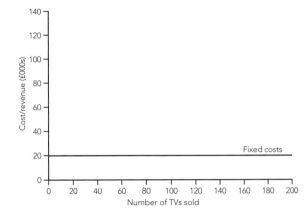

Figure 3.4: Ewan's break-even graph, Step 2

Step 3: Adding the total cost line

The total cost figure for any level of sales is made up of the sum of fixed and variable costs, so the line that represents this figure starts where the fixed cost line meets the vertical axis and represents the variable costs. Ewan has told you that each TV costs him £400. So for sales of 200 TV sets, the total variable cost would be £80,000.

Because you are drawing the total cost line, this will start at £20,000 and end at £100,000 (£80,000 + £20,000). This is because, if 200 TVs are sold, the total cost is the sum of both the variable and the fixed costs.

Draw your line carefully, making sure it ends directly above the 200 sales figure on the horizontal axis.

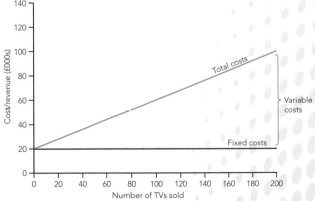

Figure 3.5: Ewan's break-even graph, Step 3

Step 4: Adding the sales revenue line

If Ewan does not sell any TVs, his revenue is zero. So, this line starts at the zero point on the graph. For sales of 200 sets, the revenue is:

£200 × 600 = £120,000

This is the end point of the revenue line: 200 sales, income £120,000, as you can see in Figure 3.6 opposite.

Remember

The fixed cost line on a break-even graph is always horizontal because fixed costs do not change with the level of sales.

Remember

The total cost line always starts at the point where the fixed cost line meets the vertical axis.

Did you know?

Plotting the lines carefully on your graph is essential, otherwise you will read off the wrong figures.

Remember

The total cost line and the sales revenue line slope upwards from left to right because both increase with the number of sales.

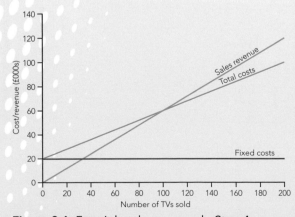

Figure 3.6: Ewan's break-even graph, Step 4

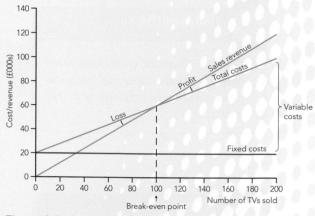

Figure 3.7: Ewan's break-even graph, Step 5

Step 5: Labelling the features of the graph

The break-even point is found by drawing a vertical dotted line from the point where the revenue and total cost lines cross to the horizontal axis. This shows that the break-even point for Ewan's proposed business venture is 100 TV sets.

You also need to label the profit and loss areas on your graph, as shown in Figure 3.7.

2.3 Reading and interpreting the break-even graph

By analysing the graph you can find out the:

- fixed cost figure
- variable and total cost figures for any level of sales
- revenue figure for any level of sales
- break-even point for the forecast figures used
- profit/loss figure for any given level of sales. Do this by measuring the distance between the lines on the graph or reading the cost and revenue figures on the vertical scale and subtracting one from the other.

Check that you can do this by working through the case study below.

Remember

The greater the distance between the total cost line and the sales revenue at the right-hand side of the graph, the greater the profit.

Case study: Ewan's Electricals – Part 2

Ewan asks you to find the following information using your graph.

1. The revenue figure if 150 TV sets are sold.
2. The total cost figure if sales are 50 sets.
3. The number of sets that need to be sold to break even.
4. The profit/loss (say which) if 50 sets are sold.
5. The profit/loss if 200 sets are sold.
6. Ewan asks you to explain what the term 'margin of safety' means. Explain exactly what this would be if 180 sets are sold.
7. For Questions 1, 2, 4 and 5, check your answers by working out the figures from the information Ewan supplied.

Assessment activity 3.2

Construct a break-even graph for a company that is planning to produce new 'Speedy Toasters' using the following information: fixed costs: £10,000; variable cost per unit: £20; selling price per unit: £50; maximum sales: 500.

Hint: The horizontal axis should go up to the maximum possible sales – 500. The vertical axis (costs and revenue) should go up to £25,000 (500 × £50).

1. When you have completed the chart, label the following items: a) the fixed cost line; b) the total cost line; c) the sales revenue line; d) the profit area and the loss area. Ask your tutor to check your graph before you continue.

2. Use your graph to identify: a) the break-even point; b) the income and total expenditure at the break-even point (they should be the same); c) the income

and total expenditure when sales are 450 units; d) from your answer to c), the profit for sales of 450 units; e) the profit or loss (say which) when sales are 400 and then 200 units.

3. Calculate the answers for Question 2 b) to e) as a double check. **P4 P5**

Grading tip

To achieve a pass, you must draw a break-even graph using the figures provided and also 'annotate' your graph. This means adding all the appropriate labels, as well as showing the break-even point, margin of safety and profit/loss areas.

2.4 Using a formula to calculate the break-even point

Another way of calculating the break-even point is to use the following formula. (This is not essential for your assessment. However, if you do know how to use it, you can check your work quickly and easily.)

$$\text{Sales level needed to break even} = \frac{\text{total fixed cost}}{\text{selling price - variable cost}}$$

For Ewan's proposed TV business, the figures used would be: fixed costs: £20,000; variable costs: £400; selling price: £600.

Using the formula, this gives:

$$\text{Sales for break-even} = \frac{£20,000}{£600 - £400} = \frac{£20,000}{£200} = 100$$

This is the same figure you found by creating your graph.

Activity: Use the formula

Use the formula to calculate the break-even point for Speedy Toasters to check you were right.

The strengths and limitations of break-even analysis

Break-even analysis is very useful. It helps business people when they are making decisions related to new ventures – the 'What if' situation you read about earlier. At the stroke of a pen, different possibilities can be tested out on paper – without investing thousands of pounds to make mistakes the hard way.

However, break-even analysis has its limitations. The main one is that it relies on people making accurate predictions about future events. They may not be very good at this. One tendency is to be too optimistic and think, 'It's a super product. I'm bound to sell thousands!' There are also problems if people are too pessimistic.

Another possible problem is that it is very difficult to predict future changes to external factors. For example, the price of oil changes quite frequently and this affects the cost of energy and fuel, as well as being the main component of plastic. Many businesses, such as airlines, are affected by these changes (as you saw in the case study on page 74). Anyone carrying out break-even analysis needs to be aware of these problems.

The main issues associated with break-even analysis are as follows.

Strengths

- Helps people to analyse situations before they are committed to spending money.
- Different factors can be changed to carry out 'What if' analysis.

Weaknesses

- Depends upon the individual business person's ability to analyse potential situations (the risks are being too optimistic or pessimistic).
- External factors, such as the price of raw materials, customers' tastes, and tax levels can be hard to predict (see also Unit 1, pages 29–30).

Just checking

1. What factors are represented by the horizontal and vertical axies on a break-even chart?
2. Which two lines cross each other to show the break-even point?
3. Between which two lines are both the profit and loss areas found?
4. How is the margin of safety found?

Assessment activity 3.3

M2

Ewan is thinking about factors that could affect his business and is looking at the options listed below. In each case, help him by calculating the new break-even point by creating new graphs or using the formula. Remember that originally his fixed costs were £20,000, his variable costs £400 and selling price £600. All the changes below are based on these figures as the starting point.

1. Ewan wonders what will happen if he reduces the selling price by £100.

2. He fears that business rates, insurance and other fixed costs will rise to give an annual fixed cost of £25,000.

3. He reads a leaflet circulated by a competitor who sells TVs for £700. Ewan wonders what would happen if he increases his price to £650.

4. He negotiates with his supplier and manages to cut his purchase price (the variable cost) by £50. He wants to pass on this reduction to his customers in full. **M2**

Grading tip

To achieve **M2**, you have to be able to analyse your graph and comment on what would happen if things changed, such as prices or costs.

3. Be able to create a cash-flow forecast

3.1 What is cash flow?

Even small businesses have several amounts of money going into their bank account each day (**cash inflows**). They normally also have a number of payments going out of their account (**cash outflows**). This movement of money into and out of business bank accounts is called cash flow. The difference between the two is called **net cash flow**. Large businesses have thousands of cash inflows and outflows each day.

If, on a particular day, a business has £1,200 paid into its account and £1,000 paid out, it is said to have a positive net cash flow of £200. If the reverse is true, and more money is paid out than is paid in, then the net cash flow is negative. If a business' net cash flow remains negative for some time, it will not have enough money to pay its bills and could eventually become bankrupt. The amount of money in a business' account at any particular time is called the **cash balance**.

For this reason, businesses must use **cash-flow forecasting** to predict the cash balance at regular intervals so that action can be taken if a problem is foreseen.

Key terms

Cash inflows – sums of money entering the bank account of a business.

Cash outflows – sums of money leaving the bank account of a business.

Net cash flow – the difference between the inflows and the outflows over a period of time.

Cash balance – total amount of money in a bank account at a particular time.

Cash-flow forecast – a prediction of what is likely to happen in the future.

Discussion point

Most businesses providing utility and telephone services offer a discount to customers who pay monthly by direct debit, rather than paying the bill they get every three months. What does 'direct debit' mean, and why do you think businesses prefer to receive money this way? Discuss your ideas as a group.

Remember

All businesses want their cash inflows to be greater than their outflows.

3.2 Cash inflow

Cash inflow is money coming into a business. It can come from many sources and for various reasons. As you have already seen, there are several methods of payment that can be used.

Capital

This term is used for large amounts of money brought into a business at a particular time. It is normally used for major projects such as:

- starting up a business from scratch where money may be needed for items such as premises, equipment, staff training and initial stock
- launching a new product
- buying/taking over another business
- expansion, which could include moving to larger premises, buying extra machines and taking on additional staff

Did you know?

The word 'cash' in 'cash flow' means any kind of money payment. It includes cheques, credit and debit card payments, and electronic transfer as well as cash.

In 2009 it was reckoned that 56 per cent of retail transactions were in cash, despite the fact most people have credit and debit cards.

Capital investment can come from several sources.

- Small businesses can be started using the owner's own money, from savings or even remortgaging their own house.

- For limited companies, people buy shares, hoping for an increase in the value of their investment (capital growth) and/or regular interest payments known as dividends.

- Loans (see below) can be taken out from banks or other sources.

Sales

This is the most common form of routine business cash inflow. It comes from customers who may be private individuals or other businesses. The two main types of sale are goods and services. Public sector organisations receive their money in different ways, such as government grants or taxation.

Where can cash inflow come from?

Activity: Investigate income

Many charities receive some income from selling goods in their shops but also from other sources, too. Choose a large charity that interests you, then explore its website to find out its different sources of income.

PLTS

Practise your skills as an independent enquirer by thoroughly searching your chosen website to find as much information about the charity's income as possible.

Loans

Banks often invest money into businesses by providing them with loans. Loans have to be repaid after an agreed length of time, with interest. In small businesses, loans can come from close friends or family of the owner. The repayments of the loan capital as well as the interest payments both have to be taken into account when forecasting cash flow.

Activity: Investigate bank loans

Split into small groups and each choose a bank from the following list: a) Lloyds TSB; b) Barclays; c) HSBC; d) NatWest. Visit the bank's website and look for the business banking section to find out about their business loans. Look for features such as:

- repayment periods
- minimum/maximum loans available
- interest payable
- any other facts you find interesting.

Compare your findings with the other groups to decide which bank you think offers the best loans overall. Note that you may not find specific interest rates quoted. Why do you think this is so?

Did you know?

- Investors and shareholders put money into a business with the aim of receiving something in return, normally capital growth or dividends, or both.

- Private individuals can take out a bank loan. A special form of this is a mortgage, where money is borrowed to buy a house.

Regular and irregular inflows

When they produce a cash-flow forecast, businesses have to allow for the fact that some amounts of money are received at regular intervals, while others appear at irregular intervals. An example of regular payments would be a customer who makes monthly purchases. At the other extreme would be a customer who disappears for months and then suddenly places an order.

Businesses prefer regular income payments since this allows cash flow to be managed more easily. This is why firms like utility companies offer discounts to customers who sign up to the direct debit scheme, as mentioned on page 83.

Timing of inflows

Businesses obviously prefer to receive the money owing to them as quickly as possible. However, most trade between businesses is conducted on a credit basis. This means that suppliers and customers have an agreement that payment will be made within a fixed period, for example, 28 days.

Unfortunately, some business customers do not pay within the agreed time period. Steps that a supplier can take to minimise this type of problem include:

- having a computer accounts package that flags up when a payment is overdue
- politely chasing up late payers with a phone call, email or text
- carrying out a **credit check** on new customers
- refusing to supply a customer until an outstanding bill is paid
- taking out **credit insurance** against **bad debt**
- offering a discount for early payment.

These activities are known as **credit control**.

A difficulty can arise when a small business has a large business as a customer. Small firms may be scared of upsetting the customer and losing their business if they press too hard to get late payments.

What is special about the cash flows of seasonal businesses?

Did you know?

- Some types of business are notorious for having irregular income. For example, **seasonal businesses** such as farmers and ice-cream producers have major fluctuations in income over a year.

- There are firms that specialise in doing credit checks and providing credit ratings on businesses or individuals, such as Experian. Visit its website to find out more. Anyone over 18 with a credit record can use this system to find and check their own credit rating.

Key terms

Bad debt – debt that is never paid and has to be 'written off' in the accounts. If this is a large amount, it could bankrupt a small trader.

Credit control – all the possible steps a business can take to identify customers who are slow to pay and the actions it can then take.

Discussion point

Many small business owners find it hard to remind customers they owe money. Would you? What would you do if a close friend or relative did not repay a loan and kept making excuses? Discuss what strategies you could use to get your money back and still stay on good terms!

Activity: Investigate credit control

Investigate one credit control system on the Barclays bank website.

3.3 Cash outflows

Generally speaking, businesses have more types of cash outflow than inflow. Typical payments include the following.

Purchases

These fall into several categories.

- Manufacturing industries have to buy raw materials and components to produce their products.
- All organisations buy **consumables** (items such as paper, printer cartridges and cleaning materials).
- Businesses also buy capital items such as computers, vehicles and machines in manufacturing industries.
- Many also **contract out** services such as cleaning, IT support and legal advice.

Loan repayments

These, and interest payments, must be included for any loan agreements that have been made.

Wages

The wages bill not only includes the money paid to employees, but also the employer's contribution to National Insurance payments and any bonuses or commissions that are paid.

Regular and irregular outflows

Regular outflows include:

- wages (most businesses pay wages on the last working day of the month)
- suppliers (who are paid towards the end of the agreed credit period)
- rent, insurance, and utility bills (which all have payment dates)
- loans (many have fixed and regular payment dates).

Irregular outflows include:

- capital purchases, such as production machinery and photocopiers
- unexpected events, such as repairs to a broken-down machine or temporary staff required to cover absence through illness
- travel expenses, particularly when employees have to travel abroad at short notice
- bonuses to employees in some businesses, particularly at Christmas.

Key terms

Consumables – used for items bought regularly by a business but that are not used directly to make the product or supply the service offered.

Contract out – pay another business to carry out support activities such as security, cleaning and payroll administration.

Did you know?

- Employers are also responsible for deducting income tax from an employee's wage and sending this to HM Revenue & Customs (HMRC). The total amount of all taxes collected by HMRC every year amounts to more than £400 billion.

- The John Lewis Partnership pays each of its 70,000 staff a bonus once a year. In 2009 this amounted to 14 per cent of everyone's annual salary – a total amount of over £100 million. This is a lot of money to find in one go!

Timing of outflows

In theory, the timing of any payment made by a business is within its control because it can delay payments if it wants. However, employees would be upset if they did not receive their wages promptly, suppliers may refuse to make further deliveries if the last one was not paid for and banks can normally demand a full repayment of a loan if interest payments are not met.

Most businesses like to control the timing of payments as much as possible with the aim of:

- hanging on to their money as long as possible so that it can earn interest in the bank

- making sure that when a payment is made there is enough money in the bank to avoid using their **overdraft** facility.

Activity: Identify your own inflows and outflows

In small groups, identify your personal inflows and outflows. How many of these are regular and how many irregular? How do you cope if you have many unexpected outflows at the same time? What could you do to manage these situations better? Compare your ideas.

3.4 Cash balances

What is a cash–flow forecast?

One useful technique for managing money is to forecast what your inflows and outflows are likely to be in the immediate future. Most businesses forecast their cash flow for at least a month in advance, but others do a forecast for a year in advance, a month at a time. They know that it will not be perfect, that things can change, but at least they can spot any obvious problems.

Note that a **cash-flow statement** is a summary of cash-flow movements that have already happened. We are concentrating on cash-flow forecasts, which predict what is likely to happen in the future.

Building a cash–flow forecast

To build a cash-flow forecast you need to have the following information.

- **Opening balance** – This is the amount of money in the business' bank account at the start of the period, say at the beginning of a month.

- **Income per period** – This is the amount of money expected to go into the bank account in that month.

Did you know?

There is an unusual arrangement in the retail trade for paying rent. Payments are made for three months in advance at the start of the period. Retailers struggle to find this amount of money all at once and are trying to have the system changed to monthly payments.

Key terms

Overdraft – an arrangement made between an account holder and a bank that allows the account holder to take more out of their current account than it contains. Banks limit the amount that can be overdrawn and charge interest for this facility. If it ever happens without a prior arrangement in place, the charges are very high indeed.

Cash-flow statement – a record of what has already happened.

- **Expenditure per period** – This is the amount of money expected to leave the account in the same month.
- **Closing balance** – This is the amount of money expected to be in the account after the income figure has been added and the expenditure amount subtracted.

The structure of a cash–flow forecast

Sam runs his own business, Superpaths, laying flagstones and blocks for paths and drives. At the end of September he carries out a cash–flow forecast for the next month.

Table 3.3: Sam's cash-flow forecast for October

Summary of October cash-flow forecast for Superpaths	£
Income for period (cash inflows, payment from customers)	10,000
Expenditure for period (cash outflows, payment for materials, wages, and so on)	9,000
Net cash flow *	1,000
Monthly summary	
Opening bank balance	3,000
Net cash flow *	1,000
Closing bank balance *	4,000

Why is Sam happy with the figures of his cash flow forecast?

Sam's forecast has two sections. The top part lists his forecast income and expenditure, and produces a net cash-flow figure. The bottom part looks at the forecast effect of a month's trading on his bank balance.

There are six figures in the forecast. Three have been entered by Sam, and the other three are calculations based on these entries. These are marked with an asterisk (*). The net cash flow is found by subtracting the expenditure from the income. This figure is repeated in the summary section. It is then added to the opening bank balance to give the closing balance figure.

Sam is happy with the figures since he is forecast to have more money in the bank at the end of the month than at the beginning. This is because his net cash-flow figure is positive.

More detailed cash–flow forecasts

Table 3.3 is a summary of a cash-flow forecast. Normally, these are drawn up in more detail.

- The income and expenditure figures are broken down into more detail. Expenditure would list items such as materials and wages. All types of income would be listed, too, such as sales and loans.
- Several months are forecast in advance. This allows time for action to be taken if problems are foreseen. It also highlights any problems due to seasonal fluctuations.

Remember

When the net cash-flow figure is positive, the business has more money at the end of the period.

Sam's cash-flow forecast in Table 3.4 shows these changes. He has broken down his expenditure to give more detail. The total expenditure (£9,000) is the same and so are all of the other figures.

The forecast also covers two months, October and November. Note that the closing bank balance for October (£4,000) becomes the opening balance for November. Otherwise all the headings and calculations are the same for both months.

Table 3.4: Sam's cash-flow forecast for October and November

	October £	November £
Income from sales	10,000	6,000
Expenditure		
Blocks	4,000	4,500
Wages	3,000	3,500
Sand	1,000	1,000
Diesel fuel	500	500
Miscellaneous	500	500
Subtotal of expenditure	9,000	10,000
Net cash flow	1,000	–4,000
Monthly summary		
Opening bank balance	3,000	4,000
Net cash flow	1,000	–4,000
Closing bank balance	4,000	0

Activity: Find a non-seasonal business

Some businesses, such as travel agents, have obvious seasonal changes. However, it is hard to think of any business that has none at all. Discuss this in a group and see if you can think of any.

PLTS

Practise your creative thinking skills. What items do you and your family buy that never change with the seasons?

Did you know?

Itemising expenditure items in a forecast means problems can be spotted more easily. For example, if fuel prices rise, this shows up quickly.

Remember

Cash-flow forecasts cover several months so that trends can be spotted and the business has time to react to potential problems.

Activity: Check Sam's cash flow

Sam is concerned that his closing bank balance for November has fallen from the £4,000 he had at the start of the month. Examine the figures to work out how this has happened and compare your ideas.

Just checking

1. Which two figures do you need to calculate the net cash flow of a business?
2. What is meant by 'closing balance'?
3. Why do businesses pay close attention to the closing balance?
4. What is meant by 'seasonal business'?

Case study
Finances at Ashford Colour Press

Ashford Colour Press produces books and training manuals for educational publishers. It employs over 130 people and has annual sales of around £10.5 million.

The finance department is responsible for checking that customers pay on time, and for ensuring suppliers are paid within the agreed credit limit period. It is also responsible for paying employees' wages after deducting income tax and National Insurance. The Finance Director says the two most important figures in the business are profit and cash flow.

To improve profit, the aim is to drive costs down and increase revenue from customers as much as possible.

Cash flow is monitored on a daily basis to make sure the business does not exceed its overdraft limit. Cash flow is forecast for six to twelve months ahead to anticipate any likely problems and allow for capital investment decisions to be made.

Capital investment falls into two categories. First, existing machinery (such as printing presses) is replaced when it becomes costly to maintain. Secondly, the firm also wants to buy new equipment that incorporates the latest technology.

Think about it!

1. Identify two variable costs and two fixed costs at Ashford Colour Press.
2. Why is it important that the business sets the credit limit for its customers at equal or less than the limit for its suppliers?
3. The company makes two deductions from employees' wages. Where does this money go?
4. Why does the business have an overdraft facility?
5. Explain why the Finance Director says that profit and cash flow are the most important figures in the business.
6. a) What financial benefits could Ashford Colour Press gain if they invest in new technology?
   b) The managers need to decide when to make this type of investment. In groups, discuss how making a 6–12 month cash-flow forecast and using break-even analysis can help them.

Work in small groups to list all your ideas.

Assessment activity 3.4

Rocket Spectacular is a business that produces fireworks for public displays. It employs seven staff and, although the market is seasonal, it keeps them permanently employed. It sells its products to businesses that provide firework displays for weddings and other social occasions, as well as Bonfire Night events. Weddings and other events tend to happen more in the summer than winter. Bonfire events happen around the fifth of November.

The information below gives the income and expenditure information for a 12-month period.

1. Use the information in Table 3.5 and the bullet list to produce a cash-flow forecast chart for the 12-month period. The opening bank balance for July is £10,000. Note that the wages bill is higher in November when a bonus is paid. **P6**

Table 3.5: Rocket Spectacular's income in £000s

Month	Jul	Aug	Sep	Oct	Nov	Dec	Jan	Feb	Mar	Apr	May	Jun
Income	20	20	18	50	60	10	2	2	4	6	10	30

Expenditure per month:

- Chemicals: £1,300
- Insurance: £1,000
- Containers for fireworks: £3,000
- Rent: £1,800
- Wages: £14,000 (except November: £20,000).

2. When you have completed the chart, ask your tutor to check it before answering the following questions.

   a) What evidence is there to show that the market is seasonal? Use figures to illustrate your answer.

   b) Would the senior managers be pleased with the forecast? Give reasons for your answer.

   c) For any problems you identified in your last answer, suggest the types of action that could be taken.

Functional skills

Practise your mathematics skills by inserting the correct number in each box on the chart and then accurately carrying out all of the calculations.

Grading tip

Managers stress the importance of 'the bottom line'. This refers to the line that shows the closing bank balance. Study this carefully when you are analysing the effect of cash inflows and outflows to achieve M3.

Did you know?

- In business, spreadsheets are used to produce cash-flow forecasts because it is easy to find out the effect of possible changes and 'What if?' calculations.

- Bank current accounts, which do not attract interest, are used for day-to-day transactions. Banks also offer interest-bearing accounts that normally have rules about withdrawing money.

The importance of cash–flow forecasting for managers

When managers carry out cash-flow forecasting, this enables them to:

- identify potential problems such as a negative cash balance in time to do something about it. This could include boosting sales, cutting costs or taking out a temporary loan/overdraft to overcome the problem
- take advantage of opportunities. For example, the forecast could show a large closing bank balance one month. The surplus could be used for capital investment or moved to an interest-bearing account until it is needed.

Did you know?

- Long-range cash-flow forecasts, such as six months or more into the future, are more likely to be inaccurate than those over the next month or two because of unpredictable events that can happen. For that reason, businesses regularly amend the forecast to take account of changes.

Managers also need to be aware that cash-flow forecasting on its own cannot solve business problems. They must act on the information that they find, for example:

- the business may be too dependent upon one or two customers
- there may be no credit control system in place so customers are allowed to owe too much money
- the business may have borrowed too much for the amount of sales it is making
- the business may be spending too much on wages or consumables.

The cash-flow forecast shows managers where their action should be focused to have the most impact on the business' finances.

BTEC ## Assessment activity 3.5

Sadia started working for herself a year ago, making handmade greetings cards for Christmas, birthdays and other special occasions. At first she worked long hours because, as well as making the cards, she also travelled around selling them to specialist card shops and other outlets such as newsagents. She was delighted when some large stores showed an interest, and she agreed they could buy her cards on credit.

As the business grew, Sadia had enough money in the bank to fund her lifestyle and thought that she had nothing to worry about. In the last few months things have changed. She knows she is owed quite a lot of money and has to take more control over her finances, especially as she wants to take on more staff and

move to bigger premises. She also wants to buy an expensive colour copier.

Sadia has asked you for your advice. Write her an email that explains how break-even analysis and cash-flow forecasting work. Evaluate both techniques and explain how they can help her to manage her business finances.

Grading tip

Evaluate each technique by giving the benefits and also identifying any drawbacks or limitations. Provide evidence to support your opinions.

edexcel

Assignment tips

- You will find it easier to explain what figures mean, and how they relate to each other, if you apply them to a real business, such as a business idea of your own or a local business you know well. Start by identifying the costs and revenue involved, how break-even analysis could help and how regular (or irregular) the cash flows are likely to be. Then think of the types of problem a cash-flow forecast could highlight and what action would then need to be taken.

- Practise doing simple calculations in your head first. Use your calculator only to check you were right.

- Do not worry about doing business calculations. If you look at them carefully, you will find most involve simple addition, subtraction and, at most, multiplication.

4 People in organisations

All businesses need hard-working, committed staff to be successful. They aim to employ people at all levels with the right skills and attitudes to help them achieve their objectives.

Before long you will be seeking a job in a business organisation. What type of job will you do? What skills will you need? How will you persuade a business that you have the ability and desire to make a valuable contribution and help them to do well?

This unit answers these questions. It also explains what people do in various job roles at different levels in an organisation. It tells you how businesses are organised internally, so you can see how each job fits into the business and how they link together to contribute to the achievement of the aims and objectives. You will see how different structures and the size of the organisation can affect the work people do and the responsibilities they have.

You will also learn about the process used by businesses to select new employees. Understanding how this works is essential when you are applying for jobs yourself. Finally, you will see how to prepare for the future career of your choice.

Learning outcomes

After completing this unit, you should:

1. know about job roles and their functions in organisations
2. be able to produce documentation for specific job roles
3. be able to prepare for employment and plan career development.

All websites referred to in this unit can be accessed via Hotlinks. See page ii for more information.

Assessment and grading criteria

This table shows you what you must do in order to achieve a pass, merit or distinction grade and where you can find activities in this book to help you.

To achieve a **pass**, the evidence must show that the learner is able to:	To achieve a **merit**, the evidence must show that, in addition to the pass criteria, the learner is able to:	To achieve a **distinction** grade, the evidence must show that, in addition to the pass and merit criteria, the learner is able to:
P1 describe the main job roles and functions in an organisation **See Assessment activity 4.1, page 102**	**M1** compare the main job roles and functions in two organisations and explain how they may differ in different organisational structures **See Assessment activity 4.1, page 102**	**D1** analyse the relationship between job roles, functions and an organisation's structure, using appropriate illustrative examples **See Assessment activity 4.1, page 102**
P2 identify different organisational structures used within business organisations **See Assessment activity 4.1, page 102**		
P3 produce a basic job description and personal specification for a specific job **See Assessment activity 4.2, page 115**	**M2** produce a detailed and relevant job description and person specification for a specific job **See Assessment activity 4.2, page 115**	**D2** analyse how effective recruitment contributes to an organisation's success **See Assessment activity 4.3, page 116**
P4 complete an application and interview for a specific job **See Assessment activity 4.2, page 115**		
P5 match current knowledge and skills to possible job opportunities using appropriate sources of information and advice **See Assessment activity 4.4, page 128**		
P6 produce a personal career development plan **See Assessment activity 4.4, page 128**		

How you will be assessed

To achieve this unit you will carry out several practical tasks. You will research the job roles, functions and organisational structures of different organisations and see how these relate to each other. You will prepare a job description and person specification for a job and attend an interview. You will also undertake activities related to preparing your own career development plan and analyse the importance of effective recruitment to the success of an organisation. The assessment activities in this book will help you prepare for this.

Farzana

I was keen to start this unit, even though I don't know what type of job I want to do yet. I'm good at finance, but I also like the idea of working in human resources.

First, we learned about different job levels and organisation structures, which I found quite hard at first. It helped that my mother works for a large company and often talks about her job and what other people do. I can now make sense of some of the things she says, and I also found it useful to ask her about it as well.

I really enjoyed researching for a job, then applying for it and attending an interview. It taught me a lot, including to sit still when I'm answering questions and to smile even when I'm nervous. Our group filmed the interviews and I got a real shock when I saw myself on screen.

By the end of the unit I knew what qualifications I would need in order to do well in finance or HR. I also found out about some other jobs that interested me, such as Trading Standards Officers. I now have a career plan that includes several options. I think I'd be more confident at an interview, too!

Over to you!

- Have you seen yourself on film? What did you notice? Did you have a shock about the way you looked or sounded, or was it a pleasant surprise?

- Does the idea of attending an interview fill you with anticipation or dread? Have you attended any interviews for part-time jobs and, if so, how did they go? Do you think you could improve on your performance and, if so, how?

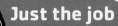 **Just the job**

1. Directors and managers of large organisations can earn a lot of money. Sir Alex Ferguson's pay packet as manager of Manchester United is £3.6 million a year. Is he worth it? How would you justify your answer?

2. Do you ever look at job adverts in your local paper? What do they tell you about the types of job available locally, the salaries and the work people do?

3. If you could choose any job at all what would you do? How much would you like to earn in five or ten years' time? What do you think you could do now to help achieve this ambition?

1. Know about job roles and their functions in organisations

Everyone who works in business has a specific job to do and each job is likely to differ in several ways, in terms of:

- the type of tasks or activities the job holder does
- the type of decisions they have to make and problems they must solve
- the level of responsibility they have and what actions they can take without anyone else's permission
- the skills, qualifications and attributes of the job holder
- the salary level and other benefits the job holder gets.

In most businesses, people are paid in relation to their level in the organisation. The more senior a person is, the more experience and qualifications they need to perform that job and the higher their pay. This is also because senior staff must take difficult decisions, which can prove expensive if they get it wrong. In effect, they are being paid to get it right.

1.1 Job roles and functions

Jobs are often grouped into different levels.

Did you know?

The most senior person in a business often has the title of Managing Director or Chief Executive, but not always. Some types of organisation use different names. Colleges have principals, schools have head teachers, newspapers have executive editors and the BBC has a director general.

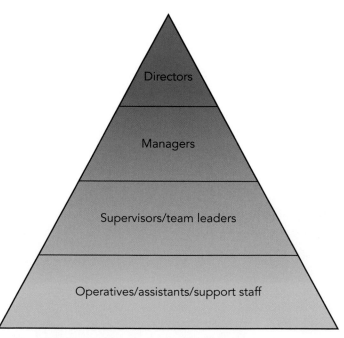

Figure 4.1: Job roles can be shown in a pyramid because there are fewer people in the higher roles and more people in the lower ones.

What do people in these levels do?

Table 4.1: Job roles and responsibilities you may find at each level

Job role	Responsibilities	This means
Directors	Looking after shareholders' interests Deciding **strategy** or **policy**	Deciding where the business is going (the strategic aims and objectives) Agreeing how it should get there (the company policies) Being successful so shareholders get a good return on their investment
Managers	Motivating staff Setting targets Recruiting and dismissing staff Allocating work Communicating Planning and decision making Problem solving	Focusing on specific objectives their department or area must achieve Organising the work to produce the required results Quickly solving any problems that may prevent this
Supervisors/ team leaders	Managing operatives Motivating their staff Allocating tasks	Allocating work and checking it is being done Solving day-to-day problems
Operatives/ assistants/ support staff	Day-to-day general work or clerical duties	Completing the tasks they are asked to do in time and to the right quality standards

Key terms

Strategy – what the business aims to do in the long term, for example, expand and recruit additional staff.

Policies – how it intends this will be done, for example, 'It is our policy to advertise all job vacancies on our website'.

Did you know?

One difference between job levels relates to time. Directors look at the long-term plans of the business, say, over the next five years. Managers focus on one or two years. Supervisors look at achieving targets over the next month, while operatives are mainly focused on their day-to-day responsibilities. One way to remember this is to think that the further you climb up the career hill, the further you are expected to see.

1.2 Organisational structures

All organisations need some type of structure to work productively. Even the smallest firm needs specific job roles for the staff to make sure they know what they are doing and do not get in each other's way. In a car dealership, for example, there may be a manager who oversees four sales staff, three mechanics, a workshop supervisor and an office administrator.

Large organisations employ more staff and organise them into different groups. The number of groups and how they are organised often varies, depending upon the size of the business and its main activities.

Hierarchical structures

Some organisations have many levels of staff. There may be a managing director at the top, then various levels of managers and supervisors, down to the staff at the bottom. You might find this type of structure in a large retail or manufacturing business.

Activity: Identify job roles

Identify the top job role in your centre. Then identify two job roles at manager level, supervisory level and support level. Discuss with your tutor the differences between the functions and responsibilities at each level. If possible, talk to some of these job holders as a group to find out more.

• Boots' five divisions are based on the format of the stores: local pharmacy, health and beauty, flagship stores, airports and Republic of Ireland.

Activity: Think about structures

In which Microsoft division would you put each of their following products: a) Office software; b) MSN Messenger; c) Xbox?

Then find out more about L'Oréal's structure by visiting its website.

Analysing organisation structures

The job roles and functions in businesses vary tremendously. In many small businesses, such as local shops, staff are expected to help out in a variety of ways, especially at busy times. In other small businesses where specialists are employed, such as vets, accountants and solicitors, staff will have more defined roles because of their training and qualifications.

In all these cases the structure will probably be quite flat. Even a solicitor's practice may only have two or three levels, from partners to support staff.

As an organisation grows in size more staff are employed, usually at the lower levels. This increases the manager's **span of control** and often makes it more difficult to supervise everything properly. To help, someone may be promoted to be assistant or deputy manager. This introduces another level into the organisation. If the business continues to grow and more staff are employed, then team leaders or additional managers will be needed to supervise their work.

Gradually the work of each person becomes more defined. Rules will be needed to keep control and to ensure everyone is treated fairly over issues like holidays and time off. People will want to receive training so that they can progress to higher-level jobs. They will also expect their pay to be reviewed on a regular basis. This means the business owner(s) need to check that they have a fair pay structure that reflects the difference between different job levels.

There are dangers, though, in having too many levels.

• Employees may consider the boss of the company has no idea how they feel or what they think.

• Information may become distorted as it passes down the levels.

• If lots of people need to be consulted about everything, then it may take a long time to make some decisions.

• Important information may not reach the people who matter if senior managers only listen to their immediate subordinates.

Why does Boots structure its operations into five divisions?

Key term

Span of control – the number of staff a manager is responsible for. Normally this is between 8 and 12, depending upon their job. It is easier to supervise staff who are doing routine operations, like packing, than it is to manage those doing very different or complex jobs.

Did you know?

Very few businesses have a structure that matches one in a textbook! You may find a combination of a hierarchical organisation with several levels and teams working on projects, too.

It is important to check that all the necessary functions are being carried out to achieve the firm's aims and objectives in the most cost-effective manner and that all job roles contribute to their achievement. This may sometimes mean the business needs to be reorganised to take account of declining areas of work and new opportunities.

The link between all these factors is shown in Figure 4.5.

THE ORGANISATION

Directors determine strategy = what it does

↓

Set aims = what the business will achieve

↓

Decide objectives = steps to measure progress

↓

Managers agree targets for their functional areas, divisions or departments = contributions of different groups to achieve objectives

↓

Individual job roles = contributions of individual staff to achieve targets

↑

The **structure of organisation** is such that all objectives can be achieved in a cost-effective way.

Figure 4.5: The link between an organisation's structure, job roles and aims and objectives

Did you know?

- The term **subordinate** means someone who is junior to you at work.

- The structure of a business is determined by its size, its activities, the industry it is in, its history and the preferences of the managers. Sometimes a new chief executive will completely **restructure** or **delayer** a business, which can be very unsettling for staff who have to get used to working in different ways with different people, or who may even lose their job altogether.

Key terms

Restructure – change the structure of a business.

Delayer – remove a layer of a hierarchical organisation, usually to save money.

Activity: Revise aims and objectives

If you have forgotten about aims and objectives, turn back to Unit 2, pages 41–45 and refresh your memory.

Just checking

1. What does the term 'organisation structure' mean?
2. Identify four types of organisation structure you may find in business.
3. Why do the types of function vary in different businesses?
4. Describe the main features of a hierarchical business.
5. Why is it important to define job roles in an organisation?

Case study: Swept away by Monsoon

Lynsey has always liked shopping at Monsoon, so when she heard the business advertises jobs online, she decided to find out more. She read about several jobs in the stores: Assistant Managers report to Branch Managers, who report to Area Managers. Below Assistant Managers are Floor Managers who lead the branch teams, consisting of Sales Assistants and Senior Sales Assistants.

Lynsey also investigated jobs at Head Office. The different functions here are buying, merchandising, design, marketing and press, retail operations, human resources, IT, logistics and support operations, property, and technical services and sourcing. She saw that if she wanted a career in buying and started at the bottom as a buyers' admin assistant, she could progress through six more levels to get to the top and become a buying director.

1. What is the title of the person in charge of a store?

2. How many levels of staff work in the stores?

3. What type of organisation structure is there at Monsoon?

4. Why do you think the head office is organised into the areas it is?

5. Lynsey works in a local gift shop on Saturdays. There is another part-time sales assistant and the owner/manager. She is fed up because it is often very quiet and she's never had a pay rise in two years, even though she does several responsible jobs, including cashing up. What differences is she likely to find at Monsoon? Discuss your ideas as a group.

6. Sketch a chart to show the organisation structure at Lynsey's workplace and then another one to show the structure in a Monsoon store. What differences can you see and how would you explain these?

7. Check out the Monsoon website. Find individual job profiles which tell you exactly what different job holders do. You may also find it useful to download a Branch Sales Assistant application form and see what guidance Monsoon give their interviewees, in preparation for the next section of this unit.

Assessment activity 4.1

Prepare an information pack on job roles and organisational structures by completing the following tasks.

1. Either investigate the Monsoon website in more detail and download the job profiles for Sales Assistants, Floor Manager, Assistant Manager and Branch Manager, as well as the information on Head Office, or choose another business where you can find similar information. This could be one where you work part-time or where a family member works. Use this information to describe the main job roles, functions and organisational structure that exists in that organisation. **P1**

2. Find out the organisation structure of your school or college. Draw a diagram to represent it and label (or list) the functions that are represented. Investigate at least two job roles at different levels in the organisation and find out how they contribute towards achieving the aims and objectives. **M1** (part)

3. Write a factsheet in which you identify the different organisation structures you can expect to find in businesses. **P2**

4. Compare the main job roles and functions in both of your organisations and explain how these may differ in different organisational structures. **M1**

5. Analyse the relationship between the job roles, functions and structure of an organisation. Illustrate your explanation with examples from your investigations into the two businesses above. **D1**

Grading tip

Analyse by identifying, and commenting on, all the separate factors that link together the job roles, functions and structure of an organisation. Support your arguments with examples from your investigations.

2. Be able to produce documentation for specific job roles

All organisations need staff to fill new jobs and to replace staff who leave. Sometimes people are promoted to a higher level job within their organisation. The advantage for the business is that the abilities of these staff are known to them. Also, because existing staff know how the company operates, they need less training. Promotion also helps to motivate existing staff to work hard and undergo training because they know they can progress.

Other times, new staff are brought in from outside. This may be because the new job is at the bottom level or because existing staff do not have the specialist skills that are needed. In addition, new staff bring in new experiences and knowledge to the business. For this reason, most organisations try to recruit using both methods.

Recruitment, though, is not easy. There may be many applicants for a job, so choosing the best one can be difficult. In addition, employment laws mean each applicant must be treated fairly and equally. Staff involved in recruitment must be aware of this and know what they can do and what they must not do. You will learn more about this if you study Option Unit 9.

Did you know?

Today many organisations advertise their job vacancies online, like Monsoon Accessorize. Your local paper may also show local job vacancies on its website but you may have to register to see them.

Is a job interview just for the employer to find out about the applicant?

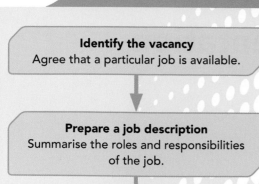

Identify the vacancy
Agree that a particular job is available.

↓

Prepare a job description
Summarise the roles and responsibilities of the job.

↓

Prepare a person specification
Identify the skills and experience required.

↓

Advertise the vacancy
Choose from a range of methods, for example, press, website.

↓

Shortlist applicants
Reduce the number of applicants to those most suitable to be interviewed.

↓

Interview
This involves one or more people and may include psychometric and/or aptitude tests.

↓

Appoint the most suitable candidate
This is the main focus of the interview.

Figure 4.6: The recruitment process

Key terms

Job description – a statement that lists the main elements of a job and the tasks done by the job holder.

Person specification – linked to the job description, it states the skills and abilities needed to do the job effectively.

Knowing how businesses go about recruiting staff helps you to understand what happens when you apply for a job yourself. It means you can prepare an application in a way that will improve your chances of getting an interview. If you know what employers are looking for during an interview, this helps your chance of being selected for the job.

 Activity: Do you get what you deserve?

Imagine your friend has started his own business and has worked day and night to get it underway. The orders have suddenly started coming in faster than he expected, customers are ringing up every day and he needs some help. He has enough income to employ his first member of staff, but getting the right person is crucial.

Work in groups to suggest the best way of hiring the best person possible. Then identify all the possible consequences of employing someone who is a complete disaster.

Compare your ideas with other groups. Keep your notes. You will find them helpful when doing the Assessment activity on page 116.

2.1 Job descriptions and person specifications

Both these documents are part of the standard recruitment process of most large organisations. This process starts when a vacancy is agreed and ends when a candidate is appointed for the job. You can see all the steps in Figure 4.6.

Applying for a permanent job is normally more formal than completing a form or attending an interview for a part-time or Saturday job, or filling in any work experience documents. This is because the organisation is making a greater commitment if it employs you. You may also find there is far more competition for the job, so everything about your application is extremely important if you are to succeed.

The more you know about the job, the easier it is to target your application effectively. For this reason, employers often send a copy of the **job description** and the **person specification** to all applicants.

 Did you know?

When someone is leaving and their job is being advertised, businesses often take advantage of this to review the job role and update the tasks and duties to include any new requirements.

2.2 Methods of drawing up a job description

This document is normally prepared before the vacancy is advertised and can be done in one of three ways.

- **By department** – Staff in the department where the vacancy has occurred may draw up a description of what the job entails. This enables any skills the department may be lacking to be identified. It also allows departmental staff to contribute ideas and suggestions.

- **By job holder** – The person who is currently doing the job may list the tasks and duties that are involved. The benefit of this method is that the current job holder will know the job better than anyone. The disadvantage is that this may not allow for changes to the current role to be made.

- **By interview** – In some cases, the current job holder is interviewed to find out what is involved. This may be carried out by the job holder's manager or by the human resources department. The advantage is that is takes account of the views of the current job holder but also allows for additional input by a specialist. This is useful if the vacancy is going to be used as an opportunity to change the job role slightly.

2.3 Contents of a job description

Job descriptions summarise all the basic facts about a particular job and the role of the job holder. They should help applicants to understand exactly what type of work they will be asked to do. They also state the salary level. An example is shown in Figure 4.7.

> What are the advantages and disadvantages of asking job holders to create job descriptions?

I knew it was a mistake to ask him to list everything he does.

SAFETY FIRST LTD – JOB DESCRIPTION

Job title	Customer Services Team Member
Location	Head Office, Main Street, Danesbury DN3 9JL
Description of organisation's business	Safety First is a provider of a wide range of safety equipment and products, such as protective clothing and safety signs.
Purpose of job	To ensure all customers are satisfied with the products and service they receive.
Main tasks	Answering customer queries by phone and by email; processing customer orders; keeping customers informed about any changes to or problems with their orders; resolving customer issues or referring these to a customer services team leader; processing customer refunds; updating customer records; liaising with other members of the customer services team; liaising with sales and finance as required.
Hours of work	37.5 hours per week (some flexible overtime may be required)
Standards required	Company policy is to respond to all customer enquiries within two working days and resolve all customer problems within one week.
Pay and benefits	£11,000–£12,500 per annum. The company operates a bonus system for all employees, based on the achievement of agreed sales targets.
Promotion prospects	After appropriate training and experience, the successful candidate may be eligible for promotion to become a customer services team leader.
Lines of reporting: **Responsible to:** **Responsible for:**	Customer Services Team Leader N/A

Figure 4.7: A job description for a customer services team member

Did you know?

- No job description can include every task you may be asked to do. For that reason there is often a 'catch-all' phrase at the bottom. It may also state that at times it may be necessary to vary or change these duties, but this would be with the agreement of the job holder.

- By law, employers can only specify particular physical abilities and personal circumstances when these are a justifiable requirement for the job.

Activity: Decide qualities and skills

Divide into groups and decide what personal qualities and skills you think someone would need to do the job of Customer Services Team Member outlined in the job description. Then compare your ideas.

2.4 Contents of a person specification

This lists the essential and desirable qualifications, skills and attributes of the person required. Preparing this document enables the employer to think about the type of person who would be best suited for the job. It also makes it easier to highlight the essential and desirable qualities clearly in the advertisement. Applications are compared and the applicants chosen for interview are normally those who have all the essential requirements and several of the desirable ones, too.

Depending upon the type of vacancy it may include information on:

- attainments, for example, qualifications
- special aptitudes, for example, numeracy
- interests of the candidate
- personal qualities/disposition, for example, leadership qualities
- circumstances, for example, whether able to travel or relocate
- competency profiles, for example, what the candidate should be able to do.

An example of a person specification to match the job description for the Customer Service Team Member is shown below.

SAFETY FIRST LTD – PERSON SPECIFICATION

Department	Customer Services	
Job title	Customer Services Team Member	
Vacancy no.	474	
	Essential	**Desirable**
Attainments	Educated to GCSE level IT literate	Level 2 business or customer service qualification
Special aptitudes	Good communication skills	Good numeracy skills
Interests	Helping other people	Solving problems
Personal qualities/ disposition	Good organisational skills Friendly personality Flexible approach to working hours	Calm and patient
Competency profile	Able to deal effectively with customers Able to contribute to the work of the team Able to work unsupervised	Able to use basic database software

Figure 4.8: A person specification for a customer services team member

2.5 Applying for jobs

Businesses vary both in the way they advertise jobs and in their application process. Because you read about one vacancy online and had to send your CV does not mean you will have to do this next time. For this reason it is very important to read all the instructions very carefully.

Activity: Decide attributes

In groups, for each attribute listed below, identify two jobs where it would be important:

a) high level of qualifications

b) good at maths

c) interest in animals

d) ability to travel and/or relocate

e) patience

f) high level of IT skills.

Then compare your ideas.

PLTS

Creative thinkers will not just think of doctors, vets and computer programmers for this activity!

Remember

The job description shows you what the job entails, whereas the person specification tells you the essential criteria.

Activity: Were you right?

Check back to the notes you made on the qualities you thought the Customer Services Team Member should have and compare this to the person specification in Figure 4.8. How many key areas did you identify?

The differences you may find include:

- you may have to phone for a job description and person specification or these may be available online

- you may also be sent an application form. This may say that CVs are not acceptable

- you may need to send your CV and a covering letter of application.

Application forms

Many organisations send out application forms, and several make these available online. Despite the fact they will be judged on these, applicants often make dreadful mistakes when they are completing them, from incorrect spellings to missing out important information, which can mean they are immediately eliminated.

Table 4.2: Dos and don'ts when completing an application form

Do	Don't
Print out (or photocopy) the form and practise on this copy	Complete the original form until your practice form is as good as it possibly can be
Read the form through first	Try to do it in a rush or if you are distracted
Collect all the relevant information, for example, examination results, before you start	Guess anything important, such as grades or dates
Check whether you can complete and submit it online or, if you are writing on it, what type of pen you must use	Use a pen that might run out halfway through or one that puts blobs of ink on the page
Check where you should use block capitals	Write your town or postcode in the wrong place – check carefully where information should go
Write neatly and think about what you are doing	Put the current year for your date of birth
Check if you need to include names of referees	Include the name of a referee without asking their permission first
Think about your answers in relation to the space you are allowed	Make any spelling errors
Check where you need to sign and date the form	Complete any section marked 'for official use only'
Ask someone whose advice you respect to check your form for you	Sulk if they criticise parts of it
Complete the original form slowly and carefully (if you are writing it); proofread it *very* carefully if you are completing it on a computer	Cross out an error you make if you are writing it – use a tiny amount of brand new correction fluid
Make a copy before you post it	Attend an interview without reminding yourself what you wrote

Curriculum Vitae

A Curriculum Vitae (CV) is a summary about you and your achievements. It must look professional so you should send an original printout on good quality white A4 paper. Your CV should be divided into different sections under clear headings to include the following information.

- **Your personal details** – Your name, address and phone number (home and mobile) are crucial. Most people put their date of birth and their email address.

Think carefully about what to include on your CV

Discussion point

Some people start their CV with their name at the top and then write a brief personal profile underneath. This is a short, opening statement that summarises their strengths to attract the reader's attention. Do you think this is a good idea? How easy would you find it to summarise your strengths in three or four lines? Compare your ideas as a group.

PLTS

Try to discuss this objectively, rather than just assuming you will find it hard. This helps your independent enquiry skills.

- **Your education** – This should be in date order with the most recent qualification/course first. Include the school or college, dates attended, qualifications obtained, or examinations taken where you are still awaiting the result.

- **Your work history** – This should also be in date order, with the most recent job first. Give a brief example of what you did. If you are a full-time learner, include part-time or temporary jobs you have undertaken.

- **Other useful information** – This section can be used to make your CV stand out from the rest. Include any positions of responsibility you have held, details of hobbies, sports, voluntary work or organisations to which you belong, and any other relevant information (for example, driving licence or fluency language).

- **Referees** – It is usual to give two names. One should be a current tutor who knows your work well. Ideally, your other referee will know how you work in business (your employer if you work part-time or a work experience supervisor). Always ask a referee for permission before you include their name.

Darren has decided to apply for a customer services assistant position at Safety First. This is his CV.

Did you know?

- It is not sensible to put a family member as a referee. Most business organisations would assume that they would be biased towards you.

- If you lie about your skills or qualifications in your application or at interview and you employer finds out, you can be dismissed as a result.

Remember

A CV is a **summary** of your background, qualifications, experience and interests. Because it is a summary it should be short, preferably on one A4 page and certainly on no more than two.

DARREN BRIGGS

Address:	14 Highcliffe Road, Danesbury DN8 6LM		
Telephone:	02931 645424	**Nationality:**	British
Date of birth:	18 June 1992	**Marital status:**	Single
Email:	darrenbriggs@athome.com		

EDUCATION

2009–present: Danesbury College, Business and IT (ECDL) course
2004–2009: Southfields High School, studying for GCSEs

QUALIFICATIONS OBTAINED

June 2010   BTEC First Diploma in business (merit grade)
                 ECDL Certificate
June 2009   GCSEs   English (B)
                                    Maths (D)
                                    Applied ICT (Double Award) (DD)
                                    Science (Double Award) (DD)

EMPLOYMENT AND WORK EXPERIENCE

July 2009–present   Part-time sales assistant at Paperstore
July 2008–July 2009   Part-time evening work at Northlands call centre
March 2009   Two weeks' work experience at Capital Housing where I carried out general office duties

ADDITIONAL INFORMATION

I am used to helping and serving customers at Paperstore and I have developed good telephone skills because of my work at the call centre. I am now doing a summer ECDL course to improve my career prospects as I know good IT skills will be very important. My hobbies include playing five-a-side football (I play for a local charity team) and going to the cinema. I am also learning to drive.

REFEREES

Mrs J Silver, Tutor, Danesbury College, Park Road, Danesbury DN2 3PR
Tel: 02931 382798

Mr T Harper, Manager, Paperstore, Key Street, Danesbury DN1 4JL
Tel: 02931 603982

Figure 4.9: Darren's CV

Activity: Advice from the professionals

Some people prefer to leave nothing to chance and pay a professional agency to prepare their CV. As a group, discuss the benefits and disadvantages of doing this. Then check out the free advice given at one agency, the CV Centre. Visit its website to find out about CVs, filling in application forms, preparing a covering letter, preparing for interviews and much more.

Letters of application

Most employers will expect you to write a letter of application, to which you will attach your CV. This letter must tempt the reader to carry on and read your CV too. In other words, you use the letter to 'sell yourself' to the prospective employer.

The key points to note include the following.

- Use a standard business letter format with your address at the top. For an example, see Figure 4.10.

- Keep the letter short (three or four paragraphs at most) with a clear beginning, middle and ending.

- There must be no spelling, punctuation or grammatical errors.

- The first paragraph should focus on why you are applying for this particular job.

- The second paragraph should give some general background information about yourself at school, college or work. If you are enclosing your CV then refer to it, otherwise you will need to give details of your qualifications and experience in the letter.

- The third paragraph should link your skills and achievements to the essential and desirable requirements in the person specification or advertisement. It should also say why you want to work for the organisation and say the contribution you can make. Provide any other information that will make your application stand out as different and interesting.

- The final paragraph should say when you are available for interview.

Activity: Check Darren's letter

Darren has written a letter to attach to his CV to send to Safety First Ltd (Figure 4.10). Read this carefully and then identify all the times when he has related his application to the essential and desirable requirements in the person specification. Could he have done any better? Discuss your ideas as a group.

Discussion point

You have seen an advert that says you must telephone for an application form. Why might an employer ask this? What would you have to think about before you rang? Discuss your ideas as a group.

Did you know?

You should expect to draft and redraft your CV and application letter several times before they are fit to send. Pay particular attention to the section that can make your application stand out from the rest, such as a special section on the application form, in the letter or the opening statement on your CV.

Remember

There are many different ways to apply for jobs. Some employers send out application packs with the job description, person specification and application form. Others make these available online. Some ask for CVs and a brief covering letter; others state that all applications must be made in writing.

14 Highcliffe Road
DANESBURY
DN8 8LM
Tel: 02931 645424
Email: darrenbriggs@athome.com

18 August 2010

Ms Sue Jones
Human Resources Manager
Safety First Ltd
Main Street
DANESBURY
DN3 9JL

Dear Ms Jones

CUSTOMER SERVICES TEAM MEMBER

I would like to apply for the position of Customer Services Team Member which was advertised in the *Danesbury Post* last Friday.

I successfully completed a BTEC First Business course at Danesbury College last month and since then have been working at the local Paperstore shop as well as taking a summer course to improve my IT skills by achieving an ECDL award. I am attaching my CV which gives full details of my qualifications and my work history.

I would very much like to be considered for this job for several reasons. I really enjoy helping customers both in person and over the telephone. I gained valuable experience when I worked at Northland call centre for a year and learned how to speak to people in a friendly and business-like way.

I am well organised and do not need direct supervision to do a good job. I have a flexible approach to working hours and often work late at Paperstore to help tidy up. I also volunteered to work two evenings when we did stock-taking recently.

I would very much like to work for your company and contribute to the work of the customer services team. I am familiar with the range of products you sell and know their importance because of my work on my business course. I would really enjoy learning more about customer services and would enjoy studying for a qualification in this area.

I am an enthusiastic and conscientious worker. I am also used to contributing to the work of a team, both at Paperstore and as a member of a local charity football team. I can attend for interview at any time.

Yours sincerely

Darren Briggs

Darren Briggs
Enc

Figure 4.10: Darren's application letter

2.6 Preparing for interviews

You may find you have a mixed reaction if you get an interview for a job, especially if it is one you really want. You may be thrilled but nervous, too. You want to do well, but may be worried because you do not know what to expect or what to do to impress your interviewer(s).

The trick is good preparation. This will help to settle your nerves and will also enable you to do your best. Then, even if you are not offered the job, you can put it down to experience and know that it must have taken someone excellent to beat you!

Preparations

Check the basics, starting with the day, date and time. Make sure you allow plenty of time to get there. This means knowing where the organisation is situated and the bus or train times. If it's somewhere unfamiliar, have a practice run to find the premises a day or so before.

Dress

Think about your appearance. Remember that the interviewer is likely to be of your parents' generation, so dress with this in mind. Choose an outfit you like and can wear comfortably, ideally something that boosts your confidence.

Research

What do you know about the organisation? What does it do? Is it local or nationwide? Have you checked the website to find out as much as possible? This should include reading any information for job applications and any press releases, which tell you its recent achievements, as well as finding out what it makes or sells.

Questions to ask

Your questions at interview should definitely *not* focus on holidays, pay or time off in lieu if you are asked to work late. Instead they should focus on filling in any gaps in your knowledge and demonstrate that you have done your research and are committed to working hard. Good examples include the following:

- Are there any times in the year when you are very busy and need people to work late?

- I saw on your website that you support the local community by doing various projects. Can all staff get involved with these?

- Would your organisation support me if I wanted to carry on studying on a part-time basis?

Question anticipation

This means thinking in advance about questions you might be asked, so that you can have some good answers ready. It also means sounding positive, never moaning or putting anyone down (such as your tutor or

Did you know?

- Some organisations have two or more interviewers on a panel, so do not be surprised if you are introduced to several people when you go into the interview room.

- In addition to making sure your clothes are freshly washed and pressed, it is important to check your hair and nails are clean too.

What would you wear to an interview?

Activity: Testing, testing

Some businesses ask candidates to do a psychometric test to check their aptitude for a job or to assess their personality. Find out if there are examples in your library that you could practice. These are better than examples online which may be too difficult unless you have been working for a few years.

supervisors on work experience) and giving responses that impress people with your future aims and ambitions. It is usual for the first questions to be the easiest, as these are meant to relax you. Later in the interview they will get slightly harder. Typical questions include the following.

- What did you enjoy most at school/college?
- Why did you decide to apply for this job?
- How could you contribute to the success of this company?
- How would you describe yourself?

Prepare a suitable answer for each question you think you may be asked and, if possible, ask someone to give you a practice interview beforehand.

Confidence

Experts say that confidence is a state of mind, but this is not much use if you are feeling just the opposite. Instead, focus on the practical.

- Wear clothes that boost your confidence.
- Rehearse so that you are well prepared.
- Remind yourself that an interview is a two-way process. Perhaps you will find out you do not want to work for the company.
- Tell yourself you can only do your best. You cannot control who else has applied.
- Tell yourself an interview is an opportunity to sell yourself to an employer. If they decide not to buy, it is their loss.

Body language

Confident people stand tall and look people in the eye. They have a firm (but not terrifying!) handshake. They sit upright and do not fidget. They smile at appropriate times. They send positive signals to people watching them. For an example of confidence in action watch Barack Obama on YouTube.

There are many things they do not do that would send negative messages from staring out of the window, to lolling back in their chair, yawning, checking their watch, studying the floor intently or talking to the wall just above the interviewer's head.

Why is a confident applicant more likely to impress an employer?

Voice

This has nothing to do with your accent and everything to do with the tone and volume of your voice and the words you use. Street slang is not appropriate; nor is muttering or mumbling or, at the opposite extreme, shouting. Your tone must be respectful, but this does not mean you have to grovel.

Activity: Your interview skills

For more hints and tips about interviews, go to the CV Centre's website or try the interview game on the BBC website.

BTEC Assessment activity 4.2

Divide into small groups of three or four. Decide upon a suitable job vacancy that would appeal and be relevant to your group. This can be a job you have found online, one you have read in your local newspaper or one you have adapted yourselves from either source.

1. On your own, use the information you have obtained about the job to decide the most likely content of a job description and person specification. Then, prepare both documents. Make these more detailed and relevant by including additional information that you think is appropriate. **P3 M2**

2. From these documents, prepare an advertisement and circulate this to the rest of your class. In the advertisement, tell applicants to apply in writing attaching their CV.

3. On your own, apply for one of the advertisements circulated by sending your CV and a letter of application. **P4** (part)

4. The group that placed the advertisement should acknowledge all applications and arrange interview times. Within your group, decide upon suitable questions you will ask the job applicants. Then hold mock interviews with your tutor as observer to give feedback both to candidates and interviewers. Write a brief review of your own experience as a candidate, which includes a summary of the feedback you received. **P4** (part)

Grading tip

You will find it easier to make your job description and person specification more detailed and relevant if you think carefully about the type of organisation where your vacancy exists and the skills and qualities you would want someone to possess if you were hiring them. Then use these documents to decide your interview questions.

2.7 The importance of effective recruitment

All organisations need skilled, committed staff to be successful and to achieve their objectives. As you saw on page 104, organisations have a specific process they follow when they want to fill a vacancy. The aim is to ensure they choose the right person first time because this provides many benefits for the organisation. Here are the benefits of having an effective recruitment process.

- The process is straightforward and easily understood by existing staff and candidates.
- It does not cost more than necessary or take too long.
- It takes account of new skills required by the business.
- It includes internal promotion opportunities to motivate existing staff.
- It is fair and does not discriminate against any groups of people.
- All legal requirements are met.

- It ensures salaries are competitive to attract suitable candidates.
- It ensures the advertisement is accurate so no candidates are misled.
- The vacancy is advertised in the most appropriate way to attract the best candidates.
- It enables the optimum number of candidates to be interviewed.
- It ensures the best person for the job is appointed.
- New employees have the basic skills to do the job properly and quickly make a positive contribution to the business.
- Any skill gaps can be identified and training put in place to fill these.
- New employees fit in with existing staff.
- **Labour turnover** is low.
- The business regularly achieves its objectives.

Signs that the recruitment process is not working properly include too few suitable applicants, people dropping out before the interview, interviewees getting the wrong impression of the work they will be doing and either not being able to do the work or leaving very quickly. At this stage, the organisation should review its processes to find out what is going wrong.

Recruitment is time-consuming and expensive. Choosing the wrong people or people who do not stay very long means repeating the whole process. Also, the process may be unsettling for existing staff, particularly if they have to do extra work while a vacancy is filled.

In some cases, organisations have additional responsibilities because of the particular industry they are in, as you will see in the case study on the following page.

Key term

Labour turnover – the rate at which employees leave a company and need replacing.

Activity: Spot the dangers

Suggest two dangers of exaggerating the work done in a fairly routine job to make it sound good in an advertisement.

Just checking

1. What is the difference between a job description and a person specification?
2. If you are applying for a job, which is the most important: the essential characteristics or the desirable characteristics required? Why?
3. Identify three ways in which applicants may be asked to apply for a job.
4. Give four ways in which you could prepare for an interview.

BTEC Assessment activity 4.3

Your friend's new business is booming and he is recruiting even more staff. You have already identified for him the dangers of employing the wrong people (see page 104). Now write an email to him in which you analyse how effective recruitment will contribute to the success of his organisation. **D2**

Grading tip

Analysing means thinking about something in detail and then making a judgement. In this case, you need to think about all the aspects of the recruitment process and how, when these are effective, the business benefits and can be more successful.

All schools and colleges need rigorous recruitment processes for several reasons. They have to find staff with the right, sometimes specialist, skills and characteristics to do the job and also have a legal obligation to safeguard their learners, so everyone who works there must have a CRB (Criminal Records Bureau) check. This finds out about any criminal background that could prevent a person working with young people.

At South Cheshire College, Sara Duncalf is the Human Resources Manager. She assesses the effectiveness of the college's recruitment and selection processes on a regular basis, for example, by asking staff who are leaving for their reasons in an exit interview and also finding out how many people drop out between the application to interview stages. Sara also has to consider any new legislation the college has to comply with. Staff turnover is low at South Cheshire, which is a good sign, and she wants this to continue.

Many schools and colleges check the range of applications they receive by collecting equal opportunities monitoring information on the application form. This asks for details of age, gender, race and ethnicity and sexual orientation. The page is separated from the application before shortlisting takes place.

Like other schools and colleges, South Cheshire College ensures that interviews are carried out by a panel so it is not one person making the decision. The questions are agreed in advance and everyone is asked the same questions.

Interviewers in schools and college usually receive training to ensure that they can assess candidates impartially against the criteria for the job. A score sheet is completed to rank candidates' responses and identify how well they fit the job description and person specification. The aim is to ensure that the best person is chosen for the job every time.

Think about it!

1. Discuss the exact recruitment process at your school or college with your tutor. Identify any differences with the process described above.

2. Why do you think equal opportunities monitoring forms are removed from the application before shortlisting takes place?

3. What do you think is the optimum number of people who should be shortlisted and asked to attend for interview? Give a reason for your choice.

4. For each stage of the recruitment process, suggest what could happen that might signal the process is not working properly.

5. Identify the consequences to your school or college of not having an effective recruitment process. Compare your ideas as a group.

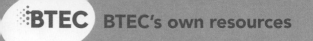
3. Be able to prepare for employment and plan career development

Did you know?

Even if you aim to continue studying full-time, it is useful to assess and record your progress at regular intervals. This enables you to benefit from opportunities to improve your skills or learn new ones.

Key term

Personal audit – a review of the knowledge, skills and attributes you have gained up to now.

At this point in your BTEC First course, you may think it is too soon to start planning for your future career and consider this section is not relevant to your current needs.

This is unlikely to be true, for several reasons. First, you cannot be sure about your current or future needs unless you have done a little self-analysis. Second, there may be several attractive options you do not yet know about. Third, planning now means you are in a better position to take advantage of any opportunities that arise and focus on areas you need to develop to achieve your goals.

3.1 Personal audit

A **personal audit** is a useful first stage in preparing for employment. It involves assessing your knowledge and skills now, then identifying areas where you are strong and areas you need to develop. This helps you then to match your knowledge and skills better to appropriate job vacancies as well as improve other areas to increase the range of opportunities available to you.

Potential employers will expect you to have proof of knowledge or skills you claim to possess, such as exam certificates, references and school or college reports. But other people's views and the experience you have gained away from school, college or work are also invaluable. So, too, are your own opinions, although you normally need to give specific examples to support your claims to convince people these are more than wishful thinking.

Your centre may issue a form on which you can carry out a personal or skills audit. The example on the following page also shows a common way of doing this which includes identifying the knowledge you have gained and the different types of skills you have acquired, for example, technical, practical, communication and interpersonal skills.

Activity: Carry out a personal audit

Carry out a personal audit, using the form shown on the following page or a pre-prepared form provided by your centre. Then discuss your conclusions with your tutor.

PERSONAL AUDIT

Name .... Date ....

KNOWLEDGE

List your qualifications here then identify knowledge you have gained from other sources, such as hobbies, interests or work experience, for example, first aid or how to do stock-taking for a retail firm.

Knowledge gained

....

....

....

....

Evidence

....

....

....

....

SKILLS

For each skill listed below, score yourself from 1–5 where 1 = I am very good at this skill, 2 = I am good but it could be improved, 3 = I definitely need to improve this skill, 4 = I would have to work hard to develop this skill, 5 = I have not had the chance yet to develop this skill.

Communication skills

Speaking to people face to face
Listening carefully
Joining in a group discussion
Using correct punctuation and spelling
Writing clearly and concisely

Speaking clearly on the telephone
Expressing own ideas and opinions
Persuading other people
Writing neatly
Composing business documents

Technical skills

Using ICT equipment
Using a range of software
Keyboarding

Using office equipment
Using the Internet
Producing professional documents

Practical and work skills

Working accurately
Finding and correcting own mistakes
Organisational ability
Being punctual
Solving problems
Thinking up new ideas
Accepting responsibility

Working with details
Tidiness
Meeting deadlines
Planning how to do a job
Making decisions
Dealing with numbers
Using own initiative

Interpersonal skills

Helping other people
Working as a member of a team
Being sensitive to the needs of others
Respecting the opinions of others

Dealing with customers
Being tactful and discreet
Being even-tempered
Being reliable

Figure 4.11: Personal audit form

Matching knowledge and skills to job opportunities

Many people apply for jobs with no chance of an interview because they do not have the necessary experience or qualifications. This is disappointing for everyone: the employer who has to read them, perhaps without finding anyone potentially suitable, and the applicants who may be desperate for a good result.

All good job advertisements clearly state the essential knowledge and experience required, as well as the desirable attributes, which are optional. These should be taken from the person specification (see page 107). This makes it easier for everyone. As an applicant, you need to check you possess all the essential attributes. You may be successful without all the desirable ones, providing you can persuade the interviewer that you are keen to develop these areas.

3.2 Types of employment

There are many different types of employment, which suits everyone.

- **Full-time employees** – contracted to work for the standard operating hours of the company. These may vary from 37 to 42 hours a week.

- **Part-time employees** – work for less than the standard operating hours, but each individual contract may be different. One employee may be contracted to work 15 hours a week and another only five hours.

- **Permanent employees** – work for a set number of hours per week from a specified start date. They will continue to work until the contract is terminated because they leave, retire or are dismissed.

- **Temporary employees** – employed for a fixed term, such as employees covering for someone on maternity leave, those employed short-term because the firm is very busy, or hired for a specific project. The final date of the contract may be stated if this is appropriate.

- **Seasonal employees** – also temporary and employed to work until the end of a specific 'season', such as the summer season for jobs in tourist resorts and the Christmas season for many retail jobs.

- **Paid work** – when employees receive a regular salary as stated in their contract of employment.

- **Voluntary work** – when people work for no payment. They volunteer their assistance for a special cause or charity, such as helping at a community group or working in a charity shop.

Remember

Carrying out a personal audit, then identifying the knowledge and skills listed in appropriate job adverts, enables you to identify the areas you need to develop to be successful.

Activity: Check out volunteering

Volunteering is a great way of developing additional skills and increasing your employability rating. Find out more about the range of opportunities available in your area on Do-it website.

PLTS

Volunteering enables you to develop as an effective participator because it benefits other people, not just yourself.

Have you ever done seasonal work?

Remember

There are several different types of employment relating to the number of hours worked, whether the job is permanent or temporary, paid or unpaid.

Did you know?

The term '**casual workers**' is used to describe workers with flexible hours who are offered work as and when they are needed. **Freelancers** are self-employed and hired by a company to do a specific task or project for a pre-arranged fee.

3.3 Sources of information and advice

Many learners have only a hazy idea about the jobs and careers that are open to them. It is all too easy to drift into a job that comes your way or to be overly influenced by family or friends. While their input can be invaluable, there are lots of other useful sources that can reveal types of work and jobs that you might not have thought about.

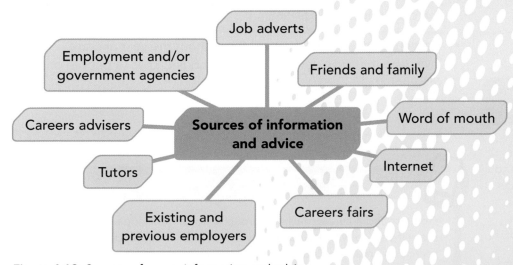

Figure 4.12: Sources of career information and advice

Obtaining information and advice about jobs

Activity: Check out Connexions

Explore the Connexions Jobs4U careers database, in particular the type of jobs listed under Admin, Business and Office Work. Are there any surprises in that list? What other work families are relevant to your course? (As a clue, there are at least six.) How can Connexions help if you are thinking of starting your own business sometime?

Did you know?

Apprenticeships enable you to work and study for a qualification at the same time. If you want to know more, go to the government's own website Directgov. You will also find links to the Apprenticeships sites in England, Wales, Scotland and Northern Ireland.

- **Careers advisers and the Connexions resource area in your school or college** – Visit this area and talk to the staff to find information about the wide variety of careers in business, such as jobs in marketing, HR and finance, which are all very different.

- **Government agencies such as Connexions or Jobcentre Plus** – Connexions provides advice if you are under 19, or if you are under 25 and have learning difficulties or disabilities. You do not have to visit a Connexions centre; you can find out about different careers and vacancies in your area online instead. Job Centres are for anyone of working age and, again, you can search for jobs and information online at the Jobcentre Plus website.

- **Word of mouth** – You may hear about a vacancy from someone you know: a neighbour, friend, relative or your tutor. Or you may be able to find out more about a particular type of work because you or your family know someone who works in this area.

- **Job advertisements** – Most local newspapers have specific 'jobs nights' – find out when these are. You should also check whether your local newspaper puts its vacancies online or is linked to a website, such as fish4jobs.

- **Local recruitment or employment agencies** – Find these in your area by checking in your local Yellow Pages or online. Agencies do not normally charge applicants for finding them a job but will charge for other services, such as helping with an application or CV.

- **The Internet** – This is changing the whole recruitment process. In addition to employers and agencies advertising jobs on their websites, other sites specialise in helping people find what they need, including jobs. Social networking sites, such as Facebook and now Twitter are also helping people to find jobs. Find out more in the case study on page 124.

- **Careers fairs** – These are held throughout the year and are invaluable because you can walk around and chat to people on the different stalls.

Activity: Job vacancies

Identify three or four businesses in your area that you would like to work for and check their websites to see if they post job vacancies online. Then check out Gumtree and 1jobs websites to search for more jobs in your own area.

Did you know?

Going round a careers fair in a group is not a good idea. You will learn more if you go with a close family member or friend and focus your search on areas that interest you.

- **Existing and previous employers** – Both are useful sources of information and advice on careers in their area of work. They may give you good ideas or confirm the type of jobs you would not like to do on a full-time basis.

- **Your tutor** – They should be your first contact and is probably the best person to give you advice about the type of jobs that link to your own strengths. Other tutors, too, may be able to provide useful information, particularly if they have an interesting or varied career history themselves.

- **Your friends and family** – They are one of the most obvious sources of information and advice because they are under your nose. If you are talking to people, check who they know who might help you.

Discussion point

Mark was desperate to work for a local advertising agency because he thought their work was fascinating. After finding out there were no vacancies, he offered to work for them during his holidays for nothing. Was this a good idea or not? As a group, discuss the advantages and disadvantages of Mark's idea.

Did you know?

'**Networking**' is the term used for making professional contacts. In some industries, such as the media, this is a major way of finding out about new job opportunities.

Remember

There are many sources of information and advice on jobs. Investigating these improves your own chances of finding a job you will enjoy.

PLTS

Being a creative thinker can help you find work more easily.

Find out about careers fairs you could attend.

Case study: All a Twitter about jobs

When your parents were young, they may have job hunted by calling into job centres, reading advertisements or perhaps checking vacancies in the windows of recruitment agencies. What people do now is often quite different because the Internet is changing the face of job hunting forever.

Social networking sites like Facebook and LinkedIn now mean that job hunters can use their profile to advertise themselves online. Some people even create their own website to do it. Twitter, too, has its advocates. With more than three million tweeters, it is a magnet for recruiters, as well as job hunters.

TweetMyJobs, TwitJobs and TwitterJobSearch all link with Twitter to make job searching even easier. These select only the jobs that might interest you, then send you an instant message to tell you.

Lucian Tarnowski, the young entrepreneur behind BraveNewTalent.com, had a different idea. This is to provide an add-on application to Facebook, MySpace and Bebo that allows users to create a separate, professional profile and then search for employers that interest them, as well as link to other job seekers with similar interests. Will this be successful? No one knows yet, but one thing is certain. The Internet has expanded the range of recruitment options, and both businesses and job applicants need to keep up.

1. **Check out three or four of the websites mentioned above to find out more about them.**

2. **Identify the major difference between LinkedIn and other social networking sites.**

3. **If recruiters could look at your profile on Facebook, Bebo or MySpace, how would this affect what you put on it? Discuss your ideas as a group.**

4. **How would you personally use the Internet to find a job? Why could this depend upon where you live and what you want to do? Discuss your ideas as a group.**

3.4 Career development

Finding out about different jobs is very useful as part of your overall career plan. Your first job is usually just the first step on your career ladder. The aim is to develop and improve your skills and abilities continuously so that you can move to higher-level, more challenging and better-paid jobs in the future.

There are two routes to moving on, and many people combine the two, as you will see below.

In the workplace

Your can start to develop your career on day one, if you have an induction programme, because this is one of several training opportunities in the workplace.

- **Induction programmes** – Enable new staff to learn the layout, policies and working practices of an organisation so that they can operate effectively as quickly as possible. During induction, opportunities for further training and career development may be discussed.

- **Training needs** – May be identified by individual staff or their managers. Certain staff may want (or need) to improve existing skills or learn new ones so that they can undertake more varied or responsible jobs. Managers may encourage staff to learn new skills because these are needed by the organisation.

- **Development plans** – Help to achieve future career aims. They should include personal targets and summarise strengths and weaknesses, and highlight specific areas of development. They also include an action plan which says how the plan will be achieved.

- **Performance targets** – Must be met if an organisation is to achieve its objectives. Staff will normally be encouraged to learn and develop skills that will help the successful achievement of targets.

- **Certificated training** – Relates to official courses, held on or away from the workplace. They may last a day or several months. A certificate or diploma confirms that a person met a certain minimum standard at the end. This document can also be used to convince future employers of continuous learning and development.

- **Uncertificated training** – Includes many in-house training sessions, such as those on health and safety, as well as informal learning opportunities, such as finding out how equipment functions or watching someone else demonstrate how to do a complicated job.

- **Personal development** – Activities you do that increase your knowledge, skills or experience, whether job related or not, such as learning a foreign language. Some organisations encourage staff to learn new things all the time, no matter what they are.

- **Flexible working** – Expected of all employees because all organisations must change and adapt to survive. This provides opportunities for staff to learn new skills and to stay up to date.

- **Progression opportunities** – Normally greater in a large, hierarchical organisation because you can plan to move up a level. In a small firm this may not be possible and the only way to progress your career may be to move sideways to learn new skills or to move to another organisation.

Did you know?

- Some organisations carry out a regular **skills audit** to identify any gaps between the skills their employees possess and those needed by the business.

- Other opportunities to learn more include **work shadowing** someone to see how they do their job, swapping work roles with someone for a short time and volunteering to help out if someone is absent.

- **Multi-skilled staff** can do a variety of tasks well. This normally means their jobs are more varied and enjoyable.

In education

You are already enhancing your career prospects by doing this BTEC First course. If you successfully complete it, then no matter what you do afterwards you will already be better qualified. Many learners go on to study at a higher level, such as on a BTEC National course, either full- or part-time. And many people continue to study on a part-time basis

Remember

It is important to think about the commitment you are making at the outset, rather than start a course and then give up.

Activity: Find a course

Check out the website of two or three local colleges and find out the higher-level education courses and professional courses availability. Look for those related to areas that interest you. For example, if you want to work in human resources, find out qualifications offered by the Chartered Institute of Personnel and Development; if you prefer finance, then look at the Association of Accounting Technicians.

Did you know?

Creating a career development plan involves finding out information relevant to your own future. It enables you to take advantage of useful opportunities when these occur.

for several years after starting work, to gain degree or professional qualifications. If you want to study on a course, you need to consider several things.

- **Qualifications need for course entry** – These are the qualifications you need to do the course in the first place. For example, if you achieve a BTEC First Diploma, then you have the qualifications needed to study a BTEC National Diploma.

- **Length of courses** – Short courses last a matter of days or weeks; others can last a year or more. It normally takes longer to study for a qualification part-time than full-time.

- **Practical experience entry requirements** – On some courses you need to prove you have relevant experience. For example, you can only study for a qualification to become the manager of a health centre or doctor's practice if you have experience of working in the health service.

- **Progression from education courses to professional training** – Education courses are broad-based and are offered at different levels. BTEC First is level 2 and BTEC National is level 3. Higher-level courses include Foundation degrees, for example. Alternatively you could study for a professional qualification linked to your area of work, such as human resources or accounting.

Preparing your career development plan

Think of your career development plan as a rough route map to the place where you one day want to be. It is 'rough' because you may change your mind several times as you progress.

It is *your* document and reflects your own aims and ambitions. Use the hints and tips below to help.

- This is your personal career path, so, although it can be helpful to chat to other people about your plans, do not be too influenced by anyone else when you prepare it.

- The aim is to plan ahead and identify what you should do next, as well as identify any gaps you need to fill to reach your goal.

- Career plans do not always focus on promotion. They can also include, for example, changing jobs or having a year out to travel or do voluntary work overseas.

- Start by assembling all the relevant information that will help you: your CV, adverts, job descriptions and person specifications of jobs that interest you, reviews from your tutor or employers and so on.

- Investigate courses, both professional and educational, that would interest you.

- Divide your goals into immediate ones, medium-term and long-term.

- Remember that your plan should be designed to be flexible. You can change your mind at any time.

The steps to follow are shown in Figure 4.13.

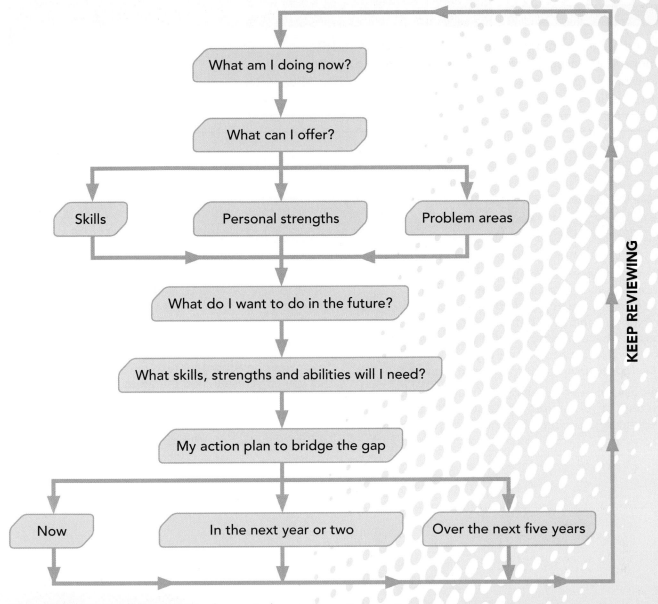

Figure 4.13: Preparing a career development plan

Activity: Draft your career development plan

In small groups, design a form for a career development plan that includes all the following items and any others of your own choice: name; date of plan; career aims (short term, medium term (one to two years), long term (three to five years)); current strengths, skills and weaknesses; strengths and skills required short term, medium term, long term. Then add a box headed 'action plan' with spaces for your activities and dates for reviewing these. Compare the forms as a class, then adopt the best one and use this to draft your own career plan.

Just checking

1. What are the benefits of carrying out a personal audit?
2. Identify and describe four different types of employment.
3. Identify five different sources of information and advice about jobs.
4. What is 'induction'?
5. What is the main benefit of preparing a career development plan?

BTEC ## Assessment activity 4.4 **P5** **P6**

1. Identify a range of job opportunities that would appeal to you using appropriate sources of information and advice. Match your current knowledge and skills to those required for the jobs you have selected. Summarise the abilities you have already and those you would need to develop to apply for each of these jobs. **P5**

2. Prepare a career development plan that takes account of your current skills, strengths and weaknesses and identifies the areas you would need to develop over the short, medium and long term to achieve your goal. **P6**

Grading tip

Your career development plan must show evidence that you have researched the areas in which you are interested and identified the qualifications and skills you will need to attain.

Assignment tips

- Use this unit to find out more about jobs that interest you and improve your own job hunting skills. Getting involved will mean that you learn more and are more likely to learn more and to achieve a better grade.

- There is a lot of information online about jobs and job application techniques. Focus your searches so that you look at areas that relate to your own career plans and jobs you would like to do.

- Your school or college will have a specific area to help people find out more about different careers. Investigate this thoroughly and talk to staff there to find out more.

6 Providing business support

Effective business support is vital for all organisations, both large and small. It is no use promoting the business to obtain orders and increase sales, and then letting customers down because the basic support functions are chaotic.

In a small firm, every member of the team needs to be able to carry out basic support activities, such as using a computer, answering the telephone and making photocopies. In a large organisation, support staff focus on activities related to their own functional area, so that in HR, for example, support staff ensure that job applications are promptly processed and interviews run smoothly. Part of this unit focuses on understanding the type of office equipment that is used and how to operate this safely.

Meetings are a feature of all businesses, both large and small. They are only effective, though, if they are well organised and if the documents recording what happened are accurate and produced promptly. In this unit you will learn about the organisation and support provided for meetings. You will also develop your own skills by carrying out business support tasks, organising meetings and preparing the documents required.

Learning outcomes

After completing this unit, you should:

1. understand the purpose of providing business support
2. be able to carry out office work safely
3. be able to organise and provide support for meetings.

All websites referred to in this unit can be accessed via Hotlinks. See page ii for more information.

Assessment and grading criteria

This table shows you what you must do in order to achieve a pass, merit or distinction grade, and where you can find activities in this book to help you.

To achieve a **pass**, the evidence must show that the learner is able to:	To achieve a **merit**, the evidence must show that, in addition to the pass criteria, the learner is able to:	To achieve a **distinction** grade, the evidence must show that, in addition to the pass and merit criteria, the learner is able to:
P1 explain the types and purposes of business support **See Assessment activity 6.1, page 134**	**M1** explain the appropriate uses of office equipment types, features and functions to suit different business purposes **See Assessment activity 6.4, page 143**	**D1** analyse the contribution that office equipment makes to the provision of business support **See Assessment activity 6.4, page 143**
P2 describe the use of office equipment to meet different business requirements **See Assessment activity 6.2, page 140**		
P3 demonstrate using office equipment safely in accordance with health and safety legislation **See Assessment activity 6.3, page 142**		
P4 draw up a checklist for a meeting **See Assessment activity 6.5, page 153**	**M2** produce all post-meeting documentation **See Assessment activity 6.6, page 156**	
P5 produce documents needed for a meeting **See Assessment activity 6.6, page 156**	**M3** explain the organisation and support provided for meetings **See Assessment activity 6.6, page 156**	**D2** analyse the organisation and documents and materials provided for a meeting, making recommendations for any improvements **See Assessment activity 6.6, page 156**

How you will be assessed

This is essentially a practical unit. This means that as well as demonstrating that you understand the types and purposes of business support functions, you will achieve the unit mainly by taking part in these activities. In particular, you will demonstrate that you can use office equipment safely, and also that you can organise a meeting and provide administrative support at that meeting. The assessment activities in this book will provide you with useful practice.

Podraig

I decided to do this unit because my brother set up his own business a couple of years ago and made a real mess of the admin side of it. He didn't have a clue what was needed, and just threw a load of papers in a tray every night and then tried to sort them out at the weekend. All he thought about was marketing and sales until he discovered there was a lot more to it. I'm hoping to learn from his mistakes.

I was a bit worried it wouldn't be very interesting, but I was wrong. Our group was given the task of choosing a charity and then doing several tasks to raise some money. This involved creating and photocopying documents, making telephone calls and holding weekly meetings. We treated our charity as the business we were supporting. It worked really well and we had lots of fun and raised £250 for our local hospice. Our final meeting was at the hospice when we handed over the cheque. So everyone gained, really, and I know if I start my own business I won't make the same mistakes my brother did.

Over to you!

- Do you know anyone who has started up their own business? How did they cope with the support activities that were required? Did they need to get someone to help them?
- What types of business support and admin jobs are advertised in your local paper? What tasks are listed and what is the pay like? At the top of the tree, senior support staff can earn over £30,000 in large cities.

Support and benefits

1. What support functions are carried out in your centre to improve the experience of both learners and staff? Discuss all your ideas as a group and ask your tutor to comment on how accurate you are.

2. Chris sells security systems to childcare nurseries around the country, and frequently travels to see prospective clients. What benefits would he gain by employing someone to carry out the business support activities? What type of tasks would this person do? Write down all your ideas and compare them as a group.

1. Understand the purpose of providing business support

Business support staff are vital in all organisations, and so are their skills. In this unit, you will learn about the purpose of business support and the tasks these staff undertake.

1.1 The purpose of business support

Business support is the lifeblood of an organisation, because it keeps the business running smoothly. This is vital in small businesses and in large enterprises for several reasons.

- **To ensure consistency** – so that support tasks are always carried out in the same way, and to the same high standards.

- **To make effective use of time** – in any thriving business there are many tasks to do. Some will be urgent, some important, a few will be both. Others will become critical in days to come. When administration tasks are prioritised and done by support staff, this enables other staff to concentrate on meeting priorities in their own jobs.

- **To support managers, teams, colleagues and departmental processes** – managers must focus on their own responsibilities. They cannot achieve targets or run their own areas efficiently if they are distracted by administrative worries. Other staff, too, will do a better job if they can rely upon support staff for assistance.

Why does effective support benefit everyone involved with the business?

- **To provide effective services to internal and external customers** – external customers may contact a business for information or advice, to complain or to buy products and/or services. Internal customers are colleagues in the same workplace who need something, such as information or a copy of a document. Both types of customer want their request to be handled promptly and professionally. If this is done consistently, the image and reputation of the business is enhanced.

1.2 Types of support

A wide variety of support tasks are carried out in organisations, all of which support the work of the business. These include the following tasks and activities.

Table 6.1: Types of business support

Admin task	Support for the business
Dealing with visitors Visitors may be other business people or members of the public. They may have a pre-arranged appointment or call in without one	Gives callers an immediate positive impression and enables visitor needs to be met promptly
Organising travel and accommodation Booking train tickets, making flight reservations, booking hotel rooms and so on	Enables staff to travel cost-effectively to meet customers and other external contacts
Managing diaries Arranging, agreeing and entering details of appointments in either a manual or electronic diary system	Enables activities to be coordinated and staff to be found quickly when necessary
Using telephone systems to make, receive and transfer calls	Enables enquiries to be dealt with promptly and accurately, improving customer relations and responsiveness
Organising and supporting meetings Preparing meeting documents, booking and preparing the room, arranging for refreshments and so on	Helps meetings to run smoothly, and a reliable and accurate record to be kept
Producing documents Using word-processing, spreadsheet and presentation packages to create letters, emails, reports and so on	Provides a written record of important information for those who need it
Processing and storing information, both manually and electronically Where documents are filed physically or scanned into an electronic filing system	Enables rapid access to records so that decisions are based on the latest available information

Remember

Support staff help a business to run more efficiently because they enable other staff to focus on their own job, knowing that important administrative tasks have been carried out properly.

Just checking

1. What are the main purposes of providing business support?
2. What differences might you find between the tasks done by support staff in small and large organisations?
3. What are six common business support activities?
4. How do these activities help the work of the business?

Assessment activity 6.1

Research the job roles of three or four business support staff in small and large organisations. Do this by talking to job holders or investigating job adverts online or in your local paper. Identify the types of support each job holder provides and the main purpose(s) of each job.

Use this information to prepare a factsheet that explains the types and purposes of business support provided in both small and large organisations. Present your findings to the rest of your group. **P1**

Keep your notes safely because you will use them again when you do Assessment activity 6.2 on page 140.

Grading tip

Make sure the jobs you investigate involve contrasting activities, as this will give you more scope in your answer.

2. Be able to carry out office work safely

Many support tasks involve office equipment. Using this correctly and safely means that you get the best results and do not risk damaging either yourself or the equipment.

2.1 Office equipment

Computers

Most offices have both desktop computers and laptops. Laptops are used by staff who travel on business or regularly work at home. Staff computers are often connected on a network. Information can then be shared easily and quickly by email or over an intranet. Each computer can access communal software, including an Internet browser, such as Internet Explorer, and packages including word-processing, database, email/diary, presentation and spreadsheet packages. Support staff need to know how to use:

* the computer system in their organisation
* the software packages needed for the tasks they have to do.

Activity: Assess your own ICT skills

List the ICT functions you can carry out easily and those that cause you more difficulty. Which software packages can you use confidently and which give you problems? Devise an action plan to overcome any difficulties that limit the type of work you can do.

Printers

There are two main types of computer printer, inkjet and laser, and there are several differences between the two.

* **Inkjet printers** are small, cheaper and usually slower. One may be provided for each user. They work by spraying very fine jets of black or coloured ink on the paper, and use ink cartridges.
* **Laser printers** are usually larger and more expensive. They are quicker and the print quality is crisper. These printers may be shared between users. Laser printers use toner cartridges.

The features and functions on a printer depend upon its type and the price paid. The main ones you might find are shown in Table 6.2.

Did you know?

The consultants in one private dental practice use instant messaging to tell the receptionist how much to charge patients, based on the treatment they have just had.

PLTS

Practise your reflective learning skills by asking for feedback from other people who know your IT abilities before you decide your action plan.

Did you know?

If you use any Microsoft Office software (for example, Word, PowerPoint, Access or Excel) and get stuck, you can get help online. Go to the Help and How-to section of the Microsoft Office Online website to see what is available. Watch a demo of something new or something you find difficult, then try doing it yourself.

Table 6.2: Features and functions of computer printers

Feature	Function
Duplex printing	Can print documents back-to-back
Media capacity	The amount of paper the paper tray holds, which can range from 100 to 850 sheets
Media size	The maximum size of paper the printer will use (usually A4)
Media type	The types of paper you can use, for example, plain paper, envelopes, labels, photographic paper
Memory	The number of pages that can be held in the printer memory
Mono or colour	Some printers also have a colour option
Monthly usage	The average number of printouts each month. Doing far more can mean the printer may break down more often
Networkable	This means the printer can be linked to several computers
Print resolution	The higher the dots per inch (dpi) figure, the better the print quality
Print speed	This is rated in pages per minute (ppm) and is slower for top quality prints. Inkjet may be 3–9, laser 6–24

Did you know?

- Many printers are multifunction devices that scan, photocopy and fax documents, too. These are ideal for many small businesses.

- Many inkjet printers are very cheap, but the ink cartridges they use are expensive. Kodak exploited a gap in the market by launching a new series of printers that use much cheaper cartridges. It claimed anyone buying one of these could save £75 or more a year. You can find out more by visiting the Kodak website.

- You can reduce the running cost of any printer by checking your work carefully, so that you do not take wasted copies, and printing in draft mode whenever possible to use less ink.

Activity: Investigate printer costs

Find out about the running cost of the printer you use at your centre. Check its features and find out how to replace an ink or toner cartridge and remedy a paper jam.

Photocopiers

Photocopiers are used to make copies of documents, such as items received in the mail and papers in files.

Photocopiers vary tremendously in terms of their size, speed and features. Some are small desktop models while others are very large machines that may be linked to the computer network. Computer users can give instructions remotely to print any documents on the system and also specify how the document should be produced, for example, whether it should be printed back-to-back.

Table 6.3: Features and functions of office photocopiers

Feature	Function
Copying speed	Can range from 15 pages a minute to over 100
Duplexing	Two-sided copying. This may be a manual operation or automatic with different options
Finishing unit	This may collate multi-page documents, hole punch or staple as required
Image density and other adjustments	Adjusts exposure for light/dark text or dirty backgrounds (for example, newspapers) to improve clarity
Image rotation	Enables crooked images to be adjusted or printed on differently orientated paper (for example, portrait to landscape)
Interrupt facility	Enables a long job to be temporarily stopped while an urgent job is done
Memory	Pages are scanned into memory before printing; routine jobs can be programmed into the machine and recalled as required
Mono or colour	Whether the copier only produces black and white copies or whether colour copies are an option
Networkable	Means it can be linked to several computers
Paper trays and capacity	Can range from one small A4 paper tray to two adjustable trays and perhaps a bypass tray for labels or transparencies
Reduce/enlarge	Enables copies to be reduced or enlarged to fixed pre-set ratios. Some machines automatically use the best ratio
Sample copy	Enables a test copy to be made
Stack	Multiple pages are inserted but each is copied and stacked separately
User ID/counter	Enables usage per user to be logged. Users must enter their PIN (personal identification number) to use the machine
Zoom	Allows more precise reduction/enlargement

Did you know?

- Photocopiers make multiple copies of computer printouts more quickly and cheaply than an inkjet printer.
- Most small businesses find it more cost-effective to have a black and white photocopier for large volume work and use a local copy shop for any colour work they need doing.

Telephone systems

There are many different business telephone systems. In a large organisation a designated person usually operates a switchboard or screen-based console that receives incoming calls. In a small business, these may be routed direct to extensions and answered from any phone.

Activity: Compare greetings

Find out the standard greeting given to telephone callers by staff at your centre. How do you think this might differ in a bank or a small retail shop? How do you answer your home (landline) phone? How do you think you should answer it and why?

Activity: Telephone features

Investigate the telephone system in your centre. Find out which features it has, as well as which are most commonly used.

Table 6.4: Features and functions of telephone systems

Feature	Function
Callback	Enables you to recall an engaged extension automatically when it is free
Caller display	Shows the caller's number plus the name and company if linked to an address book feature
Conference calls	Allows you to speak to several people at once, either extension holders and/or outside callers
Discriminating ringing	The ring tone between external calls and internal calls is different, so that you know which is which
Divert or call forwarding	Allows calls to be redirected from an extension to another phone
Do not disturb	Blocks calls to an extension while it is set
Hands free/listen on hold	Enables you to replace the handset and listen and/or talk through a speaker
Interrupt	Indicates a waiting call, usually by a bleep on the line
Last number redial	Automatically redials the last number you called
Message waiting	A light or bleep shows that a voicemail message is waiting. On a computerised system, the message pops up on screen
On hold/reminder call holding	Enables incoming calls to be held while the correct person is found to deal with the call/ gives a prompt that the caller is still waiting to be connected
Redirect	Enables a transferred call to be rerouted if the call has to be redirected yet again
Secrecy button	Depressing this means the caller cannot hear anything you say to a colleague (and is far better than covering the mouthpiece with your hand!)
Speed dial	Allows abbreviated dialling for long numbers, plus abbreviated numbers for calls made frequently
Transfer	Enables calls to be rerouted to another internal extension and on some systems to external numbers too
Voicemail	An individual answering service for each person. Callers leave voice messages in individual mailboxes when people are away or engaged on another call. Messages can be retrieved from an extension or external phone

Instruction manuals

All office equipment is sold with an instruction booklet or manual. This explains the features and functions, and includes other information the manufacturer thinks you should know. One of the most helpful sections is 'troubleshooting', which is normally near the end. This tells you what to do if you have a problem. The manual will also include safety advice, which is important if you are using electrical equipment.

Come on, it must be in here somewhere...

When are instruction manuals useful?

While it might be tempting to ignore the manual, there are several dangers with this approach. Stabbing at a few buttons and guessing what to do may mean that you make a mess of a job. Even worse, you may do something that is hazardous or that breaks the equipment.

Training in usage

The best way to learn how to use equipment is to watch an expert, though this person may make it seem very easy. You might be so busy watching you forget what you are told, so it is sensible to take notes that you can refer to when you are doing the job yourself.

Remember

- It is normally quicker and safer to check the manual to see what you should do *before* you start, not when you get stuck later on!

- All office equipment is chosen to meet specific business requirements, often relating to the production of professional-looking documents.

Did you know?

- Although you should switch off most equipment when you have finished, this does not apply to photocopiers, which are left on all day.

- Photocopier suppliers usually provide training if a business buys one of its machines. Certain members of staff will attend and other colleagues will have to contact these staff if they have a problem, such as a paper jam or if the toner is running low.

Activity: Watch demonstrations

Arrange to watch a demonstration of someone experienced carrying out a range of photocopying operations and using the telephone system at your centre. Make notes so that you remember what they did.

Discussion point

Why do you think individual staff members are discouraged from trying to solve photocopier problems on their own? Discuss your ideas as a group.

PLTS

Be an independent enquirer by deciding appropriate questions to ask to find out more.

Problem solving

All users should know the correct procedure to follow if they have a problem with a piece of equipment. In your centre, for example, if a computer printer fails to work, then you may be expected to report it to a named tutor or contact a helpdesk. However, a few basic checks, like ensuring it is plugged in and switched on, are sensible first.

 Activity: Prepare a help sheet

In groups, obtain the manuals for the printer and photocopier you use regularly. Find what to do if the paper jams, printing stops unexpectedly, the equipment stops working or the copies are unreadable, and prepare a help sheet for users.

BTEC **Assessment activity 6.2** **P2**

For at least two of the business support jobs you investigated in Assessment activity 6.1, identify the office equipment the job holders need to do their work. Then describe how using this equipment enables them to meet different business requirements. **P2**

Grading tip

Do not restrict your answer to equipment you have read about in this book. Include other equipment mentioned in the advertisements or by the job holders, too.

2.2 Working safely

Accidents do not just happen in factories and on building sites. In 2007/08, 2.8 million working days were lost because of workplace illnesses and injuries to people in administrative occupations. Safety risks include working with computers and lifting heavy items (for example, boxes of paper). Carelessness and thoughtlessness also play their part, too, such as throwing something across the room to a colleague, or leaving open a drawer for someone to bang into or trip over.

What sort of accidents might happen in the workplace?

 Activity: What about you?

Are you a safe worker or a walking hazard? As a quick check, do you leave your bag on the floor where someone can fall over it, or wear a backpack without considering the people behind you?

Using office equipment safely

Most people use computers every day. Although they look safe, they can contribute towards quite painful ailments, mainly because users can stay in one position for hours – head staring at the screen, hands on the keyboard, the rest of the body immobile, resulting in:

- musculoskeletal disorders, such as repetitive strain injury (RSI) and upper-limb disorders (ULDs) to hands, wrists, arms, neck, shoulders or back. These are caused by repetitive movements, such as keying in text or using a mouse, and poor posture

- tired eyes or migraine if the screen is flickering or unclear.

Laptop and notebook computers are even worse, especially if users rest them on their knees. The pointer is fiddly, the keyboard is not **ergonomically** designed and the screen may be hard to see in bright light. The result is a 30 per cent increase in people reporting problems with RSI, according to Microsoft's research.

Using a computer at work is covered by the Health and Safety at Work (Display Screen Equipment) Regulations 1992. These introduced minimum standards for the use of VDUs (visual display units) and the design of workstations. Users should also use their common sense to make simple adjustments for their own well-being. These include:

- sitting properly on a stable, adjustable work chair so that their back is well supported

- positioning the monitor, keyboard and mouse correctly

- putting their feet flat on the floor or on a footstool

- not straining their neck to look at documents

- taking regular breaks.

Sitting correctly with good posture can reduce strain and injury.

Did you know?

- In 2008, the TUC reported that the top three hazards of concern to office workers in Britain were overwork/stress, display screen equipment and repetitive strain injuries (RSI). Research by Microsoft in 2008 found that RSI costs UK businesses £300 million a year in lost working days.

- Your eyes need regular breaks from a computer screen. Look into the middle distance at intervals and blink more rapidly for a few seconds. Stretch your arms and wrists, and straighten your fingers at the same time.

- It is not just computer users who may suffer from RSI. Other variations include BlackBerry thumb, suffered by BlackBerry users who constantly use their thumb to type emails. Beware of this yourself if you regularly use your thumb to write texts on your mobile.

- If you use a telephone while you are on a computer, you should have a hands-free headset. This prevents you using your shoulder to hold the phone to your ear while you type, which can cause serious injuries.

Key term

Ergonomics – relates to the design of an item (such as furniture or equipment) to maximise user comfort and safety.

141

Activity: Safety at work

1. Check your own posture at a computer against the illustration on page 141. Score yourself against each item to see if you get ten out of ten or rather less!

2. Download the booklet *Working with VDUs* from the HSE website. Use this to design a poster that shows good positioning of a keyboard, monitor and mouse.

3. Investigate ergonomic keyboards and mice online, and decide which one you would like to buy. Compare your ideas with others in your group.

Do you know how to lift a box properly?

Remember

Working safely means following workplace policies and manufacturers' instructions. It also means using your common sense and concentrating when you are doing something.

Safe lifting techniques

Handling, lifting and carrying heavy objects can also cause injuries in an office, so never attempt to lift something that is too heavy. All organisations must provide trolleys or 'sack' trucks to lift and move heavy items. If the load is within your capabilities, then lift it properly: bend your knees first, not your back, so that your legs take the strain. Your legs can cope with this, your back cannot.

Following instructions

Under the Health and Safety at Work etc. Act 1974, all workers must take reasonable care of their own health and safety and that of others who may be affected by their actions. They must cooperate with their employer about health and safety requirements, which means following instructions. Businesses try to prevent accidents by providing information on using equipment and certain substances safely. These precautions are defeated if employees ignore them.

Assessment activity 6.3

In groups, choose **one** of the following guides to produce for your class using a computer, printer and a photocopier.

a) A safety guide for users of computer equipment.

b) A safety guide for the photocopying machine you use regularly.

c) A guide on safe working practices in an office environment (which includes manual handling and lifting).

d) A guide on using your centre's telephone system and good telephone technique in business.

Research the topic you have chosen. As you produce your guide, you must demonstrate to your tutor on your own that you can use different types of office equipment safely. A record of your performance will be made by your tutor as evidence of your achievements.

Grading tip

As a group, make sure that each person has plenty of opportunity to carry out each operation on the equipment and no one just stands and watches.

Just checking

1. What precautions are required to reduce the chance of RSI when you are using a computer?
2. Identify four common features of many photocopiers.
3. Explain the difference between an inkjet printer and a laser printer.
4. Suggest five features you would find on a business telephone system.
5. Explain exactly how you would tell someone to lift an extremely heavy package.

BTEC Assessment activity 6.4

Ewan, Claudia and Ashraf are expanding their successful IT consultancy and want to employ someone to provide business support.

Ewan takes coloured brochures to prospective clients, gives presentations and prepares lengthy proposal documents. Ashraf is a technical wizard and needs good-quality copies of technical documentation. Claudia runs training courses and needs high-quality handouts and information packs for participants.

However, their current equipment is not suitable. Until now they have been using a copy shop, but this is expensive so they want to buy the equipment to do these tasks in-house.

You really want this job. You have been asked to attend a second interview and do the following tasks beforehand. At the interview you will give a short presentation to the owners on the equipment they will need.

1. Identify the office equipment you think will meet their various requirements. In each case, explain the types of equipment available and how the features and functions vary to suit different business purposes. **M1**

2. Decide which equipment you think they should buy. Support your choices by analysing the contribution that each item would make to the business support you could provide. **D1**

Grading tip

An **analysis** always involves going into more detail than just giving a description or explanation. In this case, you have to apply the features and functions of the equipment to the tasks you would have to do and the outcomes you want to obtain.

3. Be able to organise and provide support for meetings

Why do many teams have regular meetings?

Getting people together for a discussion can achieve good results, especially if the meeting is well prepared and properly run. Sometimes, though, people complain nothing was agreed or the meeting was a waste of time. This often means the meeting was badly organised and supported. Doing this well is the focus of this section.

3.1 Types of meeting

There are many different types of meetings and they vary in several ways.

- **Size** – some meetings involve only two or three people, whereas others involve a large number of people.

- **Internal/external** – some meetings have only internal staff present; others include external contacts, such as customers or shareholders.

- **Formal/informal** – formal meetings have specific rules and procedures. Others are informal and may just involve a small group of people chatting together.

- **Confidentiality** – meetings are confidential when sensitive information is being discussed, such as strategy meetings where directors discuss future plans, and HR meetings about disciplinary issues.

- **The reason for holding it** – this may include keeping people up to date, generating new ideas, providing training, planning a special event or organising publicity.

The type of meeting will affect the organisational arrangements, including where and when it will be held, the number of people present, how they are invited, and the written record that is made.

Activity: Investigate meetings

Find out all the different types of meetings held at your centre, both formal and informal. Discuss with your tutor the steps that are taken at confidential meetings to ensure that sensitive information is kept private.

Discussion point

As a group, decide the problems that could arise if word leaked out that the directors in a company had held a meeting to discuss possible redundancies because of a lack of orders.

3.2 Organising a meeting

All meetings have several aspects in common. People are invited to attend, often by the **chairperson**. They are told the items that will be discussed, and these are often listed in an **agenda**. A record is taken to summarise the discussion and sent to people afterwards.

Meeting brief and agenda

The purpose of the meeting affects who will be invited, what will be discussed, how long the meeting will last and where it will be held. It also determines the budget, as you will see later.

A **meeting brief** may be prepared which summarises all the key facts. This is done by the chairperson and the organiser, often by using a checklist like the one below.

- Why is the meeting being held?
- What is the agenda?
- What is the budget?
- How long will the meeting last?
- When should it be held and what time will it start/end?
- Who should attend? Who are the key people who must attend?
- Where will it be held?
- Are refreshments required?
- Will any special equipment or other resources/facilities be needed?
- How will people be invited?
- What information/documents will they need?
- Will anyone require accommodation?
- What support activities are required (for example, taking notes or minutes)?
- What follow-up activities are required?

The agenda is often decided by the chairperson. Certain standard items are usually included and, for regular meetings, some topics may have been suggested at the last meeting. Anyone who is invited to attend may also be asked for contributions.

The agenda lists the topics in the order they will be discussed, so if someone can attend for only a short time they can work out when an item they are interested in will be raised, or where they will be expected to contribute. The agenda is often linked to the notice asking people to attend as this saves sending out two sets of paperwork (see page 148 for an example).

Checking dates

At regular weekly or monthly meetings, the participants know they are expected to attend. In other cases, the next date may be agreed at the last meeting and put in everyone's diary.

Key terms

Chairperson – the leader of a meeting.

Agenda – a list of items to be discussed at a meeting.

Meeting brief – a summary of the main requirements for a meeting.

Did you know?

During a meeting people should address remarks to the chairperson, not to each other. This is sensible. The chairperson would quickly lose track of what was happening if everyone could have separate discussions all around the room.

Sometimes the date is arranged from scratch. This is more complicated because ideally the meeting should be held when everyone can attend. This is not always possible, in which case you need to identify the key people who must be there for the meeting to achieve its purpose.

For major events at an external venue, several alternative dates may be suggested at the start because, at this stage, it will not be known whether a suitable venue is available on one particular date.

Confirming the budget

The budget sets the amount of money that can be spent on holding the meeting. Most organisations set a limit, which varies depending upon the type of meeting and its size. For a small internal meeting, the limit may be coffee/tea and biscuits. A breakfast meeting or working lunch would cost more, although this can be kept down if the catering is done internally or sandwiches are bought locally.

Meetings at an external venue, with several meals and even travel or accommodation reservations, are entirely different. The budget for this type of event must be agreed before any arrangements are made and quotations obtained to make sure the budget is not exceeded.

Choosing and booking the venue

A meeting can be a disaster if the room is unsuitable or the facilities are poor, so space, heating, lighting, ventilation and sound-proofing are very important. The room must also be clean and tidy and not cluttered with dirty cups and papers from the previous meeting.

Most informal meetings are held internally, often in special rooms kept for that purpose. Large organisations have a board room or committee room. Your centre will probably have specific meeting rooms, or use someone's office. Larger groups may meet in classrooms or other areas.

In a customised meeting room there is often a large table and several comfortable chairs, side tables for refreshments, and facilities for presentations, including blackout blinds if audio/visual equipment is regularly used.

External venues include hotels, conference centres and educational establishments. These may have specialist facilities, such as seminar rooms for group discussions, sophisticated presentation equipment, and some also provide accommodation for overnight guests.

Arranging catering, equipment and resources

- **Catering requirements** – will depend upon the length and type of event, the time of day and the budget. Usually a welcoming hot drink is offered at the start, and water jugs are placed on the table. A working breakfast or lunch usually involves finger food, from bacon sandwiches or toast to a buffet or sandwiches.

- **Basic equipment** – will include a whiteboard or flip chart to record ideas or decisions. An overhead projector or a laptop/PC and projector enables a PowerPoint presentation to be given. A radio mike and remote mouse enables the speaker to move around freely. There may be an interactive whiteboard and a video link to an external location.

- **Resources** – all the other items required. For regular meetings, these include the notice and agenda, notes or minutes from the last meeting, and supplementary documents. Discussion groups need notepads, pens and pencils. For external meetings, company literature and information packs are often given to external delegates, as well as name badges on arrival.

Discussion point

Some people say providing paper and pens is a good idea, plus soft drinks and mints or biscuits. Others disagree. They say it costs too much and people just take advantage of the freebies. What do you think?

Inviting people to attend

People can be invited in various ways. For a formal meeting, a notice may be mailed to everyone who has the right to attend, giving details of the date, time and venue. This may also include the agenda, as shown in Figure 6.1.

People are often invited to informal meetings by email. In some firms administrators use computer packages like Microsoft Outlook to check the diaries of all staff and book the first free slot available. The first 'notice' that the member of staff receives is a booking in their electronic diary.

If the meeting is at an external venue, and especially if external contacts are invited, an information pack is usually sent out. This will include a map, showing people how to reach the venue, details of any transport links (such as tube lines in London) and car parking, plus information on local accommodation. The pack should make it clear if people attending the meeting will be expected to pay for their own accommodation.

Confirming attendance and keeping a record

An accurate record must be kept of the people who will be attending a meeting for several reasons.

- Anyone who cannot attend a formal meeting should send apologies in advance. A list is kept, together with the reason for non-attendance. The chairperson can then check that everyone expected to arrive has done so and the meeting can start.

Activity: Find out about equipment

Find out the type of equipment used during meetings in your centre. Then find out the system used to book or reserve the items and the amount of notice usually needed.

Did you know?

- A key resource for many people attending a meeting is car parking. In many organisations visitor spaces can be pre-booked beforehand for attendees.

- The method(s) used to invite people must be appropriate for the formality of the meeting and the timescale. People may be informed of an urgent informal meeting by text message or phone call, as well as by email.

Remember

Anyone invited to a meeting needs to know the practical arrangements: the date, time and place of the meeting, what type of meeting it is, how long it will last, how to get there if the venue is unfamiliar, and information on accommodation, if applicable. They also need to know if they can send someone on their behalf if they cannot attend in person, as well as any costs involved.

THOMSON ELECTRONICS LTD

NOTICE OF MEETING

16 October 2010

The next meeting of the Safety Committee will be held in room T25 at 1600 hours on Thursday, 21 October.

Please contact me on extension 3280 or by email if you cannot attend.

AGENDA

1 Apologies for absence

> **1** Lists the names of those who cannot attend

2 Minutes of the previous meeting

> **2** Gives people the chance to correct any mistakes in the previous minutes

3 Matters arising

> **3** Enables people to give updates or report on action taken following discussion at the last meeting

4 Safety Officer's annual report

5 Safety exhibition

> **4** and **5** are the main business of the meeting

6 Any other business

> **6** Minor items people want to raise

7 Date and time of next meeting

> **7** The final standard item

Marta Wilcox

Secretary

Figure 6.1: A notice of a meeting and an agenda

Did you know?

At most formal meetings a minimum number of people must attend for the meeting to go ahead. This number is called the **quorum**.

- Attendees at a large meeting are often issued with name badges on arrival. These are prepared after their responses have been received.

- The number of attendees will affect the requirements for refreshments and other resources, from pens to car parking spaces. Catering requirements are also finalised a day or two before the event, when the numbers are known.

Identifying any special requirements

Some attendees may have physical disabilities or an impairment, which means they have special requirements, for example:

- wheelchair access to the meeting room and within the room itself
- a signer on the platform if anyone who is deaf will be present
- a loop hearing system for the benefit of hearing aid users
- paperwork in large print for anyone with limited vision.

Special dietary requirements can be identified by asking attendees to include these on the booking form in the information pack. Most caterers offer vegetarian options as standard, but you need to specify if anyone is vegan or has other dietary requirements or cultural/religious beliefs affecting their diet. If you cannot check requirements beforehand, the best option is a buffet with lots of salads. Remember water and soft drinks are usually served, not alcoholic drinks.

3.3 Supporting a meeting

There are several tasks to do during a meeting. Some vary depending upon the size of the event and where it is being held.

Checking the room

No one wants to start a meeting by rearranging the furniture to fit everyone in, which can happen if the room has another purpose or is a shared meeting room. Arriving early means you can make a few checks: the desks or tables are tidy and there is no rubbish lying around; any dirty glasses or crockery from the last meeting have been removed; the room is set out neatly; the heating and ventilation is appropriate; the resources you ordered, and any welcoming drinks, have arrived; there is an area where people can leave coats and umbrellas.

At an external venue you should be able to take issues such as cleanliness for granted, but it is still worth arriving early to check.

Why should you arrive early to a meeting room?

Remember

It is important to consider the needs of anyone with disabilities and to ensure refreshments take account of any religious, cultural, vegetarian and other preferences.

Activity: Investigate venues

You have been asked to investigate meeting venues in your area for a one-day seminar for 50 staff. The event will start at 9am and finish at 10pm. Three directors and two external visitors will require accommodation at the venue or nearby.

Working in groups, use the Internet to find meeting venues in your area. Check the rooms, equipment and resources, as well as other facilities, including those for disabled attendees. Find out about catering options and calculate how much the event is likely to cost.

Present your findings to the rest of the class. Then decide which venue provides the best value for money.

Functional skills

Carry out a range of appropriate calculations, such as working out the cost per person, to practise your maths skills.

Remember

Experienced organisers always arrive at a meeting early to check everything is correct, even at an external venue.

149

Checking the equipment

It can be embarrassing to start an important meeting to find the flip chart has only two pages left or the radio mike for the guest speaker is dead. Check every item methodically by switching it on and seeing that it works properly. If someone is giving a PowerPoint presentation, check the projector is focused and the screen is clearly visible from all parts of the room, even when the sun is shining.

Documentation for attendees

You will need to prepare documents to be sent ahead of the meeting, as well as those tabled at the actual event. Have spare copies of everything, because people often forget to bring important documents with them. Your set should include:

*   spare copies of the agenda and other documents sent in advance, including notes of the last meeting held by the same group

*   sets of documents to be tabled

*   the attendance list to check if all the expected people are present, and any reasons for absence you have been given

*   your own information, including details of the 'housekeeping' arrangements, such as the nearest toilets and what to do if the fire alarm sounds.

Taking accurate records of the meeting

It is normal to record what is said at a meeting to ensure that the important points are recorded and circulated promptly to those who need this information, to enable the notes to be agreed as correct at the next meeting, and to remind people what they have agreed to do.

How the **notes** or **minutes** are written up depends upon the style of the meeting and what the chairperson wants. You may write a list of numbered points or have to follow the agenda order and include an action column, as shown on page 152.

Tips on taking accurate meeting notes are given below.

*   Always include the essential information. This is: name of the organisation; date of the meeting; names of those present; names of those who could not attend; notes of what has been discussed or decided; date and time of next meeting.

*   Prepare by ruling left- and right-hand margins on an A4 lined pad. Write the essential information you already know at the top.

*   Be systematic. Put the topic or agenda heading, then the initials of the speaker in the left margin and a summary of what they say next to it.

*   The right-hand column is your action column. Put the initials here of people who agree to do something (see page 152).

*   Listen carefully to what people are saying.

Did you know?

*   There are two types of documents used at meetings. The first are documents sent out in advance, such as the agenda. The second are documents that are given out, or **tabled**, at the meeting itself. The term simply means 'put on the table'.

*   If there is no attendance list for some reason, the easiest solution is to pass around a sheet of paper and ask people to print their names on it.

*   Formal meeting notes are often known as the **minutes** of the meeting. These may be used as evidence in legal proceedings once they have been signed as correct by the chairperson.

Key term

Notes or **minutes** – a written record of the decisions made and agreed during a meeting.

Why is it important to take minutes at a meeting?

- Summarise – just write down the main points of what was agreed.

- Do not panic if you miss something. Put an asterisk (*) where the gap is and ask the chairperson for help to fill it in afterwards.

- Follow a routine, such as leaving spaces between separate items and using the same abbreviations, for example, M/c for Manchester.

- Do not over-abbreviate: see F about M on T is useless.

- Write up your notes promptly, while they are fresh in your memory.

- Use complete sentences in your final version and use the past tense, for example, 'Luke said that…', 'not 'Luke says that…'.

- Use dates, not 'yesterday' or 'tomorrow' as this will make no sense when the notes are read in the future.

- Check you have spelled names correctly.

- Be prepared to redraft your notes several times.

Serving refreshments

Ideally, serve a hot drink before the meeting starts and have jugs of water available. Try to arrange for the chairperson to pause the meeting so you can break off when the sandwiches or more hot drinks arrive. Otherwise, ask someone else to help you.

3.4 Follow-up activities

Once the meeting is finished, there are several other tasks to do.

Activity: Find out more hints and tips

Talk to a member of staff at your centre who supports meetings and takes notes. Find out what hints and tips they would give a newcomer who is doing this task for the first time.

Did you know?

An easy way of keeping tabs on who is present is to have a list of everyone you are expecting and tick the names off as people arrive.

Table 6.5: Follow-up activities

Activity	Notes
Clearing the venue	Always leave the room as you would wish to find it. Check all waste paper is in the basket, the table is clear, equipment is unplugged and tidied away, all spare papers and resources have been collected, and all furniture is where it belongs. Check, too, that no one has left anything behind.
Preparing an accurate list of those present	Check you have a list of who attended the meeting. This should be at the start of your notes, but make sure you have included any latecomers.
Apologies for absence	Check that you have noted everyone who was invited but did not attend.
Agreeing minutes of last meeting, if appropriate	The chairperson will usually ask everyone to agree the minutes from the last meeting are correct. It helps if you write up your notes in draft form and ask the chairperson to approve them before you prepare and send out the final version.
Writing minutes following meeting	Write up your minutes promptly, especially if you have any queries, or the chairperson may have forgotten what happened. Check anything controversial, such as what to write if there was an argument. An experienced chairperson will know how to word this to avoid any offence.
Action points	People may agree to do things to impress their boss, to get involved or because they find it hard to refuse a direct request. You must put what they agreed on record, to avoid arguments later. The best way is to include an action column in your notes and put the initials of anyone agreeing to do something against the relevant item (see Figure 6.2).

THOMSON ELECTRONICS LTD

MINUTES OF MEETING

A meeting of the Safety Committee was held in room T25 at 1600 hours on Thursday 21 October 2010.

PRESENT

Annika Hall (Chair)
David Blunt
Neelam Rani
Marc Salazar (Safety Officer)
Marta Wilcox

1 **Apologies for absence**
   Action
   Sean Fox sent his apologies

2 **Minutes of previous meeting**
   These were agreed as a true and correct record and signed by the Chairperson.

3 **Matters arising**
   David Blunt said he had received a quotation from Brands Electrical for new emergency lighting at a cost of £12,500. He would chase up the two quotes still outstanding.   DB

4 **Safety Officer's annual report**
   Marc Salazar circulated copies and outlined key items, in particular accident figures, which were down 8 per cent from the previous year.

6 **Safety exhibition**
   Annika Hall said this would be held at the NEC on 12 and 13 November, and Neelam Rani agreed to attend and report back.   NR

7 **Any other business**
   David Blunt said several safety signs had been vandalised at the Northfield Road depot. Marc Salazar agreed to investigate.   MS

8 **Date and time of next meeting**
   The next meeting will be held at 1600 hours on Thursday 25 November 2010.

Signed .... (Chairperson) Date ....

Figure 6.2: Minutes of a meeting

Activity: Check the names

The names of the people who attend are normally given in a certain order. Can you spot what it is?

Circulating the notes or minutes within agreed timescale

Once you know your minutes are accurate, you need to send them out. They are sent to everyone who was invited, whether they attended or not, so that they know what happened. You should aim to send out the minutes as soon as possible. This is because your minutes will remind people about the tasks they have promised to do and they will then have enough time to take action before the next meeting is held.

Activity: Read meeting documents

Try to see two or three agendas, related minutes and meeting papers for meetings at your centre, preferably in a sequence. In groups, discuss the contents and check how those who attended responded to the different agenda items and action points listed.

Assessment activity 6.5

Your friend has been asked to help a local community group by providing support for their meetings. Although willing, she has only a vague idea what this will involve.

Draw up a checklist she can use to ensure she does not forget anything. Use suitable headings.

Grading tip

You may find it easier to prepare a checklist if you use similar headings to the ones in this book, for example, meeting brief/agenda, dates, budget, venue, equipment and resources, refreshments, documents. Then put anything else under 'other tasks'.

Did you know?

- Many senior administrators keep a separate list of actions people have promised to take before the next meeting. They can then check progress has been made and give a few gentle nudges if someone has forgotten.

- An HR management survey found that 90 per cent of people reading the notes of a meeting look first to see where their name appears.

Remember

Good liaison between the chairperson and the organiser/note-taker contributes greatly towards the efficient running of the meeting.

Case study
Helping the team to win the race

Gemma Harkness works in a team of five Sports Development Officers (SDOs) and three sports coaches at St Helens Council. Their boss is Terry Bates, the Sports Development Manager. The team's aims include increasing participation in sport and physical activities, and developing clubs to support this increase. The team organises events, runs courses and liaises with national governing bodies of sports to achieve this, such as the Football Association and England Netball.

Essential admin work is done by two business support staff. This includes preparing application forms and posters when an SDO is running a sports leaders course. The support staff send these out and collate applications, then send confirmation letters and produce a work pack for each participant.

Maria Hardiman, one of the support staff, went on a course herself to learn more about supporting team meetings. One tip she learned was to sit next to the chairperson. Then if she misses a key point she can quickly ask the chairperson to ask for it to be repeated. Maria also learned the chairperson should welcome everyone at the start and introduce anyone who is new.

Maria prepares the agenda for the fortnightly team meetings. She emails the SDOs for suggestions, books the room and takes the notes. She checks these with the chairperson, Terry Bates, and also passes them around the team. On her course, Maria learned the benefits of including an action column and now does this. She was told the chairperson should check, at the next meeting, that each agreed action had been carried out. Her notes should then record exactly what had been done. A useful tip was to write notes in 'text speak' to save time, for example 'gr8'.

Maria learned a table plan was useful for a big meeting, and the chairperson and note-taker should sit where they can clearly see everyone present. An attendance register should be prepared in advance with the name of attendees and their organisations. Everyone can then check, on arrival, that their own details are correct.

Think about it!

1. How valuable do you think the work of the business support staff is to Gemma, her colleagues and their boss? Give a reason for your answer.

2. Maria learned about the key tasks to do before, during and after a meeting. Suggest three tasks that would have been included for each stage.

3. Maria was told that two important aspects of successful meetings were 'being well prepared' and 'good working relations with the chairperson'. In your own words, for each aspect, explain the actions you should take to help achieve this.

4. Some people on Maria's course work in child protection. They learned that if there was a court case, the court would study the actions promised and taken to check if anything had been overlooked. They were told to file their written notes alongside their typed minutes. In groups, suggest why these extra requirements are necessary.

Activity: Prepare to hold a meeting

Form your own meeting group(s) to prepare for your final Assessment activity. About six to eight members is best for each one. Each group has the task of organising an event, to be selected by the members. At this stage you should plan your first meeting.

- Decide when/where it will be held and make any required bookings.
- Decide what equipment you might need (for example, a flip chart).
- Ask a volunteer to be meeting organiser the first time. This duty must then be done by everyone in turn.
- The meeting organiser should prepare a notice and agenda. The notice will be straightforward. The agenda should be as follows:

1. Apologies
2. Election of chairperson
3. Rota for meetings secretary
4. Selection of event
5. Any other business (AOB)
6. Time and date of next meeting.

The first item must be done properly. Anyone unable to attend must send apologies to the organiser beforehand, with a reason.

Your group must decide a fair way to elect a chairperson. Start by thinking of the qualities a good chairperson would need. Remember the chairperson has the casting vote if there are any disagreements.

The event to be chosen is the main item of business. Do not be too ambitious or plan to spend money unless you know how to raise it. Plan on two or three months to arrange the event. Some ideas are given below but your group and your tutor may have some better suggestions.

- A one- or two-hour workshop with visiting speakers.
- An away day for the group as a whole.
- A quiz event with prizes.
- A visit to an interesting local business.
- A mini conference lasting half a day with various activities.

It is even better if you can pick an event that will help you with other aspects of your course.

If you cannot reach a decision at the first meeting, everyone should be asked to go away to think about alternatives and report back at the next meeting. This is what happens at business meetings all the time!

Finally, ask if anyone has anything to raise under AOB. The meeting's organiser must then prepare and circulate the notes, and participants must carry out agreed actions before the next meeting.

PLTS

This is a great opportunity to be an effective participator, especially when you are identifying improvements later.

Just checking

1. Identify three reasons why meetings are held.
2. Why is it important to know who cannot attend a meeting?
3. Why is an action column useful in the notes of a meeting?
4. Suggest three tasks you may have to carry out if external visitors were being invited to a venue some distance away.

BTEC Assessment activity 6.6

As part of your role in helping to plan, organise and attend the meetings of your group to arrange the event, undertake the following tasks. Remember that you must do tasks 1–3 on your own and produce all these documents yourself to achieve these criteria.

1. Produce the documents needed for a meeting. **P5**
2. Produce all the post-meeting documentation for at least one meeting. **M2**
3. After the event has taken place, write a report that explains the organisation and support that was required to hold the meetings and which you helped to provide. **M3**
4. Hold one final meeting as a group. Discuss what aspects of the meeting organisation went well and what did not. Analyse the documents and materials you all produced. This does not mean putting the blame on anyone who made a mistake.

It means identifying what could have been done better. Complete your report by summarising this discussion and making your own recommendations for improvements in the future. **D2**

Grading tips

- You might find it easier to write about organisation and support under the headings of before, during and after the meeting.

- A good way of identifying recommendations is to think about everything you have learned about meetings since you started this unit. What advice would you give someone just starting out? What do you know now that you did not know then? What hints and tips would you give next year's group?

edexcel ⁞⁞⁞

Assignment tips

- Be prepared to learn a lot from experience as you progress through this unit. If you can reflect on this and use your new-found knowledge in your assessment activities, you will do well.

- Your written English skills and your presentation skills will be on display when you are producing records of and documents for a meeting. Use a spell-checker if you struggle with spelling and take care when you are producing documents. Use good-quality paper and consider copying the layouts you have seen here.

7 Verbal and non-verbal communication in business contexts

We communicate verbally with different people every day. We talk to friends and family as well as sales assistants, waiters, taxi or bus drivers, and the other people we meet as we go about our daily lives. In your centre, you will communicate with your fellow learners, tutors and other staff; at work you will talk to your customers and colleagues.

The way we communicate is very important, both verbally and non-verbally. It can enable someone to warm to us and want to help, or antagonise and annoy them. A person with excellent interpersonal skills can usually achieve far more than someone without them. Whether on the telephone or face to face, they can gain cooperation over a wide range of issues, from booking an appointment to getting help or advice. Because they project a friendly and positive professional image, they are liked and respected by their colleagues and valued by their customers.

Anyone just starting out in their career is unlikely to project the same level of professional image and interpersonal skills as someone who has been working for several years, but there are useful tips to know from the very start. In addition, there are several ways in which you can develop your own verbal and non-verbal communication skills which will improve your confidence in dealing with people at work, but also benefit you in your private life. You will learn about all these aspects in this unit.

Learning outcomes

After completing this unit, you should:

1. be able to use non-verbal communication skills
2. understand the purpose of verbal communication in business contexts
3. be able to use verbal communication in business contexts.

All websites referred to in this unit can be accessed via Hotlinks. See page ii for more information.

Assessment and grading criteria

This table shows you what you must do in order to achieve a pass, merit or distinction grade, and where you can find activities in this book to help you.

To achieve a **pass**, the evidence must show that the learner is able to:	To achieve a **merit**, the evidence must show that, in addition to the pass criteria, the learner is able to:	To achieve a **distinction** grade, the evidence must show that, in addition to the pass and merit criteria, the learner is able to:
P1 demonstrate interpersonal interactions in a business context **See Assessment activity 7.1, page 164**	**M1** explain how interpersonal interaction skills are used to support business communication **See Assessment activity 7.2, page 171**	**D1** assess the importance of effective interpersonal interaction skills in a given business situation **See Assessment activity 7.2, page 171**
P2 explain, using examples, the purpose of verbal business communications in four different business contexts **See Assessment activity 7.2, page 171**	**M2** discuss how verbal communications can be used effectively in business situations **See Assessment activity 7.2, page 171**	
P3 demonstrate speaking and listening skills in a one-to-one business context **See Assessment activity 7.3, page 182**		
P4 demonstrate speaking and listening skills in a business group context **See Assessment activity 7.3, page 182**	**M3** carry out a review of their speaking and listening skills in both a one-to-one and group context, identifying their strengths and weaknesses **See Assessment activity 7.3, page 182**	**D2** assess the effectiveness of speaking and listening skills in supporting business operations in a given business context **See Assessment activity 7.3, page 182**

How you will be assessed

To achieve this unit you will take part in a range of activities in which you can demonstrate your speaking, listening and interpersonal interactions in business situations. Some will involve talking with people on a one-to-one basis; on other occasions you will work in a group. You will also show how you can review and assess your own skills in these situations.

Rizwan

I recently got a part-time job in a supermarket, but at the moment I prefer working in the warehouse and collecting trolleys rather than dealing with customers. I also find some of the people I work with easier to talk to than others, but I suppose that's natural.

In class, we often have discussions and I always thought that most groups have two sorts of people – those who like saying what they think and those of us who sit and listen to them! Some people just switch off at times, but it depends upon the topic. It can get really irritating if someone will not stop talking.

We found out how we should work as a group to move a discussion forwards and involve everyone. We also looked at how we communicated in non-verbal ways, and I enjoyed spotting people on TV using body language to express different emotions. And I liked watching out for different types of verbal exchanges in business when I was in shops or even buying a sandwich! Having feedback about my own performance was really useful because I knew what to do to improve – and I'm still working at it.

Over to you!

- Are you naturally talkative, or do you prefer to sit and listen, even switching off? How do you think you might need to adapt your natural tendencies at work?

- Are you aware of the facial expressions and gestures you use? Do you know when you are looking bored or irritated, and do you ever wonder how this makes other people feel?

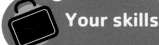

Your skills

1. You are told you are about to meet a young, successful business professional. What is the image that is now in your mind? Compare your ideas as a group.

2. Suggest three or four occasions in your private life when good verbal communication skills could help you get what you want.

1. Be able to use non-verbal communication skills

In addition to talking to other people, we communicate through our body language and presentation. In business, this means communicating the right image.

How can we communicate the right image to people we meet?

> **Remember**
>
> Customers judge an organisation on the attitude and appearance of the staff, which is why a professional image is so important.

Key terms

Interpersonal skills – the social and communication skills you need to relate to other people.

Interaction – refers to the two-way process between two or more people, for example, during a conversation.

1.1 Conveying a professional image

When you enter any business organisation, you expect to be greeted by someone who is smartly dressed, well-groomed, speaks clearly and has a friendly manner. You do not expect a scruffy, sullen individual with nose and eyebrow studs to scowl at you from behind a pile of papers.

While this may seem obvious, it is amazing how many people think they can work in businesses without thinking about their **interpersonal skills** and their **interaction** with other people. They may not think about appearing professional, yet this is very important. Conveying a professional image includes all the following aspects.

Appropriate dress or uniform to meet industry conventions or regulations

The dress code for an organisation will usually depend upon the type of industry and the overall style of the organisation. You are more likely to be expected to wear a uniform if you regularly deal with customers than if you do not. There may be a specific dress code, which regulates what you must wear, or there may just be guidelines to follow.

Even without guidelines, common sense should tell you that certain outfits are appropriate for business and others are not. If you are unsure about how casually you can dress, wear more formal clothes first and only 'dress down' if that is what everyone else does. Whatever you wear, remember it should always be clean and ironed, and your shoes should also be clean and in good condition.

Activity: Identify your working wardrobe

In groups, make a list of the clothes, footwear and jewellery which should not be part of your working wardrobe. Then compare your ideas.

In pairs, now decide what you would like to buy for your work wardrobe if you won £500. Get ideas online at DressCodeGuide and About which can be accessed via Hotlinks and compare your ideas.

Did you know?

The dress code or guidelines are usually given in the employee handbook. This is separate from strict regulations relating to protective clothing which must be worn for health and safety reasons or by staff involved in food handling. Non-compliance with these regulations can result in dismissal.

Remember

Any jewellery you wear should be subtle. If you are female, this also applies to your make-up. You also need a relatively conventional hairstyle, in terms of both style and colour.

Personal hygiene

Wearing freshly washed clothes means you are more likely to be 'nice to be near'. This is important, not just for your own self-image, but also to show your regard for the people you are with every day. It is pointless having a shower each morning if you then put on the same sweater you have worn for the last three days.

Being fussy about personal hygiene also means washing your hair regularly, making sure that your fingernails are clean and your breath smells fresh.

Sound organisational skills

Some people are naturally well organised. They deal with matters systematically and can always find what they put away. This is usually because they are good at:

- writing down anything they may otherwise forget
- making realistic plans that take into account the priority levels of different jobs

Did you know?

Some organisations refuse to allow customer-facing staff to eat curries or garlic during work days.

161

What are the strengths of well-organised people?

Activity: Your organisation skills

Check out your organisation skills. How quickly can you find a handout you got last week, a pencil and a pen? What condition are they in? If the handout is crumpled or torn, the pencil is blunt and the pen chewed, you have failed, even though you found them!

Did you know?

- Major benefits of being well organised include working more quickly, making fewer mistakes, being less stressed and keeping your belongings in tip-top condition.

- **Displacement activities** are things we do to put off starting a job we do not want to do, such as getting a drink or checking out Facebook. Which ones do you use?

- being self-disciplined and keeping to schedules

- storing information so that it can be easily found

- keeping their belongings neat, tidy and in working order

- breaking down long or complex tasks into smaller, more manageable chunks they can complete in an agreed timescale

- monitoring their progress and letting people know if there is a problem.

Good time management

Time management means being self-disciplined about the way you use your time so that you do not waste time doing unnecessary things. Good time managers normally achieve far more in the average working day. This means they meet their deadlines and commitments and do not let other people down. This is because they do jobs when they are scheduled to be done, not when they feel like it! They discourage people from distracting them when they are busy and are equally sensitive enough not to disturb anyone else at the wrong time, either.

Professional and business–like manner when dealing with staff and customers

Many types of behaviour are easy to label as 'unprofessional', including chewing gum, running down a corridor, being late, using bad language, shouting, and chatting to a friend on the office phone. The behaviour from a professional should include:

- a good knowledge of their job and the limits of their authority so you can rely on their judgement and know they will consult someone else if they need advice

Ah, I've found 16 Smiths. Now which one are you?

What type of behaviour can you expect from a professional?

- the necessary skills to do their job effectively – someone fumbling with a till or jabbing one finger at a keyboard is not a professional

- a confident, approachable, friendly, courteous manner, and giving you their full attention during a conversation

- being truthful, doing accurate work, taking responsibility for their decisions and fulfilling their promises

- self-control, particularly if things are going wrong. There are times when every business professional has had to count to ten before replying to someone!

Acting in a professional manner also means using appropriate body language (the messages we transmit by our gestures, facial expressions and posture) and where we position ourselves in relation to other people.

Did you know?

Someone who throws a 'strop' or responds aggressively to a perceived (or real) criticism is neither professional nor business-like.

What body language are these two people demonstrating?

Remember

It is no use saying one thing if your body language is saying the opposite.

Activity: Watch the masters at work

All actors are masters of body language, whether it is David Tennant as Dr Who, Dev Patel in *Slumdog Millionaire* or the entire cast of *Skins*. Find a clip of an actor/actress you admire on the Internet and analyse the body language they use. You can also find out more about body language on YouTube.

Table 7.1: The meanings of body language

Gestures Signal people or tell them how we feel	Waving hello or goodbye; touching hair/smoothing clothes when nervous; shrugging shoulders to show indifference; tapping foot to show impatience; putting hands on hips if annoyed
Facial expressions Give away thoughts and emotions	Surprise, disappointment, joy, annoyance and sexual attraction are all signalled with the eyes and facial expressions; eye contact (but not staring) shows interest in someone else; looking away indicates boredom; frowning or nose wrinkling shows displeasure; eyebrow raising shows disbelief
Posture Shows your confidence and attitude	Walking tall when confident; sitting up straight when alert and interested; slouching when bored; being hunched up indicates you are down-hearted; folded arms or crossed legs is defensive; leaning forward shows interest; leaning back means you are relaxed; cowering (literally trying to make yourself smaller) when scared
Body position Tells others what you feel and think about them	Standing closer to people you know and like than those you do not; instinctively moving away if a stranger stands too close; showing interest by turning your body and feet towards someone, tilting your head and maintaining eye contact; empathising by mirroring body language (for example, shaking your head when they do)

Just checking

1. What is meant by 'interpersonal skills'?
2. Give two reasons why time management is important.
3. Give three examples of professional behaviour.
4. Explain why a professional image is so important.
5. Give three examples of negative body language.

 Assessment activity 7.1 **P1**

Divide into groups and research dress codes and uniforms in different jobs and industries. Prepare a display that summarises what you have found and invite members of staff at your centre to see it. Demonstrate your interpersonal skills by dressing professionally for this event, greeting visitors appropriately, showing them around and answering any questions they may have. Take photos of your display to use as supporting evidence and ask your visitors for feedback, too. You could ask them to sign

a guest book and add comments as they are leaving. Your tutor will also prepare observation records to provide evidence of your achievement. **P1**

Grading tip

Remember, your skills should include being well organised and good time management.

2. Understand the purpose of verbal communications in business contexts

People communicate verbally for a purpose or reason. They also communicate in a variety of different contexts, from talking on the telephone to making a formal presentation, as you will see below.

2.1 The purpose of verbal communication

People communicate verbally for several reasons, including:

- to provide information
- to confirm an arrangement or agreement
- to make a request
- to give instructions
- to promote an idea, product or service.

Activity: Verbal communications

In groups, identify recent occasions when you have communicated for each of the reasons shown in the drawing on the left. Identify who you were talking to and what was said. Then compare your lists.

Did you know that?

This has been confirmed.

Could you?

Why do people communicate?

Key term

Business context – the business situation that applies and must be taken into consideration when people are speaking to each other.

2.2 Business contexts

Did you know?

Talking clearly and using an appropriate tone of voice has nothing to do with 'being posh'. Regional accents are attractive and perfectly acceptable. Using street slang or muttering is not!

The **business context** is the situation or circumstances that exists and affects aspects of a conversation, such as the tone of voice and the words that should be used. These will vary depending upon the formality of the occasion. Talking to a colleague over the telephone is more **informal** than speaking to a senior manager or customer; suggesting ideas at a team briefing is a more relaxed event than giving a **formal** presentation.

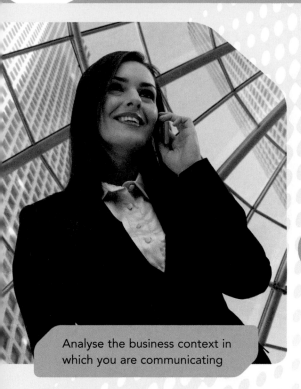

Analyse the business context in which you are communicating

Telephone contacts

Your telephone contacts at work can range from colleagues of your own age to senior staff and important customers. This may mean it is quite nerve-wracking when you first start making or receiving business calls, even if you are constantly on the phone socially. Fortunately, it is not difficult to develop a good telephone manner, with a little practice. It helps your confidence if you know your basic technique is sound, so that you appear polite and efficient to the caller no matter how you feel inside.

Did you know?

Experts say that if you smile during a call it makes you sound friendlier, and if you stand up this makes you sound more business-like.

Table 7.2: Hints and tips to make and receive phone calls

Making a business call	Receiving a business call
Make sure you know why you are making the call and the information you have to give or find out.	Answer promptly with an appropriate greeting. Identify yourself and the business or department.
List the points you have to make, or questions you must ask before you start, so you do not forget anything.	Have a pen and paper to hand so that you can make notes.
Introduce yourself clearly and explain why you are ringing.	Find out the caller's name and write this down. Check the spelling if you are unsure about it.
Do not gabble or use slang or jargon.	Next write down why the person is calling.
Speak clearly and naturally (there is no need to sound 'posh').	If you cannot help the caller, transfer the call to a colleague or take a message.
Ask the other person to slow down if they are speaking too quickly.	Remember that any information you give must be accurate and up to date.
Ask people to explain terms you do not understand and spell important words, such as their name, if it is unusual.	If you need to phone back, make sure you have the phone number and dialling code before you hang up.
Make notes of important points. Check your notes are correct before you hang up.	Let the caller conclude the call if you can.
End the call by thanking the person, if appropriate, and saying, 'Goodbye'.	End by saying, 'Thank you for calling'.
With all calls	

Never use the phone when you are chewing.
Try to use the person's name during the conversation. It makes them feel important and helps you to remember who you are speaking to.
Avoid slang, including 'OK', which sounds casual and unprofessional.
Say figures in pairs (they are easier to understand).
Do not rush a call. Give the other person time to consider what you have said.

Meetings

Your role in meetings will vary. This should affect how and when you communicate with the other people present.

- **At a team briefing,** you will be expected to listen to updates, suggest ideas, provide information when asked and help to support other members of your team. These should be positive, lively events at which everyone contributes.

- **At a formal business meeting,** you will have a reason for attending, such as to represent your department or area. Each person addresses their remarks to the chairperson, may be given tasks to do and may have to report back at the next meeting.

- **At some large meetings,** held for the purpose of providing information, most present rarely speak at all. This is similar to the situation when you are listening to a guest speaker. If there are any questions, these are usually asked at the end.

Activity: Student meetings

Find out how the meetings of the student voice or student councils in your centre are run and the role of the student representatives that attend them. Are they formal or informal, and what topics are discussed?

Technical enquiries

Technical enquiries can be made by phone, at meetings or during visits from customers. The term 'technical' means that the enquiry relates to how the products or services operate. Many businesses employ technical specialists to answer complicated enquiries, from workshop mechanics in garages to the pharmacist in a chemist shop. Here are the golden rules for dealing with technical enquiries.

- Never guess the answer. If you do not know, say so.

- Pass on the enquiry to the correct person promptly.

- Ask the speaker to spell any unfamiliar or technical words.

- Write the message down so you do not forget it.

- When you find out the answer, try to remember it for next time.

Why should the way you communicate at meetings vary?

Communicating with supervisor, colleagues and customers

You are expected to be polite and courteous with everyone you talk to, though you are likely to be less formal with colleagues of your own age than with more senior staff. Similarly, if you see a customer regularly, then you should greet them by name and may become more friendly as you get to know them. You should be more reserved if the chief executive stops to talk to you or if you have to talk to a customer you have never met before. Avoid slang and informal expressions.

In each case, there are some golden rules to stop you putting your foot into it or upsetting anyone.

- Always be courteous. 'Please' and 'thank you' cost nothing.

- Make eye contact and look pleasant and interested.

- Only provide accurate and correct information, and make sure that what you are saying is not ambiguous and makes sense.

- Never use technical terms or jargon a customer will not understand.

Complaints

Dealing with complaints can be difficult. If you contradict a customer and tell them they are wrong, you can easily make the situation worse – even if they *are* wrong! If you say your employer is at fault, the result may be a letter from the customer's solicitor claiming negligence! So what should you do?

There are two skills involved in handling complaints professionally. The first relates to the way you deal with the complaint; the second concerns the way you handle the person.

Many customers with a complaint are calm and reasonable, and just want the matter put right. Others may be more excitable or even angry. You can normally tell immediately by the customer's body language and tone of voice. The trick is to stay both calm and positive. Here are the golden rules for dealing with verbal complaints.

- Listen carefully and do not interrupt.

- Do not take the complaint personally. Think of it as a problem you may be able to solve.

- Look sympathetic and interested so the customer knows you want to help.

- Make notes if the matter is detailed or complicated.

- Apologise on behalf of your employer for the problem. This is not the same as admitting responsibility.

- Do not make any judgements about who is right or wrong and never say your organisation is at fault.

Remember

Phrase a query to someone senior as a request, not as a demand, and always think before you speak, not the other way round.

Activity: Choosing words carefully

You want to switch your lunchtime so that you can meet a friend who is in the area today. You need to ask your supervisor for permission and, if they agree, get your colleague to swap with you. In each case, decide what you would say. Then compare your ideas as a group.

Did you know?

- A young waiter confused and annoyed customers sitting outside a restaurant by telling them they must get their own food. He was actually trying to say that waiters did not take orders at outside tables so customers had to place their order at the bar!

- Many organisations have staff guidelines and procedures to ensure all complaints are dealt with in the same way (see also Unit 8, page 189).

- Use careful questioning to find out what action the customer wants you to take. Some may not want you to do anything except listen and pass on their concerns to a manager.
- If you can solve the problem then do so, but never promise to do anything that is outside your area of responsibility.
- Get help immediately if the customer threatens you or if you are losing control of the situation.

Verbal presentations

You probably have some experience of presentations because they are a common feature of many courses. This is because they give you practice at working in a team and enable you to develop your communication skills. In some companies, interview candidates are asked to give a short presentation so that both their ideas and interpersonal skills can be assessed.

Although these may be quite scary occasions, you will do better if you prepare well. This means deciding what you will wear, researching your topic, preparing your notes and practising. Here are the golden rules for giving verbal presentations.

- Start by introducing yourself and summarising the topic.
- Attract attention with an interesting opening, for example, by giving relevant facts and figures, asking a question, painting a verbal picture or using a quotation.
- Develop your theme, but remember to pause at the end of each section. It can be useful to repeat the main points here. Then tell the audience you are moving on to the next section.
- End on a high point with one interesting point or a short summary.
- Answer questions to the best of your ability and be honest if you do not know the answer.
- Never read from your notes, make out prompt cards instead.
- Be aware of your body language: stand tall, glance around at people making eye contact and, above all, smile so the audience engages with you.

Activity: Handle a complaint

Work in pairs. One of you is an assistant in a clothes shop, the other is the customer with a complaint. Decide on your own complaint, for example, no changing rooms available, something you ordered was sold when you went to collect it or the zip has broken on your new jeans. The assistant should handle the complaint and make the customer feel better about the situation so that they still have a positive opinion of the business. Then swap roles.

PLTS

Deciding upon the reason for your complaint and thinking of solutions are both good opportunities to practise creative thinking.

Did you know?

A **sales pitch** is a bid to get new business. In the creative industries, advertising and media companies 'pitch' their ideas to the client, often in a presentation.

Presentations help you practise your communication skills and prepare you for working in a team.

Case study
Locating the professional touch

Kerry Hamer (second from the right) uses her verbal and non-verbal communication skills every day.

As a branch manager for Athertons estate agency, Kerry Hamer visits the homes of prospective clients and also meets clients who want to view houses. She is heavily involved in the final stages of sales negotiations and liaises with local solicitors to ensure sales are completed promptly. Her responsibilities also include setting admin staff and negotiators their daily workload and checking jobs are completed to agreed deadlines.

Athertons staff are expected to look well presented, smart and professional at all times. Kerry also believes that looking smart means that staff feel more confident when they are dealing face to face with clients.

Kerry says that being punctual is imperative when she visits the homes of potential sellers, otherwise their immediate impression of the company would be negative. When customers are viewing a property this also must be done on time as, often, several viewings are booked together, so if one runs over this has a domino effect on the others. If staff promise to phone clients at a certain time, it is important this is done promptly, too.

New staff watch how experienced staff handle telephone calls and talk to visitors. Complaints should be dealt with sympathetically and details taken so that Kerry can get back to them later that day.

Kerry is well organised and prepares carefully for viewings, which are a type of verbal presentation. She never rushes anyone and is friendly and professional at all times. She takes notes if viewers have specific requirements or queries she cannot answer there and then. She always contacts them for feedback the day after the viewing.

Good verbal skills are essential in Kerry's job, for example, when a purchaser makes an unrealistic offer or one the seller thinks is too low. Kerry then needs to negotiate with both parties to see if she can help them reach agreement.

Think about it!

1. Identify five ways in which Kerry projects a professional image.
2. Describe two different occasions when Kerry must be punctual.
3. Explain why Kerry needs good interpersonal interaction skills in her job.
4. Identify four different business contexts in which Kerry is involved and in each case identify the purpose of her verbal communications.
5. Suggest three occasions when Kerry needs good verbal communications to do her job effectively.

Just checking

1. Identify four reasons why people communicate verbally.
2. Give one example of a context where the communication would be formal and one where it would be informal.
3. Describe how you would handle a technical enquiry.
4. Why is positive body language important during a verbal presentation?

Assessment activity 7.2

BTEC

Kerry wants to prepare a handbook on the importance of verbal business communications to give to her staff. She has asked you to help by carrying out the following activities.

1. Explain, using examples, the purpose of verbal business communications in **four** different business contexts: such as telephone contacts; meetings; technical enquiries; communicating with supervisor, colleagues or customers; complaints and verbal presentations. Use the information in the WorkSpace case study to help you. In each case, specify a specific context and then explain the purpose of the communication. Remember that this may be to inform, confirm, promote, make a request or instruct someone (see page 165). **P2**

2. Discuss how verbal communications can be used effectively in business. Do this by providing examples of different situations where verbal communication is effective in getting the correct message across to both customers and colleagues. Again use the information in the WorkSpace case study to help you. You can also suggest other occasions when Kerry and her staff will use verbal communications during the course of their work, such as talking to passers-by who call in. **M2**

3. Explain how interpersonal interaction skills are used to support business communication. Prepare for this by dividing into small groups. In your group, identify two business situations when you would communicate verbally with someone else. Then decide which skills you would need

to interact with them effectively. Role play each situation to your class twice. On one occasion, demonstrate positive interpersonal interaction skills; the other time, demonstrate negative (or zero!) skills. Then, as a class, discuss the difference and the effect on the communication. Make notes of all the different situations and keep these safely. You will find them useful when you do the final task.

When all the groups have carried out their role plays, write your own explanation about how interpersonal interaction skills support business communication and provide practical examples to support your explanations. **M1**

4. Kerry has asked you to assess the importance of effective interpersonal interaction skills at Athertons estate agency. This means explaining how these skills support the business, and you should provide practical examples. Again use the WorkSpace case study to help you. You can also refer to the notes you made in task 3, to give other examples of appropriate situations. **D1**

Grading tip

You must provide examples to illustrate each answer. Remember you do not have to limit your ideas to the information given in the case study. Any relevant examples can be used, providing they are appropriate for Kerry's business.

Why is it important to be courteous during discussions with your collegues?

Did you know?

Team briefings provide ideal opportunities for staff to make their views known to their supervisor, but they can be ruined if people whinge and moan or use them to chat.

Remember

At work it is not wise to treat your colleagues dismissively and expect them to put up with it, even if you sometimes do this with your family!

Respond appropriately to others

Most people are usually very polite with people they hardly know, but can, especially when stressed, forget basic courtesies with people they know well. Not saying 'please' and 'thank you' are two obvious examples. If you do this, reflect for a moment and note that you may not get treated politey as a result, or may get into trouble if you try it with your boss.

Table 7.5: Golden rules for responding appropriately to others

To your colleagues	To your boss or team leader
Be fair and treat everyone equally.	Be cooperative.
Be loyal and never disclose confidences.	Appreciate their priorities.
Be tactful so that you do not hurt people's feelings.	Accept their decisions gracefully – and look for the plus points.
Show extra consideration if they are under pressure or having a bad day.	Understand the stress or pressure they may be under.
Be open minded and listen to different views – you may learn something.	Respect their seniority and status.
Give praise when it is due and thank people who help you.	Report problems and difficulties accurately and promptly.
Be honest and admit your mistakes.	Do not make a drama out of a crisis.
Be a prompt, accurate and reliable communicator, no matter what the message.	

Moving a discussion forward

It is always easy to reach agreement when everyone thinks the same way. Yet sometimes people can get bogged down during a discussion and are unable to reach agreement. This may be because the issue is particularly difficult or because people hold very different views. Unless something is done they will never make a decision and, in business, this is not an option.

The problem will be worse if one person is very dominant and always shouts everyone else down, the team bicker and squabble between themselves, the leader is unable to keep order, and people are allowed to trade insults with each other.

It is easier to move a discussion forward if people do not see it as a contest that they have to win. The best approach is to treat the problem as a challenge to the team as a whole, so that everyone tries to reach the best solution possible. Often, in this way, a simple suggestion by one person can be refined or improved by the others, so that the end result is better than anyone would have thought of on their own.

You will help to move the discussion forward if you are prepared to respect other people's views and opinions, focus on solving the problem so everyone benefits, build on suggestions that have been made previously, and use persuasiveness, rather than aggression, if you are trying to win people over to your way of thinking.

If there is still deadlock, then a group vote may be the only option to decide the best way forward. You will then have to abide by the wishes of the majority with good grace and not moan and groan about it afterwards.

Did you know?

It is important to be able to **negotiate** when you work in a group. You will do this more easily if you focus on the best solution possible for everyone.

Activity: Develop your discussion skills

As a group, you have been asked to discuss a possible timetable change. You can either start one hour later each day or finish one hour earlier. Negotiate the solution the group would prefer. Remember to bear in mind the feedback you received from the activity on page 179 to improve any shortcomings the group had.

Carry out a peer review at the end, so that in addition to your tutor's feedback, you also analyse the group's performance. Then see if you all agree.

Functional skills

Remember that there is a direct link between this activity and developing your speaking and listening skills by moving a discussion forward.

Just checking

1. Explain the difference between negotiating and telling someone what to do.
2. What is a team briefing?
3. Give two examples of occasions when it is better to see someone in person than phone them.
4. Explain why it is important to respond appropriately to other people.

BTEC Assessment activity 7.3   P3 P4 M3 D2

1. Interview a member of staff in your centre to find out their views on the importance of verbal communication skills in their job. Prepare your questions in advance, listen to their answers and make notes about what you are told. Then prepare a brief verbal presentation to your group to summarise your findings. Your tutor will then give you feedback on your performance. **P3**

2. Your centre is planning to open a new student common room, which will provide state-of-the-art facilities. Each group has been asked for ideas about what it should contain. Hold a discussion, which your tutor will lead, to put forward your own suggestions and, as a group, agree on the best three to put forward. Your tutor will provide feedback on your performance afterwards. **P4**

3. Reflect upon your own performance in Tasks 1 and 2 and summarise your strengths and weaknesses in a report to your tutor. Use the feedback you have received to help you. For Task 2, you should give examples of particular points in the group discussion to support your answers. You can also refer to the strengths and weaknesses of other group members if this is appropriate. **M3**

4. Write an email to Kerry in which you assess the effectiveness of speaking and listening skills in supporting business operations at Atherton's estate agency. This means looking back at the WorkSpace case study and the leaflet you prepared for Kerry in Assessment activity 7.2 (page 171) and applying your knowledge of speaking and listening to this context. **D2**

Grading tip

To achieve a distinction, think about the consequences of having poor verbal communication skills in that context. Focus, too, on the word 'effective' and think about good examples of both one-to-one and group situations to illustrate your answer.

Assignment tips

- You will gain far better grades in this unit if you are alert to verbal communications in a business context. These happen all the time: when you are in a shop, having a snack, talking to an administrator in your centre or renting a DVD.

- If you do not have a part-time job and do not go on work placement, talk to friends and family members who work about verbal communications in their workplace, to get examples to help you.

8 Business communication through documentation

Business organisations produce millions of documents every day. They write letters and reports, send emails, and prepare agendas for meetings and purchase orders for supplies they need. They respond to enquiries and complaints, and provide information to people both inside and outside the company.

Wherever you work, at some stage your written communication skills will be on display. You will be expected to write and send emails to your colleagues almost from the outset, as in most organisations this is the most commonly used method for communicating internally with other people. If you are unable to write a proper sentence, use punctuation or spell words correctly, this will soon become obvious to everyone. It will be even worse if people cannot understand you because the meaning is not clear.

This unit will give you invaluable practice in developing your written communication skills. These are both important and useful in all areas of your life. As an example, they affect the quality of your written assignments on this course. You will also learn about the type of documents used to communicate with people in business, both internally and externally. This is invaluable when you start work as you will already be familiar with the documents you will see, read and write.

Learning outcomes

After completing this unit, you should:

1. know the purpose of written communications in business contexts
2. be able to complete and use business documents for internal and external communication in an organisation
3. know the importance of using appropriate methods of written communication depending on audience.

All websites referred to in this unit can be accessed via Hotlinks. See page ii for more information.

Assessment and grading criteria

This table shows you what you must do in order to achieve a pass, merit or distinction grade, and where you can find activities in this book to help you.

To achieve a **pass**, the evidence must show that the learner is able to:	To achieve a **merit**, the evidence must show that, in addition to the pass criteria, the learner is able to:	To achieve a **distinction** grade, the evidence must show that, in addition to the pass and merit criteria, the learner is able to:
P1 identify, using examples, the purposes of written business communications in four different business contexts **See Assessment activity 8.1, page 191**	**M1** describe appropriate methods of written communication in different business contexts **See Assessment activity 8.1, page 191**	**D1** explain the importance of written communication in an organisation in specific business contexts **See Assessment activity 8.1, page 191**
P2 produce three documents of different types to support straightforward business tasks for internal communication in an organisation **See Assessment activity 8.2, page 206**	**M2** compare your choice of internal and external documents **See Assessment activity 8.2, page 206**	**D2** justify your choice of internal and external documents explaining why each document is appropriate for its intended audience **See Assessment activity 8.2, page 206**
P3 produce three documents of different types for external communication by an organisation **See Assessment activity 8.2, page 206**		
P4 identify appropriate methods of communication to different audiences **See Assessment activity 8.3, page 210**	**M3** describe appropriate methods of written communication to different audiences **See Assessment activity 8.3, page 210**	**D3** explain appropriate methods of written communication to different audiences **See Assessment activity 8.3, page 210**

How you will be assessed

To achieve this unit you will investigate the type of documents that are prepared in different business contexts and identify their importance. You will also prepare a range of written documents yourself for internal and external contacts. The assessment activities in this book will help you to prepare for this.

Shazia

I enjoy writing but know I could improve what I write. I do not think a boss at work would be as understanding about my mistakes as my tutors have been. I would be worried about writing a document to send to a customer in case I said the wrong thing. At the start of this unit I didn't really know what documents are used in a business or how they are all set out.

If I was at work at the moment, I would be nervous about contacting other people by email, even though we regularly email our tutors at college. We keep these very short, though, and I know what I want to say.

I enjoyed doing some of the assessments in this unit, especially when we worked together as a group to plan our leavers' ball and had to decide what written documents we should use for the various tasks. Practising my writing skills has also helped me to write more clearly and think about my 'audience'. Everyone says my message-taking skills are much better, too. I feel much happier about my ability to write letters and emails now. It came in useful two weeks ago when my mum had a problem with something she had bought online. I volunteered to write an email to customer services and they arranged a replacement straight away, so I was really pleased.

Over to you!

- What written documents do you prepare at school or college? How good do you think these are?
- What benefits do you think you would gain in your private life if you felt you could confidently write many types of effective business documents? Discuss your ideas as a group.

Identify and compare written documents

1. List all the types of written business documents you have seen or heard about. Compare your lists with other people in your group.

2. How confident are you about preparing written documents for an assessment? What additional skills would help you to prepare better, more effective written documents?

1. Know the purpose of communication in business contexts

1.1 Written communication

There are four main ways of producing written communications.

- **Handwritten** documents are written with pen or pencil, such as a message you put on someone's desk. It is important you write neatly, and if your spelling is not very good, keep a dictionary close by.

- **Electronic** documents are sent from one computer to another, either as emails or attachments, such as a report or minutes of a meeting.

- **Word-processed** documents are prepared on computer using a package such as Word. These enable business documents to be prepared quickly and easily.

- **Texts** are similar to the text messages you probably send every day. In business, they are more often sent internally, but many firms now use them to contact customers.

Activity: Investigate BlackBerrys

Not even the CIA could part Barack Obama from his BlackBerry! Many other business users are just as devoted. Find out why they are so popular by visiting the BlackBerry website.

Written communication allows business people to keep in touch with their colleagues and customers.

Did you know?

- Many businesses send electronic purchase orders for goods they need, and receive invoices electronically from their suppliers after the goods have been despatched.

- Some doctors and dentists send text reminders to patients to reduce the number of missed appointments, and Ocado does the same with its home delivery customers, too.

1.2 The purpose of business communications

People in business communicate for a reason. If you have studied Option Unit 7, you will already know that these are to:

- provide information

- confirm an arrangement or agreement

- promote an idea, product or service

- make a request

- provide instructions.

The business context will affect the purpose of the communication.

Activity: List communications

Identify four written communications you sent recently, including texts and emails, and identify the purpose of each. Compare your lists as a group.

1.3 The business context

The **business context** relates to the situation that exists between the person who is communicating and the recipient. It affects many aspects, including the formality of the communication, which type of document is best, and its content. For example, writing a job application is very different from taking a message for a friend. So the type of document that is suitable, the words to use and the layout are also different.

Formal and informal communication

Communications are usually more formal in large organisations. Staff will be communicating with colleagues they rarely meet. In a small firm, everyone knows everyone else.

The type of work carried out by the firm also affects the formality of its communications. Accountants and solicitors often write formal letters, even to clients they know well, because they are related to serious financial and legal matters.

Table 8.1: Formal and informal methods of communication

	Used when	Examples
Formal	The matter is important or serious You do not know the recipient very well You want a written record	Business letters, memos and reports Job interviews Important meetings
Informal	People know each other well People are in frequent contact	Email Internal notices to staff

- **Meetings** – can be formal or informal. Formal meetings include the Annual General Meeting (AGM) of a company, Directors' meetings, and Governors' meetings in schools and colleges. The **minutes** record the discussions and actions agreed. Other meetings are more informal, such as team briefings held to update a team with matters of common interest. You will learn about meetings if you study Option Unit 6.

Key term

Business context – the business situation that applies and which must be taken into consideration when the communication is being written.

Did you know?

- Public sector organisations, including local councils, schools and colleges, are accountable to the public for their actions so they have to keep written records in case anything is queried. Because of this, many documents are worded quite formally, such as business letters and minutes of meetings.

- The formal term for a record of a meeting is the **minutes** of a meeting. If the meeting is informal, meeting notes or a summary of the discussion may be issued instead.

Have you ever seen anyone taking minutes at a meeting?

- **Notices** – internal documents that provide information or give instructions to staff. One announcing a leaving party will be more informal than a notice about health and safety. Notices must be clearly worded and contain all the details that people need.

- **Technical enquiries** – include requests for estimates, queries about a product and detailed quotations. Some are informal but many are not, such as an enquiry about the supply and installation of expensive equipment. The information is always put in writing to avoid any confusion. Any technical information given verbally should also be confirmed in writing to prevent misunderstandings.

Communicating with supervisor, colleagues, suppliers or customers

These are all different contexts. In each case you may be responding to a communication or initiating a communication yourself. The purpose and the type of recipient should influence your method of communication (for example, letter or email), as well as the words you use, the layout and your 'tone'.

Table 8.2: Internal and external communications

	Sent to	Options
Internal communications	Supervisor or colleagues within the organisation	Handwritten message or note, text message, email, memo, notice, report, agenda or notes/minutes of internal meetings
External communications	Customers, suppliers and others outside the organisation	Email, business letter, report, purchase order, invoice, agenda and notes/minutes of meetings involving external contacts

'Tone' means how you phrase your sentences. This can indicate formality or courtesy. Compare the tones on the following page.

> 'We would be grateful if you could let us have this information promptly.'
>
> 'Please could you let me know as soon as possible.'
>
> 'Can you do me a favour and let me know today?'
>
> 'Tell me now!'

The first is appropriate for a formal, external communication. The second is better for your manager. The third you might say to your colleague, and the final one, not at all!

Complaints

Customers usually complain in person to retailers, especially if they want to exchange something or ask for a refund. Other businesses may insist complaints are in writing and many record complaints in a special log. Staff may have to follow a set procedure in response. This includes replying in writing so there is a written record. This is important if the complaint could result in legal action if it cannot be resolved amicably.

Responding to a customer's complaint and writing a letter of complaint to a supplier are two different business contexts.

Activity: Write a letter of complaint

The website How To Complain provides templates for people to complete to write a letter of complaint. It also gives hints and tips. How useful do you think this is? Investigate the site and compare your ideas as a group.

Read the advice on the site and develop your own skills by writing a letter to the manager of a local taxi company. You are annoyed that the driver who took you and an elderly relative home from hospital yesterday drove like a lunatic. Invent any other appropriate details. Compare your finished letters as a group and identify the best one.

Presentations

Presentations are used to give information to a group and are more formal than a chat or discussion. The purpose can vary considerably. A safety manager may demonstrate new emergency procedures, whereas sales staff may promote products to potential customers and illustrate the presentation with a slideshow. Handouts can provide further information. The style and tone of these will vary depending upon whether the presentation is internal or external, and whether or not senior managers and/or important customers are attending.

Confidentiality

In business, you will be dealing with information that is sensitive, which the organisation does not want to be made public or maybe broadcast around the business. You will learn more about confidentiality in business on page 207.

Did you know?

It is not usual to use abbreviated words (for example, 'isn't' or 'can't') or expressions like 'OK' in business documents.

Activity: Write a note

Carrie's sister is phoning to say what time they should meet at the cinema tonight, but Carrie has to take an urgent package to the post. She wants someone to take a message if her sister calls while she is away. She writes one note for her colleague, Jack, on the next desk and another for her manager, Jo. Write both notes. Compare your notes as a group and identify the differences in tone and content between the two. Then decide which examples are best.

PLTS

As an effective participator you need to be able to propose ways forward, identify improvements and try to influence others. Use your complaints letter to practise these skills.

Remember

The business context, main purpose and type of recipient influence several aspects of a communication, including the best method to use, the formality, layout, style, content and tone.

Case Study

The importance of written communication at the Halifax

When buy-to-let mortgages were a new product for the Halifax, Sandra Crowe and her team were responsible for promoting them. As Head of Campaign Management for Halifax Mortgages, now part of Lloyds Banking Group, Sandra used many types of written communications to promote the Halifax promise of 'always giving you extra'.

First, the team wrote the communications plan and the ABC (action brief for communication) for the promotion. This sets out the communication objectives and what brochures, promotional leaflets, posters and advertising are required. These instructions go to the communications team and are sent to the agencies that will produce the literature. A purchase order is also produced to cover the work required.

Business letters are sent if a contract is being negotiated with a supplier. Another legal document, a non-disclosure agreement, must be signed by any external firm that has access to confidential information, to ensure they cannot pass this on. At the same time, senior branch staff receive information about the new product and the proposed campaign at meetings and by email.

Campaign materials are drafted and attached to emails as PDF or Word files so they can be checked and returned electronically. Leaflets are checked to ensure the information is correct, the language is appropriate and they follow organisational guidelines. Checks on press adverts are very stringent and each is officially signed off before it can be used.

Finished packs are sent to branches with written instructions on when and how they should be used. This ensures all branches do the same thing and comply with the way Halifax runs its campaigns. Sometimes, wall planners or wall hanging notices are prepared for staff rooms to help branch staff understand the new product. Text messages are also sent to staff reminding them that they can check details of the new product on the intranet.

At the end of the campaign a report is sent to senior managers, evaluating how it went. Sandra uses PowerPoint so that she can include text and the visuals (posters and adverts) that were used. Although Sandra now works in New Product Development, she still aims to ensure customers know that at the Halifax they can still get a little bit extra!

Think about it!

1. How many different types of written communication can you identify from the case study?
2. For four of the written communications you have identified, explain the business context.
3. Sandra says the aim of her communications may be: to confirm agreement, start a discussion, provide information, clarify something or provide feedback. For each purpose she has identified, describe one method of written communication that would be appropriate.
4. Select three types of written communication prepared by Sandra and explain why it is important that each one is in writing.
5. In groups, discuss why large organisations like the Halifax consider written communications so important. Compare your ideas.

Just checking

1. What is meant by the term 'business context'?
2. Why are some written communications more informal than others?
3. What is the different between 'internal' and 'external' communications?
4. Why do many organisations insist that staff reply to any complaints in writing?

BTEC Assessment activity 8.1

Your centre is holding a seminar on business communication for local entrepreneurs who have recently opened their own businesses. Your group has been asked to help by preparing handouts that will be available on the day. One part of the seminar will concentrate on written business communication in different business contexts.

1. In small groups, discuss the type of communication an entrepreneur may use or prepare in each of the following business contexts: meetings; notices; technical enquiries; communicating with supervisor, colleagues, suppliers or customers; complaints; presentations; confidential situations.

   On your own, select four different contexts from this list. Then write a factsheet about the purpose of written business communication in each of your chosen contexts. Give examples in each case. For example, you could say in the context of communicating with customers that the purpose of a poster is to provide information and to promote a product or service. **P1**

2. Prepare your own list of appropriate methods of written communication that can be used in different business contexts. For each method you identify, describe the purpose of the communication in that business context and say how this would affect the style of the communication. For example, you might say that a poster could be used by a retail business to advertise a change to the opening hours. This is an external communication because it is aimed at customers but may be quite informal. It should also be eye-catching and may include a graphic.

   Your finished work should be in the form of a table in which you identify the method of written communication, explain an appropriate context and purpose, then say how this would affect the style and content. **M1**

3. Your tutor thinks that some young entrepreneurs may think written documents are unnecessary in business today. They may think that oral and electronic communication (such as texting) will be enough. To show this is not true, prepare a factsheet headed 'The importance of written communication' which explains the difference between these three methods. Then provide examples of business contexts in which it is more appropriate that the information is provided in a written document. Use the information in the WorkSpace case study to give you ideas as well as your own experiences at your centre, on work experience or in a part-time job. You should also consider how the content of the communication will be affected by aspects such as confidentiality.

   For each example you provide, make sure that you fully explain the purpose of the communication and the wider organisational context in which it is being used. **D1**

Grading tips

- It will help you to identify and explain the importance of written communications if you contrast these to other methods, such as giving a message orally, talking to someone or making a telephone call, and think about the possible consequences of using a different method.

- Sometimes it is important to have a written record of something that took place. Look ahead to page 209 to find out more about this. You can also find out more about confidentiality on pages 207 and 208.

2. Be able to complete and use business documents for internal and external communication in an organisation

All business documents have certain things in common.

- They provide information which the recipient must be able to understand.

- External documents give an impression of the business and the writer, and for that reason must be correct in every respect.

- Internal documents give an impression of the writer, which affects that person's reputation with their supervisor and colleagues.

This section looks at the key aspects that you must observe to ensure that all your written business communications are the correct standard.

2.1 Business documents

Different documents have different features. This means that some are more appropriate for some purposes than others. Whichever type you prepare, you need to know the correct layout to use and the standards of presentation and writing that are normally expected.

Did you know?

Although the design of many standard documents such as purchase orders and invoices varies from one business to another, the type of information they contain is almost identical.

Table 8.3: Types of written documents and their main features

Type of document	Use	Main features
Letter	External	Formal, slower than electronic methods, impersonal, provides permanent written record
Email	Internal and external	Informal, rapid, other documents can be attached, can be sent worldwide very easily
Message or note	Internal	Short and informal. Usually left on recipient's desk unless absent or on holiday
Memo	Internal	More formal than email, provides permanent record if filed
Notice	Internal	Provides essential instructions or key information about event
Report	Internal and external	Gives account of an event or investigation under separate headings
Agenda	Internal and external, to people entitled to attend a meeting	Provides list of items to be discussed in order
Minutes of a meeting	Internal and external, to people who attended and those entitled to attend but absent	Summarises what was discussed, often with action to be taken and by whom
Purchase order	External to a supplier (and received from customers)	Provides official authority for the supplier to provide the goods listed at the quoted price
Invoice	External to a customer (and received from suppliers)	Includes details of the items purchased, the unit price, the VAT payable and the total price

2.2 Appropriate layouts

The layouts of different business documents have been designed with the following criteria in mind.

- **Fitness for purpose** – The type of information in a document and how it is set out must take account of its main purpose. A letter provides continuous information, an invoice summarises financial details relating to a purchase and an agenda lists items to be discussed at a meeting. The key information must be clearly seen.

- **Appropriate to the task and the audience** – Some documents serve a similar purpose, for example, both purchase orders and invoices relate to financial transactions. The layout is different because one aims to obtain goods while the other asks for payment. Letters and memos both provide information, but letters are sent to external contacts and memos are only sent internally. This affects the layout (see pages 195 and 201).

- **Use of different formats and styles** – **Format** is similar to layout. Some organisations have a **house style** that specifies how documents should be set out, and may include a template on their intranet. The instructions may include the font that should be used, as well as the style of headings, how pages should be numbered (paginated), and what headers or footers should be used. Images may include drawings and photographs. The size of these and their resolution (quality) may be specified in advance.

2.3 Writing documents for business

Writing acceptable business documents is not like scribbling a note to a friend. Quite apart from accurate spelling, punctuation and the correct grammar, there are certain other points you need to remember.

- **Use relevant technical language** – Technical language is only appropriate if the recipient will understand it. This normally means restricting it to internal communications or external specialists who work in the same industry. If you cannot think of another term in an external communication, you must clearly explain what it means.

Did you know?

Headings vary in size and style. In this book, for example, there are different sizes used at the beginning of units and within each unit. The main point is that use of headings must be **consistent** throughout the whole document or book.

Key term

Format – the design, layout and order of information in a document.

Activity: Check it yourself

On the word-processing package you normally use, check that you know how to change font styles and sizes, the different styles available for numbering multi-page documents, and how to insert headers and/or footers.

Functional skills

Being able to enter and format text to maximise clarity and enhance presentation will help you develop your ICT skills.

Discussion point

Your friend has started a new job in IT and appears to be talking in gibberish when they tell you what they do. Does this use of jargon impress, irritate or intimidate you? Discuss your views as a group.

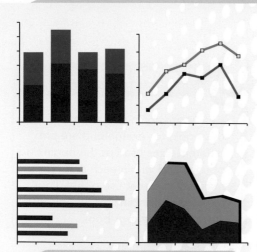

How can graphical information improve a document?

Key terms

Legible – clearly written and easy to read.

Consistency – the format is the same throughout the document in relation to typeface, style of heading, spacing and so on.

Conventions – basic principles which relate to the way certain documents are written.

- **Graphical information** – Images may be included to provide additional information. Usually these are tables, charts or diagrams, rather than images or pictures. The type and frequency will depend upon the audience (for example, internal/external, age range) and the document. Graphics often feature in notices and presentations, but not in business letters.

- **Drafting and redrafting to ensure accuracy** – Even if you can dash off an email to a friend in seconds, this is unwise if you are writing a business document. You need to check your spelling, punctuation and grammar, make sure that your information is in a logical order and nothing has been missed out, and that the 'tone' is right and your reader will understand it easily. This is likely to take a few attempts before you get it right.

- **Legibility and consistency** – Any written notes or messages must be **legible**. Jotting a note that asks your boss to urgently ring an incomprehensible number is unlikely to make you very popular. **Consistency** refers to the way the document is set out *and* the words you use. For example, if you leave one blank line between paragraphs, this must be the same throughout the document.

- **Conventions** – There are several **conventions** you must observe, usually relating to the type of document you are preparing, as you will see on pages 195–202.

- **Checking for accuracy, consistency and fitness for purpose** – Good proofreading skills are vital. Too many people think running a spell check is enough, but these miss errors where the result is another 'real' word, for example, form/from; too/two; stationery/stationary; fin/fine/find. Checking means reading through your work carefully and asking someone for advice if you are unsure about anything.

- **Meeting deadlines** – No matter how many checks you need to make, the document must be sent by the agreed deadline. If you are struggling to finish a document in time, ask for help. Never miss a deadline without warning anyone in advance.

 ### Remember

The layout and style of a business document must be fit for its purpose as well as appropriate for the task and the audience. The document must also be completely accurate, as well as legible and consistent.

 ### Did you know?

- One of the main dangers of email is that it is far too easy to press 'send'! It is better to store a first attempt in your drafts folder until you have checked it properly.

- It is unwise to have total faith in grammar checkers. If the suggestion seems odd, check it with a more experienced colleague.

- You will make a better job of checking your work if you let it 'go cold' before you read it through. This enables you to see it through the eyes of a recipient and any errors are more obvious.

- The **KISS principle** stands for **K**eep **I**t **S**hort and **S**imple! This should apply to all your written communications. Never use long or complicated words because you think they will sound impressive – they will not.

Layouts and conventions for documents

Guidelines on preparing certain business documents are given below, together with some examples.

Memos

Memos are internal documents sent between members of staff. Although many organisations now use email instead, they may sometimes be used for complex matters, and to send information to staff without email access. They are also useful when the sender wants to make sure there is a printed record for future reference. The most usual layout is shown in Figure 8.1.

Activity: Business documents

As a group, obtain a selection of business documents to compare with the examples that follow. You could ask your tutor for examples of internal documents used or received by your centre and supplement these with your own emails and business letters received at home. Do not include any that contain confidential information. Note any differences you find and, in groups, discuss the possible reasons for these.

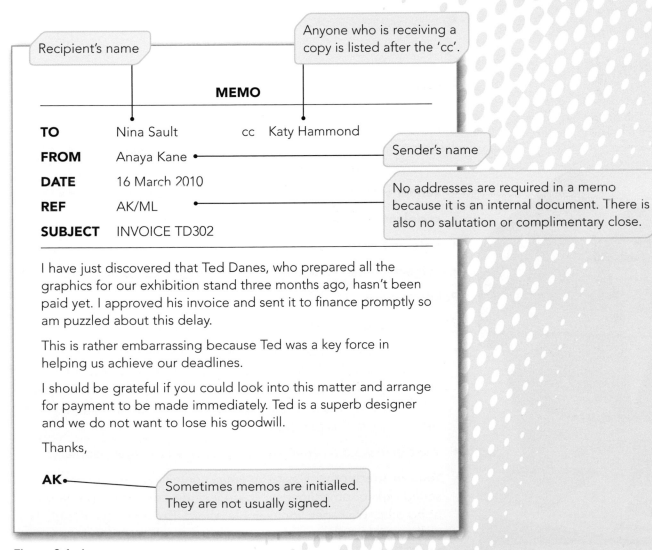

Figure 8.1: A memo

Points to note

- The formality of a memo will depend upon the recipient and the subject matter. A memo about a social event will be worded very differently from one about a serious customer complaint.

- Slang expressions should be avoided, but abbreviated words are often used, for example, 'thanks', 'I'll' or 'haven't'.

- Memos are normally quite short and concentrate on just one topic.

Activity: Write a memo

Write a memo to your tutor asking if you can be excused from class next Friday afternoon. Explain that you have a part-time job and that you have been asked to help out because of staff shortages. Reassure your tutor this is an exceptional case and that you will catch up with any work you miss if they agree.

Key term

Header – the top section of a document. The opposite is footer, which is at the bottom of a document.

Emails

Emails can be sent internally or externally. If Anaya had emailed Nina with the information in the memo the wording would be the same, but the format would be different. This is because the **header** on an email is set up by the software and includes:

- **sender's name** – inserted automatically on emails you send

- **recipient's name** – inserted automatically when you reply

- **date and time** – inserted automatically

- **subject** – enter a brief title to summarise the content.

Points to note

When you send an email, you have several options.

- You can copy an email to other people and have two choices: a) **cc copies** include the name(s) of the recipient(s) at the top so that everyone can see who has received a copy, and b) **bcc copies** which are blind copies (other recipients will not know that you have sent a copy to this person).

- You can forward an email you have received to other people.

- You can attach other files to an email containing text, graphics, sound clips or other images. These include documents prepared using other packages, for example, Word, Excel or PowerPoint, as well as original documents scanned into your computer.

- You can include a high priority level for important emails. Only use this when it really is appropriate, or people will start to ignore it.

What options do you have when sending a business email?

Email etiquette

Today, most people send emails to their friends. There are several differences, though, between these emails and those you would write in a business organisation. These are summarised in Table 8.4.

Table 8.4: Business email dos and don'ts

Do	Don't
Reply promptly to emails you receive	Use the same phrases you would use to a friend
Copy the style of salutations and complimentary closes used on emails where you work	Include confidential information
Use proper sentences and paragraphs and correct English (normal spelling, grammar and punctuation)	SHOUT BY USING ALL CAPITALS and use emoticons or abbreviations such as LOL (laugh out loud)
Get to the point quickly	Use 'Reply to All' unless it is essential
Keep your sentences relatively short	Forward and copy emails unnecessarily, particularly if they include other people's email addresses
Use bullets or numbered points for a list of items	Use technical words or jargon your recipient would not understand
Send separate emails if you are communicating on different topics	Delete the message thread – it can be useful to refresh people's memory
Carry out a spell check and then proofread for words spellcheckers miss (for example, draft/daft)	Print out messages unless it is really necessary
Check it makes sense and is error free before you press 'send'	Reply to spam
Add 'thanks' at the end if you are asking a favour	Forward chainmail or virus hoax emails
Check you are sending it to the correct recipient	Ask for a delivery receipt (it is annoying and can be ignored anyway)
Check you have included the attachments you mentioned	Assume all emails arrive. If you do not receive a response, try picking up the phone instead

Did you know?

- If you are sending a memo to a group of staff, you can put a general title at the top, for example, 'All staff' or 'Sales team'.
- If an attachment is very large, it is normal to compress or 'zip' it, using a package such as WinZip. This makes it smaller and quicker to transmit.

Activity: Email greetings

How you greet people and sign off is usually different in an external email. Instead of 'Hi' or 'Hello' you may put 'Dear' (at least on the first occasion). You may also sign off with 'Best wishes' or 'Kind regards'.

In groups, suggest what other differences you might find. Then discuss with your tutor the salutations (greetings) and endings used by staff in your centre for internal and external emails.

Did you know?

Notices for external use are usually bigger, professionally printed and called posters.

Notices

Notices are normally prepared for internal use. The style and layout will depend upon the formality of the message and how much text there is.

Notices provide information or give instructions. They may include illustrations to attract attention on a notice board.

Points to note

- Use a large, clear, short heading that says what it is about.
- Keep the text short and break up longer sections by using sub-headings or bullet points.
- Use terms and language everyone will understand.
- Include all the key details (what, when, where and whom to contact).
- Keep it simple (lots of colours and styles looks amateurish).
- Date it and put your name (people may need to contact you).
- One large illustration is usually better than lots of little ones.

Activity: Assess notices

Check notice boards at your centre and assess the notices they contain against the criteria on the left. Decide which are best and which you think are poor, with reasons. Compare your views as a group.

How will a good notice get everyone interested?

Reports

Reports may be prepared for internal or external use. They are often written after carrying out research or undertaking an investigation, or to report on an event. For example, a report could be written that said whether certain costs have increased or decreased (with reasons), or on alternative ways of updating the computer equipment.

Before you write a report, there is some preparation to be done.

- **Consider the aim** – Why have you been asked to write it? Whom is it for? What do they want to know?

- **Draft the introduction** – This is the easiest part. You simply say who asked you for the report and why.

- **Organise your information** – Put your facts into a logical order and then decide how to separate them to keep them clear.

- **Decide appropriate recommendations** – If you are asked for these, make sure that they are sensible and relevant, given the rest of your report.

Many reports today are prepared on computer and sent out as an email attachment with a covering email.

Points to note

- In all reports, the headings and spacings must be consistent, and no slang or abbreviated words must be used.

- An appropriate title should be put at the top.

- There are usually three sections: a) an **introduction**, which states the reason for writing the report; b) the **body of the report**, which gives the information you have obtained. Clear headings are essential, and numbered points are often used to separate different items; c) a **conclusion**, which sums up the information and says whether any action is needed or not.

- Only if you have been asked to provide recommendations should you put these as a final section.

- Finish with your name and the date.

Did you know?

- A report should be **objective**. This means you report the facts and not your opinions, unless you are specifically asked for these.

- It is clearer to divide up lengthy information into separate paragraphs or numbered or bulleted points. Use bullets when there is no specific order.

Discussion point

During a work experience stint at Morgan Stanley, a City bank, 15-year-old Matthew Robson wrote a report on how teenagers consume media. Matthew texted friends for ideas and wrote it in a day. The bank was so impressed, it published it. Read Matthew's full report on the *Guardian* website. Then, as a group, decide if you agree with it.

Have you read Matthew Robson's report on how teenagers consume media?

Points to note

- Slang and abbreviated words, such as 'don't' or 'can't', are never used.

- The style and tone should suit the purpose. For example, a sales letter should be upbeat, a complaint letter should be factual, and a letter responding to a justified complaint should be apologetic.

- Letters must be polite, so use the word 'please' if you want something. Avoid its overuse with other phrases such as 'we would be grateful if…' or 'it would help us if…'.

- Letters should never end with 'thank you' on its own. Instead, use a more business-like phrase such as, 'We appreciate your help in this matter.'

It is easier to write a letter if you know some standard phrases to use.

The opening paragraph focuses on the reason for writing and introduces the main topic, for example:

- We would like to invite you to the opening of our new restaurant on Friday 10 June.

- Thank you for your letter of 6 April informing us about the extended conference facilities at your hotel.

- I refer to your recent telephone conversation with a member of our staff about our interior design service.

The second paragraph goes into more detail about the information introduced at the start. If there is a lot of information, it is better split into two or more paragraphs.

- Our menus feature regional dishes prepared with food from local suppliers.

- We are particularly interested in the Grantham suite because we are planning to hold a sales seminar in September.

- We offer a wide range of services including…

The closing paragraph is often just a simple, appropriate ending that relates to what will happen or the action now expected.

- We very much hope you will be able to attend.

- We look forward to hearing from you.

- Please let us know if you require any further information.

Did you know?

Many businesses use **open punctuation** where commas are inserted only in the body of the letter to help understanding but are not used in abbreviations or at the end of address or date lines.

Activity: Write to Sonia

You are Aisha Farrell. Write a letter to thank Sonia for her report. Her address is 69 Rigby Road, Bradbury, BR3 8DL. Use today's date. Ask if she thinks the location could be having a negative effect on sales, especially as the nearest car park has just been closed. Also tell her to address her invoice to you so that you can make sure it is paid promptly.

2.4 Recording and reporting

Notes are often taken during conversations or discussions and then typed up so there is evidence of what was said or agreed. Preparing these types of records needs rather different skills from those used to compose letters or emails.

Type of record

The main types of written records in business are:

- **messages** taken on behalf of other members of staff
- **minutes (or notes)** of a meeting, often with actions to be taken and by whom.

These are not the only types. Sometimes reports are written to summarise a conversation. The police write a report when they interview someone, and sales reps often do this following a visit to a customer.

Keeping accurate and complete records of internal conversations

It is important that any record is both accurate and complete. This does not mean writing down every word, which would be impossible for most people. It does mean that the information is correct and nothing important has been left out.

Meetings and agreed actions

The notes or minutes of a meeting usually contain a brief summary of what was discussed. They also include details of the actions that have been agreed and the names, or initials, of the people who agreed to take them. This means they can be followed up easily at the next meeting.

Accurate and concise reporting in sufficient and appropriate detail

The trick is deciding which information must be included and which can safely be left out, and then writing the essential points clearly and concisely. It may take several attempts before you can do this easily.

If you are writing a message, it helps to use a printed form that prompts you to obtain the important information you need. Otherwise you will have to write or type out the message on plain paper.

Points to note when taking a message

- Write notes as you listen. Redraft them into a final message with the key information in the right order afterwards.

- Listen carefully. Ask the caller to repeat anything you do not hear properly or understand.

- Check you have all the **key facts** you need. These usually include:

  o name of the person (check the spelling if you are unsure)

  o name of the person's organisation or their private address

  o caller's telephone number and local dialling code

Did you know?

Both in court and in Parliament a verbatim (word for word) record is made of the whole proceedings. Find out more by visiting the Hansard section of the Parliament website.

Activity: Suggest consequences

As a group, suggest some of the consequences of incorrect information being recorded or important details being missed out. Start by thinking about names, phone numbers, dates and times.

Activity: Investigate agendas and minutes

Agendas and minutes of a meeting are two other important written documents. They are used for meetings held internally and externally. Examples and hints and tips on writing them are shown on pages 148 and 150–152. Read these now to learn more about them.

Why is it better to include information you are not sure about, rather than miss it out?

Activity: Write a message

Work in pairs for this activity. Decide on a message you want to give your tutor. Then tell your partner who must write it down to pass on. It is up to you whether you give the information in the right or wrong order, or deliberately leave out something important! Then change roles.

○ main points relating to the message, such as the reason for calling/visiting, details of any information requested, details of any information given to you, or action to be taken.

- **Double-check** information about dates, times, place names, product names or codes, prices or quantities (or any other numbers).

- If the message is long or complicated, read it back to check you have understood everything correctly.

- Write the final message out promptly, using simple, straightforward words that cannot be misunderstood. Include all the key facts in a logical order. Give both days and dates to be on the safe side (never say 'today' or 'tomorrow' in case the message is read on a different day from that on which it was written).

- Put your **own name** on the message and the **date and time** of the call.

- If the message is urgent, pass it on *immediately*. If the intended recipient is not available, give the message to a supervisor.

Working within given deadlines and time frames

If a document is required urgently, then it is top priority. It is useless taking an urgent message and only passing it on a day later. If you have minutes to produce, agree a deadline and then plan your work accordingly, bearing in mind your other jobs. If you take an important message, hopefully you will use your own initiative and deal with it promptly.

Reporting issues as they arise to the appropriate person

Problems or issues can arise for many reasons. A task may be harder than you first thought, you may be held up by someone else or you may not understand your own notes. The job may then take longer, so you could miss the agreed deadline.

Early in your career it can be hard to get the right balance between reporting important issues and not panicking unnecessarily. You will naturally want people to think you can cope on your own, but it is still important to warn someone if an issue could cause a serious problem. The best way to assess this is to consider the possible consequences. The worse these are, the more important it is that you tell someone promptly so they can take action.

Did you know?

- You are in danger of forgetting to do a routine job, like writing out a message properly, unless you do it straightaway.

- The appropriate person to tell is normally the person who asked you to do the work or your supervisor. Until you have notified this person that there is an issue, they will assume that everything is going to plan.

Remember

It is often necessary to have an accurate record of discussions in business, from telephone messages to minutes of meetings.

Activity: Purchase orders and invoices

Two commonly used external communications are purchase orders and invoices. Ask your tutor for examples of those sent and received by your centre, so that you can compare the type of headings and the information usually included.

Why should you report issues as they arise?

I'm sorry, too, because this is now too late to be of any use.

Just checking

1. Identify two differences between a letter and a memo.
2. Suggest three differences between a business email and one you would send to a friend.
3. Explain the steps you would take to ensure a document you produced had no spelling errors.
4. Explain the action you would take if you were worried you would not meet an agreed deadline.

BTEC Assessment activity 8.2

Your group wants to hold a leavers' dinner and ball for all BTEC First learners. Your tutor suggests this will mean:

- investigating several local venues online to see which would be most suitable by comparing features such as location, facilities, menus and costs
- holding regular meetings to make the preparations. One of the first tasks is to agree on a location and an appropriate date, time, format and dress code for the event
- booking the venue and confirming specific requirements, including the menu
- promoting and publicising the event so that all learners know about it
- making other bookings that will need to be made, such as a DJ transport and
- confirming final numbers and any special menu requirements to the venue just before the event.

Your tutor has also asked that you keep them informed throughout. This will require the creation of several documents.

1. In groups, discuss which documents would be appropriate for the tasks you have to carry out.

2. **On your own**, decide which documents you think would be the most suitable and identify which are internal and which are external. Be prepared to give reasons for your decisions (see Question 5).

3. Carry out each task and, on your own, prepare **six** of the documents that are required. It is important that at least three of your chosen documents are for internal communication and three are for external communication. **P2 P3**

4. Write a report for your tutor in which you review and compare your choice of internal and external documents. This means saying why you think each one is an appropriate choice for that particular communication. Also check that each document is grammatically correct, has no spelling errors and is fit for purpose. **M2**

5. In your report justify your choice of documents by explaining why you selected each one. Explain why you consider each document is appropriate for its intended audience by giving reasons for your choice based on that particular context. **D2**

Grading tip

Justify your choice by considering the context of the communication and its purpose. You should also think about why your particular document is preferable to another type and better than a verbal communication.

3. Know the importance of using appropriate methods of written communication depending upon audience

There are several factors to consider when deciding which method of communication to use. Some are suitable for internal use, some for external use, and some, like emails, can be used for either. Other factors to bear in mind are:

- the sensitivity of the information
- the audience and the amount of detail
- whether a written record is essential for audit or evidence purposes.

3.1 Dealing with confidential matters

Confidential or sensitive information is that which could cause worry, offence, embarrassment or even loss of business if it is made public. If you are handling confidential information, this will affect not just what type of document you should write, but also how it is prepared, stored and distributed.

Appropriate methods of communication to convey confidential messages

Business letters, memos, reports or minutes of meetings may contain confidential information. In every case, the document itself must be clearly marked as PERSONAL or PRIVATE AND CONFIDENTIAL (see example letter on page 201).

Documents containing sensitive information normally have a restricted circulation. This means only a limited number of copies are made for specified recipients. Office copies are kept in a locked file. Draft or spoiled documents are shredded, not thrown into a waste paper basket.

A message or handwritten note containing sensitive information should be put into a sealed envelope and not placed on a desk for everyone to see.

Sensitivity in dealing with confidential issues

You need to be able to recognise confidential information without being told. You must then treat it with sensitivity. This means not leaving draft documents lying on a desk, always shredding spoiled documents, and not discussing what you have read or been told with anyone else.

Did you know?

If all other factors are the same, it is also sensible to consider how quickly you need to communicate the information. For example, emails normally reach their destination quicker than business letters.

Confidential documents must be sent in a sealed envelope, clearly marked as 'personal' or 'private and confidential'.

Did you know?

- Emails are considered unsuitable for any type of confidential information, unless they are encrypted.
- Some business customers insist on confidentiality agreements being signed by their suppliers, which means they are forbidden from discussing the work they are carrying out.

Did you know?

The Data Protection Act aims to prevent information held by an organisation from being misused. This includes confidential employee data, as well as data on customers, potential customers and suppliers. Under the Act, anyone who has data held on them can formally request to see it to check it is up to date and accurate. Breaching customer or employee confidence by selling or buying personal data is a serious offence, with an unlimited fine.

PLTS

Employ your creative thinking skills when you do this activity.

Understanding of material that might be confidential

Confidential material can include:

- personal details about staff or customers (such as home address, telephone number, date of birth or age)
- payroll details, staff work and health records
- product information, plans for the future and financial information which would be of interest to competitors
- notes taken at a disciplinary hearing or the minutes of a meeting held to discuss proposed internal changes which have not yet been announced to staff.

Activity: Investigate confidential information

In groups, suggest the type of information held by your centre that you think will be confidential. Then talk to your tutor about the measures taken to ensure it is kept secure.

Discussion point

In groups, suggest the types of precautions taken by car manufacturers to prevent their competitors finding out about a new model they are preparing to launch. Then compare your ideas as a class.

3.2 Detail

The amount of detail in a communication must be appropriate for your audience. For example, you should not design a notice for young children as you would prepare one for adults.

The Fog Index

This calculates how easy it is to read something you have written. It uses a mathematical formula based on the number of words in a sentence and the number of complex (multi-syllable) words. The final number equals the number of years of education someone needs to understand it, using the US year grade system.

Did you know?

Critics of the Fog Index say that just because a word has a lot of syllables does not mean it is hard to understand. Every child knows the word 'banana' (ba-na-na), which has three syllables, whereas 'dour' has only one syllable, but fewer people know what it means.

Activity: Fog Index

Find out the Fog Index for a paragraph you have written by inputting it online via Hotlinks at the Simbon Madpage website.

The Crystal Mark

This symbol is awarded by the Plain English Campaign for documents that are easy for everyone to read and understand. An example of a document that has been awarded the Crystal Mark is the Passport Application Form. The society also issues guides on writing different types of documents, and welcomes nominations for awards, both good and bad.

Crystal
Mark
00000
Clarity approved by
Plain English Campaign

The Crystal Mark logo

Activity: Award winners

Find out more by visiting the Plain English Campaign website. Look for examples of gobbledygook, winners of Plain English awards and Golden Bulls (not a good one to win!), and check out the guides to help you improve your own written communications.

3.3 Audit

Written business documents provide evidence of discussions and actions. If your boss queries whether you ordered something, producing a copy of the purchase order is far better than saying you phoned yesterday.

An **audit** is an official check, usually by a firm of accountants, on financial claims the business has made in its accounts. The auditors check these are genuine by referring to the supporting documents. An example is an employee's expense claim that has been repaid.

Documents that may be required during an audit are kept safely. Some are kept for a minimum length of time for legal reasons, including accounts documents, accident reports, attendance records, payroll records and tax documents. Businesses are also recommended to keep various staff records and agreements for six years or more. These include disciplinary records, health and safety records, and trade union agreements.

Did you know?

At work, many people like to have evidence in writing to prove they have done something that they agreed to do, in case there are queries later.

Remember

The needs of the audience are important. Confidentiality often affects the method of communication used and all communications must be clearly written. Sometimes written copies are required for an audit or simply to provide evidence that something has been done.

Activity: Audit documents

Talk to your tutor about the type of written communications that are required and stored at your centre because they may be needed by an auditor or to prove something during an Ofsted inspection.

Discussion point

All organisations are recommended to keep copies of application forms and interview notes relating to unsuccessful candidates for one year after the interview was held. As a group, suggest reasons for this.

Just checking

1. What is the Crystal Mark?
2. Identify five types of information that are sensitive.
3. You have just taken notes at a meeting. Some of the discussions involved redundancies. What precautions would you take to keep the matter confidential?
4. What is meant by an audit?

BTEC Assessment activity 8.3

The business communication seminar for new entrepreneurs to be held by your centre will feature how the type of audience should affect the method and content of a written communication. You have been asked to prepare a handout that focuses on this.

1. Prepare a factsheet headed 'The importance of the audience' in which you identify several situations where an entrepreneur needs to consider the audience when deciding what format to use. As an example, you could consider confidential situations or when audits may be carried out. You should also think about different types of audiences, such as the very young or old, or when information must be easy to understand so that the Fog Index or Crystal Mark would be useful. **P4**

2. Add an extra section to your factsheet by describing appropriate methods you could use with different audiences. In each case identify the context in which you would use each method. For example, you could say that in your own centre, learners could receive an informal email reminder about a work project (and internal communication) but someone who attended an interview for a job would be told the outcome in a formal letter (an external communication). **M3**

3. The final section of your factsheet should fully explain how methods of written communication must be appropriate to the audience. Illustrate your answer by explaining why some types of communication that would be inappropriate in certain situations, such as when confidentiality is essential. In your answer, give further examples of organisational contexts when confidentiality or clarity is required and when audit evidence is needed. **D3**

Grading tips

- Think about the communications you prepared for your leavers' ball to think of the contexts that applied. How did you adapt your communications for different audiences, such as those to your fellow students and those to the external venue? And which types of communication would be most appropriate if you had to solve a difficult problem, such as disputing an invoice from the venue for a higher amount than you thought you had agreed?

- Look back at the WorkSpace case study on page 190 for further ideas of organisational contexts related to confidentiality, clarity and occasions when written evidence is required.

Assignment tips

- You will find this unit easier if you consider the types of written communications sent and received every day by different business organisations, such as supermarkets, hospitals and banks. For each one, consider which methods are definitely suitable, which are probably suitable and which are absolutely not. Think, too, about the consequences of using only oral methods for each one.

- You must prepare a number of well-written business communications without errors. This means checking each one very carefully and not just relying on a spell-checker. It also means taking care with your grammar and punctuation. You could try checking a friend's work while they check yours in return.

9 Training and employment in business

Wherever you work, and whatever you do, you are likely to have certain basic expectations about your employer. You will expect to be paid the amount agreed at the interview and to do the job that was described. You will expect to work in a safe place and to be treated fairly. You will no doubt hope that the job is interesting and challenging, and that you will be encouraged to gain additional skills to help you to progress in your career.

Similarly, your employer will have certain expectations of you. You will be expected to have the skills you claimed to have at the interview, to turn up for work regularly and on time (unless you are genuinely ill), to be honest, cooperative and to work for the future good of the business.

In the UK, employment laws govern many aspects of work, and you will learn about some of these in this unit. Good employers know that people work harder if they are motivated and if they enjoy doing their job. You will find out about this aspect of work as well as the benefits of teamwork. You will also learn about training opportunities that can enable you to do your job more effectively, as well as the benefits of regularly reviewing staff performance. Learning about these areas will help you to understand more about working in business.

Learning outcomes

After completing this unit, you should:

1. know the rights and responsibilities of employee and employer
2. understand how employees can be motivated
3. understand the importance of training and performance review.

All websites referred to in this unit can be accessed via Hotlinks. See page ii for more information.

Assessment and grading criteria

This table shows you what you must do in order to achieve a pass, merit or distinction grade, and where you can find activities in this book to help you.

To achieve a **pass**, the evidence must show that the learner is able to:	To achieve a **merit**, the evidence must show that, in addition to the pass criteria, the learner is able to:	To achieve a **distinction**, the evidence must show that, in addition to the pass and merit criteria, the learner is able to:
P1 outline the rights and responsibilities of employers in a chosen organisation **See Assessment activity 9.1, page 225**	**M1** explain the rights and responsibilities of employers and employees **See Assessment activity 9.1, page 225**	**D1** compare the rights and responsibilities of employers and employees **See Assessment activity 9.1, page 225**
P2 outline the rights and responsibilities of employees in a chosen organisation **See Assessment activity 9.1, page 225**		
P3 explain the importance of job satisfaction and teamwork in the workplace **See Assessment activity 9.2, page 232**	**M2** explain the relationship between motivation, teamwork and job satisfaction **See Assessment activity 9.2, page 232**	**D2** analyse the relationship between motivation, teamwork and job satisfaction, and how they contribute to organisational success **See Assessment activity 9.2, page 232**
P4 examine how employees can be motivated in the workplace **See Assessment activity 9.2, page 232**		
P5 describe the importance of training to an organisation **See Assessment activity 9.3, page 238**		
P6 explain the benefits of performance appraisal **See Assessment activity 9.3, page 238**		

How you will be assessed

To achieve this unit you will research the policies and contracts of employment to find out about, and compare, the rights and responsibilities of employers and employees in organisations. You will investigate how motivation, teamwork and job satisfaction are linked and identify the importance of training and performance reviews. The assessment activities in this book will help you to prepare for this.

Amy

This is the unit I enjoyed the most because I was interested to learn about the laws that affect people at work, and their terms and conditions of employment. It was good to learn about contracts of employment because they are so important. My brother didn't get paid recently when he was off sick and didn't know why. It turned out his contract said he only got paid for seven days in a year. He thought he would get paid whenever he was sick. Understanding his contract would have helped him to know this.

I think knowing these laws is important if I ever have my own business, which I hope to do. Learning about job satisfaction and teamwork was useful, too, because it will help me in the future whatever I do.

Although I have a part-time job we don't have appraisals, so it was interesting to learn about these and training opportunities.

I liked doing the teamwork Assessment activity because this helped me learn more about job satisfaction, the type of job I would like, and my own team-working skills, both good and not so good. It was helpful because I now know which areas I need to develop.

Over to you!

- Have you ever been appraised at work? How different do you think this would be to attending a review with your tutor?
- Do you like working as a member of a team or do you prefer to do your own thing? What benefits and drawbacks do you think there might be and why?

Your employment

1. Have you ever seen a contract of employment given to someone who has started work and, if so, did you understand it? How important do you think it is to know what it really means?

2. How important do you think it is to enjoy the work you are doing? What are the benefits for you and your employer? What factors do you think would help you to get a buzz out of the work you are doing each day?

1. Know the rights and responsibilities of employee and employer

Did you know?

- Before World War II, female teachers in Britain had to be single. If they wanted to get married they were forced to resign.

- The law tries to keep you safe, to protect you from unfair treatment at work, and make sure that you do not work for nothing.

PLTS

Practise your independent enquirer skills. Analyse and evaluate your research based on its relevance and value.

How different were working conditions 100 years ago?

In many countries, even today, there are no benefits available to anyone unable to work. One hundred and fifty years ago it was similar in the UK. An employer could dictate your pay, hours of work and working conditions, and dismiss you without a second thought. Women, disabled people and black people may never have had the chance to work at all.

After 1871, when trade unions became legally recognised, officials started to work to improve conditions. Wise employers realised, too, that treating workers properly meant people were healthier and would work better. By the 20th century, the government had started to pass laws to protect workers, and this continues today.

You benefit from all these changes. In every workplace in the UK, both employers and employees have rights and responsibilities towards one another. The aim is to prevent **exploitation** and any abuse of power by the strong over the weak. In this section you will learn about these rights and responsibilities.

Discussion point

Look up the word 'exploitation' and find out what it means. According to the TUC (which represents trade unions in England) and Citizens Advice, this continues in Britain, with migrant workers, domestic workers and home workers the most vulnerable.

In groups, research the topic on the Internet. Also check out the Gangmasters Licensing Authority website. Then discuss what you think could be done to outlaw exploitation completely.

1.1 Rights and responsibilities of employees

Statutory rights

All employees in the UK have the same **statutory rights** because these relate to the **employment laws** passed by Parliament that affect everyone in the country.

One statutory right is that you must be given a written statement of the terms and conditions of your employment within two months of starting work. The information may be given in an offer letter or in a more formal document, called a **contract of employment**.

- **Contract of employment** – This is a formal agreement about the job which includes all the important information. It is often referred to as 'legal terms and conditions of employment'. It prevents any nasty shocks when you start work, such as discovering you will be paid half the amount you expected!

You and your employer must sign the document to say you both agree with what it says. Because some information may be quite lengthy, such as details of grievance and disciplinary procedures, employers can include a brief outline only in the contract itself. They must then make sure that you know where to find the remainder, such as in an employee handbook.

From then on, both you and your employer must fulfil your legal responsibilities to each other. If one fails to do what has been agreed, they are said to be **in breach** of the law.

Here are the essential items in a contract of employment:

- o the names of the employer and employee
- o the date when the employment began
- o job title or a brief job description
- o hours of work
- o place of work
- o pay and how often payments will be made
- o holiday entitlement
- o entitlement to sick leave, and any entitlement to sick pay
- o pensions and pension schemes
- o notice required by employer and employee to terminate the contract
- o if it is not permanent, the length of time for which employment will continue or, if it is for a fixed term, the date when it will end
- o reference to disciplinary and grievance procedures
- o details of any trade union agreements that relate to the employee.

Did you know?

- One statutory right is that all employees must be paid at or above the national minimum wage rate for their age.

- Your contract of employment may enhance your statutory rights, but can never take any away. For example, many people are paid above the minimum wage rate, and their starting salary will be shown in their contract.

- Being employed carries both rights and responsibilities. You can expect certain things, but have to do certain things in exchange. Similarly, your employer must expect both to give and to get.

Key terms

Contract of employment – a written document containing the terms and conditions of employment relating to a particular person and their job.

In breach – breaking the terms of a contract.

Activity: Obtain a handbook

If you have a part-time job, or know someone who is working, see if you can obtain a copy of a handbook or other documents that give details about the terms and conditions of employment. Then as a group, compare the different types of information you have obtained.

Remember

Contracts of employment define your terms and conditions of employment and the actions that you and your employer can and cannot take. They are legally binding for both of you.

Key term

Employment tribunal – a special informal court that hears and rules upon employment cases.

goes to an **employment tribunal**, then employers may have to pay higher compensation claims. Employees who disregard the code can expect to receive a lower level of compensation.

Why are the Acas codes of practice important for all employees?

Did you know?

- If an employer ignores all procedures, then any dismissal becomes automatically unfair, no matter what the rights and wrongs of the case.

- Acas can arrange for **mediation** between an employer and employee(s). A mediator is a trained person who acts as a third party to listen to both sides in a dispute and helps them to reach agreement.

Activity: Match offences to penalties

The penalties considered by an employer at a disciplinary interview may include: verbal warning, first written warning, final written warning, suspension with pay while a matter is investigated, and summary (instant) dismissal. In groups, suggest the types of offences that would merit each of these.

- **Representative bodies** – These represent the views and rights of a group of people or organisations. They include trade unions and professional associations.

  Trade unions represent the views of employees to the employer, although some firms have works councils or staff associations instead. All employees have a legal right to join a trade union if they wish. In addition, an employee who serves as a trade union official has the statutory right to paid time off to carry out specific duties, as well as unpaid time off for training.

  Employers have **representative bodies**. Two important ones are the CBI (Confederation of British Industry), which lobbies the government if it thinks proposed new laws or regulations are unfair on business, and the FSB (Federation of Small Businesses), which has a similar role for the self-employed and owners of small firms.

Professional associations represent the members of a certain profession. Well-known ones include the British Medical Council and the Law Society.

Employee responsibilities

In return for your statutory and contractual rights, you also have several responsibilities, which link to your employer's rights.

- **Adhere to terms of contract** – Once you have signed your contract of employment, you are committed to abide by its terms. Failure to do so may result in disciplinary action and dismissal.

  Your contract contains a combination of express and implied terms. **Express terms** are those specifically listed in the contract, such as the fact that you will be paid £14,000 a year. **Implied terms** are not specifically agreed, but are terms a court would consider so obvious they do not need to be written down. Nevertheless, you still have to adhere to them (see Table 9.1).

- **Uphold business aims and objectives** – One implied responsibility is to work towards the objectives of the business. This is common sense. A business could not function if employees were undermining its efforts to achieve its goals.

- **Follow business rules** – This is another implied term. All employees must obey laws relating to their employment and cooperate with their employer over these and other business rules, such as wearing protective clothing and not taking confidential documents off the premises.

- **Respect company's property** – This means not being careless or slapdash so that you damage or break equipment, furniture or other items on the premises.

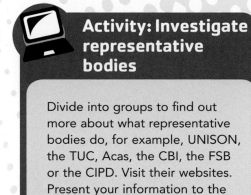

Activity: Investigate representative bodies

Divide into groups to find out more about what representative bodies do, for example, UNISON, the TUC, Acas, the CBI, the FSB or the CIPD. Visit their websites. Present your information to the rest of the class.

Can you suggest some rules this employee must follow in their working environment?

Activity: Implied terms

Table 9.1 identifies the implied terms of employment for both employees and employers. In groups, check these and discuss why it is accepted that these do not have to be expressly specified in writing in every contract. Then compare your ideas.

Activity: Decide your terms

Acas has produced a sample of a written statement online, available via Hotlinks (see page ii). You have started your own business and want to employ someone to help you. In groups, decide what terms and conditions you would offer, based on the essential items listed on page 215. Then download the statement and complete each section. Compare your ideas with other groups.

Table 9.1: Implied terms of employment

Employee responsibilities	Employer responsibilities
Comply with all the terms of the contract	Meet all the terms of the contract and notify employees of any changes within one month of these being made
Follow health and safety regulations	Provide a safe working environment
Comply with other laws related to their work, for example, not drinking and driving	Comply with all statutory employment law and regulations
	Provide appropriate training
	Allow employees to join a trade union or staff association
	Allow employees access to confidential records kept on them
In addition, the employer can expect the employee to:	**In addition, the employee can also expect the employer to:**
be reasonably competent and possess the skills claimed at the interview	treat them reasonably
be 'ready and willing' to work and do what any 'reasonable' employee would do in a situation	give them the opportunity to participate in and be consulted on company matters that would directly affect them
take reasonable care of the employer's property	never ask them to do anything that is illegal
work towards the objectives of the organisation	
carry out reasonable instructions and requests	
be honest	
not disclose confidential information	
behave responsibly towards other people at work	
be prepared to change when the job changes, for example, when new technology is introduced	

1.2 Rights and responsibilities of employers

Rights

Many of your employer's rights relate to your own responsibilities. These include the following.

- **Support the business aims** – Your employer has the right to set the business aims and to take decisions that will help to achieve them, whether these are popular with staff or not.

- **Support health and safety** – Under the Health and Safety at Work etc. Act, your employer must ensure the health, safety and welfare of their employees. You must also cooperate with your employer and take reasonable care of your own health and safety, and that of other people who may be affected by your actions.

- **Appropriate use of company equipment and time** – Your employer has the right to take disciplinary action if you spend most of the day on Facebook or take a laptop home without permission.

- **Set conditions of service** – Your employer can decide the terms and conditions that are specified in your contract of employment, such as your hours of work and pay, providing these are in accordance with statutory laws. Employers can also make minor changes to terms and conditions that may be needed to cope with changing circumstances. What they cannot usually do is to make major changes, for example, to your job duties, pay, hours of work and holiday entitlement, without consulting you first.

- **Set disciplinary and grievance procedures** – Acas have produced a code of practice for these, which employers are recommended to follow. An example is shown on the next page.

Did you know?

Many contracts contain a **variation term**. This is a short statement that allows an employer to change a condition without getting your agreement in advance. An example would be where the contract says, 'Normal working hours are 37 per week, but these may be increased if circumstances call for it.'

Activity: Investigate procedures

Disciplinary and grievance procedures for learners are often very similar to those in the workplace, because these, too, are designed to be fair to everyone. Check the disciplinary procedures in your centre and see whether they are similar to those mentioned here. Then find out what the official grievance procedures are.

It's been even worse since she got her 500th friend last week.

What can be the consequences of inappropriate use of company equipment?

During the 2008/09 recession, rather than announce redundancies, many employers asked staff to change their conditions of employment instead. Toyota cut shifts by 10 per cent, accountants KPMG offered staff the chance to work a four-day week or take 12 weeks off on 30 per cent pay, and BT offered a year's annual leave with a 75 per cent pay cut.

Would you rather take a pay cut or an unpaid holiday than lose your job altogether? Or would you prefer to take your chances in the job market and be able to claim benefits? Compare your ideas as a group.

Acas procedure

If an employee is being disciplined, Acas recommends that the employer:

1. investigates the incident

2. informs the employee of the problem in writing

3. holds a meeting with the employee to discuss it (the employee can be accompanied by someone else, such as a friend or trade union rep.)

4. decides what action to take

5. gives the employee a right of appeal.

Acas – Human Resources

Figure 9.1: An Acas recommended procedure

Responsibilities

Employers, as well as employees, have responsibilities. These are shown in Table 9.2.

Table 9.2: Employers' responsibilities

Employer responsibilities	Notes
Observe employment law and codes of practice	This is a major requirement. All employers must obey statutory laws and should abide by codes of practice that relate to their business.
Observe duty of care to employees	This means ensuring that no employee is put in danger or at risk because of actions taken by the employer. This relates to areas such as safety precautions and emergency procedures, and also covers issues such as undue stress and pressure.
Observe employees' contracts	This means that employers, too, must not breach contracts of employment by disregarding the main terms or making major changes without prior agreement of the employee.
Provide a safe workplace	All employers must abide by the Health and Safety at Work etc. Act and all other health and safety regulations that apply.
Provide procedures to protect relationships with employees	Many employers refer to Acas for guidance. In a large organisation, there may be a specific HR department that focuses on staff needs and issues. Some companies rely on firms such as Peninsula for specialist advice and assistance (see the WorkSpace case study on page 224).

Continued

Continued

Employer responsibilities	Notes
Provide public liability insurance	This covers the risk of injury to people or damage to property because of negligence or carelessness by the firm or its employees, from a driver backing into a garden wall to a major explosion that destroys nearby property. Without insurance, the business would have to pay all the costs and claims, and a small trader could never afford this.
Provide training	As part of the overall 'duty of care', all employers must ensure that employees receive essential health and safety training to enable them to work safely. This must be given at the start of their employment and later if their work or equipment changes. Employers must also provide training to employees under the age of 18, and allow trade union officials, safety representatives and employee representatives to undertake specific training for these roles.
Adhere to EU directives	An example is the European Working Time Directive (EWTD). Many UK laws and regulations originated as EU directives, and cover many different areas, including safety. They are binding on all member states of the European Union.

Activity: Investigate duty of care

Check out all the areas covered by duty of care at the Directgov website. You can use the list to check your tutor's working environment.

Discussion point

You now know that having rights protects employees. But do employers need protecting too? What if you owned a business and one employee kept taking time off, or someone else told everyone to demand a pay rise or walk out? In groups, suggest other problems employers could face, and how having rights can help them too.

Then decide how you would answer the owner of a small business who says that employment laws drive them mad as their key worker has just gone off on maternity leave and the owner is struggling to cope.

Activity: Investigate rights and responsibilities

As a group, arrange to talk to someone who works in HR at your centre. Prepare questions to find out about the rights and responsibilities of both the staff there and the employer. Ideally, find out about the main terms and conditions of employment for one particular job.

Did you know?

By law, all businesses must have employers' liability insurance and be insured for at least £5 million. This protects all employees against injury or disease – for example, a machine operator being injured because the equipment has not been maintained. It ensures any claims would be met in full.

Remember

All employers have rights and responsibilities. Their rights enable them to obtain the cooperation of their employees when they are carrying out essential tasks. Their responsibilities mean they must meet the needs of their employees in critical areas.

Joanna McGowan helps business owners meet their responsibilities as employers.

Yesterday, Joanna McGowan visited a doctor's surgery in Salford, Manchester. Not because she was ill, but as part of her job. Joanna works for Peninsula Business Services, which specialises in helping businesses to cope with their legal responsibilities. Like many business owners, the doctors in Salford want to spend their time focusing on what they are good at, which is medicine, not employment law. At the same time, they know they must meet their legal responsibilities to their staff or there could be serious consequences.

Peninsula specialises in helping businesses to put in place 'best practice policies', covering key areas such as recruitment and training, employment law and health and safety. Joanna checks the conditions of employment, prepares an Employee Handbook and makes sure all the contracts of employment are correct.

Clients pay a monthly fee to Peninsula for continuous access to expert advice and information. As well as knowing all their procedures and paperwork are correct, clients are also protected by indemnity insurance. This means that if they follow Peninsula's procedures and take its advice, then they will not have to pay any costs if there is a legal case against them.

As part of this service, clients have access to a 24/7 helpline. They must phone for advice before they take any action, such as dismissing an employee for a suspected offence, or making someone redundant. Then they must do what Peninsula says. This benefits everyone as it means employees are treated fairly and the employer has behaved lawfully. This has been important during the recession, when many employers have wanted to vary their terms and conditions of employment or lay off staff.

As a qualified HR professional, Joanna wants to help all employers, both large and small. She knows that many owners of small businesses know little about the law and struggle to keep up to date with the many changes. Neither can they afford to employ an HR manager. To improve their knowledge, they can attend one of Peninsula's short courses on employment law or health and safety, or send one of their staff instead.

Find out more about Peninsula by visiting the website before you answer the questions below.

Think about it!

1. As a group, suggest four or five actions that an owner of a small business, unaware of employer rights and responsibilities, may unwittingly take. Then compare your ideas.
2. Identify four benefits for that business of using Peninsula's services.
3. Suggest reasons why employers cannot just vary the terms and conditions of employment without consultation.
4. If Joanna was talking to your group about the importance of employee and employer rights and responsibilities, what do you think she would say and why?

Just checking

1. What is meant by the term 'statutory right'?
2. Identify three statutory rights of all employees.
3. Identify three responsibilities of an employee and three responsibilities of an employer.
4. Employers need to have rights to be able to run their business and comply with the law. Explain two rights that help them do this.

BTEC

Assessment activity 9.1

You have been asked to prepare an article on the rights and responsibilities of employers and employees. This will feature in a handbook being given out at a careers fair.

Find out the information you need by investigating the rights and responsibilities of employers and employees at a business you know. If you work part-time, then you could use your workplace or you could ask a family member or family friend who has a business. With the agreement of your tutor, you could investigate this information for your centre.

To research this task properly, you will need to be able to talk to staff and obtain a copy of any staff handbooks, an example of a contract or statement of main terms, and relevant company policies that apply.

Study the information you have obtained carefully and then prepare an article on employment in your chosen organisation.

1. In the first section, outline the rights and responsibilities of the employer and the employees who work there. **P1** **P2**

2. In the next section, explain these. This means providing more information about each one. You may also find, for example, that many of the employer's rights are the same as, or similar to, the responsibilities of the employees. **M1**

3. In your final section, compare the rights and responsibilities of both the employer and employees. To do this properly, you will need to talk to the owner or someone who represents the employer to get their view, and also talk to at least one member of staff. Read the grading tips below for more information on how to compare rights and responsibilities as well as for other sources of information you may find helpful. **D1**

Grading tips

- When you are making a comparison, look for similarities and differences. Then explain what you find.
- When you are comparing rights and responsibilities, think about how important these are and the consequences for both employees and employers if they did not exist. For ideas, check out the information on the TUC website as well as major trade union websites, like UNISON.

Why do performance appraisals benefit both the employee and the business?

Mutual agreement of objectives

The aim of the session is a frank and confidential discussion. Ideally it should be very positive and motivating for the employee. It is an opportunity to talk to their manager about their future aims, plans and preferences. It is the line manager's job to link these to the goals of the business and the departmental objectives.

Finally an action plan is agreed, which includes mutually agreed objectives. These form the basis of the discussion at the next interview.

Periodic review of progress

Because appraisal interviews are held periodically, agreed actions can be followed up. The manager will want an explanation for targets that have been missed or other unsatisfactory aspects of job performance, such as unpunctuality or lack of commitment. The important point is that the employee is aware of concerns and the need for improvement. This is not only important for workplace relations, but is essential for legal reasons if disciplinary action is taken later.

3.4 Benefits of performance appraisals

In summary, these are as follows.

- **Training needs are identified** linked to the needs of the business and the aims and ambitions of the employee.

- **Problems are revealed** and solutions can be discussed and agreed.

- **New skills may be discovered**. A line manager may be fascinated to discover some unknown interest of an employee that can be developed for everyone's benefit.

- **Communication is improved**. The chance to sit down with your line manager and talk honestly and openly, in confidence, is a rare and valuable opportunity in most business organisations.

- **Evidence is provided for promotion or dismissal**. A series of positive reviews can provide evidence for promotion. Equally, a series of negative ones can result in dismissal. The evidence documented during regular reviews would prove that the employee knew about the shortcomings and was given opportunities to improve.

- **They can lead to pay rises**. In some businesses, performance reviews are coupled with pay increases, but there can be problems trying to link individual target achievements to pay awards.

- **Performance-related pay** is easier because specific bonuses or commission payments are linked to identified targets at the outset.

- **Efficiency and effectiveness** increase. Carried out correctly, periodic performance appraisals improve both the **efficiency** and **effectiveness** of employees and the business as a whole.

Discussion point

Some experts think that pay should be kept separate from the appraisal process or employees will only agree to low targets they know they can achieve. Others say appraisals are only taken seriously if people are rewarded for their efforts. Which do you think is right and why?

Key terms

Efficiency – doing the right thing, that is, making the best use of resources such as time and money.

Effectiveness – doing things right, that is, in the right order, to the right standard and in the right way.

Activity: Hold an appraisal interview

Divide into pairs for this activity. One should take the part of the line manager, the other the employee. Decide on the following before you start: the type of business you both work for, the role of the employee, the targets set last time and performance since then. The employee must decide their personal aims and the employer must identify main business aims.

Then hold the interview. The manager should praise achievements and identify any weaknesses, motivate the employee, and identify any training needs and link these to the business aims.

The employee should try to explain any failings, and talk about future ambitions and additional skills or training they would like.

Then reverse roles. Summarise your experience and what you have both learned by doing this activity in a short presentation to your group.

PLTS

As the employee, practise your self-manager skills by showing you can work towards goals. As the employer, be an effective participator by identifying improvements that would benefit both of you.

Just checking

1. Identify four reasons why training is needed.
2. What is the difference between an in-house and an external training course? Give an example of each.
3. Explain what normally happens during a performance appraisal.
4. Identify three benefits for the employer and employee of carrying out performance appraisals.

BTEC Assessment activity 9.3 — P5 P6

Your centre is preparing a new handbook for staff and you have been asked to prepare two short articles, one on training and the other on performance appraisal.

Start by investigating the training opportunities available to staff in your centre by talking to your tutor and other staff who agree to help you. Remember that staff may also go on some courses run by your centre, so check the website and obtain any relevant course literature.

Next, find out how often performance appraisals are held and why your tutor (and other staff, too, if possible) thinks they are valuable.

Use this information to prepare your articles.

1. The first article should describe the importance of training to your centre. This means identifying why training is needed by staff at your centre (such as to update their skills or for legal reasons), what courses are held both in-house and externally and the benefits gained by your centre. **P5**

2. The second article should explain the benefits of performance appraisal. This means stating the aim of the appraisal system, how it operates and the ways in which this system benefits your centre and the staff who work there. **P6**

Grading tips

- To answer these questions properly, you need to consider what would happen if staff did not receive training for the skills needed by your centre.
- Think, too, about the consequences of not having performance appraisals.
- Then consider the effect on the staff, the business and its customers – this includes you!

Assignment tips

- This unit concentrates on people, their needs and what motivates them. You should be able to identify easily with this by thinking about your own needs and what motivates you.
- Think back to any work experiences you have had yourself, in particular what motivated you and what had exactly the opposite effect.
- Remember there is more than one opinion to consider in any debate relating to groups of people, such as employers and employees.

10 Personal selling in business

All businesses are involved in selling. Commercial organisations sell their goods and services to customers to make a profit and survive, and charities must 'sell' their cause to get donations. In the public sector, the BBC promotes its programmes by screening preview clips to tempt viewers, while your centre must 'sell' its courses, facilities and expertise to both learners and parents to meet its target enrolment figures.

Selling is also a common feature of television programmes on business. *The Apprentice* candidates must undertake several selling tasks; in *Dragon's Den*, entrepreneurs must sell both their business idea and their product to the panel. When Sir Gerry Robinson, a famous business entrepreneur, looked at investing his own money to rescue ailing businesses in Channel 4's *Gerry's Big Decision,* he constantly focused on sales and selling skills as crucial to future success. Mary Portas, *Queen of Shops*, spent time teaching the volunteers in a charity shop how to sell.

Working in sales can be fun and challenging. You need several skills, from the ability to communicate easily with customers, to a sound knowledge of the product and the policies of your employer. You also need to know basic sales techniques and be able to match the product to the customer. If you do this consistently well, everyone benefits. Customers make a great purchase, you achieve sales for your employer and get a buzz out of helping people, too. This unit focuses on the skills and knowledge you need to achieve this.

Learning outcomes

After completing this unit, you should:

1. understand the role of sales staff
2. be able to demonstrate personal selling skills and processes.

All websites referred to in this unit can be accessed via Hotlinks. See page ii for more information.

Assessment and grading criteria

This table shows you what you must do in order to achieve a pass, merit or distinction grade, and where you can find activities in this book to help you.

To achieve a **pass**, the evidence must show that the learner is able to:	To achieve a **merit**, the evidence must show that, in addition to the pass criteria, the learner is able to:	To achieve a **distinction**, the evidence must show that, in addition to the pass and merit criteria, the learner is able to:
P1 describe the role of sales staff **See Assessment activity 10.1, page 253**	**M1** explain the role of sales staff and the sales techniques they use **See Assessment activity 10.1, page 253**	**D1** demonstrate the confident use of personal selling skills when making sales **See Assessment activity 10.3, page 267**
P2 identify the techniques used when making personal sales **See Assessment activity 10.1, page 253**	**M2** compare the selling skills and processes used in different situations **See Assessment activity 10.2, page 267**	**D2** evaluate the preparation, skills and processes used in different situations **See Assessment activity 10.3, page 267**
P3 explain the knowledge and skills used when making personal sales **See Assessment activity 10.1, page 253**		
P4 prepare to make personal sales **See Assessment activity 10.3, page 267**		
P5 use selling skills and processes to make sales **See Assessment activity 10.3, page 267**		

How you will be assessed

To achieve this unit you will demonstrate that you understand the role of sales staff and the techniques, knowledge and skills they need in various situations. You will undertake several practical activities to demonstrate your own selling skills and show that you can reflect and learn from your own experiences, both as a customer and as a salesperson.

Usman

This is the unit I have enjoyed the most on my course. I learned a lot that I didn't know before I started it, such as techniques like cross-selling and up-selling. I can now spot when salespeople do this when I am buying something.

This unit allowed me to participate in role plays and then, at the end, we ran our own Charity Shopping Fair, which we all really enjoyed. We raised money for our local children's hospice and improved our own selling skills at the same time. I prefer role plays and practical work because I feel I can express myself and my work better. They also helped me understand how to use my knowledge in a practical way.

When I did the role plays I learned many helpful selling skills, for example, how to communicate with customers and keep their attention and interest. We put all these into practice when we held the fair at the end.

When we practised, I took time planning and preparing myself for the situation and worked with a partner who played the customer as I played the sales assistant.

At the end of the course I am hoping to go on to Level 3, and I also want to get a part-time job in sales. What I learned in this unit will help me to do that kind of job much better.

Over to you!

- Do you enjoy practical work and getting involved in role plays?
- Can you recognise different sales techniques when you are a customer? Do these tempt you to buy or not?

The truth about selling

There are many myths about selling. As a group, which of these statements do you think are myths and which are facts?

a) Anyone can sell – all you have to do is look smart and be friendly.

b) Selling is boring – you do the same thing over and over again.

c) Selling means persuading people to buy things they do not need.

Discuss your ideas. Then see if you have the same opinion when you have finished this unit.

Functional skills

This activity helps your reading skills by giving you practice in reading and summarising succinctly information from different sources.

Activity: Investigate consumer legislation

Divide into seven groups. One group should investigate each of the laws in Figure 10.1 in more detail, referring both to Unit 13 and useful websites, such as the consumer rights pages at Directgov. The last group should investigate the Food Handling Regulations and Weights and Measures Regulations that would affect Eva, who wants to open a wine bar selling snacks and sandwiches.

Then give a five-minute presentation about your findings to your group.

Organisational policies

Many businesses have policies that give extra benefits to their customers, such as a no-quibble refund policy. This means customers can exchange goods or get a refund, within a certain time limit, if they have changed their mind after making the purchase. The business has no legal obligation to do this, but has this policy because it encourages customer to make impulse buys, even if some are returned later.

Other examples of similar policies include the following.

- **Price matching** – this is when a business offers to match a cheaper price for the same product offered by a competitor. Normally this excludes products bought online.

- **Discounting** – discounts may be given to trade customers, those spending over a certain amount or those who pay promptly.

- **Guarantees** – a business may have a policy of offering extended guarantees on its products for no extra charge. Note that this is different from charging customers for extended warranties, which are rarely worth the money.

- **After-sales service** – this is all the extra services that are provided after the product has been purchased, such as free delivery, order tracking, free installation, spare parts and a repairs service.

Did you know?

Some companies are renowned for their discounts and frequent sales. Examples include sofa companies ScS and DFS with 'double discount sales' and other promotions.

What are the benefits for a business of offering additional services?

- **Customer care** – these are other aspects of the customer relationship, from convenient opening hours and staff availability to good signage and additional facilities/services, such as a children's play area or customer collection area (see page 266).

Reflective practice

Every salesperson will have successes and some failures. Sometimes customers may seem about to make a purchase, then suddenly change their mind and walk away. This happens to every salesperson at one time or another, although it is obviously worrying if it seems to happen to you more than anyone else.

One way to improve your success rate is to try to make sense of an encounter that went wrong afterwards, to see what you can learn from it. You can also reflect on what went right when you were successful, but this is usually less effective than learning from your mistakes.

One method of reflecting was devised by Professor Graham Gibbs. This means going through six steps, which are shown in Figure 10.2.

Figure 10.2: Graham Gibbs' model of reflection

Activity: John Lewis policies

John Lewis uses the slogan 'Never knowingly undersold'. This means if ever it knows a competitor is selling goods cheaper, John Lewis will lower its prices to match them. It also gives a free second-year guarantee on electrical products, and five years on the TVs. Investigate its other policies by visiting the customer service pages of its website.

Did you know?

The reason some sales fail is because of lack of selling skills and lack of preparation. You will learn more about these in the next section.

Activity: Reflect on your own performance

Refer to the notes you made after your experience practising the selling roles on page 248. Copy the table below and enter your findings. Then reflect on how you could improve, and have another try.

Description	
Feelings	
Evaluation	
Analysis	
Conclusion	
Action plan	

PLTS

Inviting feedback and evaluating experiences is all part of being a reflective learner.

Case study

How to change your approach – advice from an expert

With over ten years' experience, Julian Lobb knows pretty much all there is to know about selling.

From helping Carphone Warehouse customers with phone problems to selling Volkswagen cars, Julian Lobb knows the importance of changing his approach to suit each selling situation.

Julian says that selling face to face requires good observational skills in order to pick up quickly on customer reactions. Selling over the phone, however, requires good speaking skills, the ability to hold the interest of the other person, and excellent listening skills. If you hear a pause, check if the customer has fully understood. A sigh means the customer is uninterested, or even bored. If the customer gets angry, then terminate the call politely as there is no chance of making a sale.

Wherever you work, your appearance is important. Julian believes strongly that even on the telephone you are more likely to have a professional approach if you are 'suited and booted', and not in jeans and a T-shirt.

Another important factor is the type of product and its cost. In electrical retailers, like Currys or Comet, good product knowledge is vital. For many expensive items, like cars, customers are very loyal to a brand and finance is a major part of the purchase.

Julian stresses that building up a relationship with the customer is essential. He greets people by talking about anything general, such as the weather, to establish some common ground. Then he qualifies the sale by asking questions to identify the customer's needs and find out if they are a serious buyer. Next he focuses on meeting these needs and gets the customer to identify with the item by using it. This is why Julian would encourage a customer to sit on a sofa, lie on a bed or take a test drive.

The personality and style of the salesperson is vital, especially for expensive items. If the customer dislikes the salesperson they may turn their backs on a great offer and go somewhere else. Fundamentally, Julian says, people buy from people, rather than businesses!

Think about it!

1. Identify two similarities and two differences between selling face to face and over the telephone.
2. If you worked selling mobile phones and then got a job selling expensive fitness equipment, what differences could you expect to find and why?
3. What is meant by 'brand loyalty'? How would this affect the way you would sell a product?
4. Identify two different selling situations in which you would like to work. In each case, identify the techniques and skills you would need.

Just checking

1. Explain what is meant by 'product surround'.
2. Describe two ways in which you could give a good first impression to a customer.
3. Identify three sales techniques used by businesses.
4. Explain why the Sale of Goods Act is important.
5. Why is it helpful for sales staff to be able to reflect on their performance?

BTEC Assessment activity 10.1

You have recently heard that a new department store will be opening in your area, and you know that competition for sales jobs there will be tough. Your tutor has suggested you could help each other, as a group, to prepare for interviews.

1. Divide into groups. Each group will prepare and give a short presentation on:
   a) the role of sales staff
   b) the sales techniques used to make personal sales
   c) the knowledge and skills required by sales staff when making personal sales, including relevant consumer legislation.

2. From the presentations and what you have learned so far, write your own reference notes.
   a) Start by describing the role of sales staff in a business. **P1**

b) Next, identify the techniques sales staff use when they are making personal sales, and link this to the skills that are required. **P2**

c) Explain the knowledge and skills needed to make personal sales. As well as product knowledge and selling skills remember to include a broad description of the legislation that affects personal selling and the organisational policies that apply to aspects of selling such as extended warranties. **P3**

d) Add a more detailed final section in which you explain the role of sales staff and the techniques they use to promote the organisation and their contribution towards organisational goals. Then explain how sales techniques vary between organisations, products and customers. **M1**

Keep your work safely as you will refer to it again in the next Assessment activity.

Grading tips

- For P1, your description should include all the work carried out by sales staff from identifying a customer's needs to closing the sale (see also page 262).

- For P3, remember that technical skills are required by many sales people. So too is information on extended warranties, personal protection insurance, and product updates. Staff may also be expected to cross-sell or up-sell to customers and should know how to do this.

- For M1, think about all the ways in which sales staff can contribute towards the business objectives. It might help to look back to the start of the unit. You can use the WorkSpace case study to help too.

2. Be able to demonstrate personal selling skills and processes

The only way to develop your own selling skills is to practise. There are two important aspects to becoming an effective salesperson.

- **Personal selling skills** – This relates to your ability to communicate and identify with the customer so that they enjoy talking to you. It also includes your appearance and attitude.

- **Selling processes** – This means understanding what you need to do to make a successful sale and the associated tasks, such as handling a complaint or liaising with other departments.

2.1 Personal selling skills

The personal skills of the salesperson influence the outcome of many sales situations. You know this yourself. If you arrive in a store and cannot find anyone to serve you, you will probably walk out. If you get prompt service but need some advice, it is irritating if the assistant cannot answer your questions or is pushy. Even worse is someone who looks bored or messes up the sale and then needs a supervisor to sort it out. In a store where sales staff are friendly, knowledgeable and efficient, the different is startling – and they probably enjoy their job more, too!

Developing your own selling skills involves concentrating on your communication skills, assessing your own style and appearance, and learning some tricks of the trade. If you enjoy dealing with people and trying to help them, then you are already halfway there.

Communicating with customers

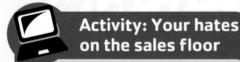

Activity: Your hates on the sales floor

In groups, list your six top hates when you are dealing with a salesperson. Then compare your list with those made by other groups to see which traits everyone finds annoying.

There are several methods of communicating with customers. The ones you use will depend upon the situation.

- **Spoken** communications are usually necessary because you need to talk to your customer, either face to face or over the telephone. Having good verbal skills does not mean being 'posh'. It does mean speaking clearly and not too quickly, and using words and phrases the customer will understand.

- **Written** communications are used to sell and promote items, such as adverts in local papers and product descriptions on eBay. You may also communicate by email, by letter and by promotional material such as leaflets. Emails to a customer are different from those written to friends, and business letters are set out in a specific way, as you will see if you study Unit 8.

- **Non-verbal** communications relate to your body language and posture – the silent signals you give all the time. You give feedback to people by nodding or smiling when you understand something or looking puzzled when you do not. To be aware of body language, you need to think about your gestures, facial expressions, posture and how you stand in relation to someone else. See also Unit 7, page 164.

- **Face-to-face** communications take place in many selling situations, including retail stores because the customer is not only listening to what you say, but also watching your expressions and your body language. It is obvious if you are pretending to be interested when you are actually bored or in a rush to get away, because your body language will betray you. Your appearance is also very important in this situation (see page 257).

- **Eye contact** means looking at the customer when you are talking to them, not staring at your shoes or at the wall behind their head. If you are dealing with more than one person, try to look at each one in turn. Otherwise, if you accidentally ignore the one who is the key decision maker, this could lose the sale. Also try to make eye contact from time to time if you are demonstrating a product.

- **Remote** communications take place when the buyer and seller are at a distance, so include telephone and online sales. Call centres want staff with good verbal skills and the ability to chat easily to people over the phone. Staff also need excellent listening skills to concentrate on what the other person is saying throughout the conversation. They must also double-check if they think they may have misheard anything.

eBay is an example of a remote selling situation. Here the customer relies upon the written description of the goods, the photograph and the rating of the supplier to decide how much to pay and whether to make a purchase.

Did you know?

- It is unprofessional to 'rubbish' the competition. This does not go down well with anyone, especially your customers.

- If you do not make eye contact with a customer when you meet them it will make you look shifty and uninterested, even if it is simply because you are shy. But remember, making eye contact does not mean staring at someone!

- Call centres are big business in Scotland and employ over 60,000 people. One reason is that surveys have shown we trust someone with a Scottish accent more than any other, particularly when money is involved.

Activity: Practise your communication skills

Turn to Unit 7, (pages 168 and 169), Unit 8 (pages 188–90) and Unit 11 (pages 285–87) to learn more about communication skills and customers. Then divide into pairs, one as the customer, the other as the assistant.

The customer wants to report a problem with a recent purchase. As customer, describe your experience in some detail and explain what you want to happen next. The assistant can make notes and ask questions but must keep the customer happy (use your knowledge of consumer legislation to help) and then report this conversation to the supervisor to find out what to tell the customer.

Your tutor will take the part of your supervisor and will assess you on your skills both talking to the customer and giving a coherent verbal message. Then swap roles and carry out another scenario.

Discussion point

You have several unwanted/ unused gifts at home you want to get rid of. You cannot decide whether to sell them on eBay or at a local car boot sale. In groups, identify the different skills you would need to sell them successfully in each situation.

Purposes of communication

Salespeople communicate for many reasons and in several different ways. These are linked to the AIDA principle, where you focus on getting the customer's attention, developing interest, creating desire and then encouraging them to take action to buy.

Table 10.2: Communication – the AIDA principle

You need to achieve...	By...
Attention	Greeting the customer positively and with a smile; inspiring confidence; pointing out relevant displays or products
Interest	Talking in a friendly, approachable manner; identifying the type of products or services in which the customer is interested
Desire	Asking open questions to find out the customer's precise needs; suggesting solutions that would meet these requirements; pointing out the benefits to the customer of different options
Action	Persuasively overcoming objections and closing the sale

- **Greeting a customer** must be done in a friendly, assured but non-threatening way so that you inspire confidence in the customer, who then feels positive about meeting you.

- **Introducing yourself** should also be done in a friendly, informal way, for example, 'Hi, my name is Anika.' In most sales situations it is a good idea to wear a name badge.

Remember

If you are selling an expensive item, you should ideally talk to the customer and establish their needs *before* you start to promote any products.

. . . and now we come to the precise way the mattress is constructed . . .

Why should salespeople present product information clearly?

- **Attracting the customer's attention and interest** means assuring the customer that you stock the products they want and know what you are talking about. You can also mention one or two unusual aspects of the product that they might not have thought about, to get them really interested.

- **Identifying and meeting customer needs** means you now need to get customers to talk about themselves. This makes them feel good (most people like to talk about themselves!) and enables you to find out what they want and why they want it.

- **Presenting product information** must be done clearly and without using jargon or technical terms a customer would not understand. The main danger is that a salesperson gets overenthusiastic and talks too much at this stage.

Appearance

You make an impression on a customer in a few seconds. In a face-to-face encounter the first thing the customer registers is your appearance.

- **Dress** – Most organisations insist sales staff wear special uniforms and name badges so that they are smart and easily recognisable. It is the responsibility of each person to make sure that their clothes are clean and ironed and their shoes are polished. The style of your hair and the jewellery you wear will also be noticed immediately. If there is no uniform then your work clothes must be suitable and in accordance with any dress code that exists. This will usually have rules that limit the type of clothes that are suitable (for example, no flip flops or crop tops, even in hot weather).

- **Personal hygiene** – It is essential that you are clean, tidy and fussy about personal hygiene so that you are always nice to be near. You may think you look terrific, but if you have splashed on too much perfume or aftershave, or just returned from a quick cigarette break, it will be immediately obvious to everyone near you. Dirty hands and/or fingernails and yellow teeth are also major turn-offs.

Attitude

Your attitude is observed from your manner and your body language. It also shows in your tone of voice, so is equally obvious to people you speak to on the telephone.

- **Positiveness** – People who stand tall and smile are always nicer to meet than those who slouch and moan about everything. They are 'can do' people who go the extra mile to try to help someone else, which is a major attribute for any salesperson.

- **Manners** – Although men no longer automatically walk on the outside of pavements or stand whenever a woman enters the room, in business these types of gestures are still important. Opening doors for customers should be second nature, as should be offering to carry anything heavy or finding a chair for someone who has to wait.

Did you know?

It is important to watch the body language of your customers carefully when you are talking to them. You should be able to tell if they do not understand, or do not agree with what you are saying.

Activity: Can you sell it?

Can you convince someone to buy something? Choose an ordinary, everyday object, such as a watch, pen, glass, shoe or bar of soap and sell it as an expensive, luxury brand such as Rolex, Shaeffer, Waterford Crystal, Jimmy Choo or Jo Malone. Present your item to the class and persuade them it is worth buying. Then decide who is best!

Discussion point

Some people think salesgirls on cosmetics counters wear too much make-up and this puts customers off. Others think they need to look glamorous to show off their products and attract customers. What do you think?

Why should good manners be second nature to salespeople?

Did you know?

- In Canada and America, salespeople automatically refer to customers they do not know as 'Sir' or 'Ma'am', which immediately makes them feel important and respected.

- A good place to start with this activity is to refresh your memory by rereading the work you did for Assessment Activity 10.1.

Remember

It is against the law to exaggerate what a product can do or to make false claims about the services you can offer.

- **Language** – Your choice of words should be different in a selling situation from when you are chatting to family and friends, even with customers of your own age. You are in a professional role, so this means speaking a little more formally than normally. If you do not hear something and need it repeated, say 'Pardon?' not 'What?'. And even young customers respond positively to being called 'Sir' or 'Madam'.

- **Courtesy and consideration** – This means putting someone else's needs before your own and should apply to all your customers and colleagues. This also relates to your behaviour with your colleagues when customers are present. Whispering, giggling and shouting to each other are all totally inappropriate.

Activity: Selling skills in different situations

You are unsure about your future selling career and where you would like to work. You have seen jobs in call centres and department stores, and know that you would need different types of skills to work in these two environments.

In groups, decide the personal skills needed by sales staff in each of the following situations: a) selling cosmetics in a department store; b) selling medicines in a pharmacy; c) selling clothes in a small boutique; d) selling holidays in a call centre; e) selling designer sunglasses at an airport; f) selling prams and cots at an exhibition of baby products; g) selling iPhones in an Apple store.

Then decide how the personal skills required by sales staff would differ from one situation to another. Compare your ideas as a class.

Keep your work for this activity safe as you will find it helpful when you do Assessment activity 10.2.

Preparing the sales area

The physical sales environment is very important for all retailers. An attractive, welcoming entrance that leads to a sales area with clearly displayed and accessible goods has many advantages. It encourages shoppers to enter, helps them to find what they want quickly, and tempts them to browse and look around, which encourages impulse buying.

The main features to consider are as follows.

- **Accessibility** – Under the Disability Discrimination Act, business premises must be accessible to disabled customers and reasonable adjustments must be made to achieve this. Signs should be clear and easy to read, a ramp should provide an alternative to steps, and access doors should be wide and easily opened. Wheelchair users must be considered when planning counter areas, as well as changing rooms and toilets.

- **Furnishings and décor** – These will reflect the image of the business and the type of products sold.

  - **Self-service and convenience stores** are clean and functional with fixed display units, a tiled or wooden floor, bright lighting and clear signage, for example, Asda and B&Q.

  - **Clothes shops** want customers to relax, browse and handle the stock, so there may be carpet, mirrors, chairs and soft lighting, for example, River Island and Next.

  - **Other shops** divide the selling area into different types of products. Staples has fixed shelving units for stationery products and a separate area for office furniture and equipment. Debenhams and John Lewis have separate areas for cosmetics, clothes and items for the home.

Remember

Cleanliness and tidiness are vital in a sales area. A neat, attractive display is worth more than thousands of pounds' worth of equipment and lighting.

Did you know?

Yellow and red are both instantly noticeable, which is why many fast food chains use one or both of these colours.

How does the Disability Discrimination Act affect retailers?

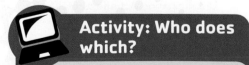
- **Music** – Used in some stores to help customers relax, to avoid silence and to mask unacceptable background noises. The music is usually linked to the target buyer, so stores like Miss Selfridge will play loud upbeat music.

- **Health and safety** – All selling environments must be assessed to ensure hazards are minimised. Sales staff must know how to act correctly in an emergency, such as an evacuation when the fire alarm sounds. This is very important in large stores where dozens of customers will not know the emergency exit routes.

Table 10.3: The sales floor and health and safety

Aspect	Key points
The building	Building regulations require safety glass in doors, handrails on steps, and non-slip flooring.
Delivery and storage of goods	Deliveries should be to a special entrance leading to the stockroom. Heavy goods must be moved using trucks/trolleys, and loads stacked safely. Perishable and hazardous items must be stored safely.
Store fixtures and fittings	Shelves must be stable, have raised front edges to prevent items falling off and not be overloaded.
Displays of merchandise	These should be created at quiet times and placed so that they cannot be knocked over. Heavy items must be stacked so they are stable.
Equipment and appliances	Freezers and chilled cabinets must be maintained or repaired by specialists. Only trained staff should use potentially hazardous equipment. Food handling staff must wear protective clothing and comply with hygiene regulations.
Cleanliness and tidiness	Cleaning should be done when customers have left or, if the store is open 24/7, at the quietest times. This should include shelf cleaning/filling and the cleaning of cabinets and freezers.
Working practices	Maintenance work should occur when the store is closed. Areas under repair during opening hours should be cordoned off and merchandise re-sited. Stock repositioning should be done at quiet times. Staff must clean up spillages and breakages quickly, and cordon off the area until it is dry and safe to walk on.

- **Competition** – All stores want to make themselves different from their competitors and can do this by:

  ○ having a distinctive image, shop front, fascia, design and layout that ensures the brand is instantly recognisable

  ○ offering special facilities, such as a coffee shop, car parking, cash machines and children's play area

  ○ offering extra services, such as help with packing, free delivery, gift wrapping and free alterations for regular customers

o opening longer hours or more days a week than competitors

o operating an integrated online and high street operation so customers who buy online can exchange their goods in store if they wish

o having regular sales promotions or reducing prices

o having a fast stock turnaround so new stock is constantly arriving in store

o being renowned for excellent customer service.

Activity: Investigate retail design

Retail design is a specialist area. Check the work of one UK consultancy, Barber Design by visiting their website. Click on the pictures of their recent work for many famous retailers to see the importance of the selling area. Take a group vote on the ones you like best.

- **The likely impact on buyer behaviour** – Buyers are influenced by many things, including their mood that day and whether they are shopping alone or with someone else, and if so, who this is. Lighting, temperature, the time of day, the weather and even the time of year affect the way we behave when we are shopping.

Supermarkets know that the smell of fresh bread or coffee makes us feel hungry; car dealers make sure their cars are squeaky clean and smell of leather upholstery. Store layout influences us, too – we normally bear right when we enter and walk faster on wooden floors than on carpet.

When a store is designed a **planogram** is prepared, which shows where every product should be situated, shelf by shelf and aisle by aisle, to maximise selling space and therefore profits. **Power aisles** are identified. These are the main aisles that lead customers to all parts of the store and will contain major displays of merchandise. At the end of each one are **power displays** where goods sell very quickly indeed. Experts claim that planograms enable them to predict 95 per cent of purchasing behaviour, which is why stores all over the world look the same! They all try to tempt us to buy non-essential items, called **discretionary spending**.

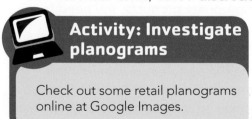

Activity: Investigate planograms

Check out some retail planograms online at Google Images.

Key terms

Buyer behaviour – the way different customers act when they are buying.

Discretionary spending – money we choose to spend on non-essentials.

Why do you think some manufacturers are prepared to pay to have their products displayed at eye level?

Activity: Check out a store

Open your eyes to a superstore near you. Walk in and check out the layout. Are sandwiches and magazines near the entrance? Is bread at the back? What products are stacked at the end of aisles in power displays? Compare your findings as a group.

Personal space

Respecting customers' personal space means not standing too close when you are talking to them or eavesdropping when a couple or a group of customers are talking together. If you are dealing with a couple, a good strategy is to say that you will leave them to talk about the various options for a few minutes, and then return when their body language shows that they have reached agreement or have further questions.

Activity: Mind the gap!

Try a simple experiment, working in pairs as customer and salesperson. The customer should ask questions about a product of interest. The salesperson must answer, and move closer each time. Then watch the customer automatically back away to keep the gap. Then reverse roles and talk about why you both did this.

2.2 Processes

Sales

The sales process consists of three separate steps.

- **Initiate the sale** – This is the first step in contacting the customer. You may be in a situation where the customer arrives and buys, such as a convenience store, or you may see a customer browsing, and approach them. If you work in a call centre, the first step may be phoning the customer and introducing yourself.

- **Make the sale** – At this stage you find out the customer's needs and describe the features of appropriate products. You need to identify the benefits for that customer of buying that product – whether it is a cat flap or a caravan!

- **Close** – The final stage is getting the customer to agree to the purchase, but there may be some **objections** you have to overcome first. Sometimes these are unspoken, but skilful sales staff know that unless they find out why these exist, the sale may be lost.

Did you know?

- You can test your own reaction to personal space when you are in a lift – for example, you will probably disassociate yourself from strangers by not making eye contact or standing too close.

- Customer objections are sometimes called 'barriers to a sale'. Finding out if a customer has any reservations that may prevent a sale should be done throughout the whole sales process, not just at the end.

Key term

Objections – reasons why a customer hesitates to commit to a purchase.

Types of objections

The main reasons customers hesitate to purchase include:

- **price** – the item may cost more than the customer plans to spend

- **timing** – the customer is in no rush to make a commitment, or not able to take delivery for some time

- **competition** – the customer may decide it is worth shopping around or looking online to see if a better deal is available

- **the item itself** – its size, colour, design, material or other features may not appeal to the customer

- **the brand or manufacturer** – especially if the customer has had a bad experience with that brand or manufacturer before.

Overcoming objections

The best way is to identify positive reasons and benefits for making the purchase at the start, for example, 'This is the most reliable make on the market and there is a free two-year guarantee' or 'We are offering free delivery and installation and will take away your old appliance free of charge.'

You will reduce the number of objections by offering one product at a time and 'fine-tuning' your suggestions to the customer's needs by discussing each one in turn. Remove rejected items to keep the sales area clutter-free. If the customer wants time to think about it, stay positive and helpful. Customers often return later to make the purchase.

Discussion point

You work in a camera shop. A woman comes in with her son who looks about 18. She asks for a simple, easy-to-use digital camera, but he is trying to talk her into a far more complex movie camera. You think he is doing it so he can borrow it himself. How would you cope with this situation? Discuss your ideas as a group.

Closing sales

Several signals show that a customer is ready to make a decision, such as asking questions about delivery, after-sales service, guarantees or credit facilities. This means the customer has moved on from thinking about the product to other aspects of the purchase. Another sign is when the customer visualises ownership, for example, 'It would exactly match the rug in the hall' or 'It would be perfect to wear at the interview.'

It is at this point that the salesperson should try to close the sale, often by using one of the following techniques.

- **The direct close** means asking a straightforward question, such as, 'Shall I wrap it?' or 'Are you happy to order now?' But note this can be high risk if you get the timing wrong and the customer says no!

Did you know?

The presence of a friend or partner can complicate a sale because the friend may point out objections the purchaser might not have thought about.

Activity: Sell a printer

In pairs, role-play a selling situation by taking the part of a customer and salesperson. The customer is interested in buying a computer printer that works wirelessly. Research the alternatives available online. The customer should decide upon other requirements they want. The salesperson should identify and describe two or three suitable options and overcome any objections that are raised. Then switch roles.

PLTS

Thinking of similar situations and deciding what you would do will help your creative thinking.

Remember

Knowing when and how to close a sale is crucial. There are several techniques you can use, but making promises you cannot keep or pressurising a customer may be unlawful under the Consumer Protection from Unfair Trading Regulations.

Did you know?

- By law, there are certain restrictions on extended warranties for domestic electrical goods. You will find out about these if you study Unit 13.

- Perry's, the car dealership, makes follow-up calls after a customer has had a car serviced or repaired to check everything is still fine.

Discussion point

Customer feedback is an important feature of eBay and Amazon Marketplace, and affects the rankings of suppliers. Do you think this is a good thing? Whom would you buy from if there were two suppliers but the higher-ranked one was asking a higher price? Discuss your opinions as a group.

- **The indirect close** is a more round-about method, such as, 'What do you think?' or 'Are you happy with this colour?' This is gentler than the direct close.

- **The silent close** involves asking a closing question and then keeping quiet. This gives the customer thinking time. You must not interrupt, which means this does not work very well if the customer also goes quiet and just stares at you.

- **The alternative close** is when you offer the customer two options as your closing question, such as, 'Would you prefer green or blue?' or 'Would you prefer delivery on Friday or Saturday?'

After-sales service

- **Delivery** – Many organisations offer a delivery service at time slots to suit the buyer. This may also be to the customer's home or workplace. If you make a sale, it will normally be your responsibility to arrange this and complete all the necessary paperwork.

- **Warranty** – Many manufacturers offer a free **guarantee**. This is an assurance that they will repair any faults or defects free of charge for a certain period after purchase, usually a year. A **warranty** is different as the customer pays for this optional extra cover. The warranty may provide free repairs and parts after the guarantee has ended and protect against accidental damage.

- **Customer care** – You should make sure your customer knows about all the aspects of customer care you can provide, such as a free customer helpline, FAQs pages on the website, and how to order new parts or spares.

- **Satisfaction** – Customers will only make repeat purchases or recommend your firm if they are satisfied with their experience. You need to check the customer is happy with how the order was processed, that the item was delivered intact and on time, and the customer is pleased with the purchase.

- **Follow-up** – This is a popular method of assessing customer satisfaction. Richer Sounds, the high street electrical retailer, calls these 'Customer Happy Calls', and staff make them two or three days after a purchase was made in a store. They phone to check the customer has had no problems setting up the equipment and that it is working satisfactorily.

- **Feedback** – Customer feedback is vital because it identifies areas where customers are happy and not so happy. Methods of getting feedback include issuing surveys – most hotels and holiday companies ask customers to complete these at the end of their stay. Comment cards are another common method, and are used in supermarkets and restaurants. Prizes can be offered to customers as an incentive to take part.

Handling complaints

It would be great if every customer said their experience was wonderful. Unfortunately the law of averages means this is unlikely to happen. It is therefore important to know:

- the procedures to follow to record and/or report a complaint
- the type of problems you can deal with yourself, and what you can and cannot do
- the type of problems you must refer to a supervisor.

If you are really enterprising, then you will use problems as opportunities to show how effective your customer care is. Quickly replacing a faulty product, promptly cancelling a missing delivery or sending a voucher to compensate your customer for inconvenience can easily earn your firm additional brownie points.

Repeat sales

Happy customers are far more likely to give you repeat orders, so maintain contact by email, phone and mail shots so that you can point out new products or special offers that may be of interest.

Up-selling

Up-selling means suggesting a better-quality or upgraded product. This can be done during the sales process. It can also be done at a later date, because contacting a customer to tell them about a new model on the market is a good opportunity to make a repeat sale.

Activity: Identify upgrades

In small groups, identify three products that are frequently upgraded or enhanced to encourage repeat business. Then compare your ideas.

Recording information

Collecting and recording customer information is essential for accurate marketing. It enables accurate customer profiles to be created, customers can be sent mail shots about interesting events and new products, and vouchers or discount offers can be sent, linked to key areas of interest. This increases the opportunities for making repeat sales.

- **Sales information** includes the date of purchase, the item and description, price charged and any discounts.
- **Payment information** gives the date, amount paid and method of payment.

Did you know?

Never ignore problems a customer mentions during a follow-up call. If you delay doing something, you will disappoint the customer twice. Always follow up the solution to a complaint, too, to ensure that the problem has been resolved to the customer's satisfaction.

Remember

You can follow up a sale in several ways, including by making a follow-up call. Checking the customer is satisfied provides useful feedback and encourages repeat sales.

- **Customer information** includes their name, title, address, telephone/mobile number and email address. For business organisations the name of the buyer/decision maker in the firm, their title, size of firm and type of business is also recorded.

Liaison with other departments

Sales staff often need to liaise with other departments that provide complementary services to customers.

- **Customer collection** points enable customer purchases to be stored safely for later collection, usually by car. They encourage customers to buy items that are not portable, and to buy more than they would if they had to carry everything. Sales staff give the customer a numbered receipt and attach a copy to the purchase before taking it to the customer collection area.

- **Despatch** may be in a separate area or even in a different building. Sometimes an item may be sent direct from a supplier. If arrangements are being made for an item to be despatched to a delivery address, then the relevant documents will be completed at the time of sale. Further details may need to be obtained by sales staff, such as ease of parking, whether the accommodation is up a flight of stairs, the best day/time for delivery, and where the item can be left if there is no one at home when it is delivered.

- **Accounts** is where details of financial transactions are held. If there is a query about a customer's payment history, if credit arrangements need to be made, or a customer's credit extended, then accounts will be involved in this process and may have to give approval before the goods can be sold. Accounts should also be able to check back on previous transactions if, for example, a customer wants to return an item but has lost the receipt.

- **Customer service** is concerned with customer welfare, so sales staff will often liaise with this department. A query or complaint about a purchase may be received by customer service, which then contacts sales staff for further details.

Just checking

1. What is AIDA and why is it used?
2. Describe the attitude of a professional salesperson.
3. Identify three health and safety precautions taken on the sales floor.
4. Identify two ways in which you could try to close a sale.
5. Explain why customer feedback is important, and describe two ways in which you could obtain this.

Assessment activity 10.2

Refer back to the notes you made for the activity on page 258 when you were investigating options for your own future selling career and comparing selling skills in different situations. In your groups, for each situation you discussed, decide how the processes used would also vary, and present your ideas as a group. Remember that 'processes' includes the sales process itself as well as after-sales service, dealing with complaints, recording information and liaising with other departments.

Then, on your own, use your notes to write a summary that compares the selling skills and processes used in different situations. **M2**

Grading tips

- Remember that differences will include the legal requirements, the amount of training staff need, the dress code, the type of advice customers require, and how information is recorded. To get a merit grade you must compare these, not just describe them.
- Look back at the WorkSpace case study (page 252) to refresh your memory.

Assessment activity 10.3

P4 **P5** **D1** **D2**

Your group must now put its selling skills into practice. Do this by holding a selling event, such as the one described below. Your group may have additional selling event opportunities, especially if your centre has its own stationery shop or holds Christmas Fairs or other selling events.

Your tutor will assess your individual performance throughout and prepare separate observation records for each member of your group, as you:

- prepare to make personal sales. **P4**
- use selling skills and processes to make several sales. **P5**
- demonstrate confident use of personal selling skills on several occasions. **D1**

You will also write your own report afterwards that evaluates the preparation, skills and processes used in different situations. **D2**

Charity Shopping Fair

As a group, you will hold a Charity Shopping Fair to sell good-quality items to learners and staff in your centre. You could invite parents and other people too, if your tutor agrees. You will also have to complete the following tasks, which involve different types of selling skills: selling the idea, getting items for the fair, selling 'events' (such as tombola stalls) and selling the goods themselves.

1. As a group, decide upon your charity and what you will do. You can gain ideas at IdeasFundraising, available via Hotlinks, and on other websites. You need to obtain goods that will be easily saleable to your target customers. These do not all need to be second-hand – people may be persuaded to donate new items to support the charity. You could also sell some themed items that link to your charity, and have other stalls with linked activities (for example, guess the number of sweets in a jar). Tell your chosen charity what you intend to do. They will often help by providing promotional information and give you ideas and tips too.

   Fix a date for the launch and for the event (allow enough time to collect goods in between) and decide where it will be held. Everyone is now responsible for contributing goods by promoting the idea to friends, family and other contacts.

2. Now plan how to prepare the sales area and make it attractive for customers. This should include your pricing policy, deciding how the goods will be organised into categories, who will be responsible for different stalls and what product knowledge/particular skills they will need. Think about your own appearance and presentation too.

continued

3. Advertise and hold your event. Put all you have learned into practice by confidently selling the goods and ensuring your customer requirements are met in full. If you are on a stall selling an experience, for example, a tombola, remember that you have to tempt people to take part. Remember also to record the money you take and which goods/ideas sell best.

4. Hold a meeting after the event to decide whether you could have done anything better. This means evaluating the preparation, skills and processes you used, both to obtain the goods and to sell them. Then write your own report that evaluates your own contribution as well.

5. Finally, as a group, arrange to present a cheque for the amount you have raised to your charity.

Grading tips

• Remember that if you decide to sell food items, then how to handle and store these should affect the processes you choose.

• Think about how visitors will identify you as sales staff – are you going to have name badges or all wear the same colour, for example?

edexcel

Assignment tips

• When you evaluate, look at the stalls that made the most and least money to see what this tells you. Use Gibbs' cycle of reflection (see page 251) to help you evaluate your own performance.

• As a consumer yourself, assess your own shopping and buying experiences, and apply this information to improve your own skills.

• If you have a part-time selling job, talk to your tutor about how you can use this to contribute towards evidence for your assessments.

11 Customer relations in business

You are a customer, and have been one for many years. So you should already know what you expect when you visit or contact an organisation. You will usually want to be dealt with by someone who is a professional and has excellent interpersonal skills so that you feel valued. You will want your needs to be met, not just at that time, but later, too, if you have a problem and need to contact the business again.

Businesses that get this right go from strength to strength. Those businesses that underestimate the importance of customer service or fail to train staff to respond to customers effectively do not. In this unit you will learn how customer service is provided, and the presentational and communication skills that staff need. You will also find out how organisations make sure their customer service is of a consistently high standard, and how they check customer satisfaction and identify ways to improve it.

You will find out about all these aspects of customer service and the benefits this provides for the business, its customers and its employers. You will also learn how to anticipate and meet the needs of your own customers in the future.

Learning outcomes

After completing this unit, you should:

1. know how customer service is provided in business
2. be able to apply appropriate presentation and interpersonal skills in customer service situations
3. understand how consistent and reliable customer service contributes to customer satisfaction
4. know how to monitor and evaluate customer service within an organisation.

All websites referred to in this unit can be accessed via Hotlinks. See page ii for more information.

Assessment and grading criteria

This table shows you what you must do in order to achieve a pass, merit or distinction grade, and where you can find activities in this book to help you.

To achieve a **pass**, the evidence must show that the learner is able to:	To achieve a **merit**, the evidence must show that, in addition to the pass criteria, the learner is able to:	To achieve a **distinction**, the evidence must show that, in addition to the pass and merit criteria, the learner is able to:
P1 describe three different types of customers and their needs and expectations **See Assessment activity 11.1, page 281**	**M1** explain how different customers' needs and expectations can differ **See Assessment activity 11.1, page 281**	
P2 outline the benefits of good customer service in a selected organisation **See Assessment activity 11.1, page 281**		
P3 demonstrate presentation, communication and interpersonal skills in different customer service situations **See Assessment activity 11.2, page 289**	**M2** display confident presentation, communication and interpersonal skills when demonstrating customer service in a range of customer service situations **See Assessment activity 11.2, page 289**	**D1** anticipate and meet the needs of different customers in three contrasting situations **See Assessment activity 11.2, page 289**
P4 explain what contributes to consistent and reliable customer service **See Assessment activity 11.3, page 294**	**M3** analyse the importance of customer service to different businesses **See Assessment activity 11.3, page 294**	
P5 describe how customer service can be monitored and evaluated **See Assessment activity 11.4, page 300**	**M4** explain how monitoring and evaluating can improve customer service for the customer, the organisation and the employee **See Assessment activity 11.4, page 300**	**D2** analyse how monitoring and evaluating can improve customer service for the customer, the organisation and the employee **See Assessment activity 11.4, page 300**
P6 outline how improvements to the customer service in an organisation could be made **See Assessment activity 11.4, page 300**		

How you will be assessed

To achieve this unit you will show that you understand the importance of customer service and will demonstrate your own customer service skills in different situations. You will also investigate businesses that provide excellent customer service to find out what they do to achieve this, and will develop your own customer service skills. Your assessments will include both practical and written tasks, and the assessment activities in this book will help you to prepare for this.

Rhiannon

Of all the units I have studied this year, I would say that my favourite was this one. This is because this unit has helped me to really improve on my communication, interpersonal and presentation skills. I have also found out what customers are like as I have never worked with customers before, and I knew nothing about how to deal with them. I especially enjoyed it when we did role plays as they gave me the chance to deal with customers and find out what they are like and what you need to do to keep them happy.

The main thing I learned from this unit was that customer satisfaction is very important. I did lots of research on the Internet, and the business book and the handouts I received were very helpful because they helped me to do well in my assignments. I found out that effective customer service benefits everyone: the customer, the organisation and the employee.

This unit has helped me to develop all the skills I need to work with customers, and I think I would now be able to work with them professionally. My confidence has improved so much that I have applied for a part-time job dealing with customers, which I want to do to be able to continue my studies to Level 3.

Over to you!

- What does customer satisfaction mean to you?
- What do you think is involved in providing effective customer service?
- What skills do you think customer service staff need to do an excellent job?

Cheap prices or super service?

Ryanair, the budget airline, is famous for cheap tickets, but charges extra for everything else including checking in online, checking in baggage and using a wheelchair. In the Money Central section of the Times Online website, you can even read 20 reasons not to use it. Stena Line, the ferry operator, claims it gains because many passengers prefer to take a boat trip to Dublin rather than fly Ryanair because its staff are so rude. Yet Ryanair continues to thrive and plans to carry 100 million passengers by 2012.

Does this mean most people prefer cheap prices to excellent service? Discuss this as a group. Then decide whether it is possible for a business to offer both.

Activity: Investigate Siemens

Siemens is a global company that provides different goods and services for its industrial and private customers. Use its UK website to find out what these are.

How do some companies address cultural differences?

- **New versus existing customers** – New customers are attracted by adverts and promotions, but their expectations must be met if they are going to become regular customers. Customer loyalty is highly prized by businesses, and many give rewards or discounts as an encouragement. Regular customers may expect staff to greet them by name and know their usual preferences.

- **Individuals versus groups or families** – Many businesses routinely deal with large groups or families, such as travel companies, hotels, theatres and tourist attractions. They often have special discounts for groups, and facilities to meet the needs of different family members.

- **Business customers versus private customers** – Some manufacturing companies only deal with business buyers. These customers will have specific needs and expect prompt and professional responses to their enquiries. They may also want special financial deals, discounts for bulk orders, and excellent after-sales service, including maintenance and spare parts. Businesses that only deal with private customers include hairdressers and hospitals. Other firms have both types of customer, but the staff who deal with them may work in separate departments and be specially trained to meet their different needs.

- **Age differences** – Some companies target specific groups: PGL provides activity holidays for families and young people, Saga provides travel and other services to people over 50, and Club 18–30 focuses on young adults. In these situations it is easier to focus on the specific needs of the target customer.

Many businesses that deal with young children provide distractions, from ball pits to toy boxes, and sometimes a crèche or play area. If you deal with elderly customers, remember that while some may be very sharp, others dislike making quick decisions. They may also need complicated information explaining carefully, particularly if it relates to hi-tech items.

- **Different cultures** – Cultural differences affect what we wear, what we eat and drink, and many other purchases, too. Some businesses cater specifically for certain cultures, such as 5 Rivers Boutique, which specialises in Indian wedding clothes, and Asia Dragon, which sells oriental furniture and clothing. Both websites are available via Hotlinks.

- **Gender** – Many studies show how men and women behave differently when they are shopping. Men are 'hunters' and focus on getting something quickly that best meets their needs. Women are 'gatherers' and like to browse longer to find exactly what they want. They are also often attracted to different features, designs and colours than those that appeal to men.

Remember

Stereotypes encourage you to categorise people wrongly, for example, thinking all old people are a bit dim, and all women love shopping. Always treat people as individuals and never assume you know what to expect.

Activity: Which phone?

Divide into different gender groups and list your top five needs if you were buying a phone. Compare your lists. Then suggest how mobile phone salespeople should take gender differences into account.

- **Special needs** – Customers may have **special needs**, especially if English is not their first language or if they have a disability. You will always do better dealing with people different from yourself if you enjoy trying to help them. Some guidelines are given in Table 11.2.

Key term

Special needs – particular requirements a customer may have, often related to a disability.

Table 11.2: The special needs of customers

Type of customer	Ways to meet their needs
Foreign customers	It may only become obvious that someone cannot speak English very well when you try to explain something to them, so: • speak relatively slowly • use simple English words (no slang or local expressions) • use short sentences • write it down – their reading skills may be better than their listening skills • do not shout, be embarrassed, laugh or show impatience • know which of your colleagues speak other languages • ask for help if you need it.
Customers who are deaf or hard of hearing	You cannot tell if someone is deaf by looking at them, but most deaf people can lip read, so: • look at the person when you are speaking • do not speak too quickly, and do not shout • if asked to do so, write down what you want to say • know whether your organisation offers the Text Relay service to deaf people who make contact by phone and has induction loops at customer purchase points.
Customers who are blind or visually impaired	Not all blind people wear dark glasses or carry white sticks, but someone with a severe visual impairment may tell you this, so: • speak to them so that your voice acts as a guide • unless they ask for assistance, do not grab hold of them • if you are asked for help, lead them gently • warn them of obstacles and stairs – say how many steps there are and whether these are up or down • tell them if there are Braille buttons on the lift or on other signs.
Customers who have mobility problems	Under the Disability Discrimination Act, all organisations must provide appropriate access and facilities for customers, so: • know the facilities that exist in your organisation, such as wheelchair access, disabled toilets and disabled parking spaces • be ready to hold open doors • do not try to rush someone or appear impatient because they are on crutches or in a wheelchair.

Did you know?

If you are struggling to communicate with someone who does not speak English, stop and think how you would feel if you were abroad, could not speak the language and had to make yourself understood.

Activity: Check out your own area

Direct Enquiries, the Nationwide Disabled Access Register, provides information about disabled access in buildings and premises all over the UK. Check out the facilities offered by businesses in your area on the website. As a group, suggest the benefits for a business of making sure they are included on the Register.

Activity: Needs and expectations

In groups, suggest at least six different types of customer who may visit a large department store. In each case, identify their likely needs and expectations. Then compare your ideas.

Remember

Organisations that provide outstanding customer service usually save money on advertising, make higher profits, have happier customers and more motivated staff.

1.3 Benefits of customer service

All organisations benefit from providing excellent customer service. Private sector businesses want to increase sales because this usually increases profits, which is cheaper to do by repeat business and by word-of-mouth recommendations than advertising. Customers who have a superb experience will be loyal to a business. In the public sector, failure to meet customer service standards may show up in league tables and be highlighted in the media.

Organisations are not the only ones who benefit. It is far more pleasant for employees to work in a business that has high standards and treats its customers well. Customers gain because they can rely on excellent service every time and have no need to shop around.

The main benefits are summarised in Table 11.3.

Table 11.3: Benefits of effective customer service

To the customer	The whole experience is pleasant and enjoyable The customer feels valued and important The customer can rely on this service every time The customer is confident about the purchase and the items bought There is less need to 'shop around' in the future
To the organisation	The image and reputation of the business is continually enhanced Word-of-mouth recommendations mean more customers are attracted at little or no cost Feedback from regular customers provides useful information that can help to improve the business The organisation flourishes as its profits and/or demand for its services increase
To the employee	The working environment is pleasant because staff know they are doing a good job and customers rarely complain All staff know that they can depend on each other for prompt and accurate information Building a positive working relationship with regular customers and working to achieve high standards both contribute to job satisfaction There is greater job security because companies with many satisfied customers are unlikely to go out of business

Just checking

1. Provide your own definition of customer service.
2. Describe the difference between an internal and an external customer.
3. Explain why many organisations set targets for customer service.
4. Give three benefits to the organisation of providing good customer service.

Assessment activity 11.1

Your friend is desperate for a part-time job and has just got an interview at a local superstore. You have promised to help her think about questions she might be asked. Write her an email in which you suggest how she should answer each of the following.

1. Describe three different types of customers you may meet in the superstore and their needs and expectations. At least one must be an 'internal' customer. Make sure that you clearly highlight the difference between them. **P1**

2. Explain how the needs and expectations of different types of customers can differ. Do this by going into more detail and fully explaining the link between the type of customer and their needs and expectations. **M1**

3. Tell us the benefits we obtain as a superstore by providing good customer service, and also outline the benefits our employees and our customers gain, too. This means thinking about the type of customer service you and your family expect in a superstore and the facilities you expect to find. **P2**

Don't forget to read the grading tips to get more help!

Grading tips

- For P1, you will find it easier if you relate it to your local superstore, and perhaps think about your own needs and expectations, and those of your family.

- For M1, you need to go into more detail and explain why different types of customers have different needs and expectations. It will be easier if you identify types of customers with contrasting needs.

- For P2, you should also think about health, safety and security as well as the information, advice and assistance different types of customers need in a superstore.

2. Be able to apply appropriate presentation and interpersonal skills in customer service situations

Did you know?

- The more your customer service skills improve, the more confidence you will have when you deal with your customers. This will show in your approach and manner, and give your customers more faith in your ability to help them.

- Some businesses provide uniforms in corporate colours to promote the company brand.

- Poor personal hygiene is not the only reason why people smell unpleasant. Someone whose clothes or breath reeks of cigarette smoke or garlic is just as bad.

Key terms

Presentation skills – your ability to look and act like a customer service professional.

Body language – the messages you communicate by using gestures, facial expressions and posture.

Activity: What to wear?

You are opening your own shop, but have decided against a staff uniform. In groups, decide what guidelines you would issue about personal hygiene, dress, hair, make-up and jewellery. Then compare your ideas and check these against the information given in Unit 7 (pages 160–61) and in Unit 10 (page 257).

It is pointless providing a wide range of customer facilities if staff are scruffy, ill-mannered or cannot answer basic questions. The attitude of staff is often remembered by customers long after they have forgotten what they bought at the time. Equally, customers are impressed if someone is very helpful and makes an effort to get them what they want.

This section deals with the presentation, interpersonal and communication skills you need to develop to deal with customers effectively.

2.1 Presentation skills

What do other people see when you approach them? Someone who looks smart and professional, or someone who looks like they fell out of bed ten minutes ago? Remember, **presentation skills** have nothing to do with good looks, but everything to do with a welcoming smile, appropriate clothes and a smart appearance.

Personal presentation

Many businesses ensure they present a consistent image to customers by issuing uniforms, such as airlines and hotels. They may also have a dress code or guidelines, especially for customer-facing staff. This may include information about hair styles, jewellery, make-up and personal hygiene. As long as these do not discriminate against different groups of people, this is perfectly legal.

Body language

You will already have learned about this if you have studied Units 7 or 10. **Body language** relates to our posture, facial expressions and gestures. If you greet a customer with a smile and look them in the eye (without staring at them!), then you will create a far better impression than if you shuffle over, mumble and look down at your feet.

Activity: Investigate body language

Learn more about body language by checking out the table in Unit 7, page 164. Then, in groups, list five negative and five positive signals you can give a customer simply by using body language. Then compare your ideas.

Working environment, work area and equipment

Your employer has a legal duty to provide a safe **working environment** and the equipment you need to do your job. It is your duty to cooperate with your employer by working safely, to keep your own work area and communal areas tidy, and follow instructions for using equipment.

The working environment also includes the way people treat each other in the workplace. Most organisations want people to enjoy working for them, so the behaviour of employees towards each other is also important for a productive working environment.

2.2 Interpersonal skills

These relate to your attitude and behaviour towards other people. Being popular with your friends does not mean you will be great to work with or employ, nor does it mean you will handle customers tactfully or skilfully.

Attitude

Your attitude is influenced by the way you think. If you are fed up or negative then this will be obvious, and even if your family tolerate it, at work people are unlikely to do so.

If you enjoy being with other people, you will be friendly. If you enjoy doing your best, you will be focused and motivated. While this is important, many employers think that the most valuable attribute is to be positive. This is because positive people are great to be with. They make other people feel better and they look at problems as a challenge and an opportunity to show what they can do. They give an up-beat image of their organisation and consistently achieve high standards.

Activity: How positive are you?

Are you a naturally positive person? If you are asked to help someone, but this involves doing something you dislike, would you answer 'yes' or 'no'? For the next fortnight, check your own responses when someone asks you a favour. If it is usually 'no', then it is time for a rethink!

Behaviour

This is closely linked to attitude because this influences what you do and why you do it.

- Positive people normally behave in a cheerful and friendly way.

Key term

Working environment – the design, layout, facilities and equipment available to staff, as well as the ethos (atmosphere) of the workplace.

Did you know?

- Being a messy worker, leaving your personal belongings lying around and borrowing things without asking are sure-fire ways of irritating the people you work with.

- Anyone can do the right thing when they feel great. Acting professionally means doing the right thing even when you feel dreadful.

PLTS

This is a perfect opportunity to practise your reflective learning skills.

- Working in a mature and professional way means not behaving in a childish or irresponsible manner, and not sulking if you cannot get your own way. It also means you understand how your behaviour affects other people.

- Many organisations insist that all staff introduce themselves by giving their name, or wear name badges. Not only is this friendly, but it also means customers know who you are if they have a complaint.

Remember

Employees are paid to behave in a professional and business-like way at work, no matter how they feel personally.

Activity: How do you shake hands?

People are often judged by their ability to shake hands properly. This means having a firm handshake, so do not grip too tightly or offer a hand like a wet rag! Check out some of the advice online through Hotlinks and practise until you get it right.

Key term

Interpersonal skills – the ability to relate to other people in a courteous and appropriate way.

- If you enjoy working with people you will be courteous and thoughtful, and respect their feelings. You will not take part in gossiping, being hurtful or misleading people to get your own way.

- If you are committed to doing a good job you will not cheat your employer, tell lies, arrive late, leave early, pretend to be sick when you are not or simply disappear when the going gets tough.

Activity: What makes a good assistant?

You are employing someone to help you to run your own business. In pairs, decide six personal qualities your assistant must possess and six that you would not tolerate. Then compare your lists with other groups and identify ten positive and ten negative attributes that everyone agrees on.

First impressions and greeting customers

Many organisations spend a considerable amount of money on their reception areas and telephone system to give a good first impression to customers, but this has to be matched by the greeting they receive from staff. There may be an official greeting you should use and rules that state how you should address customers if you do not know their names. If in doubt, be more formal than normal and use 'Sir' or 'Madam' – this should not offend anyone.

Interpersonal skills and customer relationships

If you enjoy dealing with people then you will find it easier to put yourself in your customers' shoes when you are discussing their requirements. You will be naturally interested in what they want and more likely to think carefully about the best way to help them. You will be concerned not to say anything that might cause offence or that might be hurtful. At the same time, you will realise that it is no use being caring and concerned if you make a mess of the basics. You still need to be efficient at your job to meet your customer's needs by:

- listening carefully and noting down any long or complex requests

- asking questions if you do not understand something or need further information

- aiming to give a positive response to their request. If this seems impossible, get help or advice from a more experienced colleague.

Building a relationship with a customer involves developing several **interpersonal skills**, as you will see in Figure 11.2.

Figure 11.2: Skills needed in customer service situations

Responding to different customer behaviour

Customers display different behaviour for many reasons. They may be in a rush, under stress, or be very happy with life and have time to chat. If your customers are in front of you, watch their body language as you listen to them so that you will be more aware of their mood and attitude.

It is worth knowing that some internal customers may be touchy if they are under pressure, and may react badly if you pick the wrong moment to speak to them. Again, being observant and aware of other factors which might influence their behaviour will help you to better gauge what to say and when to say it.

Activity: Develop your confidence

You have been asked to greet and assist people at a forthcoming careers exhibition. As a group, suggest four ways in which being confident would affect the way you approach and handle visitors. Then identify what you would need to know personally to feel confident yourself in this situation.

2.3 Communication skills

You have already learned about body language on page 282, but you need to speak to your customers as well, and how you do this is important. All of the following factors influence the effectiveness of your communications with customers.

Activity: Give a demonstration

In groups, identify a customer service situation (such as dealing with an enquiry or complaint) when you will have to demonstrate some, or all, of the skills in Figure 11.2. Then role-play it to the rest of your group **twice**. One time, demonstrate how it should be done; the other time, demonstrate how it should not!

Did you know?

- 'Tact' means thinking of the most thoughtful (or diplomatic) way to say something, such as, 'Could you please state your date of birth?' not, 'How old are you?'

- You will find it easier to stay calm and courteous in stressful situations if you do not take other people's behaviour or reactions personally.

Remember

You should aim to remain pleasant and courteous even if a customer is boring, annoying, sarcastic or uncommunicative. If you have serious problems dealing with someone, get help. Otherwise, silently count to ten, keep smiling and chat about it later with a confidant(e) to let off steam.

Did you know?

You can say 'yes' and sound begrudging, enthusiastic or very surprised – try it.

Key terms

Tone – the way words are spoken to reflect the speaker's attitude. Tone can also apply to the choice of words in a written communication.

Jargon – terminology or slang that is not known or understood by everyone.

Discussion point

Jed is in trouble with his manager because he told a young customer, 'Just chill. I'll give you a bell in a day or two.' Jed argues that when he is talking to someone his own age, slang does not matter. Do you agree? Discuss your ideas as a group.

Functional skills

This gives you practice in listening to information and giving a relevant response in appropriate language afterwards.

- **Tone of voice** – relates to ways in which you say something. For example, you could say 'no' in different ways to sound amazed, to sound disapproving or to make a definite refusal.

  Because your **tone** gives away your inner feelings it has an effect on the listener, who will know whether you are concerned, irritated or even disrespectful. It can soothe someone if you get it right or annoy them if you get it badly wrong, when you might get the reply, 'Don't use that tone with me!'

- **Pitch** – relates to the sound you make. A low-pitched voice is deep and gruff; a high-pitched voice can easily sound shrill. Varying the pitch makes what you say more interesting. Pitching your voice so everyone can hear means lifting your head and speaking a little more loudly if you are talking to a group of people.

- **Language** – this must be appropriate for the customer, who is unlikely to understand some of the technical terms that are used in the business. Slang expressions and **jargon** should be avoided, too. Even 'OK' is unwise when you are dealing with an important customer because it sounds too casual.

- **Pace** – relates to the speed at which you speak. Never gabble or run words together. Speak more slowly if you are somewhere noisy or if you are talking to someone who does not speak English very well. At the other extreme, never speak so slowly that your customer completely loses interest.

- **Good listening skills** – these are vital if you are to understand and respond appropriately to what your customer is saying. You can improve your listening skills through active and reflective listening.

  - **Active listening** means concentrating on the speaker so that you notice their feelings, for example, whether they are nervous, impatient or worried.

  - **Reflective listening** involves restating what you hear at points during the conversation to check your understanding.

Activity: Develop your skills

Find out more about developing your listening skills by reading Unit 7, pages 172–73. Then practise active and reflective listening in pairs. Spend a few minutes describing something you have bought, including when and where you made the purchase. Your partner should listen and try to summarise the key points back to you accurately without making notes. Then reverse roles.

Appropriateness to the customer/situation

A key attribute of customer service professionals is flexibility, because they must be able to adapt their approach to the customer and the situation. You may know that you should not shout, but if you were trying to talk to a customer in HMV on a busy Saturday, you might have to make an exception! If you are greeting an important visitor to your centre then the situation is very different. Equally, you do not need to be a genius to know that you should not speak to a senior manager at work in the same way as you would to a colleague of your own age.

2.4 Customer service situations

There are several different ways in which you may communicate with customers, depending upon your job role. In sales, on reception or in a retail environment you will usually meet external customers face to face. In a call centre or office, you may deal with customers on the telephone. You may also communicate in writing, by writing a note or sending an email. These situations will directly relate to the skills you need to demonstrate, as you can see in Table 11.4.

Did you know?

- Sometimes it can be difficult to know exactly what to do and say, because some organisations expect more formality than others. The best idea is to watch more experienced members of staff and follow their example.

- You can find out more about dealing with customers by telephone on pages 166 and 175–76.

Table 11.4: Applying skills to different types of communications

Communication	Presentation skills	Interpersonal skills	Communication skills
Face to face	Professional appearance essential Body language denotes manner and attitude	Good first impression vital Greet appropriately, be friendly and interested in meeting customer's needs	Speak clearly, use appropriate tone of voice and avoid slang and jargon
Telephone	Smiling during a conversation shows in your voice and makes you sound friendly	Use business-like greeting Attitude and concern is shown by verbal response and tone of voice	Clear voice and appropriate pace essential as gestures cannot be seen
Writing	Neatness, clear layout and accurate spelling required	All written communications must be courteous and tactful, and the wording should be appropriate for the situation	The 'tone' and degree of formality depends upon the person and why you are writing
Email	Message style and layout must follow business format		Business emails must comply with organisational rules and standards

How would you demonstrate care and concern over the phone?

Activity: Find out more

You can refresh your memory about dealing with customers with a disability by rereading Table 11.2 on page 279, and find out how to deal with customers with complaints in Unit 7, page 168.

Discussion point

After reading this section, how would you now describe 'professional customer care'? What do you think it entails, and how do you know when you are receiving it? Discuss your ideas as a group.

The type of situation should also affect your reaction. You should not act in the same way in an emergency as you would on a routine day.

- **Urgent situations** need an appropriate response, from marking an email as 'high priority' to passing on important messages immediately. In a crisis, it is important to listen carefully and stay calm.

- **Difficult situations** include awkward customers, problems you cannot solve and occasions when you are under pressure. The golden rule is not to panic and to get assistance if you need it. This is safer than trying to cope and making a mess of things.

2.5 Customers

You may also have to change your approach to meet the needs of different types of customers. Hints and tips are given in Table 11.5.

Table 11.5: Dealing with different types of customers

Type of customer	Do	Don't
Difficult or hard to please	Use listening and questioning skills to find out exactly what they want Stay positive and try to solve the problem Ask for help if you are not getting anywhere	Assume the customer is being deliberately awkward Show impatience or annoyance Try to rush or get rid of the customer
Abusive	Stay calm and try to get the customer to explain the problem Face to face: If the customer does not calm down, quickly get help On the telephone: Give a warning that unless the customer stops being abusive, you will have no option but to end the call	Argue or get angry with the customer, as it will make the matter worse Tolerate any personal insults or threats to your personal safety
Disabled	Focus on the person, not the disability	Treat them as 'odd' or 'different', or pretend the disability does not exist
Needing technical information	Write down their requirements Check any words you do not understand Pass the query to a technical expert	Try to show off how much you know Guess the answer Overestimate your own abilities

Just checking

1. Explain why knowing about body language is important for customer service staff.
2. Identify four different interpersonal skills needed by customer service staff.
3. Explain the difference between tone of voice, pitch and pace.
4. Identify the main skills you need to deal with customers effectively on the telephone.
5. Explain how you would deal with a customer who wants complex technical information you do not understand.

BTEC Assessment activity 11.2

Your group has been asked to help out before, during and after your centre's Open Night. This will involve dealing with different types of customers in a range of customer service situations.

- Before the event you will assist prospective visitors who telephone asking for information or send in email enquiries.

- During the event you will meet and show around prospective learners, parents and local employers; run the enquiry desk and provide appropriate information and literature.

- After the event you will again respond to customers who request specific or technical information in writing or by email.

Working in small groups, prepare for this task by identifying the type of presentation, interpersonal and communication skills needed to give a good impression of the centre when you are dealing with people face to face, on the telephone, in writing, and by email. Remember that you will need to respond to both urgent and non-urgent requests as well as difficult and routine enquiries. You will also be expected to deal with different types of customers, including some with disabilities. Some may need technical information, others may be difficult to deal with. You should also check you know what to do if any customer is abusive. Discuss how you can anticipate and meet the needs of all the people you will be dealing with.

You may be able to do this activity 'for real' if your centre holds open days for visitors. Alternatively, other staff or learners at your centre may take the role of visitors or callers making enquiries. Or you may be involved in playing one or more of these roles yourself during a group simulation. In this case, discuss with

your tutor beforehand the questions you should ask and what type of customer you should be.

The activity will include face-to-face scenarios as well as actual telephone conversations and preparing written answers to queries (for example, emails and short letters). When you are demonstrating your customer service skills, your tutor will conduct individual observations and record this on observation record sheets to identify whether you were able to:

1. demonstrate presentation, communication and interpersonal skills in different customer service situations **P3**

2. display confidence when demonstrating your skills in a range of customer service situations **M2**

3. anticipate and meet the needs of different customers in three contrasting situations. **D1**

Grading tips

- You will demonstrate confidence if you know what you are talking about and concentrate on meeting the customer's needs, not your own.

- To obtain a distinction, you must be able to demonstrate that you have prepared well and anticipated the specific needs of different customers.

- There may be other occasions when you can demonstrate your customer service skills, such as in a school or college shop, or when you are on work experience or in a part-time job. In this case, discuss with your tutor how you can obtain evidence, such as witness statements, to help you achieve the P3, M2 and D1 criteria.

3. Understand how consistent and reliable customer service contributes to customer satisfaction

Key terms

Consistent – offering the same standard over and over again.

Customer satisfaction – how customers feel when their needs and expectations have been met.

Activity: Job roles in learner services

Talk to your tutor about the job roles of learner services staff at your centre who handle enquiries. What limitations are there to their job roles? And what sources of information do they have about the courses on offer?

Customers need to be able to rely on consistently high levels of customer service – they are unlikely to keep using a business that lets them down or provides poor service. Wise businesses know this and aim to provide **consistent** and reliable service to guarantee **customer satisfaction**.

3.1 Consistent and reliable customer service

Most organisations provide special training to customer service staff to ensure that each person has the same approach. This is likely to focus on the following aspects of the job.

- **Scope of job role** – Staff should know what they can and cannot do as part of their job and the type of issues they must refer to a supervisor. This should not stop them using their own initiative to resolve a straightforward problem quickly, providing they do not make arrangements or promises that are outside their authority.

- **Knowledge of products/services** – You can only give customers accurate information and advise them about the best options to suit their needs if you have a good knowledge of the products and/or services available. Because you cannot always memorise these, you also need to know where to find the information, such as in a catalogue, brochure or database.

What would you need to know to sell these televisions successfully?

- **Type and quality of products/services** – Simply knowing the range of goods or services available is fine if you are selling consumable items, such as magazines. Anyone who sells expensive items or services, such as electronic equipment or package holidays, should also be able to give more detailed information and advice, based on their own knowledge, feedback from other customers and press reports.

- **Staff attitude and behaviour** – You already know that all staff should have a positive attitude and behave courteously and professionally to customers. Turn back to page 283 now if you have forgotten about this!

- **Timing** – Approaching people at the wrong time, or if they are stressed, upset or busy, can get a bad response. If you do this by accident, simply apologise and say you will contact them later. Timing also means not keeping people waiting, arranging phone calls, appointments and deliveries at your customer's convenience, not yours, and never failing to call people back as promised.

- **Accessibility/availability** – Customers are usually very irritated if they decide they want something and then find they cannot have it. This can range from an advertised product which has sold out to a room in a hotel which is fully booked. In this situation your job is to sympathise with the customer's disappointment, try to help them if you can (such as by putting their name on a waiting list) and pass on the information to your employer.

- **Meeting specific customer needs** – The skill of meeting customer needs involves identifying these by talking to the customer, and then matching them to the range of goods and services that you can offer. Further information is given in Unit 10 Personal selling in business.

- **Working under pressure** – It is easy to be charming on a quiet day. The situation is different when things are hectic, as anyone who has worked in retail at Christmas will tell you. It is also harder if you are very busy and trying to do several things at once. The first rule is not to panic. The second is to concentrate on doing one thing at a time *properly*. The third is to do the most urgent/important thing first. The fourth is to work as fast as you can while staying pleasant at the same time.

- **Confirming service meets needs and expectations** – Customer-focused businesses do not forget their customers once they have made a purchase or used a service. Instead, they check that they are satisfied. One way to do this is to make 'customer happy calls' – quick follow-up phone calls which check that all a customer's needs and expectations were met.

- **Dealing with problems** – Customer services is sometimes all about dealing with problems. You have already learned how to deal with difficult customers. Table 11.6 on the following page shows other types of situations you might meet and gives tips to help.

Did you know?

Some travel agents send their representatives on 'holiday' to different destinations each year to improve their knowledge of overseas locations.

Remember

All feedback from customers can help a business to improve. If you receive 20 enquiries for the same thing today, and disappoint 20 people, the stock levels or range of goods should be reviewed.

Activity: What would you do?

The phone is ringing, a customer has just walked in, your boss is urgently beckoning you and the postman arrives with a parcel. You are on your own. Say how you would cope by identifying exactly what you would do first, next and last in this situation.

PLTS

Sometimes creative thinking can be helpful, such as offering a customer who has to wait a drink or a newspaper to read.

Activity: Mystery customers

Find out more about being a mystery customer by visiting the Mystery Shopper website. Then turn to page 200 to see an example of a report by a mystery shopper.

Key term

Evaluate – to review the information and evidence before forming a conclusion.

- **Staff feedback** – this is invaluable, and not just because it is free. Many staff receive or overhear customer comments, both positive and negative. In addition, if staff are unhappy and leave to work elsewhere, it is sensible to find out why. They may feel, for example, they have little support if a customer becomes abusive. In this case the business should respond by drawing up a 'no tolerance' policy which all staff know and understand, and provide specialist training for all customer-facing staff, too.

- **Mystery customers** – employed to visit stores to assess staff. They may also check competitor's stores to compare service levels. They will be interested in factors such as speed of service, the attitude of staff and the layout of the store.

- **Complaints and compliment letters** – encouraged by many organisations as a form of feedback. If several similar complaints are received, there is obviously a problem that needs immediate attention. This is why organisations record the complaints they receive and then check to see if there are any common factors.

Similarly, a card or letter that praises staff is to be treasured, which is why many businesses put them on a notice board or feature them their newsletters.

Activity: Fishing for compliments!

Find out what happens to complimentary cards and letters received at your centre.

4.2 Evaluate customer service

If a business is receiving marvellous feedback from its customers, then usually it will also be thriving. If it is not, then something is obviously wrong. To **evaluate** customer service fully, it is important to look at other key business information. This is shown in Table 11.7.

Table 11.7: Methods of evaluating customer service

Key information	Trend	Method of investigation
Level of sales	Should be rising for all key product groups	Check sales turnover figures Analyse by product and by branch
Repeat customers	Customer loyalty is demonstrated through repeat business	Check customer accounts to find out reorder frequency
New customers	Numbers should be increasing	Check number of new customer accounts Should also be reflected in sales turnover
Level of complaints/compliments	Complaints should be falling; compliments should be rising	Check complaints records both for overall number received and for any trends Check compliments received
Staff turnover	Should be steady or falling	Check number of people leaving each month Hold exit interviews to find out reasons

Activity: Apply it to your centre

As a group, suggest the types of information the departments in your centre may be able to provide that will confirm whether its learner services are successful or not.

4.3 Improvements to customer service

It is pointless obtaining and evaluating customer service information if no action is taken to remedy any problems. The evaluation process should identify areas where improvements are needed.

Improvements to quality of service

Businesses have to distinguish between different types of customer service problems. An online business which uses an inefficient delivery service can easily lose customers. A high street store may lose customers if a member of staff is rude or unhelpful, and that member of staff may need retraining. It may also be necessary to discipline a member of staff who is rude or negligent.

Reliability

Reliability is essential for consumer confidence. Buying something that fails after a few days is extremely annoying, and a taxi firm that sometimes fails to arrive is unlikely to stay in business for long.

If a product is faulty, it may need to be recalled and changes made to the way it is produced. If a firm gets a reputation for unreliability this is likely to lead to a serious loss of business, profits and reputation.

Activity: Unreliable products and services

As a group, identify any products or services you have experienced that have been unreliable, how this has affected your opinion of the supplier, and what (if any) action you took as a result.

Did you know?

- DSG, the owner of Currys and PC World, introduced a new staff training programme when customer service was found to be inconsistent.

- When the makers of WD-40 wanted to find new uses for the product and expand their product range, they asked their customers, who even have their own fan club! Find out more by visiting the website.

Improvements to the organisation

Examples of **organisational improvements** include the following.

- **Improving service and/or products** – This may include making improvements to IT or distribution systems, offering different, new or improved services, or enhancing the product range. Methods of doing this include increasing training, offering incentives such as bonuses or commission, or assessing workloads and reallocating

Key term

Organisational improvements – improvements that affect the way the organisation operates and which are decided by senior managers.

We hope all staff members enjoy the new restful colours of the staff room – The Management

What can employees expect from their work environment?

some duties. Customer feedback can also be used to improve existing products or services, or to supply new products not currently made or stocked.

- **Keeping staff** – Losing good, experienced staff costs money because it is expensive to recruit and train new staff. Organisational improvements need to be targeted at areas where staff are dissatisfied, from salary levels to lack of training.

- **Attracting new customers** – This will normally be the task of sales and marketing staff. However, advertising and promotional campaigns cost money and it will be up to senior managers to decide how much to spend.

- **Increasing turnover** – It is normally cheaper to persuade existing customers to return or to spend more than it is to attract new customers. This is why many organisations operate loyalty schemes or offer rewards in the form of vouchers or points that can be traded for free goods.

- **Compliance with legal obligations** – All businesses have to comply with the laws of the land, as well as the specific regulations that relate to their type of business (see Unit 1, page 34). Failure to do so can result in severe penalties.

Improvements for employees

Staff are more likely to be polite and helpful to customers if they feel they are valued and treated fairly themselves. Improvements may be needed in two areas.

- **Job satisfaction** – Many studies have been carried out into **job satisfaction**. A famous one by Frederick Herzberg found the main factors include interesting work, having responsibility, recognition for doing a good job, a sense of achievement, personal growth and opportunities for advancement. See also Unit 9, page 227.

- **Working environment** – As you learned on page 283, this relates to the physical environment and the 'atmosphere' of the workplace. Most employees expect good lighting and ventilation, modern furnishings and equipment, adjustable heating, a lack of noise, and will work better if there is a restful colour scheme. They will expect all their legal rights to be met and not to be discriminated against, bullied or victimised in any way. You will learn more about this if you study Unit 9.

Key term

Job satisfaction – positive feelings related to the job and the workplace.

Did you know?

Herzberg's research showed that having an interesting job is more important than salary. However, most people work to earn a living, so any business that pays low wages will always be in danger of losing its staff.

Activity: Evaluating feedback at your centre

Identify the ways in which your centre obtains feedback from all its customers, as well as its staff. Then find out how it evaluates this. Work in groups to decide how obtaining and evaluating this can benefit learners, the centre itself and the staff. Then compare your ideas.

Carphone Warehouse is very proud of its customer service.

When Charles Dunstone co-founded Carphone Warehouse in 1989, he had some strong ideas about customer service and laid down five fundamental rules for all members of staff about looking after customers.

Despite this, the business has had some ups and downs. In 2006, his telecoms business TalkTalk was unable to satisfy demand for its new service, which disappointed and annoyed many people. Since then Carphone Warehouse has worked hard to rebuild its reputation, and now wants its retail stores to be number one for telecoms on the high street. This is not easy in a highly competitive market, especially as most people today have a mobile phone and may have to be persuaded to trade up or change.

To achieve its goal, Carphone Warehouse is again focusing on customer service and has made a number of changes. In 2008, it joined up with successful US electrical giant Best Buy and quickly spotted some valuable ideas for improvements. These have since included:

- introducing Customer First training for store managers and support staff
- scrapping sales commission for staff, improving basic salaries and introducing bonuses linked to customer feedback rather than sales figures. Within 48 hours of buying a phone, customers receive a text asking them to rate how polite and helpful the salesperson was. The score will be used to calculate staff bonuses
- opening new larger stores that sell laptops, gaming consoles, wireless TVs and other electrical goods
- providing technological support to customers by a specially trained 'Geek Squad'
- improving its internal communication systems so store managers only receive information relevant to what they need to do
- providing additional support for staff through the company intranet to improve customer service in store
- using Twitter in order to provide customer service alerts, support and help tips.

Surveys showed that customers soon noticed an improvement, but Carphone Warehouse is not resting on its laurels. In 2010 it plans to open more mid-sized stores and up to 80 megastores in the UK.

Think about it!

1. Carphone Warehouse is a very successful company. Why, then, do you think it wants to keep making improvements?

2. Suggest three other ways in which Carphone Warehouse may receive customer feedback besides text messages.

3. Read the five fundamental rules at the Carphone Warehouse website and check out all the different ways in which the company provides support for its customers. Then identify and analyse the benefits you think the organisation, its customers and its employees will gain from the improvements it is now making.

Just checking

1. Identify four ways of monitoring customer service.
2. Suggest two ways in which customer service can be evaluated.
3. What is the link between employee job satisfaction and customer service?
4. Suggest three ways in which a supermarket could try to increase sales turnover.

BTEC Assessment activity 11.4

(P5) (P6) (M4) (D2)

Carolyn runs her own hairdressers with a beauty salon and nail bar attached. Her husband Deon runs a car hire business that rents out cars and vans. As well as a local depot, Deon also has a rental desk at the airport. Recently both businesses have been struggling. Sales figures are down on last year and several experienced staff have left.

Choose **one** of these businesses and help either Carolyn or Deon to make improvements by writing a report which identifies the areas they must concentrate on.

You will find it easier to choose the type of business that you feel you know best. This could be because of your own experiences of hairdressers in your area or because you have visited a car hire business or other related company that provides excellent customer service.

1. Start your report with a section that explains how customer service at that business can be monitored and evaluated. **P5**

2. Next, identify how improvements to the customer service in your chosen organisation could be made. Then outline these in the next section. **P6**

3. Explain how monitoring and evaluating can improve customer service for the customer, the organisation and the employee. Use the information on pages 295–98 to help you. **M4**

4. Analyse how monitoring and evaluating can improve customer service for the customer, organisation and employees in your chosen business. Use examples from your own experience or from the WorkSpace case study or from visits you have been on to help you. **D2**

Grading tip

An analysis is more in-depth than an explanation. Now you must identify specific benefits, show how these are linked and explain the importance of each.

Assignment tips

- Use the information in the WorkSpace case study to obtain ideas for improvements in a business and think of other ideas with your group.

- You will do better in this task if you think carefully about every aspect of the business you have chosen. If you work part-time yourself, use this experience to help you, as well as your own experiences as a customer.

12 Business online

According to comScore, an online market research company, in May 2009 there were nearly 37 million Internet users in the UK. Each person goes online 21 days each month – contacting friends, catching up on TV programmes, downloading music, comparing prices, paying bills, planning holidays, researching their family tree, checking out health issues and, of course, buying stuff. According to the Interactive Media in Retail Group (IMRG), in 2008 online retail sales in the UK were worth £43.8 billion, an increase of 25 per cent on 2007.

It is little surprise, therefore, that most businesses today think that an online presence is essential. Whether the aim is to provide information, to promote the business, or to set up an online store, there are several aspects to consider, from operational issues to site security, and many potential benefits to be gained. If the business goes ahead, then planning how the website should be designed to best meet the needs of the business and achieve its objectives is the next logical step in the process.

In this unit you will learn about different online business activities and find out about the issues and benefits related to having an online presence. You will create web pages or design a small website yourself, and identify which features appeal to certain customers and which do not. You will find out about the benefits of marketing and promoting a business online and how this is done, and also have the opportunity to think about the overall effect on consumers and society as a whole as Internet use continues to grow.

Learning outcomes

After completing this unit, you should:

1. understand different online business activities
2. understand the issues relating to doing business online
3. be able to create web pages or a website for a stated business need
4. know the impact of an online business presence.

All websites referred to in this unit can be accessed via Hotlinks. See page ii for more information.

Assessment and grading criteria

This table shows you what you must do in order to achieve a pass, merit or distinction grade, and where you can find activities in this book to help you.

To achieve a **pass**, the evidence must show that the learner is able to:	To achieve a **merit**, the evidence must show that, in addition to the pass criteria, the learner is able to:	To achieve a **distinction**, the evidence must show that, in addition to the pass and merit criteria, the learner is able to:
P1 describe three different business organisations which operate online **See Assessment activity 12.1, page 311**	**M1** compare the features of three business organisations operating online **See Assessment activity 12.1, page 311**	**D1** make recommendations for a business organisation considering going online **See Assessment activity 12.2, page 321**
P2 explain how they operate their activities online **See Assessment activity 12.1, page 311**		
P3 explain the issues a business organisation would need to consider to go online **See Assessment activity 12.2, page 321**		
P4 explain the operational risks for a business organisation operating online **See Assessment activity 12.2, page 321**	**M2** analyse the benefits to businesses and customers of conducting business online **See Assessment activity 12.2, page 321**	**D2** suggest ways in which a business could deal with the operational risks associated with an online presence **See Assessment activity 12.2, page 321**
P5 create web pages to meet a user need **See Assessment activity 12.3, page 331**	**M3** explain how the website assists in achieving the aims and objectives of the business user **See Assessment activity 12.3, page 331**	**D3** justify the use of different construction features in the design of a website **See Assessment activity 12.3, page 331**
P6 describe the benefits to a business organisation marketing a product or service online **See Assessment activity 12.4, page 334**		
P7 outline the impact of online business on society **See Assessment activity 12.5, page 338**	**M4** analyse the consequences on society of an increase in online business **See Assessment activity 12.5, page 338**	**D4** evaluate the benefits and drawbacks to society of increasing business online **See Assessment activity 12.5, page 338**

How you will be assessed

To achieve this unit you will show that you understand how businesses operate online and the factors they must consider when they are planning an online presence. This includes explaining the potential issues, risks and benefits. You will demonstrate that you understand the factors to consider when designing web pages or a website for a specific business. You will show that you have considered the wider issues relating to the continuing increase of online business and how this is likely to affect society.

Chen

I'm really interested in working in an Internet-related business when I leave college, which is why I wanted to do this unit. I enjoy IT, but didn't want to specialise in it, so online business is perfect for me.

When I started the unit, I thought I knew quite a lot already, but there are many issues relating to online business that I'd never thought of, and I didn't know much about online marketing. We had a brilliant class discussion about what the online business world might be like in the future and its effect on everyone.

The best part for me was the practical task. We received a client brief and then worked on it to identify the issues and benefits, and then plan and create a website. I enjoyed making and presenting my storyboard and justifying my choices.

I am now looking forward to learning even more about online business when I start my BTEC National qualification.

Over to you!

- What activities do you carry out online? How do you think these will change in the future?
- How many different jobs can you identify related to online business? Discuss your ideas as a group.

Do you fit the pattern?

According to research, if you are between 15 and 24 you are likely to spend 14.8 hours a week online at home – slightly more if you are female. Sites or tools you use include MSN Messenger, eBay, Facebook, Google Search, Hotmail, YouTube and iTunes. You are more likely to have mobile broadband than your tutors, and more likely to want an iPhone if you are male. And this Christmas you plan to buy more online than last year.

Do you fit the pattern? If not, how do you vary? As a group, identify how online businesses can benefit by knowing all this information about you.

1. Understand different online business activities

There are many reasons for wanting an online presence, especially as the Internet continues to grow in popularity among all age groups. This section explains how the purpose of a business can affect the aims and objectives of a website, and how this relates to the features you will find on the site.

1.1 Range of online business activities

Businesses carry out a wide range of activities online. These can broadly be divided into the following categories.

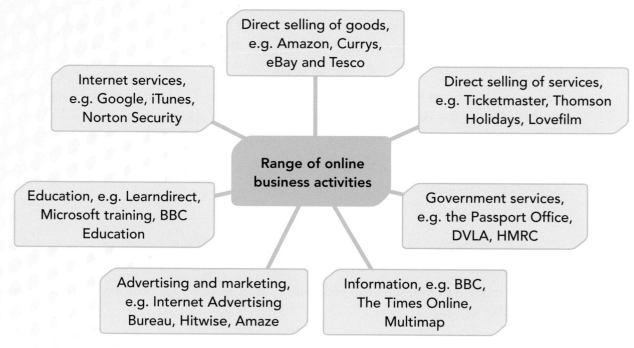

Figure 12.1: Range of online business activities

Aims and objectives of the user

The type of online activity planned by a business will depend upon its main purpose and what it wants to achieve by being online. Its aims may be to:

* sell goods and/or provide services
* supplement goods and services offered offline (for example, on the high street or by mail order)
* provide information about goods or services

- advertise and promote a brand or the business as a whole

- launch new products or ideas

- improve communications with customers

- obtain donations for a charitable cause.

It is important that a business is clear about what it wants to achieve and can also identify its target customers, because these factors will influence both its online activity and the features on the website.

Activity: Remember aims and objectives?

You first learned about these in Unit 2. Remember that a business should focus on one or two main aims, and that its objectives should be SMART. The same applies to the aims and objectives of a website. Turn back to page 42 now to refresh your memory.

Direct online selling of goods

According to Verdict Research, in 2009 online spending on retail purchases increased despite the recession, even though high street retailers were struggling to attract shoppers. So it is unsurprising that more and more businesses now want to sell goods online, from books, DVDs and clothes to household goods, groceries and furniture. The Hitwise Hot Shops List for August 2009 shows Amazon UK, Argos, Play.com, Next, Amazon, Marks & Spencer and Tesco in the top slots.

Activity: Investigate Hitwise

Experian Hitwise measures Internet data, and the information on its site will help you understand more about business online. Divide into groups and research: a) what it does; b) why firms use Hitwise; c) the information in its Data Centre; d) the benefits of competitive intelligence; e) the latest press reports/case studies. Present your findings to the rest of your class.

Direct online selling of services

The range of services online is huge. You can pay your bills, book a holiday, change your job, find a new house, bet on a horse, share your photos and keep up to date with your friends – to name but a few!

Many service providers prefer being online because it lowers their costs, such as Ryanair (which will only let you book online). Some

Did you know?

- A **microsite** is a sub-site of a larger site. It can be used to achieve an additional aim to that of the main website, for example, to advertise a new product or promote a special event. For an example of a microsite, visit the Run London site, which is a Nike microsite.

- Research has found that delivery charges are a major turn-off for online customers.

service providers – for example, electricity companies – have reduced tariffs for customers who receive their statements online because it saves on printing and postage. Major growth service areas include travel, online banking, social networking and video, including BBC iPlayer, ITV Player and 4oD.

Government services

Many government services can be accessed from the Directgov portal. You can use this site to find out about anything from student loans and benefits to applying for a driving licence. The site also has links to local council and public service websites, such as HMRC and the Highways Agency.

Information

On the Internet you can check the weather, read newspapers, plan a journey, check train times and research almost anything. Most information is free, but not all of it is reliable. Specialist information, like business research reports, is normally only available to subscribers.

Internet services

These websites provide information directly related to Internet activities, such as search engines Google and Bing, Internet Service Providers AOL and MSN, music sites iTunes and Spotify, security software providers Norton and McAfee, and email providers Hotmail and Gmail.

Advertising and marketing

A website will only promote a business if people know about it and use it. To do this successfully, many firms use specialist advertising and marketing agencies, such as Amaze (see page 330). Other firms specialise in providing competitive marketing intelligence, such as Experian Hitwise, and Nielsen NetRatings.

Education

Educational sites include those that offer training or courses online, such as Microsoft and BBC Education, information on courses of study, such as UCAS, and support, information and resources for tutors and learners, for example, Topmarks Education and Edexcel.

Activity: Find other websites

In groups, research online business activities further by finding three more relevant websites in each category. Compare your ideas as a class.

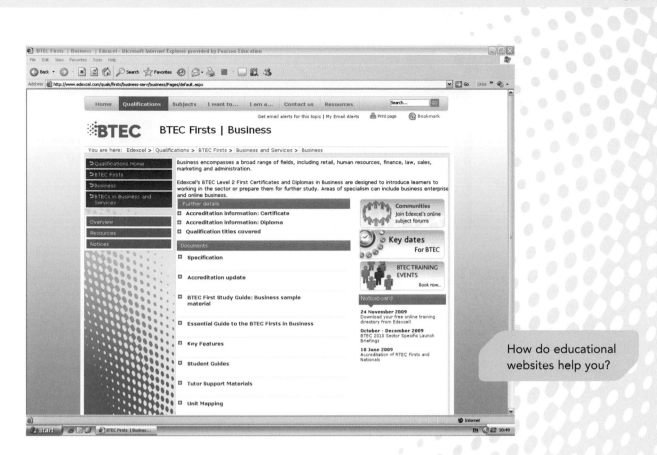

How do educational websites help you?

1.2 Sectors online

You learned about different business sectors in Unit 1. Because the type of sector affects the main purpose of the business, it also affects its aims and objectives, as you can see in Table 12.1.

Table 12.1: Sectors, aims and objectives

Sector	Organisations	Aims and objectives of websites and examples
Public	The government, its departments and agencies, local authorities, public corporations, NHS hospitals, state schools, colleges and universities	Highlight access to their services on their websites Their objectives will relate to how well they do this Examples include: Directgov, Jobcentre Plus, Met Office and NHS Direct
Private	Sole traders, partnerships, private and public limited companies	Promote their brand and products online Objectives will relate to increasing profits or reducing costs Examples include: Sarah Collins Jewellery, J.W. Mettrick & Sons Butchers, ADP and Odeon Cinemas
Voluntary/ not-for-profit	Voluntary and charitable organisations, social enterprises	Promote their cause online Objectives will relate to increased awareness and sometimes also to increased donations Examples include: The Prince's Trust, Citizens Advice, Oxfam and The Big Issue

Activity: Find the focus

Private sector businesses that do not deal direct with the public use their sites for a different purpose than those that do. Investigate some of these sites to identify their aims and compare your ideas as a group.

- Food manufacturers: Walkers, Nestlé and Heinz.
- Industrial companies: BAE Systems, Compact Instruments and Bibby Distribution.

1.3 Types of online presence

The aims and objectives of the website will determine its online presence. This may be simple or sophisticated, depending upon the size and scale of the business, and what it aims to achieve. The main options are as follows.

Brochureware

This is the most basic type of website and is designed to provide information about products or a service simply and effectively. It is used by businesses such as florists, caterers and hairdressers. It consists of a few linked pages illustrating the place and/or products – in effect, a brochure online. There may be a photograph of the staff and products, a list of prices, hours of opening, customer reviews and contact details.

Activity: Assess brochureware

Find examples of brochureware for small businesses in your own area by searching on the Internet, for example, 'caterers in XXX'. Compare four or five similar businesses and decide which sites are the most effective and why.

Complement offline activities

This is an option for businesses who want to use a website to offer additional services to customers.

- **Mail order** businesses, such as Littlewoods, now have online catalogues.
- **Service organisations** often provide additional information online, for example, Royal Mail parcel tracking and postcode finder, and Highways Agency traffic information.
- The **media** provides online news and information, and all main TV channels now offer a programme 'catch up' service online.

Activity: Film companies

Why would a film company want to go online? Investigate the Pixar, Universal Studios and Aardman websites to find out.

What are the benefits for a business of offering complementary online services to its customers?

Inviting online transactions

This means that these sites, as well as providing information, receive payments online for things such as:

- buying tickets, for example, Ticketmaster
- paying for a service such as photo prints, for example, Bonusprint
- paying a subscription for information, for example, Findmypast.com
- ordering and buying goods, for example, John Lewis.

Customers must normally register on a site and/or log in before they make a payment, for added security.

Interactive customisation

This means users can customise products online, such as at Jali where you can plan and order fitted furniture to your own design and measurements. Other variations include digital image processing sites where you can build your own photo album, such as Bonusprint and Stardoll, where little girls can create and style a virtual doll and buy virtual clothes for it. At the Sears website you can try on clothes in their virtual fitting room.

Providing information only

Your centre will have an informational website and will focus on providing details of courses and facilities to potential learners and their parents. Other examples of informational sites include:

- The Internet Movie Database (films)
- UpMyStreet (your area)
- Hoover's (business)
- Alexa (Internet information)
- Sporting Life (sport)
- workSMART (workers' rights)
- Ananova (news).

Did you know?

- Small businesses usually find it easier and cheaper to use PayPal or WorldPay to receive money than offer comprehensive site security. You can see how PayPal works by visiting the website.

- **Dynamic websites** are automatically updated from information on related databases. The BBC website uploads news reports, Amazon uploads new product information and Rightmove specialises in houses for sale.

- Useful information for all students, including discounts, is given at the National Union of Students website.

Discussion point

The Internet grows all the time. Does this mean every business should have some online presence? In groups, list the benefits you think businesses gain by being online. Then see if you can identify any businesses that would *not* benefit by being online and compare your ideas.

Activity: Does Business Link agree with you?

Check out whether Business Link agrees with the conclusions you reached after your discussion. On this site you can enter a business idea to find out whether going online is a good idea or not.

Case study: Usability and construction features

Research has shown that Internet users are very impatient. Unless the website loads quickly, is easy to follow and immediately interesting, then within 20 seconds the visitor has disappeared. The world expert on website usability is Jakob Nielsen, who says only 50 per cent of web visitors bother to scroll down the screen to see what lies below what they can see on their monitor. He recommends identifying key information and making sure this is immediately available, such as the opening hours and location, and eliminating unnecessary design and graphics.

Construction features should be chosen to help users, not to get in their way. The main ones are shown below.

- A **site search**, **site map**, clear **navigation bars**, helpful **graphics** and useful **hyperlinks**.
- **Drop-down menus** to provide additional options.
- **Complementary colours** chosen for **background** and text appropriate to the brand.
- Jargon-free **text** in a clear **font** that is easy to read.
- **Consistent page design** throughout the site.
- **Animations/video** used only to provide relevant information (such as virtual hotel tours).
- **Compressed images** that load quickly, and **thumbnails**.
- The ability to **zoom** and **rotate** images (for example, on retail and travel sites).
- Short **registration/enquiry forms** with relevant questions, and **action buttons** and a **simple log-in procedure** for existing users.
- **Hotspots** on a graphic or text to activate a function when selected, such as showing a picture or additional menu.
- **Pop-up windows** to provide additional information like terms and conditions without the user being taken away from the page.
- **Print screen** for printing informational text without graphics or adverts.
- A **Breadcrumb trail** at the top of the page so users always know where they are.

1. In groups, find examples of all the construction features shown above in bold on websites to check you clearly understand each term.

2. Frames and tables are other types of construction features, but they are complex and many web designers avoid them. Check if your tutor agrees.

3. The term 'above the fold' is used to describe what you see on your screen without scrolling down. Why do you think it is called that? How should this influence web page design?

4. The 'call to action' page is where users do something. This page and the home page are both very important. Can you suggest why?

5. In groups, research four different websites and identify the construction features of each, as well as its usability. First, though, read the checklists at Web Pages That Suck so you know what you are looking for!

Just checking

1. Describe three types of online business activities.
2. Explain why the aims of a website for a business in the public, private and voluntary sector are likely to be different.
3. Explain the difference between brochureware and inviting online transactions.
4. What is meant by 'interactive product customisation'?

Assessment activity 12.1

BTEC

Your friends Matt and Sarah both work in a family removal business called Moving Times. This has been a family business since it was founded 80 years ago. Last year, Matt and Sarah took it over from their father and are keen to modernise it. As part of this they are both trying to learn more about online businesses and have asked for your help. Matt is particularly interested in how websites link to the purpose of a business and the type of features found on websites. Carry out the following activities and produce a report for Matt and Sarah that answers their questions.

1. Choose three different business organisations from different sectors that operate online. Describe the purpose of each business and the aims and objectives of its website. **P1**

2. Explain how each of your chosen businesses operates their activities online. Use the construction features which are summarised in the case study on page 310 to help you. Then explain how these contribute towards achieving the aims and objectives you described in Question 1. **P2**

3. Identify and compare the construction features on the websites of your chosen business organisations by identifying those elements that are the same and how effective they are for each organisation. In your report, comment on how each business has used these features on its website to guide and engage the user. **M1**

Grading tips

- Remember that the aims and objectives will link to the purpose and this will link to the sector the business is in.
- For M1, you need to research the sites you have selected in detail to identify the relevant construction features and comment on these.

Activity: Your personal rights

Find out about your personal rights under the Data Protection Act at the website of the Information Commissioner's Office. Then check the privacy policy on your favourite shopping website to see what it says.

Did you know?

- The **Privacy and Electronic Communications Regulations** state businesses can send emails only to people who have 'opted in' by giving their active consent to receive these, and must allow recipients to unsubscribe at any time.

- In August 2009, Twitter was brought down by a DOS attack. The hacker also targeted Facebook. You can read about this on the BBC News website.

- In August 2009, a survey by *Which? Computing* magazine found big differences in the security offered by major high street banks. Find which are best and worst by checking out the article.

Activity: Ts and Cs

Check out the website of any major retailer and read the terms and conditions and disclaimers on its website.

Potential use of personal information

All organisations that store and process personal information must register with the Information Commissioner's Office and comply with the terms of the **Data Protection Act 1998**. This means that the data must be accurate, secure and not kept for longer than is necessary. An online business cannot put private information on its website or disclose customer details to other people. For these reasons, websites usually include a privacy policy which states how customer information is used by the business.

Vulnerability to hostile attack

All online businesses can be vulnerable to hackers or other types of cybercrime. **Financial fraud** occurs when a customer or business is deprived of money that is rightfully theirs. A customer's financial details or payments can be redirected to a spoof site, or customers can be sent 'phishing emails' asking them for personal details or bank account information. A keylogger is a virus that can be placed on an unprotected computer. This copies and transmits the user's keystrokes, including log-in details to their bank account.

Another risk is a Denial of Service (DOS) attack, which occurs when a website is overwhelmed with data, such as email messages, in a short period of time. This can be done to popular sites when they are most vulnerable, such as at Christmas when a DOS attack would lose an online store millions of pounds.

Activity: Improve your own security

Find out how to make your own PC secure, as well as what small businesses should do, at the Get Safe Online website.

Website updating and out-of-date information

Websites need updating regularly to ensure the information they provide is accurate, such as product descriptions and prices. All businesses have a legal duty to provide accurate, up-to-date information. If a customer took action based on incorrect information there may be a case to answer, although most websites have a disclaimer clause to cover this type of problem. However, this depends upon the type of website. An error by NHS Direct would be far more serious than one made by Argos or Tesco.

I'm sure it said the car was only £9.99!

What does a disclaimer clause cover?

Language problems with global customer base

Multinational businesses often operate websites in several languages. Smaller firms will not have this facility, so there is more scope for confusion with foreign buyers. Small firms can either use a local agent who specialises in overseas sales or have enquiries translated by an expert.

Hardware and software failures

All computer users depend upon their Internet Service Provider (ISP) to stay online. A technical fault will mean Internet access is lost, which can create serious problems, particularly if a business website is offline for long.

Other problems can include system failure through **hardware** malfunction or **software** becoming corrupted. Most businesses therefore have back-up servers so that they can switch if a server goes down. Software problems may be caused by programming errors or through a virus, so antivirus software and network security are crucial.

For protection against major disasters, such as a fire or flood, some businesses have their website hosted offsite in a secure location, where specialist staff can repair and restore the system quickly.

Activity: Investigate security

Find out how firms like Northgate Information Solutions and The Bunker keep systems secure by visiting their websites.

Did you know?

- Many firms including Marks & Spencer include disclaimer clauses that state the company takes no responsibility for the suitability of goods to be used abroad or any local laws that would affect the purchase.

- A UPS (Uninterruptible Power Supply) stops power surges that can damage computer hardware during a lightning storm.

Key terms

Hardware – IT equipment and components, for example, the VDU (visual display unit), keyboard and printer.

Software – IT programmes that tell the computer what to do.

Scale of the business

A business that operates on a small scale and sells only within the UK should have few problems with distribution. Those that distribute goods on a global basis have other concerns including:

- **special documents** to comply with customs and shipping regulations
- **special labelling or packaging** for perishable or hazardous goods
- **choosing the best method of transport** based on the type of goods and the destination
- **insurance** in case goods are damaged or lost in transit.

Did you know?

- Amazon has separate operations in different countries. This reduces distribution problems and enables its depots to stock the correct DVD format and most popular books for each country.

- For some types of goods to be exported, the seller must have an export licence. These include drugs, cars and flower seeds.

Activity: Investigate international operations

Check out different Amazon websites around the world at the bottom of the Amazon UK website. Then find out more about international shipping rates and restrictions at the US Amazon site or at the Amazon section of TheBigProject website.

Special types of goods

Some types of goods need special attention.

- **Fragile goods** must be packed carefully with bubble wrap or other protective material and clearly labelled.
- **Perishable goods** must be delivered promptly. They are often transported in special vehicles, such as refrigerated lorries.
- **Hazardous goods** may need to be accompanied by special paperwork, such as a Dangerous Goods Note.

Activity: Check out the BIFA

Find out what training the British International Freight Association (BIFA) offers to businesses just starting to distribute goods globally, by visiting the BIFA website. Then see how FedEx helps online businesses by visiting its site.

What extra costs are involved in delivering fragile goods?

Ease of distribution of services

Distributing services globally is easier and cheaper than providing products because there is no need to physically move anything. Apart from VAT, most costs will relate to managing and administering the service. Examples include:

- online insurance quotes for cars, houses, travel and even pets
- booking flights online and reserving hotel rooms
- downloading software.

Activity: Talk to a webmaster

Often, various functional areas contribute towards resolving online issues the business may face. IT keeps the system secure, sales and marketing provides updated information, finance obtains funding, HR trains staff, distribution despatches goods and customer service responds to complaints.

Interview the webmaster at your centre or a local business, to find out how businesses resolve the issues associated with an online presence. Make notes and keep this information safely for Assessment activity 12.2 below.

Just checking

1. Identify four kinds of planning or implementation issues a new online business may face.
2. What is financial fraud and how can an online business protect itself?
3. What type of initial investment costs would be involved with a new online operation?
4. Explain why it is easier and cheaper to sell services globally than physical goods.

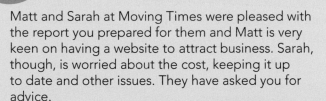

Assessment activity 12.2

 **P3 P4 M2 D1 D2**

Matt and Sarah at Moving Times were pleased with the report you prepared for them and Matt is very keen on having a website to attract business. Sarah, though, is worried about the cost, keeping it up to date and other issues. They have asked you for advice.

1. Send an email to Matt and Sarah in which you explain the type of issues a business needs to consider to go online under the headings: planning, implementation, financial, staffing and distribution. Also refer to the role of functional areas in supporting the operation of the website and say how the staff who specialise in IT, marketing, finance and customer service at Moving Times can contribute towards resolving online issues the business may face. Use the notes you made in the Activity above to help. **P3**

2. Then add a second section in which you identify and explain the operational risks associated with online business, including security breaches. **P4**

3. a) Investigate the websites of similar firms to Moving Times. Identify their aims and objectives and see how the sites are structured to achieve these. Identify the benefits you think Moving

Times and their customers could gain from conducting their business online. **M2**

b) Identify the main drawbacks and issues that Matt and Sarah will have to consider.

4. Use this information to prepare a presentation in which you summarise the benefits and drawbacks for them of going online. In your presentation, explain the methods Matt and Sarah can take to combat the risks you have identified. For each risk, suggest a possible solution. Include a reference to any legislation that applies, the possible costs involved, and the likely effectiveness of each method you identify. **D2**

5. Make a justified conclusion about whether it would be a good idea to proceed or not. **D1**

Grading tip

Many of the benefits businesses can achieve by going online are given on pages 332–36. Look ahead to these pages now to help you with your answer for M2.

3. Be able to create web pages or a website for a stated business need

Producing your own web pages or a website enables you to understand how websites can be designed to meet the needs of a client and help a business to achieve its aims and objectives. In this section you will learn how to do this and then put your ideas into practice.

The first step in designing any website is **planning**. You need to think about the design, layout and features in terms of the target audience and what they will want from the site. Then decide upon the content – the text and graphics you want to include. Many designers create a storyboard which shows the title and a brief description of each page, and how those pages link together. They then talk this through with the client before they start work.

Steps to take when producing a website include the following.

- Identify important pages and features (home page, contact details, order page, and so on).

- Create a storyboard.

- Write page content.

- Begin work on the design.

You will normally start your storyboard with your home page, then decide where this will lead to. This is the same as a site map, but in graphic form. Figure 12.2 shows an example of a storyboard for a basic website for a local florist.

Did you know?

All your pages should have an individual URL. For example, www.mysite/home and www.mysite/aboutus, because users could land on any page from a search engine and need to know where they are.

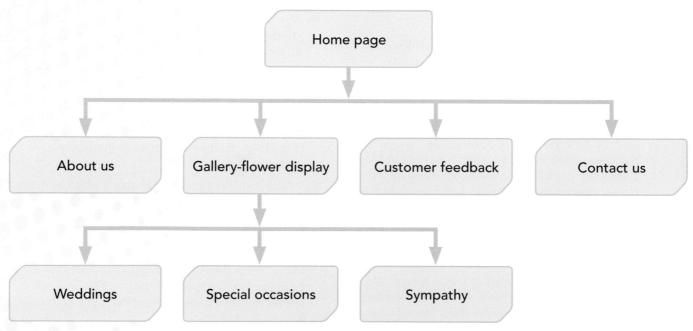

Figure 12.2: Storyboard for a florist website

Activity: Practise your skills

Look at more examples of website storyboards by searching on Google Images. Then learn how they are created by researching online. Practise making a storyboard yourself by finding a simple brochureware site and sketching what its storyboard would look like. You can also practise sketching the features of a web page, too.

Did you know?

- The 'three clicks rule' says you should be able to complete any action on a website within three clicks, for example, go back to the home page or get to the order form.

- If you are designing a company website, you may be restricted to colours linked to the brand or logo.

You also need to decide how your page will look. One method is to plan your page in grids, as shown in Figure 12.2. Good designs often include:

- a header at the top of every page, which includes the business name and logo

- a footer at the bottom, which may include additional links

- navigation in the header or down the left-hand side. On a large site it may be in both places. Navigation areas normally remain fixed when the rest of the page scrolls

- a search box at the top right

- prominent business contact details.

3.1 Web development software

To create your web pages you need special software.

- Specialist web authoring software includes Adobe Dreamweaver (the professional's favourite) or Microsoft Expression Web, which replaced FrontPage in Office 2007. These are **WYSIWYG** programmes, so show what the web page will look like as you create it.

- You can use a package such as Word, which lets you create web pages as well as document pages.

- You can use web-based technologies, such as Javascript and Flash, to add extra features to your website.

- You can write **HTML**, which is a text-based code, directly into a simple text editor such as Notepad, UltraEdit or TextPad. Text editors cannot display a finished web page, so to view a page you must load it into a web browser.

Once you start collecting graphics for your website or writing text, then you need to save them carefully. This needs excellent **file management** (see page 329). Start by creating a special website folder, and then keep all your text and graphic files in sub-folders within this folder.

Activity: Web browsers

A website must look good in all browsers. Can you name four popular web browsers besides Internet Explorer? Compare your ideas as a group.

Key terms

WYSIWYG – 'What You See Is What You Get'. The screen shows the finished web page, not the HTML code.

HTML – Hyper Text Markup Language is the language used on the web. The markup tags tell the web browser how to display each page.

Did you know?

- You can download a free web editor at Nvu.

- Even if your package writes HTML code automatically, knowing the basics enables you to create better pages (see page 326).

Key terms

Meta title – appears in the top left-hand corner and is very important for SEO (see pages 313 and 332) because it is a core area Google looks at.

Meta tag – an HTML code that gives information about different aspects of a website, such as the summary of content and author's name. They do not show on the website.

Pixel – the smallest part of a digital image. It is a tiny square that is easily seen if you increase the size of an image. The more squares an image contains, the higher its **resolution** (quality).

Did you know?

iPhone screens are only 480 × 320 pixels, so web pages designed for these (and BlackBerrys) must be much smaller.

3.2 Format and edit

Effective websites have certain aspects in common. They contain clear information, are easy to navigate and they reflect the image of the business. In most packages you will start by creating a master page or template to reflect your planned design. This shows the layout, colours, the **meta title** and **meta tags**, as well as the navigation table and links to other pages.

The size of the page must also be set. Users are happy to scroll down a web page but dislike scrolling across, so it is best to set a page size that will fit horizontally in all browser windows. In 2009, the most common size was 1024 × 768 **pixels**, and many popular websites, such as MySpace and Facebook, are just 800 pixels wide to fit smaller screens.

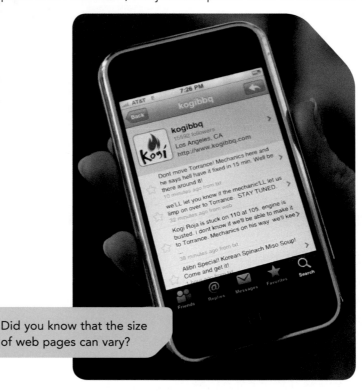

Did you know that the size of web pages can vary?

Common web functions and features

As you saw in the case study on page 310, some functions and features add to usability, such as navigation bars, and some do not, such as 'splash pages', which have to be clicked through to enter the site. On the following page are features to consider.

Functional skills

Practise your writing skills by ensuring your summary is concise and clear so it easy to refer to.

Activity: Build a good design

In groups, check out the website design pages of the Website Helpers site. Then summarise its main points to help your group when you are designing your website.

- **Bookmarks** – Adding bookmarks to a website means putting in a link that users can click on to save that page or the site as a favourite. Reminding users to do this, rather than hoping they will bookmark it themselves in their browser, means there is a greater chance users will return to the site again.

- **Hyperlinks** – Internal or **relative links** go to other pages in the website or other parts of the same page, for example, 'Top of page'. External or **absolute links** go to other websites the user may find interesting. Links must always be underlined so they are obvious to the user and change colour when they have been used. Normally they are in blue text and change to maroon.

- **Graphics, fonts and text formatting features** – The golden rule is: less is more. A cluttered web page is never a good idea and just confuses everyone.

    Graphics can be photographs (JPEGs) or drawings (GIFs). All should be checked for brightness, and many look better if they are cropped or resized. Because graphics on websites are smaller than in print, close-ups are better, as are simple pictures with a clear focus. All graphics should be compressed to reduce their file size so that they load more quickly on the page. Another useful trick is to include thumbnails the user can click on to expand.

Key terms

Relative links – internal links within the same website.

Absolute links – external links to other websites.

Did you know?

- Many websites now contain social bookmaking icons so that users can easily share content with friends.

- A **navigation bar** or **menu** is just a series of links grouped together.

- Blind people use software known as screenreaders to 'read' a computer screen. These cannot interpret graphics, but can read captions put in their place, which are known as **alternative text**.

What are the benefits of resizing photographs for a website?

Fonts relates to the typeface that is used and its size. Typefaces are of two main types: serif and sans-serif. Serif fonts have small decorative marks at the top and bottom, whereas sans serif do not. Compare the letter a in Times New Roman (serif) with the letter a in Verdana (sans-serif) to see the difference. Sans-serif is clearer and crisper on a web page, and popular options are Arial, Verdana, Tahoma and Trebuchet MS. The size should be at least 10 point, so it is easy to read.

Activity: Investigate accessibility

Find out more about website accessibility at AbilityNet.

Activity: Font options

To see more font options, visit the Code Style website.

Did you know?

- Text must be easy to read, not just for old people, but for teenagers. Research has found that because many teens multitask when they are online, they prefer larger text so that they can read it easily.

- Text content is often prepared as a Word document and checked for spelling and grammar before being copied and pasted into the web page.

- Creating many web page sections as images, even if they contain text, is bad practice because search engines and screen readers cannot see it.

- **XHTML** stands for eXtendable Hyper Text Markup Language. **DHTML** (Dynamic HTML) is used to create interactive and animated website features.

- You can spot links easily in HTML code. **Anchor tags** and `</a>` identify the start and end of the link. `href=""` tells the browser where to look and stands for hypertext reference.

Activity: See HTML in action

Check the HTML used for a web page you are viewing by right-clicking on it and selecting 'View Source'. Then check out a web guide for learning HTML, such as the one at HTML Dog.

Text formatting features that tell a browser how to display text on a web page are called **tags**. Text options include **bold** (or `<strong>` in HTML) for headings or special terms, and *italics* (`<i>` in HTML) for emphasising words. The page should start with a title, and clear headings should identify different sections. In HTML headings vary in size from h1 (the largest) to h6, but using style sheets (see page 327) enables you to set how these display on screen. Your headings must be consistent from page to page, as in this book. Text can also be formatted to display as an ordered list (with numbers) or as an unordered list (with bullets). It can also be aligned to left, right and centre, or justified.

- **Background colours and images** – The background of your web page can be any colour, but the lighter it is, the easier it will be to read dark text. This does not mean it must be white, but too much strong colour will detract from the content. You can also place an image as part of your background. This can include a contrasting colour down part of the page so that your navigation area will stand out. You then need to decide whether you want an image on every page or not, and whether you want it to scroll with the page or stay fixed while the rest of the page scrolls.

Activity: Compare backgrounds

For more information about background colours and images, visit Build Your Website.

Simple HTML

A basic knowledge of HTML is very useful, even when you are using a WYSIWYG editor like FrontPage, because you can recognise and correct errors more easily, and may also learn how to improve the coding or make changes yourself, for example, to start a new paragraph.

HTML uses 'tags' to indicate the start and end of a command, for example,

`<strong>Examples of tags</strong>`

would appear as **Examples of tags** on a web page. The opening tag `<strong>`says where bold (or strong) starts, and the closing tag `</strong>`says where it ends. Other HTML tags include:

- `<html>` which says where html starts and `</html>` where it ends

- `<body>` which defines where body text starts. This is the main text on a page, such as the text you are reading now, rather than the margin notes. End it with `</body>`

- `<p>` which starts a paragraph and `</p>` where it ends

- `<centre>` which puts a heading in the middle of the page. End with `</centre>`.

Editing and formatting tools

As you create your web pages, you will need to edit them to correct errors or add new information. All web authoring software contains editing tools to enable you to copy and paste, find text in a file, find text in multiple files, replace text in a file, replace text in multiple files, and increase or reduce indentation. You can enter commands to find text quickly, join multiple lines and so on. Similarly, in any graphics package you can edit photographs or drawings by cropping or resizing, improving brightness and correcting colours. If formatting has been done using **cascading style sheets (CSS)**, then editing is easier because these contain all the formatting elements, so a change can easily be applied to the whole site, for example, a change of background colour.

Did you know?

If you resize a graphic, ticking **aspect ratio** means you will keep the image in proportion.

Key term

Cascading style sheets (CSS) – these define how the document should look and provide formatting instructions.

Activity: Learn some shortcuts

Keyboard shortcuts help you to edit text more quickly. Next time you are cutting and pasting, use Ctrl+X to cut, Ctrl+C to copy, and Ctrl+V to paste. To replace old text, highlight it before pressing Ctrl+V.

PLTS

Remember that reflective learners are constantly on the lookout for techniques to improve their performance.

3.3 Combining information

All websites consist of a mixture of text and image files. This information can be obtained from many different sources.

- A **scanner** can be used for photographs and drawings.
- A **digital camera** (including a phone camera) enables you to take your own photos. Unless you have a good camera and understand image resolution, it is wise to stick to general shots instead of close-ups, because they would look fuzzy rather than sharp.

Why is image resolution important?

- **Application packages**, such as Word and Excel, enable you to produce text and spreadsheets.

- **Original artwork** is that you have produced yourself, which you can produce in a graphics package or scan into your computer.

- **Clip art** is available from many websites and is part of some application packages.

3.4 Checking

Regular checking of every web page is essential as you create it and whenever you make a change. It is not sensible to leave this until you have finished or you could easily have a huge task on your hands.

- **Image resolution** refers to its quality, and image editing software can usually save images optimised for the web. Remember, too, that the width (in pixels) of an image should never be greater than the size of your target site, and normally will be much lower. Useful starting values are 640 pixels across for a large image and 320 for a small one, but you should adapt this to best fit your design.

- **Colours** should be checked to make sure they are as you expected, for example, blue for links. A good tip is to check them in more than one type of browser, for example, Internet Explorer and Mozilla Firefox.

- **Internal or external links not working** can happen because you have keyed in the reference incorrectly, updated an internal page and saved it with a new name, or linked to an external website (or page) that no longer exists. Check every link as you key it in, then check them all again when you have finished the page.

- **Inappropriate content** can include jargon, wordy text, slang, inaccurate information or anything else that would be unsuitable for your customers. A false claim or allegation on a website could even result in a legal claim against you, regardless of any disclaimers. It is therefore sensible to ask someone to check your content before you upload it.

- **Text** must be perfectly correct in every detail. This means it is grammatical, every word is spelled correctly, and all your apostrophes are in the right place. Using a spell check is not enough for work that the whole world can see, so ask someone who is excellent at writing to check your work with you.

- **Formatting** means that all your headings, paragraphs, lists and other aspects (bold, italics, underlined links) are correct. Check the spacing carefully as this can be difficult to get right, especially between paragraphs. Remember that formatting must be consistent.

3.5 Review

Review your site when you have prepared all your pages.

Appropriate for purpose and audience

Test this by showing pages to several people who represent your target audience and ask them for feedback. The aim is not to get compliments about how pretty they are, but to check that the site achieves its purpose of creating and keeping interest in the business or its products. You also want to know if users are inspired to take action as a result.

Problems

Problems can include:

- **unnecessary animation** (such as splash pages)
- **inappropriate graphics** that add nothing to the content, or are the wrong size or poor quality
- **slow download speeds** because you have too many effects or large, uncompressed images
- **inappropriate font choice** that is difficult to read
- **inappropriate colour combinations** (such as red text on a blue or black background).

3.6 Publishing

When your website has been checked and reviewed you are ready to **upload your files** to an intranet or to a server (a computer that is always connected to the Internet). Large companies (and colleges) may have their own local server; small businesses will use a web hosting company.

The website must now be **maintained and kept up to date**, perhaps by using content management software, which enables staff to update a website without professional training, or by a website updating service.

Updating is much easier if you have a good **file management** system, where all files relating to your website are in named files in appropriate folders. Moving and deleting files is then far easier, as long as you check all your links still work before you upload your new version.

Did you know?

- Software to help get site feedback is available at SurveyMonkey and SurveyGizmo.

- A useful developer's tool for analysing how a web page has been built and why it loads slowly is available on the Yahoo! Developer Network site.

- Files are uploaded using a File Transfer Protocol (FTP) programme. This is part of some web authoring packages, like Dreamweaver.

Key term

Upload – the term used when website files are transferred to a web host for publishing.

As head of strategy at Amaze, Rick Curtis is at the forefront of online business developments.

Amaze is a top-ranked interactive agency and has won many awards for its expertise in creating, promoting and supporting digital business and communications. The agency has clients from every sector, and meeting their individual needs means first identifying what each brand stands for.

Amaze prepares a technical, creative and functional specification for each new website. This identifies its look and feel, and the features needed, such as ecommerce, site search or registration. An example of a feature growing in popularity is a product comparison tool. This lets buyers compare alternatives on the site, such as at Lexus, where you can compare a car with rivals like BMW. Rick explains this shows brand confidence as the firm is saying, 'We know we are best so we will make it easy for you to check this and make sure.'

Clients are shown a site map of a proposed new site and sample pages. Then a project specification is agreed which identifies the size of project, the number of pages and cost. Work then starts on building the site and deciding online marketing strategies.

Rick says the advantages of marketing online include: targeting the market more precisely, measuring conversion rates accurately, and being able to launch or change campaigns quickly to optimise opportunities. Online marketing is cost-effective and appropriate throughout the customer lifecycle, from creating awareness at the launch stage to ensuring customer retention later.

How will society be affected in the future? Rick's view is based on US research that the Internet affects how we learn. 'Content snacking' occurs when people scan several devices simultaneously for bite-sized chunks of information on screen. This may result in people no longer wanting, or being able, to read pages of text or longer articles, like this one. Rick also warns we must always be wary about trusting what we read, as so much online information is more opinion than fact.

Find out more about Amaze by visiting the website before you answer the questions below.

Think about it!

1. Amaze clients include Odeon and the Greater London Authority. Amaze has also worked with the Outward Bound Trust. What sector is each business in, and how is this likely to affect the aim(s) of their websites?

2. Why does Amaze recommend firms have a comparison tool on their site? Can you suggest two or three sites that could do this?

3. Suggest why it is important a project specification is agreed with a client before work starts on building the website.

4. Rick's research came from a US article called *Is Google making us stupid?* by Nicholas Carr. Research this as a group and suggest what could be done by parents, tutors and governments to prevent this happening. A link to the article is available via Hotlinks.

Just checking

1. Why is it useful to prepare a storyboard before designing a website?
2. Identify four ways in which you could obtain information to put on your website.
3. Describe four commonly used tags in HTML.
4. Give two reasons why links might stop working.
5. Identify four checks or reviews you would carry out before you uploaded your website.

BTEC Assessment activity 12.3

Matt and Sarah have given you the task of creating the Moving Times website. They want it to help them obtain more business over a wider area, promote the firm to young professionals and launch office removals.

1. Identify the construction features you will want to include to meet their needs. Decide on your design and layout and prepare a storyboard that shows how the website pages will link together. Then create sample web pages that will meet their needs. **P5**

2. Prepare a report for Matt and Sarah that explains how the website, its design and its features will help to achieve their aims and objectives. **M3**

3. Create a user guide for Matt and Sarah that explains the features of the web pages and how the website has been tested and checked for ease of use and suitability of purpose. **D3**

Grading tip

For D3, your user guide must justify your choice of different construction features. You might find it easier to put your reasons in the introduction or even in an attached document.

4.4 Financial advantages

An online operation enables a business to reduce costs in several ways.

- **Improved cash flow** is possible because customers pay by card as they make a purchase. The card payment is verified before goods are despatched so there is less chance the business will not be paid and less need to offer credit.

- **Low-cost locations** are possible because online businesses can locate virtually anywhere, especially if they provide a service such as writers of technical manuals or graphic designers. They may work from home and transmit their work electronically to the client.

- **Low overheads** are possible because rents and rates are cheaper out of town, and fewer specialist staff are needed for orders and enquiries. Online marketing campaigns, too, are cheaper than advertising in the press and on television.

- **Rapid payment** is a feature of online shopping. The goods will not be sent unless payment has been made.

4.5 Effects on customers

- **Convenience** is a benefit because the Internet is like a huge shopping mall. It is much easier to search and order online than travel to the shops, walk around (perhaps in the rain) and then go home again, sometimes with a good bargain, but often not.

- **Wider choice** is an obvious benefit, particularly for people who live in small towns or rural areas.

- **Flexibility** is greater because you can go online at any time of the day or night to suit yourself.

- **Lack of direct contact with products and company** is unimportant for products like books and DVDs. It can be a disadvantage for complex products, like a TV or camera when advice would be helpful. Similarly it is impossible to check the quality of fresh food online or the size/fit of clothes or shoes.

- **No goodwill element** can be a disadvantage because most online businesses are faceless operations. Even though they may provide excellent customer service they will not throw in a freebie, such as extra leads when you buy a TV, or do you a favour, such as advising you on how to get better results with your new camera when you collect your prints, whereas local shops often will.

- **Discounts** are available online through shopping comparison sites or by keying in voucher codes obtained at websites such as My Voucher Codes. Customers also benefit from being able to compare deals online, although some people may argue they prefer to haggle in person.

Did you know?

- Online businesses can save VAT by moving offshore, which is why Amazon, Tesco and HMV now operate online stores from Jersey.

- The Internet has not stopped customers visiting store sales in person to try to find a bargain.

Activity: Customer feedback online

Businesses benefit by getting customer feedback online and can use professional services to check what people are saying about them. Check out the websites of Radian6 and Market Sentinel to find out more.

4.6 Impact on society

The Internet and online business have come a long way since 1990, when emails were in their infancy, very few businesses had a website and online shopping was unheard of. What will happen over the next 20 years, or even the next ten years? Will society benefit or not?

One scenario suggests more **social isolation** as more people work from home, shop online and only communicate electronically with friends and family. This would affect many businesses: transport companies, cafés, restaurants and pubs. Villages and towns would suffer if local shops closed because they cannot compete with online rivals.

Employment could increase, leading to the **breakdown of communities** made even worse by an increase in cybercrime. A land of web servers and data centres could create massive pollution and lead to regular power failures as 1.5 billion people or more try to be online all the time. Governments could monitor everything users do by controlling ISPs, and tax broadband usage to make more money. Google could rule the world!

Alternatively, more families could benefit as parents work from home when their children are young, running online businesses or working freelance and sending off work electronically. People could save money because they know the best buys and no longer pay more than necessary. Older people and the disabled could stay in touch with their friends. Personal services could flourish because it is impossible to have your hair done or your car serviced online. Online security issues might be history and everyone might have more leisure time because routine tasks, like queuing for groceries, are a thing of the past. 'Cloud computing' could enable more mobile connectivity at lower prices, television anywhere and the end of clunky devices and problems with data storage. Google could be faced, like Microsoft was, with new challenges from up and coming online innovators.

Discussion point

How do you think online business will affect your community in the future? Research and debate the following proposal as a class: **Increasing business online will be a disaster for society.** Then decide who has the best arguments for and against, and why.

Functional skills

Practise your speaking and listening skills, and make significant contributions to the debate.

Just checking

1. Explain how operating online can help a small business compete against a much larger one.
2. How can businesses improve their level of response by operating online?
3. Explain why online retailers gain financial benefits.
4. Suggest two advantages and two disadvantages for customers of buying online.

BTEC ## Assessment activity 12.5

As a result of the class debate you held on how online business will affect your community, your tutor has asked you to each write an article for the student magazine in which you forecast the future for society. Your article should be in three clear sections, as shown below.

1. Start your article by outlining the impact that you think online business and online shopping is having on society at the moment. **P7**

2. In the next section, analyse the consequences for society as online business continues to increase. **M4**

3. In your final section, evaluate the benefits and drawbacks to society of increasing business online. **D4**

Grading tip

For P7, you may find it easier to relate this to any relevant changes in your own local community, if you think these are caused by online competition.

Assignment tips

- You can obtain data about current online usage at Hitwise. For the latest information on Internet use to help you with M4, go to UK National Statistics and enter 'Internet' in the search box.

- Use notes from the class debate you had (page 337) to help you achieve D4. Remember that you need to give a balanced view supported by appropriate evidence for both benefits and drawbacks.

Credit value: 5

13 Consumer rights

Today, we take it for granted that we have legal rights as consumers. Even if we do not really know what these are, we do not expect to buy a laptop and find the lid comes off the second time we open it, or buy a pair of trousers that shrink once they have been washed. We also instinctively know that there must be something we could do if a workman puts his foot through our ceiling, or the desk the joiner has built has nails sticking out of it.

In Britain, many laws have been passed to give consumers specific legal rights, although some only in recent times. Laws are regularly amended (updated) to try to improve them still further and make them more appropriate for modern consumer activities. For example, it is only since 2000 that consumers buying over the Internet have had legal rights to protect them from dishonest sellers.

In this unit you will learn about the most important laws that protect consumers. You will also find out about the law of contract as it applies to goods and services we buy. You will learn about these through examples of how the law can help consumers when things go wrong. You will also find out about exclusion clauses, and how consumers are protected against negligence by suppliers.

Learning outcomes

After completing this unit, you should:

1. be able to apply the law relating to consumer protection
2. know the meaning of terms in a consumer contract
3. be able to apply the law on consumer protection in a given situation.

All websites referred to in this unit can be accessed via Hotlinks. See page ii for more information.

339

Assessment and grading criteria

This table shows you what you must do in order to achieve a pass, merit or distinction grade, and where you can find activities in this book to help you.

To achieve a **pass**, the evidence must show that the learner is able to:	To achieve a **merit**, the evidence must show that, in addition to the pass criteria, the learner is able to:	To achieve a **distinction**, the evidence must show that, in addition to the pass and merit criteria, the learner is able to:
P1 explain how the law protects purchasers of goods and services **See Assessment activity 13.1, page 350**	**M1** apply the law accurately in given consumer dispute scenarios, analysing how legislation protects consumers in the purchase of both goods and services **See Assessment activities 13.3 and 13.5, pages 357 and 365**	**D1** apply the legal principles of the main areas of consumer protection by reference to statutes and decided cases in given consumer dispute scenarios, including defective goods and services **See Assessment activity 13.5, page 365**
P2 identify how the law protects consumers against negligence **See Assessment activities 13.2 and 13.5, pages 354 and 365**		
P3 identify the meaning and effect of terms in consumer contracts **See Assessment activity 13.4, page 362**	**M2** explain the meaning and effect of terms in a consumer contract **See Assessment activity 13.4, page 362**	
P4 identify how the law protects consumers against the imposition of exclusion clauses **See Assessment activity 13.4, page 362**		
P5 apply the appropriate remedy in a given consumer protection situation **See Assessment activities 13.3 and 13.5, pages 357 and 365**		

How you will be assessed

To achieve this unit you will demonstrate your knowledge of consumer law and consumer contracts to make decisions about how the law protects consumers in certain situations. You will do this by taking part in role-play activities and by assessing the correct action that should be taken by consumer service staff and others in several different circumstances.

Emma

I wanted to do this unit for lots of reasons. The most obvious is that I buy things myself, and if they do not work or something goes wrong, then it's really good to know what to do. I now know that I can be polite but persistent and, if necessary, say what my legal rights are. Just quoting the Acts I've learned often makes a tremendous difference!

I'm quite fascinated by the law and have wondered about doing legal studies at a higher level. I thought this unit would give me a useful introduction to what it's like to learn about legal matters.

It's also helped to give me confidence in my part-time job, too. I work in a clothes shop on a Saturday and sometimes we get customers who bring things back because they have changed their minds. We say they can have a full refund, but only within 28 days, and sometimes people argue with this. I now know that this is fair, legal and quite reasonable, and I can now cope better with these customers without getting worried or panicking. If I ever had my own business in the future it would also be really helpful to know about the rights my customers have.

Over to you!

- Would you find it useful to know about your consumer rights?
- How helpful do you think this would be in your future career?
- How helpful would it be in any job you do now?

Your rights

You buy a bag of crisps from a convenience store. You open it and bite into one. It is soft. You then see the packet has come apart at the bottom, so you take it back and complain. 'Your problem,' says the man at the till, 'you've opened it.' 'Rubbish,' you say, before grabbing another packet and running out. He shouts after you, 'Stop, thief!' and presses his alarm button. Is he right and what should you have done?

1. Be able to apply the law relating to consumer protection

Consumer laws aim to protect people who buy goods and services. In Britain, the first consumer protection law to be passed was the Sale of Goods Act 1893. Broadly, this stated that in any contract (agreement) between a buyer and a seller, the buyer had certain rights. Unfortunately, it allowed the seller to add special terms to the contract to restrict the buyer's rights, which virtually destroyed all the benefits of the Act. It was not until much later, in 1973 when the Supply of Goods (Implied Terms) Act was passed, that sellers were prevented from taking away the most important rights of buyers.

Since then various Acts of Parliament have improved the rights of buyers still further. Today, anyone who purchases goods or services has considerable legal rights. Unfortunately, many people do not know what these are, so do not know what action they can take if they have a problem with what they have purchased.

In this section you will learn about the main laws that protect consumers who buy goods and services.

1.1 Basic terminology

Before you can learn how the law works to help consumers, you need to understand some basic terminology and the difference between certain types of laws.

Distinction between contracts for the sale of goods and services

A contract is a legal agreement between two or more people. For example, when you start work you will have a contract of employment, and this contract is an agreement between you and your employer.

In this unit we are looking at contracts of sale relating to the provision of goods and contracts of sale relating to the provision of services. The two are treated differently in law, as you will see below.

- **A contract of sale for goods** – This is an agreement that a supplier will 'transfer or agree to transfer property in goods to a buyer for a monetary consideration, called the price'. This is the definition given in Section 2 of the Sale of Goods Act 1979 (SOGA).

  This Act is very important. Although there have been several amendments since, it still sets down the main terms relating to the sale of goods. The following important points are worth noting.

When is a consumer not a consumer?

○ The Act refers to the *sale* of goods. This is different from *hiring* goods. If you hire a DVD, then you use it only for an agreed time. If you buy a DVD you become the legal owner and can now sell it to someone else if you want.

○ To be covered by the Sale of Goods Act you must pay for what you buy.

○ It is unlawful for anyone to try to take away your legal rights under the Sale of Goods Act.

○ The sale of goods is different from the sale of services (see below), which is covered by a different Act.

You normally become the owner of the goods when you pay for them and accept delivery (or collect them). Ownership is important because the legal owner is responsible if anything goes wrong. If your frozen peas have defrosted when Tesco delivers them, then you can reject them and Tesco must replace them or give you a refund. If they defrost an hour later, because you forgot to put them in the freezer, this is not Tesco's problem.

- **Contract for the sale of services** – This is an agreement for someone to do something for you, whether it is to take your photograph, mend your car, or dry clean your best outfit. Under the Supply of Goods and Services Act 1982, these services must be carried out for a reasonable charge, within a reasonable time and with reasonable care and skill.

Unlike the sale of goods, it *is* possible for suppliers to exclude or restrict their liability if something goes wrong – but only if this would be fair and reasonable, as you will see on the following page.

Remember

- All purchases of goods are covered by SOGA, but consumers are entitled to a greater range of **remedies** than business buyers if something goes wrong or they are misled.

- In English law, a contract of sale for goods cannot exist unless there is payment.

Key term

Remedies – the methods used to put things right if you are wronged in law.

Discussion point

If you only notice the peas you received are defrosted just after the delivery man has left, why is it important that you notify Tesco immediately? Discuss your ideas as a group.

When do you become the legal owner of the frozen peas you buy in a supermarket?

Key term

Exclusion clause – a term which attempts to limit or restrict the liability of the supplier or limit the rights of the consumer.

Did you know?

When people are warned to 'read the small print', this really means 'watch out for any exclusion clauses'!

Remember

No notice or disclaimer can ever absolve an organisation from its liability to staff or customers if personal injury or death is caused through their negligence.

Key term

Statute law – laws created by passing Acts of Parliament, for example, the Sale of Goods Act.

Meaning and effect of an exclusion clause

At one time, suppliers could add all sorts of terms to a contract so that it was biased in their favour. These are called **exclusion clauses** because they limit or restrict the liability of the seller.

The law is usually very suspicious about exclusion clauses – so much so that the Unfair Contract Terms Act 1977 stops a retailer from limiting or taking away a consumer's legal rights under the Sale of Goods Act in any way. Misleading consumers about their legal rights is also a criminal offence, whether this is done as a statement in a contract or a notice in a shop. In this case, the shop could be prosecuted by Trading Standards Officers.

The only time that exclusion clauses are valid is when they are considered 'fair and reasonable'. If a jeweller loses your watch after you have left it for repair, the shop would have to prove it took reasonable care of the goods and so could not be held responsible for what occurred. If the loss or damage was through an employee's negligence, you would probably be entitled to compensation. An exclusion clause that tried to limit the firm's financial liability would be carefully examined using the 'test of reasonableness'.

Guidelines are given in the 1977 Act as to what is considered a 'reasonable' exclusion clause. For example, if you asked a joiner to make a special cupboard to hold your DVDs to your own design, and he went to some time and trouble to obtain the wood and make it, it may be considered 'reasonable' for him to want additional protection against you later deciding you did not want the item. He could do this by including a clause stating that you would still have to pay for the cupboard.

Distinction between contract, tort and criminal law

Originally in England, any disputes between buyers and sellers were settled by a judge in a court of law. The judge would make the original decision, known as a precedent, and this would apply to all future cases that had the same features. This is known as common law, or case law.

Laws can still be made this way, but the main method is now by passing Acts of Parliament. This is known as **statute law**. It is more specific than common law and defines specific terms, such as those found in the Sale of Goods Act. It also defines the actions that are a criminal offence.

- **Law of contract** – The law of contract covers agreements made between two or more people. In consumer law the contract is between the buyer and seller of goods or services. The contract does not have to be in writing. There are always certain terms that both buyer and seller have to meet. For example, all goods sold must be of satisfactory quality. So if you buy some hair straighteners and they fail to work, the seller is in **breach of contract** because the straighteners are defective (faulty). Under the law of contract, you have a claim against the seller and can ask for your money back.

- **Law of tort** – This law enables people to take action in law against people who do them a legal wrong or injure them in some way. This is mainly used when there is no contractual relationship between the two parties. The injury does not have to be a physical one. When Peter Andre sued *The People* newspaper in 2009 and won, he was awarded 'substantial damages' for false allegations about being unfaithful to Katie Price because this was damaging to his reputation. This is an example of the law of tort in action.

You may be able to sue under **civil law** if you suffered an injury. If you walked into the supermarket, slipped on the floor and broke your ankle because no warning sign had been displayed on a wet area of floor, then you may be able to claim the supermarket was negligent and sue for damages (compensation).

- **Criminal law** – A criminal is an individual who has committed an action against the interests of society. Such actions are defined in common law and statute law. In statute law they are listed as 'offences', for example, 'It is an offence to…'

The case is tried either in a magistrates' court or before a judge and jury in a crown court (or in a sheriff court in Scotland). If the defendant is found guilty, then a punishment will be given that is in proportion to the scale of the wrongdoing. If the hair straighteners you bought overheated, burnt your hand and caught fire, a prosecution could be brought by Trading Standards under the Consumer Protection Act 1987 if they found that a dangerous product was being sold (see page 352).

There are two areas where consumers are protected by criminal law:

- **defective (unsafe) products** (see Consumer Protection Act and General Product Safety Regulations 2005)

- **unfair, misleading or aggressive selling practices** (see Consumer Protection from Unfair Trading Regulations 2008).

Key terms

Breach of contract – failing to comply with one or more terms of a contract.

Tort – a wrong, injury or breach in civil law.

Civil law – concerned with righting wrongs done to individuals. Civil cases are heard in the civil courts. In civil law, the claimant is the person seeking damages against the defendant, and the remedy is usually compensation (money).

Did you know?

- When you buy goods from a shop, such as a carpet, your contract is with the retailer and not with the manufacturer. If you also buy a service, for example, you want the carpet fitted, your contract for this service depends upon whom you pay. If you pay the fitter separately, your contract for satisfactory fitting is with the fitter, not the store.

- In civil courts the case is decided 'on the balance of probability', whereas in criminal courts the case has to be proved 'beyond reasonable doubt'.

How did the law of tort help Katie Price's ex-husband?

Remember

Criminal cases are held in the **criminal courts**. In criminal law, it is the **prosecution** who is opposed to the **defendant**. The remedy is a fine or imprisonment to punish the criminal.

PLTS

Practise your independent enquirer skills by finding out as much as you can about the work of Trading Standards.

Did you know?

In 2008, Stoke-on-Trent Trading Standards seized fake GHD hair straighteners from a house. They were being sold online for half the price of genuine ones. Trading Standards found out when a consumer reported having singed hair after buying them.

Did you know?

If an item has a specific purpose then buyers do not have to say how it will be used. In **Priest v Last (1903)**, the purchaser bought a hot water bottle which burst in use and scalded his wife. The seller argued the buyer should have made the reason for purchase known. The court rejected this because hot water bottles only have one purpose.

In both these cases the supplier could be prosecuted by Trading Standards Officers, and the case would be tried in the criminal courts. The punishment would be a fine or imprisonment.

Activity: Investigate Trading Standards

Find out more about the work of Trading Standards Officers at the Trading Standards website. Use the site to find your own local Trading Standards Office and discover what it does.

1.2 Consumer protection for contracts for the sale of goods

There are two main laws that protect consumers who are buying goods. The one that applies depends upon whether you buy the item in person or not.

- The Sale of Goods Act applies if you visit the shop.

- The Consumer Protection (Distance Selling) Regulations apply if you are not physically present, for example, when you buy online or by mail order.

The main terms of these Acts, and what they mean to consumers, are summarised below.

Sale of Goods Act

Sale of Goods Act 1979 as amended by the Sale of Goods (Amendment) Act 1994, Sale and Supply of Goods Act 1994 and Sale of Goods (Amendment) Act 1995 and Supply of Goods to Consumers Regulations 2002

This states that all goods sold, whether new or second-hand, must be:

- **as described** by the seller, the package or on any display sign or in any advertisement, for example, waterproof boots must not leak

- **of satisfactory quality** in relation to the price paid, description and age of the item. The quality of the goods includes their state and condition, including appearance and finish. They should be free from minor defects, safe and durable

- **be fit for the purpose for which they are intended**, for example, walking boots should be sturdy. The goods must also be suitable for any specific purpose you made clear when you bought or ordered the goods, for example, you said you want the boots for climbing.

If these conditions are not met, the buyer can reject the goods and the seller must refund the buyer or, if reasonable, allow the buyer to opt instead for a repair or replacement. A free repair can be offered but does not have to be accepted. If it is, but is not satisfactory, the buyer still has the right to a refund. Sale goods are also covered, unless the fault was clearly obvious or pointed out at the time of sale and was the reason for the reduction.

Faulty goods can be returned by post if this is more convenient, or the customer can ask the shop to collect at its own expense. All goods posted by a supplier are at the seller's risk.

The retailer can ask for some proof of purchase, but this does not have to be a receipt. A bank or credit card statement would also suffice.

Sale of Goods Act – points to note

- The buyer's claim is against the retailer who made the sale, not the manufacturer.

- Fair wear and tear is not covered by the Act, neither is accidental damage or misuse.

- Goods cannot be rejected because of defects pointed out by the seller at the time of the sale.

- An item should be rejected within a reasonable time. Normally this is a few weeks, but it does depend upon the product and the nature of the fault.

- Defective goods must be repaired or replaced free of charge within six months of purchase or up to six years if they could reasonably be expected to last that long.

- If the buyer makes a claim within six months of purchase and the retailer rejects it, the retailer must prove the product was not faulty. If the claim is made after six months, the retailer can ask the buyer to show the fault is not due to normal wear and tear, for example, by getting an expert's report to prove this.

- If the item has been used inappropriately or more heavily than normal (for example, a tumble dryer used in a student house), then the consumer may not have a case.

- Second-hand and sales goods are covered by the Act, but it is reasonable for these not to be the same condition as new or full-price goods. Similarly, top-of-the-range goods can be expected to have a better finish and last longer than cheaper goods.

- A set of items (for example, two matching lamps) can be rejected even if only one is faulty or does not match the description.

- Self-assembly goods can be rejected if a part is missing, if there are no instructions or if these are incomprehensible.

- If the wrong number of items is delivered, the buyer can decide which to accept and which to reject, or reject them all. Accepted goods must be paid for.

Did you know?

You can only return goods that are not faulty if the retailer has a returns policy. The terms of this are up to the retailer. Most stores have a time limit for a full refund and ask for proof of purchase.

Activity: Advise Jamie

Jamie's birthday presents included a new computer game, which his sister opened before he had time to look at it, a T-shirt with his name on it and a pair of boxer shorts. He does not like any of them, but when he takes them back he is told none of them can be exchanged despite each store having a returns policy. In groups, suggest reasons why.

But do you think it's still working?

What can happen if a product is used inappropriately?

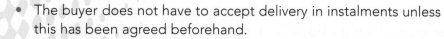

Activity: Getting your money back

Many stores insist on paying a refund using the same method as the original purchase, so if you buy using a credit card you cannot get a cash refund. Can you think why?

- The buyer does not have to accept delivery in instalments unless this has been agreed beforehand.

- Goods ordered from a sample must correspond to both the sample and the description of the item.

- If the buyer agrees the item can be repaired, this must be carried out within a reasonable time. A retailer can refuse to repair an item if this would be more expensive than replacing it. If neither a repair nor a replacement is appropriate, then a partial refund may be agreed. For example, if a coat starts to fray on the cuffs after four months and cannot be easily repaired, the seller may offer a refund that is less than the full purchase price, arguing that it has been worn all winter.

Activity: Advise Ashraf

Ashraf bought a new printer. He said it must be compatible with his laptop. He also bought an external disk drive. The next day he had an accident and was in hospital for two weeks. When he returned home, he quickly discovered the printer would not work with his laptop, and the disk drive was also faulty. When he rang the shop, the salesperson said there was nothing he could do as Ashraf should have returned them sooner. However, as a favour, he would repair the disk drive if Ashraf took it back to the shop. A month later, Ashraf is still waiting for it to be returned and still has a printer he cannot use.

In groups, identify all Ashraf's rights under the Sale of Goods Act. Decide what should have happened and what Ashraf should do now.

Consumer Protection (Distance Selling) Regulations 2000 (as amended)

Consumer Protection (Distance Selling) (Amendment) Regulations 2002 (as amended)

The Distance Selling Regulations were first passed in 2000 and amended in 2002 and 2005. They protect customers who buy goods and services sold over the Internet, by mail order, by digital television, phone or fax. The seller must:

- provide clear information to consumers on all aspects of goods being sold. This must include the name and address of the supplier, the main characteristics of the goods or services, the price and the transaction process, that is, the arrangements for payment, and details of the customer's right to withdraw from the agreement before the contract is made

- send written confirmation either by post or email after the purchase has been made

Why is there different legislation to protect consumers buying online, rather than in a shop?

Did you know?

If a seller defaults on a transaction (such as an eBay seller who never sends the goods), the customer has more protection if the goods have been bought by credit card. This is because, under the terms of the Consumer Credit Act, the credit card company is also liable providing the item cost more than £100 and less than £30,000. There are now plans to give the same protection to people who pay using a debit card.

- give customers a cooling off period of seven working days from the date goods are received or a service is requested

- give a refund if the goods are not provided by the agreed date or within 30 days from the order.

Distance Selling Regulations – points to note

- If the consumer cancels, then their money must be made available within 30 days.

- Companies are not allowed to send out unsolicited goods and services, and must offer customers an opt-out from receiving junk mail, emails and phone calls.

- Some goods and services are exempt. Consumers cannot cancel certain types of products, including perishable goods such as food and flowers, travel, and bespoke (tailor-made) items. Computer games, magazines, CDs and DVDs cannot be returned if the packaging has been opened.

- The Regulations do not apply to business-to-business transactions. The sale of financial services at a distance is covered by different Regulations.

Activity: Paying in advance

It is only lawful for an online seller to ask for payment in advance if they provide their full geographic address. Can you think why?

1.3 Consumer protection for contracts for the provision of services

Supply of Goods and Services Act

This law protects customers who have purchased a service.

Supply of Goods and Services Act 1982

These cover buyers against services such as car repairs and building work. The Act states that all services should be carried out:

- for a reasonable charge
- within a reasonable time
- with reasonable care and skill
- using satisfactory materials.

Supply of Goods and Services Act – points to note

- Any materials supplied must comply with the same requirements as those laid down in the Sale of Goods Act – for example, they should be of satisfactory quality and as described.

- If the work is done without reasonable care and skill, the buyer may be able to terminate the contract or may only be able to claim damages. It will depend upon the problem (see page 363).

- The time to be taken may be specified in the contract (see page 363). Otherwise, how reasonable it is will depend upon what is being done and whether the materials are easily available.

- The 'reasonable' price depends upon the work being carried out, but the courts can vary (change) a price they consider to be excessive. One aim of this is to thwart 'cowboy builders'.

Activity: Advise Ann

Ann wants a new kitchen. Kitchen Fit agreed to supply and fit the units, and Fred, a local plumber, agreed to do the tiling and told Ann how many tiles he would need. Ann then ordered these from RightTile. The units were a disappointment – one cupboard was missing, the doors were scratched and they did not fit properly. The tiles arrived but Fred had slightly miscalculated, so there were not enough. The rest would take another week to arrive. Ann is fed up. She wants Kitchen Fit to give her a refund and says she is not going to pay Fred. Is she right?

 BTEC **Assessment activity 13.1** **P1**

After you have advised Ann, she is very impressed with your knowledge and asks you to tell her more. Write her an email that explains how the law protects purchasers of goods and services, such as herself. **P1**

Grading tip

Make sure your explanation is clear and that you distinguish between goods and services. Identify the correct laws that apply, too.

Functional skills

Presenting information on complex subjects concisely and clearly develops your writing skills.

1.4 Negligence and consumers

Negligence takes us back to the law of tort, which you read about on page 345. If you neglect to do something, it means you do not do something you should do, or do not do it properly. Negligence in law is similar. It means either not doing something you were legally obliged to do, or doing it so carelessly that someone else suffers.

The law assumes that everyone, in the normal course of events, has a duty to avoid injuring other people. So even if a motorist is driving at only two miles per hour, if they are not concentrating and hit someone, they are negligent. Quite apart from any criminal prosecution, the person injured could take legal action in the civil courts and claim damages.

The idea of negligence has been around for a long time, but a famous case made a big difference, especially for consumers.

Remember

The tort of negligence is a breach of a legal duty to act with care.

 The snail in the bottle

In August 1928, May Donoghue was having a drink in Mellmeadow Café in Paisley. May's friend bought her an ice cream drink with ginger beer. The café owner poured some of the ginger beer over May's ice cream and left the brown, opaque bottle on the table. When her friend refilled May's glass, a partly decomposed snail fell out of the bottle. What happened next made legal history.

May was horrified. Later she complained of stomach pains and her doctor diagnosed gastroenteritis and she went to hospital. She sued the maker of the ginger beer, a Mr Stevenson, and claimed £500, partly to get back some of the money she had paid on health care (there was no NHS in 1928). She argued it was the maker's duty to ensure that snails did not get into their bottles of ginger beer.

It was only after the case reached the House of Lords that she won. One of the judges, Lord Aitkin, famously argued that people had a duty in law not to injure their neighbour. He said that a 'neighbour' is someone so closely and directly affected by someone's act, that they must think about them when doing something (or not doing something) that would affect them.

Would you want one of these in your food?

Today, this still affects all food and drink products produced in Britain. All manufacturers have a duty of care to their customers to ensure that their products are not contaminated by bacteria that cause food poisoning or by unwanted objects or foreign bodies which could hurt someone.

Manufacturers also have statutory responsibilities under the Consumer Protection Act, as you will see on page 352.

Duty, breach and damage

The law of negligence developed further in the years that followed the case of **Donoghue v Stevenson (1932)**. A three-fold test was devised to show what must be proved to succeed in a negligence action.

1. There must be a **duty of care**, as in the 'neighbour' principle. Therefore manufacturers owe a duty of care to people who use their products.

2. There must be a **breach of the duty of care**, for example, 'My daughter was playing with the doll when its arm fell off and she hurt herself on the sharp spike that was sticking out.'

3. This breach must be the direct cause of **damage** (physical, financial or emotional injury) to another and could also be foreseen, for example, anyone producing a toy with sharp spikes can reasonably expect that a child will be hurt.

Consumer Protection Act 1987

It can be difficult to prove negligence, even when someone has been hurt by a defective product. To make this easier for consumers, the Consumer Protection Act (CPA) was passed. This Act has two separate aspects, one relating to civil law and product liability, the other relating to criminal law and product safety. The Act has also been strengthened by the General Product Safety Regulations 2005.

• Product liability is the **civil** aspect. It enables someone to sue the manufacturer in the civil courts if they are hurt by a defective product.

• Product safety is the **criminal** aspect. This makes selling an unsafe product a criminal offence. This part of the CPA is enforced by Trading Standards Officers. If the producer is prosecuted and found guilty, there is a maximum fine of £5,000 and/or imprisonment of up to six months.

The Consumer Protection Act – points to note on the civil aspect of the Act

• This Act places a major responsibility on anyone producing consumer goods to ensure they are safe. 'Goods' means all types of consumer goods, as well as food.

• Someone who is injured by a product they bought could sue under the Sale of Goods Act. The CPA enables any injured person to sue, so an adult could claim on behalf of a child injured by a dangerous toy.

• If damage is caused by a defective product, then compensation can be claimed. So if you lent your hair straighteners to your friend, but they became so hot they burned her, she could sue the manufacturer. If the straighteners also caught fire and caused serious damage to the room, then in addition to claiming for the injury she could also claim compensation providing the damage caused was £275 or more.

- Court action must be taken within three years of the date of the injury and it is up to the claimant to prove that, on the balance of probability, the injury was caused by the defective product. The court would consider how the product had been sold and marketed, the instructions and any warnings that came with it, when it was supplied, and how it was used. If it was used carelessly or not according to the instructions, then any settlement could be reduced because of contributory negligence on the part of the user.

When can you claim for compensation?

 Remember

The limit of £275 is to stop silly claims for very small amounts, known as 'spurious' claims.

 Activity: Off with a bang!

Two 12-year-old brothers find a box of fireworks labelled 'for outdoor use only' in their father's shed. They set them off in one of their bedrooms. This causes extensive damage when a small fire starts, and one of the brothers is badly burned trying to extinguish the flames.

As a group, discuss what claim they would have, if any. Then decide whether this would be any different if the boys had bought the fireworks themselves from the local shop and if the outdoor use warning had been printed on a sticky label which then fell off the box.

 PLTS

Have you ever had a narrow escape when you did something you should not have done? What did you learn from it? Thinking about it can help your reflective learning.

 Activity: Recalling faulty goods

Products may be defective because of a manufacturing or design problem, or because of a faulty component. Reputable manufacturers will issue a recall notice to retailers when they discover an item is faulty and take steps to rectify the problem. This does not absolve them of liability, but is likely to reduce the number of compensation claims they may have to pay if they can show customers ignored the recall notice.

Some foreign producers may be more casual about safety, so more vigilance is needed. RAPEX is an EU scheme to get dangerous goods quickly off the shelves. Trading Standards monitor items listed on the RAPEX database so that they can check there are none on sale in their area. In 2008, the most commonly found dangerous goods were electrical goods and toys, and the main country of origin was China.

1. Find out what goods are on the RAPEX database this week by visiting the website.
2. Find out about current product recalls and the action companies are taking on the UKRecallNotice website.

 Did you know?

- If you are hurt by a product, the retailer must tell you who supplied it. Otherwise the retailer is liable. If the producer is an overseas firm, then the importer or distributor could be sued.

- A manufacturer's defence for food could be that the product had no defects when it was sold to the retailer and the contamination was introduced while it was on the shelves. In this case the retailer would be liable under the Sale of Goods Act.

Did you know?

Damages is the same as compensation, but the amount can vary. If a product is faulty, the amount normally relates to the cost of a replacement or a repair.

Consequential loss covers other losses, such as injury or damage to other property by a faulty product or other expenses, such as loss of earnings. In some cases, **additional damages** are allowed for distress, inconvenience or disappointment.

Punitive damages are awarded when a judge wants to make an example of the company.

Activity: Advise Jake

Jake buys a fish tank from Aquastuff for his lounge. He spends £500 filling it with fish at Fishstore and buys an automatic feeding system and some plants. When he is away for a week, the tank starts leaking and drenches the carpet and nearby sofa. All the fish die, which upsets him greatly. What should he claim, and from whom?

BTEC Assessment activity 13.2

Reread the tale of the snail in the bottle on page 351 and find out more about the case online (link available via Hotlinks). Then as a group, decide your answers to the following questions.

1. Why did May not sue the retailer?

2. How can an individual prove negligence?

3. Why was negligence proved in May's case?

On your own, answer the following question.

4. Identify how the law protects consumers against negligence. Use the information on pages 351–53 to help you. **P2**

Grading tip

In your answer, include the tort of negligence, and also explain how the Consumer Protection Act protects consumers.

1.5 Criminal law

You already know that manufacturers of unsafe goods can be prosecuted. Consumers also have protection from unfair, misleading or aggressive selling practices. This is covered by the following Regulations.

Consumer Protection from Unfair Trading Regulations 2008 (CPRs)

These Regulations stop traders from misleading, behaving aggressively or acting unfairly towards consumers. They prohibit any practices that deliberately set out to cause consumers to take a different decision than the one they would have made if they were dealing with an honest and fair trader. These include:

- misleading actions, such as lying about the features of a product, passing them off as another brand or advertising goods that do not exist

- misleading omissions, such as missing out important information or giving it too late to be of use

- aggressive practices that harass or coerce a consumer in some way, such as refusing to leave until a contract is signed or making threats

- specific banned practices, for example, bogus sales, falsely stating a product has limited availability and persistent cold calling.

Consumers should report a suspected offence to Trading Standards, which can take action in the civil or criminal courts. Trading Standards can apply to the civil courts for an enforcement order. Breach of the order is punishable in the criminal courts with an unlimited fine and up to two years' imprisonment.

Consumer Protection from Unfair Trading Regulations – points to note

- The CPRs apply to commercial practices that occur before, during and after a transaction. This means they also include after-sales services and the cancellation of an existing contract.

- They replaced several older laws relating to the way goods are described and sold, including the Trade Descriptions Act.

- They include business-to-business practices connected to consumers, for example, a trader supplying canned food to a supermarket must ensure its labels comply with the CPRs.

- Consumers cannot bring an action under the Act, but could use the trader's actions to end the contract and get their money back, for example, by claiming that the goods were not 'as described' or 'fit for purpose'.

Discussion point

In groups, suggest **five** types of practices you consider would be aggressive in a selling situation or would intimidate someone into buying. Then suggest **three** other misleading actions that dupe people into buying. Compare your ideas as a class.

Case study

What does it say on the tin?

Sue ensures Heinz are accurately represented.

As Labelling Legislation Manager at Heinz, Sue Semple's job is to ensure that all Heinz products (beans, soup, pasta and so on) are always accurately represented on the can.

Sue and the Regulatory Affairs team are part of the complex process at Heinz that makes sure all the legal requirements are met. These processes ensure that Heinz products are safe to eat and give you information on the label about the product.

When a new recipe is developed, for example, soup, the recipe is compiled carefully, based on key requirements. For example, is it to be low fat, low sugar, suitable for vegetarians or all three? These requirements influence the recipe and the ingredients that are used. The ingredient specifications are checked to ensure they comply with legal requirements, as well as the standards required by Heinz. Final calculations and analysis are done to ensure that any low fat or low sugar claims are absolutely accurate.

When the recipes are approved, Sue and the rest of the team pull together the information for the label. This must meet strict legal requirements and the name chosen for the product must be sufficiently precise to describe the product to consumers. This may mean that snappy marketing suggestions may be rejected in favour of a more accurate name. For example, if you buy beef and vegetable soup with chilli, you would expect it to taste of chilli and if it did, not you might be disappointed. Similarly any photos on the label must be representative of the product and not mislead the consumer.

So next time you open a Heinz can, look at the label more carefully. Now you know why it does not say 'with chilli' if it does not contain any!

Think about it!

1. You buy a can of Heinz soup in Tesco. Is your contract for the purchase with Tesco or Heinz, and what Act covers this?

2. Identify three actions Heinz takes to ensure it complies with its legal responsibilities.

3. Explain why Heinz is careful to ensure that the photographs on labels are representative of the product, and any additional claims (such as low fat or low sugar) are accurate. Refer to at least one appropriate Act in your answer.

4. Sue can overrule catchy product names suggested by marketing. Suggest why Heinz has this safeguard.

Just checking

1. Identify three key requirements under the Sale of Goods Act.
2. When do the Consumer Protection (Distance Selling) Regulations apply to a purchase?
3. What is an exclusion clause and why is it used?
4. Which Regulations protect consumers from misleading actions and omissions?

BTEC

Assessment activity 13.3

Jess has had a happy day shopping. Her purchases include a new pair of jeans and some red shoes. She also found some of her mother's favourite Dior perfume on the market, so bought it for her birthday, with a plant as well.

A week later Jess is less happy. The jeans have come apart, and the sole has come off of one shoe. The plant has died because no one watered it, and her mother has come out in a rash and says the Dior perfume smells nothing like she remembered it.

Jess's mother is also upset because her favourite dress has been ruined by the dry cleaners. There is a tear on the front and half the pretty pearl buttons are missing.

1. Jess is very upset about her jeans and shoes. What would you advise her to do and why? **P5**

2. Jess is also upset for her mother, both in relation to the perfume and the ruined dress. What action should she or her mother take? Identify and analyse the legislation that exists to protect her. **M1**

Grading tip

- For P5, remember that Jess bought the items in person.
- For M1, you will need to give more thought to the facts of each case, what the law says, and what it tells Jess or her mother to do. Remember there is separate legislation for the sale of goods and the supply of services.

2. Know the meaning of terms in a consumer contract

We all make contracts every day, although most of them are not in writing. On one night out, for example, you may 'contract' with a restaurant to provide you with food, a cinema to show you a film and a taxi firm to bring you home safely. In each case, the contract enables you to take action if something goes wrong, such as getting your money back if the cinema cannot screen the film because of a power cut.

You already know a lot about consumer rights. In this section you will see how the terms of a contract can affect them, too.

2.1 Terms of a contract

For a contract to be valid, certain basic requirements must be met.

Offer

In most contracts, the buyer must offer to buy an item from the seller. This must be a specific offer, either verbally or in writing, to buy a particular item at a stated price. It must be communicated directly to the seller. If you posted an order form to a company, the offer is not actually made until your document is received.

The retailer does not have to accept your offer, even if the goods are in the window and you offer the asking price. As long as the retailer is not discriminating against you (for example, on grounds of race or gender), there is nothing you can do if you are refused the item.

An offer does not last indefinitely. If either party dies or if there is no acceptance within a reasonable time, then the offer will lapse. The offer will also lapse if it is made subject to a particular condition which is not met. If you agree to buy a watch, but want it gift wrapped and are told this service is not available, then the offer will lapse. You can also revoke (withdraw) your offer at any time before it has been accepted.

Acceptance

If the offer is accepted, this must be communicated to the person making the offer. It may be by:

- **verbal or written statement** (for example, the company emails confirmation of your order)
- **conduct** (for example, a sales assistant wraps up the item, passes it to you and takes your money).

The acceptance must be **unqualified**. This means that it must exactly match the offer. If you offered to buy a pair of jeans for £19.99 and the sales assistant says they are really £25, then this is a **counter offer**.

Did you know?

Each person must be capable of making the contract and understand what they are doing. If someone has a mental disorder or is drunk when they make the agreement, the contract is probably invalid. If you are under 18 (a minor) there are restrictions on the type of contracts you can make.

Discussion point

The T-shirt is a bargain – Armani and only £5! At the till you are told the price is an error. The T-shirt is really £50. Can you insist on buying it at £5 or not? Read the section on 'offer' again carefully and then decide.

It is then up to you whether you offer to buy them at the new price or refuse to make a further offer.

Price (or consideration)

Here, the law in England and Wales differs from the law of Scotland. In England and Wales, a contract must involve some kind of payment or other consideration. The law is not usually interested in how much you paid. If you manage to buy a bargain, that is your good luck. Only if the price seems very inappropriate (for example, a computer for £10) might there be some concern in case undue pressure had been placed by one party to the contract upon the other party.

Express and implied terms

Some terms in a contract are express and others are implied.

Table 13.1: Express and implied terms

Express terms	Implied terms
Are specifically stated, orally or in writing They are included as a **condition** in a contract and the seller must comply, for example, a specific date for delivery The correct phrase to use is 'time is of the essence'	Are those the courts are prepared to accept are the clear, but unexpressed intentions of both parties For example, it is implied you will pay a reasonable price for an item – you cannot expect to receive it for nothing Terms can also be implied by Acts of Parliament

Did you know?

Another basic requirement is that you actually want to enter into the transaction. The legal term is '**intention to create legal relations**'. In a business agreement, such as buying something from a shop, the courts will always presume this unless it can be proved otherwise.

Remember

A **condition** in a contract is a vital term.

Obligations of the buyer

The buyer's obligations will depend upon the item or service being bought, but will usually include obligations to:

- pay the agreed price. If the buyer is being allowed credit, the terms will be specified in the contract. At what point the buyer will become the legal owner (for example, on the first or last payment) is also a term of the contract

- take delivery of the items (or collect them as arranged). After this point the buyer will be responsible for the goods and for any damage to them (think back to the frozen peas on page 343)

- make certain provisions – for example, to allow access to an area or to empty a room of furniture. As another example, if you are having a Sky Box installed, you need to provide a telephone socket nearby

- gain any necessary licences or permissions – for example, to get a licence for a rubbish skip or a licence from the council for building work to be carried out that will affect a public footpath.

Activity: Buyer obligations

In groups, suggest six passenger obligations an airline will specify in its contract. Compare your ideas and then see if you are right by visiting the Monarch website.

Discussion point

You buy a second-hand car from someone and the police arrive to tell you the car was stolen. What happens next? Discuss your ideas as a group.

Remember

- All the conditions stated in the Sale of Goods Act are implied into a sale of goods contract whether they are specified or not – for example, satisfactory quality.

- All the conditions stated in the Sale of Goods and Services Act are implied into a service contract.

Did you know?

- Many service contracts run for a fixed term, including mobile phone and broadband contracts.

- 'Force majeure' means 'greater force'. As a contractual term it specifies major situations under which the seller would not be liable for non-supply, such as a holiday being cancelled because of a hurricane or outbreak of war.

Obligations of the seller (of goods)

For the contract to be valid, a seller can only sell goods that exist and which they legally own. The contract will then include a full description of all goods to be supplied. Other obligations may include:

- packing and delivering the goods safely
- delivering by a specific date, if this is a condition of the contract
- delivering goods that correspond to the description and in the right quantity
- charging the agreed price.

Obligations of the provider of services

The contract should include a full description of the services to be provided so that it is clear what is and is not provided in the contract price. There may also be a payment schedule which shows what the service provider will do, at each stage, before payment is made. The obligations will also include:

- providing the services as stipulated
- starting and finishing the work on time
- using reasonable care and skill
- using suitable materials.

A service contract is also likely to include information on how any disputes will be settled and the rights of the buyer to terminate the contract (see page 363).

2.2 Types of contract
Standard form contracts

Many small businesses use a standard form for a contract because these are quicker, easier and cheaper than drawing up individual contracts. They contain standard clauses under several headings and specific details are entered into the blanks.

Table 13.2: Typical headings and terms in standard form contracts

Term	Meaning
Price	The amount to be paid
Payment terms	When/how payment will be made
Specification of goods and/or services	Full description, including quantities and quality
Delivery	How and when this will be made
Customer's obligations	What the customer must do
Supplier's obligations	What the supplier must do
Limitation of liability	What the supplier will not be liable for
Cancellation and refunds	Under what conditions the buyer has the right to cancel

Verbal contracts

We all make verbal contracts every day. If you buy a sandwich or a bottled drink, this is a verbal contract of sale. Most are fine for straightforward arrangements. Complex or expensive goods or services are better contracted in writing so there are fewer opportunities for arguments or misunderstandings.

One problem with verbal contracts is that people do not realise there can be a penalty for breaching them. For example, if you book a dentist's appointment or a table in a restaurant, these are both verbal contracts. If you fail to turn up in either case, you could be charged.

Did you know that when booking a table in a restaurant, you make a verbal contract?

Activity: Suggest the reason

A dentist would be more likely to charge you for breaching a verbal contract than a restaurant. Can you suggest why?

Online and mail order trading contracts

In any mail order catalogue you will find the terms and conditions that apply. Often these are in summary form at the back and will tell you to go online to get more information. The information will include details about delivery, postage and packing charges, prices, product guarantees and the returns policy.

Exclusion clauses

You learned about exclusion clauses on page 344. These are terms introduced into a contract by the seller to try to limit their liability if something goes wrong. You should remember that the Unfair Contract Terms Act prevents sellers from avoiding their liabilities under the Sale of Goods Act and the Supply of Goods and Services Act. If a written contract contains an exclusion clause, the seller must bring this to the attention of the consumer.

The Unfair Contract Terms Act also helps to protect customers. For example, a garage which accepts a car for servicing cannot limit its liability for being negligent and damaging the vehicle; neither can the travel agent who promised you a holiday in Turkey suddenly say they have the right to switch this to Spain instead. This is because, under the Act, neither would be 'reasonable'. But this does not mean that all exclusion clauses are considered unreasonable. For this reason, consumers should always check a contract carefully to identify any exclusion clauses that would apply.

Activity: Check out a contract

You can check out an example of an online/mail order contract by visiting the Great Little Trading Co. website.

PLTS

Carefully checking out any contracts you are asked to sign demonstrates your ability to be a self-manager.

Activity: Investigate extended warranties

In 2005, new legislation was passed called the Supply of Extended Warranties on Domestic Electrical Goods Order 2005. This was needed because so many consumers were being misled by retailers about extended warranties, sold to give extra protection against items like washing machines breaking down. Often they contained exclusion clauses that meant many parts that could break were not covered by the warranty.

Which?, the Consumers Association, has said that most extended warranties are not worth buying, but customers should still know their rights. Check these out by going to the *Which?* website. Then prepare a notice that would tell someone the key facts about these warranties you think they should know.

Just checking

1. What is a 'contract'?
2. You decide to buy a bar of chocolate. Does the shopkeeper have to sell it to you? Give a reason for your answer.
3. Give two obligations usually expected of a buyer.
4. Identify the Act that determines implied terms of a service contract.
5. Suggest one example of an exclusion clause that would be void and unenforceable.

Assessment activity 13.4

BTEC

In groups, obtain a consumer contract. This could be a contract:

- for a holiday (normally printed at the end of the brochure)
- to buy goods online or from a mail order catalogue (look in the catalogue or on the website)
- you have yourself, such as your mobile phone contract.

Identify all the main terms that apply, including the obligations of the buyer and the seller. Then check for any exclusion clauses.

On your own, and using the contract as your reference, write a summary for yourself about the main terms that you can use in the future. Do this by carrying out the

following tasks. Remember that you can also use the information on pages 358–60 to help you.

1. Identify the meaning and effect of the terms the contract contains for consumers. This means identifying the meaning and effect of some of the specific terms in the contract. **P3**
2. Identify how the law protects consumers against the imposition of exclusion clauses. **P4**
3. Explain the meaning and effect of terms in a consumer contract. This should build on Question 1 and look at the reason for certain terms and their intended effect. Use the information on pages 358–60 to help you answer this question. **M2**

Grading tips

- Before you answer Question 2, turn back to page 361 to refresh your memory about exclusion clauses.
- Remember that identifying and explaining are different. Identify by finding something and giving a description.
- Your explanation for Question 3 should provide further details, including the impact of unfair exclusion terms in a contract.

3. Be able to apply the law on consumer protection in a given situation

In the first section of this unit you had practice in solving various consumer problems. You have seen that there may be different situations when a buyer is unhappy and requires a remedy to put things right. The different situations and remedies available are summarised below.

3.1 Situations

The buyer wants to end the contract

You cannot just cancel a contract because you feel like it. Many contracts contain specific information about cancellation, so you need to check the terms that apply in each case. Other points to note are given below.

- If you did not make the contract in person, then under the Distance Selling Regulations you have a cooling-off period of seven days. This applies from the day after you receive the goods or agree to receive the service. Therefore, you can use this period to end the contract if you change your mind.

- If the goods arrive late, you can cancel if you stated that 'time is of the essence' (see page 359).

- If you signed a contract for a minimum term (like a mobile phone or broadband contract) you will have to pay a cancellation fee to end it prematurely. This can be expensive. After the minimum term is up, the contract will state the amount of notice that must then be given (usually a month).

- You have 45 days to end a contract for an extended warranty if you change your mind after buying it, and within that time you will get your money back.

Activity: Time is of the essence

Suggest three occasions when it would be important to state that 'time is of the essence' on a contract for the sale of goods.

Where goods are defective

If the goods are unsatisfactory and do not meet the terms of the Sale of Goods Act, the seller has breached the terms of the contract. You can therefore reject the goods, ask for a refund and end the contract. The same applies if you bought goods under the Distance Selling Regulations.

Where services are not provided

Under the terms of the Goods and Services Act, if a service is not provided by the date agreed or to an acceptable standard, then the buyer may be able to cancel the contract and could be able to claim damages.

Did you know?

- You cannot claim damages for distress or disappointment unless the aim of the contract is to provide pleasure, for example, a holiday.

- Rescission is an **equitable remedy**. Equitable remedies are alternative methods of solving a dispute where damages or compensation would not be appropriate.

Activity: Advise your sister

The photographer who took your sister's wedding photographs claims his camera was faulty so they are all out of focus. He argues the contract she signed says that he is not responsible for any problems caused by faulty equipment.

In groups, decide whether this exclusion term is reasonable or unreasonable. Then decide what your sister should do and what damages she might be able to claim. (Refer back to page 361 before you answer.)

3.2 Remedies

Rescission

Sue always wanted her own business. When she saw a local sandwich shop for sale she immediately went to chat to Martin, the owner. He told her she would make a good living from the business, just like him. What he did not tell her was that he was selling because another sandwich shop was about to open round the corner. Sue bought the business. Two weeks later the other shop opened and took most of her trade. Sue was desperate until her solicitor told her she could take action to rescind the contract.

In this situation, both parties are put back into the situation they were in before the contract existed. Sue no longer owns the sandwich shop and gets her money back, and Martin gets the shop back again.

Termination

In this case, the contract has happened and then it is ended. An example is cancelling a mobile phone contract which has been running for several months.

A contract may be terminated because of breach of contract, such as being sold faulty goods. In this case the contract did exist, and if the buyer suffered a wrong during this time then action can still be taken to remedy this. This may include claiming compensation/damages.

Alternatively a contract may be terminated by mutual agreement when there is no breach.

Damages

As you have already learned, damages can range from a basic refund to punitive damages, set at a high level as a warning to other firms.

	Sandwich	Bap or Baguette	Vienna
e & Marmite	2.40	2.60	2.45
ssalata	2.40	2.60	2.50
us	2.20	2.40	2.30
	2.20	£	30
ange Egg Mayo	2.50		
do & Onion	2.50		
Salad	2.10		
t Butter & Banana	2.40		
Salami	2.20		
s + One	3.50		
llings	3.20		
Fillings	3.60		
Prices Available			

Baguettes · 3.40
Guacamole & Crispy Bacon
Mozzarella, Tomato & Basil
Ham & Olive Pate
Cambozola & Grape
Egg Mayo & Anchovy

What action can Sue take?

Activity: Which is which?

In groups, identify which situation below equates with: a) termination and breach of contract by one party; b) termination by mutual agreement; c) termination and breach by both parties. Then discuss if either of the parties would be able to sue for damages. Compare your ideas.

Mr and Mrs Smith book a mini-break. They do not pay in advance.

1. When they arrive, they decide they do not like the location of the hotel so pack up early and leave without telling anyone.
2. When they arrive they are not happy with their room. They agree with the owner to leave a day earlier than planned.
3. Without unpacking, they walk out because their room is nothing like the photo on the website and does not even have a window.
4. During their stay the food makes them ill and Mr Smith is taken to hospital with food poisoning.

Just checking

1. You want to end a written contract. How would you know if this is possible?
2. What does 'breach of contract' mean?
3. What is consequential loss?
4. Give one example of a situation where the seller cannot object to you ending a contract.

Assessment activity 13.5

 BTEC

 P2 P5 M1 D1

This is your opportunity to put your knowledge of consumer rights to the ultimate test! Read the scenarios below and then answer the questions that follow.

Sasha is distressed. She and her husband, Baz, recently moved into their first house with their baby son Zak. It was an old property, and quite cheap, so they could afford it. They had great plans to do it up and to celebrate Zak's first birthday but all sorts of things have gone wrong. Can you help them?

Sasha's shelves

The local joiner has made a total mess of putting up some shelves. Nails are sticking out, and Baz cut his fingers so badly he had to go to hospital. This has proved serious because Baz is a musician and cannot work until his hand has healed. The joiner says there is nothing wrong with the shelves and refuses to repair them. He has also refused to refund the money they paid him.

Your task: Email Sasha to tell her what she and Baz should say to the joiner and what statutes they could quote. In addition, explain the legal action Baz could take relating to his injury.

Zak's birthday

It is Zak's first birthday. His grandparents have bought him a painted wooden farm and animals from a local toy shop. Sasha has bought a cake from the local bakery and invited three little children of her friends to a small party.

During the party, all the children play with the farm. Being toddlers, they put the animals in their mouths. To her horror, Sasha suddenly notices that they have brown paint on their mouths and tongues. She quickly puts the animals away and makes all the children wash their hands and faces.

The little group blow out the candle on Zak's cake and Sasha takes it into the kitchen to cut it into slices and put them in the party bags. She can't resist taking a bite of a slice herself. Even though it is a sponge cake, she suddenly crunches something in her mouth – and spits out part of her tooth and a small screw. In panic she puts chocolate biscuits and sweets into the party bags instead and moves the cake out of reach of the children. She also keeps the screw.

Later that night Zak is very ill with tummy ache. She also has phone calls from her friends. Their children are also ill. One is being violently sick and has had to be taken to hospital. Sasha is also in pain, with terrible toothache, and distressed that the party has been a complete disaster.

Your tasks: Sasha wants to take action about the defective farm and about the cake. You are meeting her tonight so write notes you can refer to during your conversation.

1. Your notes about the farm should focus on the statutes and common law claims that apply in this situation and what legal remedies are possible, in both civil and criminal law. When you are considering this, remember that the people who were ill were *not* the people who bought the farm. Quote a famous case where someone was ill when they used a product bought by someone else to explain to Sasha about the type of remedies available and tell Sasha what action she should take to prevent other parents buying the product in the future.

2. Your notes about the cake should include what Sasha should say when she visits the bakery. Sasha is concerned the bakery may argue she never told them she wanted the cake for a children's birthday party. Again quote a decided case and tell her the statute that applies in this situation.

3. Finally, use these examples to explain to Sasha how the legal remedies available put pressures on businesses to comply with the law.

Grading tips

- Take each problem in turn. Then refer to the legal principles you have learned and the appropriate statute where it applies.

- Remember you would normally take action under the Sale of Goods Act or the Supply of Goods and Services Act if you were the purchaser because there is a contract between you and the seller/service provider. If you are hurt by a product someone else bought, you have to do things differently.

- A legal precedent is set when a court decision made in a case becomes the rule for similar cases in the future. Identifying a relevant case gives you guidance on the outcome in the same or similar situations.

- Consider the fact that some goods have only one specific purpose – hot water bottles and biscuits are two examples.

- Look back at the WorkSpace case study to remind yourself about some of the precautions Heinz takes to ensure it complies with the law. Then think about what toy manufacturers do as well as other actions taken by food producers.

edexcel

Assignment tips

- Do not expect to remember everything you have read. Check back to the pages that summarise the statutes and the contract law you have learned.

- It is often helpful to use your common sense in matters of law. If something seems reasonable or unreasonable, it often is.

- Do not forget that consumers can be negligent, too. If this happens when they own the goods, then they cannot blame anyone else!

- Remember that the main law to think about if someone has purchased goods is the Sale of Goods Act, and for services it is the Supply of Goods and Services Act.

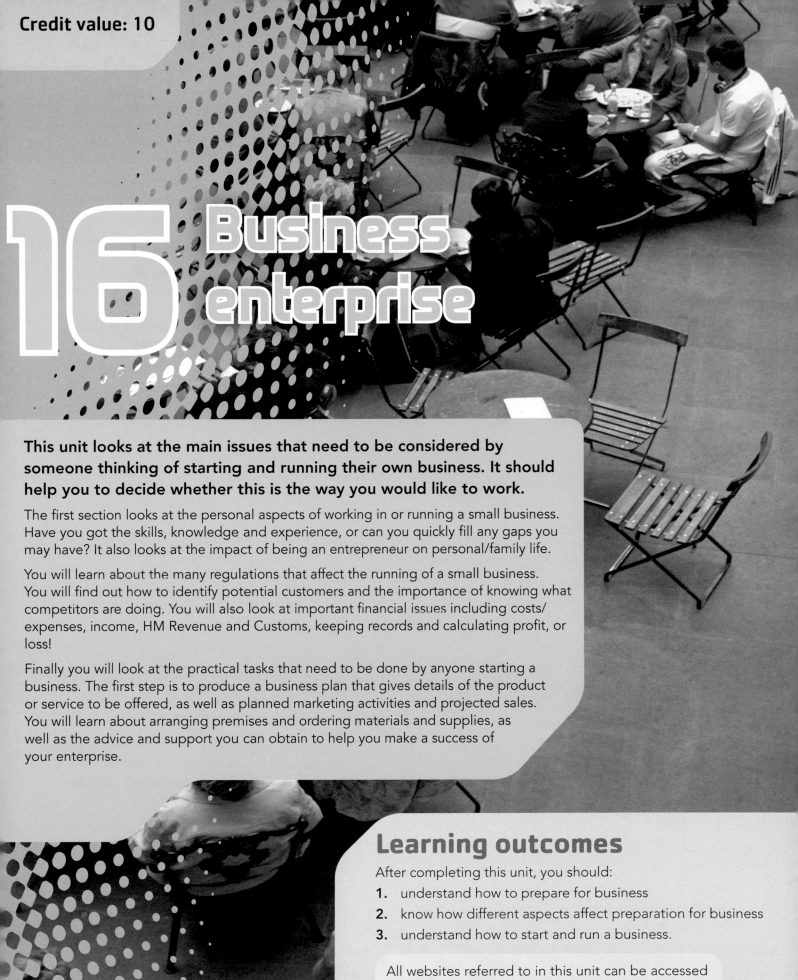

16 Business enterprise

This unit looks at the main issues that need to be considered by someone thinking of starting and running their own business. It should help you to decide whether this is the way you would like to work.

The first section looks at the personal aspects of working in or running a small business. Have you got the skills, knowledge and experience, or can you quickly fill any gaps you may have? It also looks at the impact of being an entrepreneur on personal/family life.

You will learn about the many regulations that affect the running of a small business. You will find out how to identify potential customers and the importance of knowing what competitors are doing. You will also look at important financial issues including costs/ expenses, income, HM Revenue and Customs, keeping records and calculating profit, or loss!

Finally you will look at the practical tasks that need to be done by anyone starting a business. The first step is to produce a business plan that gives details of the product or service to be offered, as well as planned marketing activities and projected sales. You will learn about arranging premises and ordering materials and supplies, as well as the advice and support you can obtain to help you make a success of your enterprise.

Learning outcomes

After completing this unit, you should:

1. understand how to prepare for business
2. know how different aspects affect preparation for business
3. understand how to start and run a business.

All websites referred to in this unit can be accessed via Hotlinks. See page ii for more information.

Assessment and grading criteria

This table shows you what you must do in order to achieve a pass, merit or distinction grade, and where you can find activities in this book to help you.

To achieve a **pass**, the evidence must show that the learner is able to:	To achieve a **merit**, the evidence must show that, in addition to the pass criteria, the learner is able to:	To achieve a **distinction** grade, the evidence must show that, in addition to the pass and merit criteria, the learner is able to:
P1 explain how knowledge of personal strengths and weaknesses can be applied to preparing for and contributing to a business **See Assessment activity 16.1, page 379**	**M1** explain, using examples, the benefits of starting a business **See Assessment activity 16.1, page 379**	**D1** evaluate the issues that need to be considered when starting a business **See Assessment activity 16.5, page 399**
P2 identify how regulations and laws for small businesses can affect preparation for business **See Assessment activity 16.2, page 386**	**M2** analyse the different aspects that will affect preparation for business **See Assessment activity 16.5, page 399**	
P3 describe how small businesses prepare to market and sell products or services **See Assessment activity 16.3, page 394**		
P4 describe the financial issues that can affect preparation for business **See Assessment activity 16.4, page 399**		
P5 outline the contents of a business plan when starting and running a business **See Assessment activity 16.6, page 410**		**D2** justify recommendations made for starting a business **See Assessment activity 16.6, page 410**
P6 explain the sources of advice and support available when preparing for business **See Assessment activity 16.6, page 410**		

How you will be assessed

To achieve this unit, you will investigate several aspects of starting a business, such as the benefits and issues that must be considered, including the legal aspects, marketing and finance. You will focus on a specific business you would like to start and run, if you had the opportunity. You will develop your ideas to create a business plan, and then evaluate this to see whether you could justify a decision to go ahead.

Nikki

I find my part-time job in a supermarket very boring, although I like dealing with the customers and making my own decisions where I can. I've always thought that I would work in a medium/large business in sales, but this unit has made me wonder if I could work for myself. My sister set up her own business six months ago. She is a trained physiotherapist and has worked for the NHS. She converted a room in her house to a treatment room and works as many hours as she wants. She enjoys herself and makes plenty of money.

Before I started this unit, I didn't know how much preparation was needed to start a business. The first section we did made me think about my own strengths and weaknesses. I think that I have what it takes to run a successful business. I like the idea of being independent and my people skills would help me to sell, but I would need help on financial aspects. It's good I now know there are several sources of advice available for small business in my own area. When I finish my studies, I'd like to get some experience working for someone else before trying to start out on my own.

Over to you!

- Do you know anyone who runs their own business? Could you talk to them to gain some background information for this unit?
- In a group, decide on a type of business which one of you could start. Then make a list of all the things you would have to spend money on before the business could open and start trading.

Think about small businesses

Your assessment for this unit is partly based on a business you would like to start in the future. You will find this easier if it is based on a business you know something about.

1. Identify businesses you know well because you have worked there or know someone there who would help you.

2. In groups, suggest ideas for small businesses. Do this by identifying the types of business that are successful in your area.

3. In groups, suggest how you could find further information about the business idea of your choice.

1. Understand how to prepare for business

1.1 Your own strengths and weaknesses

When you discuss your future career with an adviser, you probably talk about subjects you are good at and how these link to different jobs. If you enjoy working with figures, for example, you may look at accountancy as an option. What you may not discuss is the size and type of an organisation you would prefer to be in. Do you prefer jobs where you are with other people, or do you like the idea of travelling and working on your own?

This section looks at the personal skills and attitude needed to start and run a small business. It gives you an opportunity to think about your own talents and how suited you may be to this type of work.

Personal circumstances

People who opt to work in organisations have a steady income, fixed working hours, regular pay, paid holidays and payment when they are off work ill. Within reason they should also have a job that is fairly secure – in other words it is unlikely that they will be sacked or made redundant. On the other hand, self-employed people have no job security, no guaranteed income and no paid holidays or sick pay. They also usually work long hours, which means less time to spend with family and friends. For example, self-employed people have to find time to keep financial and other records, as well as paying suppliers and collecting money from customers. However, they have the freedom to choose what kind of work they do, what hours they work and are rewarded if the business is a success.

The financial aspects of running a small business have a strong effect on personal circumstances. For example, starting a business normally requires money to be **invested**, which can come from the owner's own savings, family, friends or a bank loan. Whichever way this happens, the money is an investment and there is a **risk** that, if the business gets into trouble, it cannot be repaid. In some cases the owner may lose their home. This is a worry when household payments such as mortgage repayments and grocery bills have to be met. In addition, when **start-up capital** comes from savings it may not be possible to afford family holidays and other luxury items. This is also true if the income from the business is low, particularly in the early months and years.

Did you know?

- Newspapers are delivered to newsagents at about four or five o'clock in the morning. So, to be a newsagent, you have to be prepared to get up early.

- Some small businesses grow and grow to the point where the owners become very rich. Others go out of business and the owners lose money. In between these two situations, many small businesses survive but do not make much money for the owners.

Key terms

Invest – to put money into a business with the expectation of making a profit.

Risk – danger of losing money in a business venture.

Start-up capital – amount of money needed to set up a business.

Case study: Starting to Go Ape!

Tristram Mayhew was a tank commander in the army but, after getting married, left the army as he did not want to have to keep relocating his family. He then worked for two big companies, but found this boring after the excitement of army life.

On a holiday in France he visited a forest adventure course and was very impressed. He decided to set up a similar business in Britain. He negotiated an exclusive deal with the Forestry Commission and sold a flat which his wife owned to pay for the start-up costs.

The first site was a success, but he was ambitious and expanded too quickly to the point where, if he had not been able to borrow some money from his mother, the business would have folded. After that he was more cautious, but the latest figures show him making a profit of £750,000 before interest, tax and depreciation, on a turnover of £8.3 million.

1. **What personal circumstances led Tristram to start his own business, particularly the type of business he chose? Do you think that his army background affected this?**

2. **What aspects of the business have affected his personal finances?**

3. **Find out more about Tristram's business by visiting the Go Ape website.**

Business enterprise ideas can be very varied.

Experience

Obviously it is helpful if someone planning to run a small business has had some relevant experience(s). Two types of work experiences are useful.

- **Working in a similar type of business** – such as someone setting up a domestic alarm business who has worked for an alarm company.

- **Working in a small business** – seeing how it is run on a day-to-day basis, perhaps even helping with some of the paperwork and dealing with customers.

Did you know?

- There are several terms used if a business runs out of money and ceases trading. These include 'going bankrupt', 'going bust', 'becoming insolvent', 'failing' and 'folding'.

- Most people who start small businesses admit that they made mistakes in the early days. The secret of success is to learn quickly from the mistakes so as not to repeat them. This is called learning from experience.

Key terms

Skill – ability to carry out certain tasks after training. For example, a florist would become skilled at flower arranging after training and practice.

Knowledge – information that has been learned. For example, a business owner needs to know which aspects of the law apply to them.

Ability – natural talent. For example, some people find it easy to relate to people and sell products; on the other hand some people are creative and imaginative.

Aptitude – the potential a person has to develop skills and acquire information. For example, a Premiership football club scout will watch schoolboys playing to spot youngsters who look as if they have the aptitude to develop into Premiership-class players.

Mentor – a person who gives support and confidential advice to another person. Mentors normally have a lot of experience in the type of business concerned.

What are the technical skills of a plumber?

Skills, knowledge and abilities

These terms all relate to the qualities that individuals need to successfully start and run a business. For example, someone starting a plastering business should have the **skill** to work out the price to charge for a job so that they make a reasonable profit. They would need the **knowledge** of the cost of materials to carry out this task. Finally, they would need the **ability** to communicate easily and clearly with customers to find out exactly what they want, and to agree what realistically can be done. They should also have the ability to make useful suggestions and the skills to do the job correctly.

All these personal qualities fall into two categories:

- technical skills of the trade or profession. For example a plumber needs to have the skill to make a joint in a pipe which does not leak

- business skills to start and run the operation successfully.

This section is concerned with the business skills you would need. The attributes which fall into this category are:

- being able to promote and sell the product or service effectively

- having good organisational abilities so that work is planned efficiently and customer deadlines are met

- understanding how to record and analyse financial information

- good communication and personal skills for building customer relations.

Later in this section you will have the opportunity to assess your own **aptitude** to start and run a small business (see page 379).

Areas for development or improvement

People can acquire the skills, knowledge and abilities needed to set up and run a small business in different ways.

- **Skills** can be learned by practice, possibly supported by a **mentor** and/or written information.

- **Knowledge** can be acquired in many ways, including talking to people (for example, customers, people in the same kind of business), published material and the Internet.

- **Abilities** cannot be learned, as such, but they can be hidden and need to be recognised. The simple answer is to try new things and see how you get on.

Most small business managers will say that they learned a lot by doing the job. There are three things which can assist this process.

- **Learning from experience, particularly mistakes** – This means thinking about things that go wrong to work out why they happened and then deciding how to do things differently to avoid the same problem in future.

- **Using any advice/guidance that can be found** – You will learn about the sources of advice that are available to small business owners on pages 407–9.

- **Doing an appropriate course at college.**

Suitability for self–employment or a small business

Not everyone is capable of running a small business. This should not be seen as something negative, but merely evidence that people are different and have different aptitudes. If no one wanted to work in a large organisation, there would be no hospitals or supermarkets. On page 379 you will be able to complete a questionnaire which will help you to assess your own aptitude for running a small business.

1.2 Contributing to a business

Own contribution

If you work for an employer, your contract of employment states what is expected of you. Broadly, you will be expected to contribute:

- skills, knowledge and expertise relevant to the job

- your time during working hours

- enough effort and commitment to get a job done to a certain standard and in a reasonable amount of time.

If you run your own business, the contribution you make will be over a much broader range, including the following.

- **Personal time** – For the self-employed, there are no fixed working hours. Most often say that they are rarely 'off-duty' and that the business is their life.

- **Money** – Owners often have to dig into their savings to fund the start-up of their business. In addition, businesses often take time to become established and produce a reasonable income for the owner. In the early days, the owner may have to survive on very little income.

Remember

There is a saying, 'The person who never made a mistake never made a decision.' Business people have to experiment with new ideas. If the decision goes wrong, they should work out what went wrong and try something different next time.

Discussion point

Can you think of a situation where you learned from experience? Try to think of something which is not too embarrassing so that you can discuss it with your group.

PLTS

Practise your skills as a reflective learner by discussing how you have learned from your mistakes.

Did you know?

If a small business produces and sells cakes or other foodstuffs, the owners often use their own kitchen to make the products.

Why do small business owners often have to work long hours?

- **Space** – For some types of business, separate premises are not needed and owners use part of their own home, perhaps a spare bedroom.
- **Ability** – Running a small business requires a broader range of skills than are needed if working for an employer, for example, marketing, accounting, administration, scheduling, purchasing.

Personal savings

All businesses need money to get started. This is known as start-up capital. Money might also be needed for living expenses until the business starts to make enough profit. The business owner can look at several sources of money to fund this and you will learn more about these on page 395.

Availability of time

People who run small businesses often work long and irregular hours. Even those who have a shop which opens from 9 am to 5 pm work in the evening catching up with the paperwork, such as ordering stock, paying suppliers and updating financial records.

This may mean sacrificing time spent with children or socialising with friends. However, they must be careful to build in time for relaxation and exercise to remain fit and healthy.

Impact on working and personal life

Many people start a business while they still have a full-time job. The advantage is that they still have a guaranteed income which they can use to pay household bills until the business becomes established. The disadvantage is that they have to use their evenings and weekends to start and run the business.

People who do this need to consult their family and close friends to work out how their lives will be affected by the decision to start a business.

Barriers to starting/running a successful business

Anyone who starts a business needs to be both optimistic and pessimistic at the same time. Optimism is required to have the courage to take a chance and start the business. Pessimism is needed to be realistic about the hurdles to be overcome. Typical potential barriers are:

- not enough time
- lack of both technical and business skills
- too few customers
- not enough start-up money.

Barriers should be recognised and steps taken to overcome them. For example, if shortage of time is a problem, perhaps a relative or friend could help.

Professional help

One way of overcoming barriers is to seek professional help. This means getting advice from people who know how to run a small business. There are many sources of this kind of support and you will find out more about these on page 408. Important sources include the following.

- **The Business Link network** provides support and information on all business activities, such as marketing and finance. The government finances this because businesses boost the economy by providing employment and paying taxes, as you learned in Unit 1.

- **Local enterprise agencies** provide help locally to entrepreneurs (see Unit 1, page 20).

- **High street banks** employ specialist advisers who work with entrepreneurs who need to borrow money. Obviously, the banks want to make sure that the business is profitable so that the loan and interest can be repaid.

Unfortunately, people are sometimes too proud to ask for advice because they see it as a sign of weakness.

Did you know?

- There is no definite answer to the question of how many businesses fail within a year of starting, but most people agree that the answer is at least a third fail in the first year. Restaurant business start-ups are three times as likely to fail as other types of businesses.

- The reason the recession of 2008/09 was called the credit crunch was because banks ran out of money to lend, both to house buyers and to small business owners.

Why would a mentor be a good source of advice?

1.3 Benefits of running a business

Although there are several problems and pitfalls associated with running a small business, there are also some potential benefits.

Personal objectives

There are several reasons why people want to run their own business. Most **entrepreneurs** would say there is more than one which applies to them. The main ones are:

- to make money. Some people aim to get rich, others just want to make enough to provide a reasonable standard of living. Others want to save enough to retire early

- spotting a business which is up for sale and deciding to buy it

- having a good business idea. Some entrepreneurs start businesses because they have tried to obtain a product or service and found that they could not, so they fill the gap

- a change in circumstances, such as being made redundant or inheriting money

- having the personal satisfaction of seeing the successful results of their own work

- to have more control over their own lifestyle. Some small business owners work for two to three days a week and still make a decent living

- to turn a hobby into a business

- to provide work for family members.

Key term

Entrepreneur – person who uses their own money to start a business enterprise with the aim of making a profit.

Did you know?

Sir Richard Branson's first business venture was a publication called *Student*. He quickly moved into the record business. He is now worth over a billion pounds.

Why does the richest man in the world keep on working?

Activity: Personal objectives

As individuals, think of a small business owner you know. Then, from the list of personal objectives above, pick three which you think would most apply to them. Then share your ideas as a group.

Discussion point

Bill Gates is reckoned to be the richest man in the world and Richard Branson is worth billions. Why do they keep on working? Discuss this as a group.

Business objectives

In Unit 2, you learned that setting targets or objectives can help businesses to focus on what is important and to make progress (see page 42). Examples of possible business objectives include:

- to make a profit of £30,000 in the next year
- to sell £20,000 worth of products in the next month
- to move to premises which have a cheaper rent
- to provide the highest-quality service
- to keep the stock level of consumables down to two weeks' usage.

These are just examples to illustrate a point. Each business will have its own unique set of objectives.

Profitability of the business

You learned about profitability in Unit 3, page 71. The same basic principles apply to small businesses as they do to large organisations. The main points are as follows.

- The profit is found by subtracting the total expenditure from the total income.
- The profit made can be used to pay the owners an income and for reinvestment to improve or expand the business.
- The balance between how much profit goes to the owner(s) and how much is reinvested in the business is an important issue. In the early years, some owners take as little as possible for themselves so that the business can develop and grow. This should mean that the business is more profitable in the future.
- Tax has to be paid on the profit. Exactly how it is paid depends on the legal status of the business (see page 381).
- The profit figure is probably the best way of measuring the success (or otherwise) of the business.
- If profits are low or, worse still, the business consistently makes a loss, it will eventually fail.

Other considerations

Other potential benefits of setting up and running a small business are often personal to the individual. These include:

- being able to choose their own working hours, particularly if a person's experience of previous employment has included shift work or weekend working
- choosing working hours that help with family arrangements
- feeling more in control of their lives and being less stressed
- doing a type of work they have chosen, which means that the work is enjoyable, particularly if it started as a hobby.

Activity: SMART objectives

Good objectives are SMART (see Unit 2, page 42). Identify the objectives on the left that are SMART and those that are not. Justify your choices.

Did you know?

Some entrepreneurs expand their businesses slowly by reinvesting profit rather than borrowing money from the bank. They say that they feel more in control this way.

Case study

360° Solutions: the all round solution for two entrepreneurs

Sam and Oliver were determined to be their own bosses.

Until 2003, brothers Sam and Oliver Marsden both worked for telecommunications companies. They wanted more control of their own 'destinies' and decided to resign from their jobs to set up a business. They called their enterprise 360° Solutions. In 2009, it had a turnover of £3 million and employed 11 people. Its focus is to provide state-of-the-art technology to solve clients' communications problems, particularly when employees are away from the office.

Sam and Oliver set up their business because they were fed up of working for someone else. They both had marketing/sales skills and found this invaluable in their new venture. In addition, they had an in-depth knowledge of the technology involved, such as VOIP (Voice-over Internet Protocol). Looking back they admit that they knew little about managing staff, organisational skills, finance, administration or web design. They had to pay for help in these areas but consider their expertise in selling, customer service and technical know-how are the main factors that made the business successful. They demonstrated commercial awareness by keeping costs down and focusing on selling the range of services they could provide, not just the products.

Both admit they work very hard, at least 50 hours a week, but feel it is worth it for the rewards they gain. They enjoy being independent and, in some ways, feel this gives them greater security than being dependent upon decisions made by other people, especially in a recession. Some of the statements the entrepreneurs make are:

- 'Even when I'm not at work, I find it difficult to switch off. I continually check my BlackBerry for emails.'
- 'Our biggest problem was finding funding to fulfil our early orders.'
- 'The biggest reward is when we successfully complete a customer installation and they recommend us to other people.'
  - 'We made lots of mistakes, but that is all part of the learning process.'
    - 'If you feel that you have it in you to run a business, then you must find a way to do it.'
      - 'Remaining positive is most important.'
        - 'I continue to read books relating to running a business.'
          - 'I'm always thinking of ways to improve the business.'

Think about it!

1. Suggest one advantage and one disadvantage of two people jointly starting a business, as opposed to one person doing it on their own.
2. What motivated Sam and Oliver to start a business?
3. What strengths, skills and abilities did they have that helped them start up on their own?
4. In what areas were the owners weak – and how did they overcome these problems?
5. Overall, what benefits do the brothers think they gain from working for themselves?

Just checking

1. Ali is thinking of taking over a newsagent business. How might his decision be affected by his personal circumstances?
2. Joanne is thinking of setting up a website design business. Suggest three types of experience which would be useful for her to run the business successfully.
3. What types of professional help are available to small businesses?
4. Give three benefits of running a small business as opposed to working for a large organisation.
5. Suggest three drawbacks of running a small business as opposed to working for a large organisation.

Activity: Aptitude assessment

Assess your aptitude to run your own business by deciding whether each statement is true or false. In each case, justify your answer by giving an example of your behaviour as evidence.

1. I am prepared to take a reasonable risk, even if it could lose me money.
2. I am good at finding people who can help or advise me.
3. I can take criticism and learn from it.
4. I generally feel confident and able to overcome problems.
5. Having a variable income would not bother me.
6. I can work long hours (evenings and weekends) if necessary.
7. My family and close friends would support me if I needed them.
8. I can handle money and always have enough for essentials.
9. I can usually persuade people round to my way of thinking, so I should be able to sell my product or service.
10. I am well organised and rarely or never lose things.

PLTS

Practise your skills as a reflective learner by thinking carefully before you decide on your answer to each of the statements.

Activity: Check out your ideas

Before you start Assessment activity 16.1, talk to your tutor about your suggestion for your own start-up business to make sure that your idea is both appropriate and practical.

Assessment activity 16.1

1. Using the WorkSpace case study and your answers to the aptitude assessment above, explain, with examples, why it is important for you to know about personal strengths and weaknesses when preparing to set up and run a business. **P1**
2. Thinking about the business you plan to set up, prepare and deliver a five-minute presentation explaining the benefits you expect to have from starting your planned business. Again, you may find rereading the WorkSpace case study useful to give you some ideas. **M1**

Grading tips

- To gain **P1**, you must be able to explain why entrepreneurs need to know their strengths and weaknesses. When you are doing this task, it might help if you think about what could happen if someone was not aware of their own weak areas.
- To achieve **M1**, it may help to imagine what a typical day would be like if you were running your own business, rather than working for a boss in a large organisation.

2. Know how different aspects affect preparation for business

2.1 Regulations and laws for small businesses

All businesses have to abide by the laws of the land as well as specific regulations that apply to their type of business. Although there are too many different laws and regulations to list here, this section describes the most important.

Legal status

There are several different types of business ownership (see Unit 1, pages 5–9). The most appropriate options for an entrepreneur are usually sole trader, partnership or private limited company (Ltd). Each of these has different advantages and disadvantages, which are shown in the table below. In each case, the choice affects the legal status of the business and the owner, which affects the way the business must be run.

Table 16.1: Advantages and disadvantages of types of legal status

Legal status	Advantages	Disadvantages
Sole trader	Freedom to do things the way you want to Minimal reporting to government bodies	**Unlimited liability** Can be lonely existence if work completely alone Need to have a wide range of skills (marketing, finance, and so on)
Partnership	(As for sole trader) Shared problem solving More money to invest	(As for sole trader) Risk of disagreeing on key issues One partner may not work as hard but still take 50 per cent of profit
Private limited company (Ltd)	Liability for debts limited to the amount of money invested (**limited liability**) Opportunity to attract more money from additional private shareholders Seen as a more solid enterprise by banks and customers	Additional regulations and paperwork. In some cases accounts may have to be independently audited Accounts have to be sent to Companies House as well as HM Revenue and Customs

Key terms

Unlimited liability – if a business fails, the owners can lose their personal assets, for example, their savings or houses, to pay off their debts.

Limited liability – if a business fails, the owners will only lose whatever money they have invested in the business. Their personal property is safe.

As a sole trader or a partner you will be self-employed. You will not pay income tax on a **PAYE** (pay as you earn) basis like employees. Instead you must complete a self-assessment tax return each year and then pay the income tax you owe for a year in two instalments.

The process for starting a business legally

All businesses have to inform one or more government bodies about their business at the time it is being formed, or shortly afterwards. HM Revenue and Customs (HMRC) must *always* be informed because tax is due from profits in some way or other.

- **Sole traders** must inform HMRC within three months of starting the business and have to complete an annual self-assessment tax return and pay income tax on their profit. In addition, they pay a fixed rate National Insurance contribution called Class 2 and another contribution based on their profit called Class 4. Sole traders who use their own name for their business do not need to register this, but owners who wish to trade under a different business name must also include their own name on their business information. A sole trader is personally liable for all debts incurred by the business.

- **Partnership** must follow the same procedures as sole traders, and the partners must notify HMRC of their existence. Although not compulsory, it is advisable for a Partnership Agreement to be drawn up by a solicitor. This will state the share of the profit each receives (important for tax purposes) and also what decisions both partners have to agree on. One form of partnership is where one (or more) partners invest money in the business but play no active role in day-to-day decision making and is called a '**sleeping partner**'.

Key term

PAYE – short for pay as you earn. It applies to all employed people. They receive a pay slip showing how much tax their employer has deducted from their pay.

Did you know?

- A small private limited company pays corporation tax, not income tax. This is due to be paid nine months and one day after the end of its accounting period.

- National Insurance is a form of tax that was set up originally to fund benefits such as the NHS and the State Pension. In reality, it is just another general tax such as income tax and VAT.

What is the meaning of 'sleeping partner'?

Activity: Forming a company

Read more about company formation on the Business Link website. In addition, you can learn about businesses that help you to set up companies 'off the shelf' by typing 'business incorporation UK' into a search engine. Find out what these businesses charge.

- **Limited companies** must be registered with Companies House. The documents required are a Memorandum of Association, which sets out the structure of the company, and the Articles of Association, which explain how it will operate. At least two people must set up the company by investing money in it. They are called shareholders because they each own a 'share' of the business. They are also directors and one is the company secretary. They will receive a dividend payment based on the number of shares that they hold. They will probably also work for the company as employees and receive a salary. Limited companies with an annual turnover of over a certain amount must have their statutory annual accounts audited and send a copy to Companies House. In 2009, this figure was £5.6 million. Returns detailing directorships and shareholdings also have to be submitted each year.

Remember

People who start a business have to decide which kind of legal status they want to have and notify HMRC of their existence. If things do not work out, they can change their minds later.

Activity: Companies House

Companies House regulates all limited companies in two ways. It requires the business to be registered when it starts, then it requires annual company accounts to be submitted. Find out about the information it provides on UK companies by visiting the website.

Regulations

All businesses are affected by some forms of legislation, as you saw in Unit 1 (see page 34). These can be divided into six broad categories as shown in Table 16.2.

Table 16.2: Laws and regulations applying to almost all businesses

Category	Examples
Business formations and operations and the payment of tax	Partnership Act, Companies Acts
Health and safety in the workplace	Health and Safety at Work Act, Workplace (Health, Safety and Welfare) Regulations, Health and Safety (Display Screen Equipment) Regulations
Employing staff and discrimination	Employment Act, Employment Relations Act, Working Time Regulations, Race Relations Act, Disability Discrimination Act, Sunday Trading Act
Paying staff	National Minimum Wage Act, Equal Pay Act
Information and data handling	Copyright Act, Data Protection Act
Selling goods and giving credit	Sale of Goods Act, Consumer Protection Act, Trade Descriptions Act, Consumer Credit Act, Distance Selling Regulations

Why are there special Regulations for food-handling businesses?

However, there are many more specific laws and regulations that might apply depending upon the type of activities being carried out by the business. A few examples are given below.

- All establishments that deal with food handling have to comply with food safety laws and those that apply to food labelling, weights and measures, and food handling.

- Road haulage and distribution companies have to monitor and regulate the hours their drivers spend driving and comply with laws relating to safe loads.

- Organisations that deal with large amounts of money, such as travel agents and solicitors, have to comply with money laundering legislation.

- Businesses that operate a website to sell or market their products must comply with regulations such as the E-commerce (EC Directive) Regulations and the Distance Selling Regulations.

- Many businesses have to comply with environmental legislation relating to air, water and noise pollution, the disposal of waste materials and the use of packaging (see page 394).

Activity: Red tape

Many business owners complain about the amount of legislation or 'red tape' they have to comply with. The organisation that puts pressure on the government about this and other matters is the Federation of Small Businesses. Find out more about this by visiting its website.

Activity: Environment legislation

Find out about how environmental legislation relates to businesses at the NetRegs website.

Did you know?

Most firms that employ staff must have employers' liability insurance. This protects the business against claims for injuries or health problems that might occur as a result of employment.

Licences

Licences give businesses permission to carry out various types of activity. Businesses need a licence to sell alcohol and tobacco. Licences are issued by local and national government bodies. For example, a takeaway food shop starting up may need to contact:

- the local authority if the business is located in a restricted parking zone to have permission to park a trade vehicle, or if chairs and tables are to be placed on the street outside a café

- the local fire authority for a fire certificate

- the Information Commissioner if customer details are kept or a CCTV is used.

Activity: Licences

Go to the website of your own local authority and search for 'licences' to find six types of organisation/situation which need a licence.

Did you know?

- The Licensing Act 2003 means that licences are required for premises that sell alcohol or provide entertainment. Personal licences are required for those who run these establishments.

- All documents relating to a tax return such as bank statements and receipts have to be kept for at least six years in case HMRC wants to carry out an investigation.

Formal records

All businesses have to keep records. Large organisations probably record millions of facts every day ranging from customer purchases to staff accidents. All records fall into two main categories: those required by law and those that help to run the business. Some of the more important records which need to be kept are given below.

- **Leasing arrangements** – Rather than buy large items of office equipment, premises or vehicles, businesses sometimes lease them. This means that the business does not have to find the money to buy the item outright. Instead a fixed amount is paid monthly. Sometimes maintenance is included in the leasing arrangement and this will be stated in the formal contract.

- **Tax returns** – Self-employed people complete a self-assessment tax return and send it to HMRC once a year. The form has space for allowable expenses which are deducted from the income to calculate the amount of tax due. HMRC has the right to investigate people's finances if it is unhappy with the information supplied. For this reason, many businesses employ professional accountants to complete their tax return. It is also essential that businesses keep complete, detailed and accurate records of *all* sales and purchasing transactions, including salaries paid.

Activity: VAT threshold

Check out the current VAT registration threshold by visiting the HMRC website.

- **VAT returns** – Value Added Tax (VAT) is a tax charged on most sales transactions. VAT-registered businesses can reclaim the VAT they pay on most purchase transactions. Businesses with a turnover of (currently) more than £67,000 must be VAT registered and send a VAT returns to HMRC, normally every quarter. The business can be visited at random by a VAT inspector to check the financial records and VAT account.

- **Health and safety** – All businesses with premises have to inform either the local authority or the Health and Safety Executive (HSE) area office that they exist and give the name and address of the business. If the business employs five or more people, then a formal risk assessment has to be carried out and the results recorded. Businesses of this size also have to produce a written safety policy. All businesses have to report serious accidents and incidents under the RIDDOR regulations (see Activity, right). An HSE inspector can visit any industrial premises to investigate an accident or complaint, or to carry out a random inspection. Offices and shops are visited by an environmental health officer employed by the local authority.

Activity: RIDDOR

Visit the HSE RIDDOR website to find out more about this legislation. It relates to the type of workplace accidents and incidents which have to be reported by law.

Activity: Regulations

In Unit 1, you learned that you can search on the Business Link website to find what regulations would affect you for your chosen business. Refresh your memory about this by rereading page 34 and then search the site for your current business idea.

Did you know?

- It is the responsibility of all business owners to find out which laws and regulations apply to their particular business, and obey them. Even the smallest business may need one or two licences allowing it to trade. All businesses must keep accurate and complete records and submit them as required.

- In some organisations, most, if not all, documents are scanned and stored electronically. Many standard computer packages allow businesses to store customer, supplier and financial information. As an example, find out more by visiting the Sage website.

Keeping and submitting business records

Because businesses have to collect and store several types of records, the first step is to ensure that the information is stored systematically so that it is easy to retrieve, which normally means a manual or electronic filing system. Many types of records can now be submitted online, such as tax returns, VAT returns and accident reports.

The importance of completing and keeping correct records

It is important to complete and keep correct records for legal reasons, but there are other reasons connected with the efficient running of the business, such as:

- monitoring financial performance, such as profitability and cash flow on a regular basis

- monitoring sales trends – for example, are some products selling better than others?

- checking that customers are paying their bills on time

- ensuring that the business pays its own bills on time.

Discussion point

'Small businesses need to be as free as possible to get on with their work. Rules and regulations get in the way of this.' Discuss this in your group.

Just checking

1. What is meant by the term 'legal status of a business' and what options are available to the owner of a small business?
2. Give two types of formal records that a business should keep.
3. Which government department needs information on the profit made by a business?
4. What regulations and licences might apply to a small café near you?

BTEC Assessment activity 16.2

Identify how regulations and laws for small businesses can affect preparation for business. Do this by identifying the legal status you would prefer for your own chosen business (with reasons) by researching the regulations and laws that would apply and by listing the records you would plan to keep. **P2**

Keep your work safely as it will form part of a presentation you will make relating to your preparations for business (see page 399).

Grading tips

Try to talk to entrepreneurs who have set up a business similar to the one you are planning, to find out their views about legal status and obtain more information on laws and regulations.

2.2 Marketing and sales

Marketing is involved with attracting new customers and then keeping them. In small businesses, the owner often meets customers face to face, which means that good interpersonal skills are essential.

Reaching and retaining customers

When businesses provide a personal service, such as plumbing or hairdressing, the owner is often in direct contact with the customer. The main issues in these businesses are how customers find out about the business and how they decide which business to choose from the options available.

When a business supplies a product, there are more ways of getting the product to the customer. These are sometimes referred to as **sales channels**. The main options are as follows.

- **Direct selling** – either by having a shop or visiting customers. Normally, for a shop to be successful, it has to be in a good location with plenty of passing trade. Visiting customers has the advantage of face-to-face contact, but is expensive and time-consuming.

Key term

Sales channels – ways in which businesses sell and distribute goods to customers.

- **Selling to wholesalers** – this reduces distribution costs but there is no direct contact with customers.

- **Distance selling** – using the telephone, direct mail and/or the Internet. This has the advantage of being inexpensive but there is less opportunity to interact with customers and there are several regulations about this type of selling.

Businesses could use a combination of these channels. Once a customer has made a purchase, it is important to encourage them to buy from the business again. This is where using different sales channels are useful. For example, a customer could make an initial purchase via the Internet and then be informed about new products by direct mail as well as by email newsletters.

Customer care

Customer care means looking at every aspect of the business that can affect the customer and trying to make the customers' experience as good as possible. For example:

- the product or service exactly matches customers' needs

- customers get value for money

- orders/services are delivered promptly and efficiently

- people in contact with customers are professional and friendly

- customers are kept up to date with developments

- excellent after-sales service, including advice when needed

- complaints are dealt with promptly, courteously and thoroughly.

Marketing information

Marketing was first covered in Unit 2, page 57. It relates to everything that a business does to identify and satisfy potential customers. Whereas market research (see below) mainly relates to finding out about potential customers, marketing information applies to all information relating to the market as a whole. This can include:

- the actions of competitors in the market

- the views, thoughts and actions of existing customers (Tesco runs its loyalty scheme to analyse customer spending habits)

- external research about trends in the market, such as that undertaken by Mintel or Euromonitor.

Did you know?

- In addition to having a user-friendly website, many businesses also use electronic methods to promote their products or services, such as text messaging, email or online marketing. This is known as **e-marketing**.

- Many businesses use the marketing information they obtain to carry out a SWOT analysis. This analyses the strengths, weaknesses, opportunities and threats relating to the business.

Activity: Customer care

In small groups, choose a type of business and write down all of the factors that contribute to good customer care. Then compare notes with other groups to find similarities and differences. Aim to choose a range of small businesses such as a driving school, a clothes shop, a takeaway and a newsagent to see how they compare.

Activity: Marketing mix

Turn back to Unit 2, pages 57 and 58, and refresh your memory about the **marketing mix**, particularly the four Ps.

Key term

Marketing mix – combination of decisions which a business makes about key areas which influence sales: product, price, place and promotion.

What are the benefits of a loyalty scheme for companies such as Tesco?

Key terms

Key customers – people who contribute to most of the profits of a business.

Primary research – information obtained from existing and potential customers.

Focus group – small group of people representing the range of customers a business has. They give opinions on issues related to the business.

Secondary research – information obtained from published data.

Did you know?

Many organisations recruit customer feedback groups online to answer questionnaires sent by email.

Remember

The more a business knows about its customers, the better its chances of improving profitability.

Market research

Market research is concerned with finding information about existing and potential customers. This is particularly useful when someone is planning to start a new business. The aim is to build up a profile of **key customers**. The information required will depend on the product or service being offered and may include:

- personal factors, such as age, gender, culture, occupation, income, family size, lifestyle and leisure activities
- location
- attitude to price
- the products/services they currently use
- the potential size of the market.

There are two main ways to carry out market research.

- **Primary research** is where information is obtained directly from customers. Methods include interviews, questionnaires, analysing purchase records, feedback and **focus groups**.
- **Secondary research** uses published information such as electoral rolls, Yellow Pages, newspaper reports and articles in trade journals.

Activity: Market research reports

Find out about the type of market research reports published by large organisations online by visiting the websites of Mintel and Euromonitor International.

What are the benefits of getting information direct from your customers?

Activity: Customer questionnaire

In small groups, design a short questionnaire to discover what people think about a local cinema. Then exchange it with another group. Complete and assess the other group's questionnaire and decide its effectiveness by evaluating how useful the information would be to the manager. Give feedback to each other and see if this can help you to improve the questionnaire you first designed.

Analysing and meeting customer needs

Businesses need to analyse the results of their market research to identify the needs of their key customers. This helps them to decide the best composition of the marketing mix for their particular business by asking questions focused on the four Ps, such as the following.

- Is the product or service what customers want? Could it be improved or should additional facilities or enhancements be introduced?

- Is the price right, bearing in mind our customers' expectations and our competitors? You may think that customers always want prices to be low, but this is not always true. It may be possible to increase the price and attract the same number of customers.

Did you know?

Businesses with no competitors are called monopolies. The government believes that this is not good because competition is better for the economy and consumers. The Competition Commission monitors this area and tries to prevent any one firm dominating a market. Find out more by visiting its website.

Activity: Competition

Working in small groups, choose two competing businesses you know well – for example, two mobile phone companies or two sandwich shops. Use the marketing mix four Ps to decide in which areas they compete. Then decide which is the better of the two in each area. Be prepared to justify your decision(s).

- What is the best place (or places) to reach our customers? Is it best to open a shop, sell online, use mail order or do all three?

- How do we promote our product or service? Is it best to use posters, local or national papers, specialist magazines, Yellow Pages or advertise online? Many small businesses rely mainly on word of mouth to attract customers.

Competition

Very few businesses operate without some form of competition. For that reason, businesses need to know as much as they can about their competitors and their operations, such as the following.

- How many competitors are there and where are they located?

- What are their products/services and how do they compare?

- What prices do they charge?

- What is their customer service package?

- What is their customer profile?

- What is their sales turnover?

- What is their unique selling point? (See page 392.)

Some of this information is easier to find for large organisations, which are the subject of market research reports (see page 388). Entrepreneurs competing against smaller firms may find it better to use the following methods:

- reading competitors' adverts or leaflets

- checking press reports

- issuing questionnaires

- noting comments made by a competitor's customers or sales staff

- checking out their website

- visiting the competitor as a 'customer', if possible.

Building customer relationships

All businesses aim to convert casual customers into 'regulars' who buy frequently and, hopefully, are high spenders as well. It is particularly important that these customers feel that they have a special relationship with the business.

This does not mean that all customers should not be treated well. What it does mean is giving extra special attention to loyal customers who are also high spenders, particularly those who also pay their bills promptly. This could include:

- keeping valuable customers informed of new developments

- taking them to lunch periodically

- getting to know them personally, such as finding out about their family, holidays and so on
- giving them slightly better discounts
- dealing with any complaints personally.

Cost and price of products or services

Financially, the two important features about a product or service in which a business is interested are the cost and the price.

For retailers, the cost is the amount they pay their supplier for the product plus the costs incurred in running the store. Similarly manufacturers must allow for direct and indirect costs (see Unit 3, page 68).

The main considerations when the price is set are as follows.

- The price charged must be more than the total cost, that is, the direct plus the indirect costs. The difference between the selling price and the total cost is profit.
- Some businesses, such as retailers, may just add a percentage to their purchase price to arrive at the selling price. This is known as 'mark-up'.
- Sometimes the selling price is based on value to the customer. This is the case when customers are prepared to pay a high price because of special circumstances (such as a shortage of supply) or because the item is a luxury good, such as designer clothes.
- Competition reduces prices because fierce rivals have to make sure that their prices are competitive.
- Sometimes pricing is tactical – to get customers to spend more overall.

Remember

- In most businesses 80 per cent of the income comes from 20 per cent of the customers. It is particularly important for the business to fully understand the needs of these customers.
- A major consideration in setting prices is that the business must make a profit in the long term.

Did you know?

Buying food and drinks in cinemas and at festivals and music events often costs more than in ordinary shops. This is because customers cannot buy anywhere else if they are hungry or thirsty, so the value of these items is higher than it is outside.

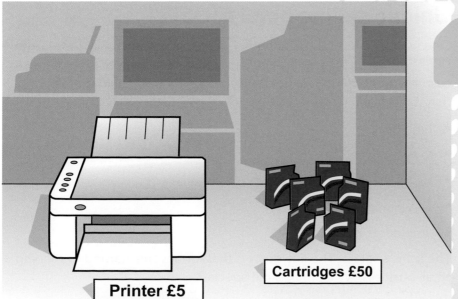

Expensive ink cartridges make up for cheap printers sold at a loss.

Cartridges £50

Printer £5

Key term

Promotions – methods of bringing a product or service to the attention of customers with the aim of persuading them to buy.

Discussion point

Write down the names of three businesses that you know. They could be local, national or multinational. Now, against each one, write down what you think their USP is. Discuss your ideas as a group to see if you agree.

Promoting products or services

While promotion is one component of the marketing mix, many firms talk about their promotional mix. The best mix will depend upon the type of product, the target market, the actions of competitors and the budget available. The main reasons for promoting the business include:

- providing information about the location of the business and its contact details

- giving information on products and services, stating their attributes and the benefits associated with buying them

- explaining about changes and improvements

- publicising special offers or events, including competitions or sales

- building up a positive image of the business.

Table 16.3: Common promotional methods used by small businesses selling locally

Advertising and brand marketing	Direct and promotional marketing
Adverts in the local press and trade/professional journals Commercial radio Billboards and posters Bus and Tube advertising New media, for example, Internet adverts, emails, text messages Cinema adverts	Sales literature, for example, leaflets, brochures, catalogues Point-of-sale materials, for example, posters, display stands, LED displays, free samples Calendars Carrier bags CDs and DVDs Clothing and bags Give-aways, for example, pens, key fobs, badges, stickers

Unique selling points (USPs)

One way of assessing the potential of a business is to ask, 'What is its USP?' The idea is that every business must have *something* that makes customers choose it over its competitors. The USP could be many things, such as:

- high quality

- lowest prices

- being the only shop of its type in the area

- very friendly staff

- ample free parking.

The list is endless. The key point is that for anyone starting or running a small business, 'What makes me special?'

Selling techniques

The most obvious selling technique is where customer and supplier meet face to face to negotiate the deal. However, sales transactions can also take place over the telephone, over the Internet, by mail order or by the customer completing a newspaper or magazine coupon. Business-to-business sales are sometimes carried out by a formal presentation followed by individual contact by a salesperson when prices and other terms are discussed. Selling techniques are covered in more detail in Unit 10 (see pages 247–48).

What skills do you need to sell an idea to the Dragons?

 Activity: Pitching

The term 'pitch' is used by some service providers, such as marketing firms, when they put a sales proposal to a client. Check out some pitches from *Dragons' Den*, where potential small business owners have five minutes to pitch their ideas to get start-up money, on YouTube. Visit YouTube or the *Dragons' Den* website and decide which pitches would tempt you to part with money and which would not.

 Functional skills

When you watch the pitches, pay attention to people's speaking skills, and how clearly and persuasively they can present their information and ideas.

Personal selling

This occurs when customer and supplier are face to face or speak on the phone to discuss the transaction. Sometimes salesmen can adopt an aggressive approach, but there are sound principles which apply to face-to-face selling.

- If you are dealing with someone from a large organisation, always ensure you are dealing with the person who has the authority to make the purchasing decision.

- If you get a 'yes' answer to your first question, this starts things off in a positive way.

 Did you know?

The Doorstep Selling Regulations protect consumers who buy in their own home by giving them a seven day cooling-off period, during which time they can change their mind without any penalty. The Regulations also apply to goods bought by telephone, mail order, fax, digital television or on the Internet.

- Try to keep eye contact during face-to-face discussions and listen carefully to what the customer has to say.

- It is often better to concentrate on the benefits of the product or service, not the features. Say, 'The iPhone is compact, easy to use and you have quick access to every feature' rather than, 'The iPhone now lets you cut, copy and paste.'

You will learn more about personal selling if you study Option Unit 10, see page 239.

Environmental issues

According to a survey by the Department for Environment, very few small businesses have taken positive steps to limit their impact on the environment. Many, too, did not know about the Environmental Protection Act, which affects most businesses, or about the Duty of Care Regulation, which applies to all businesses producing or disposing of waste.

Most did, however, recognise that there was a link between doing things properly and increased sales, as well as reduced operating costs. They also knew that bad publicity as a result of being prosecuted for breaking environmental laws was unlikely to attract more customers.

Activity: Environmental issues

Find out more about information and advice on environmental issues by visiting the NetRegs and Envirowise websites.

Remember

Most businesses carry out some type of promotional activity, even if it is only placing an entry in the Yellow Pages. Every business needs to publicise a unique selling point that makes customers prefer it to its competitors.

Just checking

1. Name three methods that businesses can use to attract the attention of potential customers.
2. What are the 'four Ps' that make up the marketing mix?
3. What steps can a business take to retain existing customers?
4. What is meant by 'USP'?
5. What investigation should a person planning to set up a business undertake in relation to potential competitors?

Assessment activity 16.3

BTEC

For your own chosen business, describe how you will prepare to market and sell your products or services. Do this by considering how you will attract and retain customers, find out about their needs, build customer relationships and promote/sell your products or services. **P3**

Keep your work safely as it will form part of your presentation (see page 399).

Grading tips

Remember that the methods you choose must be appropriate to the type of business you would like to start. You may want to begin by thinking about your USP and the needs of the customers you aim to attract.

2.3 Financial issues

The ultimate test of the success of a business is how much profit it makes. Profit is needed to give the owner sufficient income and enough money to reinvest into the business to help it prosper. If the business makes a loss for some time, it will cease trading. If the financial health of the business is watched closely, action can be taken at the first sign of trouble.

Sources of finance

All businesses need money to get them started and for running costs for the first few months. The main sources of this are given below.

- **Own savings** – Many entrepreneurs have savings from previous employment, money they have inherited or redundancy money. A major advantage of this source of money is that interest does not have to be paid. Relatives and friends can sometimes be persuaded to lend money, but they may want interest to be paid and will almost certainly want their money back at some stage.

- **Entering into a partnership** – There are then two sets of savings to use.

- **Bank overdrafts** – An overdraft is an agreement with the bank where the customer can 'overdraw' money from the current account. Interest rates are higher than those for a loan but are charged on the balance each day. They are far lower for an arranged overdraft than for one that has not been previously agreed with the bank.

- **Bank loans** – Money is borrowed for a fixed period and repayments (including interest) are paid monthly. Banks usually want some personal security, such as the owner's property, which they could claim if the business defaulted on the loan. The government has set up a Small Firms Loan Guarantee system to help businesses that cannot provide security. Often, banks will offer new businesses incentives to open an account, and provide an adviser.

- **Grants and loans** – There are several types of grants and special loans available from local, national and European governments.

What is the ultimate test for a business?

Did you know?

- Sole traders and partnerships that fail go bankrupt, but companies go into liquidation. This is because they have to be formally wound up as a legal entity.

- Loans and grants are an example of the government's attempts to encourage more people to start their own business because sometimes they grow into large organisations employing hundreds of people.

Activity: Grants and loans

Research the section on grants and loans at the Business Link website to find out what is available. Then visit the Prince's Trust website and find out about funding available to people under 30. If you are Muslim, you should note that the Prince's Trust support for new businesses complies with Shariah law.

Functional skills

Summarising the key facts about funding from different websites is good practice for reading and selecting appropriate information.

Key term

Activity: Operating costs

In a group, think of a small business which you may wish to start. Think of as many possible operating costs as you can. If you are feeling adventurous, think how much each item would cost for a month.

Can you think of different operating costs?

Start-up costs

Businesses need money to get them started – these are **start-up costs**. There are two basic costs associated with starting a new business: capital costs and start-up working capital.

Capital items are those that will last for a long time. Start-up capital is needed for items such as:

- purchase of a building or rental deposit
- equipment for production, office equipment, such as a computer or photocopier, any vehicles required
- the refitting of a building, such as installing shop display equipment or a shelf.

Start-up working capital is needed to buy stock for production and/ or resale and consumable items such as office stationery and cleaning products.

Operating expenses and income

Operating costs are the routine costs incurred to keep the business running. Typical examples include staff wages, materials for production or resale, utility bills (for example, gas, water, electricity), telephone and fax bills, rent and business rates, insurance, and any interest payable on a loan.

Income is discussed in Unit 3, page 70. It mainly comes from customers paying for goods or services.

Organising and controlling expenses and income and cash flow

This topic is covered in more depth in Unit 3 (page 72). The main points to remember are as follows.

- **Cash flow** is the measurement of how much money flows into and out of the bank account of a business.
- The critical factor is the **closing balance**, which gives the final amount of money in the bank at the end of the period. If it is negative, the business may not have enough money to pay its bills and could be in serious trouble if the situation continues for some time.
- Businesses should monitor creditors (those who owe them money) to encourage them to pay their bills promptly. This is called **credit control**.
- **Expenses** should be monitored to keep them to a minimum.
- Businesses should **forecast** cash flow to see if there may be a problem.

Financial records

Businesses must keep a record of all financial transactions. You have already learned about the legal requirements of keeping records on page 384. Businesses also keep financial records so that they can analyse them to check on their performance. This enables them to take timely action when it is needed (see Unit 3, page 91) and check that no unexpected problems are occurring, such as fraud by staff or customers.

External organisations

The main external organisation that has the right to be given detailed information about a business's finances is HM Revenue and Customs (see pages 381–82). This information is needed for tax purposes.

As you have also seen, Companies House receives a summary report of the finances of a limited company. Anyone can read these for a small fee.

Measuring financial success

The financial success of a business can be measured in several ways. The following are the most important.

- **Cash flow** – The closing bank balance is a measure of a business' ability to pay its debts on time. If it does not do this, suppliers may become wary and refuse to provide goods.

- **Costs and income** – Businesses aim to minimise costs and maximise income. You can learn more about this on page 72.

- **Profit** – This is the figure arrived at when costs are subtracted from income. Businesses normally only formally measure profit once or twice a year.

- **Assets** – These are also known as capital items. They could include buildings, equipment and furniture. The value of all of these would be taken into account when calculating a selling price if the business was sold.

- **Financial state of a business** – The overall performance of a business can be measured by producing a profit and loss account and a balance sheet. The first summarises income and expenses to produce an overall profit figure. The second shows how all the invested money has been spent. Businesses with limited liability have to provide this information.

Financial priorities

Almost all small businesses aim to make a profit, but some entrepreneurs have different priorities to others. They link to the different business aims and objectives you read about in Unit 1.

- One entrepreneur may want to earn as much as possible as quickly as possible, with the aim of retiring while still young.

Activity: Specialist services

Many specialist organisations help new businesses to form companies and provide other specialist services. Visit the Duport services website to find out the type of help that is available.

Did you know?

- When a business is sold, all of the assets have to be valued to help agree a selling price. However, there is sometimes an intangible asset called 'goodwill'. This item is made up of aspects such as a loyal group of customers, equally loyal suppliers, as well as a reputable brand name.

- Profit can be measured as a percentage of the amount of money invested in a business. This is called Return on Capital Employed (ROCE). This figure should be higher than the interest on bank savings accounts, or the owner is better off investing any savings and taking it easy.

- Many business owners say that earning money is not their main objective. They enjoy meeting challenges, being in charge of their own destiny and seeing the results of their own efforts.

What are your financial priorities?

- Another may prefer a quiet life and just want to earn enough to live comfortably.

- One may be prepared to work long hours to earn enough money to expand the business.

- Another may have no wish to be rich or powerful and just invest enough to keep the business running.

Risk

All businesses run some risk. Some of the potential problems encountered in running a business are given below.

- **Losing money** – If the business fails, money invested and more can be lost, particularly if the owner has unlimited liability or has secured personal property against a loan.

- **Security of income** – Most employed people receive a regular salary each month. People who run small businesses have no such security. A business owner's income depends on the success of the business and will vary from month to month. They are also unlikely to receive any payment if they are ill or when they take a holiday.

- **Other financial changes** –Setting up and running a small business often means that personal financial planning becomes more difficult. For example, banks often prefer proof of a guaranteed steady income for someone applying for a mortgage.

Did you know?

Under the Enterprise Act 2002, the penalties for responsible business owners who go bankrupt are less harsh than those where the owner has been negligent or reckless. To find out more, visit the Insolvency online website.

Just checking

1. Explain the meaning of the following terms: expense, income, cash flow, profit, assets.
2. What are the main risks involved in being a sole trader?
3. Identify four start-up costs for your own business idea.
4. State two ways in which you could measure your financial success.

Discussion point

Some people want to make as much money as possible. Is this a good idea? How might it affect the way they run their business? Discuss your ideas as a group.

BTEC Assessment activity 16.4

Describe the financial issues that can affect preparation for business. Do this by identifying the financial issues that relate to your own business idea. This includes identifying the likely start-up costs and sources of capital and start-up working capital, as well as how you would control the finances of the business. Remember, too, the importance of cash flow and profitability! **P4**

Keep your notes safely for your presentation below.

Grading tip

Many new entrepreneurs underestimate the amount of money they will need. When you are identifying all your planned expenditure, try to think of everything you might possibly need to spend money on.

BTEC Assessment activity 16.5

You are preparing to give a presentation to a possible sponsor for your new business, such as the Prince's Trust. Use the notes you have prepared in Assessment activities 16.2, 16.3 and 16.4 to help you prepare for this.

1. Your presentation should start with an analysis of the different aspects you need to think about in preparation for starting up your own chosen business. **M2**

   It must include:

   a) the legal status you would choose, with reasons, and the regulations and laws that would apply

   b) a marketing plan that says how you intend to promote and sell your product/service. Include ideas on how you would identify and analyse your competition

   c) how much money you would need to start the business and where the money would come from. Give reasons for your choice.

2. Complete your presentation with an evaluation of all the different issues that people need to consider when they want to start and run a business. This must include a review of their own strengths and weaknesses. **D1**

Grading tips

- An analysis means looking at each aspect that would apply to your own business and explaining the effect of each one.
- To obtain a distinction grade, forget your own views and ideas. You must now look at all the issues you have learned about so far and give clear, objective reasons why it is important that each issue is considered.

3. Understand how to start and run a business

The main focus of this section is the production of a business plan. A business plan is a comprehensive list of all the factors that need to be considered by anyone planning to start a business. It should include the product or service to be provided, type and number of customers, proposed location and forward plans. Almost all of the factors that must be considered have already been covered in this unit. The business plan brings them all together. Note that the assessment for this section requires you to produce a business plan for your chosen business idea. Make sure that you keep all your notes related to the business idea safely in a folder.

3.1 Business plan

All high street banks provide templates for a business plan with space to add information under the various headings. If you can obtain one of these, you could complete it as part of the assessment for this unit. Alternatively, a template you could use is given on page 410.

The business idea, products or services

Although your business plan is not meant to be put into practice, you should aim to make it as realistic as possible, particularly as you will also have to evaluate it to decide how likely it is that your plan would succeed.

The first step should therefore be to think of a business you would like to set up and run, and then think about the feasibility of your idea. Some ideas of how to identify a possible business include:

- identifying a shortage of goods or service, such as something you wanted but could not obtain
- thinking about small businesses you already know, such as a shop where you have worked part-time
- identifying a growing market where more and more products/services are being sold
- having a new or novel idea, like Ruth Amos' StairSteady (see Case study)
- thinking of opportunities linked to your skills, strengths and preferences, or even one of your hobbies.

One basic decision to make is whether to sell goods made by someone else, make your own product or provide a service. Generally, making products requires manufacturing equipment, which means the start-up costs are higher.

Did you know?

At the start of a business plan, you should identify your personal goals (see page 376) and also the proposed legal status (see page 381) of your business idea.

Case study: Ruth Amos

Ruth Amos designed a cheaper alternative to a stair lift as a project for her GCSE coursework. A conventional stair lift is a chair that transports people with disabilities up and down stairs. With the help and support of her tutor, whose father was disabled, Ruth designed a mechanism that provided a rod that people could hold on to which helps them to climb stairs.

Ruth used her own savings and money provided by family members to develop a prototype which she entered in the Young Engineers Competition. She won first prize and then took the idea to an engineering firm called Advanced Engineering Techniques. Reg Copeland, the director, was impressed with the idea and encouraged Ruth to patent it. The Young Engineers team also offered advice and support. In addition, they put Ruth in touch with Tanya Budd, a previous competition winner, who gave extra support.

The product was launched at the 2008 Naidex exhibition, where exhibitors demonstrate products designed to help people with disabilities. Ruth says, 'Running a business is a big responsibility. It is also a rewarding and life-changing experience. You do not want to regret it in later years that you never took the plunge.'

What do you think the unique selling points of Ruth's product are?

1. Where did the original idea come from?
2. What sources of funds did Ruth use and why would these be better than taking out a bank loan?
3. List the sources of help and advice Ruth used. Do you think it is a good idea to have several sources?
4. Find out more about Ruth's product by visiting the StairSteady website.

Activity: Choice of business type

Write a statement about deciding on the type of business you have chosen, then present it to your group. Be prepared to answer questions and to justify your ideas. Make a note of the questions you are asked as they may help you to improve your proposal. Then listen to other people and challenge their ideas if you spot any gaps or weaknesses in the ideas they present.

Remember

New businesses start with someone having a business idea that they think will attract plenty of customers and make money.

Possible customers

This was discussed on page 386. Part of the new business planning process is to build up a profile of potential key customers and try to find out how many might be persuaded to buy the products or use the services.

Customers' needs

Having identified potential customers, it is then necessary to work out the best place and time(s) to deliver the product or service. Both will depend upon the nature of the business. For example, those providing a personal service such as hairdressers and personal trainers often have to operate in the evenings and at weekends.

Sales targets

Targets or objectives are discussed on page 376 and in Unit 1, page 42. Targets are standards of performance which the business owner aims to achieve in the future. They are useful because they help the entrepreneur to focus on what needs to be achieved and work out a plan to achieve them. Sales targets could be set in terms of number sold in a month, number of new customers found or number of repeat orders.

Targets or objectives are discussed on page 376 and in Unit 1, page 42.

What will be the targets for your business?

The need for forward planning

'Forward planning' means planning for the future. This is needed because action often needs to be taken weeks or months before a planned event can happen, and sometimes additional resources are required, such as extra finance. For example, a business that wanted to expand its premises may need to get planning permission before building work can start. It may also need to borrow money to pay for the work and would have to apply to the bank for a loan. All this would take time.

3.2 Starting and running a business

There are several aspects to consider when you are planning to start a business.

The needs of a business

All businesses need resources. These include:

- premises or, at least, space in which the owner can work

- equipment, such as a cash register or computer

- raw materials or stock, if goods will be made or resold

- someone to deal with customers or process enquiries (it may be the owner or additional staff may be needed)

- basic consumable items, from carrier bags to printer paper.

The owner needs to list the resources that are required and work out the likely cost of each to calculate the start-up costs and to decide what tasks must be done in what order before the business can start trading (see page 396).

Research techniques

You have already undertaken several research techniques in this unit – for example, to find out about laws and regulations that apply to particular types of business. There are basically three methods of carrying out research.

- **Asking people** – Primary research (see also page 388). You can ask people face to face, by issuing questionnaires, or by carrying out telephone research. However, it is important to ensure that the people you choose represent your key customers so that their opinions would be representative of the prospective customers you are trying to attract.

- **Reading publications** – Secondary research (see page 388). This can include local and national newspapers, trade journals and leaflets, and brochures or catalogues produced by competitors.

- **Online** – A particular type of secondary research. This is the easiest way of obtaining information from the agencies and organisations that offer advice on business start-ups (see pages 407–9). Studying competitors' websites also provides useful information.

Did you know?

If passing trade is important, then the location of the business can be critical. It is less important if the business will mainly trade online.

Activity: Resources needed

List the resources that you would be likely to need for your proposed business and estimate the cost of each one. Remember that you may be able to save money by buying some basic items of equipment second-hand or leasing instead of buying.

Activity: Business ideas

Access the websites of two competitors, or two businesses that carry out the same activity you plan to do. Note down any ideas you can borrow or adapt for your own business.

Planning ahead and planning techniques

The importance of planning ahead was explained on page 402. Your plans state what you intend to do in the future. It is important that your plans are realistic and link to your financial targets. Planning techniques include:

Did you know?

Forgetting an arrangement or commitment in your social life or even at college may be overlooked. In business it would cost you money.

- thinking about what you want to achieve in 12 months' time, then identifying the steps and resources necessary to achieve your goals

- identifying key times in the year for your business, such as Christmas for all retailers, and then planning activities linked to this

- using a wall planner to enter key events and preparations for these

- recording all commitments and 'to do' lists in a diary or personal organiser so that nothing important is ever forgotten.

Controllable and uncontrollable aspects

Controllable aspects of a plan are those parts over which the owner can take direct action. These would include:

- reducing prices to sell off surplus stock to achieve sales targets

- hiring temporary staff to cover for staff absences due to illness

- rescheduling work to meet an urgent deadline.

Uncontrollable aspects are factors that can affect the plan over which the owner has no control. Examples include:

Key terms

Uncontrollable factors – events that can affect a business and over which it has no control.

Contingency plan – a business plan to be brought into effect if a predicted possible event occurs.

- changes in interest rates which affect loan repayments

- competitors launching a new product or service

- the local authority introducing new parking restrictions or a one-way system that reduces passing trade

- suppliers increasing their prices.

Although **uncontrollable factors** usually involve an element of surprise, effective business owners try to be prepared. They do this by asking themselves, 'What could really hurt my business?' They then decide if there are any precautions they can take to protect themselves and what action they would have to take if the situation occurred. This is known as a **contingency plan**.

Of course, some uncontrollable factors may change in a way that helps the business. Interest rates could fall or a competitor could go out of business.

Activity: Changes

Changes to traffic layouts, car parking and even road works can have a huge impact on local businesses. Identify any changes like these that have taken place in your own area, the businesses that have been affected and in which way(s).

Timing

Many markets are seasonal or have quiet times and busy times. Most new businesses like to open in time to benefit from particularly good times, such as retail stores opening in September or October in time for Christmas, and tourism-related industries in time for the summer season. Adequate time must be allowed, though, for the business owner and staff to find their feet and for the business to get established and customers to find it. It is not a wise idea to open at the height of the busy season.

> **Remember**
>
> People starting a business may want to do so in a quiet period to give them time to get used to running it.

The work that needs to be done to start and run a business

There are two main stages in planning to start and run a business.

- **The planning stage** – having the idea, researching it, preparing a business plan and obtaining finance. Until this stage is complete, the business is an idea, not a reality. Figure 16.1 shows the main steps involved in this process.

- **The preparatory stage** – putting these plans into action after finance is agreed. Most businesses plan to start trading on a certain day. Before this, several tasks must be carried out so that everything will be ready on time. These will depend upon the nature of the business, but for a small retailer they may be similar to the list shown below.

Preparatory tasks for a small shop:

- obtain premises
- agree lease/rental terms
- check water, gas, electricity connected
- paint/clean premises
- install shop fittings and fixtures
- buy and install equipment, for example, cash register
- install telephone/fax line/Internet connection
- buy stock
- appoint and train staff
- advertise opening.

Start business and monitor progress. Set targets but be flexible. Learn from experience.

If the plan is feasible, obtain and prepare premises.

Write your findings into a business plan.

Identifiy the possible sources of finance.

Work out the start-up costs.

Have an idea. Research resources and skills required.

Figure 16.1: Steps in planning a business

Your business cannot start trading until you have completed the planning and preparatory stages.

Remember

People who are starting a business need a comprehensive and detailed written plan of everything which needs to be done.

Activity: Preparation for business

Prepare your own list of jobs that would need to be done before you could start your chosen business. Then convert these into an action plan by putting them into the most appropriate order for completion and deciding how long you would need for each one.

Key term

Lead time – time period between placing an order and receiving the goods.

Next, the owner needs to convert the list into an action plan, using either a wall chart, a computer or a diary. The plan should also take into account the possibility that things could go wrong, such as stock being delivered late.

When the start date approaches, the owner needs to think about the day-to-day activities that will have to be carried out to keep the business operational, such as paying bills, monitoring sales and reordering stock or consumables.

Materials and supplies

If a business produces goods, it must regularly purchase raw materials. If goods or services are bought ready to use or sell, they are called supplies. In both instances, businesses need to find cheap and reliable sources (see Unit 3, page 73). They also need to decide how often to reorder materials and how much to order. This decision would depend on a number of factors, including:

- the storage space available
- the effect on the cash flow of paying for large quantities of goods
- possible discounts for bulk purchases
- the length of time from ordering to delivery. This is called **lead time**.

Did you know?

Materials are costs to an organisation and so purchases should be made very carefully to get the best value for money.

What does 'lead time' mean?

3.3 Advice and support

People setting up new businesses need to learn a lot of new skills very quickly. Because of this, they need advice and fortunately there are many sources.

People

People who can give you advice include professional specialists, such as business advisers who work for organisations like the Prince's Trust, and people who have experience of setting up their own business. Talking to several people will give you a wider range of views than simply talking to one or two, as they may have quite fixed views on certain aspects of business.

You will also often hear professional people talk about the benefits of **networking**. This happens when an individual builds up a number of contacts of people who have knowledge and skills which they are prepared to share. They could be other business people (though not necessarily in the same type of business), suppliers or customers, for example. Note that it is unlikely that any direct competitors will want to share their knowledge and skills with you!

Did you know?

Clever business people build up a network of contacts of people they can turn to for advice and support. You can find out about business networks in your area by entering 'business advice networks' and your town, city or area into a search engine.

Key term

Networking – developing your business contacts to learn more and increase your business opportunities.

Agencies and organisations offering advice or help

There are several agencies and organisations that offer help and/or advice to small businesses. The main ones are listed below.

- **Business Link** is a government-sponsored organisation providing a range of support facilities to business, as you have already seen. They can recommend specialist agencies as well.

- If someone approaches a **bank** for a loan to start a business, they would normally be invited to meet a specialist adviser to discuss their business plan. This person would also be available for consultation in the early days of the business.

- **Your local authority and/or local enterprise agency** is likely to offer a range of advisory services and may also offer funding for new business start-ups.

- **Solicitors and accountants** can give advice in their own specialist areas, but they may charge a fee.

- **Local Chambers of Commerce** can also give advice and could be useful for building up networks of contacts.

- **Online enterprise sites** such as BizHelp24, Startups and the Entrepreneur section of Times Online are also useful sources.

Did you know?

- If you are aged 16–30 and live in London, you may qualify for support by the Bright Ideas Trust. Visit their website.

- One trade association is the British Institute of Professional Photography. Check out the support it can offer someone setting up in business as a photographer by visiting the website.

Activity: Advice available

Go to Startups.co.uk and investigate the advice given for starting up your chosen type of business. Visit the NFEA website for the address of your local enterprise agency.

Technical support

The type of technical support and specialist advice required will depend upon the type of business. An online business will require the expertise of a web host which can advise on security aspects, and a website designer who can help to devise an appealing website and advise on how to monitor and market the site.

Specialist advice can often be obtained from a **trade association**. There is usually a membership fee to pay, but this is well worth paying because of the specialist support available. This would typically include legal advice, special insurance deals, marketing advice and so on.

Activity: Trade associations

Find out if there is a trade association or professional body for your chosen type of business by entering your type of business followed by 'trade association' or 'professional body' into a search engine. Make sure you are only accessing sites from the UK. Then explore the website to discover what services are available. Alternatively, look through the trade associations and regulatory bodies lists on the British Services website.

Why would you be better to hire a photographer who is a member of the British Institute of Professional Photography (BIPP) on a special occasion?

Education and training available

Some courses are useful for almost anyone entering business, such as IT skills and web page design, marketing or accounting. Others are specific to certain trades or industries and concentrate upon technical skills. Often the first step is to carry out a training needs analysis to find out what skills you have and what skills you need to acquire. You can find out more on the Business Link website. Other sources of information include Learndirect, your local college, any trade associations or professional bodies for a particular industry and your local Chamber of Commerce.

Did you know?

Barclays Bank, in conjunction with the NFEA, hosted a series of successful seminars in 2008/09 called 'Let's Talk Business'. These were run to help people thinking of setting up in business. Check the NFEA website to find out if these seminars, or others, are still available.

Assessment activity 16.6

P5 P6 D2

You now need to create your own business plan for your chosen business. To do this you will need to use a template. You can use one provided by any of the major banks or the one below. Discuss this with your tutor.

Template for a business plan

a) Names and address(es) of owner(s) and business name

b) Personal objectives

c) Nature of the business and USP

d) Long-term plans for the business

e) Legal status

f) Skill(s) of owner(s)

g) Description of market, types and planned number of customers

h) Analysis of competitors

i) Marketing plan – advertising

j) Financial forecasts – sales revenue, income and forecast profit/loss for first three months

k) Resources needed – start-up capital and working capital

l) Sources of finance

m) Information on suppliers

n) Start-up plans.

1. Using the business plan template, you should outline the information you would give against each heading for your own business. For example, under heading e), state what legal status you have chosen, for example, sole trader, partnership. **P5**

2. Identify and describe the sources of advice and support you would use to help you to plan your business. Say why you have chosen each one and what kind of help and support you would expect from them. **P6**

3. Prepare a presentation based on your business plan, highlighting any strengths and weaknesses you feel that it has. Give your presentation to the rest of your group and ask for questions. Make a note of the questions and use these as part of a final evaluation (strengths and weaknesses) of your plan. You should end with an objective statement as to whether or not the plan is viable, giving full reasons. **D2**

Grading tips

- When you are compiling your business plan, use the information given in this unit as a guide. Do not expect the document you produce to be as comprehensive as a business plan would need to be if you were applying for a bank loan. The aim of the assessment tasks is to allow you to demonstrate that you understand what it is like to plan to start a business.

- For the D2 task you may, in the end, decide that the plan you have produced is not going to work. This is quite acceptable, provided that you give logical reasons for this recommendation.

Assignment tips

- List all your sources of information as you go so you can refer back to them easily at any time.

- Think of your business plan as a work-in-progress and be prepared to keep amending it as you find out more about your business idea.

- New entrepreneurs often use one word when describing their new business idea – passion! Sam and Oliver Marsden (see page 378) are passionate about new technology. What are you passionate about? If you can identify this, and research it thoroughly, this will help your grade for this unit.

19 The marketing plan

Every business needs customers to be successful, so knowing how to attract customers and persuade them to make a purchase is essential. The way in which a business intends to do this is identified in its marketing and promotional plans.

The marketing plan and promotional plan are important parts of the business plan, which you will already have learned about if you have studied Unit 16 (see page 400). The marketing plan identifies the target market, which is the main group of customers to whom the business aims to sell its goods or services. The promotional plan then identifies the best ways of communicating with these customers based on the budget available.

Large businesses, such as McDonald's or Tesco, can afford to spend large sums of money on marketing, but must plan carefully to get the best results possible for this expenditure. This is also vital for any type of small business, whether this is a micro business, with ten or fewer employees, or a social enterprise (see Unit 1, page 7), where any profit or surplus, is used to fulfil its social objectives.

Any small business is very reliant on the marketing skills of the owner or manager to help it succeed. In this unit you will find out how to develop these skills. You will learn about marketing concepts, or theories, and apply these to your own business idea. You will also carry out research to identify the most appropriate marketing tactics to use. You will then prepare a marketing and promotional plan for your own business.

Learning outcomes

After completing this unit, you should:

1. understand marketing concepts used by business
2. be able to plan marketing and promotion.

All websites referred to in this unit can be accessed via Hotlinks. See page ii for more information.

Assessment and grading criteria

This table shows you what you must do in order to achieve a pass, merit or distinction grade, and where you can find activities in this book to help you.

To achieve a **pass**, the evidence must show that the learner is able to:	To achieve a **merit**, the evidence must show that, in addition to the pass criteria, the learner is able to:	To achieve a **distinction**, the evidence must show that, in addition to the pass and merit criteria, the learner is able to:
P1 assess own business proposition using marketing concepts **See Assessment activity 19.1, page 427**		
P2 justify types of promotion for a micro start-up business drawing on evidence of success or failure in the marketplace **See Assessment activity 19.1, page 427**		
P3 plan marketing for a micro start-up business that is relevant to customer needs **See Assessment activity 19.2, page 432**	**M1** explain how marketing principles have been used to develop a marketing mix for a micro start-up business **See Assessment activity 19.2, page 432**	**D1** develop a cost-effective coordinated marketing mix and promotion plan to meet the needs of a defined target market **See Assessment activity 19.4, page 438**
P4 plan a costed promotional activity for a micro start-up business that is appropriate for customer groups **See Assessment activity 19.3, page 437**	**M2** produce a cost-effective promotion plan that communicates consistent messages to prospective customers **See Assessment activity 19.3, page 437**	

How you will be assessed

To achieve this unit, you will investigate businesses that operate in your local area and nationally to gain an insight into the type of promotional activity that they carry out. Your assessment could include both practical and written tasks as well as presentations. The assessment activities in this book will help you prepare for this.

Leroy

I really looked forward to this unit because I have always enjoyed thinking of new ideas and being creative. I liked finding out about marketing when we did Unit 2 and learning about the marketing mix. Working through this unit helped me to understand more about this concept and also to learn new ones.

During this unit I was able to find out more about the different types of promotional activities used by businesses. I already knew about advertising in the local paper and on radio and TV, but I now know there are many other important ways to attract customers, such as having a catchy name and a good website. I also learned how to compare the costs of different types of promotions. This was very useful because I would like to start my own business in the future, and I was able to think about which promotional activities would be the most cost-effective.

It was also helpful to find out about the research that needs to be done to make sure that any promotions are appropriate for the target customer. I enjoyed comparing successful promotional campaigns with those that have failed, and finding out the reasons for the difference.

My favourite part of the unit was listening to a local entrepreneur who owns a successful business. She talked to our class about marketing and the promotions she has done. It was interesting to hear about her successes and also hear about what had gone wrong – and the lessons she learned as a result.

Over to you!

- Promotional messages tempt you to spend money. Can you identify three promotional messages you have noticed recently, and where you saw or heard them?
- Think of a small independent shop you visit regularly. How does it promote its activities? Are there any other methods you think it could use?
- Why do you think organisations should research and plan their marketing and promotional activities carefully?

How much does marketing affect you?

Think about the last item of clothing that you bought for yourself. Where did you buy it from? What made you pick that store or website? Did you buy on impulse, go to a favourite store or shop around on the high street or online? How influenced were you by advertising, offers, emails or other types of promotions?

Discuss your findings in small groups. What common themes can you identify? How much do you think the marketing affected what you bought and where you bought it?

1. Understand marketing concepts used by businesses

Activity: Choosing a micro business or social enterprise

Work in pairs to think of a micro business or social enterprise that you would like to start. You can use an idea from another unit, use mind mapping or check out business opportunities in your area online at BizSale for more inspiration. You will then apply the marketing concepts you learn in this unit to your chosen business idea.

1.1 Marketing concepts

Marketing concepts are the ideas and techniques used by businesses to make customers aware of their product or service and tempt them to buy. They relate to:

- how buyers decide what they buy
- what makes one product or service different from another
- how different groups of customers can be targeted according to their needs
- the marketing mix – considering the price, product, place and promotional activity that will attract customers.

Understanding these different areas means a business can identify which groups of customers it should target and how it can tempt them to buy.

Buyer decision-making process

Every time you buy something you go through a certain process, although you are probably unaware of this. You normally buy something to satisfy a need or to solve a problem. You want food when you are hungry and a winter coat to keep you warm. But how do you decide which product or service to buy, and where to buy it from? Research has identified several 'models' or theories for how people do this. One of these, the AIDA(S) model, is shown in Table 19.1.

Understanding how people come to decisions helps all businesses because they can match their marketing and promotional activities to each part of the process.

Did you know?

Businesses that are **marketing-led** put the customer first in everything they do. This is often called 'looking at the business through the customer's eyes'. It means considering how every decision could affect the customers.

Remember

If you have studied Unit 10, you will already have learned about AIDA(S) in relation to selling. The model below is a slightly different version.

Table 19.1: The AIDA(S), model of decision making

Stage 1 Attention	Quite obviously, you must be aware of a product before you can buy it. Marketing brings products and services to your attention in many ways, including adverts, posters, leaflets, store displays and striking packaging.
Stage 2 Information	Your next step is to find out if a certain item will meet your needs. To assess this you need more information. You can get this in various ways – for example, by reading the label or packaging, asking your friends, searching online, collecting brochures and/or asking sales staff.
Stage 3 Decision	You may decide to buy immediately or you may want time to think about it, particularly if the item is expensive. You may want to check what alternatives are available and where you can get the best deal. This is when excellent sales staff and good customer service can influence your decision, as well as special offers and 'extras' like free delivery or extended warranties.
Stage 4 Action	The next step is to find a shop that stocks the product you want. Delaying action can mean you run the risk that the item you want is no longer available or a special discount offer has ended. In either case, sales staff may try to convince you to still make a purchase by suggesting suitable alternatives.
Stage 5 Satisfaction	If you like the product and it meets your needs, then you may become a regular customer and/or **repeat purchaser**. If you think another product would have been better, you will probably switch brands next time. If the item was expensive, you may worry that you could have got a better deal. Customer guarantees aim to convince you that you have made the best choice, such as the John Lewis slogan 'Never knowingly undersold' and price match promises. Other firms encourage you to return with incentives such as future discounts or loyalty rewards.

Discussion point

As a group, discuss how and why your buying behaviour may vary:

a) when you are shopping with a group of friends

b) when there is a sale on at your favourite clothes store

c) when you are looking for a very expensive item

d) when you are buying a routine product, such as a can of drink.

Did you know?

- Delaying taking action to buy a popular product can be risky. In 2007/08, demand for Nintendo DS Lites, Wiis and Wii Fits was so high that high street retailers sold out. Buyers could only get one quickly if they were prepared to pay much higher prices to some online suppliers.

- Word-of-mouth recommendations are very valuable because they are a free type of marketing. Satisfied customers who tell their friends will help to increase sales and profits.

Activity: Promotions and buyer behaviour

In small groups, identify how the following promotional methods link to the AIDA(S) model of buyer behaviour:

- trailers for television programmes

- double-discount furniture sales

- leaflet/menu drops for a local takeaway

- Christmas catalogues with free delivery for immediate orders.

Key term

Repeat purchase – when a customer goes back and buys another product or service from the organisation again.

Key terms

Mass market – all the consumers in a market.

Segmentation – when a market is divided up into different sections of customers who each have their own needs.

Did you know?

A **niche market** is a narrowly defined group of customers, like left-handed people. Examples of niche market retailers are ballet shops and vinyl record stores. Satisfying the needs of a niche market can be ideal for small firms because the market is usually too small to be of interest to large organisations.

Unique selling point (USP)

A product or service has a unique selling point, or USP, when it has something that makes it distinctive from its rivals. This might be the way the product or service is offered, or a difference in the product or service itself. It is also sometimes called the unique selling proposition.

Having a USP means there is a very good reason why a customer should buy from you, such as:

- **a unique mix/product**, for example, the Apple iPhone or the facilities available at Alton Park or SNO!zone centres

- **quicker, friendlier or cheaper products or services**. Some city centre hair salons offer an express service for busy professionals; travel firms may offer a free, friendly transport service to/from the airport; pound shops focus on everything for £1.

Segmentation and targeting

Products designed for the **mass market** are aimed at all consumers, such as washing powder and chocolate. Other products target more specific markets, such as environmentally friendly washing powder and diabetic chocolate. Some retail outlets also do this, such as Long Tall Sally stores, which focus on the clothing needs of tall women. These are examples of customer **segmentation**.

Segmentation means dividing up the market into different groups of customers. Each group thinks in the same way or has similar needs. The business then targets this market in terms of the products it stocks, its facilities and its sales promotions. This enables the business to identify and meet the needs of its customers more accurately. It will do this by taking into account the needs of its target customers when it identifies its marketing mix (see page 418).

Table 19.2: Examples of segmentation in consumer markets

Segmentation by...	Which means some businesses focus on...	Example businesses
Age	Babies and toddlers, others on the teen market or older customers	Mothercare, Plum Baby and Disney Stores focus on babies and toddlers
Gender	Gender-specific items including toiletries, cosmetics, clothing and magazines	Bobbie Brown produces make-up for women
Culture	Relates to people's religion, language, customs, ethnicity and dietary habits	Halal butchers are promoted to Muslim people
Income	Luxury goods are made for high earners, whereas other businesses target those on a budget	Luxury goods businesses include Harvey Nichols, Selfridges, Gucci
Lifestyle, hobbies and interests	Lifestyle relating to the way we live. People will also spend money on their hobbies and the interests that take up their spare time	Hobbycraft targets people who like arts and crafts
Location	The local market. Often, these businesses are small. An exception is firms that trade online, for example, eBay retailers	Local businesses include greengrocers, hairdressers, sandwich shops and dog walkers

Activity: More examples of segmentation

In groups of two or three, suggest two more examples of businesses for each type of segmentation shown in Table 19.2.

Discussion point

The Garlic Farm on the Isle of Wight is the only garlic farm to have an annual Garlic Festival. The farm offers anything and everything to do with growing, cooking and eating garlic, and once a year hosts the festival to celebrate the harvest and garlic cuisine. This is one of the things that The Garlic Farm offers that is different and distinctive from similar businesses.

1. In small groups, explore The Garlic Farm website and identify its USPs.
2. Why do customers keep returning to the organisation?
3. How does The Garlic Farm promote its activities?
4. What are the benefits to the farm of holding the festival?

Functional skills

Practise your speaking and listening skills by listening to other people and also contributing relevant and useful suggestions to discussions.

Defining typical customers

Small firms that make a product or provide a specialist service must decide whether to deal direct with consumers or to deal only with other businesses. For example, a specialist car body workshop may prefer to receive referrals from local garages rather than advertise its services to the public. In other cases, a small firm may decide that it wants to attract both private and business customers. An interior designer may work on show houses and hotels, and have private clients as well.

A business that operates in a niche market or in a specific market segment will find it relatively easy to identify and define its typical customers. Most businesses, however, will have a broader mixture. For example, your centre may have learners who attend during the day and others who attend in the evening. Some may be full-time and others part-time. Their ages will vary and the needs of each group may need to be met in different ways.

One way to find out about customers is to carry out market research to create customer profiles for different groups. This can be done through issuing questionnaires, by talking to customers, by asking staff for feedback or by analysing a customer database. The aim is to find out more detailed information, such as where customers live, which papers they read, what other products they buy and their leisure interests.

Did you know?

Customer Relationship Management (CRM) software helps businesses to find out more about their customers. Website monitoring provides information on online visitors. Both enable a business to define and target its customers more easily.

Targeting groups of potential customers

The business can use the information it obtains to target groups of potential customers through its promotions and marketing activities. For example, many fast food businesses promote their activities through a leaflet drop to nearby houses. This would not be effective for a wedding photographer, who would do better attending wedding fairs or advertising in wedding supplements in the local newspaper. You will learn more about different types of promotions on pages 421–22.

Did you know?

- Asking new customers how they heard about your business helps to target future marketing and promotions more effectively.

- The new PlayStation 3 console, which was launched in September 2009, was slimmer and lighter than previous consoles. It was also cheaper and included more software than previous models. The benefits of the changes to the PlayStation's features were lower levels of noise when using the console, lower power costs as it used less electricity, and it was better looking due to its smaller size.

Activity: Your USP and target market

For your own business idea, decide on an appropriate USP and the market segment you would be targeting. Then decide how you could find out more information on your target market. Keep your notes safely.

Benefits versus features

Gillette launched its new Fusion razor with the message that it gave a more comfortable and closer shave than the Mach3. In other words, Gillette concentrated on the *benefits* of buying the Fusion, rather than the features. Marketing messages that stress the benefits attract our attention because they appeal on a personal level. We can then find out more information by reading a leaflet or looking online. This is why Gillette explains the features on its microsite, available via Hotlinks.

Using this technique, a non-iron shirt gives you more time to relax, drinking green tea provides many health benefits and using this book helps you to achieve your BTEC First qualification more easily!

Activity: Benefits to the customer

For each of the following products, create a marketing message that highlights the benefits to the customer, rather than the features.

a) Odourless garlic; b) self-cleaning windows; c) crustless bread; d) battery-operated candles; e) solar lighting that illuminates when dark; f) automatic pet feeder.

Key term

Marketing mix – the four essential elements of marketing, also known as the four Ps: product, place, price and promotion.

Remember

You first learned about the marketing mix in Unit 2. Turn back to page 58 now and refresh your memory before you continue.

Marketing mix

The **marketing mix**, also known as the four Ps, is central to the marketing activity of any business. Many businesses have failed because their marketing mix was wrong, so getting this right is crucial to your future success.

Product or service

The **product mix** is the range of products that is going to be made and/or sold by a business – getting this right is vital. The business needs to identify what its target customers need and will buy. The owner of a sandwich shop may research customer needs and find that many people would like soup, hot bacon sandwiches, pies or salads. Offering these will increase sales and profits. Offering products no one wants, or which have expensive or unnecessary features, will do the opposite.

Place or distribution

Place or distribution refers to how and when your customers will obtain the product or service. Will they want to buy online, in a shop, by phone or have all these options? Will they want to look through a brochure or catalogue? Will you visit them? This is essential for some services, such as fitting burglar alarms. Small businesses such as catteries or dog kennels can improve business if they also collect animals, rather than insisting the customer always brings in their own pet. Others can increase sales by opening longer hours than their competitors.

Many firms that sell to other businesses employ sales reps to visit potential customers to explain the product or service and obtain orders. They may 'cold call' potential customers (see page 247) or follow up customer enquiries received by phone or email.

Price

Deciding on the selling price of a product or service can be difficult for a small business. There are several reasons for this.

- The price must enable the business to make a profit (or surplus), but must also take account of competitors' prices, the type of product being sold, its image and/or quality, and the amount the customer will expect to pay. If a service is being provided, the price charged must take account of the materials used, the time taken and the appropriate hourly rate for doing the work bearing in mind the skills needed.

- Large businesses can practise **differential pricing**, when different prices are charged to different sets of customers (for example, rail fares for first class, standard and student travellers). This is harder for a small firm as all customers will expect to be charged at the same rate.

- Most small businesses choose a cost-plus pricing strategy, but this is not always the wisest choice, especially for luxury goods such as handmade jewellery. Other alternatives are shown in Table 19.3.

Key term

Product mix – the range or variety of products made or sold by a business.

Did you know?

- Many makeover television programmes focus on improving businesses by reviewing their product range. Mary Portas 'Queen of Shops' reviewed the stock at retail shops, and Gordon Ramsey changed the menus of many small restaurants in *Ramsay's Kitchen Nightmares*.

- A good location is crucial for businesses that depend upon passing trade, and specialist businesses, like estate agents, are often grouped close together to attract customers. Changes to the road layout or the closure of a nearby car park can have a devastating effect on trade.

Did you know?

A **loss leader** is an item priced below cost price to attract people into a store.

Key term

Differential pricing – charging different prices to different customer groups.

Did you know?

Most small businesses have to pay more for their supplies than large firms because they cannot buy in bulk, so cannot compete on price. They are therefore wiser choosing a different USP, such as personal service.

Pricing strategy	How it is used
Price skimming	Pricing a product as high as possible in order to 'skim' off the profits. This is only appropriate if the product is special or unique in some way or in short supply
Cost-plus	Adding a percentage to the cost of making a product or buying an item for reselling to cover overheads and make a profit
Price penetration	Having a low price in order to enter the market and build up customer loyalty. Once loyalty is established, the price increases
Competitive pricing	When the price reflects what the competition are doing and the product or service is priced competitively
Psychological pricing	Prices such as £1.99 seem psychologically cheaper than £2.00, even though there is only 1p difference
Predatory pricing	When the price is set in a way to deliberately damage competitors. This may result in a 'price war'

Activity: What method to use?

In groups, decide what method(s) of pricing each of the following small businesses should use. Then compare your ideas.

a) A nail bar

b) A shop that makes cakes to order for special occasions

c) A card and gift shop

d) A taxi firm.

> I only suggested collecting them because I thought you could drive

Key term

Promotional mix – the mix of promotional methods a business chooses to use to attract customers.

Promotion

Promotion is that part of the marketing mix that makes customers aware of the product and includes advertising, personal selling, sales promotions and publicity campaigns. You will learn more about this later in this unit. However, it is worth noting now that getting the **promotional mix** right is very important, otherwise a business will waste money trying to attract customers because it is using the wrong methods.

Other important aspects of the marketing mix

There are three other important aspects to remember when you are considering the marketing mix for your own business.

- **The marketing mix must be designed to meet customers' needs** – This means thinking about each aspect from the customer's point of view. What products (or services) do your target customers want to buy? Where will they want to buy them? What price will they expect to pay? What are the best ways to bring your business to their attention?

- **All aspects of the marketing mix must be coordinated** – Jack wants to provide luxury transport for business VIPs. Dev focuses on taking family groups to the airport. Their target customers are very different, and so is the marketing mix of each one. One buys a Mercedes and wears a uniform; the other has a people carrier. One charges a higher price because he knows he must allow plenty of time to meet his customers' needs. The other checks the rate of rival firms to make sure he is competitive. One gives out cards to travel agents and advertises in the local newspaper, whereas the other promotes the business on a website and through a network of business contacts.

You do not win a prize for guessing which person has which marketing mix! The point is that each person should be successful because they have considered their target customer and this has affected every aspect of their marketing mix.

- **Importance of costing a marketing mix** – Some marketing methods are more expensive than others. Employing sales reps, holding a large stock of products or locating in a popular shopping mall are all expensive decisions that must be considered carefully in relation to their potential benefits. The price of promotional methods can also vary hugely, as you will learn on page 422.

Activity: The good, the bad and the...?

1. The Oldest Sweet Shop in England is in North Yorkshire. It opened in 1827 and is still very successful, selling a huge range of sweets, toffees and chocolates. Investigate its marketing mix by checking out its website. In groups, identify how it has coordinated the four Ps of product, place, price and promotion to stay successful.

2. As a class, identify two local businesses that are successful and two that are not (or that have had to close down). Divide into groups to investigate each one in more detail. Your task is to find out how its marketing mix contributes or contributed to its success or failure. Then present your findings to the rest of your class.

Activity: Your marketing mix

For your own business idea, start to consider the marketing mix that would be most appropriate for you to meet the needs of your target customer. Make notes and keep them safe.

1.2 Types of promotion

All businesses are regularly involved in promotional activities to launch new products or services and to make sure that customers do not forget about their existing ones.

There are many types of promotion. The methods that are the most appropriate and cost-effective for a business will depend upon its target customer, the type of product or service it is supplying and the other factors in its marketing mix.

Advertising

Advertising is one method of communicating information to potential customers. Where the advert appears, and its content, will depend upon the type of product or service, the target customer, the cost of using that type of **media** and other aspects of the marketing mix.

Did you know?

Adverts are written to persuade or inform, though some do both. A persuasive advert sells an image, whereas an informational advert gives the facts. Try to find examples of both to see the difference.

Key term

Media – methods of communicating with the public either offline (for example, newspapers and TV) or online (for example, Internet and text messages).

Did you know?

- The best night to advertise in a local newspaper is often on the day that job vacancies appear because sales are higher.

- P&O Ferries have run many successful campaigns using local radio to encourage people to travel across to France for special occasions.

- **Newspapers** – There is a huge variety of newspapers, from local regional papers, such as the *Daily Echo* in Southampton, to national newspapers such as *The Times*, the *Sun* or the *Independent*. Businesses should only advertise in a newspaper that is read by their target customers.

- **Radio** – This is a popular method of advertising. The costs vary depending on the type of radio station and the area to which it broadcasts. Some radio stations operate as not-for-profit organisations for the local community; those run as commercial enterprises are likely to charge more for advertising.

Activity: The Park radio station

The Park is a community radio station that broadcasts in the New Forest area. It advertises commercial and not-for-profit organisations during its broadcasts and via its website.

1. Find out what community radio stations are in your local area.
2. Can you think of any campaigns you have heard on your local radio stations? How successful do you think they were?

- **Television** – The cost of this type of advertising used to be very expensive but has fallen as more specialist channels come on air. Aspects that affect the cost include: the channel that is chosen, the target audience, the size of the audience, the length of the advert and the time of day or year. At the time of writing, one of the most expensive advertising slots was during *The X Factor* final when a 30-second ad cost as much as £250,000.

- **Cinema** – There are two major cinema advertising companies in the UK: Digital Cinema Media and Pearl & Dean. Each arranges for advertising material to be shown in UK cinemas.

Activity: Cinema advertising

Find out more about Digital Cinema Media, Pearl & Dean, and the role that they play in your local cinema by visiting their websites. On your next trip to the cinema, note the type of local businesses that advertise there. Decide whom the adverts are aimed at and why they are showing with that particular film.

- **Magazines** – There are more than 2,800 different consumer magazines in the UK. They are targeted by age, gender, interests and location – such as *Seventeen*, *Men's Health*, *Amateur Gardening* and *Solent Life*. They all have different prices for advertising and a different audience that they are trying to attract.

- **Outdoor** – Outdoor advertising can take many different forms including billboards, bus shelter adverts, posters in train and Tube stations and on ferries.

- **Flyers** – Paper-based advertising such as leaflets or booklets can be sent to specific targeted customers or given out with other information, such as free newspapers delivered through your door.

- **Internet** – Many people now buy goods and services online. In 2009, spending on online marketing was greater than on offline media for the first time ever. You will learn more about this if you study Unit 12 Business online.

Personal selling

If you are studying Unit 10 Personal selling in business, you will know that **personal selling** is the most effective promotional method for some products. Customers buying an expensive or complex item such as a car or a computer usually want to discuss their options before making a decision. If you are buying a new outfit or a special present you may have a favourite store where you can chat to an assistant. Personal selling is also a feature of markets, trade fairs and exhibitions.

Promotional activities

There are many different **promotional activities** that businesses carry out to raise awareness of their product or campaign. They include competitions, money-off coupons, free gifts with purchase, tasting sessions, demonstrations and fundraising activities.

Activity: Promotional activities

In groups, write down some promotional activities you have seen recently. Include the name of the business and a brief description of the activity. Organise your information according to whether these activities were competitions, money-off coupons, free gifts, tasting sessions, demonstrations, fundraisers or any other type.

1. Which promotional activities are the most popular?
2. Which promotional activities are the least popular?
3. Can you think why these activities are most/least popular?
4. Which types of business use the most promotional activities?

Direct marketing and direct mail

Direct marketing is when a business communicates its promotional message direct to the potential customer by mail, email, text message or telephone. **Direct mail** is when organisations send out information to customers about their latest products or offers, often with a brochure or leaflet enclosed. Many charity appeals are promoted this way.

Catalogue and Internet shopping

Traditionally, catalogue shopping was the main method by which customers could buy goods without leaving home. They looked through a catalogue, decided what they wanted to buy and placed their order. You can see the range available today at the British Catalogues website.

Key terms

Personal selling – when a product or service is sold to a customer through personal contact, usually face to face.

Promotional activities – activities that make customers aware of a product or service, or give them an incentive to buy.

Did you know?

- Online marketing methods include emails, SMS or text messages, podcasts, viral marketing (see page 58) and Internet adverts, as well as search engine optimisation (SEO) which focuses on ensuring a website is ranked highly by search engines such as Google.

- Many charities carry out promotional activities, such as walks, races, cycle rides and overseas treks, to raise awareness and money at the same time. Find out more at the Rocket Charity website.

PLTS

Practise your creative thinking skills by suggesting some different promotional activities which charities could carry out.

Did you know?

Most direct mail is unsolicited (not asked for) and is often called **junk mail**. Businesses often exchange databases, so customers who show an interest in one product or charitable cause then receive similar mail shots.

Today these businesses offer customers the option to buy online as well. So, too, do many high street stores and other businesses involved in online retailing. eBay and Amazon Marketplace enable small firms to sell goods online without needing to have their own website.

Sponsorship

Commercial sponsorship mainly concentrates on sports, the arts and TV programmes. Simply saying 'The Barclays Premier League' or the '2010 Virgin London Marathon' immediately promotes the sponsor's name. Both sports teams and sports personalities attract sponsors. Tennis player Andy Murray has several sponsors, and some football teams have many more. The benefit for the team or player is the additional money; the benefit for the business is the additional publicity they obtain.

Sponsorship can also help small firms as it is a relatively cheap way of promoting the name and enhancing the business profile. 360° Solutions, which was featured in Unit 16 Business enterprise (see page 378), sponsors Draycott and Hanbury cricket club. Sam Marsden, one of the owners, says this has several benefits. Everyone connected to the club tells them about local business opportunities, they have gained additional customers, and the business is now highly regarded in the community. Which is very good value for the £300 they paid!

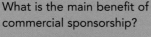
What is the main benefit of commercial sponsorship?

Activity: Sponsorship deals

Find out who sponsors your favourite sport team or television programme.

1. How much do you think the sponsorship deal increases awareness of the business?

2. What are the advantages and disadvantages of using sponsorship in the example you have chosen?

Compare your ideas as a group.

Public relations

The aim of public relations (or PR) is to form good relationships with the outside world. This includes making contacts to gain free publicity, so it is an important promotional activity for all businesses. Sometimes it involves getting a reporter to write about the firm or its products and print the information in an article in a newspaper or magazine.

An alternative method is to plan a special event, write a **press release** that describes this and send it to the press in advance. For a small firm, this normally means the local paper. If the event is newsworthy, such as when Richard Branson dressed up as a Virgin bride, a photographer and journalist will cover it and obtain more details.

Large organisations, political parties and celebrities sometimes hold a **press conference** to make an announcement or give an explanation to the media. You may have seen these on television and seen the press asking questions, sometimes quite intrusively.

Networking not only enables entrepreneurs to make contacts, it also enables them to gain support and advice, to share and exchange information and to make friends as well. Professional bodies, trade associations, the Chambers of Commerce and the Federation of Small Businesses all provide networking information and contacts as well as many other regional and local groups. Online options are also available including LinkedIn, a networking site similar to Facebook, but designed specifically to make business contacts.

Cost-effectiveness of method and plan

Whichever methods of promotion are used by an organisation, they must be cost-effective. This means that they obtain the best results as cheaply as possible. Measuring outcomes as part of the marketing plan means that the business can tell if the activity is successful or not. You will learn more about this in the next section.

Activity: Investigate PR and promotions by your centre

Interview a senior manager at your centre to find out their thoughts on public relations and ways that they might obtain free publicity. Also find out what other promotional methods they use that they consider to be cost-effective.

1.3 Evidence of success or failure in the marketplace

You should now have some ideas about why some marketing campaigns are successful and others are not. The case studies of Divine Chocolate and Glasses On Spec should help you to learn more about this.

Key terms

Press release – a prepared statement released to the media to let people know about plans, events or newsworthy changes.

Press conference – a meeting to which representatives from the media are invited to learn about a new product or other development.

Networking – business networking is building relationships with other business people with the aim of helping each other and promoting each other's businesses.

Did you know?

- PR people also have the task of managing press enquiries when something bad happens and the business needs to respond to it.

- You can find out more about PR and networking online, at sites like Entrepreneur and Business Link available via Hotlinks (see page ii).

Case study

Divine Chocolate and Glasses On Spec

'45% farmer owned, 100% Fairtrade'

Divine Chocolate was the idea of a group of cocoa farmers in Ghana who started to pool together resources to help each other. They had created their own cooperative, Kuapa Kokoo, and decided to set up their own Fairtrade chocolate company in the UK. This social enterprise was then supported by organisations including The Body Shop and Comic Relief, and the Divine chocolate brand was born. Divine has used various ways to promote the organisation, including public relations activities such as endorsements by famous personalities, and running their own national poetry competition judged by famous writers such as Anthony Horowitz.

Divine Chocolate is a leading Fairtrade brand in the UK, and demonstrates how social enterprises can be extremely good at marketing. Find out more about current campaigns by accessing their website, available via Hotlinks (see page ii).

Glasses On Spec was launched by Bob Ward in April 2005. He worked out that he could supply glasses for just £9 per pair online – much cheaper than most high street retailers.

He started marketing his business by using public relations methods such as featuring in local newspapers and on radio programmes, telling everyone that they could buy glasses from him instead of from their optician.

Bob invested £9,500 in radio advertising and £4,000 in consumer magazines. He thought he had done everything right, but he noticed that after these activities he did not get more visitors to the website. His campaign had not worked because people hearing his radio adverts could not write down its name and so forgot it.

Bob decided that he would have been better spending the money on promoting his website through a search engine like Google. You can read how to do this in Unit 12, pages 332–33.

Buying glasses online often saves money.

Think about it!

1. Divine Chocolate is a social enterprise. It focuses heavily on the personal involvement of its supporters to promote it. Use its website to find at least six examples of these activities. Then suggest why the business favours this type of promotional activity.

2. Why does Glasses On Spec need to be ranked highly on Google? How can the business achieve this, and would it also benefit from 'pay per click' advertising? Research this online before you answer.

3. Explain how the promotional activities of both businesses enable them to reach their target market in a cost-effective way.

Just checking

1. What are the four elements of the marketing mix?
2. What does AIDA(S) stand for in relation to buyer behaviour and why is understanding this so important?
3. What is meant by public relations and how can this help a business?
4. Name four different methods of advertising that would be appropriate for a small business.
5. When might it be appropriate to use personal selling?

BTEC Assessment activity 19.1

For this unit you must develop a marketing plan for a planned micro business or social enterprise. If you have taken Units 16 or 17, you may find it useful to refer back to the learning and assessment work that you did for these units. You should also use the notes you have made in this unit to prepare for marketing your own business.

Then prepare research notes for your marketing plan by carrying out the following tasks.

1. Apply the following marketing concepts that you have learned about so far to your business idea.
   • The AIDA(S) model of buyer decision making
   • USP
   • Segmentation
   • Target market
   • Marketing mix.

Assess your business idea against each of these concepts. **P1**

2. Apply the following different types of promotion that you have learned about so far to your business by saying how you would use each one.
   • Advertising – including online methods
   • Personal selling
   • Promotional activities
   • Direct marketing
   • Sponsorship
   • Public relations and networking.

Justify types of promotion for your business, drawing on evidence of success or failure in the marketplace that you have learned about. If you reject some, then give reasons. **P2**

Grading tips

• Keep researching other activities that might be suitable while you are preparing your assessment work. Check out other ways in which markets are segmented; find out more about online marketing and new ideas for promotional activities. Reference your ideas in your work using a bibliography.

• Make sure you include clear reasons why you think something will or will not work when you are answering these questions. This helps you to make choices and justify them.

2. Be able to plan marketing and promotion

To put together a marketing plan and promotion plan properly for your assessment, you need to use the right headings and content. In this section you will also develop your skills by putting your work from Assessment activity 19.1 into more formal plans.

2.1 Sections in the marketing plan

There are nine key sections in a marketing plan. Learning about what goes into each will help you put the right content in your plan.

Market definition and opportunity

Before a business can plan any marketing, it must find out as much as possible about its target market. Defining the market means identifying exactly which group(s) of people, or businesses, will buy from you. The total 'market' means the total number of people who could be sold the product or service. By working out the value of total possible sales to this market, you can calculate how many people could be your potential customers. Small firms, like micro or social enterprise businesses, will not try to sell to the whole market, but knowing its size and value, and trends in the market, enables them to assess future opportunities and predict future sales patterns.

Proposed target market segments

As you already know, a business will target particular customer groups, or market segments, that it considers are most suitable, such as young adults between 14 and 25. It will identify its aims for selling to this target market with objectives that can be followed, so that at the end of the plan the business can measure its success against what it set out to do.

Did you know?

The bottled sauces market in the UK in 2008 was estimated to be worth £474 million, with key players such as Heinz and Hellman's dominating the market. Demand is increasing, particularly for specialist and ethnic products, such as Caribbean hot pepper sauce.

Why should a business gather market information before launching a marketing plan?

Activity: Segmenting your market

There are many different ways that a market can be segmented, and for your assessed work you will need to segment your market. In pairs or small groups, discuss the market for your micro business or social enterprise. How could it be segmented? Refresh your memory by looking back at page 416.

Ways include: job/occupation, education level, family size, size of purchase and sexual orientation. You may have other ideas that could be considered too.

Demand for product/service

After you have researched the size of your market and decided which segment(s) to target, you then need to find out if there is a demand for your product or service. You can do this by checking demand (and sales) for similar products or by asking potential customers whether they would buy it.

Activity: Would you buy it?

Look at the products listed below and decide whether there is a demand for them or not. Carry out research into whether they exist, and then in small groups discuss why they are successful or not.

a) Garlic ice cream; b) chocolate courgette cake; c) chocolate teapots; d) cabbage-flavoured fudge; e) parsnip crisps; f) Brussels sprout-flavour boiled sweets.

PLTS

Practise your team-working skills by taking responsibility for your own work and being fair and considerate to other people in your group.

Competition

Competition is something all businesses take very seriously. If you have many rivals offering similar products or services, then you need to offer something different to attract customers. The first step is to find out as much as you can about both your offline and online competitors, and then identify what you can do that will be different.

Other external influences

Trends relate to the market itself (such as the bottled sauce market) or to overall consumer spending patterns. These changes can occur for many reasons, such as technological advances, lifestyle changes and economic factors. Although these are outside the control of businesses they can have a dramatic effect on sales, as you learned in Unit 1 (see pages 29–30). For example, the credit crunch and the weakness of sterling, which made foreign holidays expensive, meant many British people took their holidays in the UK in 2009, so hotels and holiday letting agencies did well. In the same year, health issues, such as concerns over swine flu, led to an increase in sales of alcohol hand sanitisers and other cleaning products.

Legislation (the laws of the UK and European Union) can affect whether or not products/services can be sold and where they can be used. Examples include the ban on smoking in public places in 2007 in England, and the change in the purchasing age of smoking materials from 16 to 18 (see also Unit 1, page 34).

Remember

Having a unique selling point (USP) means you have identified a way in which you will be different from your competitors. Turn back to page 416 to remind yourself about a USP. Then check back to the notes you made on how this could apply to your product or service.

Did you know?

Bamboo Clothing is made from real bamboo in an environmentally friendly and ethical way. This is a trend in the way that clothing is made.

Did you know?

Guerrilla marketing is so called because it is quick, cheap and targeted – ideal for small firms. Tactics include increasing sales to existing customers first, rewarding customers who provide referrals, networking (online and offline), forming business alliances, and direct marketing campaigns (for example, by email newsletter or leaflet drops).

Activity: Decide tactics

In pairs or small groups, think of some creative ways to market your business and present these to the rest of your class. Vote on the best suggestions.

Did you know?

Mintel is one of the largest market research companies in the UK. For the past 30 years it has predicted industry trends and produced highly detailed reports.

Remember

Sales are important, but profits are essential if you are going to make your living from the business. Anyone can forecast high sales if they sell very cheaply, but they are unlikely to stay in business for long!

Marketing tactics

Marketing tactics are the methods an organisation uses to bring its product or service to the attention of potential customers. Small businesses cannot afford to advertise and promote their products in the same way as large firms, so have to be more creative. They also need to start making sales quickly, so they need to use tactics that will enable them to do this.

- One way is to **use the marketing mix** (see pages 418–20) to achieve this, such as by working longer hours at the start, having a competition to attract interest or holding an event that gains free publicity to launch the business. The trick is to select the best methods to get noticed quickly within budget.

- **The image** of the business and the target customer will dictate the most appropriate tactics. Distributing garish red and yellow flyers will make you look cheap and cheerful – and be spot on if you are offering a bargain product! Posting a video on YouTube could be the best way to attract younger customers, and start a viral campaign. Holding a champagne reception for invited guests may be more appropriate for luxury goods or for the business market.

Marketing research

Marketing research is an important part of your plan. You will need to detail:

1. the **method** that you are going to use. There are lots to choose from, for example, a study of websites, reviewing articles, handing out questionnaires, conducting interviews, getting together a focus group and so on

2. the **scale**, which is the size of the research, that is the number of people you are going to ask, or the amount of research that you are going to collect and analyse

3. the **findings**, which are the things that you find out from the research. The findings need to be analysed – for example, how many people would be prepared to pay between £2 and £2.99 for the product?

4. the **conclusions**. Here you should write a summary of what you think overall about your findings. You should back this up with other information that shows your plan is likely to work.

Sales forecasts

Your sales forecasts are your predictions of the level of sales you expect to achieve and must be based on sound research, not wild guesses.

Anyone who is considering buying an existing business, such as a beauty salon or fast food outlet, will find information on the average weekly takings in the advert. These, plus scope for expansion or improvement, will form the basis of the sales forecast.

If you are setting up a new business from scratch then you need to use your research on the potential market, and current trends, as your basis. Many market research companies produce reports that analyse markets in depth. These can be expensive but will provide valuable information to support (or contradict) your own findings.

It is also invaluable to find out average levels of sales (and profits) made by similar businesses in your area. Business Link advisers and local accountants should know the average level of sales, and profit, that you should be able to make for your investment. If these are not within realistic levels then they would suggest that you rethink your ideas.

Support material

Support material is evidence you obtain to prove that you have done your research properly. This can include:

- **industry studies**, such as market research reports and other data you have found both online and offline, such as articles from industry journals and government statistics on consumer trends. You can supplement this with press reports and articles relevant to your proposed business idea

- **letters of support**, which can be valuable if they are from a reputable source, such as:

  - a business adviser who knows how thoroughly you have researched your market and how committed you are to the idea

  - an accountant who considers your forecast sales are accurate

  - customers who consider your work or product to be high quality and popular

  - an entrepreneur who runs a similar successful business (but not a direct competitor), such as someone carrying out the same trade in a different area, who knows about your skills and expertise, and can vouch for your potential to do well.

I agree all these letters are impressive. The fact they are from four ex girlfriends, your mother and sister is not.

Activity: Social enterprises

Suggest the type of support material that would be useful if you were setting up a social enterprise, rather than a profit-making business. Compare your ideas as a group.

How the success of your marketing will be measured

How will you know if your marketing efforts are successful? You need to state how you will measure this in your marketing plan. The best way is to identify a few key performance indicators that you will check at regular intervals, such as:

- **stock turnover**, which will enable you to identify which items (or services) are slow to sell and which are very popular. This will enable you to review your product mix effectively

- customer satisfaction (including complaints and comments), such as the additional items/services they want you to offer, their views on your prices and other improvements they want you to make

Key term

Stock turnover – the speed at which different items are sold.

- sales levels. A month-by-month analysis will identify seasonal patterns and show when you need to take action to boost sales

- sales conversion rates from enquiry to firm order.

You will also need to assess the effectiveness of your promotional activities, as you will see on page 436.

Assessment activity 19.2

For this activity you will create a formal marketing plan for your own business, using the work you did for Assessment activity 19.1. Before you start, look back through that assessment to see if you can improve your research notes because of new ideas or information you have had since then.

1. Produce your plan for the marketing of your micro start-up business or social enterprise. Make sure this is relevant to the needs of your customers and use the headings below. **P3**

   - Market definition and opportunity
   - Other external influences (for example, trends and legislation)
   - Proposed target market segments
   - Marketing tactics, including the marketing mix
   - Demand for product/service
   - Marketing research
   - Competition
   - Sales forecasts and support material
   - How success will be measured.

2. To develop your work further, explain how you have used the principles of marketing when you have developed the marketing mix for your micro start-up business. Make sure you include at least two concepts in your answer to explain how you have developed your marketing mix. **M1**

Grading tips

- For P3, you need to create a clear plan using the headings provided. Keep looking back through the work you created in Assessment activity 19.1 to help you develop the best ideas for your plan.

- For M1, you should apply two of the marketing concepts to your marketing mix and explain how you did this, making sure that your answers are clear.

2.2 Promotion plan

In a promotion plan there are also nine sections. Again you need to plan carefully what you will write under each heading.

Coordination with the rest of the marketing mix

You already know that promotion is an important part of the marketing mix and that all aspects of the marketing mix must be coordinated. This includes your promotional methods. Each must be chosen to reach your target customers, so if you open a children's shoe shop your choices will be very different from if you plan to start a mobile car valeting service.

Image to be developed and costs

A promotion plan must reflect the image the business aims to portray: luxury, basic, environmentally friendly, and so on. Matching the promotion to the image is very important for a successful campaign.

However, no business can ignore the cost of each promotional method. Some are free, while others are very expensive. The skill is to spend the available money wisely, and this means selecting promotional methods and promotional messages that will appeal to your target customer. Your choice then comes down to what you can afford. If the cost is high but the benefit would be small, then an alternative method must be found.

Schedule for proposed promotion campaign

A promotional campaign usually happens for a special reason, such as the launch of a new business or new product. A schedule should list the different aspects of the campaign and say when each will take place, ideally in date order. You will need to think about the following.

- When will the campaign start?

- How long will it run for?

- Which resources are needed and when?

- Is there anything that may stop or delay it and how can this be avoided?

- How, and when, will you evaluate the campaign?

Type of promotional materials

The type of promotional materials you choose must be appropriate for the target customer group. For example, money-off coupons might appeal to one customer group, but not to another. The choice will depend upon the buying habits of your target customer and where they will look for information.

A poster will attract the attention of the travelling public, whereas a leaflet is more appropriate to promote a local service. An advertisement may be an option, but you have to decide where to place it – on local radio or in your local paper. Alternatively, if your customers will look online for information, you may prefer a listing on Google Local, or have your own website.

Did you know?

- A cheap but effective way for many local firms to get noticed is by advertising on their business vehicles. Find out more by visiting the Century Signs & Graphics website.

- It is sensible to have a fixed start and end date for a campaign, then you can evaluate its success before you decide whether to repeat it or not.

- You can find out more about the benefits of having a website or a listing online in Unit 12.

What are the benefits of carrying out an unusual promotional activity?

Activity: St Ann's Manchester Midnight Walk

Each year, the Manchester Midnight Walk raises money for St Ann's Hospice so they can provide care for patients over the age of 16 who are living with a life-threatening illness.

In March 2009, they used a 'flash mob' promotional campaign to highlight the 2009 walk that took place in June. Around 100 pyjama-wearing people gathered outside Manchester Town Hall to hold a pretend race and reconstruct the event. People taking part were recruited through social networking sites and did the walk to the theme tune from *Rocky*.

You can find out more about the 'flash mob' promotion by visiting the Manchester Midnight Walk website.

In small groups, research and discuss other types of promotional activity that you have heard of like this.

Nature of the promotional materials

Promotional materials need to attract attention and create interest. This means choosing colours and visual features, such as graphics or photographs, that will appeal to the target group. Colour can be used effectively to reflect an image, which is why many environmentally friendly businesses use green or brown lettering.

The wording must be appropriate and the style of text, and its size, should be appropriate. Writing effective promotional messages is a skilled task because too much information can have a negative effect. So, too, can any basic errors in spelling or punctuation.

Name of the product/service and company

There are two aspects to choosing a business name. The first relates to the legal aspects, the second to its promotional appeal.

Anyone can start a non-limited business and trade using their own name. The situation is different if you want to use another name or become a limited company. The law then stops you from using a name that would be offensive, a name that already exists as a recognised brand (for example, Tesco) or a name that is identical to an existing registered company. Company registration firms advise on this and can provide lists of available names that might be suitable.

You then need to choose a name that is appropriate for your business, easy to remember and, if you will have a website or will be starting an Internet business, available as a web address. If your business name also makes it clear what your business is about, such as SportsDirect or LoveFilm, then you have the ideal name!

Branding or logo

Some companies and their products are instantly recognisable by their brand names and/or logos: McDonald's and its 'golden arches', the Nike tick and the Apple image are well-known examples.

Developing a brand is a major asset for any business because it helps people to remember the business (or product) and also associate specific qualities with it, such as reliability, value for money, honesty and professional expertise. This saves money on marketing in the long run, because customers stay loyal to a brand they know and trust. It is also easier to launch new products or services under an existing brand.

It is just as appropriate for a small business to develop a brand as a large one. It means considering how you want customers to think about your business and then promoting your name and your product or service consistently, using these values. Adopting a memorable logo and using this on all your stationery, business vehicles and promotional materials also helps. Choosing or designing this image is a skilled job and, obviously, you must not copy anyone else's. Obtaining professional advice is usually sensible to avoid any problems.

Did you know?

UKTV G2 went from 29th to 10th most watched channel after changing its name to Dave to reflect its image and target market.

PEARSON

A logo is often immediately recognisable and usually representative of a company, brand or product – why is this?

Activity: Check out designers

Find out about graphic design companies that create logos and carry out related work in your own area.

Key term

Functionality – the features on a website, such as a search facility or order form, and how easy these are for someone to use.

Website design and functionality

Most businesses today have some presence on the Internet, even if this is just a listing on a website directory. The vast majority prefer to have their own website, even if this is quite a basic site which simply summarises what they offer and where they are. At the other extreme are vast interactive sites with millions of pages, such as Amazon or the BBC website.

The aims of having a website must be considered carefully and these will affect the design and the **functionality**. The design relates to what the website looks like, and this should obviously link to the brand or image of the business. Functionality relates to the features on the website and how you use them, such as whether you can order online and how easy it is to do this. Usability is a key issue for all websites – there is no point having lots of features available if they are slow to load or difficult to find.

There is also no point in having a website if no one knows about it. For this reason, putting the address on all your stationery and business vehicles is essential. So, too, is learning about search engine marketing and search engine optimisation so that you are ranked highly by search engines.

Reasons why the promotional material is appropriate

In your promotion plan you need to justify your promotional material and say why this will suit the target customer group. The message and any graphics you use must be clear and appropriate and communicated using the most appropriate media. For example, if the target customer group is people aged between 14 and 18, messages or blogs on social networking sites, text messages and YouTube videos may be a good idea. Many cinema and radio adverts are also targeted at young people, whereas older people are more likely to read newspapers. You could also take advantage of seasonal events or memorable events to create a special promotion, such as Easter or the 2012 London Olympics.

Remember that if your promotional material is not appropriate to the customer group, the message may not reach them, and if it does, it may not interest or attract them.

Measuring the success of promotions

The final part of a promotion plan should state how you intend to measure the success of your promotional activities. This should also take account of the proposed cost of each. The more expensive the method, the better the results you can reasonably expect to achieve. In addition to increases in sales or profits, some businesses use the following to measure the success of a campaign:

- amount of press coverage they get
- the number of new enquiries received by phone or email
- the number of new customers who visit the business
- the increase in visitor traffic to the website
- the number of text message responses received
- the number of responses to a competition or promotional vouchers redeemed.

Just checking

1. What is a market?
2. What does it mean to segment a market?
3. Name two external influences that might affect a marketing plan.
4. What are two benefits of branding?
5. Name three ways in which you could measure the success of a promotional activity.

BTEC   ## Assessment activity 19.3

Use the work that you completed for Assessment activity 19.1 and convert this into a promotion plan by doing the following tasks.

1. Prepare a promotional plan for your proposed micro start-up business. Include at least one sample promotional activity that would be appropriate for your customer groups. Include details about the proposed cost and your suggested timing for the activity.

   Include these headings within your plan:

   - Coordination with the rest of the marketing mix
   - Image to be developed
   - Costs and schedule for the campaign
   - Type of promotional materials
   - Nature of the promotional materials

   - Name of the product/service and company
   - Ideas for branding or logo
   - Website design and functionality
   - Reasons why the promotional material is appropriate
   - Measuring the success of promotions. **P4**

2. Develop your work further by producing a cost-effective promotion plan that communicates consistent messages to prospective customers. Your plan should be developed enough so that it could actually be used and include the choice of media that you would wish to use.

Grading tips

- Remember to keep going back through this unit to check your understanding, which will improve your assessed activity work.
- For M2, you will need to make sure that your promotion plan matches your marketing mix effectively so that everything is coordinated.

Assessment activity 19.4

D1

The final part of the assessed work for this unit is set at distinction level, so this requires the higher-level skills that you have been developing.

Develop a cost-effective coordinated marketing mix and promotion plan to meet the needs of a defined target market. You must include a full description of the attributes and needs of your target customer(s). **D1**

Grading tip

For D1, each aspect of the marketing mix and promotion plan must complement the others and be designed to appeal to your potential customers. You will need to include judgements within your work and research the costs and the marketing mix very effectively. You should also review your work on the target market to ensure that it is defined well enough to help you with this task.

edexcel

Assignment tips

- Do not forget that the marketing plan and the promotion plan are very different activities. You will need to plan each one carefully and complete the relevant sections.

- Marketing and promotion are all about being as creative as you possibly can be. Keep looking around for new and unusual ideas that will inspire your work.

- Start to look for the many marketing or promotion messages that are around us every day. Consider how many you would normally take notice of, how many you would ignore and why.

20 Managing personal finances

BTEC First is concerned with several aspects of business, but this unit is special because it relates to your own personal finance. There are two good reasons for learning about this.

- If you are good at managing your own finances, this will help you to manage business finances.

- If you run, or work hard in, a business to earn money, it is sad if you cannot use the money you earn wisely.

The first section of this unit looks at managing your own money. You will learn how to avoid getting into debt, how to bank online and open a current account, and the importance of keeping financial records.

In the next section you will find out about the organisations that provide financial services, including banks, building societies, independent financial advisers and several others. You will also learn about various financial products including savings accounts, insurance, loans and mortgages.

Finally, you will learn how to prepare a personal budget. You will do this by working out the best way to plan your income and expenditure, and then construct a budget to help you use every penny you get in the best possible way.

Learning outcomes

After completing this unit, you should:

1. know ways to manage personal finance
2. know common financial products and services
3. be able to produce a personal budget that takes account of personal remuneration and expenditure.

All websites referred to in this unit can be accessed via Hotlinks. See page ii for more information.

Assessment and grading criteria

This table shows you what you must do in order to achieve a pass, merit or distinction grade, and where you can find activities in this book to help you.

To achieve a **pass**, the evidence must show that the learner is able to:	To achieve a **merit**, the evidence must show that, in addition to the pass criteria, the learner is able to:	To achieve a **distinction** grade, the evidence must show that, in addition to the pass and merit criteria, the learner is able to:
P1 outline ways of managing personal financial planning and accurate record keeping **See Assessment activity 20.1, page 453**	**M1** explain the reasons for budgetary decisions **See Assessment activity 20.3, page 468**	**D1** justify reasons for financial planning decisions **See Assessment activity 20.3, page 468**
P2 identify sources of advice for ways of managing financial products and services **See Assessment activity 20.2, page 462**	**M2** analyse the different features of financial products and services relating to current and savings accounts **See Assessment activity 20.2, page 462**	
P3 describe financial products and services appropriate to self **See Assessment activity 20.2, page 462**		
P4 construct a personal budget that takes account of personal remuneration and expenditure **See Assessment activity 20.3, page 468**		

How you will be assessed

To achieve this unit, you will demonstrate that you can plan and manage your personal finances and keep accurate records. You will be asked to explain what financial products and sources of advice are available, as well as research and identify the best financial products for your own needs. You will also prepare a personal budget and explain how you have constructed it.

Sammy

I enjoyed this unit because I gained extra knowledge of how to manage my finances. I also found it useful to learn about the differences between store and credit cards, and personal loans and overdrafts. I wanted to learn how to work out a budget because I thought it would benefit me in later life.

I'm not bad at planning my own finances. I'd give myself five out of ten, because when there's something I want to buy I will save my money to get it. On the other hand, if I have nothing to save my money towards, I usually end up spending it with nothing to show for it.

I enjoyed planning a budget for myself and finding out about different financial products, as well as making decisions about them. In our group we sometimes talk about what it would be like to live away from home, and think that rent and living expenses would cost more than what we would earn, even if we moved in together. Now we can prepare a budget properly, it will help us to check if this is really true.

Over to you!

- What would you score yourself out of ten on planning your finances and why?
- How do you think your spending habits may change over the next few years, and how could financial planning skills help you?

Discussing personal finance

1. Work in groups to find out the cost of insuring a car at 17. Choose a make and model you might realistically own and get a quote for third party insurance from a comparison website such as Go Compare or MoneySupermarket. Compare your results with other groups.

2. In your group, discuss if any of you has a part-time job, and if so, why. Also discuss how you allow for money needed for birthday presents and other irregular expenses.

1. Know ways to manage personal finance

1.1 Managing personal finance

The importance of managing personal finance

There are several good reasons why it is important to be in control of your personal finances.

Avoiding getting into debt

Being in **debt** means that you owe money to another person or to a bank, credit card company or other lender. The word debt means that you have to pay the money back, usually with **interest**.

There are two types of debt: 'good debt' and 'bad debt'. Good debt is when people (or businesses) borrow money that they can easily repay, even when the interested is included. This situation can occur, for example, when someone takes out a loan to buy a car. The debt is 'good' if the person earns enough to easily afford the repayments.

Bad debt is when people borrow money that they cannot afford to repay. When the term 'debt' is used in this unit, it means bad debt.

Key terms

Debt – money owed to someone else or a financial organisation.

Interest – the cost of borrowing money, normally a percentage of the amount borrowed.

Did you know?

People sometimes use the slang expression 'maxed out' when they have spent up to their maximum limit on a credit card. It really is not a good thing to do.

What is the difference between good and bad debts?

You can avoid getting into debt by:

- doing very careful calculations about repayment *and* interest before signing any loan agreement. Can you afford to repay?

- being very careful about using credit cards. People often lose track of how much they have spent until the statement arrives

- saving up for major expenses, such as holidays, so that you can pay for them outright and avoid having to pay interest

- avoiding becoming overdrawn at the bank to avoid any bank charges (see page 459).

Controlling costs

For most people, the amount of income they receive is fixed. This could be spending money from parents, income from part-time work, salary from full-time employment or (eventually) a pension. The main way of managing money is to control costs. You will look at this in more detail later in this unit (see page 467). Here are some tips which should help you keep costs to a minimum.

- Shops want you to spend as much as possible. They may appear to be 'friendly' by having sales and special offers, but they are after your money, whether you can afford to buy something or not.

- Avoid '**impulse purchases**' where you buy something on the spur of the moment. Shops encourage this by stacking sweets and gossip magazines near the checkout.

- Before you buy something, ask yourself three questions: 'Will I use it?', 'Is it worth it?' and 'Could I get it cheaper somewhere else?'

- When you go out, only take with you the money you will need that day.

- Plan your spending by having a budget (see page 464).

Activity: Impulse buys

Gok Wan proved that most of us have lots of clothes we never wear. What about you? Choose something you hardly ever use or wear and think back to when you bought it and work out why you did so. Is there a lesson for you about how you could avoid making the same mistake again?

Remaining solvent

Someone is solvent when they have enough money to meet their commitments. There is a difference between owing money and being **insolvent**, as you will see from Samia's and Jason's living expenses in Table 20.1 on the following page.

Did you know?

- A mortgage is a **secured debt**. This is because the loan is secured against the house. It means that, if people cannot keep up the repayments, the lender could take possession of the property. You will learn about secured and unsecured debts on page 459.

- In 2009 it was reckoned that the total personal debt in the UK was **£1.4 trillion**. Because of this it was thought that four million people would seek debt counselling.

- One of the most common reasons for people spending more than they can afford is because credit cards are so easy to get and use (see page 459).

Key terms

Impulse purchase – an unplanned purchase. It often indicates a problem as the purchaser may not really need the item. It is said that impulse purchases are made using emotion rather than reason.

Insolvent – when someone becomes legally insolvent, they do not have enough money to pay their debts. The people or businesses they owe money to can go to court to have them declared bankrupt. This means that they can lose their property, possessions and any savings to pay off the debt. Note that bankrupt is another word for insolvent.

PLTS

Practise your reflective learner skills by being realistic about something you have bought which you now see as a mistake.

Table 20.1: Samia's and Jason's expenses

	Samia	Jason
Monthly income	£1,200 after tax	£1,200 after tax
Monthly expenditure	Flat: £400 Living expenses: £400 Loan repayment on small car: £250	Luxury flat: £700 Living expenses: £500 Loan repayment on sports car: £300
Total monthly expenses	£1,050	£1,500
Result	Samia can meet all her commitments. She is solvent. She has £150 for holidays, clothes, savings, and so on.	As he only earns £1,200, Jason cannot pay his way and is therefore insolvent.

A major aim of managing personal finance is to avoid becoming insolvent by carefully monitoring income and expenditure.

Saving

Savings is money that is not spent but is saved to use on a major item, for example, a holiday, a car or the deposit on a house, or in case of emergency. Savings should be kept in a bank account, preferably not a current account, but a special savings account. There are two reasons for this. First, the money is separate and not as easy to access, so there is less temptation to spend it on an impulse buy. Also, savings accounts pay interest, so the amount saved increases over a period of time.

Money put into savings can come from two main sources.

- **Regular savings** – surplus money not spent on daily living expenses (see Samia in Table 20.1). The easy way is to have money transferred each month by standing order before you have the chance to spend it.

- **Saving additional income** – such as money given as birthday and Christmas presents.

Did you know?

Most people forget about money automatically put into a savings account from their wage and soon get used to living on the lower amount. And £10 saved each week gives you over £500 at the end of a year, plus interest!

Activity: Interest rates on savings

In groups, choose one of the main high street banks, access their website and check the interest rates offered on their savings accounts. Find the best one and see if MoneySupermarket agrees with you.

Discussion point

Are you a saver or a spender? If your uncle won £10,000 on the lottery and gave you £500, would you:

a) immediately buy an iPhone or some new clothes

b) save it for something special, like a holiday

c) save half and spend half?

Or should your uncle make it a condition what you spend it on? Discuss your ideas as a group.

Where can savings come from?

Maintaining a good credit rating

When someone applies for credit, the business that can lend the money will almost always have a credit check carried out.

The checks are carried out mainly because the lender does not want to lend money that the borrower may not be able to pay back. There are three main **credit reference agencies** in the UK; they are Experian, Equifax and Callcredit.

Activity: Get a credit score

Go to the loans sections on the MoneySupermarket website and carry out a credit rating check by answering ten questions. You can choose to be a fictitious person if you want. Read the explanation with each question to learn what factors are taken into account to get a credit rating. Make a note of these because they tell you how to keep a good credit rating, for example, only have the minimum number of credit and store cards. If someone has credit cards they do not use, they are still considered to have that amount of credit available.

Key term

Credit reference agencies – companies that collect information on people, and assess how much of a risk they are to businesses that lend money.

Did you know?

You are 'applying for credit' when you ask for a bank loan or overdraft, apply for a credit card or mobile phone contract, or ask to pay your car insurance monthly.

Keeping financial records

How much did you spend last month, or last week, or even yesterday? The chances are you cannot be sure. That is why keeping financial records is most important. They should be stored in a safe place and filed in date order so you can find information quickly. The main types of records that you need to keep, and sometimes check, are as follows.

Bank and credit card statements

Current bank account holders normally receive a printed statement each month. The same is true for credit card holders. Both types of statement show the amount in the account at the start of the month and then the amounts withdrawn and amounts entered (paid in). Finally, the closing balance shows the result of all the entries.

Activity: Check out a bank statement

Check out the sample bank statement at the NatWest MoneySense website and answer the questions below to make sure you understand it.

Discussion point

Banks and credit card companies are now trying to persuade customers to have online statements only. They say this will save paper and help the environment. Could there be another reason? And is this really in the customer's interest? Discuss your ideas as a group.

Did you know?

- It is illegal for a financial institution (for example, a bank) to lend money to anyone under the age of 18. So you cannot have a credit card, take out a bank loan or have an overdraft until you reach this age.

- The use of cheques is falling as more people switch to credit/debit cards and online banking. Some shops refuse to accept cheques at all.

Cheque stubs

Sometimes people use cheques to pay for goods. The cheque is given to the person who is due to receive the money and the counterfoil (the part on the left-hand side) is kept by the person giving the money. If you use a cheque book, you should check that the entries on these match those on your bank statement.

Discussion point

In groups, discuss why the use of cheques is declining, in particular why shops prefer other forms of payment.

Activity: Complete a cheque

You can practise completing a cheque at the NatWest MoneySense website.

Activity: Compare receipts

In small groups, collect a few receipts and compare notes on what information they contain. Who has collected the one with the most items of information?

Receipts

When you pay for goods in a shop, you usually are given a receipt. This is important when you pay cash because the receipt is the only proof that you have paid for the goods.

If you buy goods that you may have to return, for example, because they are faulty, it is important that you keep the receipt as proof of your purchase. If you pay by debit or credit card, the receipt doubles up as a record of the card transaction and you need it to check your statement.

Why should you always ask for a receipt in a shop?

Bills

Your family will receive utility **bills** for gas, water and electricity. As well as the total amount owed, they usually have a breakdown of how the figure has been calculated. Bills give the date when the money must be paid. Many people pay their bills by bank transfer, which includes direct debits and standing orders (see pages 448–49).

Pay slips

When you go to work, your employer must by law give you a pay slip (sometimes called 'pay advice') to itemise your earnings and deductions. You will normally get this at the end of a week or month, depending on how frequently you are paid. The document will contain several types of information, including your unique employee number and your total pay to date for the financial year. The most important entries need checking carefully. These are:

- **your gross pay** – the amount of pay you would receive if there were no deductions (see below). If you are paid on an hourly rate, you should check that both the hours you have worked and your rate per hour is correct

- **deductions** – such as income tax and national insurance

- **net pay** – the gross pay figure minus deductions.

If you are paid by electronic transfer (BACS), you should check that the net pay figure appears correctly on your bank statement.

Contingency planning

'If I'm not at Starbucks by half-past-two, I'll see you outside Vue at a quarter to three.' This is an example of contingency planning –

Key term

Bills – documents issued by organisations stating how much money is owed for a certain product or service. Another word for a bill is an invoice.

Activity: A pay slip

If you have never seen a pay slip then check out the interactive one online at Ceridian to find out how one is set out and what the entries mean.

Did you know?

BACS stands for **B**anks **A**utomated **C**learing **S**ystem. It is a system that allows for direct debits and salaries to be transferred from one bank account to another.

planning for something that may not happen. In personal finance this means allowing for unexpected events, such as having to contribute to an unexpected present or night out. Having a contingency plan means having enough spare money to do this.

There is a strong link between having a financial contingency plan and saving, because some savings could be used to pay for unexpected events.

Personal taxation

As you learned in Unit 1, the government provides many services for us including education, the health service and the road network. To pay for these, it raises money through taxation, such as VAT and excise duty.

Most taxes are collected by HM Revenue & Customs (HMRC).

People who are employed pay income tax and National Insurance, as well as tax on any income from investments, for example, interest from a savings account, and rent from property.

Income tax is deducted automatically by an employer before you are paid. This is known as PAYE – pay as you earn. The tax is calculated in bands, so how much you pay depends upon how much you earn. Everyone has a personal allowance, which is tax free. After that, income is taxed at the basic rate of 20 per cent and a higher rate of 40 per cent, which only applies to earnings of more than £37,400 (in 2009/10). A third rate of 50 per cent applies only to earnings above £150,000, as you saw in Unit 1 (page 23).

National Insurance Contributions (NICs) are also paid on earned income. The contribution counts towards certain state benefits, including the state pension. NICs are paid by everyone earning more than the weekly earnings threshold. Again, the more you earn the more you pay.

Security of money

Direct debit

Justin receives a bill from E.ON, his electricity supplier, every three months. He used to send a cheque in payment until one was lost in the post. Justin had to contact the bank to cancel it (the bank charged him for this), and then had to send a replacement. Because of this hassle, he set up a monthly direct debit instead. Now E.ON take the money automatically from his bank account. They have to tell him if the amount they take changes, but otherwise Justin knows he is paying the same, agreed amount every month. He can easily check the amount is correct by looking at his bank statement. If there was a problem, he could contact E.ON immediately to sort things out.

The main point about direct debits is that the organisation that is owed money can withdraw **variable amounts** of money from the customer's account, provided that they tell the customer in advance.

Did you know?

- There is a payment threshold for both income tax and NICs. This means that up to a certain minimum amount you do not pay any tax. For 2009/10 the tax threshold is £6,475 a year, and for NICs, it is £95–£110 a week. The difference between these two pay rates is important. If you earn £94 a week you do not pay NICs, but do not get any benefits either. If you can persuade your employer to pay you £109 instead, you get an NI credit but still do not pay any contributions, so for NICs this is the best pay rate of all!

- Employers are legally required to deduct income tax from your gross wage as soon as you start working for them. If you take on a holiday job and are unlikely to earn more than your personal allowance for a year, you can complete a form P38(S) to stop tax being deducted.

Activity: Tax and NICs

Find out more about tax and national insurance at the Directgov website. You can also find out about National Insurance. Then check out current income tax bands and rates by visiting the HMRC website.

Standing order

Justin also belongs to an angling club and pays his quarterly subscription of £15 by standing order. Justin set up this arrangement direct with his bank. If the subscription changes, he will have to inform his bank. The angling club has no control over the timing or amount of payment.

Discussion point

One danger of paying by direct debit is that people can end up 'saving up' with their supplier. For example, if Justin uses less electricity than E.ON has calculated they will not refund him, or change his payments, for quite some time. They will argue this is because Justin could easily use more again. But what could be the other reasons? And what should Justin do? Discuss your ideas as a group.

Remember

Although direct debits and standing orders are similar at first glance, they are fundamentally different. For direct debits, the organisation receiving the money controls the amount and timing of the payment. For standing orders, the reverse is true – the person making the payment is in control.

ATMs

ATM is the official name for cash machines. They have facilities linked to current accounts and credit card accounts. You gain access by inserting the appropriate card and typing in your **PIN**. To access your current account you enter a debit card. Most people use the machines to withdraw cash (and print a transaction record), and to check their account balance. The machines may also enable you to: print a mini statement, order a bank statement or cheque book, change your PIN, pay in cash or cheques, pay bills and top up mobile phones.

Transactions can be done at any time, but there are a couple of negative sides to ATMs. Some machines charge for withdrawing cash no matter which card you use. And any cash withdrawn using a credit card has interest charged on it immediately, and at a high rate. This is something you should only ever do as a last resort.

Did you know?

- Many suppliers charge a lower rate, or tariff, to people who pay by direct debit because it costs them less to administer the payments.

- A current bank account is the one used for everyday transactions. Most people have their wages paid into their current account and pay all of their bills from it.

- You can top up someone else's mobile phone from an ATM. Hopefully, if you do this, your friend will pay you back!

- **ATM** stands for **A**utomated **T**eller **M**achine. 'Teller' is the old term for a bank clerk who sits at a counter and deals with customers face to face. You may also come across other terms such as 'cash point' and 'hole in the wall'.

Key term

PIN – Personal Identification Number you use to gain access to various accounts.

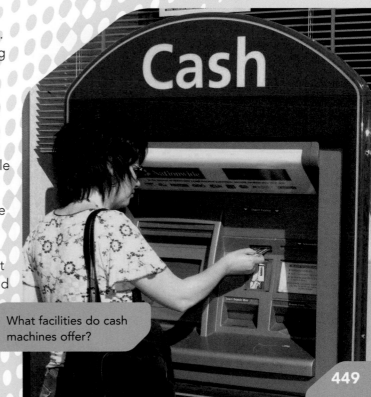

What facilities do cash machines offer?

PIN security

If someone got hold of your debit/credit card and knew your PIN, they would have access to your account via any ATM. For this reason, the following security measures should be followed.

- Keep your card in a safe place and, if you lose it, report the loss immediately.

- Do not choose a birth date or other obvious number for your PIN.

- Do not let anyone borrow your card, and never tell them your PIN.

- Make sure that no one standing behind you at an ATM can see you enter your PIN.

- Do not insert your card into an ATM if the card slot looks odd in any way.

Online banking

Virtually all banks and building societies offer the option of carrying out most banking activities online. Registered users gain access to a secure section of the bank's website provided they correctly enter their password and PIN. Most online banking systems offer the facilities to:

- check balances and view statements

- download transactions into personal records using specific software

- transfer money between own bank accounts

- pay money owing to other people and businesses, including credit card bills

- set up or cancel standing orders and direct debits

Why is online banking convenient for many people?

- carry out administrative tasks such as ordering cheque books, amending addresses and email address, and activating a new debit card

- apply for loans, overdraft facilities and credit cards.

Skills needed to manage personal finance

Problem solving

A problem is an unexpected difficulty. In finance, this normally means you need extra money for something unexpected, like tickets to go to see a favourite band play and money for the minibus to get you there. This will cost £35 for the ticket and £20 for the transport, and you only have £5 until you get paid from your part-time job in a week's time.

A key aspect of problem solving is to think of as many alternative solutions as possible. For example, if you had the problem above, you could:

- not go and stay in instead

- ask the person who is collecting the money if you can pay in a week's time

- ask a family member if you can borrow the money

- try to sell some stuff you do not want on eBay

- ask your family if they have any jobs you can do in return for payment.

Did you know?

You can tell when you are in a secure (encrypted) part of a website because you see 'https' in the address line and a padlock at the bottom right of your screen.

Discussion point

In groups, how many more solutions to the problem can you think of? Compare all the ideas and identify their strengths and weaknesses. Then decide on the top two or three options.

What do you do to earn extra money?

Discussion point

You lent £10 to a friend who hasn't repaid you and is now avoiding you. What would you do and how would you learn from this?

Key term

Decision – a decision occurs when there is a choice between two or more courses of action.

You should set time aside to manage personal finance.

Risk taking

Sometimes financial decisions involve an element of risk taking. For example, if a friend asks to borrow £10 you have to decide on the chances of getting it back. Or you may see something being sold very cheaply – yet it could be badly made or faulty. Finally, as you progress in life, you may have money to invest, and then you will have to decide how safe different types of investments are.

There is no hard and fast rule about how to assess this kind of risk. However, if you have doubts about something, you could ask yourself if you could afford to lose the money if things go wrong. If the answer is 'yes', you might want to take the chance. If the answer is 'no', it is probably best to forget the idea.

Decision making

Decision making means choosing what to do when there are several options, as in the case of staying in or going to see a band play. In this situation, the following suggestions should help.

* Have you thought of as many courses of action as possible? For example, when you are thinking of buying something, is there anywhere that sells it cheaper?

* Do you have to decide now or is there time to think about it? Often delaying a decision, perhaps only to the next day, can make a difference. This is why people sometimes say they will 'sleep on it'.

* If the decision is important, it often helps to talk it over with family members or a close friend. Explaining it to someone else often helps to clear your thinking.

Time management

Managing personal finance takes time and should not be rushed. It is good practice to set aside time every week to:

* collect and file all receipts and statements (bank statements and credit card statements) in date order so that you can find them easily

* check each entry of every statement to make sure that they are correct, for example, that your cash machine withdrawals match the receipt that you got

* carry out a rough cash-flow check for the following week to make sure that you have enough money to cover planned expenditure.

And always shop around for the best price for expensive items, such as a new pair of trainers.

Activity: The role of CAB

The Citizens Advice Bureau (CAB) is a charitable organisation that provides free information and advice on legal, money and other problems. It also influences policy makers when they think that something is unfair.

CAB gives information and advice through face-to-face meetings, telephone, email and online. There are over 100 advice centres in England and Wales, and over 20 in Northern Ireland.

Watch CAB's video clips in the 'Changing young lives' section of its website. In groups, identify the points made that link to the topics you have covered in this section of the unit.

PLTS

Talking about the problems the young people discussed in the CAB clips allows you to practise your effective participator skills by discussing issues of concern and proposing solutions.

Just checking

1. What does 'getting into debt' mean?
2. What is a person's credit rating, and why is it important?
3. What is the difference between direct debits and standing orders?
4. Why is time management important for managing money?
5. Why do you need to keep receipts and statements?

BTEC Assessment activity 20.1

Asif receives his wages from a part-time job each Saturday, and by Tuesday it has all gone. He then borrows money from people to get him by until the next pay day when he pays back the loans. Then the whole cycle starts again.

Write an email to Asif giving him hints and tips on managing his finances. Include, in your suggestions, information on the type of records he should keep. **P1**

Grading tip

A good response will include advising Asif to review his finances regularly by keeping records and checking statements and other documents he receives.

2. Know common financial products and services

There are a number of financial products that you will need at some stage in your life and several types of organisation provide them.

2.1 Financial services providers

Banks

When people talk about banks, they normally mean the main 'high street banks'. These are the large banks in most major towns, which provide a wide range of services. Some, though, offer only an online/telephone service, such as first direct.

Activity: Find the banks

Read through the list of high street banks on the UK Net Guide website. How many names do you recognise as branches in your nearest high street?

What are 'high street banks'?

Discussion point

Most banks offer incentives for students to open an account with them. Can you think why? Find out more about the incentives offered by visiting the Student Finance website, and decide as a group which are the best offers.

Building societies

Today, building societies are almost identical to high street banks in terms of the products/services they offer. When they began they were quite different. Groups of people got together to pay money into a central pool and used money from this to buy houses for the members. Because of this they were called 'mutual societies'. They were often named after the district where they started, such as Halifax or Cheltenham and Gloucester.

Gradually, many of these societies 'de-mutualised' and became banks. Even those that did not do this now offer similar services to banks.

Independent financial advisers (IFAs)

Independent financial advisers are not tied to any particular provider and should know about all the products available to suit their client's needs. They mainly advise on pensions and investments, and some also give mortgage advice. Some financial advisers are 'tied' to one provider. For example, if you visit a local bank, their adviser will advise you only on that bank's products.

There are two ways in which IFAs are paid. One is by charging an hourly rate and the other is by being paid commission from the supplier of the financial product. If you are contacting an IFA, make sure that they are working under FSA regulations.

Financial companies

There are many different types of financial company. Some specialise in one particular type of product, others offer two or more. Examples of the wide variety of financial products/services available include:

- mortgage providers
- consumer finance companies
- debt management companies
- credit card companies
- bankruptcy specialists
- insurance companies
- pension companies
- pawnbrokers.

Retailers

In addition to specialist financial companies, many large retailers also offer financial services and store (credit) cards. They can only be used in that particular store. To tempt people to have one, the store may make discounts and special offers available only to card holders. The catch is that the interest rates are very high, so they are best avoided unless you can always pay off the full amount owing when it is due.

Did you know?

- The government may stop IFAs from taking commission as payment from 2012 because it thinks some advisers may be biased to offer products that pay the most. If this happens, all IFAs will charge an hourly rate.
- **Loan sharks** is the name given to unscrupulous people who lend money at very high rates.

Activity: Finance companies

In groups, choose one type of financial company and research it online to find out more about what it offers. Then prepare a short presentation in which each person takes part, to tell other groups what you have found.

PLTS

Practise your skills as an independent enquirer by finding out the benefits and disadvantages of using each type of company.

Why do stores promote their store cards to customers?

Discussion point

Debenhams staff are trained to ask all customers if they would like a Debenhams store card if they offer a different payment method. Why do you think this is done and do you agree with it? Discuss your ideas as a class.

Key term

Debt consolidation – combining several debts of a homeowner into one, normally secured against the house. The overall result is that there is less to pay, but the borrower is likely to lose their house if things go wrong.

Functional skills

Reading promotional leaflets and adverts on financial products gives you the ideal opportunity to practise detecting **implicit meanings** and **bias**.

Some retailers of expensive items, such as furniture and cars, also offer personal loans. These loans are often made through a finance company or bank, with the retailer acting as agent. As with any loan, the conditions (interest rate, repayment period and so on) need to be investigated carefully before deciding what to do, as you will see on page 459.

Purpose of financial services

Giving financial advice on managing money

People seek financial advice for several reasons. A student going to university might want advice on student loans and accommodation. A young couple might not know whether to rent or buy a house. A young family man might want to have insurance in case of a serious accident that prevents him from working. Another couple might want to check they are saving enough for their retirement. Banks and IFAs are the most obvious sources of advice, although you must remember that each bank can only offer its own products.

In either case, the advisers should obtain all the financial information related to their client including wages, investments and commitments, such as an outstanding mortgage. Only then can they offer comprehensive advice to suit that person.

Other types of service provided

Other types of financial services include:

* providing savings or investment accounts
* providing insurance against death, sickness or loss
* lending money subject to specific criteria.

You will learn about these on pages 457–59.

Other sources of information/advice

Although banks and building societies are the main sources of information on financial matters, there are other sources available.

* Some solicitors can give advice on investment.
* CAB advice centres provide information on benefits and debt counselling (see page 453).
* Some financial companies advise on **debt consolidation**. People have to be careful about using these firms as they are in the business to make money, not to help their clients.
* Several Internet sites give independent comparative advice on financial products, as you will see on page 461.

Activity: How true?

Your sister thinks that bank staff and financial advisers are very clever and trusts everything they say. You know that this is not always true. How would you convince her to be cautious about the advice she receives and the information she reads in their leaflets and adverts?

2.2 Types of products and services

Features

Although there are many types of financial product, there are a few features that are common to several of them.

- **Borrowing** – Several products enable customers to borrow money. These include loans from banks and finance companies, overdrafts, credit cards and mortgages. All loans have specific requirements, such as interest to be paid and a timescale to repay the amount borrowed.

- **Saving/investing** – This is where money is deposited in an account and is available for later withdrawal. Normally interest is paid.

- **Risk** – Some types of savings, such as company shares, involve the risk that some or even all of the money invested could be lost.

Benefits and charges

Current or savings accounts

Most people have a current account, if only because their employer insists on transferring wages directly into one. Current accounts also allow money transfers, such as direct debits, standing orders and cheque payments, to be made. Banks normally offer these services for free, and some even pay a small amount of interest if your salary is paid in. If you are likely to need an overdraft, these charges must be investigated carefully.

Banks often fail to warn students who start work that they are no longer eligible for the special terms and conditions of their student account, so be careful. Do not expect your bank to look after you.

Savings accounts are designed for people who want to put their money in a safe place. In addition, the bank pays interest to the savers. The main features of a savings account are as follows.

- Generally, the greater the amount of money saved, the higher the interest rate paid.

- Banks also encourage regular savings by offering higher interest rates.

- Some savings accounts restrict the number of withdrawals in a given period, say a year.

Banks often offer new savings accounts with attractive benefits such as a high interest rate or bonus. They then cut these at a later date and rely on people's inertia to leave their money where it is.

Banks make much of their own income by lending money at a much higher rate of interest than the rate they pay to savers.

Insurance protection

Insurance is a way of avoiding hardship if something disastrous happens, for example, if your car is stolen. Typically, you pay a regular premium

Did you know?

- One student forgot to check her student current account balance during her exams and went overdrawn by £2.15. The bank charged her £48 for doing this and ignored all pleas to get the amount lowered.

- **Cash ISAs** are special savings accounts where the interest is tax-free. The government allows these to encourage people to save. Remember that normally people pay tax on the interest they receive.

Remember

Banks are in business to make money. They try to tempt current account holders to 'upgrade' to a special account for which they pay a fee. These are rarely worth it.

Did you know?

- You can insure against almost anything! For example, the producers of an outdoor event can insure against bad weather spoiling it. Famous singers can insure against losing their voice, and footballers can insure their legs!

- By law, car owners have to insure against damage to other people and their property (for example, another car). This is known as third party protection. They can increase the premium to pay for comprehensive insurance which covers their own car as well.

- In 2009, a city financier who had lost all of his money in the credit crunch had his house repossessed. It was valued at £11 million.

and the insurance company pays the bill if the disaster occurs. There are many forms of insurance, including:

- cars and motorcycles
- houses, buildings
- house contents
- income protection (some specifically protect mortgage payments if you become disabled and cannot work)
- travel insurance
- life insurance (see also next section on life assurance).

What are the benefits of travel insurance?

Remember

A mortgage is a form of secured loan. This means that the lender can reclaim the house if the borrower falls behind with payments.

The insurance market is very competitive, so it is important to shop around. It is also important to check that everything you want is covered, such as how much your travel insurance will pay out if your suitcase is lost, and whether it would pay for an air ambulance home if you were seriously hurt.

Life assurance

There is an important difference between life *insurance* and life *assurance*. In the case of life insurance, in return for a premium the insurer will pay an agreed amount if the insured person dies within a set period. If the insured person lives beyond that time, nothing is paid out.

With life assurance the policy always pays out. The policy includes an element of investment and can be cashed in early if required.

Mortgages

When you want to buy a house or flat, you will almost certainly need a mortgage, unless you have a very rich relative! A mortgage is a form of loan that requires a deposit and monthly repayments for several years.

When you are choosing a mortgage lender, the critical factor is the interest rate. Other factors to consider include the cost of transferring to another lender at a later date (called the exit fee), the lender's solicitor's fee, the property valuation fee, and an application fee that is charged by some lenders.

Pensions

At some stage most people retire from employment and rely on pension income to cover their expenses. Pensions are obtained by making contributions from earned income before retirement. There are three main types of pension.

- **State pension** – paid to everyone who has made National Insurance contributions. Your pension entitlement can be checked by contacting the Pension Service.

- **Occupational pension** – organised by an employer who deducts an amount of money from your salary, and often contributes a percentage as well. Some schemes pay a pension based on final salary, but these are very expensive and becoming less popular.

- **Personal pension** – pension schemes taken out by individuals from banks or other pension providers. The government allows tax relief on some contributions. A special kind of provision is Stakeholder Pensions. These are regulated by the government, which limits the amount of management charges that can be deducted.

Pensions are very complex. People should review their pension provision every few years throughout their working life. The Pensions Advisory Service gives independent general advice, but people wanting a personal review should talk to a reputable, independent financial adviser.

Activity: Fixed or variable?

See if you can work this out for yourself: if interest rates are likely to increase soon, are you better with a fixed or variable mortgage? And what if they are likely to fall?

Activity: Pension ages

The government is gradually raising the retirement age for both men and women. This is the age from which you are paid a state pension. Check the Pensions Advisory Service website to find more about pensions and how old you will be before you get a state pension.

Risks and benefits of borrowing money

There are several ways of borrowing money.

Table 20.2: Advantages and disadvantages of borrowing money

Method of borrowing money	Description	Risks	Benefits
Secured loan	Money borrowed against an asset, such as a mortgage or car loan	Losing the asset if the borrower gets behind with payments	Easier to get, and interest rates lower than an unsecured loan
Unsecured loan	Money borrowed without security	Loan can be recalled if borrower falls behind with payments	No immediate risk of losing a personal asset
Overdrafts	Drawing more money from a current account than is in it	Interest rates are high and get a lot worse if the agreed limit is overshot	Interest paid on a daily basis
Credit cards	Plastic card used for payment. Statement of account details sent monthly	High interest rates if balance not paid in full. Interest paid on cash withdrawals straight away	Easy to complete transactions. Interest-free provided balance is paid in full

Key terms

APR – Annual Percentage Rate. This figure tells you how much interest you are being charged on a loan (including a credit card).

AER – Annual Equivalent Rate. This is the best way of comparing savings accounts as it takes into account when the interest is paid. Choose the account with the highest AER.

Discussion point

In 2009, O2 Money, in conjunction with NatWest bank, launched Load & Go, a prepay Visa card for 13 to16-year-olds, and Cash Manager, a similar card for adults. The difference is that parents load up their children's card, whereas adults normally load theirs from their own earnings. Critics felt Load & Go would enable teens to splurge online, while others thought it was a good idea and safer than cash. What do you think?

Comparing options

Whether you want to open a current account, take out a loan or obtain a credit card, there are always options. This is the most important point about financial products. If you are buying a car, the dealer will be an agent for a finance company and can offer you an instant loan. The terms may be poor compared to those offered by your bank, but it is tempting to go for convenience and drive away the car that afternoon.

The solution is simple. You should always compare the key factors on any financial product, such as the **APR** on loans and credits cards, and **AER** on savings accounts. One way is to draw a chart, similar to the one below. Another is to use a comparison website, as you will see on the following page.

Table 20.3: Sample chart to compare key factors of financial products

Key factors	Provider 1	Provider 2	Provider 3
Factor 1			
Factor 2			

Making suitable choices based on accurate information

Comparing products should help you to make a suitable choice. Do be careful, though, if you are using information from providers' websites and TV or newspaper advertisements. Banks may advertise a savings account with a high interest rate, but this might only apply to very large deposits and you may have to leave the money untouched for at least a year. A travel insurance company could offer a good rate, but only offer low compensation for lost luggage. Because of this, many people find it quicker and easier to use an impartial comparison website instead.

Simon Nixon wants us all to know enough to live in a rich man's world.

Simon Nixon wanted people to see how different products compare in price by putting the information online. At the age of 29, he launched MoneySupermarket.com. Eight years later, in 2007, the business floated on the stock exchange for a cool £800 million.

He started with mortgages, but the site now covers current accounts, insurance, utilities (electricity and gas), broadband, mobile phones, flights, holidays, car hire and even general shopping. It is also the most comprehensive site. This is why it claims to be the number one price comparison site, and why, if you ever go for less than the best deal, it certainly is not their fault!

Ian Williams is Director of Communications at MoneySupermarket. Can he help to make you richer? He is certainly happy to try. His advice is to open a current account the minute you start work and have your salary paid into it. Then get a cash point/debit card. It is no surprise that he says you should use MoneySupermarket to find the best deals on current accounts.

Ian recommends you save until you have at least three months' income in reserve. This is vital in case you lose your job or are too ill to work. Get into the habit of saving, he says, then you will always have money for Christmas and holidays.

Every employer has to offer a pension scheme, and you really should join, even if you think you are far too young. Time is your friend, Ian says, and the earlier you start saving the more money you amass. If your employer pays in contributions then you get extra 'free money' as well!

Simon Nixon still owns 53 per cent of the business, and works one day a week at the company's base near Chester. The rest of the time he is developing other new ideas. In the meantime, 460 employees are working hard to keep the site up to date so their 120 million visitors a year can look after their finances better. Does that include you?

Think about it!

1. Why does Ian Williams recommend that you open a current bank account when you start work? What features of this type of account would you find useful?

2. You have inherited £1,000 and decide to save the money. You cannot work out whether to save it for a fixed length of time or be able to withdraw some or all of it at any time.
   a) What are the advantages and disadvantages of both options?
   b) Decide what you would do and then check out the MoneySupermarket website, to find the best deal. Compare your ideas as a group.

3. How much does it cost you to live each week? How much would it cost if you did not live at home? As of October 2009, the state pension for a single person was just under £100 per week. Could you live off this? If not, what cuts would you make?

4. Ian Williams recommends planned saving. This means saving a certain amount of money as soon as you get paid. Why is this better than just saving the money you have left over at the end of each week or month?

5. What are the benefits and drawbacks of using MoneySupermarket to obtain information rather than consulting a financial services provider or IFA? Discuss your ideas as a group.

Just checking

1. Suggest three important questions you should ask a financial adviser about the way they operate.
2. Name one advantage and one disadvantage of taking a store credit card.
3. What do APR and AER mean, and in what circumstances do they apply?
4. What is the difference between an overdraft and a personal loan?
5. Why do many people have both current accounts and savings accounts?

BTEC Assessment activity 20.2

1. Your cousin, Jessica, is 22. She has recently been offered a job away from home on a much higher salary than the one she has at the moment. If she rents a flat or house, she will have to find money for a deposit. On the other hand, she is thinking about buying a flat or a small house. She will also need a car so that she can come home at weekends to see her boyfriend. Jessica has asked you to suggest where she can turn to for advice on the various financial issues she faces. What would you recommend? **P2**

2. After completing your studies, you will either want to get a job or you may think about going to university. If you decide to go to university, you might want to stay at home and travel each day, or live away from home. Choose the options that you think you would prefer and then describe the financial products and services you may need if you did this. **P3**

3. Your brother has just started work and his employer has insisted that he opens a current bank account. He does not know what this means and is even more confused because the bank he has approached has suggested that he should open a savings account at the same time. Explain to him what the difference is between the two accounts by describing the features and services in relation to each one. **M2**

Grading tips

- For Question 1, think about all the financial implications of moving away from home – write a list. Then use this to decide how Jessica would find the information she needs.

- When you answer Question 2, remember to write one or two sentences saying what features of each product are important and relevant to you.

- For a merit grade you will find it useful to check out the websites of one or two major banks to obtain the information you need.

3. Be able to produce a personal budget that takes account of personal remuneration and expenditure

3.1 Personal budget

Some people always seem to get through money quickly and often run out long before their next pay day. Others always have money left over at the end of the month – if this is you, then you are good at budgeting, even if you never write anything down.

A **personal budget** is a financial plan showing where your money comes from (income) and what you intend to do with it (expenditure). This may sound easy, but many people spend money without thinking or do so on impulse, which can get them into trouble as a result.

Did you know?

Some people think teenagers should get their spending money monthly, not weekly, to prepare them for when they start work. Do you agree?

Key term

Personal budget – a list of planned income and expenditure for a particular period in the future (for example, a week). You can also use this to compare your actual spending with what you planned to do.

Are you ever tempted to spend more than you intended?

Purpose of a personal budget

The main reasons for having a budgeting system are:

• you can make sure that you do not spend more than your income and so avoid getting into debt

• writing it down means you can study where your money comes from and where it goes

• you can see if there are any ways of increasing your income.

- you can see if there are any ways of reducing your spending, such as by cutting down on something or not buying it at all

- you can divide your expenses into essential and non-essential categories to make the most of the money you spend.

Construction and key elements of a budget

Weekly budget planning chart

Study the budget planning chart (Table 20.4) carefully and note the following points.

Table 20.4: Weekly budget planning chart

	Planned income/ expenses £ (I)	Actual income/ expenses £ (J)
Income (A)		
Spending money		
Wages from part-time job		
(Other)		
(Other)		
Total income (B)		
Essential expenditure (C)		
Travel		
Lunches		
(Other)		
(Other)		
(Other)		
Total essential expenditure (D)		
Disposable income (B - D) (E)		
Planned savings (F)		
Available for optional spends (E - F) (G)		
Snacks		
Magazines		
Meals out and cinema		
T-shirt		
(Other)		
Total planned savings and optional spends (H)		

- The first part of the left-hand column (A) lists the items of income. At the end of this part, the total income is calculated (B).

- The second part (C) lists suggested items of **essential expenditure**. This is unavoidable expenditure necessary for day-to-day living. In your own budget you should enter items that are personal to you. The total for this section is shown at (D).

- The difference between income and essential expenditure is your **disposable income** (E), that is, the amount available for saving or spending on optional expenses. These are items, such as leisure activities, that you could avoid if you had to.

- The next section enables you to specify the amount you plan to save out of your disposable income (F). It is important that you set aside an amount to save before looking at optional spending.

- Then you can list the optional items that, in your budget, would be personal to you (G).

- The total of your planned savings and optional expenses (H) should be equal to or less than the amount available (E). Another term for 'optional expenses' is discretionary spending (money you can choose to spend or not).

Completing the budget

This is done in three stages.

1. Enter the items personal to you in the first column below each heading.

2. Think about what you will receive and what you plan to spend at the start of the week. Then complete the second column 'Planned income/expenses £' (I) with these figures.

3. At the end of the week, complete the final column 'Actual income/expenses £' (J). Make a note of any differences between the second and third columns. The time to worry is if you do not have enough income to cover your essential expenditure or if you are spending all your disposable income each week and never saving a penny.

At first sight, this chart may seem complicated, but after a little practice you should find it is quite straightforward.

Activity: Prepare Alex's budget

Alex sits down on Sunday and plans his budget for the week. He enters the following figures on a weekly budget planning chart:

- spending money £25
- wages from part-time job £80
- travel expenses £15
- lunches £20
- savings £10
- snacks £10
- meals out and cinema £15
- computer game £25.

Copy the chart above, inserting only the words in bold, and then add the planned income and expenditure figures.

On the following Sunday, Alex reviews the week's finances and finds the following.

- His aunt gave him an extra £10 to boost his spending money.
- His wages were as normal.
- His brother gave him a lift into college, so his travel expenses were £5 less.
- He spent the amount planned on lunches, but £5 more on snacks.
- He went to the cinema and ate out more times than planned and this cost him £30 in total.
- The computer game was £10 more than expected.
- At the end of the week Alex had no money left to put into his savings account.

Complete Alex's budget chart by adding the 'actual' figures and then complete the totals as before. Now comment on the differences between the planned and actual figures. What is your opinion of Alex's budget system?

Did you know?

If you are familiar with spreadsheets, you could set one up to work on the budget exercises in this section.

Functional skills

Practise your maths skills by completing the chart accurately and ensuring that all of the calculations are correct.

Regular and irregular income and expenditure

When you are planning a budget, some entries are fairly predictable since they happen on a regular basis. Other items of income and expenditure are irregular, and in some cases not predictable at all. See the next section for examples of both kinds.

When preparing a budget, it is difficult to allow for irregular income and expenditure. You could put all irregular income into a savings account with your regular savings. This can then be used for irregular expenditure.

Sources of income

At the moment, your income may be limited but, as your life progresses, you could well have additional sources.

Table 20.5: Main regular (R) and irregular (I) sources of income

Source of income	Notes
Wages (R)	Term used for money paid for manual work, for example, a waiter/waitress (normally quoted as an hourly rate)
Salary (R)	The annual amount paid for non-manual work. Both wages and salaries are subject to income tax (see page 448)
Overtime (I)	Payment for additional hours worked on top of contracted hours
Tips (I)	Normally associated with a personal service, for example, waiting or hairdressing
Fees (R)	Money paid for a professional service, for example, an architect or solicitor
Bonus earned (I)	Money paid on top of a salary for achieving an agreed standard of performance
Commission earned (I)	Mainly applies to salespeople who receive a percentage commission on everything they sell
Allowances (I)	Extra money provided by an employer for certain items essential for work, for example, safety shoes or the dry cleaning of a uniform, a meal allowance, expenses paid if you travel
State benefits (R)	The state gives money (benefits) to people in certain circumstances, for example, bringing up children, being disabled, being unemployed
Grants (and loans) (R)	The government gives grants and loans, such as the EMA (Education Maintenance Allowance). University students can also get a student loan
Interest on savings or investments (R)	Money paid by a financial provider as a reward for saving with them. Interest is normally paid annually, but can sometimes be paid monthly
Gifts (I)	Includes monetary gifts for birthdays and other special occasions
Inheritance (I)	Money you have been left in a will that has been made by someone who has since died

Did you know?

- Everyone who is employed must be paid a minimum hourly rate, known as **minimum wage**. If you study Option Unit 9 you will learn more about this.

- People who are paid commission often only receive a low basic salary, and sometimes none at all. Therefore, they depend on their commission to bring their earnings up to a reasonable standard.

- People write their will to say what should happen to their property (money, house, jewellery and so on) after they have died. Normally they want it shared between children, grandchildren and other close relatives. If someone dies without a will, their possessions go to their next of kin or, if there is no one, to the government.

Activity: Grants and loans

To find out about student grants and loans, go to the Money to learn section of the Directgov website. To find out about State benefits, visit the Money, tax and benefits section of the site.

Types of expenditure

The way people spend their money varies a lot from one person to another. Table 20.6 lists some examples.

What are your most common types of expenditure?

Table 20.6: Main regular (R) and irregular (I) types of expenditure

Types of expenditure	Notes
Accommodation (R)	Cost of living in a house/flat (rent or mortgage)
Tax (R)	Expenditure you rarely see! Income tax is taken from your wage before you are paid. VAT and excise duty are added to the price of things before you buy
Household expenses (R)	All the costs associated with running a household, for example, utility bills, maintenance and council tax
Travelling (I)	With public transport, travelling expenses should be easy to assess. With a car, it is more complex as it includes fuel, insurance, road tax, maintenance and depreciation (how much the car loses in value each year)
Food (R)	Day-to-day expenses on groceries (excluding eating out)
Clothing (R)	All forms of clothing, including footwear
Communication (landline, mobile, Internet) (R)	Purchase of equipment, rental of landlines, all mobile charges (on a contract or Pay As You Go)
Leisure activities (I)	Hobbies, visits to the cinema, holidays, meals out, and so on.
Insurance (R)	There are several types of insurance (see pages 457–58)
Savings (R)	Planned savings that you intend to make from regular income and gifts
Special occasions (I)	Holidays and other events, for example, theatre, cinema, weddings, parties (where you have to buy a gift)
Credit card payments (R)	You may pay off the full amount owed every month, but even if you make the minimum payment, this still has to be allowed for
Loan payments (R)	Fixed by the terms of the loan agreement; usually made monthly

Just checking

1. Give three benefits of preparing a personal budget.
2. Explain what is meant by the following types of income: overtime; tips; fees; bonus; commission.
3. If you take a job that means you have to live away from home, list three types of additional expense you will have.

BTEC Assessment activity 20.3

P4 M1 D1

1. Plan your budgeted expenditure for a week and then check the results. Copy out the budget planning chart on page 464, including only the words in bold. Then insert your own personal items under the income, essential expenditure and optional spends headings. Enter an amount against each one, suggesting how much you think you will spend that week.

   At the end of each day, write down all the items you spent money on, and how much. At the end of the week, use the records you have kept to complete the budget chart by filling in the last column. Then attach a short commentary in which you explain the importance of the different aspects of the budget. **P4**

2. Review the format and the structure of your budget. How could you improve this to make it better for your own use? Look at the headings and the items you have entered. Do these clearly give you the accurate information you need? Make any changes you feel would improve your budget and then write a commentary which explains why you have made these decisions. **M1**

3. Now reconsider each item you have entered in your budget and justify its inclusion. This means saying why you felt each item of essential expenditure is necessary and why there are no alternatives. In your optional spends section, you will need to include the alternatives you have considered and why you chose to include these particular items. **D1**

Grading tips

- To start your commentary, look at the main headings in your budget and your calculations to identify what you now know about your spending habits that you did not know before.

- To get a distinction, you need to be able to justify all the decisions you made when you were doing your financial planning. It will help if you include your sources of information to support your arguments.

Assignment tips

- Before you start your budget, it is also helpful to keep a record of what you spend your money on for a few days. This will help you to make it as accurate as possible.

- If you are making changes to the format on a spreadsheet package, it can help to save your earlier versions rather than overwrite them, then you can go back if you need to.

Glossary

Ability – the natural talent, skill or aptitude to do something.

Advice (for customers) – guidance on the product or service that would best meet the customer's needs.

AER – **A**nnual **E**quivalent **R**ate. The method of comparing savings accounts that takes into account when the interest is paid. The best account is the one with the highest AER.

Agenda – a list of items to be discussed at a meeting.

APR – **A**nnual **P**ercentage **R**ate. The amount of interest charged on a loan (including a credit card) each year.

Aptitude – a person's potential to develop skills and acquire information.

Bad debt – debt that is never paid and has to be 'written off' in the accounts.

Bankrupt – a person who has been declared **insolvent** by a court.

Bills – documents that state how much money is owed for a product or service. Another word for a bill is an invoice.

Body language – the messages communicated by using gestures, facial expressions and posture.

Breach of contract – failing to comply with one or more terms of a contract.

Break-even – covering the costs of making the product and running the business, but no more. Businesses break even when income and expenditure are equal.

Business context – the business situation that applies and which will influence the choice of communication method, its tone and style.

Business discussion – an informal debate between a group of people to reach a joint agreement.

Business meeting – an arrangement for people to meet to discuss specific business issues.

Buyer behaviour – the way different customers act when they are buying.

Cash balance – total amount of money in a bank account at a particular time.

Cash inflows – sums of money entering the bank account of a business.

Cash outflows – sums of money leaving the bank account of a business.

Cash-flow forecast – a prediction of what is likely to happen in the future.

Cash-flow statement – a record of what has already happened.

Chairperson – the leader of a meeting.

Civil law – concerned with righting wrongs done to individuals through the civil courts.

Competently – being able to do a job properly, in the correct way.

Complementary skills – skills that go together to enable jobs to be done more efficiently.

Consistent – offering the same standard or using the same format every time.

Consumables – items bought regularly by businesses but not used in making the product or supplying the service, for example printer paper.

Contingency plan – a business plan brought into effect if a predicted possible event occurs.

Contract of employment – a written document containing the terms and conditions of employment relating to a particular person and their job.

Contract out – paying another business to carry out support activities such as security, cleaning and payroll administration. (See also **outsourcing**.)

Conventions – basic principles which relate to the way certain documents are written.

Conversion rate – the number of website visitors who take action, for example by registering or making a purchase.

Cost of sales – the money spent by a business on materials for manufacturing or resale.

Credit control – all the possible steps a business can take to identify customers who are slow to pay and the actions it can then take.

Credit reference agencies – companies that collect information on people and assess how much of a risk they are to businesses that lend money.

Customer objections – reasons why a customer hesitates to commit to a purchase.

Customer satisfaction – how customers feel when their needs and expectations have been met.

Debt – money owed to someone else or a financial organisation.

Debt consolidation – combining several debts of a homeowner into one, normally secured against the house.

Decision – choosing between two or more courses of action.

Deflation – when the prices of goods are falling.

Delayering – removing a layer of a hierarchical organisation, usually to save money.

Differential pricing – charging different prices to different customer groups.

Direct costs – money paid out in direct proportion to the number of items produced and sold. Also called **variable costs**.

Discretionary spending – money we choose to spend on non-essentials.

Discrimination – treating someone differently and unfairly because of a reason unrelated to their job.

Disposable income – amount left from wages after paying taxes and essential bills.

Diversify – to carry out a different business activity, instead of (or as well as) the original one; to broaden the range of products made or activities undertaken.

Dividend – the reward paid to shareholders for investing in the business, similar to interest on a bank account.

Domain name – the unique name that identifies a website.

Economy – the financial situation of a country as a result of all the items that are produced and consumed there.

Economies of scale – savings made by large businesses that can produce or sell items with lower unit costs than small businesses.

Effectiveness – doing things right, i.e. in the right order, to the right standard and in the right way.

Efficiency – doing the right thing, i.e. making the best use of resources, such as time and money.

E-marketing – relates to electronic and online promotions, such as email newsletters, website competitions or advertising on search engines.

Employment tribunal – a special informal court that hears and rules upon employment cases.

Entrepreneur – person who uses their own money to start a business enterprise with the aim of making a profit.

Ergonomics – designing or adapting the job, equipment and working environment to meet the needs of the person or user.

Ethical – to be fair and to act according to moral principles.

Exclusion clause – a term which attempts to limit or restrict the liability of the supplier or limit the rights of the consumer.

Fixed costs – costs that do not vary in relation to the number of items produced. Also known as **indirect costs**.

Focus group – small group of people representing the range of customers a business has. They give opinions on issues related to the business.

Format – the design, layout and order of information in a document.

Functionality – the features on a website, such as a search facility or order form, and how easy these are for someone to use.

Gross Domestic Product (GDP) – the total value of all goods and services produced by a nation in a year.

Gross profit – the amount left over from revenue when the **cost of sales** is deducted.

Hardware – IT equipment and components, for example the VDU (Visual Unit Display), keyboard and printer.

Header – the top section of a document. The opposite is footer, at the bottom of a document.

Hits – the number of requests made for an element on a web page or graphic.

HTML – Hyper Text Markup Language is the language used on the web.

Import duty – tax paid on imports from non-EU countries.

Impulse purchase – an unplanned purchase.

In breach – breaking the terms of a contract.

Indirect costs – see **fixed costs**.

Industrial sectors – the primary, secondary and tertiary sectors by which all business activities in the UK are classified.

Industry – a group of businesses undertaking the same activity and offering the same or similar products, for example the advertising or catering industries.

Inflation – where the prices of goods are increasing.

Information – details about a product or service.

Insolvent – when someone becomes legally insolvent they do not have enough money to pay their debts and may be declared **bankrupt**.

Interaction – the two-way process between people, such as during a conversation.

Interest – the cost of borrowing money, normally a percentage of the amount borrowed.

Interpersonal skills – the social and communication skills needed to relate to other people.

Invest – put money into a business with the expectation of making a profit.

Jargon – terminology or slang that is not known or understood by everyone.

Job description – a statement that lists the main elements of a job and the tasks done by the job holder.

Key customers – people who contribute most to the profits of the business.

Labour turnover – the rate at which employees leave a company and need replacing.

Lead time – time period between placing an order and receiving the goods.

Legible – clearly written and easy to read.

Limited liability – the owners cannot lose more than they invested in the business if it fails.

Loan – amount of money lent to a business to help it to grow or to improve cash flow.

Logistics – planning and controlling the movement of goods.

Market – all the possible consumers who might buy a product or service.

Market share – the share of customers that buy from a certain supplier, or purchase a specific product or service.

Marketing mix – the four essential elements of marketing, also know as the Four Ps: product, place, price and promotion.

Mass market – a large, non-targeted market for consumer goods.

Media – methods of communicating with the public such as newspapers, TV and the Internet.

Meeting brief – a summary of the main requirements for a meeting.

Mentor – a person who gives support and advice to another person.

Micro business – a business with ten or fewer employees.

Minutes – the official written record of the decisions taken at a meeting.

Mission statement – explains the main purpose of the business and the activities it is doing to achieve this.

Multi-skilled – having several skills.

Net cash flow – the difference between **cash inflows** and **cash outflows** over a period of time.

Net profit – the amount left when the operating expenses are deducted from the gross profit figure.

Network – a system of linked computers that can communicate and share information.

Networking – developing business contacts to increase potential business opportunities.

Outsourcing – hiring an outside firm to do a specific job, such as distribution or security.

Overdraft – an arrangement with the bank that an account holder can withdraw more from their current account than it contains.

PAYE – short for **Pay as You Earn**, is income tax taken from an employee's wage by their employer.

Person specification – linked to the job description, it states the skills and abilities needed to do the job effectively.

Personal audit – a review of the knowledge, skills and attributes a person has gained.

Personal budget – a list of planned income and expenditure for a future period.

Personal selling – selling a product or service through personal contact, usually face to face.

PIN – **P**ersonal **I**dentification **N**umber used to gain access to various accounts.

Pixel – the smallest part of a digital image.

Press conference – a meeting to which representatives from the media are invited to learn about a new product or other development.

Press release – a prepared statement released to the media to let people know about plans, events or newsworthy changes.

Primary market research – information obtained from existing and potential customers.

Primary sector – industries involved in growing, extracting or converting natural resources.

Private ownership – relates to businesses owned by individuals who aim to make a profit.

Productivity – amount of output produced by a person or industry.

Product mix – the range or variety of products made or sold by a business.

Profit – the amount left from sales revenue after deducting the cost of producing or supplying the goods or service.

Profit maximisation – making as much profit as possible.

Promotional activities – activities that make customers aware of a product or service or give them an incentive to buy.

Promotional mix – the mix of promotional methods used to attract customers.

Promotions – methods of bringing a product or service to the attention of customers with the aim of persuading them to buy.

Public ownership – relates to businesses owned by the government.

Publicity campaign – a linked combination of marketing activities.

Remedies – the methods used to put things right if a person is wronged in law.

Restructuring – changing the organisation structure of a business.

Revenue – the total amount of money going into a business.

Risk – danger of losing money in a business venture.

Sales channels – ways in which businesses sell and distribute goods to customers.

Sales turnover – amount of money the business obtains by selling its goods and services.

Scale of a business – relates to the size of its operations and whether it sells on a large scale, globally, or on a small scale, to just a local area.

Secondary market research – information obtained from published data.

Secondary sector – industries that manufacture or construct goods.

Segmentation – dividing a market into different groups of customers, each with their own needs.

Server – a computer that allows access to files and programmes stored on a computer network.

Size of a business – relates to its physical size, number of employees and value of its sales turnover.

Skill – the ability to carry out certain tasks after training.

Social enterprises – businesses that use any profit, or surplus, to fulfil their social objectives.

Software – IT programmes that tell the computer what to do.

Span of control – the number of staff a manager is responsible for.

Start-up capital – amount of money needed to set up a business.

Start-up costs – the costs incurred before the business begins to operate.

Statute law – laws created by passing Acts of Parliament, for example the Sale of Goods Act.

Strategy – what the business aims to do in the long term, for example expand and recruit additional staff.

Stock turnover – the speed at which different items are sold.

Surplus – in the voluntary sector, the amount remaining from donations, fund-raising and commercial activities after essential expenses have been paid.

Targets – short-term goals which motivate people to try harder.

Team briefing – regular staff meetings to discuss information relevant to the team.

Tertiary sector – industries that provide services to other businesses and private individuals.

Tone – the way words are spoken to reflect the speaker's attitude. Tone can also apply to the choice of words in a written communication.

Tort – a wrong, injury or breach in civil law.

Total costs – all the fixed and variable costs added together.

Uncontrollable factors – events that can affect a business over which it has no control.

Unique users – the number of individual visitors to a website.

Unit cost – price of making or selling each item.

Unlimited liability – a business where the owners may lose their personal assets to pay off their debts if the enterprise fails.

Value for money – belief that the price paid was fair.

Variable costs – see **direct costs**.

VAT – **V**alue **A**dded **T**ax, a tax added to the selling price of many goods and services.

Vision statement – explains what the business is hoping or planning to do in the future.

Voluntary organisations – not-for-profit organisations that provide a service and are run by professional staff and volunteers. These include charities.

What if? – questions asked by business managers to assess the options open to them and the potential outcomes.

Word of mouth – customers telling their friends and colleagues about their experiences.

Working environment – the design, layout, facilities, and equipment available to staff, as well as the ethos (atmosphere) of the workplace.

Index

The

EMBROIDERED
BOOK

DRAMATIS PERSONAE

❧

THE HOUSE OF HABSBURG-LORRAINE

MARIA THERESA . . . . . . *sovereign of Austria, Hungary, and Bohemia, and, by marriage, Holy Roman Empress. Widow, statesman, fanatic, matriarch.*

JOSEPH . . . . . . *eldest son of Maria Theresa. Holy Roman Emperor and co-regent of the Habsburg domains. Thwarted philosopher.*

MIMI . . . . . . *formally Maria Christina, favourite daughter of Maria Theresa.*

LIESL . . . . . . *formally Maria Elisabeth, most beautiful daughter of Maria Theresa.*

AMALIA . . . . . . *most terrifying daughter of Maria Theresa.*

JOSEPHA . . . . . . *most terrified daughter of Maria Theresa.*

LEOPOLD . . . . . . *son of Maria Theresa. Grand Duke of Tuscany.*

FRANCIS . . . . . . *son of Leopold.*

CHARLOTTE . . . . . . *formally Maria Carolina. Said to be the daughter of Maria Theresa most like her mother.*

ANTOINE . . . . . . *formally Maria Antonia. Known for her sweet nature and charm.*

MAX . . . . . . *Maria Theresa's youngest child, more than a little spoiled.*

AUSTRIA

ANGELO SOLIMAN ......*soldier and scholar. Friend of the Emperor Joseph.*

PRINCE LOUIS DE ROHAN ......*nobleman with titles in France and the Holy Roman Empire.*

COUNTESS LERCHENFELD ......*governess: first to Charlotte and Antoine, then to Charlotte alone.*

COUNTESS BRANDEIS ......*governess to Antoine.*

GENEVIÈVE ......*a mysterious visitor to the Austrian court.*

NAPLES

FERDINAND ......*young ruler of Naples and Sicily, third son of King Carlos of Spain, terrible reputation.*

FILIPPO ......*Ferdinand's older brother, ineligible for the throne because of a lifelong medical condition.*

BERNARDO TANUCCI ......*corrupt lawyer, Ferdinand's chief adviser and former regent.*

CATERINA DE' MEDICI, MARCHESA OF SAN MARCO ......*lady-in-waiting who knows everything that happens in Naples.*

FRANCESCO D'AQUINO, PRINCE OF CARAMANICO ......*Neapolitan noble who refuses to appear at court.*

VINCENZO LUNARDI ......*secretary to the Prince of Caramanico, inventor.*

ALESSANDRO CAGLIOSTRO ......*magician and 'count' from Sicily.*

ISAAC LARS SILFVERSPARRE ......*Swedish nobleman and violinist.*

WILLIAM HAMILTON ......*British ambassador, lover of antiquities and volcanoes, owner of a monkey.*

EMMA HART ......*Hamilton's mistress, famous for her performance art.*

JOHN ACTON ......*expatriate Englishman, naval commander.*

ANGELICA KAUFFMAN ......*successful Swiss painter.*

HORATIO NELSON ......*captain in the British navy.*

FRANCE

LOUIS-AUGUSTE, DAUPHIN OF FRANCE ...... *orphaned heir to the throne.*

LOUIS XV ...... *King of France, the Dauphin's grandfather.*

JEANNE BÉCU, COMTESSE DU BARRY ...... *mistress to King Louis XV.*

LOUIS-STANISLAS, COMTE DE PROVENCE ...... *the Dauphin's arrogant brother.*

CHARLES, COMTE D'ARTOIS ...... *the Dauphin's charming brother.*

ÉLISABETH ...... *the Dauphin's devoted sister.*

PHILIPPE D'ORLÉANS ...... *royal cousin and prince of the blood.*

'MESDAMES' ADÉLAÏDE, VICTOIRE AND SOPHIE ...... *eccentric unmarried daughters of Louis XV, the Dauphin's aunts.*

ANNE D'ARPAJON, COMTESSE DE NOAILLES ...... *'Madame Etiquette',* dame d'honneur, *principal lady-in-waiting at Versailles.*

HENRIETTE CAMPAN ...... *lady-in-waiting at Versailles.*

MARIE-THÉRÈSE LOUISE DE SAVOIE ...... PRINCESSE DE LAMBALLE, *beautiful widowed French noble.*

YOLANDE GABRIELLE DE POLASTRON, COMTESSE DE POLIGNAC ...... *equally beautiful married French noble.*

JOSEPH BOLOGNE, CHEVALIER DE SAINT-GEORGES ...... *brilliant composer, violinist and fencer.*

GILBERT DU MOTIER, MARQUIS DE LAFAYETTE ...... *young French noble bent on revenge for his father's death at the hands of the English.*

LÉONARD AUTIÉ AND JEAN-FRANÇOIS AUTIÉ ...... *collectively* 'MONSIEUR LÉONARD', *hairdressers at Versailles.*

AXEL VON FERSEN ...... *Swedish count.*

THE CHEVALIER D'ÉON ...... *French spy living in exile after a falling-out with Louis XV.*

ÉLISABETH LOUISE VIGÉE LE BRUN ...... *successful French painter.*

LOUISE-ÉLISABETH DE CROŸ ...... THE MARQUISE DE TOURZEL, *French noble.*

PAULINE ...... *daughter of the Marquise de Tourzel.*

CHARLOTTE'S CHILDREN

TERESA ...... *born June* 1772

LUISA ...... *born July* 1773

CARLO ...... *born January* 1775

MARIANNA ...... *born November* 1775

FRANCESCO ...... *born August* 1777

MARIA CRISTINA (LITTLE MIMI) ...... *born January* 1779

GENNARO ...... *born April* 1780

GIUSEPPE ...... *born June* 1781

MARIA AMALIA ...... *born April* 1782

MARIA ANTONIA ...... *born December* 1784

CLOTHILDE ...... *born February* 1786

ENRICHIETTA ...... *born July* 1787

CARLO ...... *born August* 1788

LEOPOLD ...... *born July* 1790

ALBERTO ...... *born May* 1792

ISABELLA ...... *born December* 1793

ANTOINETTE'S CHILDREN

MARIE-THÉRÈSE ...... *affectionately 'Mousseline', born December* 1778

LOUIS-JOSEPH ...... *born October* 1781

LOUIS-CHARLES ...... *born March* 1785

SOPHIE ...... *born July* 1786

PART ONE

1767 TO 1768

CHAPTER ONE

The Empress Is Unmoved — You, Lucky Habsburg,
Marry — Charlotte Voices an Opinion — Death and
Decay — The Embroidered Book — Sacrifices

If only Antoine could find a love spell. A potion, a ribbon, a ring. With the right magic, she'd open Mama's heart, and save her sister from marrying the beast of Naples.

It's not as if the Empress Maria Theresa, sovereign of half of Europe, is incapable of love. She loved Papa so fiercely that she tallied every minute she spent with him in her diary. And after Papa's death, the year before last, Mama loved her daughter Mimi enough to let her marry the man of her choice.

Charlotte says that Mama was just relieved that Mimi did fall in love with a man, since her only romance before that had been with her sister-in-law. But Charlotte is uncharitable.

It is undeniable that Mama shows no signs of bending when it comes to Josepha. Josepha must go to Naples. It has been decreed.

Bella gerant alii, tu felix Austria nube. The family motto. *Let others wage war; you, lucky Habsburg, marry.*

Even Antoine, who has not studied much Latin, knows *nube* is in the imperative case.

At her sigh, Mama looks up sharply.

3

Mama has brought Antoine and her sisters to do their needlework in the Porcelain Room today. All the unmarried archduchesses, except for pretty Liesl, who is away visiting cousins. The remaining girls work furiously, silently, like mice trapped inside a teacup. Shadow-coloured plaster vines climb creamy walls on indigo trellises, between masses of gold-framed drawings.

Josepha is sixteen, which is very grown up, but she looks terrified. Her eyes go wide at Antoine's sigh, but she doesn't lift her head. She pokes her needle into the cloth in her lap.

Charlotte is slightly less grown-up at fifteen, but she looks angry. Dear Charlotte. She's the only one who's a match for Mama, and she thinks Mama hates her for it. But hasn't Mama said she plans to send Charlotte to marry the heir to the French throne? The most important of all the alliances? Only Charlotte could manage that, because she is just like Mama, though Antoine would never tell her that for fear of the look Charlotte would give her.

Antoine, at eleven, is still young enough to sigh and get away with it. She should be more prudent, though. Everything depends on Mama's love.

'Are you worried about your performance tomorrow?' Mama asks Antoine.

'No, Mama,' she says with her best smile. 'I've practised and practised. I just hope the ambassador likes it.'

The Neapolitan ambassador. The man who wants Josepha to marry his horrible king.

'Don't frown, Josepha,' murmurs Mama. 'Your forehead.'

Josepha smooths her expression, but her eyes go feral, like the cats the groom chased away from the stable last year. She stares at the cloth, unable to see where the threads went awry.

'You've pulled a thread clear through, Josepha,' Mama says.

'Ah. Thank you, Mama. I don't know how I didn't notice that.'

'Distraction is not a luxury we can afford,' says Mama. She sips her coffee, out of a cup the same colours as the walls.

Mama, as a young woman, drank coffee in secret, defying her father's ban on the drink during the wars with Turkey. Now Mama drinks coffee openly, because she is the Empress and can do what she likes. Only she will decide what can and cannot be done within the walls of Schönbrunn Palace in the year 1767.

Including everything her unmarried daughters do and think.

'Josepha,' Mama says, 'I suspect you're still nervous about your upcoming marriage. You should accept God's will. Pray for the strength to do so.'

'Yes, Mama,' says Josepha. Her face goes white.

Charlotte coughs.

'You have an opinion, Charlotte?' Mama looks at her. 'Say it plainly, if you do. I will have no coughers and tutters among my children.'

Charlotte looks at the white gloves in her lap, at the tiny knots of white silk thread in the monograms. 'I have heard nothing good of King Ferdinand of Naples. People say he is a monster.'

'He is a sixteen-year-old bachelor king,' says Mama. 'Of course he is a monster. His whole life he has been surrounded by flatterers and, and . . . Italians. He needs a good Christian wife to keep him away from the brothels and turn his mind towards his responsibilities, that's all. And we need Naples on our side.'

'Why me and not Amalia?' Josepha whispers, her face red. 'She is stronger than I am, and older. She is downright terrifying.'

'Ferdinand refused her,' Mama retorts. 'He doesn't want a wife five years older than he is. Not even Liesl, despite her beauty. Which is all to the good, as your brother and I have several possibilities in mind for Liesl. Anyway, Amalia will do for Parma. We must all do our duty, Josepha.' She pauses, and raises one formidable finger. 'The current Empress of Russia began life as the shabby daughter of a shabby soldier in a shabby town. But her mother made her a good marriage. And now Catherine rules an empire!'

'Catherine rules because she had her husband killed and seized his throne for herself,' Charlotte says with a little smile.

'Well,' her mother replies with a wave of her hand, 'Russians.' For Mama, it sufficed to say 'Italians' or 'Russians' to explain events in other lands. 'And she would not have had a throne to seize, had she married some local count's son who called her pretty.'

'Mimi married the man she loves,' says Charlotte, quieter, and without the smile.

Why test Mama? She'll only anger her. Antoine holds her breath.

Nobody speaks for a moment; the only sound is thread moving roughly through muslin. Nobody disputes, least of all Mama, that Mimi has always been Mama's favourite.

'The circumstances were different,' Mama mutters, her voice sinking so low that Antoine stops pulling her thread, to hear. 'We need Naples, and Naples has a king of marrying age. Josepha will be queen of the lower half of the Italian peninsula, and Sicily besides. It is not such a terrible fate.'

Charlotte lifts the white glove she's been embroidering, and looks at Antoine pointedly. Charlotte has been insisting on trying an enchantment to change Mama's mind. Trying to direct Mama's thoughts seems awfully dangerous, and Antoine has been arguing against it. But what choice do they have?

If only Antoine could find a love spell.

She starts to sigh again, and realizes halfway through, and tries to stop it, but it turns into a cough.

'Goodness,' Mama says, dropping her embroidery into her lap and raising both hands to God. 'All my daughters are coughing today. I'll have the cooks prepare my thyme tea for all three of you tonight. We can't afford any more illness in this family.'

The first death Charlotte remembers was her brother Charles. Smallpox. He was the same age Charlotte is now; he made desperate, horrible jokes right to the end, and she wishes that wasn't how she remembers him.

Not long after that, their governess, Countess Ertag, was murdered.

The next death was her sister Johanna. Johanna and Josepha were a pair, just as Charlotte and Antoine are. There are so many siblings in the family that their ages stretch over two decades, with ten-year-old Max at the bottom. And there are some gaps, from deaths. So the children tend to be closest to one or two of their siblings who are nearest to them in age. Johanna and Josepha did everything together and were always merry.

Johanna didn't even seem to mind being betrothed to Ferdinand of Naples; but then, she was young, and Ferdinand hadn't yet made his reputation as a beast. The year after Charles died, smallpox took Johanna, two days before Christmas. Josepha took it hardest; since that time she's never looked anything but afraid. And now she's heading off to Naples in her sister's place, if Mama gets her way.

The next death was their father's. Two years ago, a messenger came to say Papa had died – suddenly, of a stroke – far from home.

Their brother Joseph lost both his wives to smallpox: the first, he passionately loved (while she passionately loved Mimi). The second wife, poor woman, he did not love at all; and now she lies in the family crypt too.

The girls are powerless over death.

But Mama was not. When Joseph's second wife fell ill, so did Mama, but Mama got better. Let Antoine believe it was the ribbon enchanted 'for mending' they put under Mama's pillow; Charlotte knows it was sheer stubbornness. And when the Empress heard that her daughters had been crawling under hedges in the garden (they were looking for dropped coins, for sacrifices), she declared that Charlotte was an unfortunate influence on her younger sister. From then on, they were to see each other only at dinners or with other family present. Different governesses from then on, and different tutoring sessions, and rooms at opposite ends of the children's wing.

They found ways of coping, of meeting in secret at night to talk about magic.

But they still have no spell that will save a life.

Charlotte opens Antoine's door, softly and soundlessly, and steps in.

Antoine is standing at her dressing table, with a pewter powder box in her hand. 'There you are,' she says brightly. 'Did you bring it?'

Charlotte nods, and pulls the book with the embroidered cover from the false pocket sewn inside her nightgown, the pocket that can hold a vast quantity of things (so long as each is, itself, a pocket-sized thing) and still seem empty from the outside.

Antoine kneels and sprinkles ash from the powder box.

'I'm glad you have ash,' says Charlotte, pulling the items for the sacrifice out of her pocket. 'It's been so hot lately that there's nothing in the fireplaces and the kitchens are always crowded.'

'Herr Bauer gave me some.'

'Who?'

'The gardener. He puts ash into the soil around the roses. He is very clever and shows me all the new roses he invents.'

'People don't invent roses,' Charlotte says, before realizing she knows nothing about it; perhaps they do.

She opens the embroidered book. On the thirtieth page, there is the spell she needs, in her long-dead governess's patient and frilly handwriting:

For an item of clothing, reproducible and inexhaustible, to confer on the wearer persuasion of a listener's mind beyond the natural, these proofs have been found: convaincre ⇢ convainore ⇢ ooovaioore ⇢ oooaaioore ⇢ oooaaiooue. For the prime magister, these were the sacrifices corresponding to the letters of power, in sequence dextral: ooo, for the love, an affection, written; aa, for the body, clippings of all fingernails; i, for the hope, a passing fancy or appetite, written; oo, for the second love, a fondness, written; u, for the memory, one jape or trifle, written; and at the last, e, for the treasure, a clipped groat.

'It's mostly writing this time,' Charlotte murmurs. 'You have pen and paper? I brought the other things.'

The other things are a velvet coin-purse filled with her own fingernail clippings and a small copper coin, with the shield of Austria on one side and '1 HELLER 1765' on the other. She doesn't have a clipped groat, and she hopes this will do.

She goes now to Antoine's dressing table, where her sister has laid a few scraps of paper, an inkwell, and a quill. Charlotte has already decided on the hope: for chocolate cake tomorrow. A passing fancy or appetite. The memory, small as it is, is harder than she thought it would be: the people who used to tell jokes were Papa and Charles, and they are both dead, and she doesn't want to sacrifice her memories of them. Finally, she remembers the way her little brother Max dramatically lifted his coat-tails to sit down at dinner the other day, in imitation of a certain cousin. She smiles and writes that down.

The loves are difficult. For the fondness, she writes the name of Mops, Antoine's little pug. It's hard to imagine not being fond of Mops, with his perpetually confused face and delightful little ears. The affection is a little trickier, but ultimately she settles on Lerchenfeld, her new governess. She's been a good governess, even something like a friend.

9

Charlotte folds the papers, so that Antoine won't see what she's written. They do this to spare each other.

Into each point of the star, she puts her sacrifices, walking around twice clockwise so she can place them in order as they are in the spell.

Then Charlotte pulls the final item out of her pocket: the long white gloves with her monogram on them. Mama says it is a waste for the unmarried archduchesses to monogram anything; soon they will have new initials, once they're married. But Charlotte likes to mark the things that are hers.

She steps gingerly over the ash lines of the star, places the gloves in the middle, and steps back.

'I give these things,' she pronounces.

She takes a deep breath, pulls out a handkerchief and puts it to her nose. She can hear Antoine doing the same. But she smells nothing, sees nothing.

Perhaps the sacrifices aren't worth enough. The coin is wrong, or the memory too trifling. Or they misunderstood the spell altogether. They've never tried this one before.

Then, small but real movement: the little pile of fingernail and toenail clippings darkens and shifts. The coin rusts and wears, going green and then bright orange and then brown. The bits of paper become ragged and thin and, as with every spell, there is a horrible moment when the words come off the paper, in a stream of ink that rises into the air as if someone were tugging on them. Little currents of dark ink in the air, dissipating, gone. The paper itself is a pile of brown threads, and the pile of nail trimmings is now a kind of sludge. Everything goes brown, eventually. The coin, the paper, the nails.

It's working.

Charlotte watches it all with her usual fascination. It distracts from the fact that she is losing things, including some she will not remember. No matter how small, these losses are deaths, unnaturally hastened. They have given

10

death more than its due. But now she is fifteen, and she has need of important magic.

There it is at last: the smell of decay and death. They hold their handkerchiefs tightly to their faces, but the smell fills Charlotte's nostrils anyway.

The coin lasts the longest. For several minutes, the pile of brown dust remains, smaller and smaller, until a breath of unseen wind takes it. The items in the points of the star are gone, as if they never were. She doesn't care what they eat for dessert tomorrow, and Lerchenfeld is just an old sycophant in a bonnet. She glances at the pink-lined basket where Mops is snoring gently, disgustingly.

As for the memory, it was there – a moment ago – but it is gone. She can see her hand setting down the words, but her mind's eye can't make sense of what she wrote. Her breath catches – it always comes with a lurch, this loss of memory – but she is fairly sure that it was nothing of any importance, this time.

The embroidered book is still lying open on the floor. Charlotte closes it gently, gratefully. The stitches of the book's cover are familiar to her fingertips: the hard knots at the centres of the forget-me-nots, the feathered chain stitch of the vine at the edge. She can even feel the slight change in the length of the stitches where her own work begins.

Countess Ertag was governess to both Charlotte and Antoine when they were young. She had been working on the embroidery for a book cover for months. A week before she died, she stitched the worked canvas onto the binding, and sat staring at it, resting her hand on it, as though it were the portrait of one dead.

'It isn't finished,' Charlotte said; she was then nine years old. 'Look, the bottom right corner is empty.'

'I left that to finish later. See how I've left it open here, just a little flap? I'm going to put a poppy there, the same design as the petticoat I made for you last year.'

11

A week later, a servant found Ertag with her throat cut in her bed.

The children were not supposed to know, but Charlotte and Antoine overheard. They listened at keyholes. All of Ertag's possessions were found strewn about her room: her petticoats and prayer books and letters. Everything stained with blood. Her window, a palace window, wide open to the cold air.

Nobody talks about this now; Mama must have covered it all up.

The embroidered book was still in the needlework basket, which was in the nursery, so nobody noticed it. One day, Charlotte took it out, and flipped through the blank pages. Then she closed it and laid her palm on the cover and sat with it, just as her governess had done.

'Why don't you finish it?' Antoine suggested. Charlotte can still see Antoine as she was then, at six years old: her taffeta skirt spread around her on the nursery floor, her golden ringlets tumbling. Antoine has a way of making herself into a picture, of sticking in the memory that way.

And she has a way of being wise about things. Charlotte did finish the embroidery, in memory of her governess. She filled in the poppy, just as it was on her petticoat. She stitched the corner of the embroidered canvas to the binding. What would she do with those blank pages? What had Ertag intended to do? She'd opened the book again, idly, and then dropped it.

It had filled, somehow, with Ertag's handwriting.

Spell after spell, written in a style that was nothing like the way Ertag spoke.

And on the first page, a five-pointed star drawn in golden ink, with the word 'cindres' written across the bottom, and in each point of the star, a word: 'l'amour', 'le corps', 'l'espoir', 'la mémoire', 'le trésor'.

This was a book Ertag kept secret, and Ertag was killed, her possessions examined. Charlotte and Antoine have never told anyone about the book, and never will. They don't even need to discuss it. They simply know.

The spells are written confusingly. There are dozens of them – it's hard to say how many, as some have variations, and it's difficult to say where one leaves off and another begins. Some spells stretch on for pages of notes and commentary, even bizarre drawings. Only thirteen of the spells make the slightest sense; with the rest, Charlotte and Antoine aren't sure what item one is meant to enchant or how. The sisters haven't even tried all thirteen that do make sense – there is one for a shroud to remember the dead, which Antoine finds frightening even to read. And some of the ones they've tried, they can't make work.

Still, they've enchanted dolls and ribbons and silk fans. They can remember a pretty speech without memorizing it, cause a twinge in each other's hands, and cool a hot ballroom, a very little bit, on a summer night.

Now they can add one more spell to their list of successes: the spell for an item of clothing that makes the wearer persuasive to listeners.

'It worked!' Antoine stands up and claps her hands. The smell of rot lingers, but they know it will be gone in minutes.

'It worked,' Charlotte agrees, plucking the gloves off the floor.

'Are you sure this is a good idea?' Antoine asks, flopping onto the bed. 'Remember what happened when you enchanted Wolfgang Mozart's shoe.'

One of the first spells Charlotte ever managed. 'I do remember. He tripped, which was just what I intended. So the spell worked perfectly. And the little beast got plenty of attention, not to mention mollycoddling from you, so it did him no harm.'

'He could have tripped in front of a carriage, or off a cliff. You promised me then—'

'Believe me, Antoine, I won't do any harm to anyone. I'm

trying to prevent harm, remember? Do you really want Josepha to go off to marry that horrible boy?'

Antoine bites her lip. 'Just be careful.'

'I will be. And anyway, unlike Mozart's shoe, I'll be the one wearing these. I'll be the one in control.'

Charlotte pulls the gloves onto her arms, one after the other. They look just the same as they did, but now they are enchanted. Now they have power.

'Tomorrow,' Charlotte vows, 'we'll make Mama see reason at last.'

CHAPTER TWO

A Conversation with the Emperor —
Unbreakable Ciphers — Charlotte Tests her Gloves —
Consequences — Pandora Dolls

Charlotte has never seen her brother Joseph looking more content than he is behind his desk, writing. The oldest son of Maria Theresa, Holy Roman Emperor since Father died.

Joseph has been a grown-up for nearly as long as Charlotte can remember. She learned how to navigate the court and manage her mother from the older siblings closer to her in age: Amalia, for example, is the one who told her and Johanna what to expect from their monthly courses, which all the girls in the family call 'the General', for mysterious reasons. Before he left for Tuscany, Leopold advised her to think of her eventual marriage to the Dauphin as freedom, a chance to make a life of her own. Joseph has never given her any advice.

But she needs to understand politics, and she can't think of anyone else who can explain it to her.

The glove spell promised *persuasion of a listener's mind beyond the natural*. But it can't tell Charlotte what, exactly, she should *say* to Mama. Persuasion is not command, and she wants to give the magic the best possible chance of working. Mama doesn't seem to care about Ferdinand's terrible reputation, or Josepha's ill-suited character. She only cares about alliances and pacts. So it is time Charlotte learned to speak that language.

Her governess frowns when she asks for philosophy books, saying Charlotte wouldn't understand them anyway. But she does understand. Her chess teacher, Joseph's friend Angelo Soliman, gave her a copy of Montesquieu's book *The Spirit of the Laws* and she understood it perfectly. Besides, she has eyes and ears and a brain. She understands that if there's land to be worked and people to work it, nobody should be hungry. She understands that the alliances Mama wants so badly are no protection against war; all the alliances in Europe have changed in the course of her lifetime and she's only fifteen years old. She understands more than any of them think – or she could, if they would only tell her more about what's really happening.

'What is it, Charlotte?' Joseph asks. He looks tired, irritated.

She steps into the big, red-walled room, her hands behind her back. 'I have some questions, about the Empire. Shall I come back at another time?'

'Some questions about the Empire.' He looks at her as though she's just said something ridiculous, holding his pen just off the paper. 'Don't you have tutors? A governess?'

'Yes, but they won't tell me any of the things I really want to know.'

'And what is it you really want to know?'

She swallows. 'Why must we marry Bourbons?'

At that, Joseph actually smiles, and lays down his pen. 'We don't always marry Bourbons. My second wife was not a Bourbon.'

'But so many of us are promised to members of that house.'

'Yes, because Mama wishes it, and I leave that business to her.'

'But why does Mama wish it? She says we need the alliance, and I understand that much, but why is that one alliance so important that we must repeat it over and over again?'

'Well, if you ask me, it isn't,' Joseph says abruptly. 'But with Britain and Prussia plotting against us, the House of Bourbon seems a natural friend. So Mama looks south and west, to France, Spain, Italy.'

'But you disagree, Joseph,' she encourages him.

'I don't disagree, exactly, but I think we should look eastward, too, to Russia and even the Turks. And, most importantly, we must strengthen our own dominions. We can't rely too much on any of them.'

Charlotte considers this. There's an argument, then: we can't rely too much on the House of Bourbon. She can make that argument, and Mama will listen, because Charlotte will be wearing enchanted gloves. But she needs to know more.

'And how do we make ourselves stronger?'

He looks at her for a moment, as if considering his words. How he must see her as a child still. 'We've brought in some new laws in Hungary, which might make things better.'

'Laws to free the serfs?' Charlotte has heard that this is something Joseph wants.

'Not yet.' The smile he had when she asked her first question has faded with every answer, and it is entirely gone now. 'One day, soon, I hope. I'm trying to convince Mama.'

Charlotte purses her mouth. She knows what that's like. 'I think that if the serfs were free, they would make their own food. Montesquieu says—'

'Montesquieu! I didn't know you were reading him. Do you know Hume?'

Charlotte shakes her head. 'Montesquieu is the only philosopher I've read.' She feels embarrassed, and then angry at being embarrassed. Is it her fault her governess doesn't teach her any of the things she'll need to know?

Joseph seems to read some of this on her face. 'Well, borrow my copy of Hume, then. You can't go out into the world having read only one book, for God's sake. Worse than reading none at all. Borrow all of my books, any time you like, and maybe you'll make better use of them than I can.

There's so little I can do – in my current situation. But at least I can get out, travel, see how things are. I'd advise you to do the same, Charlotte. When you go to France, when you're queen there one day, you must be sure to get out and see how the common people are living, so you'll know what is really happening. Don't trust anything but your own eyes. And don't trust anyone, either.' His face relaxes a little, and he holds up the piece of paper. 'That's why you must cipher everything. Even the silliest letter, about Christmas presents or what-have-you. Because if you only cipher the dangerous letters, spies will know immediately which letters, and which relationships, are dangerous. You do know how to cipher, don't you?'

'I know the kind where one letter substitutes for another,' she says uncertainly.

'Yes, but that one's easy to crack. That one's for children. Mother hasn't had you taught to do it properly? Of course she hasn't. Charlotte, listen to me. You mustn't wait for Mama to allow you to do anything. You wait and wait and then one day you realize that there could have been a time when you might have—'

Joseph runs his hands over his close-cropped head – she likes seeing him without his wig. He's only twenty-six years old, but he talks like a bitter old man. She would like to tease him about it, if she knew him better.

He is rummaging in his desk. At last he finds a steel ruler, with which he marks a blank paper along both the top edge and the left side; then he uses the ruler to make a grid. He writes the letters of the alphabet along the top, and then down the left side, in neat rows.

'Here,' he says, holding the paper out to her. 'You do the rest. For each row, write the alphabet in order, but start with a different letter each time. So, the first row starts with A, then the next row starts with B, then C, and so on.'

Joseph sits and opens a book while she works at his desk. Her letters are uncannily like his, she notices. How strange, that simply being brother and sister would give them the same handwriting.

When she has finished writing the table of letters, she hands him the paper.

'This is the *tabula recta*,' he says. 'That just means a lined tablet.'

That Charlotte knew, although she doesn't say so. She's gone many times to the Latin grammars and dictionaries in the children's library. She went looking for *magister* and found 'a teacher or leader, a master, as of the arts, an authority, or an owner or keeper; rarely, an instigator or author' and, further down the page, '*magistra*: a female teacher'. A governess might be called *magistra*, then, but though the book was Countess Ertag's, the word in it is always *magister*.

'This cipher is unbreakable, but a little tricky to learn,' Joseph says. 'Say, for example, you wanted to write the word Charlotte – that's the message you want to send. First you write the letters of a keyword over top – let's make the keyword, oh, *mot clef*. See, write *mot clef* over Charlotte, at the bottom of the page, and see what you get. Just start again at *mot* when you run out.'

She does so.

'See? In the place of C-H-A-R-L-O-T-T-E, you get M-O-T-C-L-E-F-M-O.'

'But the L is still L.'

'That doesn't matter. Now match each letter in "Charlotte" to the letter of the keyword you have written underneath it, and you'll get the coded letter. See, find "C" on the left-hand side of the table, and "M" at the top, follow your finger along . . . *voilà*. The first letter of the enciphered text is now "O". Do you see?'

She stares at the letters. It reminds her of the letter substitution in the embroidered book, of how a word in French becomes something that looks like nonsense, but is really magic. Where did they come from, these 'proofs' that turn words into spells? Surely Countess Ertag didn't think of them all herself.

'Charlotte?' Joseph prods. 'Do you understand?'

She frowns. She doesn't understand – not enough. Still not enough. 'But if everyone knows what the *tabula recta* is, can't anyone decode it?'

He shakes his head. 'Everything depends on the keyword. You see, nobody would really use *mot clef*. They might use anything. The last letter I had from Leopold used *cheval*. If you don't know the word, you can't break the code.'

She nods. 'I'll practise. And I'll teach Antoine. Shall I?'

'Good girl,' Joseph says, and folds the paper into a paper dart, and sends it flying. It hits an ugly landscape painting, and his eyes go wide in mock horror.

The private theatre at Schönbrunn rises to a gilt-framed painting of the heavens. Charlotte always feels a little vertigo here, though the imperial box is not so terribly high. Everything seems poised on an edge, from the strains of violins tuning in front of the stage, to the rustle of conversation. It's warm. From her seat, Charlotte can see through to the backstage, where Antoine and little Max stand, fidgeting. They're dressed in Turkish style, bright as parrots with beads and feathers, and Antoine in an orange turban.

Charlotte feels as though she's in costume herself. Ordinarily, the archduchesses would not wear full court dress to an evening of family entertainment, but Mama insisted tonight, because the Neapolitan ambassador is here. So Charlotte stands stiffly in a rustling skirt that juts out a full foot on either side. Her hair has been teased and tugged so tightly that even her eyebrows are reluctant to move.

She doesn't actually mind it, this costume that flattens her, forces her to be the image of Her Imperial Highness the Archduchess, rather than a mere living girl.

But the panniers and powder can be annoying. And here,

in this golden room, she feels restless. The theatre always feels as if it is opening onto the world, somehow; perhaps it's the blue sky and clouds of the fresco on the ceiling, although the palace is full of such scenes. Perhaps it's the backdrop on stage, the landscape reaching into some imaginary distance.

Mama is dressed in her perpetual black; she will never stop mourning Papa. She looks angry.

'He's late,' she murmurs. 'I don't like this ambassador. He knows I can't afford to be anything but kind to him. They've been more than patient with us, God knows. After dear Johanna died, Ferdinand could have chosen a new bride then, and he didn't. So, now the Empress waits for the ambassador, and will not frown when he arrives. Put your gloves on, Charlotte. Are those the ones you've been embroidering? They're not suitable with that dress.'

Charlotte looks down at the long white gloves in her hand. She thinks they're very suitable. She thinks they're fit for a queen.

She draws them on, pushing each finger right to the end, holding them out like a conjurer. 'Mama, I think we can afford not to send anyone at all to marry Ferdinand of Naples.'

Josepha's mouth gapes.

Mama's mouth twists upward and, for a heartbeat, Charlotte believes she's succeeded. But the smile is not agreement.

'Is that so, Charlotte? You think we can afford that, do you? That we can afford to lose the support of half of Italy and also of the entire Bourbon family? To make an enemy of the King of Spain?' Mama closes her eyes, a sure sign she's losing what passes, with her, for patience. 'Good God, I really am alone.'

Charlotte lifts her chin and carries on with what she rehearsed. 'I think we ought to look to the east, and to our own dominions, to make sure that our own people are well fed, well trained and able to fight for us. We cannot rely too much on a single ally, which the House of Bourbon really is. We should draw our strength from many sources.'

Mama stares at her, astonished. Charlotte has never seen her mother speechless before. Is this the effect of the gloves?

It doesn't last long.

'Charlotte, you are speaking about things you don't understand. I am ashamed. Ashamed and disappointed. What has possessed you?'

Joseph walks into the imperial box at just that moment, and tightens his mouth, nodding briefly to his mother before squeezing past the wide skirts.

'He's here, Mama,' Josepha whispers, and indeed, there is the Neapolitan ambassador. Grinning as he comes into the imperial box behind Joseph. Showing no shame at all for being late, he kisses Mama's hand, and greets the archduchesses.

Behind the ambassador stands a young man, richly dressed. When he bows, a crucifix swings from his neck. As he stands up, he looks fixedly at Charlotte. He has a very smug expression on his face, accentuated by the peaches-and-cream of his make-up and the pale curls of his wig.

'Your Imperial Majesty, Your Imperial Highnesses,' says the ambassador, 'may I present Prince Louis de Rohan, Bishop of Canopus and Co-adjutor of Strasbourg.'

Mama holds out her hand for Rohan to kiss. Charlotte tries not to scowl and then gives up, deciding she doesn't care enough to make the effort. Was there something more she needed to do to make the gloves work? Some magic word or gesture?

'I have heard so much of the talents of the archdukes and archduchesses of Austria,' says this Rohan, still looking at Charlotte.

She looks pointedly at the back of Mama's head, but Mama is focused on the ambassador, and impervious to pointed stares, as to everything else. What went wrong? The gloves should have had some effect!

Charlotte has memorized the titles of every courtier who might greet her at a ball, especially the ones who have something to do with France, where she'll be sent in a year or two. She knows well enough who Rohan is. He's usually in Paris, but he comes to Vienna from time to time. 'Prince' means very little in his case; the Rohan family is a branch of a branch of a family that might once have been kings in Brittany. But he's in line to become Bishop of Strasbourg, and that city is an ecclesiastical principality within the Empire, so then he'll have something to rule. Charlotte can't imagine a worse way to run things, for either the Church or the state. At the moment, Rohan has nothing but his name, and whatever scraps the Church gives him to make it look as though he has some use in the world.

He's smiling at Charlotte now, altogether too benignly. She decides she dislikes him.

'The dance is about to begin,' says Mama, clapping her hands, and they take their seats.

Charlotte sits to the left of Mama, and glances with a little envy over at the right-hand side of the imperial box, where Joseph sits with a few people he's invited: the young composer Antonio Salieri, who looks nervous; the scholar Angelo Soliman, in a golden turban and long silver coat; and the comfortable, pink-and-white face of Christoph Gluck, Antoine's music teacher. Joseph glances at her, and gives her a conspiratorial, apologetic smile, as if to recognize that she's stuck at Mama's end of the box.

Charlotte feels as though everything happening in the theatre is on the outside of a glass box that surrounds her. She is a person of no consequence and her actions have no effect. How could the gloves not have worked? Perhaps the effects are subtle. Perhaps Mama is simply too stubborn to be convinced, even by magic. Or perhaps magic doesn't work on Mama at all. But how? Why? Mama is no magister – of that, Charlotte is sure. Maria Theresa would consider it unnatural and un-Christian, no doubt, but it's not only that. If the

Empress knew about magic, she would do whatever it took to make sure her daughters never used it.

So what, then, is the solution to the riddle? The spell didn't work, but the gloves are enchanted. The sacrifices vanished, and every time the sacrifices have vanished before, the object in the centre of the star has been enchanted.

Charlotte breathes heavily, which the stomacher of her gown does not allow, so she breathes noisily. Mama flicks her gaze her way, just once, as the lights dim and the music skirls.

The concertmaster walks in and takes his position before the little orchestra, bows to the Empress, and the violins begin.

Max and Antoine enter the stage from opposite sides, Max mincing out like a miniature potentate. Over their heads, the red stage curtains hang heavily, their golden fringes seeming to mimic the loops of ribbon on Antoine's sleeves. Charlotte nearly forgets about the gloves, about everything, watching her sister dance as though nothing in the world weighs anything at all. How does Antoine make the angles of her elbows match so perfectly, through every change of her arms?

Charlotte clasps her gloved fingers together in amazement. Her little sister has grown up lately. She moves with such precision. She never falters, never forgets. Is it tiresome to be so perfect all the time? To have to be so perfect? What would it be like if Antoine were to . . . Charlotte unclasps her fingers, and lifts one index finger, and half imagines before she can form the words—

Antoine stops her pirouette abruptly, and stands as lumpen and perplexed as a milkmaid transported to the opera house from some alpine pasture.

The family stays perfectly quiet and composed, as if they are under a spell too. For this is a spell; no doubt about it. This is not Antoine. The gloves work, damn them. Damn them! Max frowns at Antoine, and the moment stretches on. The ambassador coughs, not precisely politely. Charlotte tears the gloves off, finger by finger, getting them stuck.

The French Prince de Rohan is staring at her. Let him stare.

Then too late, too late, she realizes what to do, and she shoves the gloves back onto her hands. What must she do to make them work? She didn't do anything before, only let a stray thought enter her mind. *Come on, Antoine! Move!*

At last, Antoine glides into a chassé. She performs every move perfectly, but her mortification is like a roar in the ears. The dance continues, and everyone pretends not to take any notice. But Mama is frowning, and Antoine's cheeks are scarlet.

Charlotte is already out of bed when she feels the sudden twinge in her hand that means Antoine has stuck a pin into the Pandora doll. Not the first time she's regretted giving that doll to her sister!

They began life not as toys, but as miniature models that dressmakers brought to court as samples, to show the Austrian ladies what the ladies of Paris were wearing, and to offer the same fashions for sale. Somehow, these two prim-faced dolls had gone unclaimed at some point, and ended up in the nursery.

Charlotte enchanted one to represent herself, and the other Antoine. A pin in the hand of the doll means pain to the hand of the girl. So they always know when one of them needs the other. It's a panicky, unmoored ache that causes her to clutch her elbow as though her whole arm is rebellious, but when she forces herself to identify the pain, calmly, to locate it, it's bearable.

Perhaps not the best mode of communication between sisters. Especially not when one of those sisters doesn't take the pin out right away.

Charlotte grits her teeth and slips through doorways in silent shoes that won't wake her governess, past ushers and guards trained to mind their own business.

She opens the door, and Antoine's face is hard, all bunched

up like a batch of bad knitting. But the moment her eyes meet Charlotte's, her expression softens and she pulls the pin out. The pain softens too.

Charlotte comes to the bed, sits next to her. 'You didn't have to use the doll. I was already on my way to apologize.'

'No need,' says Antoine. 'I'm sure you had a reason for testing the gloves that way. Rather than in private, I mean.'

'I didn't. That's the thing. It was an accident.'

Antoine's brows bunch together. 'You were wearing the gloves and you—'

'Had a thought. Half a thought, really. The gloves work. They work much better than I realized. I never would have done that to you on purpose, Antoine. Please believe me.'

Antoine purses her lips. 'I believe you. You didn't intend – I did tell you, you know—'

'I know.' Charlotte puts her arm around her sister and pulls Antoine's head onto her shoulder. They sit for a moment, the doll on Antoine's lap that looks a little like Charlotte did a few years ago, dressed in the fashions of 1764.

The fashions of Paris, where one day, Charlotte will live, as dauphine, as queen. As a sovereign, she won't be able to travel much – there are dangers on the road, and worse dangers in leaving one's country unattended – but if Antoine marries one of the French princes, she will have many opportunities to come to see Charlotte. All will be well.

But, in the meantime, they must save poor Josepha from having to go to Naples, beyond the Alps, to marry a king who already has a worse reputation at sixteen than most men manage by sixty.

And somehow they have to do it without the gloves, for it seems they won't work on Mama. Charlotte tells Antoine about her efforts to affect Mama's behaviour.

'There's no changing her mind, not even through magic,' Antoine says sadly. 'Why do you think she's so cruel to Josepha?'

'I don't think she intends to be cruel. She's just so used to being afraid.'

'Afraid!'

'Papa was Holy Roman Emperor. And now Joseph. But Mama is the one who rules, even so! It's quite the trick she's managed, especially when you consider that all the powers of Europe tried to stop her, when she first took the throne. I think she always keeps herself ready in case someone comes along and says, Now wait a moment, Frau Habsburg, things don't seem to be in order here. We're not just her children. We're her weapons. But we have weapons of our own, don't we, sister? And nobody expects us to have any, that's the thing.' Charlotte pulls the embroidered book out of her secret pocket. 'Nobody looks in the needlework basket.'

Antoine takes the book from her and smiles. 'All right. I'll try to think of my needle as a weapon. It might make my embroidery go better.'

'Your embroidery is perfect, like everything you do.'

Antoine casts her gaze down, disbelieving.

'Everything is perfect when your meddling sister doesn't ruin it. Am I absolved, Antoine?' Charlotte asks, putting her hand on Antoine's shoulder. 'May I go? Or will you summon me back with the pin?'

'I didn't summon you here to absolve you, Charlotte. I wanted to see the book, in fact.'

'The book?' Charlotte frowns. She only brought it because she always carries the book with her when she leaves her bedroom at night, for safekeeping. 'What spell do you want? It's late, Antoine.'

'I don't want to do a spell tonight. I just want to see something.' She flips through the pages. 'Ah, here it is. I thought I remembered—'

Charlotte reads the page upside down: 'For an anointment to confer resistance, a simple spell, to be performed only on a clean vial containing no matter saving the liquor found in the inner coffin of a human inhumation . . .'

'Clever girl,' Charlotte says. 'That must be it!'

'It?'

'The reason the gloves didn't work on Mama. Isn't that why you thought of it?'

'Yes, that's it, of course. Horrible, isn't it? The liquor – what is that, exactly, Charlotte?'

'The liquid remains of a rotting corpse, I suppose. I can't imagine Mama willingly anointing herself with such a thing. Perhaps someone did it without her knowing?'

'Or perhaps there's a similar spell that's less gruesome. I don't think Countess Ertag knew every spell in the world. There must be other magisters, with other spellbooks, and perhaps one of them sent Mama a present. Perfume, or something.'

'That must be it. Oh, Antoine, I feel so much better. Knowing, I mean. Why the gloves didn't work.'

'They didn't work on her. They worked on me. Because I'm not resistant.'

Charlotte nods, slowly, and puts her hands over Antoine's to close the book. 'We'll find out. Somehow, we'll find out what made Mama resistant, and we'll get some for ourselves. But first, we have to find a way to change her mind. Josepha is set to leave in less than a month.'

Antoine nods. 'But if magic won't work on Mama, what can we do, Charlotte?'

What indeed? 'Let me worry about that. Am I absolved, then?'

Antoine's face falls into a mockery of a jowly old priest as she says, dramatically, '*Ego te absolvo.*'

Charlotte kisses her quickly on the cheek and slides the book back into her apron pocket.

CHAPTER THREE

The Empress Lectures — The Court Moves — Noises in the Crypt — Magic Lantern Demonstration — A Tilt in the Axis of the World

The next morning, Antoine waits, straight-backed on the newly upholstered settee in Mama's anteroom, until Josepha comes out of Mama's study. Josepha's face is pale except for two irregular patches of red on her cheeks, like rouge applied by a monkey.

'How is she?' Antoine asks, stepping close to Josepha so she can speak without the door usher or Mama's secretary overhearing. But Josepha just widens her eyes, breathes deeply, and shakes her head. She pulls a copy of *Don Quixote* out of her apron pocket and opens it in front of her to read while she walks out of the room and into the corridor.

Mama is still recovering from the smallpox she had in the spring; she still begins work early in the morning, but she does it from her bed, with heavy curtains drawn and standing orders that she is not to be disturbed until after Mass. But she summoned Antoine and Josepha first thing, today.

Antoine steels herself and goes in.

The golden room is as dark and sour as a dough-cupboard. Mama is sitting up, but even so it is strange to see her in bed. Mama, who always said no one needs more than six hours' sleep a night.

'Antoine,' Mama says.

'It was an error, Mama. I am mortified.'

'No doubt. Antoine, you are nearly twelve years old. You do not dance to please yourself, or even to please me. Soon enough, ambassadors will be sending reports back to their princes of your suitability.'

'Yes, Mama.'

'I can't think what came over you. I've been negligent, I see. I've left you too much in the hands of governesses and cousins, and they all fawn over you. Of course they do. You're a beautiful child, and you're sweet-hearted and good by nature. Everyone loves you, as well they should. But you also need proper instruction and sternness of character, and there, I've failed you.'

'Oh, Mama—'

'Don't contradict me, Antoine. I have. You were always your father's favourite, so I've tried to keep you little, for his sake. My last sight of him was when you ran after him as he left, and he came down off his horse to embrace you. So for him – I thought I'd have time to – but you're growing up so quickly. You must make yourself beyond reproach in everything. Good heavens, girl, don't look so stricken. Manage yourself.'

He came down off his horse. Down off his horse? Antoine has no memory of her father saying goodbye to her. The family's last sight of him was of an embrace with Antoine, and she has forgotten it.

She has sacrificed it, surely. Her father's final touch, a moment of desperate affection for her alone. And she can't even remember what she bought with that sacrifice.

'Mama, I am so, so sorry.'

'You've said so. Don't repeat yourself and never make yourself craven with apologies. What you must do is be more attentive in your lessons, and remember that in everything you do, you affect the reputation of this family.'

Antoine bows her head. This is the moment for the request that she rehearsed. She knows she looks sorrowful and remorseful, and she has good reason for that, better than Mama knows. And she knows, guiltily, that her real pain will serve her purposes well now, and she wishes that she could for one moment separate the Antoine who *is* from the Antoine who performs, but what would happen if she did?

'Mama,' she whispers, her head still bowed, 'I shall ask God to help me be a more attentive student.'

'Good,' says Mama, leaning back, satisfied. 'Tomorrow you will attend Mass twice.'

Antoine nods solemnly. 'Perhaps I should pray in the crypt, as you do?'

There's a silence, for two beats of Antoine's sparrow heart. The imperial family crypt is in the heart of Vienna, near the Hofburg palace, where the family spends its winters. It's nearly October, and the servants are already packing for the move. One of the first things Mama does, every autumn, is visit the dead.

'I don't think that's necessary,' Mama says uncertainly.

'When Papa said goodbye to me,' Antoine says, hating herself with every word, 'I wonder if he knew . . . what was to come. I would like to ask for his help. I need his help to be a better daughter.'

It's a perfect performance, and it's entirely genuine. How can both be true? She looks up and sees Mama's face. It looks different, suddenly. The lined face of an old woman, though she's only fifty. Without rouge, in her black sleeping bonnet in the dim room, the Empress looks as pale and worn as a market woman. And she looks tired in her eyes, too: tired and sad.

'Very well,' Mama says at last. 'We're scheduled to move to the Hofburg next week. After we're settled there, we'll go to the crypt together to pray for the late Emperor's soul, and that of dear Joseph's lately departed wife, and the others we have lost in these last terrible years. Josepha will come with us.'

Antoine holds her face steady and thinks as quickly as she can. Poor Josepha. The last thing Antoine wants is to put her through anything more!

'Josepha?' she asks. 'Couldn't it be just the two of us, Mama?'

Mama is resistant to more than magic. She shakes her head, so that her bonnet ribbons flap. 'Josepha has great need of courage and faith. She needs, as you need, to be reminded of her duty to her father and to the Empire. Dear heavens, what – Come forward, Antoine. Come, come, so I can see you.'

Antoine does a subtle *pas de bourrée en avant*. She reaches the foot of her mother's bed.

'That hairline,' Mama says. 'Has it always been so crooked? We'll have to find another way of dressing it in the front, hide it somehow.'

Try as she might to avoid it, Antoine always adds to Mama's burdens. She puts her hand to her hairline.

'Don't touch your face, dear,' the Empress commands. 'You're nearly of the age for pimples.'

There are only five miles between Schönbrunn and the Hofburg palace, but to Antoine the annual move from summer residence to winter always feels like a tilt in the axis of the world. Antoine prefers Schönbrunn, surrounded by nothing but gardens, open and bright. The Hofburg is in the heart of Vienna, all shadows and whispers.

She does like the plain, cheerful Capuchin church just outside the palace, but the crypt beneath the church is neither plain nor cheerful.

On the morning after the move, Antoine, Mama, Josepha and a half-dozen servants with lamps file through the quiet nave and down the stone steps, and enter the vault where the dead lie. Antoine's grandfather's sarcophagus looms great and terrible in dark metal, with death's heads on each corner bearing the imperial crown. They walk past, and the newer vault opens before them, its ceiling soaring high overhead.

Antoine tastes marble and metal. There is the tomb of her brother Charles. She tries not to think of him lying there, of his heart in a silver urn in another church, where the Habsburg hearts are kept. What will happen to the hearts on the last day? She would like to ask someone, but Charlotte will think it's a silly question, and anyone else will scold her for asking it.

At the sight of her sister-in-law's sarcophagus, with a portrait of Maria worked in a bronze disc at its head, Antoine stops short. What a terrible notion this is! Surely she can't open a tomb. It's unthinkable. The price is too high. She can live without the corpse liquor, without the spell. Can't she?

Without it, a magister could work a spell on her at any time. She knows now what that feels like, to be powerless. It felt like losing herself entirely.

She closes her eyes, and shudders. No. She must be strong. She must do this, for Mama and for Austria, if not herself. Antoine is not like Charlotte or Mama. Not clever like them. She has no weapons other than her smile and her dancing and her wit. If someone can take those away, she has nothing, and she will let everyone down.

She opens the vial of enchanted oil in her pocket and shakes one drop on a marble finial near the entrance to the current vault as they walk past. No one sees. She knows the oil works to make metal and stone pliable; she and Charlotte made it early in their experiments with the spell-book, but have found few good uses for it, and after they mangled a gargoyle in the courtyard outside the Hofburg chapel last winter, they haven't used it since. A single drop is enough.

Mama kneels by the tomb where Papa lies, where Mama will one day lie too. Josepha and Antoine kneel behind her. Antoine waits, trying to pray for strength.

A grinding sound, unlike anything from this world, comes from behind them, from the entrance. Antoine's oil at work.

'What in God's name?' Maria Theresa rises and follows the servants to the source of it, bustling back the way they came. Antoine takes her chance. This must be Maria's tomb; Joseph's second wife was put to rest within a few hours of her death, with no embalming, because no one wanted to handle her smallpox-riddled body. Antoine shakes one drop of her oil onto a lion's face sculpted on the side of the sarcophagus.

The lion yawns.

Out of the lion's mouth trickles a dark umber liquor, into the bottle that Antoine tucks back into her pocket as the servants and courtiers return.

Maria Theresa is annoyed. 'Come, Antoine. It's nothing.'

'Rats,' whispers Josepha, wide-eyed.

As they kneel again to make their devotions, Mama cries out, and points at Maria's sarcophagus. The lion's face is motionless now, but its mouth remains slack, and something drips from it.

'It isn't sealed properly,' Maria Theresa says, and stands, covering her mouth with her handkerchief. 'Come, girls, quickly. Good God.'

Charlotte can think better at the Hofburg. At Schönbrunn, everything is built to Mama's specifications. But there is no single mind behind the cluster of old buildings at the heart of Vienna, the dark rooms and connecting courtyards, busy with soldiers and horses.

The servants' passageways behind the rooms also make it easier to sneak to Antoine's chambers. All day, it's been clear that something new is bothering Antoine. She sat listless at dinner, and she and Josepha both looked stone-faced as they sat embroidering with Mama. At last, Charlotte has a chance to ask her, sitting in her room by the light of a few candles.

She can hardly believe the answer.

'You opened a coffin? Antoine, what were you thinking?'

Antoine's mouth is set. 'We had to get it from somewhere.'

Charlotte sits next to her on the narrow bed, stares at the tiny vial in Antoine's shaking hand, and wrinkles her nose. 'I know you're angry with me over the dance—'

'It's not only that.' Antoine's cheeks are flushed. 'Charlotte, Ertag was killed because she knew about magic. Don't you think? Why else would anyone kill a governess? And whoever killed her got past the palace guards and through her window on the second floor. Someone out there knows about magic, and probably knows how to do magic. What if they find out we have the book?'

Charlotte looks away. These are thoughts she's had before, but she never spoke about her fears with Antoine. Her sister was too young, before, to understand the danger. No longer.

The sky outside the window is soft indigo, and outside it, only a few guards and walls between them and Vienna. The palace can't protect them; Ertag's death is proof of that. A few weeks until Josepha is set to leave for Naples, if Charlotte fails. Mama has been playing three different suitors off each other for the beautiful Liesl but that will have to end soon, as Liesl is getting old at twenty-four. And in a year or two, Charlotte will leave too, off to marry the Dauphin of France, leaving Antoine here alone. Antoine and Max, the two youngest children, are the only ones whose marriages haven't yet been arranged.

Antoine's blue silk dressing screen casts one corner of the room in shadow, and the candlelight catches on the silver basin on her washstand. They're sitting on the little bed in the middle of the room, and knowing that there are guards at the doors, that their governesses are not far, doesn't bring much comfort. They were sleeping near Ertag when she died.

Charlotte looks back at her sister's earnest face. Antoine is so clever, though she never realizes it. She's the very best girl in the world, and Charlotte loves her. She'll do anything to protect her. Charlotte looks again at the vial of unspeakable liquid in Antoine's hand, and shudders.

'All right,' Charlotte says, opening the book. '"For an anointment to confer resistance . . ."'

The spell is simple enough, and the sacrifices decay. Then it's a matter of determining what the embroidered book means by 'anointing', whether a dab on the forehead would be enough. They decide to start with that, and then they will test the gloves on each other.

It doesn't feel like protection when they dip their fingers in and touch a drop to each other's brow. It feels like penitence, and Charlotte is oddly grateful to share in it. The girls both shudder, and Charlotte has to block out all thoughts about what they've just touched, or she'll retch. It's lucky there's such a tiny quantity, barely enough to wet two fingertips.

They try the gloves, eventually dissolving into nervous giggles as they try to make each other walk like chickens or speak poetry. Nothing happens. They are immune.

Charlotte feels strangely powerful. She can't change her mother's heart, but she can find a way to stop Josepha's marriage. She has almost a month. There's still time.

The move to the Hofburg always exhausts Mama, who has to oversee every reinstallation of wood panelling, every arrangement of paintings. So when the bustle of the first few days has quieted, Mama goes to her private rooms, and there is a day or two of peace. She has a tiny chapel built onto her bedroom here, so even morning Mass at the Hofburg chapel is a quieter affair, without the presence of the Empress.

Joseph pulls Charlotte aside as they're leaving the chapel.

At that moment, he doesn't look like a twice-widowed emperor. He looks like her oldest brother, those familiar watery blue eyes smiling down at her.

'Will you bring Antoine and Max to my study after breakfast? I've sent word to your governesses. Angelo Soliman is coming by to show me a new kind of magic lantern – it has a stronger lamp inside, and projects clearer images on the wall. He suggested the youngest members of the family might like to see it. You can ask Josepha too if you like, but she's in bed with a headache, last I heard.'

Charlotte nods. 'Antoine loves magic lanterns. She'll be pleased.'

Joseph steps in closer, quieter. 'And will you make sure to tell Max to behave himself? I'm trying to convince Soliman that royal children aren't so bad.'

Charlotte suppresses a grin as they walk past the font, the crush of people ahead slowing them down. Angelo Soliman has been a friend of Joseph's for years; he organized everything for Joseph's first wedding, seven years ago. He heads the household of the Prince of Liechtenstein, whose palace is a short walk from the Hofburg, so Soliman has been a fixture in the children's lives. Charlotte likes to play chess with him and Antoine loves it when he takes her to see the warhorses.

'Has Dr Soliman developed some new fear of us?' she asks, joking.

'Keep this to yourself, but Soliman's leaving Prince Wenzel's household soon. He's getting married and he'll need some new employment. I've been trying to convince him to tutor Max.'

Charlotte duly gathers her two younger siblings and they traipse through the middle of several vast rooms and into Joseph's study. It's a square room, with the Emperor's desk in one corner, and one of the Hofburg's ornate white stoves in another. Smaller and duller than his study at Schönbrunn, but this one seems to suit Joseph better. The stoves are fed from the passageways behind the walls, so servants seldom come into the rooms at the Hofburg, unless they're called.

Joseph closes the doors as Angelo Soliman, standing in the middle of the room, bows to the children. Antoine gives her pretty curtsey, and Max a military bow. Soliman catches Charlotte's eye, with an expression of camaraderie.

Charlotte likes Soliman. He doesn't frown when Charlotte talks, or warn her against being prideful, or tell her there are only certain things she needs to know. In that, he is unlike all her teachers and her governesses, and certainly unlike her mother.

And today, he's brought his sabre, which pleases Max mightily. Max pulls it out of the scabbard and brandishes it, baring his teeth. Joseph has to put out an arm to protect his prize astronomical clock from the sabre's dull edge.

'Did you take this from a Turk, Dr Soliman?' Max asks, breathless.

Soliman smiles. 'No, Your Highness. I bought it so that I'd look dazzling at your brother's wedding. The war with Turkey was before my time. I fought against the Spanish, the Neapolitans, and the French, in the war over your mother's succession.'

There's an odd smell in the room: familiar but misplaced. A smell like wet leaves or old coins. Something musty – perhaps it's the magic lantern on the cart in the corner, although it looks quite new, all painted in red and yellow. It's a smell like – like the one that comes when sacrifices decay, Charlotte realizes. The smell of magic.

She glares at Antoine, looks her up and down, but doesn't see any enchanted items on her that she knows about. Antoine looks back at her, a little grumpy at being glared at. She looks nervous, though, too. Surely if she were up to something magical, she would have told Charlotte? Or is this something furtive like the business in the crypt all over again?

Charlotte takes a breath, and decides that she's imagined the smell. She, Antoine and Max take the chairs Soliman indicates, all in a row.

Joseph leans back, his elbow on the back of the unoccupied, upholstered yellow chair next to his, his fingers playing at his mouth. 'Max, Dr Soliman fought at the Battle of Piacenza, our great victory over the Bourbon forces.'

Max's eyes go wide.

'That was twenty years ago, when I was a young man,' Soliman says in his slightly accented German. 'But that was where I met His Highness Prince Josef Wenzel, and I have been in his service ever since.'

'But why are you in Vienna?' Max asks, his sabreless hands now at his hips. 'Why don't you go home?'

Soliman frowns slightly. 'Oh, I see. It's confusing, I know – my master is Prince of Liechtenstein, but he doesn't actually live in Liechtenstein. I don't believe he's even been there. He's always lived here in Vienna, and since I am head of his household—'

'No, I mean . . .' Max pauses. '. . . you come from Africa, don't you?'

'Ah,' Soliman says, and looks at Joseph, who makes a half-apologetic gesture. 'I was born in the Bornu Empire, but I was taken from there when I was a little younger than you are now. Do you know where the Bornu Empire is, Your Highness?'

Max does not.

'I've told you, the palace tutors are abysmal,' Joseph says. 'And geography's not even their worst subject.'

Soliman turns to Antoine and Charlotte, his expression quizzical.

Antoine says, 'I'm afraid Countess Brandeis doesn't emphasize such things in the education of girls.'

'What do governesses teach, I wonder?' Soliman asks Antoine, looking at her quite seriously.

It's an innocent question, but it makes Charlotte nervous all the same. Antoine glances at Charlotte, but she doesn't look nervous – she's only looking to her for commiseration. Charlotte had Brandeis for a governess until recently too.

'Oh, all sorts of rules.'

'Rules, Your Highness?'

'How one ought to greet a count, or how to signal that an audience is at an end, or what sort of rewards to give for service. That sort of thing.'

Charlotte has been trained in these things too, though at least she knows to what end. She has heard that Versailles has even more rules than Schönbrunn.

'Ah,' Soliman says, the shoulders inside his golden jacket relaxing slightly. 'Well, Your Highness, that does sound tedious, but necessary training for imperial children.'

'I don't see why,' Max says, still petulant.

'Because', Charlotte says, 'rules help everyone understand what to expect. Without rules, everything happens according to the monarch's whim, and that's despotism.'

Soliman turns to her. 'I see you've been reading your Montesquieu, Your Highness.'

She nods, partly in thanks for his gift of the book. She wants to say more about it – to discuss the definition of 'civic virtue', which she never feels she has quite understood – but she has learned not to show off. Soliman, at least, isn't looking at her as though her intelligence is a problem to be managed. She doesn't know quite how he's looking at her. There's satisfaction, but also . . . what? Not quite sadness. Reluctance. Perhaps there's something else he wants to say, too.

Or perhaps she said something wrong, and he doesn't want to embarrass her.

Soliman pulls the cart with the magic lantern into the middle of the room. He picks up a bundle of wooden slides, each of them with painted glass set into it. In his other hand, he holds a bit of chalk. 'You must each mark your slide, according to which one you think will be the most spectacular, and then we'll see who chose best.'

Antoine takes the chalk first, and looks through carefully, finally marking a pretty 'A' on a long slide that contains four pictures of animals. Max marks an 'M' on a slide with a stick protruding out of it. Charlotte chooses one with a windmill and a round pulley. She can smell magic again; she's sure of it.

Soliman takes a spill out of the vase, lights it in the fire and touches it to the small lamp inside the magic lantern. Joseph closes the window shutter and they are in darkness, save a circle of blurry light on the far wall, one of the few plain walls in the palace.

'We begin with His Highness's tightrope walker,' says Soliman with a grandiloquent manner. As he moves the stick, the figure walks across the rope, and Max claps his hands.

'This one', Soliman says, 'has an oddity to it. You do see that bird, above the tightrope-walker's head, all of you?'

'Of course,' says Max, pointing.

There is no bird on the image. The sky over the tightrope-walker's head is plain blue paint, not a spot on it.

Antoine opens her mouth, but Charlotte nudges her ankle under their chairs. She can smell magic, and she can sense a little too much interest in the set of Soliman's shoulders as he waits for their answers. Better to say the same as Max.

'You mean that little one, there,' she says. 'Oh yes, I think I see it. You see it, Antoine?'

'Of course,' Antoine says tightly.

Soliman's shoulders relax. 'Sometimes people can't see it from certain angles. The way the light bounces off the paint just there, a small chip in the glass, I suspect. Well, shall we move on to these handsome bears and leopards?'

There's a bang of a servant's rod outside the door, and it swings open, and the image of the tightrope-walker fades in sudden light from the next room. At the door stands Countess Brandeis. For a moment Charlotte thinks: We summoned her by gossiping about her; but then she sees the expression on Brandeis's face.

'Your Imperial Majesty, Your Highnesses,' Brandeis says. 'The Empress would like to see you immediately.'

Joseph rises. 'What's the matter?'

He goes to the door of the study, speaks quietly to the countess, then turns back, his fingers to his temple and his eyes downcast. 'It's Josepha. Her headache – it's smallpox.'

CHAPTER FOUR

*Red Curtains — Notes from a Harpsichord — The Empress
Changes Her Plans — Recriminations —
A Conversation Overheard*

The court adopts its familiar smallpox practices for the second
time that year. Performances and balls are cancelled, not
only at court but throughout the city, because, in Vienna,
when there's an outbreak in one there's an outbreak in the
other. Everyone eats alone in their rooms, and when they
pass in the halls, they keep their distance.

The doctor is old fashioned. Every time Charlotte passes
Josepha's room, she sees covered porcelain pans being
removed. Blood. She can't see her sister in the dim room;
all she sees, in those brief moments when the door opens,
is red. Red blankets, red curtains. Why the colour red ought
to have any effect on smallpox, she can't say, but the doctor
always does it. Ties bits of cloth around people's arms and
necks.

A week passes like this, and Charlotte speaks very little
to anyone. Antoine stays away from her, even at night. Maids
dress her quickly, from behind, and leave again. She spends
a lot of time looking out of the window and reading: sometimes the embroidered book, sometimes Montesquieu,

sometimes Hume, thanks to Joseph. She thinks about the smell of magic and Dr Soliman's questions, and the more she thinks about it, the more she convinces herself it was all her imagination. But sometimes she lets herself wonder if perhaps he is a magister after all, if her decision to lie to him may have been a mistake. Perhaps he wants to teach them! But then again, perhaps he would tell Joseph or, worse, Mama, and they would take the embroidered book away.

She does not see Josepha ever again. Josepha dies on 15 October, the very day she was meant to leave Vienna for her new home in Naples.

Mama calls her children into her study at the Hofburg the day before the funeral, to say a prayer in private together. It's a warm room full of gilt and wood, and the air is stuffy. Everyone is in black. Even now, they stand some distance apart, like guards arrayed in the courtyard.

Charlotte has a tune in her head, a set of five notes, rising, falling. Harpsichord notes – it's a piece Josepha used to play. The notes light, melodic, almost frivolous. The harpsichords are silent – no one would dare play while the court is in mourning – but the notes press into her mind all the same, dampening everything else. Mama's red eyes, red knuckles on the edge of her desk. Josepha always held her hands so prettily at the harpischord, her left little finger crooked; Charlotte can see it.

Not all the children are here. Liesl is unwell and still in bed; she has caught smallpox too but is expected to recover. The doctors say that Liesl will be horribly scarred, though. Pretty Liesl.

Joseph loved Josepha so; she was his favourite. He holds his own little daughter close to him, the only two people in the room who aren't standing apart.

Charlotte. Antoine.

Max, whose ten-year-old face is red and puffy.

Amalia, who, as an unmarried and unscarred Habsburg of

twenty-one, is on borrowed time, stands like a soldier near the door, as though she expects an ambush.

But the first shot is directed at Joseph.

'I'm told there's a delegation of Protestants come to meet with you,' Maria Theresa says, levelling her gaze at the Holy Roman Emperor.

'They will wait until after the funeral, of course.'

'They will wait longer than that.'

'They wish to discuss the restrictions on their own worship, Mother. Restrictions that are in dire need of reform.'

'Joseph, you think everything is in dire need of reform.'

He says nothing, which says a great deal. His little daughter stands upright, looking at his face, while he looks at the Empress.

'If we were not Catholic monarchs of a Catholic nation, what would we be?' Maria Theresa says, spreading her delicate hands wide. 'Despots. There would be no higher law, no restraint, and men could do as they liked. We must be humble before God, in this sacred hour. We must take refuge in Him, and put our Empire fully in His hands.'

Joseph raises his chin. 'Then I'll tell the Protestants to go away, and perhaps while I'm at it, we can expel the Jews from Prague again.'

Charlotte freezes, and everyone in the room freezes too. Mama's deportation of the Jews happened before Charlotte was born, and she knows little about it, or how it ended.

'I have agreed that was an error,' Mama says evenly. 'I am fallible. I make mistakes, but I put my faith in God, and I ask him to guide me to do better. What do you use for guidance, Joseph? Faith? I don't think so. No, with you it's all books and bons mots. Wit! All your clever, barbed conversations, but there's no decency in any of it.'

Joseph burns; Charlotte can feel it, and she burns on his behalf. She breathes heavily, wanting to defend him but seeing the pain on her mother's face too. Mama blames herself for Josepha's death. Indeed, the whole court blames Mama. The story of the improperly sealed tomb, leaking unspeakable liquors, has made the rounds. Josepha caught smallpox from her dead sister-in-law, people say, because of the Empress's obstinate piety.

'I will send the Protestants away,' Joseph says, even more quietly than Mama. Their voices always get lowest when they are angriest; it is the Habsburg way.

'Good,' Mama says. 'We have problems enough without going looking for more. I have had letters from all the Bourbons, who send their condolences. We cannot much longer delay the wedding with Naples.'

'But Josepha is dead!' says Max. 'How can she be married?'

'Max, it's time you learned to hold your tongue and think,' snaps Mama. 'I have other daughters, do I not?'

Sixteen years, Josepha lived. Sixteen years, she smiled with her hand over her mouth, and played quietly with Max on the floor with his toy soldiers, and ran through the gardens with her favourite sister, who's now in the crypt with her.

Charlotte remembers, pointlessly, the name of the piece Josepha used to play, the one that is playing now in her head, the notes rising and falling mockingly. The Sarabande from Handel's Suite in D Minor.

In the doorway, Amalia puts her hand to her waist, as if she wears a sword there rather than a pannier.

'Amalia, be at ease. Ferdinand of Naples does not want a bride five years his senior,' snaps Mama. 'Charlotte, it is Naples for you, I'm afraid. Amalia is too old and Antoine is too young.'

Charlotte . . .

The final notes of the Sarabande.

. . . it is . . .

The right hand reaching, the left hand pulling back.

. . . Naples . . .

Josepha's hands poised over the keyboard.

. . . for you.

Charlotte hears the 'No' escape her lips before she thinks the word. In her head there's no more music.

No.

Charlotte was never meant to go to Naples; she has always been promised to the Dauphin of France. She's trained for France! All her planned enchantments, starting with the gloves, are for diplomacy. She's prepared for politics, not whatever the boorish King of Naples might want of her. Decoration? Submission?

'No?' Mama asks in a whisper.

Charlotte breathes, and starts again. 'God has taken away the bride you prepared for the King of Naples, Mama. Perhaps He considers the matter closed.'

'Oh, it's blasphemy now, is it?' Mama says. 'Charlotte, I expect you to do your duty. Naples was ruled by Austrian Habsburgs when I was a child. Now you have a chance to win it back for us: in fact, if not in name. You can do what an army cannot, and all you need do is be pleasant, stand up straight, bear children, whisper wisdom into your husband's ear, and speak prudently on those rare occasions when you must speak in public at all.'

If only there were an odious substance she could paint on her body to protect herself from this. But Mama doesn't need magic to do her harm.

And Charlotte doesn't need magic to survive a wound. She lifts her chin, opens her mouth, and asks, 'When must I go?'

Mama shrugs. 'The King of Naples knows you are bereaved. They won't insist that you come right away. But we can't leave it too long.'

For once, Antoine's face is not a mask. She is stricken. And well she should be. If Charlotte could be angry with her, this might be easier for both of them. Charlotte makes an attempt at petulance, says, 'Send me to Naples, then, and forget me.'

She isn't speaking to Mama but to Antoine.

Mama snorts. 'This is not a pantomime, Charlotte. Spare us your dramatic speeches.'

'We are left with the question of who will marry the Dauphin,' murmurs Joseph.

Mama spreads her black-taffeta arms wide. 'Amalia is for Parma. Liesl, poor dear, will never lose her smallpox scars. She will make an abbess, and pray for all our souls. Antoine is the only one left to me. Antoine will have to do for France.'

'But she is . . .'

'Antoine is eleven. The Dauphin is thirteen. We have a year or two to get Antoine into condition.'

Charlotte can barely look at Antoine, for fear of what she'll see on her face.

Charlotte, it is Naples for you. Antoine will have to do for France.

The word of the Empress.

For once, Charlotte is glad that she is separated from Antoine for the hour before dinner, when they each are meant to take their exercise. She tells her governess she's going out to the gardens and while Lerchenfeld is fussing with her cloak, Charlotte runs ahead into the bright cool air.

The Hofburg is just inside the walls of Vienna, an irregular ring of bastions and open slopes that separate the old city from its suburbs. Unlike Schönbrunn with its acres of orangeries and lakes, the green spaces here are mostly tucked inside the palace, in courtyards or squares. The one place to get a good walk is the narrow strip of private garden outside the palace proper, and just inside the fortifications. A central path leads from one section to the next, each laid out with trees, topiary and neat hedge walls.

It's cold today, wonderfully cold, though the grass is still green. The world smells like moss and bark: an October smell. Nobody's here. Charlotte strides towards the little maze at the centre of the garden, pauses for a moment, and then runs into it, her black cloak streaming behind her. She turns down one path and then another. For a moment, at least, she'll be alone.

It's a childish thing to do but Charlotte can't bear anyone looking at her or talking at her now. She's too angry to think straight, and what might happen if, for once, Charlotte did or said something without thinking?

She sags against a statue of Minerva. She's worn out, panting from more than the sharp October air. It takes everything Charlotte has to anticipate the blows before they come, from her mother, from the grinning, looming courtiers, from governesses and teachers. To find ways to fend them off, or cushion them, or heal the wounds they leave. She works all the time; she watches all the time. She doesn't have the energy to do all that and not be angry.

Josepha is dead. Josepha deserved better; she deserved a moment to sit and read a book or play her harpsichord in peace. Charlotte would have gladly taken Josepha's place to save her from going to Naples, but now she is taking her place and it saves no one, helps no one. No one but Mama and her schemes and alliances.

Charlotte puts her hands to her cheeks.

Rage is a relief. Easier than some other possibilities. And here, for a moment, she can be angry in peace, and hurt no one. The hedges are half a foot higher than her head, and thick. A maze is a kind of magic: a way to escape without leaving; a way to hide under the dove-grey sky.

A crunch on the gravel: a footstep. She whirls and sees Antoine, holding her black skirt in both hands and looking nervous. As though she's found a monster in the middle of the labyrinth.

'You'll get a lecture, Antoine, if Mama finds out we've been together. My terrible influence and all that.'

'What more can she do to us?' Antoine asks, her voice a mix of bright and sweet and sad.

'She'd think of something.'

'Charlotte, I'm so—'

Charlotte shakes her head. 'Antoine, leave it.'

'But – but Charlotte, I – How horrible that you—'

Charlotte feels the words surging at her teeth, demanding escape. They fly like knives. 'Stop. Just stop.'

'You'll be a wonderful queen, Charlotte,' Antoine says earnestly. 'You'll be just like Mama. A great ruler.'

Charlotte winces. 'I am *nothing* like her. I'm nothing but one of her spare parts. And you – you're not even that yet. Try to remember it, before—'

'Before I get anyone else killed.'

Charlotte turns to her then, and the anger, damn it, dissipates. Why wouldn't Antoine leave her alone? Antoine is shivering, her arms wrapped around herself.

'I didn't say that,' Charlotte says. 'And you must not think it. Not for a moment. You and I painted that – that horrible – If the infection came from the coffin, you would have taken ill too. Perhaps Josepha was sick before she even went into the crypt, and it has nothing to do with you.'

Antoine looks down the gravel of the path, at a brown leaf caught in an eddy of wind. It flies past her toes and catches on the base of the statue. 'Mama thinks I had a mild case as a baby. Perhaps I'm immune to smallpox. I was a vain little beast, to be so upset by making a mistake in the ballet. And now Josepha is dead and you – I'm so sorry, Charlotte. I can't tell you how sorry I am. I don't have words for it.'

The air has gone out of Charlotte, the anger, the hurt, everything. She feels nothing but grief.

She and Antoine sink to the ground, their skirts on the damp gravel, and hug tightly, black taffeta cold in each other's arms.

They are just putting their hands to the ground to raise themselves up when they both freeze. They hear adult voices, passing by on the path that encircles the maze, and Charlotte puts her hand out to stop Antoine.

'Dr Mesmer and Dr Hell are always going to be at each other's throats.' The voice is familiar, someone speaking Parisian French. Charlotte kneels, cranes her neck and catches a glimpse. Louis de Rohan, the French prince-bishop. Charlotte half forgot he was still in Vienna; she hasn't seen him since the move from Schönbrunn. He says, 'Take my advice, Soliman, and don't let Mesmer spout his reformist ideas. Before you know it, you'll have rogue magisters performing spells in every alley in Vienna.'

Soliman! Charlotte catches a glimpse of a red turban, and then they've walked on, past them.

She crouches back down with Antoine and whispers, 'Come on. I want to hear what they're talking about.'

Antoine's eyes go wide, but Charlotte doesn't stop to argue. She creeps along the hedge, silently cursing the crick in her back. This little maze is nothing like the grand labyrinth at Schönbrunn – if they'd been standing, Rohan and Soliman would have seen them. She creeps to the corner and looks; the men are farther along the path, up on a raised circular court surrounded by a low stone wall. She can see them, their backs to her.

Charlotte gestures to Antoine and they run across an open area to the wall, crouch below it. She doesn't think the men have seen them, but she can hardly hear over her heart.

'I'm sure of it, Brother,' Soliman says, his voice low. 'My chalk left no mark on their hands. It would have, if they had done any magic within the last month. Five years I've watched them, and I've found no evidence. I had a suspicion, yes, after that strange moment during the ballet performance, but now I know it was wrong.'

Antoine grasps her arm, but Charlotte avoids her gaze, her own hand to her mouth.

'Perhaps the girls fooled you somehow,' Rohan says. 'Perhaps they've put a spell on you.'

'They can't put a spell on me, of course.'

'Well, how am I to know what your practices are here?' Rohan retorts. 'You've said yourself it's as much as you can do to keep everyone in line. And whether the governess told the children anything or not, the fact remains she was a rogue magister in the imperial court. You and your Vienna friends must decide whether you are a chapter of the Order of 1326 or just another nest of rogues.'

'I would have handled that whole business with the governess differently,' Soliman retorts. 'But what was done was done, and I have done my best to make sure it left no trace.'

'There's still too much we don't know about that governess, and you've had five years to find out.'

'It seems there isn't much to find out. She was what rogue magisters always are: unlucky enough to find out something they should never have known. I don't think she had many spells. We know she didn't make herself immune.'

'That's true enough,' Rohan says, with an edge to his voice Charlotte dislikes. 'You don't suppose the girls, though—'

'I think it's highly unlikely they could have obtained what they need, even if they knew about it. Anyway, I tested them for that as well; they saw an illusion they would not have, if they were immune.'

'Well, we'll lose our chance to take their memories soon enough, and it'll be death or nothing, if you're wrong. They'll be anointed when they're crowned. One for Naples and one for France, I suspect. Our last chance to make sure of this business without mess.'

Death or nothing. Rohan looks out at the garden, over the girls' heads. They crouch as low as they can.

'If we act,' Soliman says, 'if we intercede to take their memories, that too presents a risk of discovery. I believe that risk is unnecessary and imprudent, given the lack of evidence. They were very young when Countess Ertag died. Even if she did say something to them, it would be no more real to them now than fairy tales. And I don't think she said anything.'

There's silence for a few moments, and Antoine's breathing so loudly. So is Charlotte, for that matter. They should get away, but they don't dare move. She grips Antoine's hand in her own.

'All right,' Rohan says at last. 'An end to it, then, Dr Soliman. You'll be glad to spend your time on more important things, I'm sure. I'll make my report to Paris. And I'll take that illumination spell, too, thank you, although I think something other than shoes . . .'

The two men are walking again, away from the girls, and their voices trail off.

Charlotte and Antoine look at each other with wide eyes, holding each other's arms, their breath fogging together. There are magisters in Vienna, right in the very heart of the imperial court, and they have spells to share and opinions to debate. They knew about Countess Ertag. And they have been watching Charlotte and Antoine, for years, watching for signs that they know something they should not.

CHAPTER FIVE

*Black Silk — The House of Bourbon — Antoine Is
Twelve — Charlotte's Trousseau — Leave-takings*

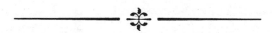

A few days after Josepha's funeral, Mama calls Charlotte into
her study. One wall is cluttered with the children's landscape
paintings. When Charlotte was small, when Papa was still
alive, all the children used to come in here and chatter away
while Mama signed papers, a smile on her face.

Now, Mama and Charlotte face each other in black silk.
Mama is standing, so Charlotte stands too.

'You must stop,' Mama says, without so much as a greeting.
'Charlotte, from this moment forward, your complaining
stops.'

There's no point in arguing. 'As you say, Mama.'

'You are fifteen and yet you act like a child. The world
does not conform itself to your wishes, and it never will. It
would be best if you resigned yourself to that fact now, before
you do your family and your country damage.'

'I am sorry, Mama.'

Charlotte is only half listening. She is thinking, as she has
been thinking for days, about what spells Angelo Soliman
might have. Would he be able to explain the mysterious
spells in the embroidered book? If not him, well, he and

Rohan spoke of other magisters. Of 'rogues'. Perhaps the world is full of people who know about magic.

Mama comes around the edge of the desk, closer. 'Naples is very beautiful.'

'So I have heard, Mama.' Charlotte can't help adding, with a little smile to show she's not entirely serious but also that she is not going to forgive anything, 'The volcano must keep it interesting.'

Mama's mouth shows her disapproval of irony, but she stays in diplomatic mode. 'And not only the city. The whole southern portion of Italy is yours, my dear, and Sicily too.'

'Mine? I don't think the House of Bourbon will see it that way.'

'You always knew you would marry into that family,' Mama says sharply. 'Do not act as though this has surprised you.'

'I believed I would marry the Dauphin, and go to France. You always told me so.'

'Surely one Bourbon is as good as another.'

She's shaken out of thinking about magic, now. Irritated. 'But, Mama, the King of Naples does everything his father tells him to do. Naples is ruled from afar by the King of Spain. In France I could be of some *use*. Some purpose.'

'In France, your purpose would have been to hold the Bourbon alliance and hold the support of France and Spain for Austria and the Empire, against our enemies. England is rising, and Prussia will never be satisfied. Your role in Naples is the same: to cement the compact between the families, and rear children who will ensure the continuation of the Empire.'

'But, Mama, if the King of Spain is the true power in Naples, I'll be powerless.'

Mama turns away, looks down at her desk, at the perpetual stack of papers, the coffee set, the inkwell, the engraved brass globe.

'I know what it's like to have one's childhood expectations

exposed as the fragile things they are. My father spent the last years of his life bartering with every European power, getting promises that they would recognize me as his heir. Oh, the treasures he traded away for those promises! I was twenty-three when he died and, immediately, the vultures descended. This king and that king, all portioning up my lands for themselves, claiming to be horrified at the thought of a woman inheriting. Monsters. Most of Europe was against me. My father had left me a handful of promises but he had not thought to leave me much of an army. Do you know what I did?'

'You went to Hungary.' Charlotte has always liked this story.

Mama grips the side of her desk, as if for support, and indeed she is shaky on her feet these days. 'I went to Hungary. I rode a black horse up to the top of a hill and I brandished my sword and I swore to defend Hungary to my last breath. I gave myself to Hungary in return for an army. And with that army, I won back nearly everything. But do you know what it says on all the official documents, my daughter?'

Charlotte frowns. She doesn't know this part. This is a departure from the usual tale. 'I don't, Mama.'

'It says that I am *King* of Hungary, and Austria, and Bohemia, of all my other lands. I am king. Because one cannot be both a woman and a sovereign at once, you see. And as for emperor, well, I had to ask your dear papa to take that title on for me. Do you know what they shouted in Hungary, when I rode my black horse? "Our lives and blood for King Maria Theresa!"'

Mama is a king. Just as Charlotte is not a magistra but a magister.

Mama steps forward and puts one hand on each of Charlotte's shoulders. 'You will not be powerless in Naples, my dear daughter. Power is not something you are given. Power is something you take. When you are a woman, it is a little more difficult, that's all. You have to give people a

57

way to believe they don't see you taking it. Your power, as a woman, is in submission, as I submitted to Hungary.'

Charlotte bends her head, in acknowledgement, if not submission. 'Mama,' she says, quietly, 'will Antoine be all right?'

'Better than all right. They say the Dauphin is very sweet, by the standards of thirteen-year-old boys.'

'Well, perhaps it is for the best, then,' Charlotte says with a grin. 'I couldn't stand a sweet husband.'

'No, indeed!' Mama lets her hands drop from Charlotte's shoulders. 'All of France will fall in love with Antoine. Our dear little pet. How could they not adore her? Of course, we have a great deal of work to do to make her ready. All her tutors are unsuitable, and I shall have to send to France for others. French history, etiquette, deportment. And then there is the matter of her spelling. I had thought of asking Angelo Soliman to take over her language instruction, because Joseph speaks so highly of him, but he's run off to get married, so I'll have to find someone else.'

Charlotte blinks. 'Run off?'

'Yes, my dear. Joseph tells me she's a Kellerman, so from a good family, and widow of Countess Harrach's secretary – what was his name?'

Charlotte should be relieved; she doesn't need to worry about Soliman discovering them, with him gone from Vienna. Instead she feels strangely desolate.

'I didn't know he was going so soon.'

'Mmm, so soon after your sister's funeral. It would have been better to postpone it.'

Very quietly, Charlotte asks, 'And my wedding? When is that to be?'

'We'll perform it here in April, at the Augustinian church, with one of your brothers standing as proxy for the groom. That gives you a full six months to prepare. Then you'll travel to Naples, and I'm sure they'll want to have another ceremony there after you arrive.'

'And Antoine? How long before she goes to France?'

'I think we can make it two years at least. The Dauphin is young too, and not yet king. There is time for them. Speaking of churches, I have an idea. The Abbé Vermond might be able to help Antoine with her French. I think she'd do very well if she only applied herself.'

'I'm sure you're right, Mama,' Charlotte says, and means it. She kisses her mother on her powdered cheek, and to her surprise, she means that too.

Antoine turns twelve while the court is still in mourning. She feels terribly old, now that her marriage is being arranged.

In February, they ask Joseph about Soliman as casually as they can, and he says Soliman's wedding took place, very quietly with just a few witnesses because the Prince of Liechtenstein did not approve. Soliman has, in fact, left the prince's service at last, and taken his wife travelling. He said something about Trieste.

Mama sends for a new doctor, to inoculate Joseph's daughter and Max against the smallpox; the older children are deemed to have been exposed to it often enough. The inoculation is dangerous: the doctor takes a scraping of a smallpox sore from an infected person and places it inside a cut in the skin of the healthy patient. For several days, the only reports anyone makes about anything are the latest count of pustules, the incidence of fever. But both children recover, and Maria Theresa declares that she will begin a programme of inoculation for anyone who wants the procedure and cannot afford it. Gradually, the balls and concerts resume, as smallpox abates again, for months, years if they're lucky.

While all of this occupies the Empress, Charlotte and Antoine make the most of their time together. In the six months between Josepha's death and Charlotte's proxy wedding, they do as many spells as they can, making Charlotte a kind of magical trousseau, with all the weapons she might require.

She has some things already: a fan that can cool a room, the Pandora doll and, now, her white gloves. She won't be taking her childish old nightgown with her, the one with the enchanted pocket on the inside where she hides the embroidered book. She and Antoine enchant a new pocket for her, a portable one of the kind they wear under their skirts. A pale, rose-coloured pouch of plain linen, with ribbons for tying it around her waist. They also attempt a couple of new enchantments: a thimble that can break something – a thread, a piece of fabric – into even pieces, and a spell to make the contents of a book seem like the contents of another book to anyone but its owner.

They do the enchantment to make a little more of the oil that makes metal and stone pliable, in case it's useful.

There is a spell they've never been able to make work, for crumbs that show a path, and they try it again, with no success. Magic mending is of no use to them at the moment: they have nothing to mend. As for the shoe that rises in the air, which Charlotte once used to play a prank on Mozart, it seems of little use now.

That leaves only two spells that they can make sense of. One is for a drink that confers loyalty, but its sacrifices are unimaginably high. The other is the enchantment for 'a shroud to remember the dead', which is not something Charlotte wants in her trousseau.

The fourteenth spell they puzzled out, for immunity, is something Charlotte only needed once.

They've never found the spell for the embroidery within the book itself. Antoine thinks it's probably there, written so confusingly that she and Charlotte have no idea what it does. There must also be a way to make secret writing appear. What wonders might be in the book, but hidden to them! Perhaps there's even a love spell, somewhere?

Charlotte and Antoine put off the work of deciding how they will continue to share one book between them, with a mountain range in the middle.

So, on their last night together, a spring evening, they sprawl on the floor of Antoine's room, each with a pen and an inkwell and a sheaf of papers, copying out spells: the ones they understand and the ones they don't.

'I wonder where Ertag found these,' Charlotte says. 'The way they're written – she wouldn't have written them that way herself.'

Antoine copies the words that appear in nearly every spell: 'these proofs have been found'. What does it mean? It sounds as though spells are things that magisters can discover, or even invent. She thinks of saying something about it, but remembers Charlotte chiding her, months before: *People don't invent roses.*

Charlotte stops, puts down her pen and sits up, sighing.

'What is it?' Antoine asks. She's still lying on her front, copying out spells.

'All of this,' Charlotte says, gesturing at the piles of paper. 'So much we don't understand. What do we have? Fans and dolls and ribbons.'

'We puzzled out the immunity spell. Maybe we'll puzzle out these others too.'

'Maybe. But this is only one spellbook! We know there are other magisters in the world, and they must have amazing powers. We know they keep magic secret, and they don't seem to want us to know about it. If they were to find out, Antoine, what would they do?'

Antoine thinks of Countess Ertag's bloody bedsheets and shudders. 'They won't find out.'

'We must be very careful, and not ever mention magic to anyone. Antoine, if someone comes to you and says they're a magister, asks what you know, you must not say anything about it. Don't do any new magic that might go wrong in ways you can't predict – yes, I'm thinking of the gloves. If you see Rohan, write to me. When Soliman comes back to Vienna, if he talks to you about anything at all, write to me. Do you promise, Antoine?'

'Of course. We've kept it secret this long.' Antoine looks over the papers filled with strange instructions. *Fans and dolls and ribbons*, Charlotte said. 'But how will we ever learn any new spells if we can't do new magic?'

Charlotte pauses, and gives voice to something she's hardly allowed herself to think about until now. 'Do you remember Rohan saying, "They'll be anointed when they're crowned"? When we're queens, they wouldn't dare act against us. Maybe there's something they've done to Mama and Joseph, but Mama and Joseph didn't understand it, but we will. I'll find out what I can. Perhaps there are books about it in Naples. Once I have a son, I'll be on the Council there, and then I'll be able to order all sorts of scientific enquiries, as queen. Perhaps when you are a queen, you can do the same. But for now, we must be careful. I promise, I won't let anyone find out about you. And whatever you do, keep the book hidden.'

'Aren't you taking the book, Charlotte? I think you should. You're the one travelling.'

'You'll be travelling too, dear, soon enough.'

'But you were the one who finished the embroidery. It's yours. It's always been yours, really. I don't think it would be right if it stayed with me.'

Charlotte leans closer on one elbow and kisses Antoine's cheek. She seems glad; she has always been protective of the book. 'All right. You keep these copies, then, and I'll take the book. But you must be very careful to keep them safe. Put them inside an enchanted pocket and put that under the floorboards. No one must ever see them.'

Antoine nods. 'I don't know what I'll do without you, Charlotte. I can't imagine it.'

'You won't be without me,' Charlotte says, and takes her hand. 'Not ever. Don't forget. If anything ever happens, if you need help, I will help you. Always. Even if you're in the wilds of America.'

'I'm not going to the wilds of America,' says Antoine,

giggling. They used to play at living simple lives in nature, or at exploring strange islands and ruling pirate bands, but she's too grown up for that now. 'I'm going to Paris.'

'All the easier for me to reach you, then. No matter what, I will help you. I promise.'

Antoine purses her lips, and nods. 'I promise too.'

They have always known they would be separated one day. They have known it as they have known that one day they will die. That doesn't make it any easier.

Charlotte stands in the grey morning courtyard, looking at her sister in her blue jacket and dress. Antoine looks older, suddenly. A dauphine in the making.

'I wish I could climb into your pocket,' Antoine whispers, 'and go with you.'

'Climb in,' Charlotte whispers back. 'This is my enchanted one.'

At that, Antoine grins. Then: 'If something happens in Naples,' she says, her smile gone, 'if—'

'Write to me often. Always use the cipher. The one that Joseph taught us. And change the keyword with each letter; do you remember the order?'

'*Amour, corps, espoir, mémoire, trésor,*' Antoine recites.

Charlotte wants to say that everything will be fine, but she can't. It isn't true, and she can't hide it from Antoine. Antoine is, despite her smart little jacket and pile of curls, not a child any more. They're being sent away like packages to the men who've ordered them, and nothing will ever be entirely fine now.

Charlotte holds her sister close, warm in her arms. Then she looks one last time into Antoine's cornflower eyes and wonders which of them will sacrifice this memory. She turns. She walks away.

Countess Lerchenfeld, their old governess, is waiting by the carriage that will deliver Charlotte to Naples. She packs Charlotte in with her attendants and her furs and books. For the next three weeks, this carriage will be Charlotte's world, taking her over the Alps and down into Italy.

'Lerchenfeld, I have one request, for when you return here without me,' Charlotte says. She's seated now, but the carriage door is still open, and Lerchenfeld is holding her gloved hand.

'I will make a good report of you to your mother and brother.'

'You're very kind. But would you also . . . write to me, often, and please be sure in every letter to send word of Antoine. Write the smallest details: what she says, what she does, almost what she thinks. If anything happens, tell me.'

Lerchenfeld looks at her quizzically.

'She will soon be a bride herself,' Charlotte supplies, because Lerchenfeld seems to want an explanation, 'and I wish I could prepare her for the ordeal. She is so young and so soft-hearted. Please – please love her, for my sake.'

Lerchenfeld nods. 'I will be a friend to your sister. And I will write you letters, every week. More.'

Charlotte nods, absently, as Lerchenfeld closes the carriage door. Charlotte puts her hand to the window-glass to cover the small figure of Antoine, her warm-hearted sister nothing but a cold, blue blur.

Then she opens the carriage door and runs out, before they can stop her, before she can stop herself. She gathers Antoine into her arms and they fall into tears, shaking, laughing at each other between their sobs.

PART TWO

1768 TO 1775

CHAPTER SIX

Charlotte Travels to Italy — Conversations with Leopold —
Conversations with Ferdinand — The Wedding —
The White Gloves

Maria Theresa, to her credit, is a formidable negotiator of
marriage contracts: as soon as Charlotte bears an heir, she
will be given a seat on the Council of Naples. The better to
do what the Empress expects of her daughter: protect
Austria's interests and keep her mother and brother apprised
of what the Bourbons are doing. This, along with the rearing
of good Catholic children, is what Maria Theresa expects.
She has made that clear over the course of the last six months.

Charlotte has quietly used these six months to read all of
Joseph's philosophy books and decide what sort of queen
she can be and will be, in Naples. It's true that she can't
count on her position giving her as much respect or influence
as it might have in France. But Charlotte knows she can be
more than the protector of Habsburg interests. She can be a
great queen, and she intends to be one.

And Joseph, in his conversations with her over the last
few months, has given her some practical advice.

'Nobody pretends that the King of Naples is anything but
a figurehead, so his advisers report directly to the King of

Spain,' Joseph said after she returned his copy of Hume's *Treatise of Human Nature* and gave him her impressions of it. 'That's a problem, but also an opportunity. Think of the people in Naples who will feel aggrieved and neglected. The writers and artists and philosophers who have no royal patron. The local nobility, who have been told they don't matter. You can be the champion of those people, and they'll love you for it.'

So Charlotte has been preparing, when she wasn't spending time with Antoine, mining Joseph for all the information about wars and diplomacy that she could, or asking the Italians at court about customs and history. Now she has a journey of 873 miles, and she still has work to do. By the time the carriages reach Salzburg, she has a notebook full of comments on the opera, which Neapolitans are said to love, and she has memorized the names of all the King's relatives and advisers.

Salzburg is the border of the Alps, and marks the place where Antoine's future journey will diverge from Charlotte's. Charlotte's carriage turns to the south, towards a horizon that ripples and rises.

At Innsbruck, Charlotte writes to Lerchenfeld and asks for news of Antoine. It's a beautiful city, all cold whites and blues even on the sunniest spring days, surrounded by snow-capped mountains. She prays in the room where her father died, now converted into a chapel by Maria Theresa. She makes a list of expressions she likes in the Neapolitan language. *Ô paese mio*: in my country or in my opinion. *Meglio sulo ca male accumpagnato*: better alone than in bad company.

By the time they reach the Brenner Pass, she is spending more time than she likes staring out of the window, her thoughts wordless, as fanciful as the sinuous clouds and the sparkling veins of quartz in the cliffside. The people watch the imperial carriage train as if it were a stray dog; they wear coloured feathers in their hats.

The convoy stops at an ugly inn, and by morning she has

her paper and pencil in hand again. She makes an inventory of the sacrifices she can make, as the carriage rattles down-hill into a land of hillside vineyards. Hopes she would rather bury; affections that hurt.

One day, it's warm enough in the carriage that she wishes she had her enchanted fan, which cools down any room so nicely. But it's wrapped inside a fur deep in one of her trunks, because it cools down everything around it even when she doesn't want it to. She always wears gloves when she uses it, because it's like ice to the touch. Yet another girlish enchantment that is of very little use.

In golden Florence, she meets her brother Leopold and his Bourbon wife, who is a sister of Charlotte's new husband. She hasn't seen Leopold in three years, not since he became the Grand Duke of Tuscany. More importantly, he hasn't seen her in three years, and he treats her almost as if she were a stranger, a visiting ruler who needs to know the lay of the land. She loves him for it.

Even better, Leopold and his wife accompany her south to her new home. She sits in a carriage with her brother as they roll on to Rome.

'Your wife is lovely,' she says. 'Such beautiful blue eyes.'

'Yes, she's very good.'

'Not like her brother then.'

Leopold laughs shortly. 'Ah, no. Not much like her brother. They both have the same long nose, but I must admit it suits Luisa much better.'

'Is he awful?'

He shrugs. 'Your husband? Ferdinand is a nonentity. An irritation. You'll have no difficulty getting around him, so long as you don't have any unrealistic expectations.'

'Love, you mean.'

He looks out of the window, where the trees are bright with green. 'Ha! Yes. Love. But I meant, well, common decency, really. Reason. Respect. He's not . . . sound. Do you know what I mean? He's rotten to the core. But as long as you don't try to lean on him, he can't hurt you too badly. I think.'

'You fill me with hope, Brother.'

He looks back at her, very serious. 'Hope is something we all have to set aside, sooner or later, if we're realists. You'll get on all right, Charlotte. There's a mountain range between us and Mama now. We can make our own lives here. And I won't be far. Don't worry too much about Ferdinand. Give him enough freedom to keep himself occupied and he won't get in your way. The man you really have to watch out for is Bernardo Tanucci.'

'He was the head of the council of regency when Ferdinand was still a minor, yes? The Tuscan lawyer.'

Leopold nods. 'Tanucci is still the real ruler of Naples, though he reports to Ferdinand's father in Spain. Any policy that keeps money flowing into the coffers, and thus Tanucci's purse, is the official policy of Naples. There's no military to speak of, because that would cost money. And anyone who *has* money must give it up or shut up. Taxes upon taxes. The people don't like it, but there's not much they can do about it, and Ferdinand being such a vulgar oaf protects him from criticism – the King is a man of the people, you see. The Church is another matter. Tanucci's practically at war with the Pope – His Holiness had the gall to think himself above him.'

Charlotte's expression says something like: 'Well, well.'

'So the question is', Leopold says, crossing his legs, 'whether you want to be Queen of Naples in reality, or just in name. I recommend the latter course as the easier option. But somehow I doubt that's the path you'll take.'

She smiles. 'If I weren't a queen, what would I be?'

Leopold shrugs and grins. 'Charlotte, I suppose.'

She shakes her head, but she's grinning too. 'I left that waif behind on the road, somewhere north of the Alps.'

They've been told to drive straight through Rome, because of Tanucci's troubles with the Pope, but Charlotte insists they stop long enough to have at least a look at Saint Peter's. They sleep in Marino that night, and she stays up late and writes a letter to Antoine.

Three days, and they reach Terracina, on a warm day. Everything smells like rotting fish. On one side, mountains; on the other, the sea. On a tiny spit of land surrounded by marshes, a pavilion waits, with her husband inside it. No escape.

Ferdinand is not as ugly as his portrait led Charlotte to believe. He looks insouciant, almost dashing, in his bright blue coat, thick with medals and sashes. It brings out his eyes, which are intelligent enough, or perhaps it's only that they are appraising, and confident. He looks her up and down when she enters the pavilion.

She does as she's been taught: she kneels before him. He snorts. What does that mean? What is he snorting about? She's done something wrong, or – no, he's breaking the formality to keep himself comfortable. He takes Charlotte by the hand and lifts her to her feet, and grins at her.

Another eight hours by carriage to the Palace of Caserta, and this time she cannot ride with Leopold. Charlotte and Ferdinand change out of court dress and into travelling clothes; Charlotte wears a dove-grey Brunswick, the jacket flaring nicely out over the slim skirt. No more panniers today, thank God.

They put her into a carriage with the man who is technically already her husband. Charlotte has already married him once, by proxy in Vienna. But they'll have to be married again, tomorrow. That way, both countries get a wedding. She'll have to go through it all twice: the standing, the swearing, the music in the streets, the nauseatingly long party.

The doors close; the carriage rolls.

'Well, Carolina,' he says in Neapolitan. 'How do you think we'll get on?'

'Charlotte,' she says. 'My family calls me Charlotte. We use the French versions of our names. Our father was from Lorraine, you know.'

He cocks his head, as though surprised to hear her speak Neapolitan back. She's been studying.

'But you're in Italy now,' he replies.

'And yet I remain Charlotte.'

'Are you a virgin?' he asks, switching into French.

She nearly chokes. 'What?'

He laughs, and looks out of the window. 'I can see we'll have great conversations.'

She was caught off guard, not embarrassed, but there's no way to tell him that now, and why does she care what he thinks, anyway? The bully. But she should at least try not to make an enemy of him. A nonentity, Leopold called him.

The road skirts the coast, along a dark green promontory named for Circe. She pulls a book out of her velvet travel bag. Thanks to the enchantment she and Antoine did, it looks like a French translation of Smollett's *Travels Through France and Italy*. It is, in fact, Joseph's copy of *Candide*. He can get another, when he finds it missing. Maria Theresa would never approve of her daughter reading Voltaire, least of all this irreverent book.

But Charlotte isn't really reading it at the moment. The carriage turns, and she shifts in the seat, bringing her husband into view.

He drops his tongue out of his mouth, a glazed pink monstrosity, and she drops her book.

He laughs hysterically, bends and picks it up. 'Thank you,' she says, anticipating. But he doesn't straighten. He takes the opportunity to seize the hem of her skirt in both hands and agitate it, flapping and worrying it.

She flinches, pulling her legs as close to the edge of the seat as she can. Ferdinand lets go, with a grin on his face, and leafs through the book, lazily, not taking care with the pages. He reads aloud: '"The old philosopher, whose name was Martin, embarked then with Candide for Bordeaux. They had both seen and suffered a great deal . . ." Looks boring.'

Then he tosses it to her. He leans back.

'You'll have to learn how to have a bit of fun, *Charlotte*.'

She stares at him, stunned. He seems not to have recognized what he was reading, but he was reading it all the same: *Candide*. He should have seen a travel diary. The enchantment on the book had no effect on him.

Charlotte goes cold. Surely Ferdinand cannot be a magister.

'I'm looking forward to meeting some of the natural philosophers in Naples,' she says, in French, casually, as though the book has given her the thought. 'In Vienna, many proofs have been found of fascinating theories, of late.'

She emphasizes *proofs have been found*, in case that is a common formula for magic spells; Ertag would certainly never have come up with such a phrase on her own. But Ferdinand's face just wrinkles into a bemused, mocking expression.

'Great conversations,' he mutters.

No, he cannot be a magister. But, like Mama, he seems to be immune to magic. She remembers Rohan saying, *They'll be anointed when they're crowned*. But Ferdinand seems to know nothing of magic, any more than Mama or Joseph did. If they've been anointed to make them immune, they were unaware. The thought makes her shudder. In any case, if Ferdinand is immune, she won't be able to use her gloves on him, or anything else. She has never felt so powerless, and she has felt powerless all her life.

They ride on in silence for a painful hour, and at some point she realizes that he is, mercifully, asleep.

It's nearly midnight when they arrive at the top of a low hill, with a starless night above a vast façade of pale stone in all the colours of a blushing bride. Caserta Palace. They show her to a room with walls and paintings she does not know, and sheets that do not smell of home. She falls asleep at last, reciting the exports of Naples and Sicily: olive oil, wheat, silk, wool, sulphur, wine.

At the wedding supper, Charlotte sits on a dais beside her husband. She's glad to be out of the stiff armour of cloth of silver she wore for the ceremony, and the heavy purple cloak, lined with ermine. A queen's wedding finery. Now, she's in one of the ninety-nine silk gowns from her trousseau, but it's still a court dress, stiff, with wide panniers. Blood red. She doesn't sit so much as arrange herself, with plumes on her head. And she's not hungry.

It doesn't help that there's no table. Everyone sits against the wall, balancing their plates on their knees.

'Spanish etiquette dictates that no one else may eat at the King's table,' says Leopold, on her other side. 'And they follow Spanish etiquette here. So Ferdinand did away with tables altogether, so he could eat with his friends. You'll get used to it – eating without a table, I mean. And the rest.'

Charlotte's husband, at her side, is not looking at her. He is looking at the men at the further reaches of the room, and laughing with most of the arm of a braised octopus falling out of his mouth. Her husband's face is florid – the wine, perhaps. His nose is not as big as she was led to believe – she had heard that the people call him King Big-Nose – but it will soon be covered in red veins if he keeps carrying on like this.

She doesn't want him to look at her, as a man looks at a horse he bought for too much money.

'I've heard the Jesuits have all left Naples,' says Ferdinand. 'Who will the Pied Piper lure away next? Maybe all the lawyers, eh, Tanucci?'

Bernardo Tanucci, sitting across the room from Charlotte, does not touch his food either. He watches everyone from under his terrifying eyebrows.

'I am afraid I cannot do anything about the lawyers, Your Majesty, because a man cannot act against his own interests,' says Tanucci with an evil little smile. 'But yes, I've rid the city of the Jesuits. They were too powerful.'

'Surely everyone is only just as powerful as I allow them to be.'

Charlotte sips the white Tuscan wine in her glass. It's sweeter than she likes.

Tanucci inclines his head. 'Of course. But these not-so-secret societies think they run Naples, and we must remind them from time to time that they do not. The Freemasons, the Jesuits – they're no better than criminals.'

'I suppose you're right, Tanucci. You know best. Though I do stick my nose in, from time to time, eh?' Ferdinand looks around, basking in the laughter at the joke he has made at his own expense.

Charlotte clears her throat. 'Begging Your Majesty's pardon.'

'My wife speaks!' Ferdinand crows, looking at her. 'The German mouse squeaks!'

Everyone laughs.

Charlotte smooths a rumple in the white glove on her left wrist. Time to see whether the white gloves work on anyone here. There's a lump in her throat. The last time she used the gloves, inadvertently, they needed only a passing thought, and that thought froze Antoine in place for what seemed forever. She must be very precise, and very deliberate.

'I wonder who will run the schools,' she says in her most persuasive tones, 'if the Jesuits are gone. Expensive, aren't they, schools?'

Tanucci, she thinks. *You will agree.*

'Expensive, aren't they,' Tanucci says woodenly. 'Schools.'

His face is impassive as he says it, and afterwards his mouth quirks into a short, nervous chuckle. He's surprised by what he just said.

But everyone else interprets it as mockery, his parroting her own words back to her as though they are ridiculous. They think his little smile at the end was triumph, not nerves or surprise. They laugh, and she fights the urge to pull the damned gloves off her hands.

'You don't have any scars,' says Ferdinand, peering at her.

'I'm sorry, Your Majesty?'

'I mean, I knew the smallpox killed half of Maria Theresa's whelps, so I expected you to be covered in bumps when you arrived. But perhaps that is what those two little lumps are there, under your bodice.'

As the hall fills with laughter again, he reaches across and puts his hand on her breast. She tries to pull away, but the heavy, carved chair doesn't move.

The laughter stops.

'You have no right to pull away from me,' he says, his voice low.

Then he turns and looks around the silent room, and Charlotte thinks for a moment she has misheard the next thing he says, because the blood is beating in her ears.

'I need to take a shit,' Ferdinand groans, his hand on his belly. 'Who's coming to keep me company?'

A half-dozen men rise dutifully from their seats and follow the King down the corridor to his close-stool.

The only magic she has doesn't work against her husband, and it hasn't been much help with Tanucci, either. She sits alone in the room full of discarded plates and glasses, the ushers at the door not meeting her eyes.

The wedding night.

Charlotte sits in bed in her nightgown and thinks as hard as she can. For a few days out of every month, at least, she can send word to Ferdinand that she is unwell. Will he know what she means? God knows what he calls the General. It might not even put him off, but some men don't like blood, her sisters have told her, and he might give her five days' peace out of every month. A week's peace? Can she get away with that?

If only there were some spell to make him believe, falsely,

that he's been in bed with his wife. She can see nothing like that in the embroidered book, though, and she needs to give birth to an heir. When she has a son, she gets a seat on the Council of Naples. And then she can start doing something real with her life.

Three weeks out of every month. That's not so bad. And maybe it won't be every one of those nights. He will have mistresses, no doubt, and so long as they don't try to legitimize their children, Charlotte is happy to let them take some of the burden.

Perhaps, all in all, it will be bearable. She folds her hands in her lap and looks at the courtiers giggling at the doorway, waiting for the King. Courtiers whose names she does not know, giggling about her private life. About what's going to happen, any moment now.

Or, perhaps, giggling because it hasn't happened yet. Where is Ferdinand? Passed out drunk somewhere? God damn him: he seems intent on embarrassing her. If she'll have to get it over with some time, it might as well—

The door opens, and the room is full of people. Liveried people, except for Ferdinand, who swaggers in to general applause.

Charlotte goes over everything her sisters told her in her mind. What to expect. It won't hurt too badly, they said.

She expects Ferdinand to undress, but he just leaps at her, making a show for the audience. They all roar with laughter as his first kiss lands like a blow on her mouth, as he puts his hand on her leg and pushes her onto her back.

'Go on, leave us!' he roars, laughing.

She stares at the interlaced gold crowns that decorate the underside of the top of the bedstead.

Ferdinand attaches himself to Charlotte, every one of his kisses draining her, his arms binding her.

Then he pulls back, and says, 'I haven't forced anyone in my life. If you're unwilling, there are plenty of other fifteen-year-old girls in the palace.'

She hesitates; then she says, 'I am your wife.'

He grins, and for a moment she can understand why he thinks himself handsome. 'You are. Carolina.'

Charlotte tries not to freeze, but can only bring herself to return a fraction of his kisses. She gives him her cheek, her neck. She sings songs in her head.

She cries out once, from the pain. And then Ferdinand leaves, mercifully, and she weeps, alone.

CHAPTER SEVEN

The French Ambassador – Antoine's Shortcomings –
Alliances – A Very Good Likeness – Turpentine
and Blood

The new French ambassador to Vienna, the Marquis de Durfort, has the most amiable expression Antoine has ever seen. It's so beatific, with such rosy cheeks and sparkling eyes, that she feels sure he could send men to their deaths and they'd go happily. She tries to copy it, discreetly, as she sits across from him at dinner, but she's sure she isn't getting it right.

Durfort has made it perfectly clear, without ever saying so, that Antoine is unsatisfactory.

Antoine knows the list of her shortcomings as well as she knows the Ten Commandments.

She speaks French with a German accent, the tutors say – and when she protests that she speaks the same French as her father and has since she was a baby, her tutors say, well, but the late Emperor was from Lorraine! Entirely the wrong vowels. Her written French is even worse.

She is too short, and short-sighted. She gets pimples. Her bosom is too small. One shoulder rides above the other. Her hairline is too high – and if that were not bad enough, she's losing patches of hair along her temples from the wool band that scrapes her curls back under the constructions of her hairstylists.

Most painfully, her teeth are crooked. For three months, a doctor has been adjusting them, pulling on some of the bottom teeth with a set of pliers called a pelican, and wrapping golden wires around the top. Her jaw aches all the time, but the teeth haven't moved.

'After dinner, I will show you my collection of French royal portraits,' says Maria Theresa, her soup spoon quavering. She's been shakier of late, and heavier on her legs. The soup spoon clatters down into the bowl as she raises one finger to make her next point. 'I have every member of the royal family now, and they are all quite recent and done by the very best painters. The King of France has been very good to me. I'd like to reciprocate. We shall have one made of Antoine for him, especially if she is going to marry his grandson. No doubt the young Dauphin wants to have a look at her, too.'

'What a gracious offer, Your Imperial Majesty!' Durfort beams. 'Perhaps next year, when the subject is a little older? There is no rush.'

Did Antoine imagine that before he said *older*, he let his gaze linger over her disappointing lack of bosom? She blushes, which is not the end of the world, even though it is not quite for the reason they'll all assume.

Mama does not smile. Despite what Durfort says, she is indeed in a rush.

Austria and France used to be enemies, before Antoine was born. Then France finally took Austria's side in the most recent war against Prussia and England. France came out of that war poorer and with fewer colonies. Many French people blame Mama and hate Austrians.

But Mama's old enemy, Prussia, has allied with England, and rich England has gained territories in America and Africa.

So Mama must seal the French alliance. Antoine understands this very well. France may be a bankrupt and reluctant friend, but Austria needs all the friends it can get. Besides,

France is ruled by Bourbons, and Mama is joining Habsburgs to Bourbons all over Europe.

But the French King has been non-committal about the plan to marry Antoine to his grandson Louis.

'It takes time to make a good picture,' Mama says.

'Indeed,' says Durfort, tenting his fingers and leaning back to regard Antoine. 'I know of a painter with just the right touch. Joseph Ducreux. Yes, I think it must be Ducreux.'

'He's in Paris?' Mama asks dubiously.

'And very sought after there. But I'm sure he would wrap up his affairs and travel here, for such a commission. It would be a mere matter of months, and in the meantime . . .' He smiles indulgently, and pauses, and says, '. . . the archduchess can only grow more beautiful.'

Mama stares for a long time at the finished portrait of Antoine. She stands, breathing heavily, scowling.

'It's a very good likeness,' Countess Lerchenfeld ventures at last. She's standing on one side of Mama, and Antoine on the other. They're alone in the Mirrors Room, where Mama can get a sense of the portrait from a distance. On an easel, the girl in the painting waits.

'Is it?' Mama asks. 'Hmm. I don't see why the painter couldn't have moved that shoulder down. She looks as though she's cringing. You didn't cringe, did you, Antoine? Your smile is strange.'

She did not cringe, all through the many hours of sitting still. The smile is strange because of the wires, although it is some mercy at least that formal portraits never show the mouth open. Still, Antoine's mouth looks as uncomfortable as it feels.

'It doesn't have . . .' Maria Theresa waves her hand. '. . . her sweetness.'

'Yes, well, she's growing up,' Lerchenfeld says encouragingly. 'She's to be a bride. The King will see how sweet she is, certainly, but he will also see that she's no longer a child.'

'Indeed, indeed. Antoine, Lerchenfeld tells me you've had your monthly courses! Is that so?'

Antoine blushes. 'Yes, Mama. Just yesterday.'

'What is it your sisters call it? The General? Ha. Well, that's good news at last. I'll inform the ambassador. But this painting – no. We can't afford a bad impression. We'll have to have a new one. Or perhaps that French painter can fix it. Have it put in storage, Lerchenfeld, until we can find out what can be done. What a shame.'

Mama will ask the painter to try again. Which means Antoine must sit for more hours. And it won't ever be good enough. Antoine knows as well as anyone that it is impossible to please Mama entirely. No human painter can make this portrait match the image in Mama's mind.

She feels a sudden warmth of feeling for Wolfgang Mozart, who played for her once in this very room, when they were children. Now she is nearly thirteen, and off to be married. And he has written an opera, which was meant to be performed this past spring, but it keeps being postponed. The reasons aren't entirely clear. Some people say it's because it's so very bad – what can one expect from a twelve-year-old boy? Others say the problem is the opposite, that it is so good, it must be a fraud, written by the boy's father, perhaps. Making fools of everyone in Vienna.

Antoine is caught in a similar bind: the painting shows that she is not pretty enough, but if she were to use magic to make the painting show a beautiful woman, nobody would believe it was her.

But perhaps there is a way to make the painting just a *little* different. Antoine imagines asking Mama to take a second look; imagines the Empress cocking her head and saying, 'Perhaps I was unfair. It does catch the eye, doesn't it?'

There is one spell about paintings in the embroidered book, but it's confusing and it says nothing about the desires of the beholder: 'For a painting to preserve the subject as he is, these proofs have been found, with the prime magister's later warning that the body will indeed age, although it may seem otherwise to observers, and thus the reversal spell that follows may be employed . . .'

The subject as he is? That's no help. A painting that showed Antoine as she really is, flaws and all, is the last thing Mama wants. In fact, she wants the opposite.

Antoine bites her lip. Tonight, when she is alone, she'll read the spell again. She can feel an idea forming in her mind, and only needs the courage to put it into action.

The painting spell is a costly one. By the light of one candle, the sacrifices in the star around the painting rot, curl, disintegrate.

Some of these sacrifices are harder than others, but they are all losses.

Antoine's baby teeth yellow and crumble. The embroidered leash for Mops that Charlotte gave her as a farewell gift rots and withers.

A scrap of paper turns to dust and, with it, the memory of a French essay she'd written, covered in a second shade of ink where her tutor has corrected her spelling.

She can't look at the paper that contains her hope of seeing her family again once she leaves for France. Why not? She wants to lose that hope; it will be easier without it. And yet she can't look at that one, or the one containing her affection for her little brother Max.

How can the love in her heart just disappear, as if it never was? Can love be a thing, a substance, independent of its causes? And if so, why can't a spell create it, out of nothing?

She shivers, and then coughs. She'd forgotten about the smell and does not have a kerchief to hand. Never mind. She gets to her feet and walks over the lines of ash to the easel in the centre of the star. The sacrifices disappeared. The painting is enchanted.

It does look more like her, strangely. The shoulder is even higher, and, look, there is a pimple that did not exist when she sat for the painting. Even if it had, the painter would have left it out. This is Antoine as she is, and as she will always remain, if the reversal spell doesn't work the way she hopes it will. What has she done? She shivers again.

And she opens her paintbox.

Like all of Mama's children, Antoine has been taught painting. Her perfectly adequate landscapes grace one wall in the nursery wing still. She is no genius, but she doesn't need to be, for the tiny alterations she has in mind. Nothing that anyone will find impossible. Little changes that an observer, even one as eagle-eyed as Mama, might believe they simply hadn't noticed before.

She mixes a silvery colour, a fat paint with plenty of oil in it, so it will dry properly over the layers below. With the tiniest brush, she fills in her high, uneven hairline, just a little. She feels a sting on her forehead, as though someone had dragged nettles across it.

Antoine rushes to the wall hung with many mirrors and checks. Yes, her hairline does look smoother now. She can change herself!

The next thing is the right shoulder, which is higher than the other. Ducreux chose an angle that would disguise that, but it's still perfectly apparent to anyone who looks closely. Antoine takes up the palette knife and scrapes a tiny line away from the top of her shoulder.

That pain is not stinging, but deep. Her bones shift and shudder. A crack like lightning racks her body. She's on the floor, writhing, and she doesn't even know whether she's cried aloud, or whether it's only in her mind. She's bitten the inside of her lip, the rough patch created by the ends of the wires on her teeth.

If they find her like this, what will they do? She can barely bring herself to care through the red haze of agony.

After a very long while, the ache subsides enough for her to get to her feet. She's still alone. But she can walk; she can stand.

There's a pale line above her new shoulder, on the painting. It will always be there as a ghost image, but luckily Ducreux painted a sort of glow around her, fading into the darker background. When Antoine (using her less sore left arm) paints a thin line of darkness onto the canvas, the ghost of her flesh becomes a bit of *sfumato*.

It's a more difficult matter to change the teeth, which weren't showing in the portrait anyway. She settles for trying to shift the jaw a little, to reduce the thrust of her bottom lip. A little dab of white there and a curve of shadow there—

And she's holding her mouth to stop from screaming in pain as blood runs out between her lips. She grabs a rag and holds it, breathing in the smell of turpentine as she collects the blood on her palette. Blood is a useful sacrifice, and it must never go to waste.

The reversal spell is simpler, but feels just as momentous. Antoine almost convinces herself she can feel the change when her link to the painting disintegrates. She stares for a moment at the girl on the canvas, then does a small test. A red dot on one arm of the painted girl; nothing appears on Antoine's own arm. It worked! Exactly as she'd planned. She figured out the spell and made it work, all on her own.

To be certain, she scrapes a dress-pin across the back of one hand, making a red line she can cover with gloves until it heals.

The perfect girl in the painting shows no sign of the scratch. They are no longer linked. Antoine bids her goodbye.

CHAPTER EIGHT

Charlotte's Plans Are Frustrated — A Long Winter —
Letters from Home — A Glass of Nocillo — Allies

Charlotte does not understand her husband. Unlike Joseph, Ferdinand doesn't have to contend with a fractious empire, a patchwork of laws and languages. He is king; he could make his country into a place where doctors can save the lives of children, where great writers and artists work without interference from superstition and cant, where the streets are clean and safe, where laws and treaties create peace where before there was tribalism and violence. She straightens her shoulders and breathes more freely, just thinking of it. If she were king, she would do all those things, and more. She *will* do them. After all, Mama made herself king, despite being a woman. Charlotte can see that future for herself, hiding behind every marble pillar or shadowed doorway in the palace, tempting her to run after it.

Her ladies-in-waiting don't see that future, she's sure. They see a stiff, reserved sixteen-year-old who speaks their language haltingly and doesn't laugh at anyone's jokes. The only one who smiles at her is Caterina of San Marco.

Caterina is twenty-one years old, five years older than

Charlotte. She has brown curls, a sharp nose, a slight smile, and heavy-lidded, appraising eyes. A Medici on both sides, she is married to a marquis forty years her senior. Forty years! Charlotte can hardly imagine it. Caterina, it seems, can hardly imagine it either, because she is engaged in a very public and unabashed affair with the dashing Austrian envoy. That connection with Austria is one reason Charlotte asks Caterina to sit with her one rainy afternoon, in her bedchamber. They embroider flowered needlecases and look out of the window at the expanse of grey sky and green slopes, marked with pale pathways. Caserta is vast, bigger even than Schönbrunn. Charlotte feels very far away from everything here.

'When do we move to the Palazzo Reale?' she asks.

Caterina pulls her needle through a piece of silk. 'In October, usually, but it changes every year. Everything is smaller there, and older of course, but I like it better. I like to see Vesuvius when I look out of the window.'

Charlotte laughs, surprised. 'The volcano doesn't make you nervous?'

'No, it's fascinating. But what I like the best is on the other side of the palace: the Phlegraean Fields. The craters there smoke all the time, and I've picked yellow sulphur off the ground, pieces as big as my fist. Do you know about Laura Bassi, the first woman who graduated from the University of Bologna? She explained to me the workings of the acid in the boiling mud pits there. And there's a mountain that's only as old as our great-grandfathers, at least by Mr Hamilton's estimate. But I'm boring you, Your Majesty.'

'Not at all!' Charlotte protests. 'I'm afraid I don't know as much as I'd like about the natural world, but I hope to encourage its study. That's one of the things I would very much like to do, as queen.'

Caterina gives her a look she can't interpret. 'Yes, well, the Phlegraean Fields are best known at court for their wines

– there are vineyards at the mouth of the underworld. Isn't that a beautiful thought? But the wines the palace buys are always terrible. Favour-trading and old contracts, you know. If you'd like the best for your own rooms, Your Majesty, I'm happy to help. I know a supplier of Maraschino from Venice: half the price and twice the quality.'

Charlotte laughs again, out of sheer amazement. The world of Naples is not as constrained as it feels.

She sends out invitations to the half-dozen notables on the top of the list she made so carefully on her journey.

The Neapolitan nobility and the intellectuals: that was Joseph's advice. She already has a list a dozen names long of the people she wants to meet: poets, philosophers, the heads of ancient families. She gives the list to the Superintendent of the Queen's Household, only to be told that all events within the palace must be approved by the Master of the King's Entertainments. The Master of the King's Entertainments informs her that the calendar is, alas, full for the foreseeable future.

So she sends invitations one at a time, starting with Francesco d'Aquino, the Prince of Caramanico, a Freemason with an interest in natural philosophy who stays in his own town and does not come to the palace. That means he is outside of Ferdinand's orbit, and a potential ally.

But she receives only a polite refusal with the vaguest excuse about the needs of his estate.

The problem is that those who avoid Ferdinand's court have no reason to believe his new queen is worth changing that practice. She could try to explain in letters, but that's risky, even with ciphers.

She asks Caterina for an explanation, over coffee in her rooms.

'Your Majesty, court life is not for everyone,' Caterina says, her usually staccato speech uncharacteristically slow and careful. 'The prince does not come to the palace.'

'Because he doesn't like my husband. But I am not my

husband.' She picks up her coffee cup, but her hand is shaking, and she puts it down again. 'I could write him a letter, but would it convince him?'

And, she thinks, *would ciphers be enough to keep it private? I don't know who I can trust, if anyone.*

'Your Majesty, of course I am happy to speak to the prince and anyone else, on your behalf. But . . . may I speak frankly?'

'Always.'

'Those who don't come to the palace survive by staying out of Tanucci's way. If they were to accept the Queen's invitation, after refusing the King's . . . Well, Your Majesty, it would be poking the bear.'

Charlotte grits her teeth. 'Do what you can, please, Caterina,' she says.

She asks for Tanucci to come and see her, but the request is ignored. Finally, she corners him in the King's antechamber one day, as members of the Council stream past: men with stern jowls, watery eyes, and sharp noses, who make the smallest possible courtesies to her as they race away to run her kingdom.

Charlotte stands before Tanucci and demands to know why the Queen may not see people.

'You may invite anyone you like, Your Majesty,' he says smugly. 'Of course, it is not within my power to make them come. You must understand that you are new to this country, and its customs.'

'I would like to get to know it better,' she retorts. 'Soon enough I'll have a seat on the Council. I need to learn all I can.'

He smiles, almost conspiratorially, and lowers his voice as he sneers at the old men now on the far side of the room. 'Your Majesty, the Council's business is not very arduous. I would not worry about it requiring much of you.'

Of course. He's taken power away from the Council, too. The one thing she has been clinging to, naively.

Now he's looking at the papers in his hand, impatiently,

as though he has better things to do than talk to a sixteen-year-old girl. Than talk to the Queen.

'May I at least have a carriage to go calling on people?' She doesn't like the pleading tone to her own voice. She wanted that to sound colder, more confident.

'Whenever the expense of outfitting the proper guard for such an outing can be justified, of course. I don't know how things are done in Vienna, Your Majesty, but here even the royal family must consider the palace budget before acting on their whims.'

She grits her teeth. She might try the gloves on him again, to force him to approve an outing or a salon, but what would stop him from rescinding the approval the moment she was out of the room? Besides, her last attempt to control him didn't work very well.

'It is not a whim to wish to speak to someone other than my ladies-in-waiting,' she protests.

He spreads his arms wide. 'Your Majesty, there are card parties and billiards parties, dances and masquerades, several nights a week here in the palace. Is that not sufficient entertainment for you?'

And all of them filled with Ferdinand's lackeys. She gives Tanucci a brittle smile and leaves him smirking at her.

That night, Charlotte draws the blue and gold silk curtains around her bed, and opens the embroidered book. The rough paper feels so familiar to her fingers. As a child, she had thought all the world's possibilities were open before her. One day she would be a queen, and she was already a magister. But both of those titles are paper crowns.

Her life will be what her mother always planned it to be. It's so simple, so plain before her eyes now. Years upon years of letting Ferdinand into her bed and body, of standing beside him for portraits and ceremonies. Watching the flames of Enlightenment gutter in Naples as anyone with a brain leaves, while those who have no choice but to stay starve in body and mind. Her brother Joseph will have no partner here for his plans. Leopold seems content to merely survive in his own kingdom. And Antoine—

And Antoine is going to Paris, where anything might await her. Where Prince de Rohan is. Charlotte had assured her sister that they would learn more about magic, once they became queens. But here she is, Queen, and she knows nothing and no one.

She flips through page after page of spells that she can't decipher. Reads them over again, reads them aloud, in dry whispers. If she could work even a few more spells in this book, what might she be able to do then?

There must be magisters in Naples. She hears Rohan's voice in her memory: *You and your Vienna friends must decide whether you are a chapter of the Order of 1326 or just another nest of rogues.* If this Order of 1326 is different in every place, who's to say whether the same Order in Naples would be a danger? But who's to say that it wouldn't? And she promised Antoine to keep it secret.

She also promised that when they were queens, they would be safe.

Charlotte's ignorance gnaws at her, but she has no way of finding anything out. Her only accomplice is Caterina, but she can't say anything to Caterina about the Order without breaking her promise, and risking discovery. The marchesa is a pleasant companion – and Charlotte's only friend in Naples – but the moment Charlotte spoke the words, everything could shatter. She could put Caterina in danger. Or, more likely, she could give Caterina the tools to betray her, in a court where she has no influence at all of her own.

She makes claws with her hands in frustration, and hot tears rim her eyes. Roughly, she turns the pages, until her eyes land on a spell that she and Antoine had never quite understood and never dared to try:

For a pearl to be dropped into one-third of one demiard of eau-de-vie then to be quaffed equally by two from a single cup, exhaustible, to confer on the second drinker eternally pain pro tempore on the threshold of betrayal of the first, these proofs have been found.'

She thinks about it for five days. The threshold of betrayal. If Caterina could not betray her, that would be the same as trust, the same as secrecy. Wouldn't it?

The spell requires minor sacrifices when it comes to love, hope, treasure, and memory. The body sacrifice, though, is a more difficult matter.

The embroidered book says that the prime magister sacrificed 'a flaying of the skin'. If it's to be of any size, and it must be, according to the long string of 'a's in the spell formula, then Charlotte would require some explanation. She is willing to fake a carriage accident or something of that kind, but the trouble is that if the initial amount of skin she takes is wrong, or from the wrong part of the body, then it will all be for nothing.

She and Antoine have made other substitutions for the sacrifices the book lists as those of the 'prime magister' for any spell: hair when they ran out of fingernail clippings; two copper coins for a silver one. Once or twice, they simply couldn't get a spell to work no matter what they sacrificed. But in general, they have found, substitutions *can* work. Perhaps the only question is quantity.

So Charlotte starts bleeding.

Mama's doctors used to bleed her when she was ill; she knows how to do it with a razor and a pan. But it will take a few tries, she thinks, to get enough for this spell. She'll have to keep the blood somewhere in the meantime.

There are many drawers that lock in Charlotte's rooms at Caserta: inside her massive jewellery cabinet there are three alone. But she doesn't keep those keys. The only key she has is to a document box of ebony that Joseph gave her, which she keeps on her writing table. It's just big enough inside for a slightly elongated ashen star, and for her enchanted fan, to keep the blood cold.

In the centre of the star, one perfect pearl, for the enchantment. In one point of the star, she keeps the pan of blood, and adds to it day by day, as much blood as she dares. She speaks the words.

But the sacrifices do not decay.

She almost can't remember, now, what it feels like not to be tired, to have headaches. She can't bear noise and has great difficulty bringing herself to eat. When she walks, even a few steps, she gets dizzy and her heart races.

The court moves to the Palazzo Reale, and she insists on carrying her document box on her lap in the carriage. The old palace is a maze and she doesn't know where anything is. She walks through room after room, looking at the people in them as though they were portraits on the walls.

People don't keep their voices low enough when they murmur about how the King will have to take a new wife. Ferdinand, to his credit, looks genuinely concerned, although most of the time he's out hunting and whoring as usual.

Just after Christmas, the doctor offers to bleed Charlotte, and she laughs in a manner that seems strange and desperate even to her own ears. She insists they leave her the blood. And when she takes it, resting after every step, her heart dancing a bourrée, and adds it to her pan, at last the blood dries and rots, and the bits of paper and silver coins decay, and Charlotte has lost a little more hope and memory, and she crawls back to bed with the pearl clutched in one palm.

For months, she rests.

1768 turns to 1769. The winter passes into spring. The court returns to Caserta.

Charlotte remains in her bed, because she lacks the strength to get out of it.

10 June 1769
Antoine to Charlotte

My dear Charlotte,
 My teeth and shoulder are much straighter now and the French ambassador has made the formal offer for my hand at last. Mother is pleased. So am I, of course, if a little terrified. At least I have your good example to show me how to be brave.
 I hope you are feeling less unwell now and I'm so sorry your husband is such a beast. Once you have a child and get onto the Council of Naples, things will change.
 Now that the General has arrived for me, Mother says her youngest girl has grown up and is ready to do her duty. I will do my best to prove her right!
 Please don't sacrifice any memories of me, if you can help it. I'm going to be very lonely in France. Do you think they'll like me?

 Your loving
 Antoine

Charlotte is a little stronger every day. Ferdinand is getting impatient; these are months gone to waste, months when she could be giving him his heir.

By October, she's well enough to sit up most of the day and even take short walks. She asks for Caterina of San Marco to come sit with her and talk, to bring her a bottle of this year's nocillo, so she can see what all the fuss is about. Charlotte is in her bedroom, wearing a white lace dressing gown. She takes the edge of it between her fingers, thinking of the hours of women's work that lace represents, and how quickly it would tear, or take a stain.

Caterina comes in, and tells the guard to wait outside the door. They're alone in a room that has very little of Charlotte in it: her bed, with coverings and curtains she still doesn't quite recognize when she wakes; two upholstered chairs and a walnut table; and two long silk settees in dark blue. Charlotte, for the first time in a long while, is on the settee rather than the bed.

Caterina quickly covers up her expression of concern. She's brought a glass bottle full of dark liquid; she does as she is told. She comes forward, puts the bottle on the little round table at Charlotte's side and kneels, taking Charlotte's cold hands in her own.

'I'm overjoyed to see you looking so well, Your Majesty!'

Caterina is the picture of health, and suddenly Charlotte feels as if their ages have reversed.

'Please, sit, Caterina,' says Charlotte, indicating the place next to her on the settee. They speak French together, which is a relief. 'What are they saying about me? About my illness?'

'The palace has managed to keep the secret rather well, for once. The common people know nothing, although the rumour is that you're with child and ill from that, and the palace does nothing to dispel that idea. As for the courtiers, well . . . Two of them will argue, and the following day they'll have the same argument but will have switched sides, forgetting what they thought the day before. You know how it is, Madame.'

'Well, soon I'll be back at my regular duties and they'll have to find something else to argue about. Is that the nocillo, Caterina?'

'It is, Your Majesty. As you asked. The first of this year's bottling. My mother is a great believer in its medicinal properties. It ought to perk your appetite. Shall I pour it for you?'

'Let me,' Charlotte says, and takes out the stopper. There is already one small crystal glass on the table. Charlotte pours the nocillo in, up to the line she measured.

Caterina explains that the walnuts were green when they went into the spirits, but the resulting concoction is as dark as ink, as viscous as blood. It smells sharp, spicy, like pine trees and cloves. Charlotte surreptitiously drops the enchanted pearl into the glass, and it dissolves, as though it were made of sugar.

She turns to Caterina with her best attempt at a bright smile, and takes a sip. It's smooth, herbal at first, then nutty. Bittersweet.

'Very good,' she says.

She starts to offer Caterina the cup, but then hesitates.

The only power Charlotte has is in magic; that is her only advantage over Tanucci. But she can't find other magisters on her own; she can barely leave the palace. She needs Caterina.

Pain, the spell promised. What sort of pain, and how much? Of course, Caterina will have nothing to fear so long as she is loyal, and is loyalty not something she has already promised, as Charlotte's lady-in-waiting? Still, it seems only fair to give her something like a choice.

'My father', Charlotte says, thinking as she goes, 'came from Lorraine. Sometimes you can hear it in my French, I'd wager. He said they had a tradition there that the second person to drink from a cup would suffer great pain if they ever betrayed the one who drank first.'

'A quaint belief,' says Caterina. 'Then again, people here eat snails to keep their friends loyal, so we all have our stories, don't we?'

'We do. Would you drink from my cup, Caterina, if that were true? If you knew you would suffer if you ever betrayed me?'

In answer, Caterina curls her fingers around Charlotte's, and takes a sip. 'Most willingly,' she says.

It's done, Charlotte thinks, and she puts the nocillo down on the table.

'I do trust you, Caterina,' she says. Her heart hammers. It is so difficult to step over the line and speak of the things she's kept secret forever. Even now, even after the magic is done and Caterina can't turn on her.

But the secret is not only hers; it is hers and Antoine's, and she promised to keep it between them.

'I have a commission for you,' Charlotte says, her voice low. 'Have you ever heard of a society that calls itself the Order of 1326?'

'I have not, Your Majesty. I thought Tanucci had banished all the secret societies. Are they like the Freemasons, or like the Jesuits? Are they in Naples?'

'These are the questions I need answered. Will you go out into the city for me, and find out what you can? And, Caterina, you must not breathe a word to anyone about my interest in this. Gather what information you can, but don't let them realize I've sent you. And if you find them, keep yourself safe. Don't let them think you know anything.'

Caterina smiles. 'But I don't know anything, Your Majesty.'

'It's a strange task, I know. But I will be most grateful.'

Caterina nods. 'If they're in Naples, I'll find them.'

24 January 1770
Joseph to Charlotte

My dear Charlotte,

I believe Antoine told you in her last letter that my daughter, my darling Thérèse, had contracted pleurisy shortly after the new year. Yesterday, she died. She was seven years old and I don't think I will ever be happy again. I was at her side, holding her fevered body in my arms, and praying to God to give me my daughter back. It was only later, when I got to my own room, that the full horror of it struck me, and I think I shall carry that horror with me until I die.

On New Year's Day, she gave us a puppet show all about her grandmother's reign, and now, not a month later, she is gone.

I'll write to Leopold and ask him to come to Vienna for a few weeks. He's the heir now – I won't marry again – and he will need to be ready to rule this empire.

How odd it feels to not be a father any more. So often, these last years, I have felt as though that was all I had, my one joy and comfort.

I am sending you a few of her little writings and drawings, as you always liked to see those. I know your first years in Naples have been difficult ones, and you haven't been able to establish yourself there as you planned. We can't control our fates; we can only keep going as best we can.

Finally, I will give you a report on Antoine because you will chastise me if I don't: she is healthy and well and, by all accounts, studying very hard for her life in France.

With all my devotion,
Joseph

CHAPTER NINE

The Court Grieves — The Court Sees a Marvel —
Concealments — A Gold Watch

The spring of 1770 is a desperate one in the Austrian court.

Antoine could not save Joseph's little daughter, any more than she could save her sister Josepha. What can she do that is of any use to anyone? She can practise matching the correct forms of address to the long lists of names the ambassador has given her. She knows what to say and how to move, and she makes an appearance at masquerades and balls, half of them in her honour. Even Joseph, grim and grieving, does his duty as emperor and hosts a magnificent feast, with supper served in shifts of one hundred courtiers each. There are plates and flags and drawings everywhere in Vienna, praising the nuptials between France and Austria in the most poetic language.

Every day, her mother tells her how vital it is that Antoine impresses the French: she will be the embodiment of Austria and the alliance.

The Marquis de Durfort, the French ambassador, sits with Antoine and Mama one day to report on the vast trousseau being assembled for her in Paris.

'I think you'll find it quite sufficient, Your Imperial

Highness,' he says, smiling as he shows her several Pandora dolls wearing the latest fashions.

'I have a new *robe à l'anglaise* almost exactly like that one already,' Antoine says, pointing to a pink silk confection.

'But of course, the Dauphine owns no such gown,' he says with a twisted smirk.

She lets her confusion show. 'I will be the Dauphine, will I not?'

'And the Dauphine will bring no item with her from Austria. Not so much as a ring or a dressing gown.'

Now it's alarm, not confusion, but she still doesn't try to hide it. 'Mama?'

Mama nods. 'You must remember, Antoine, that an entire generation of French people were brought up to hate Austria.' She spreads her knobby hands, as if to say that it is one more inexplicable French quirk. 'It seems strange to you, I know, as your papa was French. Both countries have always been part of your heritage. But to them, you are an Austrian, and they need to believe you are not a spy. You will have to renounce all claims of inheritance through me, and you will have to bring nothing with you, to show that you are ready to become a French dauphine, entirely.' She pauses. 'I'm afraid even little Mops must stay here with me. Oh, just for a little while. Don't look so stricken. I'm allowed to send you gifts, my dear. After you've been in France for a few months, I'll send Mops to you, and any little items here you particularly want – a prayer book, that sort of thing. But for now you must take nothing. And . . .' Mama pauses, and looks at Durfort.

'And?' Antoine prompts. 'What more is there, Mama?'

'When you enter into French territory, you are not to bring even the clothes on your back. You will undress, in the presence of a few noble ladies of the court, before crossing the border.'

Nothing. Naked. Naked? Antoine shivers, as if she's already stripped. She must think. Her enchanted items may be few

102

but she sacrificed so much to create them! And the spells themselves, which she is working so hard to understand. She keeps them safe with her at all times in her pocket. Travelling without them would be unthinkable.

What can she do? Can she memorize all the book's spells in the few weeks that remain before she must leave? She can't leave them behind. She could destroy them, ask Charlotte to recopy them and send them on to her in France. But what courier could Charlotte trust with such a mission, even if the spells were ciphered? Between Naples and Versailles, there is a great deal of road.

And those weeks on the road, without any magic and without the spells that might give her some small advantage. Heaven knows she has few natural advantages, as Mama and Durfort make plain at every opportunity. Those first months in France, when she cannot put a single foot wrong, lest the whole alliance suffer, and the people of Europe fall back into war and hunger. It's too much to ask of her. It should have been Charlotte; France is too important for Antoine.

'My dear, it's natural to be nervous about it, but the ladies will dress you again quickly,' Mama says kindly.

It's barbaric, Antoine wants to spit, but she holds her tongue, because the French ambassador is present, and Mama wants the French ambassador to tell his king that Mama is sending France an angel.

'I'm only a little surprised,' Antoine says, and puts on her sweetest smile. 'I didn't know.'

Countess Ertag used magic herself to hide her spells, to keep them safe. Surely Antoine should be able to do the same. But if there are spells that could help her in the embroidered book, they're hidden in words and phrases she can't understand. She reads them over and over anyway, looking for some thread she might grasp and begin to unravel.

It's tricky even to know what item a spell is meant to

enchant. There is a spell 'to test gold', but does the gold itself go into the centre of the star, or some instrument? There's a spell 'for a winnowing basket' but with no clue as to what the enchantment might be; perhaps the basket would simply winnow better.

And then there are the sacrifices, some of which are written as references to other things. 'For the love, a sacrifice equal to twice that of the whetstone enchantment', reads a spell for creating an accurate map, but there seems to be no whetstone enchantment in the book. The book reads like a collection of scattered things, found at random, and perhaps that is precisely what it is. Antoine wonders, often, how many of the spells Countess Ertag managed to make work herself, and, always, whether the spell for the embroidery is somewhere among them, in words that disguise its meaning.

Finally, she catches a tiny thread-end of meaning she hadn't noticed before. There's a spell for a 'cap of Hades, to steal shadows' and, in desperation, she asks Joseph for a book on Greek legends. There she finds it, in the Perseus story: a hat that renders its wearer invisible.

The sacrifices, though, are written in equally obscure phrases. Still, Antoine puzzles over them, and makes notes as she tries the spell every night. If she cracks it, that might help her understand the other spells, or show her some way to hide them. The more magic she does, the more she will understand. It's only a matter of hitting on the right sacrifices, and that is only a matter of doing the work. But she is running out of time.

Three weeks before Antoine's proxy wedding, everyone is in the Small Gallery at Schönbrunn, waiting for a spectacle to begin.

It's a bright room, thanks to the gleaming white walls broken only by gilt sconces and large windows that let in the daylight. A painted sky opens above their heads. Courtiers wait on their chairs, an army of dolls in their finery. Antoine is wearing her robin's-egg *robe à la française*, her skirt spilling beyond her chair. Perhaps the reason the French ambassador whispers so loudly to Mama is that it is hard to get close to any woman wearing panniers.

Antoine feels alone, apart, despite the crowd in the room. She's losing everything and everyone, very soon. She would like to be in her room, studying spells, reading them over to try to commit them all to memory even if she can't make them work. But she, like the rest of the court, was commanded to witness a marvel.

A young engineer called Wolfgang Kempelen wants the contract to redesign the water pipes at Schönbrunn. The Empress asked to see some example of his work.

So here is the engineer, looking rather uncomfortable in stiff new jacket and breeches, opening the door from the adjoining Round Chinese Cabinet Room. He bows low to Maria Theresa. The courtiers gasp, not at Kempelen but at a turbaned dummy in an ermine robe sitting inside a cabinet on wheels.

The turban makes her think of Angelo Soliman. He's known for his skill at chess, and ordinarily he would be present at any scientific demonstration. But he often accompanies Joseph on his travels, and her brother the Emperor has been travelling a great deal lately. He's always inspecting provinces or going to diplomatic meetings. Antoine suspects Joseph is unhappy at court, with the reminders of the people he's lost. He and Mama seem to be ever more irritated with each other, and Joseph doesn't get along well with Leopold either.

Since that day in the garden at the Hofburg, Antoine has only seen Soliman once or twice, in crowded rooms, after he returned to Vienna with his wife. It's a relief, of course, because it means he isn't spying on her any more, or so she hopes. But it also makes her feel even more that magic is slipping away from her, that soon it will all be a half-remembered childhood lark. She will be stripped, remade, powerless.

On the surface of the cabinet is a painted chess board.

'Behold, my artificial man!' says Kempelen, his voice breaking. 'Will anyone here challenge the Turk to a game of chess?'

Automata can do marvellous things. A Frenchman named Vaucanson built a metal man who could play the flute thanks to a system of bellows. But to play a game of chess?

Antoine's brother Max stands and bows histrionically to the audience for a laugh. Antoine, irritated, doesn't smile along with everyone else, until it occurs to her with a jolt that she might be smiling if she hadn't sacrificed her love for him. Then she does smile, falsely, though no one is looking at her anyway. Max walks to the open area of the gallery, where the Turk sits. He walks around the Turk, bending down to look below it. Then he moves a pawn.

The Turk moves an opposing pawn.

The audience applauds lightly.

'Well, but it can't really play,' says Max. 'It doesn't understand.'

Max lifts up a knight and moves it diagonally across the board, as if it were a queen or a bishop. An illegal move.

There's a pause, then the Turk slowly shakes its head.

Everyone gasps.

Someone in the crowd says, 'Perhaps there's finally someone in Vienna who can beat Angelo Soliman at chess.'

Someone else shouts, 'There's room for a man in that cabinet. A monkey, at least!'

The engineer bows his head. 'I'd be delighted to show the court the inner workings of my machine.'

He flings open one small door covering about one-third of the cabinet. Wheels and spiked cylinders fill the space. Kempelen throws open a door at the back of the cabinet and waves a candlestick behind it, so they can all see that the space extends to the back.

Max's face is red.

Antoine leans forward in her seat. It must be magic! Surely

there is no other explanation. An enchanted automaton – the thought makes her shiver. Or an enchantment to conceal someone inside? Any spell that hides a thing or a person could be useful to her.

'If Your Highness would like a closer look,' says Kempelen loudly, and sweeps his arm, bowing. He's looking at Antoine.

They are all looking at Antoine.

She must know more. Antoine looks at Mama for permission and Mama sighs. Good enough. Antoine stands and says nothing; she got into the habit of keeping her mouth closed when her teeth were wired.

She approaches the cabinet with a surreptitious sniff, wondering whether she might smell magic the way Charlotte thought she did in Joseph's study, when Soliman showed them the magic lantern. But this room is big and airy, and Antoine smells nothing.

It looks ordinary. There is no magnet she can see, no strings. Kempelen showed them the inside, and there didn't seem to be room for a hidden compartment. If Kempelen is a magister, it would be dangerous to reveal that she knows anything about magic. And she promised Charlotte. But surely it's safer to be sure of who is and who isn't?

She knows so little. But she knows her own skills, at least; they are listed in every diplomatic document between Austria and France.

She can dance, at least when her sister is not putting spells on her. That will not help her here.

She paints competent portraits. More competent than anyone knows. That will not help her here.

She sings and plays both harp and clavier.

She is clever at games of cards.

She can bluff.

Antoine moves a pawn, saying lightly, 'I think you must be a magician, Herr Kempelen.'

The Turk takes the pawn as Antoine glances quickly at Kempelen's face, to see if she can see a secret on it.

What Antoine sees is a momentary glance beyond her, over her shoulder, at the little room off to the side of the Great Gallery. The room where Kempelen made his preparations. The Round Chinese Cabinet Room.

Antoine shrugs prettily and walks through polite laughter back to her seat.

And when the crowd moves to the Grand Gallery for dinner, she manages to slip into the little adjoining room, alone.

The Round Chinese Cabinet Room is empty.

The only furnishings are a few large porcelain vases, and two upholstered chairs. The room is its own adornment, its walls covered in gilt-framed lacquer panels, and its floor a pattern of inlaid exotic woods: black, orange, yellow, every shade of brown. It dazzles the eye, but there can be no doubt: the room is empty.

Antoine turns, about to open the door to exit, when her mind catches up to her eye. An imperfection in the pattern of the variegated wood on the floor. She turns slowly, looking down.

In the centre of the floor is a six-petalled, stylized flower, from which linear patterns stretch to fill the floor. Just to one side of that flower, a crack between a dark strip of wood and a light one is slightly too wide.

Antoine catches her breath, remembering. She and Max used to play here, until Mama caught them. The line must show where the floor used to open up to allow Mama's 'conspiracy table' to rise through. Antoine barely remembers what it used to look like; Mama had this room redecorated when Antoine was a small child, and the table has not been in operation since. This room was for private conversations – very private, with Mama's counsellors, ambassadors, allies. So that they would not be overheard, not even by servants, Mama would have the servants place all the food and dishes and even the candles and flowers onto a table far below, on the ground floor of the palace. Then an apparatus would hoist the table up in the midst of the dinner guests. The name *table de conspiration* survived despite Mama's efforts to have everyone call it the *table d'union* instead.

There must still be a gap, under the floor. The secret to the workings of the Mechanical Turk, perhaps? She is probably wrong, but if she is, there is no one to mock her for it. She can test her theory.

Antoine forces herself to breathe, to think, as she quietly walks through the door. She leaves the room. But she doesn't walk back to the crowd in the Great Gallery. Instead, she grabs her skirts and runs lightly down the small staircase to the floor below.

The chamber underneath the Round Chinese Cabinet Room is much plainer, and dim despite the pale plaster walls. In the centre rises a thick rectangular column of cheap, plain wood. Covering the old workings of the table? One panel is swinging free at one side.

'I know you're there,' Antoine says, though she doesn't.

The panel swings open to reveal a woman holding an open fan before her face: a fan with round glass lenses in each blade, like a peacock's tail.

Antoine reaches into her pocket, searching for something that could protect her, and she pulls out the thimble that breaks small items into pieces. What will she do with that? She knows as she holds it out that it's ridiculous, and puts it back in her pocket as the woman drops her fan, and looks at Antoine.

She's older than Antoine; perhaps about forty, with a strong nose and a sweet, wry little mouth.

'A magister,' the woman says. 'Aren't you? I'm not going to hurt you, child. I do like a surprise.'

Antoine takes refuge in diplomacy. 'I'll keep your secret if you keep mine,' she says.

'We have an agreement,' says the woman, and puts out her hand.

⁑

After she says her prayers, Antoine sneaks back down to the room beneath the Chinese Cabinet Room. She half expects it to be empty. But she is still there: Geneviève. The only name she would give. They didn't get much past introductions before Antoine knew she'd be missed upstairs, and left, swearing to return.

Her other promise, to Charlotte, weighs on her heart. But if this woman wanted to do her harm, she could have done it already. And she already knows, or suspects, something about Antoine, so surely it would be more dangerous to let her get away from the palace without learning something about her?

Geneviève has procured a bottle of red wine and two glasses. Antoine, at fourteen, is allowed to drink wine at meals and balls, but she doesn't much like it. She keeps a little in her glass for toasts and otherwise drinks mineral water. Still, for a clandestine meeting with a magister, she nods in a grown-up fashion and Geneviève pours into both glasses. They sit on the floor, their skirts spreading around them, tucking their feet to one side.

'*Voilà*,' Geneviève says, holding up her glass. 'To my health. I need it more than you do, my dear. Sitting on the floor reminds me of my age.' She speaks French with a Parisian accent; how Antoine wishes she could learn that from her, as well as all the other things she wants to know. She will sound like a foreigner when she goes to Paris, or so the French ambassador says, even though she's been speaking French all her life.

'So you are not here for me?' Antoine asks before she sips. 'Are you not a . . . member of the Order of 1326?'

Geneviève's mouth twists. 'I most certainly am not. I am what the Order calls a "rogue". As you are too, I think? Believe me, my dear, there are worse things women can be called, and I've been called them all.' She takes a sip of the wine, closes her eyes, leans back.

'Then you are hiding from them too,' Antoine says conspiratorially.

That makes Geneviève smile. 'The Brothers are aware of me, but their attempts to deal with me have been, shall we say, more trouble than they were worth. I keep my activities out of public view so as far as those pompous asses are concerned, I don't pose a very great threat. Their biggest fear is that magic will become public knowledge, you see. So if I were to start being open about my abilities, well, then suddenly I would find myself declared insane, or something of that nature. It is a détente.'

Antoine wishes she understood more of this. She frowns. 'And they don't ask you to join them?'

Geneviève snorts, which is all the answer she gives.

'Hmm,' Antoine says. 'I didn't know that one could be a magister and not be in the Order. I mean, I did know, but I thought—'

'You're a magister and not a Brother. You asked if I was one, remember?'

'Yes, but I'm an accident.' She smiles. 'And they don't know about me. I think. And I don't know any other magisters, Brother or otherwise.' Charlotte, of course, but she must keep that secret. A thought occurs to her, about her future, about the journey she is soon to take. 'Are there many rogue magisters in Paris?'

'Paris? Yes, there are rogues in Paris, of course, but how many, I can't say. I haven't been there in some time.'

Geneviève's snort sends the long white lappets of her bonnet flapping. On each one there is a large, furry moth embroidered in many hues of brown and gold. It gives the effect of two moths flying about, as Geneviève is rather animated when she talks.

'I thought – your accent—'

'I am French, yes,' Geneviève says, 'but I live in London now. Where I have very good friends and, yes, some rogues are among them. But everyone's trying to kidnap me in London at the moment. It's very tiresome. So, sometimes I find it pleasant to disappear for a few weeks. Kempelen needed help, and I have always had a gift for machines and devices. He doesn't know I'm actually doing magic. It drives him mad, not knowing how I do it.'

'And how *do* you do it?' Antoine asks, leaning closer and matching Geneviève's wry smile.

In answer, Geneviève pulls her fan lorgnette out of her pocket. 'All the lenses of this fan show me somewhere different, you see. They let me see certain places, even when I am not precisely there. But the trouble with it is that one has to be quite close to the place one wants to see; I can't look through a lens and see Constantinople, for example, though believe me I have tried. This one in the middle lets me see through a similar lens, disguised as a jewel in the Turk's turban. I also have a glove that acts as a kind of possession spell: whatever one glove does, its twin does as well. So I keep a chessboard in front of me, and whatever I do, the Turk does.'

Geneviève gets to her feet, groaning a little and putting a hand on her hip. She swings open the panel on the side of the column in the middle of the room, the one that once held the workings of Mama's table. Inside, Antoine can see the space where Geneviève was concealed. There's a smell of oil and metal. Two great wheels gleam on either side, in the dark. The vestiges of the mechanical table.

'It's not a terribly comfortable spot, but it serves the purpose. I didn't count on a magister snooping. What sort of spell did you use to find me?'

She says it admiringly, and Antoine feels, for the first time, as though magic is something she can be proud of, not just a secret she loves and has to hide away. As though she's done something of merit, although of course she hasn't. She was simply lucky. Still, she would like to do something of merit. She likes the feeling of being admired for something other than her dancing and her posture.

'I didn't do any spell. I just guessed.'

'Guessed! It seems Maria Theresa's youngest daughter is

intelligent as well as beautiful. Oh, yes, I keep up with the great families of Europe. Old habit. And you're off to Paris, if my gossip is up to date? To marry the Dauphin? Well, that's a waste. They won't know what to do with a young woman of intelligence there.'

'Geneviève, how long are you staying in Vienna?'

She makes a non-committal shape with her mouth, shrugs one shoulder. 'Not for long, but I don't have to leave right away. A few days, perhaps. If you will visit me, perhaps I can convince Kempelen to stay a little.'

Antoine nods, eager to please her new acquaintance. A magister! She may be able to teach Antoine how to decipher the rest of the spells in the embroidered book. She may even be able to find a way for Antoine to take the book with her to France. 'Please stay as long as you can. I will bring you anything you need from the kitchens.'

Geneviève lowers her face, raises her eyebrows and looks at her as though she ought to know better. 'My dear, I can get whatever I like.'

For three nights in a row, Antoine meets Geneviève at midnight and talks until close to dawn. Antoine is beyond tired, but she's hungry for more of these conversations, and afraid that Geneviève will vanish as inexplicably as she appeared.

Antoine doesn't ask Geneviève how she gets in and out of the palace for their meetings; she has so many other questions to ask. Tonight, Geneviève has spread a rug on the floor with a candelabrum, a plate of fresh bread and strong cheese, two glasses, and a dark bottle of port. Antoine doesn't ask about them either.

Geneviève looks at every page of Antoine's spells with great interest, and points out a few places where Antoine might try something she hadn't considered. But she says most of the spells are new to her too.

'I don't know anything about this governess of yours.

113

Which may mean she found out about magic not from another rogue, but in some way she wasn't supposed to. Perhaps she stole spells from one of the Brothers, or happened upon them by accident somewhere. Of course, it's possible she did know other rogues, and I just never heard about it. We don't all know each other. Unlike the Order, we don't work together very well, and it is often safer to work alone. And you have managed to keep these spells secret all these years?'

Geneviève looks at her shrewdly, arching an eyebrow.

Antoine hasn't mentioned the embroidered book, because she can't think of a way to explain why she made the copies and doesn't have the book any more – a way that doesn't point to Charlotte.

'Angelo Soliman and Prince Louis de Rohan were suspicious, but I overheard them say they had found no evidence that my governess had taught me.' She changes the subject, quickly, and asks about the Order.

'The Order of 1326 is a cult of secrecy and snobbery,' Geneviève says bluntly, pouring the port. 'They want to make sure that only the people they approve can do magic. No one else. So the Brothers hunt the rest of us, as if we were animals. They take our memories of magic away, if they can, but that is tricky. Sometimes they find it more useful to undermine a magister's reputation, so everyone believes them to be a fraud, or insane. But if the Brothers truly want to do away with a difficult magister, and if they think it's worth risking the attention that murders tend to draw, they kill them.'

Antoine's eyes go wide.

'I've stood over the coffins of several of my friends,' Geneviève says, pointing her bejewelled finger at Antoine's chest. 'They kill. They hunt us and they will not hesitate to kill us. Who do you think killed your governess? A rogue magister dies in a locked room in a palace, and nobody seems to remember it afterwards or speak of it ever again? I'd say that was the Order's work.'

114

Antoine can't imagine Angelo Soliman as an assassin. She remembers his voice in the garden: *I would have handled the whole business differently*. It isn't Angelo Soliman she has to fear. It's Rohan, and who knows how many others. These Brothers could be anyone, anywhere. She shivers. She's so sick and tired of being afraid. In France, she must be the perfect dauphine, secure the alliance, and keep herself safe from unseen magisters. It's too much.

'Geneviève, I need to find some way to learn more magic, to help me when I'm in France. At the very least, I need some way to carry my spells with me.'

'What do you mean?' Geneviève asks sharply, a piece of cheese halfway to her mouth. 'Why wouldn't you have your spells?'

'I can't bring anything of my own with me. Not even the clothes I wear. I'll be stripped at the border. So that I'll be entirely reborn as French.'

'Ah,' Geneviève says, and puts down the cheese. 'I'd forgotten how fucking ridiculous they are at Versailles. More rules and rituals than the Order. Poor child. You're going to travel without any of your enchanted items? Without your spells? Good God. I'm not sure anything could induce me to do that, in this dangerous world. You want so desperately to go to France?'

Antoine hasn't ever thought about it in those terms. She must go *somewhere*; unmarriageable archduchesses go to abbeys. It would be lovely, of course, to be closer to her family. The French royal family does not travel much outside the borders of France, and she knows full well she might never see Austria again. But what cold comfort it would be, to be near to everyone, and watch helplessly as the French alliance faltered, as Prussia invaded, as Joseph and Mama were dethroned and the Empire dismantled.

'I want to be *worthy* of France,' she says.

Geneviève snorts and pulls up her Belgian lace engageantes, as if she's about to begin work on something, but

115

instead she just pours another glass of port for each of them.

'France will be lucky to have a magister as its queen.'

'Well,' says Antoine, 'I'm hardly a magister at all.'

Geneviève grins. 'We'll see about that.'

CHAPTER TEN

Farewell to Austria — The Pavilion at the Rhine —
The Invention of Marie Antoinette —
Lorrainers — An Old Enemy

Distant shouts of coachmen. Antoine's gilded carriage rolls to a stop. After two weeks on the road, they have reached the edge of the Habsburg universe: the Rhine.

It's nearly May, but no warmer than when they set out. Her last sight of her mother was a dark blur of widow's clothing through a carriage window fogged with Antoine's own breath, through rebellious tears. She still feels guilty that she wasn't able to manage a smile and a wave for the people who lined the streets to say goodbye to her; it was so kind of them to come out so early on such a cold morning.

Now all her tears are dry and Vienna seems very distant and long ago. She gave away most of her things. Books and embroideries to her siblings. Clothing to the daughters of courtiers. A self-portrait for Mama. Her enchanted items wait in a chest to be mailed to her after her arrival at Versailles: her Pandora doll, her thimble, her book ribbon. The treasures of a girl, worthless to a world that does not know about her sacrifices.

Fifty-six coaches and carriages accompany her, carrying

256 people. None of them will go with her into France.

She kisses the two cousins who have come all this way, playmates from childhood, and they all wipe tears away. She holds her dog Mops to her heart. It hurts to leave him behind, after all. She doesn't love him – she sacrificed that – but she knows she should, and that is nearly the same.

Antoine steps out of her jewel-box carriage of gold and glass. She steps onto the hardened mud and looks at the trees, all slanted rays of bleak sunlight and green shadows, like a wood between worlds.

Three Frenchwomen, pinch-faced, drop to their knees. She raises them up and embraces them, and their faces become even more pinched. They say their names but she immediately forgets them; Geneviève gave her a spell for earrings that will whisper a forgotten name, but Antoine cannot wear those today.

The women lead her into a wooden pavilion. She'll enter from the Holy Roman Empire, and emerge into France.

The thin walls are hung with tapestries in rich colours, showing pale faces staring off at something unseen. The tapestries do nothing to warm the air that whistles through the slatted walls.

A woman wheels over a cart bearing Antoine's new French clothes. The *grand habit*, the court dress, for the handover. She's wearing a beautiful new *robe à la française* already, and it was even made in France, but the ritual is what matters.

The first things they strip from her are the muslin cap on her head and the satin shoes on her feet. One woman unpins her gown, and then her stomacher. Someone, standing behind her, is unlacing her stays. A woman in front of her unties the silk gown petticoat, then the hip roll. Then the modesty petticoat, and she is standing in her chemise, shivering, as a woman kneels before her, unties her garters, rolls down her silk stockings.

'Soon you will meet your husband, Your Royal Highness,' says one of the ladies, trying to distract her from her own

118

nakedness, perhaps. 'How exciting! You will call him Monseigneur le Dauphin and he will call you Madame la Dauphine.'

Durfort has briefed her on French etiquette, and she bristles at the reminder she did not need. But these women are kind. They are trying to help.

'I hope in private he will call me Antoine,' she says with her warmest smile. 'Do you think that would be all right?'

'In France, you will be Marie Antoinette,' says one. 'Much more suitable. Much prettier.'

She hesitates, then nods. Is she not here to be pretty and suitable? What does it matter what her name is?

Poor Joseph's second wife never did make a place for herself, and she was miserable throughout their marriage. Antoine won't make the same mistake. She'll make her husband love her. She'll make everyone love her. Antoine has a perfect hairline now, and straight teeth. Her jaw aches as she smiles.

She glances at the cart to see what they'll dress her in. A chemise. A tightly boned golden bodice with lace trim. Wide panniers. Hooped petticoat. Cloth-of-gold skirt and stomacher covered in gemstones and silk bows. Lace engageantes for her arms, gold-embroidered silk stockings for her legs. Diamond-buckled silk shoes with little heels. A gold brocade train to go over the skirt.

Gold is not the prettiest colour on her, but gold means power. Gold means *we can*. A shining new dress, an enormous dress, conforming to the traditions laid down as gospel by the Sun King.

All of this is magic of a kind.

Pots of powder and rouge, which will at least help hide the effects of her shameful crying.

Outside the pavilion's thin walls, there's distant thunder and the rumble of men's voices.

The tears threaten, the tears she has stifled at such great pain on her journey, in her glass box.

One woman takes her old clothing back out through the German door, to give to the cousins, Antoine's final gifts to them in gratitude for being her last friends on Habsburg soil.

For one last moment Antoine stands as Antoine, naked. But not quite naked. She smiles.

Invisible for the moment, around her neck, hangs the golden device that Geneviève created for her. The one bit of gold that no one can see. Its heavy, cold weight lies just below her collarbone.

They worked together, for three nights. The workings came out of Antoine's big gold watch, which had been a present from her mother. Inside, Geneviève affixed six copper wheels. She has access to all of Kempelen's instruments, and some enchanted ones of her own. With a magic pen, she engraved tiny numbers on one wheel, and wrote letters of sacrifice on five wheels beneath it. Each of the numbers corresponds to one of the spells in Antoine's papers, plus seven that Geneviève has given her.

Antoine wrote a legend on a little scroll in tiny handwriting, to show which number goes with which spell. The scroll fits inside the glass watchcase. Most of them are still mysterious to her, but she notes them down anyway, in the hope of a day when she can use them.

A book, made of gears. Now if Antoine wants to know what sacrifices go with which spell, she need only consult her watch. And, most importantly, Geneviève even enchanted it so that it can become invisible at the touch of a tiny button on the side. Geneviève made her own sacrifices for that; it is the best gift Antoine has ever received.

The night after the watch was finished, Geneviève was nowhere to be found. Kempelen had stopped showing the mechanical Turk to the court, and had moved on to his commission to change the water system. Geneviève left no note, no vestiges of her presence.

Antoine holds back tears, sniffing as quickly and discreetly as she can; she has no handkerchief. She smiles violently and holds up her arms as the new chemise drops over her head, and the world, for one brief moment, goes white.

Strasbourg, just over the border, is the first city to welcome the new Dauphine. They let off fireworks and there is a magnificent ball. It seems strangely sombre, all the same, but perhaps people are more sombre here. Antoinette greets everyone – the local girls and boys in shepherd dress, the officials, the nobility – just as she has been taught. There are mountains of flowers and the whole city is alight.

In the episcopal palace, she comes face to face with Prince Louis de Rohan, and she stops breathing for a moment.

'Your Royal Highness,' he says, bowing low. 'I welcome you to France.'

A hundred people are watching them. She tries not to look like a magister. How does one look like a magister, or not like a magister? She tries not to look wary, but she is.

'The people of this country appreciate the sacrifices you have made,' the prince says lightly. 'We appreciate that you have left your family behind. Although of course you have the examples of your sisters ahead of you.'

She must say something.

'If I am pleasing to the people of France, that is all I desire.'

He smiles, not prettily. 'How could they not be pleased?'

'They don't look pleased,' she says, looking around, and realizing that she's spoken too frankly. Oh well. Frankness can be one of her charms. Let him think she wants to be friends, that she has no reason not to want to be friends. She steps closer to the prince, and says almost conspiratorially, 'Everyone looks a little sour here today.'

'Ah, well, as to that, Your Royal Highness, there is an explanation,' says Rohan. 'His Majesty in his wisdom gave a princess of Lorraine, about your age, the honour of the first dance after the royal family's. This broke with precedence and half the nobility threatened to boycott. They're here but they're still not happy about it.'

'About when a princess dances?'

'About whether it has anything to do with our new dauphine being a daughter of Lorraine on her father's side,' he says. 'And whether her being a daughter of Austria, on her mother's side, will affect the way the King of France does business. Today, it's which princess dances first; tomorrow, it may be which side we take in the next disastrous Habsburg war. The great families of France make it their business to understand the significance of the slightest change to etiquette. Your arrival has set the cat among the pigeons.'

She feels cold. 'I did not know about any of this. The King only meant it as a kindness, I'm sure.'

He shakes his head, smiling. 'Of course. Between you and me, Your Highness, these are pigeons in urgent need of a visit from a cat.'

She smiles back, and the line of people who want to speak to her is moving, pushing the Prince de Rohan away from her. He seems content to be pushed, making his farewell. Perhaps everything will be fine.

The King of France is handsome, Antoinette decides. The ballroom at the Château de Compiègne, the last major stop before Paris, is full of eyes watching her: eyes couched in feathers and powder, lace and rouge. Antoinette dances perfectly in dove-grey silk shoes, pointed in the front with a small but sturdy heel.

There are eight dancers in the contredanse allemande, and the rest of the ballroom observes, with drinks in their hands. A walking gavotte step now; a sprightly rigaudon, and back to the refrain. She feels light in every vein, like going downhill on a sled in the snow.

The King is handsome, yes, but in the way of old men – he must be sixty if he's a day; she should know his exact age: it was in her notes – with a fine nose and dark eyebrows beneath a very plain, powdered coiffure. He has been king since he was a child – France barely remembers any other – and he seems to wear it as if it is a part of him. Every one of his feelings appears on his face; why should he bother to hide them? He is king, and his feelings are everyone's business.

His grandson, Antoinette's husband, doesn't seem to have any feelings at all. The Dauphin greeted her very nicely, and the two of them danced a minuet, before everyone, perfectly. But he has not spoken much to her since. He is dark-haired, big-featured, heavy-set. He watches everything in a stolid way that Antoinette has decided is the sign of great intelligence. He keeps his thoughts to himself; and isn't that wisdom? No one seems to pay him any mind, but he is the future king, and perhaps they are showing deference.

She rotates on the ballroom floor, her arms interlaced, her hands resting lightly in those of Philippe d'Orléans, a man she just met. One of her husband's highest-ranking cousins. The music stops, and they separate.

D'Orléans's face is florid, and he bows stiffly, his expression sour. She wonders what she could have done wrong. She is sure she got all the steps right. As she's puzzling it over, he slips away into the crowd.

Antoinette has a moment to rest, now. She steps out of the way of the dance floor and into a group of women. She smiles at the young Princesse de Lamballe, who was presented to her earlier. Madame Adélaïde, the eldest surviving daughter of the King, says that Antoine danced beautifully. She and the Dauphin's other three aunts at Versailles are unmarried. She's terrifyingly beautiful, with piercing grey eyes and glowing skin. Antoinette feels like a child next to her.

'I'm afraid I have to keep reminding myself to dance the Parisian way, and not the Viennese,' Antoinette says with a friendly smile. 'Some of the steps are a little different. I hope I remembered.'

'You've shown them all how to dance in the Austrian

style, Your Royal Highness,' says Adélaïde. 'Soon they will match their steps to yours, and not the other way around.'

That wasn't what Antoinette intended at all, but she can't think of a way to say so.

'Everyone was quite dazzled,' Madame Adélaïde continues. 'You must not pay the slightest attention to Philippe. He's as bitter as a lemon, and has been from birth. If your husband and his brothers were to die childless, he'd be *it*. He never forgets that. Not for one moment. After all, stranger things have happened, haven't they? My father was fourth in line for the throne one moment, and then smallpox and measles did their work, and there he was, king at five years old.'

'Thank you,' Antoinette says, a little befuddled but genuinely grateful. 'I studied very hard, but I'm afraid I still have so much to learn.'

'Do you? Then you must ask me for help. Come, don't be shy, I like nothing better than gossip. What do you want to know?'

'Well, I did wonder about that very elegant woman with the high voice, there by the King.'

The woman in question, as if she's heard, turns her doe-like gaze and perpetual half-smile in Antoinette's direction.

'And well you might wonder, my dear, well you might. That is Jeanne Bécu. She calls herself the Comtesse du Barry.'

'Calls herself?'

Madame Adélaïde makes a dismissive gesture that might mean anything. 'She's the illegitimate daughter of a seamstress. A shop assistant and errand girl.'

Antoinette frowns, trying to frame her question. 'But why is she here?'

'She's here because she pleases the King.'

Antoinette smiles. 'I should like to please the King too. I suppose I'll be her rival!'

Madame Adélaïde snorts, and covers her face with a bit of lace as she laughs. It's only after the fact that Antoinette realizes, to her great embarrassment, what Madame Adélaïde meant by 'pleases'.

Everyone around them is listening, and people who didn't hear are whispering to their neighbours, asking what the Dauphine said.

The Princesse de Lamballe is not staring or whispering. She is one of the prettiest creatures Antoinette has ever seen, with laughing eyes and a wry little smile under her pointed nose. She's a little older than Antoinette but she's as tiny as a girl in her mauve bodice all covered in shining ribbons. She's so thin that the force of her weight comes as a surprise when it smacks into Antoinette's shoulder as the princess falls to the floor.

'She's fainted!' one of the women says.

'She does that quite a lot,' says Madame Adélaïde wryly.

Louis appears at Antoinette's side and offers Lamballe a hand. 'Are you all right, my dear?'

'I'm quite all right, thank you, Your Royal Highness. It's only a bit warm in here, isn't it? Oh, I'm so sorry, Your Royal Highness!'

This last is addressed to Antoinette, for hitting her on the way down.

'You must think no more of it,' she says to Lamballe, as they both stand and smooth their skirts. She steps forward and embraces her, saying in her ear, 'In fact I think I shall love you forever for rescuing me from my embarrassment.'

'Sometimes we simply need a distraction,' Lamballe whispers back with a faintly Italian accent. She turns to the other women, reassuring them and smiling and taking the offered water.

Louis, overhearing, takes Antoinette's arm lightly, and speaks in her ear. 'Is everything all right?'

How lucky she is, to have such a gallant and perceptive husband!

'I'm afraid I am tired, and danced badly,' she says.

'No,' says Louis very seriously. 'You dance with such grace. I'm quite jealous. Everything you do is perfect.'

CHAPTER ELEVEN

A Man Who Talks in His Sleep — Meetings in the
Palazzo Reale — Promises — Roman Ruins — Risks

Caterina meets Charlotte in the garden at Portici, on the slopes of Vesuvius, on a spring morning in 1770 when the air is full of moisture and the cries of sea birds. They walk together on an open path lined with orange trees, where they can see others coming.

'It has been slow,' says Caterina. 'I didn't want to be seen to be investigating, so I only dropped the phrase here and there. I let people think I'd encountered it in an old book. But no one ever reacted to it in the slightest. I was starting to despair. And then I had lunch with my cousin.'

Charlotte stops walking and turns to her. 'Your cousin—'

'Knows nothing,' Caterina says, holding up one hand. 'But he has a tendency to fall in love with the beautiful men who come through on the Grand Tour – you know, the foreigners. Diplomats. Artists. He had his heart broken by a German scholar named Johann Winckelmann, who came here to study the ruins at Pompeii a few years ago.'

'He had just come to Vienna when I left,' Charlotte says. 'If I'm thinking of the right man. Isn't he the one who was murdered in Trieste a couple of years ago?'

Caterina nods. 'Not by my cousin, I hasten to add. But this Winckelmann was a man inclined to talk in his sleep or in his drink, my cousin says. He used to mutter about the Order of 1326. My cousin once followed Winckelmann to a Freemasons' lodge, but he said he never came out, and he thought Winckelmann had simply been trying to elude him. I found the lodge; it is still meeting in secret here in Naples.'

'Despite Tanucci?'

'Despite Tanucci. I found a place where I could see the entrance, watch them come and go. And I saw a very peculiar thing. Three of the people who went into the Masons' meeting did not come out again. At least, not by that door, and not at the time when everyone else did.'

'Their names?'

Caterina looks slightly smug. 'One of them is the Prince of Caramanico.'

Charlotte puts her hand on Caterina's. The very man she invited to the palace when she first came to Naples; the one who snubbed her.

'He's the grandmaster of the Masonic lodge, you see,' Caterina says.

'And you are sure it was him? He doesn't come to court, you said.'

'I've met him several times at demonstrations and lectures. I'd know him anywhere; he has a very recognizable profile.' Caterina lifts her face into an impression of a haughty aristocrat. 'It doesn't surprise me that he would be a member of any society that's thumbing its nose at Tanucci.'

Caterina seems to have made some assumptions about the Order, which Charlotte ignores.

'And the other two men?'

'The prince's friend Vincenzo Lunardi, a handsome young clerk – I've seen him at lectures as well. The third man I didn't recognize, but he wore a very distinctive cloak with stars embroidered on it – not the best way to be inconspicuous. I gave his description to a few actresses I know, and they said he's a Sicilian alchemist, recently arrived here with his young wife after they left Rome under some sort of scandal. He calls himself Alessandro Cagliostro, and claims to be a count, but I know all the noble families of Sicily. Whoever he is, he did not begin life as Count Alessandro Cagliostro.'

Charlotte thinks for a moment. The sun is hot on her face, and the air smells clean. 'Well, Caterina, I want you to find out everything you can about these men – their families, their interests, their debts, their desires. You've found the Order of 1326. I have no doubt.'

'And what is this Order, Your Majesty? What do they do?'

Charlotte feels a surprising affection for Caterina in that moment, giddy with the knowledge that she has an ally, that she can discover things about the world beyond Ferdinand's palaces, beyond her mother's reach. Something terrifying is happening beyond those walls, but Charlotte is going to terrify it right back.

So she pulls an enchanted thimble out of her pocket and, with it on her thumb, flicks a silver piastra coin in the air. It falls to the earth in a shower of 120 grana coins; the thimble splits anything into its constituent parts, literally or figuratively, unpredictably and wonderfully. She has not quite found a good use for it yet.

'They do magic,' she says, answering Caterina's question, enjoying the look of astonishment on the marchesa's face. 'Would you like to learn?'

Charlotte sits in the library at the Palazzo Reale and grips the smooth dark wood of the chair's armrest, trying to hold on, to make reality stay in position.

Three stuffed heads – a pine marten, a quail, a badger – look at her, unimpressed. The old library is horrible, but it serves her purpose for today. No fear of Ferdinand or his friends turning up in a library, least of all this one. It's a dingy room with more taxidermy than books, and with little brown landscapes on the walls. It was last decorated in the time of Ferdinand's father, before the old man left Naples to take up the throne of Spain.

More importantly for her purposes, it has three doors: one leading to a stairwell, one leading into the suite of royal antechambers, and one leading out into the galleries and ballroom. She can have her conversation with each of the three men alone, without giving them any time to consult each other in between.

With Caterina's help, she arranged to have the Prince of Caramanico brought in through the gallery door, while Vincenzo Lunardi waited in the immense and richly decorated antechamber. The prince agreed to her proposal, kissed her hand, and left through the door ahead of her, and then Lunardi came in from the door on her left. He, too, was persuaded, and left how he came in.

Now that only leaves the man waiting beyond the door to the right, in a stairwell, but that couldn't be helped, and besides, it is a very grand stairwell, even if it is only a minor one stuck in a corner of the palace. Everything here is grand, and Count Cagliostro can wait very nicely, surrounded by pink and blue marble, gold finials and inoffensive oil landscapes rising far above his head. 'Count' Cagliostro. Caterina says that he makes his living by frightening superstitious old ladies who take one look at his spangled blue robe and heavy amulet and hand over their money.

Today, at least, he has the good sense not to be wearing the robe. He's dressed in sober indigo velvet, with lace at his throat. He's younger than Charlotte expected, stout, with a face that is pleasant enough. He doesn't look as though he is in touch with the dark forces of the universe. Is that good or bad for his business? Caterina ushers him in and waits by the door; they have sent away the footmen so there is only the guard outside the room's main doors.

And then the meeting proceeds as it did with Caramanico and Lunardi.

'Will you take something?'

Caramanico, as expected, requested a glass of his favourite wine, the sweet golden Constantia, imported from Africa at great expense. Lunardi, as expected, enjoyed a sweet white as well, but in his case the Italian Picolit.

It's warm in the room – summer now, as it took some time for Charlotte to make her plans and send her letters. It's a thirsty sort of day for a man who's been kept waiting.

For Cagliostro, it's champagne, in a thin crystal flute. The table is arrayed with silver plates carrying each man's favourite cheese and nuts, and Cagliostro takes a few chest-nuts in his beringed fingers.

'I will save Your Majesty from saying it directly,' the count says, once he has swallowed. 'I would be overjoyed to supply an elixir. For fertility, or . . .?'

Charlotte nearly laughs. She's still exuberant from the easy success of the other two interviews. 'I do not want an elixir, Count. I will do you the same courtesy you showed me, and speak directly. I am a magister, and I wish to join the Naples chapter of the Order of 1326.'

Cagliostro almost chokes on a chestnut. 'Your Majesty,' he says, recovering, 'I must confess my ignorance.'

She waves a hand, and turns away from him, and launches into the explanation that worked so well with the other two. She has some spells of her own, but she wishes to learn more. She wishes to work with other magisters for the good of the country and the world.

The prince objected here, helpfully telling Charlotte more about precisely what rules she was breaking. It was forbidden for anyone to use magic who had not first been initiated.

To which Charlotte replied that she had learned magic before she knew of such a rule, and now she wanted only to regularize her position.

More than that, though, the prince explained, there was a rule against monarchs being members of the Order, lest they become too powerful. And besides – here he paused, and she had to prompt him – there had never been a female member of the Order, at least not in living memory.

By the time Cagliostro makes these same objections, Charlotte has her argument rehearsed. In a way, the fact that she represents the breaking of two rules at once makes the one cancel out the other: she is a monarch, but she is a woman. She cannot easily overstep. Her husband is the King of Naples, and the Queen will swear a solemn oath never to breathe a word about magic to the King.

But she can give the magisters of Naples access such as they have never had – such as no magisters have.

This is where she told Caramanico that, as queen, she intended to make the court of Naples the centre of the diplomatic world, as it ought to be, with men such as the prince given key positions. What wonders magic could work in spycraft – but of course, few have ever been able to attempt it, because of the rules against monarchs knowing anything about magic. It would take someone bold and intelligent to put magic to use in ways no one ever has. A departure, certainly, but are these not extraordinary times?

This is where she told Lunardi that in this golden age, magic ought to work in concert with the other arts and sciences. Charlotte explained her intention to make the court of Naples a beacon to the world's best artists, writers, composers, and natural philosophers – and she would need Lunardi's help in that. Perhaps magic could be put to use in unrolling the ancient papyrus scrolls found in Herculaneum – the King would have to agree to grant access, of course. Perhaps a new Academy of Sciences, with Lunardi as royal adviser?

Cagliostro, who seems to want nothing but to defraud fearful housewives, presents a more difficult problem. Charlotte swallows, turns back to look at him. 'And of course we must do something about the charlatans with their oils and nostrums, preying on the simple. I understand, of course, that you, Count Cagliostro, are nothing of that kind, despite appearances.'

132

'I use my gift to help people,' he says, his voice thick and cautious.

'Just so. But as you are known for your gift with elixirs, you might very well be caught up in the King's efforts to rid the city of such people, unless you had someone at court willing to ensure your name was kept off all the lists.'

Cagliostro downs what remains of his champagne and sets the crystal flute back on the table. 'The King has no interest in anything but hunting and whores. He doesn't care about me or anyone else, so long as we pay the right bribes. He might be very interested to find that his little German wife fancies herself a witch.'

The world stops, spools, tangles. Caramanico agreed, kissed her hand, went out through his door to the gallery. Lunardi agreed, kissed her hand, went out through his door to the anteroom.

Cagliostro isn't meeting her eye, and not out of respect. He simply can't be bothered.

'Let me be plainer still,' she says. 'The King is occupied with the business of state, and I am the business of state. The King loses a great deal if he loses me: good relations with the Habsburg Empire, for one thing. My position is not at risk, but yours is, Count. I will make it my business to hunt down every peddler of superstition in Naples, if you try to thwart me.'

She's shaking now; it's a brazen lie, or close to it. Without more magic, Charlotte will remain powerless, and Ferdinand could well make her life even more miserable than it is. She can only hope Cagliostro will think she's shaking out of anger. He does look at her then, still exuding a cultivated arrogance, but she can tell he's uncertain now.

'If the people look to their superstitions for a little hope,' he says, 'a little distraction, is that such a bad thing?'

'We will replace their counterfeit hopes with truer stuff,' she says.

'We,' he repeats.

'I am already welcome among your "Brothers" here in Naples. I brought you here as a courtesy and to give you a warning. If you cause me problems, I will cause you problems. I think you may find that a queen makes a better ally than an enemy, *Count*.'

He pauses, and then nods, just briefly. 'Indeed, Your Majesty. I have never put much stock in the hidebound rules of our Order.'

'No, I thought not.' She smiles, trying not to show her relief. 'How did you come to be a Brother?'

'Ah,' he says, bowing. 'We magisters must keep some secrets, even from each other. I will expect Your Majesty at the next meeting, then. If Caramanico, Lunardi, and Hamilton have already agreed, who am I to cause trouble?'

Charlotte nods tightly, thinking furiously. Hamilton? There is another member of the Order of 1326 in Naples. A Brother she didn't work into her plans, who has no reason to accept her. No reason not to treat her as the Order treats any other rogue.

William Hamilton has been the British envoy to Naples for several years. His official residence is in Naples, but he also has a beach house in Posillipo, and a villa at Portici, on the slopes of Vesuvius, close to the ruins of Herculaneum. He spends a lot of time at the ruins, it's said, and so Charlotte takes an interest in them. This is, apparently, the sort of thing a young queen is supposed to want to do, and when she asks to go, she encounters no trouble about carriages or guards.

Running into him at the ruins will also help avoid any misconceptions on Hamilton's part, or on the part of any onlookers. This is not a diplomatic matter.

The Roman town, buried since the eruption of AD 79, now looks like a building site, with ramps carved out of the dirt, and bits of pediments and other masonry lying here and there as if waiting to be set in place. There are trees on the slopes nearby, but here everything is open, between Vesuvius and the sea.

Hamilton's a sharp-faced man, middle-aged, his coat dusty. He scrambles up out of a shallow hole with a bit of broken pot in his hand. But he doesn't look surprised to see her.

'I have expected you, Your Majesty,' Hamilton says evenly. 'Caramanico told me.'

She shades her eyes against the sun, to see him better. 'Can we speak here?'

'Oh, certainly.' He gestures at the open space around them. The nearest person is Charlotte's footman, waiting back at the carriage. 'This place used to be a hive of activity, but since the discovery of Pompeii, everyone has moved there – shallower, you know. I don't mind. They've left me all sorts of wonders. This was a temple, I'm certain of it.'

She peers into the hole. 'May I see it closer?'

He taps the bit of pot against his hand. 'I should like to know, Your Majesty, whether you have any plans to undermine our Order, to spread its secrets abroad, or use it to work against the interests of King George.'

'I do not.'

'Then by all means.' He steps down into the hole and offers her his hand. There's not much more she can see, only some stones that seem to form the bottom of a wall. She takes his hand, but she's on her guard.

'Mr Hamilton, you seem remarkably unconcerned about the fact that I've asked to join the Order.'

He smiles. 'I would not say that, Your Majesty. But it seems the choices before me are few, and none of them good. I am not an assassin or a fanatic. I joined the Order because I am interested in all aspects of the natural world.'

'Do you think of magic that way?'

'Of course!' He puts a hand onto the ruined wall. 'It's all one: magic, science, even religion, or at least the stories thereof.'

'Surely the Church is not—'

He waves his hand. 'The Church is quite opposed to magic, whenever it is forced to acknowledge it exists. For everyone's sake, we try to prevent that from happening as much as we can. But the stories – "In the beginning was the Word", we're told in the Gospel of John. Words are will, intention, decision. Many cultures have a story about language as a medium of creation, or destruction for that matter. Magic is, fundamentally, the first law of nature.'

Charlotte's reading has tended more to political philosophy than natural. 'Hobbes says the first law of nature is peace,' she ventures uncertainly.

'Rot,' says Hamilton, shaking his head. 'That's the first law, the only truth. Rot. Decay. When anything is left to itself, it decays, and changes into any number of possible states. Some of those states are more likely than others. Magic is, simply, the choice to force a highly improbable condition. But there is, in all things, an equilibrium. Forcing one possibility, at the expense of others, has a cost: the sacrifices decay. And so, to some degree, does the magister who made those sacrifices. So perhaps Hobbes is right after all. Perhaps decay is a kind of peace. Some people think a volcano is violent, but I think it is the most peaceful thing there is.'

She looks towards Vesuvius. An insect is trilling in the trees nearby. She feels, suddenly, a kind of homesickness, a lost feeling, like nostalgia soured, but she has nothing to be nostalgic for. Everything is ahead of her, and nothing is behind.

'Thank you for explaining,' she says, turning back to him. 'I have a great deal to learn about magic.'

'Will I see you at the next meeting, Your Majesty?'

She nods. 'I wasn't sure you were in the habit of attending. My spies did not see you.'

'Ah,' he says. 'That's because I am careful. Underneath Naples, there are tunnels – no one knows how many. Some were quarries, so the builders could get tufo – not this stuff, this is mostly ash, here – but the volcanic rock, you know, oddly light. Some were aqueducts. Some were for secret doings. There is an entrance to the cavern beneath the Masonic lodge through the tunnels.'

'And if I were also to find my way through the tunnels, would I find the entrance there open to me?'

'One simply speaks the password,' Hamilton says. '"*Omnia mea mecum porto*". There are doors into the tunnels throughout the city. There was even an entrance beneath what is now the Palazzo Reale, so it is said. Don Pedro, a viceroy of the sixteenth century, mentions in his letters a "vexatious stair" that was uncovered during building work – it must have interfered with his plans, but he was loath to brick it up, in case he needed it to make an escape from the people he ruled.'

She nods with what she hopes looks like mere polite interest. No need for Hamilton to know that the Queen is desperate to find a way in and out of the palace that doesn't require permission.

CHAPTER TWELVE

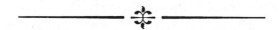

*Secrets of the Palace — Under Naples — The Moon
Waxes — Rituals — Rules Are Broken*

Caterina shows no outward sign of surprise or curiosity when
Charlotte asks her about the stair to the tunnels. They each
have needlework in their laps, and there are other ladies
scattered about the room. So they speak in low voices, as if
they are gossiping.

'There's no such stair that I know of, Your Majesty, and I
would venture to say that I've had occasion to sneak into
every dusty staircase and dim corridor in the palace.' She
smiles a little at that, thinking no doubt of her Austrian lover.
Then she adds, as her needle moves, 'Well, except one.'

'Except one?'

'The Haunted Staircase. Haven't you heard the stories?
The ladies love to frighten each other with them. Young
courtiers used to dare each other to run up it, I'm told, but
it's been locked for years anyway.'

'*Up* it?' Charlotte repeats.

Caterina nods. 'It can't be your stair to the tunnels. It's in the
undercroft, beneath the chapel, but it leads up, back to ground
level. It probably led to a vault or a sacristy; perhaps someone
started the haunting story as a way to discourage theft.'

'Well, if it's the only staircase you haven't seen, let's have a look.'

It's easy enough to go to the chapel that evening, and neither Ferdinand nor Tanucci are ever there outside their obligatory appearances at Mass. In fact, the place is quite empty, and Caterina and Charlotte slip behind an arcade and into the plain door that leads down to a small stone undercroft.

There are several heavy wooden doors, all with locks. Caterina strides to one, picks the padlock with a hairpin (Charlotte does not comment) and it swings open.

The pale stone steps do indeed rise, straight into a brick wall. Charlotte sighs. She tells Caterina she will just test the bricks, and she steps onto the first riser.

And the staircase inverts, Charlotte lurches down; the world is a ship in a storm. She clutches at the walls and feels as though she's about to tip forward.

'What's wrong?' Caterina whispers.

'It's magic,' she says. 'Look!'

'I don't see anything.'

Charlotte turns, and looks up at Caterina – while Caterina is looking up at her. It's quite impossible, and makes her dizzy.

'The stairs do lead down after all. They were here two hundred years ago, Hamilton said, but I suppose they must have been built long before that. The Order must not know they're here, or it would have covered it up with something better than a flimsy lock and a story. Come, you'll see!'

She stretches out her hand, steps down, and Caterina puts her foot on the first step. Then she nearly falls on Charlotte, begging her pardon and laughing with embarrassment.

Instead of a brick wall, these stairs go on and on, down into depths too dark to see. When the time comes, they'll need to bring a light.

But they have three weeks to wait. The meetings of the Order follow the phases of the moon. There is, from what

140

she can tell, no magical reason for this inconvenience, no real reason whatsoever.

Every morning, Charlotte wakes up grateful that no one has slipped a knife between her ribs, and she runs over her memories of magic, of Antoine, to make sure they are intact. Soliman and Rohan may have been ready to kill her for her knowledge, but these magisters are not. She has gambled and won.

She has not yet told Antoine, for fear her sister will worry. Once she is a member, and safe, she'll write all about it.

On the appointed night, she and Caterina both retire early, then meet in the chapel. Charlotte does not think she will be in physical danger, but she brings a stiletto and a number of other useful items in her enchanted pocket, nonetheless.

They open the lock, and Caterina holds up a lamp to the stairs that seem, once again, to rise.

'There is no map of the tunnels, but I know some of them already, and I have friends who know others, and it didn't take me long to find a route,' Caterina says. 'We will never have to go near the street. How funny that the Order meets beneath a Masonic lodge. If Tanucci sends his thugs to investigate, he'll find nothing but silly men comforting themselves with empty rituals.'

'While beneath the surface, there are silly men comforting themselves with empty rituals,' Charlotte says, smiling slightly. 'And performing magic.'

'Are there rituals?' Caterina says with mock nervousness that may be partly real.

'Something the prince said led me to think so. We are to be initiated, Caterina. But just think of everything we'll learn. They must have more spells. Everything they've kept so carefully hidden. I intend to put all of it to good use.'

They walk into the darkness, Caterina carrying the lamp and walking ahead. Charlotte doesn't look into the darkness behind her.

Some of the tunnels are built of hewn stone, with archways

to rival any village church. Some are carved roughly out of the rock itself, with ancient wooden lintels marking what passes for a ceiling. Some are mining shafts, with ciphers of workers long dead scratched into the stone walls. The city of Naples is built on this volcanic yellow stuff, and built out of it.

They come at last to a dead end, a mere hollow in the rock. Water drips from above.

'"*Omnia mea mecum porto*",' Charlotte mutters. For a moment, she thinks the password Hamilton gave her was a feint, and that they've been tricked, that they'll be trapped here, underground.

But then the rockface dissolves into an open archway.

This is the world she's always known must exist, and it is real, and she is entering it as a magister and as a queen.

Charlotte steps over the threshold.

In a cavern lit by torches stand Hamilton, Caramanico, Cagliostro and Lunardi. But tonight, they are dressed in black robes, and all are wearing red silk caps, loose at the top so that they droop in little peaks. They would look ridiculous anywhere other than this cavern, where they are dressed in shadows too.

'Your Majesty,' says Caramanico a little nervously. 'We have broken with long practice here tonight, but we hope to build a better world, and a stronger Brotherhood in Naples.'

He speaks a smooth, cosmopolitan Italian, not the Neapolitan of the palace. She wonders about that last bit, and it occurs to her that they agreed to her proposal to join them rather easily, and that four magisters does not seem very many for a city this size. Then again, what does she know about this Order of 1326? There is only one way to find out.

They bow, Cagliostro more slowly than the others, and she looks at them each in turn, trying to get the measure of them. Charlotte realizes that Lunardi has two other caps in his hand. She takes one, and hands the other to Caterina. They fit uneasily over mounded hair, and they itch.

'There's a ritual, to begin with,' whispers Hamilton with an avuncular smile.

Caramanico, looking annoyed at Hamilton's lack of solemnity, addresses Charlotte: 'These are ancient symbols, and we begin the meeting with the ancient rite. Do you come in darkness, and leave in silence?'

It seems to be the moment for her to take her vow. Should she elaborate on what she intends to do? She thinks not, somehow. 'I do,' she says, and Caterina repeats it.

'Then I admit you to the Order of 1326. From this moment you are bound to keep its secrets, to protect its ancient knowledge, and to serve the greater good of mankind.'

They stand in a loose circle, and Caramanico produces a goblet from somewhere. He spits in it, says, 'I give this to my Brother magister,' and hands it to Cagliostro. He does the same and passes it to the Lunardi, who follows suit and passes it to Charlotte, who does not look at the contents of the goblet. 'I give this to my Brother magister,' she says, and spits, hard, to make sure nothing dribbles. She feels more than a little ridiculous, more like a schoolboy than a queen, and more than a little concerned that there will at some point be an expectation to drink. She passes the goblet to Caterina.

When Caramanico has taken it back, he pulls a piece of bright blue silk out of some pocket, flourishes it, and lays it on the floor. It's a large star made of silk, woven in blues and reds and trimmed all around with silver thread. The lines that make up the pentacle are silver too. It's quite beautiful.

Caramanico dips a reed into the goblet and places three drops of the liquid inside into each of the five points of the star, intoning, 'From seven to five to three to one, the harmonies of the universe indivisible. The gifts of my Brothers' bodies I have taken for my own gifts. Every drop of my Brothers' blood I treasure. I give them now, to purify our craft, to keep it eternal, to keep it undimmed, to keep it for those who honour its mysteries.'

143

He's still speaking a variety of Italian, the words rolling out of him in a way that makes Charlotte shiver despite his pomposity. But there's nothing in the middle of the star; if he's trying to work an enchantment, what is he working it on?

'I give these sacrifices,' he whispers.

Charlotte flinches as an orange flame rises with a pop in the centre of the silk star. The star itself is the item, she realizes, with a sick drop in her stomach as the flame eats black-rimmed holes through the gorgeous weaving. The smell – like burning hair – is stronger than whatever odour of decay might come from a few drops of spittle. In moments, the star is nothing but a pile of dark ash on the floor.

Lunardi stoops and, with a little straw whisk, brushes the ash carefully into a silver pan. He hands them each a squat glass vial, into which the prince pours the ash using a little silver funnel.

'We have spells to share, and work to perform,' says Hamilton, 'but none of that is as important as the historic step we have taken here today. Her Majesty is now one of us, and no doors are closed. We must proceed with wisdom, carefully, but it is a moment for joy. A moment of possibility.'

He turns to her, and Charlotte has the unusual sensation of realizing that people are waiting for her to speak. 'I will keep the Order's secrets, and work for the betterment of my Brothers and for all mankind. And it begins here, today, underneath the city of Naples.'

As if to illuminate her point, the torches on the wall flicker. She rehearsed that speech, and it came off rather well.

She glances up at the wall, where a skull is embedded – somehow – in the rock, grinning down at her. How perfect, and how ridiculous. What would that skull see? A soon-to-turn-eighteen unsatisfactory bride, whose chin tends to double but whose lip never trembles. She glares at it.

'For today's business, I believe Count Cagliostro has a report,' Caramanico says, turning to him.

'The trouble is taken care of,' Cagliostro says.

There's a pause.

'You can speak freely among your Brothers,' Caramanico reminds him.

Cagliostro heaves a sigh. 'It was as we suspected. The midwife was a rogue magister. She will do magic no more. I took a few papers from her, and it includes a spell we did not have before. For enchanting a dog collar so that the dog never runs away. It could be useful to us, especially if it works on things other than dogs.'

'Could it be a trap?' Lunardi says. 'Remember what happened to our Brothers in Turin.'

Hamilton explains for Charlotte and Caterina: 'The rogues of Turin planted a spell that filled the room with a poisonous gas when the Brothers of that city tried to use it.'

'I have tested it,' Cagliostro says.

As odious as Cagliostro is, the prospect of shared spells makes Charlotte eager. 'Where are the Order's spells kept? Is there a library?'

'Oh indeed, Your Majesty, of a sort.' Hamilton smiles, and makes a gesture like a man pulling a cloth off a birdcage, but there is no cloth. Still, once he has finished, Charlotte sees a small dark table standing beside him, and, on it, a book thicker than a bible. 'This is the *Reconditus*. It is a single book, that exists in every place where there is a chapter of magisters. It cannot be removed from this cavern; the Freemasons' lodge was put here to disguise a place that already existed.'

'May I . . .?' Charlotte walks to the book, puts her hand on its cover. It is plain yellow leather, with no words or markings.

She puts her finger on the edge of the cover, but the book will not open. Then her whole hand, but she can't prise it apart, and is hesitant to use more force.

'It requires at least two magisters,' says Vincenzo Lunardi, stepping forward with a slight smile. 'May we show you?'

He takes the book, then looks past Charlotte to Caramanico, and asks, in an odd tone of voice, 'What is the virtue of five?'

'The virtue of five is to point in no direction,' Caramanico says, and steps forward to put his hand on the cover next to Lunardi's.

'Who is at the bottom of the grave?'

'The head, the heart, the hand, the eye, the voice.'

'What is the call?'

'The call is chaos.'

'What is the call?'

'The call is creation.'

'What is the call?'

Nobody says anything for an uncomfortably long time, and Charlotte wonders whether she is meant to say or do something. She shifts, opens her mouth, and Lunardi puts his finger to his lips.

Then there is a faint sighing: a creaking sound, as if somone has opened an old door very far away. The two men remove their hands and step aside, and gesture for Charlotte to open the book.

It opens smoothly, and the vellum pages turn stiffly in her hands. She sees all sorts of writing, from plump medieval majuscule to delicate copperplate, in all shades of ink. She sees German, and Russian, and some round languages she doesn't recognize.

'The Five Questions are a sort of key or password,' Hamilton says. 'In fact, the *Reconditus* only appears in a place for the first time when each of the Five Questions are asked by a separate magister. Once any magister has participated in calling the *Reconditus* into existence, that magister can never do so again, and any manifestation of the *Reconditus* can never be moved. This is why each chapter of the Order is to have five members.'

They all look around, at the six people gathered in the cavern.

Caramanico puts his hand to his mouth and coughs lightly; then he says, 'Having already broken with the traditional ban on magical monarchs, we saw no reason to restrict our numbers in these difficult times.'

'The Naples chapter has so much work to do,' Lunardi adds. 'The challenges we face are new, and so our response must be too.'

'Challenges?' Caterina asks mildly.

'Rogue magic is proliferating out in the world,' Hamilton explains with a vague, sweeping gesture. 'But within the Order, we hold ourselves to rules that hamper us to no good purpose. The original intent, I suspect, was to help keep magic secret, but in Naples, the effect of the rule of five has been to keep our numbers lower than they ought to be, as we lose members to other places quite often.'

In response to her questioning expression, Caramanico says, 'Because Naples, and in particular intellectual Naples, is a city of travellers. Perhaps that will change soon.'

Charlotte decides to accept this answer, and turns the pages of the *Reconditus*. Spell after spell that she has never seen before. What wonders could she perform! It makes the embroidered book look like a sampler.

She has so much to learn, but first she wants answers to basic questions, such as how the spells relate to the words from which they are derived, and how that can be when humanity speaks so many languages. Most of the spells seem to be in French or Latin.

Lunardi explains that the letter-substitution is a way of translating intention, that most magisters can only use spells derived from languages they speak.

Every answer begets more questions, but the relief of finally having answers at all makes Charlotte giddy.

'And how can it be a single book, in more than one place at once?'

'The magic is old and beyond our knowledge to replicate,' says Caramanico uneasily. 'When any of our Brothers, anywhere, writes a spell in it, the book grows to accommodate it. We may copy spells from it, but not, of course, remove the book.'

'Impossible to move the book,' Cagliostro mutters, and he rather looks as though he's tried.

'New spells will appear in our copy, but only when we add one of our own. Cagliostro, it's your turn to add a spell. Your dog collar one will do nicely.'

Cagliostro coughs. 'I thought we might keep it out of the *Reconditus* for a little while, Caramanico. Give Rome a little surprise.'

Rome? Charlotte thinks at first they mean the Holy Father, and she's seized with a worry that the Order's relationship with the Church might be more openly hostile than Hamilton had led her to believe.

'It isn't in the spirit of the Order to keep spells out of the *Reconditus*,' Lunardi says.

'It isn't in the spirit of the Order to steal magisters away, but that's what Rome has done to us,' Cagliostro snaps. 'Three of our best magisters in the last year.'

'They use Naples to get into the Order,' Caramanico explains, 'and then they go to Rome, where the five members might as well be five hundred, as they'll share the contents of the *Reconditus* with anyone claiming to be a Brother.'

Ah. Charlotte thinks. *There it is. A rivalry between chapters of the Order.*

'They didn't steal them,' Caramanico says smoothly. 'Those magisters left of their own accord. They found Rome attractive. As many magisters will find Naples attractive, especially now that we have many reasons for magisters to come here, reasons beyond dog collars.'

They all look at Charlotte.

'Perhaps,' Cagliostro says. 'Perhaps the other chapters would be interested to know about Her Majesty. If, that is, they don't try to kill her, which would be unfortunate.'

Caterina steps closer to Cagliostro. 'You'll keep her presence here a secret, or you'll find yourself in a collar of your own.'

Caramanico raises his hand. 'There are no secrets among Brothers, Marchesa. The other chapters will learn soon enough, but there is nothing to fear now that you have both taken the oath. I'm sure of it.'

No secrets among Brothers. Charlotte thinks of Antoine: a secret she has no intention of divulging to any Brother.

'All the same,' Charlotte says uneasily, 'perhaps for now—'

'At least one chapter is already aware,' Caramanico says. 'Brother Angelo will be arriving in a few days from Vienna.' Caramanico looks around at all their faces. 'If we are to restore Naples to her former position in the Order, we must demonstrate that we will not be trifled with. Cagliostro, you need not worry. The Brothers of Rome will be knocking on our door soon enough.'

Caterina is quivering like a harp string, and Charlotte feels sick. 'Brother Angelo,' she says. 'Angelo Soliman?'

'The very same.'

CHAPTER THIRTEEN

A Tragedy and a New Name — The Alchemist —
A Visitor to Naples — Factions — Confessions

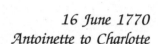

16 *June 1770*
Antoinette to Charlotte

Dear Charlotte,
  You have no doubt heard about the accident with the fireworks display that greeted us in Paris. One hundred and thirty-two people trampled or burned to death. My husband and I have agreed to pay all our personal allowance over to the families of the dead, and I have been visiting their families. It isn't enough, but I don't know what more to do.
  Surely magic must exist for some good purpose. In that terrible fire, the screams and the burning, everyone was powerless. Could they have saved themselves if they had enchanted their clothing to be fireproof, or enchanted the fireworks themselves not to be faulty? What if the manufacturers of fireworks, the smiths who shoe horses, the bakers of bread, what if they all could do everything with just a little more certainty of success? I can't solve their problems for them — I am nobody — but I am their dauphine,

151

and I wish I could do something for them. I wish I could understand more of our spells, or learn some new ones.

Don't worry; I won't stop being careful. I am doing as we agreed, and burning all your letters that refer to magic, never trusting to encryption alone.

What can I tell you that is happier? I admit I smile to see the words 'my husband' above in my own handwriting! The Dauphin seems very nice. He has been very gentlemanly towards me, and, though he doesn't talk much, when he does he always speaks to me like a true friend. I feel quite sorry for Louis (as he has agreeably asked me to call him in private), since he lost both his parents. His grandfather, the King, is very cheerful and brilliant but quite intimidating. The wedding and the journey were tiring for both my husband and me, and there was no rest when we arrived at Versailles. We must eat our meals, many of them, with people watching.

Mama will want to know that Louis has truly made me his wife but I'm afraid nothing of that kind has occurred. I don't know what to tell her. I suppose there is some mercy in the fact that she will know without me telling her; I have no secrets here, other than magic.

After all of this settles down, I'm sure the Dauphin and I will be very content together.

You asked me about Louis de Rohan. I did see him briefly as we went through Strasbourg, and we stayed in his uncle's house there. He was friendly towards me and I think he's satisfied that I am not a magister.

Which brings me to my confession. I didn't want to keep this from you, and I began to write this so many times on the journey, but I couldn't see a way to begin. So if it is disjointed, or makes no sense, just remember how jumbled I get when I'm nervous.

Courage!

In Vienna, I met another magister. Nobody else knows. Her name I swore to keep secret, but I don't even know all

of it anyway, or where she is now. I wanted to tell you but I was afraid . . . I don't know of what. That you would send someone to keep her away from me or something. I wanted to find out all I could about her. She is not a member of that Order of 1326 – she said they would call her a rogue.

She guessed my secret, but I didn't tell her anything about you.

She was a friend to me when I needed one most, and gave me a way to keep my spells close and safe.

Not that it matters; I can't seem to find a way to be alone for ten seconds at a time, so I have made very few sacrifices since I left home. Versailles is full of people, all the time, even in our very rooms. I have nowhere to do magic, or even to think.

I'm very lonely, sister, and I'm making so many mistakes.

All my love,
Antoinette

P.S. I've been told I must sign Antoinette now, being French. I almost forgot, which was why the pen blotted.

A few days after the meeting in the tunnels, Caterina brings Charlotte news that a widowed old countess is telling everyone that she is plagued by a mischievous spirit, that not even the indefatigable Count Cagliostro's repeated attempts to communicate with the spirit and send it away have prevented strange occurrences in her house. The spirit has taken several of her most treasured possessions, to torment her. But Cagliostro has sworn to defeat it, and really he has proven himself to be a powerful alchemist, and so kind-hearted.

'Cagliostro will just grow bolder in his crimes now,' Caterina says. 'He thinks he has royal permission.'

He does not have Charlotte's permission. It wouldn't help him much if he did; she has very little power to protect her

friends or harm her enemies. She can't imagine what she can do about Cagliostro, other than continue to warn and threaten him. And in the meantime, she has a greater worry on her hands.

Angelo Soliman is in Naples.

He calls upon the Queen, as though he were simply a visiting scholar from Vienna calling upon the local Habsburg. Charlotte receives him alone in her antechamber, the better to protect Caterina, if it comes to that.

Soliman once made it his business to make sure that Charlotte knew nothing about magic. Now he knows that he failed in that task, and he may have a new solution to the problem in mind. Perhaps he won't appreciate the Naples chapter taking matters into its own hands. Hamilton has told her that there is no head or centre to the Order, that every chapter is equal to all the others, at least in theory. But the way the Brothers of Naples speak about the Brothers of Rome, and the way they speak about Vienna with a mixture of resentment and reverence, tells her that the truth is more complex.

Soliman kisses her hand and takes the seat she indicates for him. She sits opposite, back straight, and has a look at him. For the first time, they are meeting as two adults. He looks a little older now – he must be nearly fifty. There are a few bits of grey escaping his black turban.

Well, she thinks. *The only way out is through.*

'Have you come to Naples to kill me, Dr Soliman?'

At that, he laughs with genuine surprise, although his eyes are still sad. 'I have not, Your Majesty.'

'But the Order has rules against magister-monarchs.' She says it defiantly, plainly, poking at the sore spot. She wants to test precisely where she stands with him.

'We do. However, we also have strict rules against causing bodily harm to members of our Order, of which you are now one, I understand. Besides, the deepest purpose of our Order is to prevent magic from coming to public notice and changing

the course of nations. The assassination of a queen would be, as it were, an even greater mess to clean up. If you'll forgive me for speaking plainly.'

'Please do speak plainly, always,' she says, and means it. For a moment, she considers mentioning Antoine, to ensure her safety too, but if Soliman has not asked, perhaps it's better to leave it. Antoine – Antoinette, she must get used to that – does not have the protection of the Order, after all.

'Then if you are not here to kill me,' she says, 'why have you come?'

'I have come to reckon with the consequences of mistakes I made.' His face is grave, his hands folded on his knees. 'I intend to make sure that this set of circumstances does not tear our Order apart, or cause harm to innocent people. I have come to make sure, frankly, that it does not ruin me. I am, you may have gathered, the senior member of the Vienna chapter, and there are many both in Vienna and outside it who would like nothing better than to see me ruined. For more than one reason. And I have a wife, now, to protect.'

'I never did have a chance to congratulate you on your marriage,' she says.

He inclines his head. 'Magdalena is the joy of my life. We have set up house in Vienna – I left Prince Wenzel's service, as you know. But I have begun tutoring the prince's nephew, and Magdalena is kept busy getting our house in order.'

The room they are sitting in has nothing of Charlotte in it. The walls are covered in patterned, burnt-orange silk, hung with gloomy landscapes of places she's never seen. She likes the marble chequerboard floor. But she feels wistful at the idea of *getting a house in order* – a magister's house, full of books and enchantments.

'Your wife knows nothing of—'

He shakes his head. 'Nothing. The Order's rule of secrecy is absolute.'

'So is its rule against magister-monarchs.'

155

'Indeed.' He sighs. 'It goes right to the heart of what the Order does. Do you know why it's called the Order of 1326?'

'Hamilton told me the Order was formed in that year.'

'Yes, when Pope John XXII issued a bull declaring witchcraft to be heresy. Before that, you see, Europe had its sorcerers and witches, all sorts of rituals and beliefs. Most of it was mere folklore or superstition, but not all. When magic became heresy, a secret Order took shape in Europe, with the goal of protecting scholars of magic, by keeping its study out of the public eye. It codified one particular way of working spells, and it improved its methods year over year. The Order has been, for reasons that may be obvious, the dominion of very powerful men; either they came into the Order because they were powerful, or they gained power because of their membership in it. Some very powerful men indeed.' He pauses. 'But not royalty.'

Charlotte shifts her arms, clutching one elbow protectively. 'Why not royalty?'

'Because magister-kings have proven to be dangerous. It had something to do with Sviatopolk the Accursed, in the eleventh century. For a long time, though, the Order was fairly lax about it, and succession being a difficult game to predict, some men who were already magisters became kings. One of your ancestors, Frederick III, had the motto AEIOU. Have you ever wondered why?'

She has seen that on family plaques, tapestries and portraits, but never drew a connection to the letters used in her spells. 'He was a magister?'

Soliman nods. 'And a king, because the Order didn't expect him to become king and didn't put a stop to him. He wasn't a very good magister, but after him, we became more careful. Rudolph II had some inkling about magic, from somewhere, and spent his life trying to find the truth, but we made sure he never did.'

Charlotte gets up, and he stands as well. She hasn't offered him anything; after all, he might have come to do her harm.

But he came as a friend, or as a potential friend, at least. Soliman makes her think of Joseph, of books and maps and the conversations of men. She pours brandy into two heavy cut glasses that fracture the light. She hands one to Soliman, and they stand near the window, with sunlight catching tiny motes in the air between them. How ridiculously grown-up it is to be here offering her brother's friend brandy and talking of societies and emperors. She sips to stop a nervous smile, to feel the warm sting on her tongue.

'I have no desire to become the sort of monarch who is called "the Accursed",' she says at last. 'I want to use magic to improve – I think we have a duty to use it for the good of humanity. To use it in service of science, education, agriculture. Don't you agree?'

'I do.'

He says it simply, without the slightest surprise. All those years he was watching her, checking to see whether she was working magic. He must have seen that she shared his friend Joseph's interests and ambitions. He gave her Montesquieu's book, after all.

'But you said you came to make sure that this set of circumstances – and by that you mean me, I take it – does not tear the Order apart.'

He sighs. 'The Order has never been completely successful in hiding magic here in Europe, but there was a time when it was fairly easy to find rogue magisters and prevent them from doing any harm. That time has gone. Ships crisscross every ocean, carrying people to and from this continent every day. There are those in Vienna – most notably, the doctor Anton Mesmer – who say it's no longer possible or even wise to put all our efforts into keeping magic contained to our little groups of five. Mesmer says we should develop new rules, for a new world. But many see him as a—' He stops, and smiles. 'Well, as a sort of heretic, one might say. As the senior member of the Order in Vienna, I've tried to keep the peace between the Brothers there as much as

possible, but I admit I incline to the Mesmerite view. If we cannot control magic entirely, how can we best ensure it's used safely and to good purpose?'

'Exactly,' she says, waving her glass of brandy in her excitement. 'I have so many things I want to do. I don't see why magic should be used only for the benefit of a few learned men.'

He coughs. 'Well, yes. But the conservatives in the Order argue that there are good reasons why we keep magic out of the hands of the mass of people, and though I disagree with their insistence on following every rule laid down centuries ago, I admit they have a point. Magic is dangerous.'

'Why is it more dangerous for a rogue magister than it would be for you?'

'I have been trained to know the costs, and I am protected by the Order. I am not driven by desperation. The temptation to sacrifice beyond what is wise, for example. Imagine a poor woman, desperate, hungry, with mouths to feed. Imagine she found a spell that required some terrible sacrifice.'

Charlotte considers this. 'But even if the people were ignorant of it, magic could be put to secret use for their benefit. And perhaps one day, with the proper controls, more people could use it themselves.'

He nods slowly. 'Precisely the sort of approach I think we must take. You are a queen. You are a magister. What secret uses might you consider? What do you intend to do with your magic? That is the question I came here to ask.'

Charlotte has notebooks full of facts and problems, though she has very few solutions to any of them. But there is a fat book in a cave below the city, full of spells, and surely some of them must be of more use than the few tricks Charlotte and Antoinette managed to learn. What would Joseph do, if he could do anything he wanted?

'I want to show the world that it is possible to feed a nation without the use of forced labour or serfdom.'

Soliman nods again, a tutor's nod. 'Yes.'

She gazes into the distance, thinking of her other siblings: of Josepha, of Amalia. 'I want to make sure no woman ever has to marry without her consent. I want wars to cease. And all children to be educated and – to live. To be free from disease. To begin with.'

She snaps her gaze back at him, afraid she's being childish in the scope of her ambitions, but he doesn't laugh at her.

'I can't promise you any of that is possible,' he says. 'But this is a new age, with new arts and new sciences. And new magic, perhaps! The Order is ossified, weakened by its own fears. Perhaps a magister-queen can show it the way forward into the modern world. I think perhaps you are in a good position to start. I know that your husband is, if I may say so, rather tractable.'

He might have said rotten, rather than tractable. He might have used any number of words. But he doesn't know yet how Charlotte feels about her husband. She keeps that to herself, for now.

'But I don't even have a seat on the Council yet. Bernardo Tanucci controls everything. And I gather these Brothers of Naples are dilettantes.'

'Ha, yes. Alas. The ambitious magisters in Italy go to Rome, or to Turin. Those chapters have lost members recently, because rogue magisters have turned to violence to try to steal spells. So they tempt magisters from elsewhere. The ones who stay in Naples put their own interests above the Order's rules, as you've already discovered. But it also means Your Majesty is working with dull clay here.'

'And with at least one member who'd stick a letter-opener in my ribs the first chance he got,' she says.

'Cagliostro?'

'Cagliostro. He wants to be left alone to prey on old ladies, and sees me as a threat to that. He resents me and will try to turn the chapter against me, but I can't just ignore him.'

'No indeed. His reputation has reached Vienna. One of Prince Wenzel's great-aunts has made over her will to him

in gratitude for his recognition that she is the incarnation of the goddess Isis, and the family is not taking it well.'

Charlotte makes a fist. 'He will attract attention and hamper all my plans.'

'And the Naples chapter will be distracted and ineffective,' Soliman says.

He explains that he has seen the effect of dissension within the Vienna chapter: not because of a charlatan, but because of a theatre director and scion of minor nobility named Theodore von Graben. Graben is a traditionalist who argues that if the Mesmerites get their way, rogue magic will spread like a rash across Europe. In search for evidence for their point of view, Graben and an easily led Vienna Brother have started seeing rogues behind every curtain: every irritating neighbour, every rival at court, every upstart prodigy must surely be a dangerous rogue magister. They recently concocted a conspiracy theory about the Mozart family and managed to stop the performance of the boy's opera. All Soliman's efforts to bring the chapter to a consensus have failed. For some time, he has suspected that the only way to bring peace to Vienna is for one side or the other to take over the chapter – and he knows which side he would prefer.

Now, he says, Charlotte has forced the question.

'Mesmer will see this as an opportunity, as I do. A chance for the Order to evolve. And I dare say Mesmer would sway the rest of the chapter if it weren't for Graben. Graben will never accept a magister-queen. He's a conduit for the conservative views of his friends in Paris.'

She frowns. 'Paris?'

'Prince Louis de Rohan is intent on preserving magic as a secret privilege. He can do as he likes in Paris, but I've had enough of his influence on Vienna.'

Charlotte is not so sanguine about Rohan, given that his path is likely to cross Antoinette's frequently. 'Are the Brothers of Paris all very traditional, then?'

'They're all the sons or grandsons of former Brothers. It's

become an inherited privilege, in Paris, and so perhaps they cling to it differently. But it's not the same elsewhere in France. In Marseille, the Brothers are quite scholarly, and take no interest in political debates. I think it would be the safest place for someone like Cagliostro. He could do little harm to the Order there. I could prevail on the Brothers I know in Marseille to summon Cagliostro, to replace a Brother who died last year.' Soliman stops, and thinks for a moment, tapping one finger against his brandy glass. 'We may be able to help each other, Your Majesty.'

He explains that Theodore von Graben has an invitation to go to Stockholm to run a new theatre there, but he's resisted because the Order in Stockholm already has its five Brothers. It would be a great relief to get him out of Vienna, Soliman says. The Stockholm chapter already inclines to Graben's views, but they're so enmeshed in the mess of Swedish politics that they won't bother too much about the rest of Europe.

'The lone Mesmerite in Stockholm is a young man named Isaac Lars Silfversparre, who has been miserable there. If Your Majesty would consent to welcome Silfversparre to Naples, Stockholm would have room for Theodore von Graben.'

'Why not simply bring this Silfversparre to Vienna, Dr Soliman? An even trade for Graben?'

'If Graben suspects I've had anything to do with it, he'll stay in Vienna out of spite. Silfversparre is about the age for the Grand Tour, so it will all seem perfectly natural if he comes to Italy. I think he could be a great help to you here.'

Charlotte nods. 'All right, then. Isaac Lars Silfversparre to Naples, Theodore von Graben to Stockholm, and Cagliostro to Marseille.'

With a smile, she thinks of how nervous she was when Soliman arrived. Even within the Order, there is politics – and she is good at politics. At last, she sees a path ahead. She has allies and plans.

She considers asking more about Paris and Louis de Rohan, but then decides she does not want Soliman's thoughts tending to Antoinette. She trusts him now, but Antoinette's secret is her own to keep.

14 August 1770
Charlotte to Antoinette

My dear, I have a confession. First, let me tell you that there's no reason to worry about me, though I know you will! I met with Angelo Soliman recently. He now knows I am a magister, and so do five others, here in Naples. The Order of 1326 has a chapter here, and they have admitted me.

Sweet sister, I did not make this decision lightly. This palace is a prison: my husband is a lout and his chief adviser stops me at every turn. I need to learn more magic or I'll be useless here, and useless to you. I need to learn what I can, about magic and about the Order, so I can keep you safe in France. Please forgive me, Antoinette, but believe that I'm safe and I've done what I think is best for both of us.

I have sworn to keep the Order's secrets. I consider that vow to cover its rituals, its spells, and its magical processes, but I will tell you anything else I can, of course! I haven't told them you're a magister, and I don't intend to. But as the other chapters across Europe learn about me, new suspicion is sure to fall on you. I'm sorry about that. Please be careful, especially if you encounter Prince Louis de Rohan. I don't think they will hurt you – and I will do whatever I can to keep you safe – but be careful. I'll find out what I can about the state of things in Paris.

My heart hurts when I think of how overwhelmed you must be in your new life. How I wish I were there to help you.

One last bit of advice: surround yourself with mirrors wherever you can. Mirrors have a scattering effect on magic, which can keep a room safe from outside magical influence. It isn't a sure protection, but it helps.

Apparently most of the kings of Europe, including Mama, have been advised to use mirrors by people they thought were decorators.

Be well. I will be thinking of you on your journey. You are never alone.

Your sister,
Charlotte

CHAPTER FOURTEEN

*The Queen's Pocket – How Spells Are Added to the
Reconditus – The Brothers of Naples – The Problem
of Tanucci – Honesty*

Under her panniers, the Queen of Naples wears a capacious
pocket, a pale rose-coloured pouch of linen. Inside, depending
on the day, she may have: her white gloves, an enamelled
pot of rouge that will not fade until it is touched with a rose
petal, a gold snuffbox that buys favours, a silver-handled
hairbrush for taking memories, a rosewood box of face
powder, a comb of ivory that enhances her ability to do
arithmetic, a velvet mask that makes it difficult for people
to recognize her, a silver-handled folding knife, a map of the
world, an earring that lets the wearer understand any
language spoken, and other things.

She is not the girl who left Vienna.

The summer of 1771 arrives, and the court moves to the
sprawling Caserta Palace, a few hours' carriage ride outside
the city. It always reminds Charlotte of childhood summers
at Schönbrunn. Up on a high hill, and the skies overhead
as dramatic as those of a fresco. The gardens are so vast that
she almost gets lost in them.

Half the rooms at Caserta have chickens and ducks running

through them at all hours of the day and night, and the other half have Ferdinand's mistresses lurking behind the screens and tapestries.

But Charlotte has some privacy now, thanks to the spells in the *Reconditus*.

She has an enchanted candlestick that will gutter three times if someone comes into a room while it is lit: a guard against intruders. Another spell, on a candle itself, can dampen the sound in a room. She has seen a spell for a sword that will point to any hidden passageways; Charlotte, alas, does not have a sword, but she can work on that.

The firescreen spell seems the most useful of all: a way to hide a room. It requires a treasure sacrifice, but Charlotte still has a few things from her trousseau that no one will miss but her, including a gold and sapphire brooch in the shape of a cross, which belonged to her grandmother. It breaks before it decays; the sapphires roughen, darken, and crack, as the gold pits and darkens into a lump that lasts a long time, while her little bathroom smells like the deepest, darkest pit in the world. It's three in the morning, and no one will come unless she calls. All the same, her heart is pounding.

But then there is nothing but a stain where the brooch was, and nothing but void where she had written 'I hope to see Antoinette again'. The sacrifices are gone; the spell worked; the room is hidden. For a price in treasure and hope, Charlotte has a little privacy.

The firescreen is one of her own embroidery projects, a pastoral landscape with apple-cheeked farmers, inside a simple wooden frame. It isn't very large and not very good at keeping the heat and sparks off, but it's very portable. She can take it to any room and that room will suddenly drop out of everyone else's memory, as if it never existed.

The Palace of Caserta has rooms to spare. Ferdinand's father was jealous of Versailles, and undertook to build a palace so enormous that it is still under construction two

decades later, with some wings filled with dust and the shouts of workmen – but no noisier than the habitable sections, with Ferdinand's standing invitation to the local animals and his many bosom friends. The painted ceilings soar; every room could be a cathedral. The walls are covered in patterned silk from the nearby factory at San Leucio, in yellows, greens, reds.

At first, she places the enchanted firescreen in her state bedroom, forgetting that it would make it impossible for servants to get to Ferdinand's adjoining rooms that way. They all went the long way around, causing incredible delays in his routine one night, which made her smile, but realize that she must be more careful.

So for her secret room she chooses a small boudoir at the very corner of the palace, a room that no one would pass through to get anywhere else, a room that connects only to her own apartments. The walls are bordered with mirrors. Gilt candle sconces jut out from them like wizened branches, beckoning the unwary on a forest path. On the floor of multicoloured stone, she draws an ashen star.

No one knows this room exists; she can come here and perform magic without being disturbed. She can take the firescreen with her when the court goes to the Naples or Portici palaces. She has a place of her own.

She may not have a child yet, or the respect of the King, or a seat on the Council of Naples. But she has magic and magisters to help her.

And since Ferdinand is usually either hunting or with his mistress, she has time to work.

In the mornings, she reads the reports of Ferdinand's ministers, procured for her in secret by Caterina using a duplication enchantment. In the evenings, she reads whatever Soliman sends her to further her education in all things, although she prefers the books on statecraft. This summer she is reading the *Nakaz*, Catherine of Russia's new statement of principles for a modern nation.

In between, she practises using her gloves, persuading her ladies-in-waiting to do small things with no consequence: to put their embroidery down and look out of the window, or to say something about the weather. She's getting better at it.

She's also studying spells from the *Reconditus*.

It is a book that takes sacrifices. Since new spells from other magisters in other parts of the world only appear when it is fed, every magister must take a turn, at each monthly meeting. Caterina doesn't hunt rogue magisters, the way that Cagliostro and Caramanico do, but she seems to find spells nonetheless; she has friends everywhere, and sources for everything. Charlotte takes her turns every sixth month, adding a spell from the embroidered book. (The unreliable shoe and the doll pin are already there.) Many of the spells that Countess Ertag found somewhere, which the Order did not know about, were women's spells: thimbles that divide, ribbons that mend, pockets and fans and gloves. What might Ertag have taught her, had she lived?

But Ertag did not have the spells in the ever-growing *Reconditus*. The strength of the Order is not in the individual magister. And so Charlotte makes her sacrifices, so that she can learn more and more and more.

In a letter, Soliman told her there have been magister-scholars who spent their lives travelling from city to city, noting down the order of the spells in each manifestation of the *Reconditus*, tracing the pathways of magic through the generations. The debate about which spell was the first to be placed in the *Reconditus* has grown so heated over the years that at least one magister's death in a duel can be attributed to it. Likewise the infamous rivalry between the chapters in Barcelona and Madrid, he writes darkly, saying no more about it.

Thanks to the *Reconditus*, Charlotte has so many new spells now, and she reads them over and over, making notes about what sacrifices she might make for each one.

The Brothers of Naples come to Caserta frequently, between official meetings, to sit in the gardens and discuss magic and gossip. Charlotte likes this better than the damp cavern with the silly red hats and rituals; the only reason she can see for visiting it every month is to check for new spells in the *Reconditus*. Instead of being an interloper at the palace, now she can play host, and she likes seeing her Brothers here: Hamilton with his battered notebooks, the sleek and sophisticated Prince of Caramanico, Vincenzo Lunardi pacing excitedly and examining the limestone walls in the grotto for fossils.

And the new member, the replacement for Cagliostro, whom Soliman successfully spirited away. Isaac Lars Silfversparre is a blond man in his early twenties, with a soldier's bearing and a gift for the violin. Sometimes in the evening, he plays for them, setting the instrument between his chin – always gilded with stubble – and his broad shoulders. Caterina is quite smitten with him, but Charlotte is merely grateful. He is a committed Mesmerite and wants nothing more than to put magic to some use – apparently the Brothers of Stockholm have been nearly as fractious as those of Vienna, and Silfversparre is relieved to be among people who, as he puts it, 'want to do more with their time than lock up midwives and fortune tellers'.

At every meeting of Brothers, Charlotte argues that Naples must demonstrate to the rest of the Order how magic can be put to use in a state project. No other chapter can do that. It would be a clear signal that Naples is the future of the Order.

To begin, she wants to turn the former Jesuit schools into royal institutions, with proper uniforms and teachers and books. And students, for that matter. Even the Jesuits had trouble convincing the parents in the poorest villages that their older children ought to study rather than work. Unlike Maria Theresa, Charlotte has neither the power nor the inclination to solve the problem with a mandatory education

decree. The Brothers will have to find some way to compensate and support the families, and persuade them to send their children. Lunardi is excited to try something he calls a 'Pied Piper spell', so Charlotte leaves that with him.

She has enough to worry about: Charlotte needs the King to agree to use the school buildings. She will need to do something about Tanucci.

The Red Room at Caserta is one of her favourites.

Here they come to drink coffee in the evening with Tanucci sometimes, when Ferdinand has decided he should check on what's happening in his kingdom. Usually, this follows a letter from his father, the King of Spain. Ferdinand approaches these conversations resentfully, knowing that Tanucci only humours him when it comes to matters of state. But it is something he forces himself to do. And he invites Charlotte, more and more. At first, she thought it was so that he'd have someone to make feel small. But increasingly, he invites her because she asks clever questions of Tanucci, and so takes the pressure off him.

Tonight she watched her husband, all through dinner, gearing himself up for it.

Tanucci and Ferdinand are drinking port in chairs facing each other.

She sits to the side, with her needlework, maintaining a demure posture.

Charlotte's needle finds the hidden space in the weave, pricks apart the weft, leaves behind its scarlet thread. She is embroidering her monogram, to adorn a cushion. She will put her monogram on every surface she can find in this palace. She will brand this place with her mark.

As Tanucci runs through his list of new grievances against the Church and his worries about expenses, Charlotte stays quiet.

'Well, what are we going to do to bring in more money, Tanucci?' Ferdinand asks, covering his lack of intelligence with brusqueness as he always does.

'Luckily, Sire, the confiscated Jesuit property should bring in some income, once it's sold. I've written up an inventory.'

'What about the schools?' Charlotte asks mildly.

'Everything can be sold,' Tanucci says.

Charlotte clears her throat. 'There are so many children in Naples—' she begins.

Ferdinand interrupts. 'Of course there are! Most men in Naples don't have frigid Germans for wives!'

Tanucci smiles indulgently while Ferdinand laughs. Charlotte's face burns. She thrusts her needle into the cloth and leaves it there for the time it takes to breathe in and out.

'It is a question of how best to invest what the state has recovered from the Jesuits, it seems to me,' she says. 'You have exiled the Jesuits; you say they taught superstition and cant. Fine. Then we should put in new teachers. More schools. I don't see why the schools can't continue just as they are, with secular instruction.'

Tanucci smirks. 'Your Majesty is newly arrived here, and unfamiliar with our customs. The poor children of Naples learn best from their masters, where they have them, and from Nature, where they do not. They are simple people.'

'They have been kept that way,' she snaps. 'Do you want a nation of masters, or a nation of the mastered? I wonder.'

Then she takes her white gloves off the armrest of the gilded chair and draws them up over her arms. She tugs the ends of the gloves up over her elbows, smooths the satin over the backs of her hands.

Charlotte has never been one to move her hands as she speaks. She generally holds herself still, aware always that she was born to be an image, painted and posed, meeting the gaze of the world's unblinking curiosity. But now, deliberately, she waves her hand.

'Tell us the truth, Tanucci. Tell us what you want.'

And he does.

'What I want is for all you Bourbons and Habsburgs to go

off and amuse yourselves and let me do as I see fit in Naples,' Tanucci says. As his mouth forms the words, the rest of his face contorts, as if he's having some kind of stroke. His eyes go wide and a vein bulges in his forehead. He claps his hand over his mouth, like a child, and Charlotte can't help but laugh, louder and longer than she's laughed for a long time.

Ferdinand stares at Tanucci, and then stares at Charlotte.

Tanucci says, 'I didn't mean – Your Majesty, I didn't mean to say that.'

Ferdinand growls, 'This Bourbon wishes to use the Jesuit schools for the good of the kingdom and make the people love us. See that it is done, Tanucci.'

Tanucci nods, his face red. 'Excuse me, Your Majesty. I must – I am unwell.'

He stands and stumbles out of the room.

Charlotte smiles. All the practice with the gloves was worth it. At nineteen years old, at last, she sees the life that she was born to live stretching out in front of her.

CHAPTER FIFTEEN

Vincenzo Lunardi Is Frustrated — A Visit to San Leucio —
The Smell of Wet Silkworm — Ethics — A Letter
from Vienna

Having Ferdinand agree to use the Jesuit schools as secular institutions was only the first step. How much easier it would be if she had a seat on the Council! But for that, she needs to bear Ferdinand a son, and despite the depressing regularity with which he visits her bed, she isn't pregnant yet.

So Charlotte has to find a way to ensure someone hires the teachers and stocks the schools with supplies. It takes some magical duplication of ledgers and letters — with a few key alterations — and some subterfuge on the part of Caterina, but at last the Brothers manage to get some funds into the hands of Vincenzo Lunardi, who now appears as head of the education programme in the official documents, if anyone were to look. Lunardi grumbles somewhat at the work, but it gives him a chance to try his Pied Piper spell and to test a few others, such as a memory spell. And the Prince of Caramanico makes it very clear that such a position would be beneath him, and Hamilton is a foreign envoy, and Charlotte needs Caterina by her side.

The schools open and, bit by bit, the plan is a success.

But Lunardi is frustrated. It isn't enough, he says, to persuade the children and their parents (through magical means or otherwise) that they ought to be in school. The older children can't leave their jobs, not only because their families need the money but also because someone has to do that work.

So Charlotte decides to pay a visit to some working children, to see what might be possible.

The village of San Leucio is just a short drive north of Caserta, up in the hills, where the water runs down to the palace in a long aqueduct. There's a stately hunting lodge, a square of creamy buildings set against the olive-green hills, with palm trees in the courtyard overlooking a wide view down to Vesuvius.

Ferdinand's father, finding himself richly endowed with hunting lodges, decided to put the place to better use. He planted mulberry trees and founded a silk factory there, converting parts of the old lodge into lodging for the families of the workers.

Charlotte is well aware that gossips at court refer to the silk-works as her husband's 'harem'. Like most of the gossip about Ferdinand, it's plausible because of his character, but overestimates his energy. She hasn't known him to go up to San Leucio once. But it's obvious why the rumours started. Many of the weaving and twisting tasks are the domain of teenage girls from destitute families. They work en masse, separated from their family members who are out doing the other labour to maintain the silkworms and keep the colony running.

Charlotte can come and go as she likes these days, between her new skill with the white gloves and the fact that Tanucci seems less eager to cross swords with her. She drives to San Leucio with Caterina. They take a cold lunch in the drab, underused royal apartment, and after the dusty drive, Charlotte wishes she could take a proper bath, but doesn't relish the idea of a wooden tub and servants she doesn't

know. Perhaps she could build a bathhouse here on this open hillside, in an ancient style, with frescoes on the walls.

In the meantime, there is work to be done. The superintendent takes them out of the main complex and shows them one of the connected cottages, with a little loom in the front room, and a kitchen in the back, bedrooms upstairs. The cottage's occupants, a family of four, stand quietly during this inspection. The youngest girl gives Charlotte a posy of orange blossom, the little white flowers shining as tightly as silkworm cocoons.

The cocoons themselves do not smell as nice. There's a strong, fishy smell of dead silkworm in one of the long, low buildings attached to the old lodge. Girls pull the shining white threads onto bobbins, and younger children run back and forth, resetting parts of the machines.

A matching building holds the big looms. It's a place of wooden gears and metal hinges, of girls in drab dresses, punctuated by swathes of bright woven silk: yellow fleurs-de-lys on a red background, bottle-green with dark vines, deep robin's-egg blue. It's as if parts of other rooms, in other places, have intruded here.

At least two dozen girls work the looms with strong arms and set expressions.

'As you can see,' says the superintendent, a minor noble who must have done something to annoy Tanucci to be given this job, 'the whole process is here, from the trees to the cloth. It's a self-contained world; the families have garden plots, and their marriages are even performed in the church.'

'And where are the school buildings?'

'The children are trained alongside their older siblings.'

'But where do they learn to read and write?'

The superintendent gives her a tight smile. 'The priest runs a small school once a week to help them with their names and that sort of thing.'

That won't do, Charlotte thinks. In Prussia they've had universal primary education for nearly a decade; it is not

impossible. Parts of the lodge are empty, and can easily be converted to school buildings. But she's already having trouble supplying the former Jesuit schools. Creating more schools for these factory children means yet more money Charlotte will have to redirect from the state finances, hoping that no one notices. Tanucci may be a corrupt incompetent but the cold fact is that he's not wrong about the state of Naples' coffers.

There is one spell that could help: the duplication spell in the *Reconditus*, which Caterina uses to copy documents. It's a simple one, and can multiply nearly anything, but it requires a little sacrifice every time. To multiply a ream of paper or a bottle of ink, one would have to sacrifice a small quantity of blood, and the human body only has so much blood in it at any one time.

If they had more magisters – or if the students could manufacture their own supplies . . . A self-contained world.

She looks at the girls working the loom, those hard-working girls who have nothing but their labour and the glints in their eyes. Charlotte has said all along that she wants to use magic for the benefit of all. But the problems of government are problems on a scale that dwarfs the sacrifices any single magister – or even a half-dozen magisters – could make. To remake the world using magic, she will have to remake the way the world does magic.

1 October 1771
Angelo Soliman to Maria Carolina

Your Majesty,
   Your question about having non-magisters perform small sacrifices for the public good, without full understanding of what they were doing, is an interesting one. It may not work at all; intention is key. Leaving that aside, what are the ethics of it? Can an action be good if it treats a human being as a resource, even if no material harm comes to that person?

176

David Hume would argue that 'public utility is the sole origin of justice'. We can say that an action is good if its consequences are good.

That last point is key, I think. The rule against non-magisters knowing anything about magic is there for good reason. A desperate person may make a desperate sacrifice, and so knowledge of magic could do harm. Which brings us from philosophy to the rules of our Order, of course, which we have already begun to break, and to change, and to re-form. Is this such a rule? Can the very bodies of the people be put into the hands of their sovereign?

One might say that they already are; the roads in some countries are built by their labour, which is taken as due and necessary. Sovereigns require their people to kill and die; why not require them to contribute to the public welfare? Informed consent would be, arguably, a greater danger to them than ignorance, until the Order and the world evolve.

If the question is not mere philosophy, I urge you to be careful. The idea holds many risks – and if you embark on it, you must take pains to make sure no Brothers outside your trusted circle know about it. A desperate person may make a desperate sacrifice, as we have discussed, and the same is true of a desperate magister, who may choose to denounce Your Majesty over something like this – or worse, to copy it, but without safeguards.

I suggest you take some time to consider these questions, and not act too hastily.

With my sincerest respects,

> Yours in fraternity,
> Angelo Soliman

CHAPTER SIXTEEN

Married Life — The Grand Corps — How to Walk at
Versailles — A Planned Encounter — An Unplanned
Encounter — The War Room

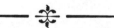

Antoinette's mornings begin with a dozen strangers dressing her. The Comtesse de Noailles, her *dame d'honneur*, supervises all of this with thin lips. Madame Etiquette, Antoinette calls her, although she doesn't mean it unkindly. And Madame Etiquette corrects Antoinette several times a day, although she doesn't mean that unkindly.

And every day ends as every day begins, with strangers stripping her and watching her wash. Antoinette stands rigid as the court takes its due from her body.

Sometimes she feels as helpless and manipulated as she did when Charlotte used her gloves on her, that moment on stage when she was unable to move except as directed by an outside force. What is left of her, here? She is a doll to be dressed and undressed, a marionette.

For the briefest of moments, undressed and in bed, she is almost alone. But she hears footsteps. She takes a breath.

Louis comes to her bed as his attendants close the door on them. It is a ceremony, every time he makes the attempt,

179

although now that a year has passed since the wedding, the mood of the attendants is more funeral than charivari.

They lie next to each other in their night clothes by the light of one candle, the sheets tucked over their chests.

Antoinette leans on one elbow and looks into her husband's face. She tries to look beguiling without looking intimidating.

'My dear, you are so lovely,' Louis says.

He caresses her hair: her real hair, unpowdered and loose, darker than it was when she arrived in France, now more brass than gold.

It is not exciting, but it warms her. Antoinette snuggles closer to him, puts her hand on his chest. Beneath the night-dress, his chest is soft, not well muscled. It is her husband's chest, her dear husband's.

'Shall we try?' she whispers.

In answer, he kisses her, and she rolls onto her back. He rolls on top of her and fumbles at their two nightdresses until they are both up to their chests.

She feels the pressure of his penis against her. With her hands on his back, she holds him to her, rises against him.

He rolls off. 'I'm sorry. Not tonight.'

She swallows, nods. For a little while, they lie next to each other in silence, watching the candlelight flicker across the carved ceiling. Antoinette has done everything she can think of to make herself lovable, and yet here she lies, unloved.

After a while, Louis kisses her cheek, bids her goodnight and uses the semi-secret passageway to go back to his own room, and she is alone in the dark.

31 October 1771
Maria Theresa to Marie Antoinette

My daughter,
In two days' time, you will be sixteen years old. I look often at the miniature you sent, though I see there someone

without the blush of youth that you had when you left
Austria. You will never be able to rely on beauty, so you
must use the other gifts God has given you, such as
sweetness, charm, and patience.

My ambassador, Count Mercy, writes that you put those
gifts to good use among the circle of courtiers that you call
friends, that you have a gift for making everyone think you
are speaking directly to them, with every remark you utter.
This is all to the good, but he also writes that you never
speak a word to important people, and that when the crowds
come to watch you at mealtimes, you eat little and say
nothing. You must take care that people do not lose the
esteem they had for you on your arrival, when you made
such a favourable impression. They will forget, so easily,
if you let them.

Where is the full list of the books you are reading? I hope
you are getting good advice in that matter. You mentioned
your husband's love for David Hume's History of England;
yes, I think that would be fine for you to read, if only to
please the Dauphin, although you must remember it was
written by a Protestant.

Joseph has been travelling for weeks, trying to see what
can be done about the famine; we have had three years of
crop failure, and I fear that whatever we do, many will die.
Meanwhile, I watch very pretty manoeuvres and hope that
our troops will not be needed for another war. I don't know
how much you know about the current difficulties over
Poland – you do not meet with the ambassador often
enough. I have taken back a few small territories on the
edge, which were once part of the Kingdom of Hungary.
The rest of the country will soon be divided between
Austria, Prussia, and Russia.

Your task is to ensure that this does not threaten our
alliance with France, which has a friendly relationship with
Poland, and may look unfavourably on the partition – a
partition that is absolutely necessary to check the growing

power of Russia, which has absorbed so many lands from its Ottoman war. The warm feeling between the Bourbon and Habsburg families may be all we have to prevent another conflict in which so many young soldiers would die on the field, come home wounded or diseased; in which the already barren fields of the Empire would be stripped bare. Your sister in Naples would find herself in the territory of the enemy.

Speaking of Charlotte, I will share with you how overjoyed I am that Ferdinand has made her his wife, completely, right from the wedding night. My contentment at the affairs of all your siblings is overshadowed by my concern for you. I do not think you understand the seriousness of your situation — or you choose not to understand it.

Sending you my best wishes on your birthday,

I remain,
Your loving mother

10 November 1771
Charlotte to Antoinette

My dear Antoinette,

I have wonderful news: I'm expecting a child at last. If it is a boy, I will have my seat on the Council, and an official role in the governance of Naples.

My dreams have been terrible, and no wonder, as I try to sleep wrapped around one pillow to save my poor hips and with my head propped on three more so I can breathe through a nose that seems to have swollen at least as much as my feet have.

(If only there were spells for all these aches, for the heartburn. I suppose magisters have focused on more important matters; or, at least, the magisters whose spells ended up in Ertag's hands and in those of my fellow Brothers.)

My heart aches to hear that you have nowhere to do magic, nowhere to be safe. Please do not ask where I learned these spells, and you must not tell anyone else about them, not even your rogue friend. I have enclosed the firescreen spell for the secret room. And the spell for the candle that dampens sound in a room when lit, but it requires a significant memory sacrifice, and of course the candle burns to nothing like any other, so do use it sparingly. After all, I have three years and three months more memories than you do, little sister.

I have the utmost faith that you will conceive, Antoinette. The difficulties with your husband will solve themselves soon enough. He is young and awkward, that's all.

Enjoy your peace while you can.

Your loving
Charlotte

Antoinette knows she has to reconcile with Madame du Barry, to start with. In fact, it piques her a little that there's a need to reconcile at all; she's been too nervous to speak to the woman, with her impertinent little smile and the cultivated blankness of her stare. But everyone thinks there's a feud, and that will make the King unhappy with Antoinette. Perhaps even unhappy enough to send her home, with the marriage still unconsummated.

She worked herself up to speak to Madame du Barry one day in the presence of the King, when all the courtiers were milling about. But all Antoinette could think to say was, 'There are a lot of people at Versailles today.'

How cold the Dauphine is to the Comtesse du Barry, people think! But it is not coldness; it is a terrible heat, a burning inadequacy. It, whatever it is, has taken on a life of its own.

And her husband's aunts, who bear no love for the royal

183

mistress, supplanter of their influence with their father the King, have done their best to help nurture it.

Twice, Antoinette has been scheduled to meet with Madame du Barry, and twice, Madame Adélaïde has helpfully created some minor emergency and called Antoinette to her rooms. Only afterwards, when Antoinette arrived pink and flustered, did she recognize the conspiracy.

So, on this evening, Antoinette has prevented that by asking Madame Adélaïde and her sisters to assist her while she gets dressed for the encounter. They assist by sitting on chaises, watching and making comments.

She tries very hard always to think of them as Mesdames Adélaïde, Victoire and Sophie, although the entire court calls them Aunt Rag, Aunt Pig, and Aunt Grub.

The King's daughters might have lost the childish nicknames that he gave them, had they married and moved away to other countries, other courts. Antoinette, after all, lost her name, and chose another. But Mesdames never married.

Adélaïde decided she was too good for any foreign prince, and as there was no French man other than her brother or her nephew high-ranking enough for a daughter of France, that was that.

Victoire and Sophie, two nervous rabbits raised in a nunnery, do what Adélaïde tells them to do.

All three aunts are married, in a sense, to the court: they know Versailles not only at the superficial level of etiquette, as Madame de Noailles does, but in its guts and workings. While the aunts are present as Antoinette prepares for her meeting with Madame du Barry, it's Madame de Noailles who dresses her.

'Such white skin,' says the *dame d'honneur*, lacing her into her stays. 'One can hardly tell where it ends and your chemise begins. It would show through the stays so nicely, in a *grand corps*.'

Antoinette sighs at the mention of the French instrument of torture, the corset that puts other corsets to shame.

'I can't move my arms in a *grand corps*,' she says.

'Well, one doesn't need to move one's arms a great deal,' says Madame Victoire.

The other aunts titter. In reaching middle age unmarried, they have achieved a sort of dispensation that allows them to flout the fashions of the court. Many days they spend in their adjoining rooms wearing comfortable old mantuas. When the time comes to greet the King, in moments when etiquette demands it, they step into panniers, tie a sort of false train around their waists with strings, and throw black taffeta cloaks over everything. Antoinette envies them.

'The *grand corps*', says Madame de Noailles, 'might help with the shoulders.'

The blasted shoulders. Despite all the pain she went through with the painting, or perhaps because of it, there's still something not quite right about them, it seems, and all of Versailles can see it.

'Oh, yes,' all the aunts say at once. 'The shoulders.'

Madame de Noailles frowns. 'Mesdames are teasing you, Your Royal Highness. After all, they are past thirty.'

The aunts groan and pretend to be offended.

'But His Majesty is very strict about the dress and figures of young women at court,' the *dame d'honneur* continues. 'He follows the rules set down by the Sun King.'

'Louis XIV had very particular ideas about the figures of young women,' says Madame Sophie.

Antoinette sighs as the *dame d'honneur* puts the final pin in her bodice. 'Well, luckily I am not off to see the Sun King tonight. I am only going to speak for a few minutes with Madame du Barry before bed. A chance encounter.'

'I hope you're prepared,' says Madame Adélaïde. 'She will be.'

It is fitting that this very carefully arranged chance encounter is to take place in the War Room, on the far side of the Hall of Mirrors from the Dauphine's apartments. They have chosen

a moment late in the evening, when the activity of Versailles is concentrated in the smaller rooms, and the Hall of Mirrors is empty save for a few guards. Madame de Noailles follows – Antoinette hardly ever moves through Versailles alone – but at a long remove, to give Antoinette an opportunity to speak to the Comtesse du Barry woman to woman.

The corridors of Versailles are perilous to the absent-minded, but Antoinette has perfected the art of avoiding dog dirt and scraps of food. A woman walking in panniers is liable to waddle, unless she perfects a certain gliding stride.

Antoinette, taking no chances, wears a new set of shoes she enchanted that allow her to walk on just a quarter-inch of air. When they were very young, soon after they received the embroidered book, Charlotte used the same spell to make Wolfgang Mozart trip. It was a prank; the girls had learned for themselves that walking in the shoes takes practice. Mozart was a child of six, and didn't seem to mind falling into Antoinette's arms. She and Charlotte used the shoe spell to help them sneak into each other's rooms. Here in Versailles, Antoinette finds it useful for helping her walk gracefully, room to room, past the liveried ushers and uniformed guards. She never tangles in her skirt and she never waddles.

An unusual effect, though, is that she makes no sound of footsteps when she walks. She's never noticed it before now; usually there are so many people around, so many wooden heels on wooden floors. Tonight, she glides like a ghost towards the War Room, and she can see through the arch that the du Barry is not alone.

She's with the King, and another man, seated at three sides of a small table. None of them are facing the Hall of Mirrors, so they don't see her approach.

Their voices carry so far that she hears them before she's even at the door.

'She doesn't wear the *grand corps*.' Madame du Barry's velvet voice. 'Her shoulders are a disaster. Is it that one is higher than the other? I'd heard that about her and I swear

it's so. I don't know why she doesn't wear the *grand corps*. Her figure is going to rot.'

'She doesn't wear it because she couldn't give a shit about Versailles, or about her husband, or about France,' says another voice, and Antoinette's hand goes to her throat. It's Rohan!

She'd heard that Louis de Rohan and Jeanne du Barry were friends. Why is he here? Charlotte has promised to tell Antoinette if the Order learns about her knowledge of magic; she has promised that Antoinette need not worry about them. But perhaps Charlotte doesn't know everything there is to know about everything. Unlikely, but Antoinette has to admit the possibility. It seems so reckless of Charlotte to reveal herself to the very Order that spied on them as children. Charlotte has said that Rohan and the other Brothers of Paris have no power over her, but they do know Charlotte's a magister.

'Husband, ha,' Rohan is saying. 'We all know it's in name only. And can you blame the boy, really? With her dressing like a country countess, and getting a matronly stomach without ever being a real wife?'

'But can she be sent back?'

The worst blow of all: the King's voice. The King! Antoinette looks down at her *robe a l'anglaise*; it's a beautiful shade of yellow, but it's not formal enough for a meeting with the King.

'Anything is possible,' says Rohan. 'The boy's revulsion for his bride may be a blessing. Gives us a chance to annul, now, before it's too late.'

The usher is trying his best to pretend he hasn't heard a thing. She could turn and leave. She could return to the aunts, to Madame de Noailles's dour ministrations. She could accept that she is unloved and unwanted, that she has failed in the one thing she came to France to do.

Antoinette sweeps into enemy territory.

Being inside the War Room is like being inside a sculpture of dark marble and bright gold, with soaring paintings over-

head and an enormous bas-relief of the Sun King dominating one wall. It's a terrifying place, even without these people in it.

'Ah,' says the King as she enters and curtseys. 'My grandson's lovely bride. Please, come in, Antoinette. I was just wondering whether you've heard anything from your mother. I haven't had a letter lately, and I wondered if all was well.'

No one says anything about the fact that this was to be a meeting with Madame du Barry alone. The mistress's face is the usual mocking mask. Is it a trap, or simply a misunderstanding? In any case, if they won't acknowledge it, then neither will Antoinette.

Antoinette does not let her voice waver. 'Your Majesty, I had a letter just this morning and she is very well.'

'Ah. Good, good. I thought if anything were wrong, you'd be the first to know.'

The du Barry makes a face Antoinette cannot interpret; or maybe it's just the weight of her hair.

'Indeed, Sire,' Antoinette says slowly. 'My mother would not let three days pass without a long list of instructions to me.' She sucks in her stomach and wishes she could see herself in a mirror to know whether her shoulders are aligned.

But she has said the wrong thing, after all; Rohan's eyes roll upward, and then towards the King, as if she's said something horribly significant. And then she realizes it: they do not want her receiving instructions from Austria. She's confirmed their fears.

She looks from face to face. The old King's pitying grimace; the Prince de Rohan's sneer; the Comtesse du Barry's wide-eyed disinterest.

And there, above them all, the pale bas-relief as round and big as the sun, the Sun King on horseback, crushing his enemies.

It was he, a century ago, who put all the rules in place that govern Antoinette now: the hierarchy of ladies who

take her clothes off and put her clothes on, the titles and forms of address, even the clothing (the dreaded *grand corps*; she should have worn it). He was all stage glamour and cheap tricks, but his ghost cannot be dislodged from this place.

Well, she won't be dislodged, either. She won't be a ghost before her time. *Be so good that the people of France will say I have sent them an angel,* her mother said. Antoinette isn't Charlotte; she doesn't know how to make people respect her.

She only knows how to make them love her.

Antoinette can't go back to Austria, a failure, a disgrace. Louis might never make her a wife, but by God, she will be a queen anyway. So they want her to wear better clothes? She will wear *such* clothes. A country countess, indeed. She will make all the people love her. It can be done. She has so much left to sacrifice.

'Your Majesty, you are most kind,' she says, carefully looking only at the King, as though Madame du Barry and Louis de Rohan do not exist. 'I hope you will come to one of my card parties some day. I have made it my goal to beat the Comte d'Artois at whist, and it will be a moment to remember.'

She smiles her most brilliant smile at her enemies.

CHAPTER SEVENTEEN

*The Hairdresser – Antoinette's Wardrobe Book – A Card
Party – Gifts and Wagers – The Chevalier Plays
the Violin*

Léonard Autié is a legend among hairdressers. The Marquise
de Langeac claims him as her lover but can't lay claim to his
exclusive services; Madame du Barry, apparently, receives
him in her bath.

Antoinette has several hairdressers already, and the
morning ritual is daunting enough. But now she must have
the most fashionable hairdresser, the best dresses. She must
become perfect.

*She couldn't give a shit about Versailles, or about her husband,
or about France.*

None of these accusations is true. The trouble is that
Versailles, Louis, and France don't care enough for her. She
has not made any of them fall in love with her. She has
failed, and the alliance hangs in the balance. But she will not
fail for much longer.

Versailles is the easiest territory to conquer. She has been
too dowdy, too plain. Very well: she will become the most
fashionable woman at court.

She is awake, sitting on the edge of her bed in her morning

191

gown, when Madame Etiquette and the court ladies arrive to perform the rituals. Antoinette holds up her hand, then points at one of her ladies-in-waiting.

'Madame Campan will help me arrange my hair first, in my private dressing room,' she says. 'And I have sent for Léonard Autié to join me there to assist.'

Madame Etiquette goes beet red.

Campan, though, is smiling. 'You've destroyed her, Your Highness,' she whispers as she closes the door on the little antechamber, all robin's-egg blues and whites.

Antoinette laughs. 'She is indestructible.'

Monsieur Léonard arrives only a little late, breathless. Deliberately so, probably: maintaining his reputation for being always in demand, and always fleeing husbands. He looks like a performer of some kind – a stage magician perhaps. Between his sharp nose and chin, a curling red mouth. On his head, a wig of layered, fat white curls.

He bows low, and the wig does not shift.

'Your Royal Highness,' he says. 'I thought this day would never come.'

He speaks with the round, deliberate syllables and thick consonants of southern France, so different to the broad, smooth Parisian accent.

She inclines her head. 'I didn't want to impose on you. I know you're busy.'

'Never too busy for Madame la Dauphine.'

'Have you always worked at Versailles, Monsieur?'

He shakes his head. 'I came to Paris from Bordeaux, penniless, only two years ago.'

'Two years! From penniless to the most sought-after hairdresser at court!'

He steps forward and whispers. 'I have a secret.'

'Indeed?'

'When I arrived, I had nothing, and no prospects. But then I had a stroke of luck. I found something on the street,

discarded. A tortoiseshell comb. It was pretty, so I picked it up and washed it. It was fate, you see.'

'And that comb inspired you?'

'More than that. It was magic. I swear it was. It gave me abilities, ideas, I never had before. You will laugh, Madame.'

'No,' she says, but not too seriously. 'I do not laugh. So, it is this magical comb that creates these wonderful coiffures?'

'The comb began it. It gave me confidence. It showed me what was possible. It taught me. The comb may have been magic, but I—'

'Yes?'

'Well, I am the magician.'

He looks self-satisfied, and she can't help but smile. 'Good. Tell me, then, magician. If I were to say to you, do whatever you like to my hair – create whatever you like – what would you do?'

He puts one hand to his lips, and cocks his head. Then he opens the black bag he brought, and pulls out a long piece of pink gauze.

Antoinette has taken Madame Etiquette's instruction on the proper thing to wear each day. No longer. She has her ladies bring her a wardrobe book each morning, page after page with little snippets of cloth from each of her dresses pasted in, and notes written beside the fabric about the style of the dress. She sticks a pin into the one she chooses. Sometimes it's a tentative stab, as she used to do with the Pandora doll when she wanted to speak to Charlotte. Sometimes it's deliberate and workmanlike, as though she's putting her needle back into a pincushion. Some mornings, it's almost savage.

Her hair and clothing are only part of the problem. She has made too many enemies, because she prefers the company of sweet, loyal women like Lamballe over the gossips and wits like Philippe d'Orléans.

How could Antoinette not love Lamballe? She's twenty-

two, six years older than Antoinette, but she's never snooty. And she's always, eternally, cheerful. She was born in Turin; at seventeen she was packaged off to France to marry one of the Sun King's grandsons, a cad who made her miserable for a year before dying of the libertine's disease. Instead of the romance she deserves, the princess has had only fearful marriage and careful widowhood. And yet her smile has no bitterness in it. Only sweet love of life.

But Lamballe has no influence, so she doesn't count. Very well, then. Antoinette will go out of her way to befriend the people who gossip, who intrigue, who most clearly don't like the Dauphine.

As for her husband, she is at a loss. She had thought perhaps that his sixteenth birthday would be the moment he would consummate the marriage, but he did not. Mama is adamant that if Antoinette increases her caresses and adoration, all will be well. Patience and charm, Mama says. Very well: she will be patient and she will be charming.

France poses its own problems. Many people see Antoinette at Versailles, at the public dinners and presentations, and sometimes at affairs of state. She travels a little, to Fontainebleau or the Tuileries. But the common people have not truly seen her since her journey through the country to the wedding. *They will forget, so easily, if you let them.*

If only there was a love spell in her golden watch!

There is a spell of Geneviève's, though, about a lute-key that will turn music into a reminder. If nothing else, she can make sure the people who hear it will think of her. They will remember her, and they will remember her arrival, when they all cheered so loudly. Who would dare to send away one whom the people of France have welcomed so warmly?

There's an underused bathroom in the queen's apartments, very cold and damp, no one uses it now, there being no queen, and no one passes through it to get anywhere else. There, Antoinette enchants a firescreen; there, she is hidden from view at last.

After long labours, she finds a way to adapt the lute-key spell, to make it work on a violin bow. The enchantment on the bow is a simple one, and most of the sacrifices are minor memories. She is sixteen and has memories to spare. Now she only needs a violinist, and she has one in mind. She invites the Chevalier de Saint-Georges to a card party. And after a moment's thought, she invites Philippe d'Orléans too.

Antoinette's anteroom is lit with twenty-four candles and twelve lamps with golden glass shades. Everyone at the card party looks beautiful, and everyone is.

The Chevalier de Saint-Georges is the sort of handsome that crackles through the air of whatever room he enters. And he enters all the rooms. That's why she needs him; he travels all through France, and he plays his violin.

'Madame la Dauphine and I were discussing the Sun King earlier,' says Saint-Georges. 'I think I see a little of him in your face, Monseigneur.' He looks at Philippe.

Philippe snorts. 'You should. I'm descended from him on both sides. When my father dies, I'll become First Prince of the Blood: next in line.'

'After my husband and his brothers,' says Antoinette.

'Of course,' says Philippe. He looks down at his cards. 'Why are we talking about this? So tiresome, all these titles and bullshit.'

'We weren't,' says Lamballe mildly. She's practically family to Philippe: his wife is the sister of her late husband. 'Bad hand, Philippe?'

'The worst.' He throws it down, looks up at Antoinette, smiles. 'Why don't you sing, Madame? Sing for us.'

Antoinette shakes her head. 'It's kind of you to ask, Philippe, but I'm not in form tonight.'

'Not in the mood, you mean.'

'Isn't it the same thing?'

'We have the best musician in the world with us,' says Lamballe, saving her. 'Oh, do play for us, Chevalier. I'm sure

we can procure a violin for you. Or will you only play your own?'

'Saint-Georges could get a tune out of anything,' says Philippe, his teeth shining in the candlelight. 'Bring him a bit of sausage casing and he'll play you a sonata.'

Saint-Georges smiles. 'No need for that, Monseigneur. I was bold. I brought my violin.'

But Philippe isn't finished. 'In fact, I will make you a wager, Monsieur. I will wager that you can't play a perfect scale using . . . a horsewhip for a bow. Footman, fetch us a horsewhip!'

Antoinette and Lamballe look apologetically at Saint-Georges, but he smiles.

'I am used to being the subject of wagers. I grew up proving myself in the streets of Paris. I can prove myself in Versailles quite happily.'

'Proving yourself, Chevalier?' Lamballe asks.

'The other students bullied me, called me mulatto, taunted my mother in the streets.'

'And your father did nothing?' Philippe asks.

'My father?' the chevalier snorts. 'I don't think the man who enslaved and raped my mother cared about what unkind things people might say to her. He left her to watch over my education in Paris and then went back to Guadeloupe.'

Antoinette hardly knows what to say; her conversational-etiquette training prepared her for such pinched and narrow circumstances and sets of people, and she's never had a friend like the chevalier before. 'I'm sorry, Chevalier. Is your mother still alive?'

'She is. And I learned to fence so I could draw the blood of anyone who insults my mother.'

The footman returns with a horsewhip on a red cushion. Philippe takes it, and holds it out to the chevalier, looking a little chastened. It's a rich, black-handled thing, with the whip wrapped around the bottom unused, by the look of it.

Lamballe laughs and claps her hands. 'Yes, let's see it!'

Saint-Georges obliges. The whip-handle rubs against the strings, bouncing awkwardly. The first note is uncertain, and the second squeaks. But every note is true, and on the eighth the chevalier plays a grace note, hops away from the group a little, and then brandishes his whip with a crack while the final note is still sounding.

'You see?' Philippe crows. 'I knew it.'

'Shall I play something with my real bow, now?'

'Wait a moment, please, Chevalier,' says Antoinette. She runs over to the side table, pulls out a long drawer that holds the enchanted bow.

For a moment, she holds the bow in her hands. The weight of it. The smoothness of the dark wood, the perfect tautness of the horsehair. With this bow, the chevalier will play in every city and town in France. He will play for every mayor and factory owner.

And with every arpeggio, every grace note, people will find themselves thinking of Marie Antoinette, the Dauphine. They won't know why. But they will think of her. She will be in their thoughts, and she will not be dislodged.

She turns and presents it to him. 'A small gift, if it would please you – I know musicians are very partial to their old instruments, but perhaps – It was made by the best, I'm told.'

'What a wonder!' The chevalier takes it from her with a short, chivalrous bow. 'I thank you, Your Royal Highness.'

'I hope it won't interfere with your playing.'

'Let's find out.'

Saint-Georges puts the bow to the strings with a little bounce, and then starts in on a low, slow tune Antoinette does not recognize. The sound of love stirring in the gut, the sound of an unrequited lover turning in cold sheets. And then a high note comes in, and the tune speeds up, until it is a whirl, a dance, a flirtation, a long deep chord.

The bow comes away from the vibrating strings and the chevalier holds it for a moment. No one claps; no one says

a word. Antoinette realizes she has been staring, unfocused, at the floor. She looks up and sees Philippe staring at her, and Lamballe, and Saint-Georges. They have never stared at her that way before. She has been lost in the music, and they have been lost in thought – about her.

The enchantment works.

She claps and, as if it breaks a spell, the others applaud, too. Philippe puts his hand on Saint-Georges's broad shoulder.

'Do you like it, Chevalier?' Antoinette asks. 'It would bring me great joy to know you were using it, as a reminder of our friendship, even when we're far apart.'

'I think it will suit me very well,' Saint-Georges says. 'I'll use no bow but this one, from today forward, so long as I can do so without breaking my obligations.'

He will play, and people will think of the Dauphine. And, as Mama said, she made such a good impression when she first arrived. Just let Louis de Rohan and Jeanne du Barry try to send her away, when she has a home in the hearts of the people of France.

15 March 1772
Antoinette to Charlotte

My beloved Charlotte,
  I have succeeded in adapting a spell meant for one sort of musical instrument to another, and then I thought, if I can adapt the item to be enchanted, why not adapt the enchantment as well? The rogue I met in Vienna told me that this is how most rogues in Europe get their spells: they trade among themselves when they can, but also, they invent them. Once one knows, for example, that both 'c' and 'n' can be replaced with 'o', or with 'i', it is possible, through a great deal of trial and error, to hit on a combination of sacrifices that will translate the magister's will in the magister's language.

I have been having very little luck and getting rather wet with 'fontaine de jouvence' so I think I'll try my hand at 'surprendre'.

I'm wearing these horrible French corsets and dressing my hair more fashionably. Mother will complain about my décolletage and my 'frivolity', but I can't win. She tells me to do what the French court expects? Well, this is what the French court expects. I need to do more than be a good girl to make them love me here. I have decided to take the Sun King as my model, and shine so brightly that without my presence the plants in the Versailles gardens would wither. Do you think I can do that? It's that or disaster, I think, so it had better work.

My little card and music parties have become quite the success. My husband's youngest brother, the Comte d'Artois, is very good at cards and we are friends already. As yet, I have not found anything in common in the Comte de Provence, the King's other brother, but his youngest sister, Élisabeth, is a charming child with the sweetest nature. How lucky I am in both of my families!

No consummation of my marriage.

> *I kiss you, my beloved.*
>   *Antoinette*

CHAPTER EIGHTEEN

*Little Caps and Shoes, Done in White Lace — Hunger
and Want — Letters and Plans — Ambitions —
Many Small Sacrifices*

1 July 1772
Joseph to Charlotte

My dear Charlotte,

I was overjoyed to learn of the birth of your first child —
I had just returned to Vienna after another journey into
Bohemia, of which more in a moment — let me be brother
first and emperor second. I know that you hoped for a boy —
we all did — but the day will come, and you will take your
place as the mother of the heir to the throne, and your seat
on the Council of Naples. I would give my life in a moment
for one more glimpse of my darling daughters, and I never
wished them other than what they were.

And of course you have named your firstborn girl, as we
all have, for our mother — it was very good of you, though
I admit I suspected you might follow Amalia's path and put
another name ahead of it! Amalia has stopped writing to
Mama altogether, and has surrounded herself with young
male bodyguards instead of ladies-in-waiting. She is by all

accounts the real ruler of Parma. Your Ferdinand and hers are of a kind, I gather: two of the worst men the House of Bourbon has produced.

The news of the arrival of your little Teresa was a moment of hope amid great sadness. For months, I have been saying that the situation among the serfs is untenable, that we must curb the rights of the landholders. Three years of drought has left our empire barren, and now the mice and worms eat what is left. You must take care in Naples – grain will be dear everywhere, I suspect. In India, I hear, there are millions dead from famine – they can blame that vampiric British East India Company, but here in the Holy Roman Empire we can blame only our own bureaucrats. Mama has finally sent a commissar to take note of the situation – when she might have saved the man time and bother by simply listening to me.

What we need to do, most urgently, is distribute food and other aid. The supplies and the methods of distribution will occupy us for some time, while many die, and I anticipate uprisings before too long.

I cannot spend too long in Vienna – I am off to see our friends the Turks, increasingly our bulwark against Russia.

Mama has built a new gloriette in the gardens at Schönbrunn, and I have asked for another showing of Salieri's latest opera – it is very popular. Perhaps we all need a little comedy in such times.

I have sent some of my own Teresa's little caps and shoes, done in white lace.

> *With love,*
> *Joseph*

Caterina has told Charlotte about the famine that hit Naples and Sicily in 1764, a few years before Charlotte arrived. People died of hunger, and Tanucci tried to divert anger away from the King by blaming local merchants and officials, saying

they were storing grain to try to make a profit. This caused violence in all the towns, and people stormed the storehouses, only to find them empty anyway. Then the gallows went up, to try to restore order.

Eventually, the kingdom bought enough grain from elsewhere, but the laws keeping the prices down had killed the local market, and so many people wanted to leave Naples that Tanucci brought in penalties to prevent emigration.

It is, Charlotte thinks, precisely the example of how not to run a country. She has that example before her, and she has the example now to the north of her mother and brother, trying in vain to feed an empire.

But she is not her brother or her mother. She has magic.

The question of whether to have people perform sacrifices without their knowledge has been haunting her thoughts for months. Ultimately, she sent a single teacher to San Leucio, deciding that it wasn't worth the risk just to save money.

But famine is another matter. If there is simply not enough food in Europe, surely that is a problem Charlotte must solve. The duplication spell, on a vast scale, would do it. It would simply require the same sorts of sacrifices that any labour requires: a little time, a little wear on the body. It won't hurt the unwitting magisters, and it may save their lives.

She makes the decision. The copying spell will become the loaves-and-fishes spell, and ensure her kingdom will not suffer as the other nations of Europe are suffering. Never again will Naples suffer a famine, not if Charlotte is here to prevent it.

In the centre of each pentagram on the hidden factory floor at San Leucio, a flour sack slumps. Each student is enchanting their sack to refill once it is empty.

Charlotte leans against the railing of the raised platform that runs the length of the factory. Her second pregnancy weighs heavily on her.

'How many sacks, now?'

'Five hundred,' says Caterina.

'That's enough. Any more and they'll drive down the price. You know what to do with them?'

She nods. 'Yes, Your Majesty. I have a man who picks up the empty sacks and delivers them to a place of my choosing nearby, where I have someone else pick them up a few days later.'

The flour must be put to market, or it will spoil, and they will have five hundred bags of spoiled enchanted flour, always refilling. They learned that early on, after a batch went bad. But no one must know of the magic, and they can't disrupt the ordinary flour market to any significant degree.

She's found a way to improve education and the food supply. Charlotte is on her way to becoming the secret King of Naples. Being a secret king is probably not nearly as satisfying as being a real one, but for her, for now, it will have to do.

'Good,' she says. 'Good. Next week, you can start the students on the beans, if you think they're ready.'

'They're ready.'

The girls file out of the factory and into a room where their supervisor, a prim lady Caterina found somewhere who sees nothing, directs them to clean themselves for dinner, where each of them must (by order of the Queen) brush their hair with a hairbrush they've been supplied. A hairbrush enchanted to remove a very particular strand of memory each time.

And each morning, they return to their posts at the looms to find the day's instructions waiting.

It is all managed with great care.

Charlotte and Caterina walk out into the dirt courtyard. It's warm for March, even for Naples. A bead of sweat trickles down her temple.

A movement draws her gaze: a student walking the path to the privies. A young woman, hair bundled into a cap, gaze low, clothing as simple as an oblate's.

They must have little to give up, these girls. But the spell

doesn't ask for much. Each sack of flour takes one set of fingernail clippings, a coin, and a kiss on a handkerchief. The Crown pays them the coins in advance and supplies the handkerchiefs. They lose nothing.

And in return, the girls gain a place to live, two meals a day, classes in reading and arithmetic.

Charlotte has been able to write to Soliman and tell him they have a real experiment to consider, now. To test the question of how an enlightened monarch can direct their subjects' sacrifices.

Charlotte guides her belly down the steps after Caterina.

Charlotte's second daughter, Luisa, comes into the world at the cost of great pain to her mother, and the recovery takes weeks. But at last the day comes when Ferdinand decides he's waited long enough to visit her bed.

Ferdinand comes down on her like a lamprey. She dodges his lips, tucks her chin up at his shoulder while he pounds away at her. He whispers in her ear: 'Charlotte. Charlotte, you make me want to be better.'

Damn, if only he wouldn't talk. She flips him over and gets on top, finishes him off. Then she gets off the bed as fast as she can. He has never hit her after sex, but there is a first time for everything, with Ferdinand.

She turns away from him and pulls on her stockings. She's been repressing a shudder for the last twenty minutes, and she is trying to repress it just a few minutes longer, long enough to get herself dressed enough to make it to the privy closet, but her shoulders shake and she gags on nothing. Perhaps he doesn't see.

He lies, panting. 'You know, the courtesans have no trouble kissing me. It's only the low-class whores that turn their faces away. Like you.'

Ferdinand crawls naked out of the bed and picks up the white glove lying on the back of her chair. She reaches for it but he holds it up, teasing her with it.

Then he opens the window and throws it out, cackling. Her white glove. She'll have to retrieve it, or make another. Damn him.

A few more days of him coming to her room for their monthly reproductive duty. After this, he'll be some other woman's problem for a few weeks. It is an arrangement she can live with; an arrangement she can survive.

30 August 1773
Charlotte to Antoinette

My best beloved sister,

Your letter of 30 July arrived safely. I can't tell you how much I look forward to each one, Antoinette. You must write to me as often as you can, even if it's only a few words. I read every letter ten times or more, not counting the deciphering!

The new baby, Maria Luisa, is a healthy little thing. Her sister loves her dearly and calls her 'doll'. Teresa can say seven words now. (I write each one down on its own sheet of paper. I am such a miser: I hoard memories I hope never to spend.) She and my Luisa will be as close as you and I were, I'm sure, although perhaps they will get into less trouble. There is plenty of trouble to get into here. The ducks and pigs run through half the rooms of the palace, and Teresa was nearly mauled by a goose last week.

Sometimes I'm sure I will teach my girls magic, when they are old enough to keep the secret. But would it be wise to add a reason someone might want to hurt them? I'm not enough like our mother, I suppose.

You might have your heir before I do, if I keep having girls. Any progress on that score? Is the General still arriving with its usual promptness?

Wouldn't it be wonderful if we could have children without the interference of husbands? What sacrifices would that spell require, I wonder?

I'm so lonely here, my dear Antoinette. I'm able to see friends now, and have been gathering people, holding salons when I can. But most of my friends are scholars or diplomats, and I cannot deal with either at the moment. The world is on fire, and they argue about the temperature of the flames. I want to see you.

With love,

Your sister,
Charlotte

CHAPTER NINETEEN

*A Masquerade – A Duel – The Mysterious Swede –
An Attack*

The carriage to Paris seats four: the Dauphin and Dauphine, and two chosen comrades: the Princesse de Lamballe and Philippe d'Orléans.

Antoinette still doesn't like Philippe; perhaps it's because he's several years older than her and Louis, and conveys the impression he'd have nothing to do with them if they didn't outrank him. But he's important at court, and Louis is wise – wiser than Antoinette used to be – in choosing his friends.

Not even Philippe's perpetual sneer can ruin this night. Day after day of being on display at Versailles, and tonight, for a change, she'll be behind a mask. A masquerade! At the opera house! In Paris! As the carriage rolls through the city streets, she peers out at the women walking in plain dresses with babies on their backs or baskets in their arms. They frown slightly at the carriage but nobody throws flowers or gawks, not tonight. Tonight the Dauphin and Dauphine are travelling incognito.

They are out, in glorious Paris, and nobody knows who they are. She can breathe; no need tonight for the *grand corps*. No need to say the right thing, to impress the court,

to serve the alliance. She feels frighteningly free, as if anything might happen.

Antoinette dons the black feathered mask she enchanted with a dazzling spell – courtesy of Geneviève in one of her recent letters. It makes her identity harder to fathom. Philippe glances at her with a slight frown. She's getting something wrong, no doubt; she's always getting something wrong.

'Do you think it will be a good night?' Antoinette asks nobody in particular, brightly.

Lamballe lifts her chin, her slightly knobby nose high in the air. 'I think it will be a remarkable night,' she says.

Antoinette leans forward and puts her hand on the princess's knee, then glances at her husband.

Louis is nice. The warmth of him next to her is nice; it is January, and cold, despite the furs in the carriage. How fortunate she is to have a nice husband, when poor Charlotte has to live with a beast. Louis is stout and solid. His one passion is for locksmithing, of all things. He spends his days at his foundry when he isn't hunting. All things considered, he could be so much worse.

The carriage stops at last at the Palais-Royal, where the newly rebuilt opera house occupies one wing.

'They're all here,' says Philippe, peering out of the window at the bright people scattered all over the steps of the Palais-Royal. His breath fogs the glass. 'They know we're coming. They're waiting to attach, like leeches.'

Antoinette does not much like that *we*. But she says nothing. She does not have to like Philippe; it is of no consequence whether she likes Philippe.

The door opens, the cold air swirls in, and the Dauphine takes the footman's hand. People look at her, but curiously, not appraisingly. She could be anyone. She's taking up no more space than any other member of France's sprawling court.

She and Lamballe gambol hand-in-hand to a knot of people in harlequin silks and feathered masks, lounging on the steps

of the opera house near a brazier. The heat of it ripples the air. One lanky character sits on the stairs, stretching his legs and whispering into the ear of the lady next to him. He'd be recognizable by his somewhat dark skin in any event – he's wearing only the slimmest of masks on his eyes, as if he doesn't care to bother pretending to hide – but there's also little mistaking the shapeliness of those legs.

'Chevalier!' Lamballe cries out as they approach. 'I know you.'

The Chevalier de Saint-Georges stands, and bows, and looks her over. Lamballe pirouettes obligingly.

'And I know you, Madame la Princesse de Lamballe,' he says. 'Which means this must be, ah, Your Royal Highness.' He bows to Louis. 'And Monseigneur le Duc. And Her Royal Highness the Dauphine? I would not have known you, Madame, if it had not been for your companions.'

Philippe nods absently; he's scanning the crowd, frowning as though he's looking for someone in particular, but not finding them. But, then, he always has that line between his brows; Antoinette resolves not to try to interpret it.

A snowflake kisses her forehead, and she looks up to see tiny pricks of white, falling from the black sky. They do not even hiss on the brazier; they melt before they touch the ground.

'We so seldom see you at Versailles these days, Chevalier,' says Lamballe. 'When will you play your violin again for us?'

'I beg your forgiveness. I've been travelling with Monsieur Gossec's orchestra.'

'I've heard you're very good, Chevalier,' says Louis encouragingly.

'Good?' says Antoinette, taking the chevalier's arm. 'I say today, with absolute confidence, that this man will be the next director of the Paris Opera.'

'I did not know Madame la Dauphine could see the future,' says Saint-Georges with a sad smile. There is something

happening there; she will have to take him aside later and figure it out.

'Just the other day,' Lamballe says, 'I heard someone call you the Black Mozart.'

'My darling,' says Antoinette with a laugh, 'I have met Wolfgang Mozart, and I can say with confidence that he would be fortunate indeed to be described as the White Saint-Georges. The chevalier is the best violinist in France.'

'It doesn't seem fair,' says Louis, smiling, 'that the best violinist in France should also reputedly be the best swordsman.'

Louis's cheeks are red, not only from the rouge but also from the cold. Everyone is shivering but no one wants to go inside, not just yet.

'The best swordsman!' says Philippe with mock horror. They have his full attention, now, at last. 'Oh, no. You've gone too far. He knows you're not serious. It's cruel of you to mock him.'

He's smiling, but now the chevalier is not.

'I have never said I am the best anything,' the chevalier says.

'No, no, but your friends do. I admit your prowess with the violin, but I haven't yet had a chance to test the other thing.'

Philippe's rapier glitters in the light of the braziers and torches. Women gasp.

The chevalier bows low. 'Monsigneur. Forgive me. I cannot join swords with you.'

'Ah, you haven't the stomach for it. The quality of a musical performance may be argued, but there is no denying the victor in a duel.'

Saint-Georges sighs heavily. 'There is no way for me to win. I must not wound a prince of the blood, so I lose even if I win.'

'Then we'll fence for points. Come now, Saint-Georges. Surely you have enough control over your weapon to avoid spilling my blood?'

The chevalier cocks his head. 'It is not in me to refuse a challenge, Your Highness.'

He pulls his rapier free, and the two men clatter down the stairs to open ground. A crowd gathers with a great rustling of skirts.

For once, everyone is watching someone else, and Antoinette hangs back, one of the crowd. No one seems to recognize her; the enchanted mask is doing its work.

A red-cheeked young man beside her is staring at the duel, following every cut and thrust. His elbow meets her ribs and he starts.

'I'm sorry,' he says.

'Not at all,' she says, thrilled by anonymity. 'It's a dangerous sport. Who are you cheering for?'

'The chevalier, of course.'

'Of course. You are absolutely right. Are you a swordsman?'

He bows his head. 'I am a musketeer of the guard.'

'I had thought they were older!' she says.

'I'm sixteen, Mademoiselle,' he says, his cheeks getting redder. 'In fact, I'm about to be married.'

'Lafayette!' someone calls, and the red-cheeked boy turns his head. 'We're over here!'

The boy bows deeply, and he's gone.

She sees something at the corner of one eye: among the many powdered heads, a glimpse of a brown moth, embroidered on a lappet, hanging from a high white bonnet.

Her breath catches and suddenly, she can't breathe in the winter air.

There could be more than one such bonnet in the world. This is a masquerade, after all; people are wearing all sorts of strange costumes.

But Antoinette has only ever seen a moth like that on the bonnet Geneviève wore back in Vienna, in their secret meetings under the Chinese Cabinet Room.

Could it be Geneviève, here in Paris? Antoinette had a

213

letter from her just last week, and she made no mention of a visit here. She always says that she hates Paris.

Mumbling excuses, Antoinette jostles through the crowd, pursuing the bonnet as it bobs and dips away from her.

The opera house is nearly empty; everyone is outside, watching the duel. Antoinette moves easily through the empty foyer, past couples lolling against pillars. She glimpses the bonnet at the far end of the foyer.

Antoinette runs after it, down a small staircase.

An empty corridor.

On her right, a door is ajar. She pushes it open. The light from the candelabra in the corridor falls inside, casts a diamond of light. The room is painted with the same elaborate gilt and heroic frescoes as the rest of this vast place, but it's small. Too empty to be a dressing room.

Ah, there is a harpsichord near the back wall. A practice room, or something like that.

She peers into the shadows.

'May I help you, Mademoiselle?'

She steps back, surprised. A young man steps into the light from behind the door.

His French is good, his accent slight. Swedish, perhaps. It makes her conscious of her own regional accent, which she's worked so hard to purge. She knows some people call her *l'Autrichienne*, emphasis on *chienne*. The Austrian bitch.

'I was looking for a friend,' she says, which is the truth.

'You've found one.' He bows. 'I am at your command.'

She grins. A Swede, definitely. 'What makes you think I command my friends?'

'I am sure you don't, Mademoiselle. But I serve mine.'

'How far?'

'Unto death.'

She raises an eyebrow, wondering if the careful line of it shows above her mask. 'Then I hope for your sake, Sir, that your friends are few and good-natured. Why are you hiding?'

214

She looks again into the shadows, but there is no woman there – no man either.

'I needed a quiet place to think. It's very bright and noisy here.'

'Well, one does expect a little sound and light at a Paris ball.'

What a funny thing he is! Even with the mask over his eyes, he looks handsome as Saint-Georges, or nearly, and he seems to be Antoinette's own age.

To her surprise, he takes her hand, draws her into the room and pulls the door nearly closed again. It is very dark now but they are close enough that she can see the line of his face, and the rise and fall of his chest as he breathes. He's wearing a red and black damask coat, with brocade all down the front. His mask is black, shining silk.

'I beg your pardon, Monsieur. If you think—'

He puts his fingers to his lips. 'Someone is coming.'

'We have no reason to hide.'

'We do. You just don't know it yet.'

Her stomach flips. It isn't a sin, is it, to wish that some portion of this kind of fire might spark between her and her husband? The only man allowed to touch her, from now until the day she dies.

Antoinette drops her voice to oblige the stranger. 'I am married.' She didn't mean to make it sound like a complaint.

'I am not seducing you, Madame. As much as I might like to. Please, let us be silent for a moment.'

He's watching the door and seems to have forgotten that he's still holding her hand, not in the way of lovers, but in the way that one holds the hand of a child who can't be trusted not to run in front of a carriage.

She pulls her hand away.

Footsteps in the corridor.

The man takes her hand again and pulls her back, deeper into the shadows. He draws her behind the harpsichord and they both crouch down. She should be giggling, or, more

wisely, leaving, but he seems so serious that she does neither. He smooths her voluminous skirts, pulls them out of sight. There's a slim gap beneath the lid of the harpsichord; Antoinette peers through it.

The door creaks open. A hand wraps around the edge of the door.

Antoinette sees a man standing there, dressed in black, sleek as a cat.

Prince Louis de Rohan.

She stops a cry of surprise in her throat. The Swede's arm comes around her shoulder, his hand over her mouth, gently. A reminder, not a threat.

Rohan has something in his hand, something black – a cross, made of gleaming ebony – no. No, it is a stiletto with a black hilt and crossbar, and the edge of the thin black steel hardly catches the light.

'My lord Bishop,' comes a voice from the corridor beyond. The stiletto disappears into Rohan's clothing as he turns.

'Monseigneur,' he says lightly.

It's Philippe's voice. 'I had thought you were in Vienna, finding out what you could about the partition of Poland and the proclivities of Viennese girls.'

Rohan chuckles, and closes the door, saying, 'I've recently returned. I was looking for someone.'

'Aren't you always?'

The door clicks shut, the room is dark, and their voices fade.

Antoinette waits in silence for several breaths, the Swede's hand slowly loosening at her mouth, the tips of his fingers grazing her cheek, and then he is no longer holding her. She turns and looks at him. His face is inches away.

Somehow, Rohan knows she is a magister. It's the only explanation. She feels as though she might vomit all over the handsome young man's shoes. Would Rohan have killed her?

'Thank you for hiding me,' she whispers.

The man looks at her. 'I would love to take credit for

gallantry, but the fact is, he was looking for me. An old enemy of mine. He set a trap for me, and I very nearly fell into it.'

She's astonished, speechless.

'It's best we get back out into the crowd,' he continues, standing up. 'Always the safest place.'

He walks forward, opens the door and looks out.

She stands, cursing the pins and needles in one calf, and staggers beside him, out into the room.

He takes her arm, and she blushes. Of all times!

'It's only pins and needles,' she says. 'You don't need to help me.'

He shakes his head with a grin. 'Unto death, remember?'

Her heart, her fool heart, is beating again. Let it beat.

They walk out into the corridor, and her leg finally comes to its senses. The Swede gestures for her to step out. For a moment, she almost takes his hand in their shared enterprise, but she stops as their fingers brush each other.

Lamballe comes running down the corridor, laughing, her face red. 'The chevalier won, of course – what is it?' she asks, seeing Antoinette, looking at the Swede. She was laughing: the duel with Saint-Georges must have ended without casualties. And with Philippe coming looking for her? Or for Rohan?

'Until the next time, Madame la Dauphine,' says the Swede with a small bow, and strides away from them, down the corridor.

Lamballe says portentously, 'I see you've met Axel von Fersen.'

Antoinette's face is hot, and she only realizes after he turns a corner and is out of sight that he should not have known who she was. Perhaps he recognized Lamballe, and put it together, as the chevalier had. Or perhaps he knew all along, while he was holding her hand and calling her Mademoiselle.

But if he knew all along, that means her enchanted mask didn't work on him.

CHAPTER TWENTY

The Newest Brother of Naples — A Puppet Show —
Expectations — The Empress Is Irritating —
A Game of Chess

Charlotte holds the latest letter from her sister in both hands, willing her eyes to focus. She thought she could keep Antoinette safe by keeping her magic a secret, by saying that she, Charlotte, had been the only girl who learned magic at Schönbrunn. But this incident with the mysterious Swede and a knife-bearing Rohan has unsettled Antoinette, and no wonder. Louis de Rohan is a bishop, a prince, and a Brother of Paris. And he is skulking around in dark corners with a knife.

She puts the letter into the candle flame, then writes a short response, telling Antoinette not to worry, but to be careful. She writes another letter, even shorter, the quill leaping and jumping on the page, this one to Soliman.

At her signal, the usher shows in Isaac Lars Silfversparre.

The newest Brother of Naples walks into the room like a man of the world – a sailor, or something like that – though he's only twenty-one, and the only travel he's done is between Sweden and Italy. He's here to report on his work making connections with the intellectuals of southern Italy, but Charlotte's glad to see him for other reasons. He's more

cautious than Caterina, better connected than Lunardi, and more pragmatic than Caramanico. He has just the sort of circumspect confidence Charlotte needs right now, when she is ready to cut out a bishop's heart with sewing scissors.

More than all that, he's a Swede.

Silfversparre bows, and she gestures that he should sit. A footman brings brandy and two glasses, and then Charlotte dismisses him and the usher.

She sips, and says, 'How is our list of writers and musicians coming?'

'Very well. It's true that many of the bright young men of good family have gone elsewhere, lately, but if we look beyond the bright young men of good family, Naples has many people whose talents have been overlooked.'

What a good choice he was. She must remember to tell Soliman how grateful she is.

'I know this takes you away from your other work,' she says.

Part of that work is the hunting of rogues. Already the Naples chapter has shown itself to be more tolerant and enlightened, only concerning itself with rogue magisters who have shown themselves to be a danger: to themselves, to others, or to the state. And now, when they find them, her Brothers merely discredit the rogues, or remove their memories of magic with enchanted hairbrushes in the night. No killing, if they can help it.

There are, even so, enough dangerous rogues in southern Italy to supply them with spells, to feed the *Reconditus*, to keep it up to date. Sometimes, Charlotte wonders whether some Brothers – not in Naples, of course, but elsewhere – hunt rogues more out of a need for their spells than out of any principle. The *Reconditus* makes its demands. The rogues always seem to be coming up with new spells, while the Order has little practice with that.

'Searching for talented people to support is a pleasant change,' Silfversparre says wryly. 'I've found it fascinating,

in fact, how many bright young artists and scholars there are in Naples. I have been meaning to bring to your attention Eleonora Fonseca Pimentel. She wrote a poem on the occasion of Your Majesty's wedding – you may recall.'

'A lot of people wrote poems on the occasion of my wedding,' she says grimly. 'Was hers particularly good?'

He shrugs. 'I think she has talent. She corresponds with Voltaire now, and he has dedicated a poem to her. She has a rich dowry, and has been engaged for years to her cousin, but I don't think that's going to come off. All in all, I think she ought to be at court.'

Charlotte considers. 'A correspondent of Voltaire's – I do find myself in need of a librarian. I am going to replace this monstrosity.' She gestures at the room around her, the old King's dusty and dismal nod to literature. 'But do you think appointing a woman would draw criticism?'

'A signal of enlightened ideas, of newness. I'll have her come for an interview, if you like.'

'Good. Soon Naples will be the light of the world. I hope you'll never regret leaving Stockholm to join us.' She smiles.

'I think that is most unlikely, Your Majesty. I didn't get along with the Brothers there.'

She looks down at her glass, swirls the dark brandy. 'Did you ever meet a young man named Axel von Fersen?'

Silfversparre stiffens. 'Has he turned up in Italy?'

She shakes her head, gauging him. 'In Paris. I heard some rumour of trouble between him and our Brother Louis de Rohan.'

'Ah.' Silfversparre sits quietly for a moment, thinking or remembering. 'Fersen was once like a brother to me. He comes from an old family – he's the field marshal's son. We joined the Order at the same time, in Stockholm. Barely more than boys. Our fathers are magisters, so we were made magisters.'

'He's a Brother, then?'

He shakes his head. 'Not any more. He left the Order

shortly before I came here. He was sympathetic to Mesmer's ideas, like me, and he never had the stomach for hunting down rogues. But Fersen is more hotheaded, and he never knew when to give up, or how to have patience. They made his life miserable in whatever ways they could, until one day he simply stopped coming to meetings.'

'*Can* one leave the Order?'

Silfversparre gives a little shrug. 'Not officially, though they don't consider him a member of the Stockholm chapter. And I suppose that's why they didn't bother him too much, or treat him like any other rogue they knew about. As far as they're concerned, he's a Brother, just not a very active one.'

He's holding something back; his jaw moves strangely.

'But you know otherwise.'

A breath, and then the shoulders relax under the blue jacket. 'Some rogues are organizing themselves. They're creating new magical societies, or at least loose associations. I'm not sure how far any of it has gone – it must be difficult to hold an orderly meeting when your magisters are peasant midwives, back-alley fortune tellers, God knows what else. But I have heard that Fersen was interested in that – in the possibilities. He's a Mesmerite through and through.'

'Some might say the same about our chapter,' Charlotte says quietly. 'Yet you didn't leave the Order.'

'I thought that if we worked and waited, the Order would begin to change. And I have been proven right. Not in Stockholm – not yet. But here, and in Vienna. While they round up witches in Sweden, here I round up musicians and writers, and study magic. I believe the Order can change. Fersen does not. In fact, he argued that the Order is fundamentally opposed to change, that preserving secrets is its only reason for existence. I can't say I blame him, but I don't feel the same. I believe the Order is what we make it.'

'Indeed.' Charlotte considers. 'And if not the Order, then what?'

'Fersen liked to talk about the possibilities of teaching magic to anyone who wanted to learn, without the restrictions of any Order. But he doesn't fully grasp the dangers. It may begin with food in the belly of the poor, but how long until the poor are sacrificing their blood and bone for money? If you give magic to all, whole cities could be ruined.' He pauses, and sips his drink. 'All the same, Fersen was my friend, and he was treated badly by the Order. I have never forgiven myself for not . . . I don't know. For not being a better friend to him, for helping him find his way. He went on the Grand Tour not long ago, I heard – that's why I thought he might have been here.'

'He may have been,' Charlotte says, thoughtfully. 'I don't remember every young man who comes through Naples. Handsome?'

'Successful enough with women, anyway.' He pauses. 'Come to think of it, that may be the explanation for any argument he would have with Rohan. I hear the good bishop is quite the philanderer. Or it's possible Rohan thinks Fersen is a danger. The Order in Paris is quite opposed to reform.'

The Brothers of Paris holding knives, rogues in Paris trying to organize themselves, and Antoinette caught quite literally between them. Charlotte suddenly feels older than her twenty-one years. She has done too many sacrifices lately; there are so many spells in the *Reconditus* that are useful to her.

Little Teresa, Charlotte's firstborn, is a darling at nearly two years old in the spring of 1774. She squeals in gleeful terror and points at the stage, where the Devil now sits on her father's right hand.

On Ferdinand's left hand, Pulcinella squats, oblivious. The boor in the white suit and black mask, the favourite puppet of every stage in Naples. The puppet looks up, down, in every corner of the stage except where the Devil is. Teresa stands on her chubby legs, approaches the stage, and touches the puppet.

223

Pulcinella turns, and sees the Devil, and the wooden spoon in his hand becomes a weapon. Thwack! The Devil bows beneath Pulcinella's blows, but still the masked man hits him, to the sound of Ferdinand's high-pitched giggles from behind the stage.

At last, the red Devil puppet slips off his hand and floats down to the floor, where Teresa picks it up. She runs as fast as her little legs will take her, around the edge of the stage, to show her father what she has found.

King Ferdinand emerges from his puppet stage, red in the face and crawling on all fours, and all the courtiers applaud.

The King's latest mistress, a black-haired dancer called Isabella, lets out a long, loud whistle, and stands, her skirts swishing.

Charlotte pats her belly. Not yet swelling, but she knows. If it's a boy, Charlotte will finally get her seat on Ferdinand's Council. She'll have influence. He can't deny her her place on the Council if she has a son; it's in the marriage contract.

She does love her two little daughters, though. Maria Luisa crawls on a mat on the floor, while Teresa laughs with her father.

The King picks up Teresa and twirls her around, kissing her and flipping her upside down. How Charlotte wishes he wouldn't do that! One day the oaf will drop her.

When Charlotte was eight, Father took the youngest children to a puppet show in the village near Schönbrunn Palace. Antoine and Max both gasped at the Faust puppet with his ratty grey beard, his beetling eyebrows, his sorcerer's robes.

'No,' laughed Father, lifting Antoine up so she could see better, 'Faust is not the frightening one. Look, see his scholar's hat? He is just a man. If you are frightened by Faust, what will you do when Mephistopheles appears?'

Antoine pouted, and hid her face in Father's neck. But Charlotte, standing a little behind, could see that her sister's eyes were dry and she was smiling. Antoine never saw the horned figure appear, not then. But Charlotte watched it all,

because she was a bigger girl, and Father's shoulder was already occupied.

Ferdinand puts his daughter down, and holds his back with an exaggerated groan, play-acting as if he were a much older man. Then he looks straight at Charlotte, the only adult in the room not standing.

His face is as serious as her own and his expression is a command.

So she smiles, bows her head, claps.

He smiles back, and leads his parade of fools to dinner.

Maria Theresa's weekly letters demand that Charlotte do something about Antoinette.

Antoinette, whose husband is not yet *truly* her husband. As though Charlotte could do anything about that! Worse, word reaches the imperial ears of ridiculous hairstyles and late-night card parties. All eyes in Paris are fixed on Antoinette, watching for the slightest pretext to tear her apart in print. *In print, and perhaps more.* Doesn't Charlotte know there have been riots in France? Right up to the doors of Versailles? What will Antoinette do about that? What will Antoinette do next?

Charlotte has no intention of changing Antoinette's mind about anything. Let Antoinette be. Let her live.

Meanwhile, Joseph explains that Mama, always so intent on her subjects' moral character and industry, has made education mandatory for all children in her dominions – despite the lack of schools and teachers, something he's been warning her about for years. Mama may not have educated her daughters to rule but she's a constant example of mistakes to avoid.

Charlotte's letter to Antoinette reassures her that the dis-agreement between Rohan and Fersen had nothing to do with Antoinette, and warns her sister to avoid them both and continue to keep her magic secret. Charlotte shakes pounce onto the letter to set the ink, taps it off in a fine

cloud, folds it, lights her sealing-wax taper and pours a scarlet drop. Presses her seal. Done.

She glances up at Ferdinand, huddled over a chessboard, alone but for dregs of wine. He's playing a game with his father, King Carlos of Spain, by mail. In every letter, one move. Ferdinand is losing, of course.

He's had his father's last letter for a week but hasn't sat down to make his move until now. There's a pestilence in Naples and everyone has gone to ground, leaving Ferdinand without much company but his wife's.

Charlotte stretches her neck to see the board better.

'Christ on the cross,' Ferdinand mutters. 'I'm buggered in this game, I think. More wine!'

She stands, walks over to the board. Ferdinand's lost a lot of blood in the game, but he's far from doomed.

'You see?' he moans. 'I can't move anywhere good.'

'You could move your knight here.' She points to an open area at the edge of the board, within striking distance of King Carlos's knight.

Ferdinand glowers up at her. 'Are you mad? It threatens nothing there and would be completely unprotected. His knight would take mine and I'd get nothing in return.'

'But then you could take that pawn on the other side; the knight he moved to take yours wouldn't be protecting it any more.'

He scoffs. 'A fucking pawn.'

'But that gap puts you into a better position to get at your father's king. It makes him vulnerable.'

'Hmm,' says Ferdinand. He sees it now, sees how the sacrifice could be worth the cost; he would be clever if he weren't so resentful of anything that spoils his fun. He leans back and laughs as the footman pours wine into his cup.

'Isn't it astonishing?' he gestures, addressing the footman. 'My wife knows everything.'

This is one of his more dangerous modes, when he speaks

of Charlotte as if she were a prize addition to his menagerie. She takes a step back from the board.

The footman nods, retires. Charlotte's parents knew about the lives of all their servants and spoke with each of them privately, in interviews they scheduled. They never spoke to them while they were serving. Ferdinand is the opposite; he doesn't know any of the servants' names but he talks at them whenever he needs an audience.

'I'm tired of these games with my father,' says Ferdinand, and walks over to the mantel, lifts the lid off a box of snuff. 'Tired in general. And I have to meet those tedious Americans tomorrow. Remind me what they want, Charlotte.'

'The tedious Americans are about to go to war with the British, which serves your father's purposes. If the British Empire gets one or two of its tentacles lopped off, the whole world will breathe a little easier.'

'Oh, well, if Father wants it,' Ferdinand says sardonically.

There's no point in talking to him, but sometimes he's the only one in the room.

'There is such a thing as the national interest,' she says.

He's not listening. 'Do you know what Isabella said the other day? It was adorable. She said she thought the wars had ended, and now there was peace, we should look upon Britain as our ally. Do you know, as innocent as she is, I see a kind of wisdom in it?'

Charlotte's throat closes. She doesn't disagree with that, as far as it goes. And she is content – happy, even – to let Isabella into Ferdinand's bed. But the woman must not worm her way into his counsel. Charlotte has weakened Tanucci's position in Ferdinand's confidence; once she bears a son, she'll replace him completely. None of the King's mistresses can be allowed to step into that gap instead.

She must say something, do something. It is dangerous to chide Ferdinand, or even to disagree with him, but she must take the chance.

'I suppose when a woman learns statecraft on her back,

it is natural that she should get things backwards,' she says mildly.

'You are jealous, my wife,' says Ferdinand. The look on his face is a warning. She chooses to ignore it.

'Pfft,' she says. 'I don't care who you fuck. Just remember that the King is fucking her; the state is not.'

She has seen him move like this twice before, with this terrifying speed, over the past five years, and she knows what is coming.

Ferdinand grabs her arm, hard, and pulls her towards him, as if she were a child who will not obey. If she were a child, her arm might break when he twists it, bending the elbow the wrong way. But her bones are strong.

He pulls her close to him so that she can smell the wine on his breath. Even a queen knows there is always one man in the world who could hold her like this, hurt her like this. A queen has to obey her king; a wife has to obey her husband. Those are the rules and the rules are set.

'You do not tell me what to do,' he says. But there's doubt in his face; he is ashamed, now. She has indeed told him what to do and he is just clever enough to know it.

Charlotte is running the schools. She's collecting the brightest young minds. She's controlling part of the food supply. She reads all the diplomats' reports and knows more than anyone about how matters stand in Europe and around the world. One day, soon, Ferdinand will wake up to find that he is the King of Naples in name only, that his wife is the true king, and there won't be a damn thing he can do about it. On that day she will dance.

CHAPTER TWENTY-ONE

The Departure of Madame du Barry — The King Is Ill —
Louis and Antoinette — Changes

11 March 1774
Geneviève to Antoinette

My dear friend,

I am sorry to hear that you were so badly frightened by
that villain Rohan. He's on his way to England, I'm told,
and I'll keep an eye on him while he's here.

And you needn't worry about Axel von Fersen, either. He
is a friend of mine, and was in Paris at my behest. The
trap they laid — the gall of anyone copying my bonnet! —
was for him, not you.

Let them do their worst. The days of the Order hunting
us down are numbered. We — my friends and I — are
working on great things, my dear.

But so are you! I am impressed with that perfume spell
you invented — the idea of different scents creating different
emotions is genius. However, I wonder if it's too difficult to
control? After all, we can't always know who might be
smelling us, or even our letters or flowers. What if you
found a way to put it into food instead?

*I look forward to your next letter. In the meantime, I'm
enclosing a spell of my own, for a bottle of ink that will make
your letters rearrange themselves into ciphers as you write
them. I know ciphering gives you a headache! But be warned
that it doesn't make very much, and takes a heavy sacrifice,
so you must save it for the days when you are very tired.*

I embrace you,

Your friend,
Geneviève

What Antoinette likes best about the exterior of the château
of Versailles is not the sensuous grey stonework, or the red
brick that glows like the cheeks of a freshly scrubbed
schoolboy, or even the golden fleurs-de-lys that rise from
the railings against the azure sky. No, what she likes best
are the windows. Sometimes they are as dark as deep water;
sometimes, at a certain angle, they shine in jagged white,
reminding Antoinette of the sugar on a slice of *Gugelhupf*,
the cake Papa used to love.

And sometimes, like now, the sun glazes them golden,
opaque, like the top of a *Linzertorte*. It makes her smile.

Out in the royal courtyard, little knots of people walk in
the gentle sun of an early May morning. And her coach is
waiting, its robin's-egg panels painted with mythological
scenes, and four white horses ready to go visiting.

On a day like today, she cannot believe that Prince Louis
de Rohan or anyone else wishes her harm. He's gone to
England, anyway. Everything may not be for the best in the
best of all possible worlds: her marriage is unconsummated
and Mama is always disappointed in her. But the sun shines
on Versailles.

Antoinette lifts one sage silk shoe to step into her coach,
when one of the four horses snorts and the other stamps.
Another coach comes rattling past, passes by Antoinette's
and then rolls to a stop.

It shines in black and gold, the horses roan and bay, their coats glossy.

The footman opens the door, and out comes the Comtesse du Barry, in a dark green polonaise, with a *bergère* straw hat tilted down over her face. When she turns her gaze on Antoinette it looks wide-eyed and dazed, rather than, as is usual, studiously blank.

'The King is dying,' she says.

Antoinette steps back down to the grey stones of the courtyard. The King has been ill with smallpox for more than a week, but everyone said he was improving.

'Surely—'

'He has sent me away, so he can confess all his sins without the little additional sin of me on his conscience. Oh, I know, he did that with another mistress once, but this time I think he won't recover, and I won't return.'

'May God help him,' Antoinette prays. But what will happen if the King dies? Now? Today? 'The Dauphin – he's in his foundry.'

'They'll send someone to tell him. Now that I'm out of the way.'

Antoinette doesn't know what to say. 'His Majesty's love for you—'

'Ha,' the comtesse interrupts, staring at something invisible just over Antoinette's shoulder. 'Ha. For Louis, love flowed one way, like taxes. He collected as much as he could from as many as he could and he's still dying bankrupt.'

Madame du Barry looks at Antoinette then, just for a moment, and turns and gets back into her lacquered coach.

The shoes that carry Antoinette elegantly over the floors of Versailles don't manage well on uneven ground. She skids across silvery stones. Up the stairs to the Marble Courtyard, where the black and white diamonds unbalance her. It's crowded. She's trying to find Louis, her Louis. Nobody seems to know where he is, or to quite care.

She sees Madame de Noailles and runs to her.

'Your Highness,' the *dame d'honneur* says, and for once she doesn't flinch from Antoinette's embrace.

'Do you think it's really true?'

Madame de Noailles nods, and whispers, 'They say the King's face is as dark as bronze from the disease.'

'I must find my husband.'

'The Dauphin is in your rooms, waiting for you.'

Dear Louis! The last place she would have looked.

The King's valet comes trotting out into the courtyard, his face red with rouge and activity. 'The Comtesse du Barry!' he gasps. 'His Majesty calls for Madame du Barry.'

'Gone,' someone says.

'Her coach just left,' Antoinette says. 'I saw it. She can't have got far.'

The valet shakes his head. 'There isn't time.'

But there is time, as it happens. For several hours, Antoinette and Louis sit with a few of their closest servants and friends, and no one comes to advise them. The doctors want no one in the room with the King for his final breaths; they don't want the contagion to spread. Louis examines the workings of a barometer. Antoinette writes to Mama, to Charlotte, to Amalia, to her brother Joseph. She reads out loud for a while from a novel, *L'Histoire d'Ernestine*, but she can tell that Louis isn't listening, and she stops, letting the book fall onto her lap. She looks out of the window.

'Do you think that I should write to anyone?' he asks at one point. 'The King of England, or the King of Spain, or—'

'I'm sure someone will tell you what is best,' she says.

'Mmm.'

Louis, who can always eat, calls for bread and cheese.

The sunlight moves across the patterned carpet on the floor until mid-afternoon, when they hear a noise like

thunder: it is dozens of hard heels tromping across the Hall of Mirrors, running from the rooms of the dead King to the room that holds the living one.

She and Louis take each other's hands and stand ready.

The door opens and the people rush through. There are a few murmurs of *'Vive le roi!'* And Madame de Noailles greets them both as majesties.

Antoinette doesn't remember, later, which of them moved first to kneel, but both she and Louis were on their knees, hand in hand still. And Louis, King at nineteen, said, 'May God guide us and protect us. We are too young to rule.'

The labour pains start just after the new year celebrations that welcome 1775, when it seems everyone other than Charlotte in the Caserta Palace is asleep with a headache and a sick stomach. Charlotte walks up and down the empty corridors; the walking distracts from the pain, although it does not soften it. She prays for her baby.

She writes instructions to the doctor that every bloody sheet, the placenta, the cord, must all be kept. In the event of her death, the cord is to be kept in a lead box and bequeathed to the baby, should he live.

He?

Yes, *he*, after a short but painful labour that gives Charlotte enough of her own blood for many spells. A little scowling duke, with tiny balled fists.

The doctor orders broth for Charlotte and hands the little bundle to the wet nurse – a potato-faced woman, matter-of-fact, with eyes only for the baby. Charlotte likes her at first sight.

When Ferdinand comes, he takes his son gently out of the nurse's arms, holds him up in the crook of one arm to have a look at him.

'Carlo,' he says.

Charlotte nods. The name was never in question: as their

first daughter was named for Charlotte's mother, their first son is named for Ferdinand's father. Their children are not merely children; they are states in waiting.

'Naples has an heir,' she says. He is, in a way, the fulfilment of duty, but those tiny fingernails, the smallest things in the world, require a greater duty still.

'And you have a seat on the Council,' he says, smiling at her in a way that is not quite friendly, but not cruel either. The smile of a stranger who doesn't quite understand. 'I wish you joy of it. Tedious, but I know you wanted it. This little one has changed your status, wife.'

'All my children have changed me,' she says.

She calls for Teresa and Luisa and her two girls, rising three and two, toddle in, each holding the hand of their nurse. They meet their brother, and kiss his little furrowed forehead. Teresa says he smells like cake, and Charlotte smiles. Her ladies are fussing to put pillows behind her back but she shoos them away. No need for that; she doesn't care. She watches her children, three healthy children, and she doesn't care about anything else.

A day's rest. And then she gets to work. During her confinement, she has people bring her the records of the Council to read. Now that she doesn't have to rely on Caterina finding and copying only the most important, she wants to read everything. And there is so much to study! All the financial records are a mess, probably by Tanucci's design. There are so many complaints: reports of subjects seeking justice and receiving nothing for months on end, presumably until they bribed their local officials. The schools are improving, but the university needs support if it's to keep any of its scholars. The country's manufacturing and agriculture are thirty years behind the times. And then there are foreign matters: the American colonies have stopped all trade with Britain and there will be war before long, which could drag in Spain and, perhaps, Naples too. She can't make a wrong step once she takes her Council seat. This is her one chance to do what

she's good for, and at last nobody can tell her not to do it. She is queen, and magister, and minister, and she's going to set all the wrongs right.

PART THREE

1775 TO 1777

CHAPTER TWENTY-TWO

The Baker's Wife — A Hope Sacrificed — The Comtesse
de Polignac — The Petit Trianon — Private Life

Now that they are king and queen, Louis and Antoinette are always on display. Some of their dinners together are public performances, and even the private dinners have people coming and going: not only servants but nobles clinging to their rights to wait upon the King, because personal service as a mark of royal favour is codified to the smallest degree at Versailles. Everyone at court is anxious to make sure they won't lose anything, under this new sovereign.

The nobles have reason to worry. Louis appointed Jacques Turgot as his minister of finance. Turgot is a reformer, and has already replaced forced labour with taxes on property owners, cut spending everywhere, and abolished many of the expensive sinecures that keep the privileged loyal to the Crown.

But the reform that shook the whole country is free trade in grain, because bread is everything.

It has long been the duty of the King of France to make sure there is bread on the table. Farmers grow approved amounts of wheat, and sell for an approved price, to the approved people, at the approved times, by order of the King.

Philippe tells her that the common people call the King 'the Baker', and her, Antoinette, they call 'the Baker's wife'. He mentioned it, she suspects, to puncture some of her happiness over the way the people have shown their love through paintings and poetry and letters, during this first year of her husband's reign.

At least there are no murmurs now that Antoinette will be sent away. She asks Geneviève what rumours she hears from England; she asks Charles and the Princesse de Lamballe what people say in the salons. Nothing. It has all faded away, the talk of getting rid of her. A dauphin's stumble into an annulled first marriage with a forgettable foreigner would be a minor embarrassment; it's unthinkable for a king beset with problems, whose wife is the subject of gossip and speculation in every village in France, thanks to the chevalier's violin. She has survived.

The newspapers call her beautiful, and indeed, on the coronation day, she knows that she was. She and Louis shone in the rays of God's approval.

But Maria Theresa's approval has been harder to win, especially since Louis keeps choosing advisers who are wary of the Austrian alliance. And what is Antoinette to do about it? She is just the Baker's wife; she does not set policy.

Turgot argues that the best way to ensure a steady supply of grain is to allow landowners to make profits, some of which they will invest, allowing France to produce more grain.

'It might still work,' Louis says glumly, pulling her bed sheets up over their legs for warmth. 'If this year's harvest is better than the last.'

Sometimes Louis comes to Antoinette's bed with intentions to consummate the marriage, though it never happens. They sit in their night clothes, backs against her lace pillows, and discuss the business of the day. It's the only time they really can talk, alone.

The first harvest of Louis's reign was a disaster. With a

shortage of wheat and Turgot's policies in place, the grain suppliers stockpiled and sold only to those who could pay the highest price. Louis bought grain from other countries; he opened the royal storehouses, set caps on prices once again. Still the people starved, and there were riots in the spring, all over France. In Versailles salons, people called it 'the Flour War'. Turgot, once so insistent that the police should have better things to do than enforce the price of wheat, ordered the police to restore order.

'It seems to me that it doesn't matter what might work in theory,' she says, gently, not wanting to overstep. She likes the fact that Louis talks to her about politics. 'What matters is what happens in practice.'

Louis sighs.

The next day, Louis's sister-in-law, the Comtesse d'Artois, goes into labour. Anyone with any rank is expected to attend the birth, so Antoinette is there, watching, as her poor sister-in-law screams and sweats and bleeds in front of everyone. She is there when the baby is born: a healthy boy, named Louis-Antoine.

There is a boy for the royal family, and Antoinette is no longer quite as necessary. She turns in one direction and sees something on Philippe d'Orléans's face: an expression of empathy? How dare he try to make common cause with her over this? She does not begrudge her sister-in-law her happiness, not one jot of it. She's not envious. She is worn out from being useless.

She whirls in the other direction and walks out through room after room after room, into the Hall of Mirrors. There are always crowds at Versailles – anyone who's dressed decently can come into some parts of the palace – but on a day like today, with a royal birth, the place is packed from wall to wall. A knot of plainly dressed women calls after her as she walks. 'When will it be your turn? When will you give us a boy?'

She doesn't breathe until she reaches the enormous, panelled guardroom that marks the entrance to her own chambers. She wipes her tears – a waste – and her shoes carry her on an inch of air into her secret room.

She collapses onto the floor, here where no servants can see her. How can they be angry with her, these strangers, for something that is not her fault? Why do they take such delight in taunting her?

The women of every market square in Paris expect only one thing from their queen, and that is something Antoinette cannot provide. Her body is of little use to France. She is not a mother, and even her occasional utility as a pretty spectacle is fading in these hungry times. Turgot has made it clear the state coffers have already been scraped bare. She is omnipresent in the thoughts of everyone in France, but what do they think of, when they think of her?

Antoinette slows her breathing. She is not without skills. She may not understand politics but she knows hearts, and Louis likes to confide in her. But every word Antoinette speaks in favour of a policy or a politician is as good as poison; she is *l'Autrichienne*, a foreign influence.

She is no Charlotte but she needs allies and plans of her own. It is time to stop losing her breath and her wits over what she cannot change. Some hopes are better sacrificed.

Antoinette goes to the little writing desk her mother gave her. She keeps it in her secret room because its many drawers hold small treasures and pots of ash. Under the gold watch are her notes about the new emotion spell: not perfume but, as Geneviève suggested, something to eat. She has a little sack of flour, given to her on a goodwill tour of a mill the month before, a mill that had been the target of a mob. Perhaps it wasn't wise, when so many are hungry, but she couldn't very well refuse. She told the miller it was a treasure greater than any riches, and she meant it. Antoinette had asked to keep the flour herself, and everyone seemed to forget she had it.

She could ask for cakes to be made of it. Louis's chief trouble is that his advisers squabble among themselves over their pet theories; what if magic made them all a little more tractable, compassionate, pragmatic?

But every time she has tried to enchant the flour, the sacrifices do not decay. She hasn't been able to bring herself to write down a hope that would suffice. Perhaps Antoinette has hardly known what to hope for, these days.

The one hope she has clung to, she will sacrifice willingly now. She will throw her vision of herself as mother onto the fire and watch it burn. Why hold onto the hope for a child, five years into an unconsummated marriage? What good does it do her? It only hurts.

Antoinette writes it down and places it in the star. Three coins for treasure, and one affection. The fifth sacrifice is of the body. There's a bag of hair clippings out of the desk. She's been collecting them every time Léonard cuts her hair. She shakes them out onto the floor, where they look sad and dirty and alien. For good measure, she takes her silver scissors out of her desk drawer and cuts one long tress, near the crown, where it won't show when her hair is dressed, then it curls down on top of the rest, a slightly different colour because of the powder.

She places the sack in the centre of the star, thinks for a moment of the housewives fighting each other for flour in Paris, and steps back, covering her nose.

'I give these things.'

The sacrifices do not vanish. It is not enough; she has not given enough. Her most painful hope has been found wanting. Is that it? Or is it the body? Has she not punished it sufficiently?

She grasps a chunk of hair from the top of her head and yanks it out. The ripping sound of it is what stuns her, astonishes her, stops her face from contorting into thwarted sobs. Her head stings and her fingers trail long powdered strands, a fistful of hair, a sacrifice from the root.

She throws it onto the point of the star as if it were a spider, and as the last strand floats down onto the pile, the paper with the hope written on it begins to curl, the coins to rust, the hair to rot. There's a smell like dead animal and Antoinette stands, numb. The desire for a child is in her memory, a thing that she used to want. But time passes, doors close, and some things will be only for others, not for her.

16 September 1775
Geneviève to Antoinette

My friend,

I must admit I received your last letter with a mixture of pride and trepidation. You write that you wish to do more with magic; well and good, so long as you're careful. You ask me for the names of rogues you might befriend. There, I can't help you. Paris may be full of rogues but none of them are friends I trust, and even the ones I know of aren't the sort of people who could visit you at Versailles without attracting attention.

Rohan's travels in England and Austria are at an end, I hear, and he is determined to ingratiate himself with your husband. He's ambitious in his own right – or greedy, anyway, and certainly won't take well to Turgot's reforms. And the Paris chapter of the Order no doubt wants to get its tentacles into everything, to make sure they can find and discredit any rogues in the army, the scientific and artistic academies, anywhere they might appear. So Rohan is even more dangerous these days, and you mustn't do anything to make him wonder whether Soliman was wrong about you all those years ago, whether your sister is not the only magister in the family.

Count Axel von Fersen, by the way, is quite chagrined about drawing you into danger that night at the opera house. Yes, I know you were probably thinking of him when you asked me about rogues, but he can't be your ally in Paris,

as he's stopped travelling for the moment too. He's returned to Sweden, and is working to protect some friends there from the Stockholm chapter, which has become especially vicious in the last few years. I've told him to stay away from you anyway, to prevent any more close calls, and now the poor man is afraid even to write to you, lest he cause you any danger by association. But he asked me to give you the spell I've enclosed, for a candle that dampens sound in a room. An offering in apology for endangering you, he says.

If you wish to have magister-allies, my dear, you will have to create them. Find some people you can trust, people of high enough birth that they'll have access to you and you to them. Find a safe place where you can meet.

Antoinette, you told me once you wanted to be worthy of France, and I am not surprised that you haven't dropped that ambition. You are stubborn, in your own way! But remember that being worthy of France, and being welcomed by it, are different things. Nobody will take kindly to a queen meddling, and the Order has spies everywhere.

I remain,

Your friend,
Geneviève

Antoinette orders cakes to be made of her enchanted flour that will make whoever eats it more compliant, temporarily. She's eager to try another batch; perhaps one to make Louis's advisers wary of new schemes and persuasive rhetoric. At last, she may be able to have some influence, to help nudge things in useful directions for Louis even when he can't himself. She may be able to help Louis's advisers stop pulling the cart in six different directions, each of them arguing only for their own pet projects. Even Turgot may learn to be a little more practical.

But the cakes will only work on the people she can feed them to, and her circle at the moment does not include many

245

people with the ear of the King, or even the ears of his advisers. She has to be careful about how people perceive her. Perhaps it's because she's a daughter of Maria Theresa, or for some other reason, but she knows that Versailles is always liable to interpret her smallest move as an attempt to take power away from her husband.

So she needs allies, which, it seems, means telling a few people about magic, and teaching them how to do it. A thrilling and terrifying thought! And she needs somewhere to speak to those people, where they won't be overheard. Her little secret room at Versailles, hidden by the firescreen, is quite unsuitable and it would attract too much attention to have people disappearing inside.

When Antoinette was a child, and not yet destined for France, the old King began construction on a retreat for his mistress at the time, Madame de Pompadour. It was not finished when she died, but it was ready and waiting for the new mistress, Madame du Barry, to occupy as she occupied everything else. Then the King died, and Antoinette's husband became Louis XVI, and the Comtesse du Barry was packed off to an abbey to cool her heels.

King Louis XVI has no mistress, nor any desire for one. He has had to stop people from putting women forward for the position. Antoinette occupies the positions of both wife and mistress; or, rather, she occupies neither.

And thus, the Petit Trianon falls to Marie Antoinette.

If one meanders through the gardens, keeping the Palace of Versailles at one's back, veering to the right and walking down a tree-lined road, one comes upon it almost by accident. It is a simple, classical rectangle, five windows at the front and five at the back, adorned with columns and pilasters, and a balustrade around the top. There is a bit of open lawn beside a stream, behind, which looks like a good place for children.

So it is there that she invites Gabrielle de Polastron, Comtesse de Polignac, and her two young children, to enjoy

some lemonade made with fresh juice from the greenhouses at Versailles.

The daughter is seven, and the son is four, and they are charming, with red cheeks and dark curls and polite expressions. When they have permission to run and play, they go to the stream and bend over a pile of rocks, happily oblivious.

Antoinette and Polignac sit on a sheet of white muslin and drink lemonade. Here they are free, not only from Versailles's gossips and spies, but also from its tedious etiquette.

Polignac looks perfectly comfortable, her long legs folded beneath her, her simple lavender dress the same colour as her eyes. She has a calming presence, with the same lovely dark curls as her children, and a stillness to the way she holds herself – not taut, not slack, simply present.

Polignac is second on Antoinette's list of people she may be able to trust with the secret of magic. The Princesse de Lamballe is at the top, of course. But Lamballe has always moved in the same rooms Antoinette does, and knows what Antoinette knows. Polignac is different. Though Antoinette doesn't know her well, she finds her fascinating and would like to know her better. And Polignac seems like a rather clever choice as a magister-ally, Antoinette thinks a little smugly. She has deliberately separated herself from the daily intrigues of court life, and doesn't seem to care about politics.

Polignac is the last person anyone would suspect of meddling in the government's affairs.

'I suppose the late King must have planned these gardens,' says Polignac politely. Between the little slope where they're sitting and the building, there are rows of black earth, line after line, with a hodgepodge of plants.

'They're botanical. The arrangement is a bit ugly, isn't it? More like a classroom than a garden. Do you have gardens at Claye, Madame?'

Polignac smiles a little. 'Mainly for vegetables. It's a very simple place, Your Majesty, but we are – how shall I say it?

Self-sufficient there. We have, over the last few years, sunk into the habit of hardly ever coming to court.'

'I hope there's nothing keeping you from us. If I can resolve anything, I will.'

'Oh, no. Thank you, Your Majesty. We're simply happy where we are, and we are quite on the other side of Paris, of course, so it is a drive to Versailles. It seems a world apart, sometimes. We have a quiet life.'

'Do you not miss the parties and dances?'

'I do not miss the scheming and sniping. Our private life may be dull but at least it's not painful. I protect myself, and my children. That's the main thing.'

Antoinette nods, looking over at the children under an overhanging willow. 'I envy you. I have no private life here. I am dressed in public, I pray in public, I eat in public, and I sleep in public. I have found . . . little ways to carve out space in Versailles, and I guard my little ways like a miser.'

'Kings and queens must carve out their private lives for themselves, if they are to have any at all,' the countess agrees. 'That is why this place is here, isn't it? A private place for a mistress. But now it is yours, Madame. And you have no mistress.' The violet eyes twinkle.

'No, indeed, though some of the pamphleteers spread all sorts of rumours about Lamballe!' Antoinette smiles, all the way to her eyes. It's true, she thinks, that the Crown now pays Lamballe, as new Superintendent of the Queen's Household, precisely what the King used to lavish on Madame du Barry. 'I suppose at least I can come here myself to be alone from time to time. What I want is not loneliness, though, but a small piece of private life, like the one you've managed to create.'

'I think you could do that here, Your Majesty. It would need some work, of course, but you could have a few friends here, for days at a time if you liked. It's distant enough from the palace that one could be quite informal here. It's a place for secrets, after all.'

It's a place for secrets.

'You're right, Madame,' she says, trying to keep her excitement out of her voice. 'I do have a place of my own, now. And it's mercifully small – so small I could only have an intimate circle of friends at any one time. One would have to do something about the gardens, but at night – with lanterns – it would be lovely here.'

'Sometimes it takes a little work to fall in love,' says Polignac indulgently. 'Armand! You're getting your knees wet.'

How clever the Comtesse de Polignac is! How capable!

'It takes sacrifices, too,' Antoinette says, testing.

But Polignac's expression doesn't change; her shoulders don't tighten. She merely nods, still gazing after her child. 'We make our choices.'

'And I believe our choices can remake our worlds, or at least our own small parts of it. To help us do our duty better.'

'My duty is there,' Polignac says, looking out at her children.

'And so is mine,' Antoinette says with cold determination. 'My duty to God and to France is to ensure that every child is protected from harm, that every mother can feed her babies.'

'That is the duty of us all, surely,' Polignac says, turning to her with a kind smile. 'But some of us can run away from it more easily than others. Most days I don't think beyond protecting my own family, my friends.'

'Then your friends are very lucky to have you.' Shyly, she adds, 'I would like to count myself among them.'

Polignac's smile brightens, as though she's amused. 'Your Majesty, I am at your service.'

'But you must have some rooms at Versailles, so you can be here with me sometimes,' Antoinette says, in a rush. 'I'm sure we can find something suitable. For you and your family.'

Polignac inclines her head. 'I thank you, Your Majesty,

but I'm afraid it's very expensive to live at Versailles. There are other reasons I don't come to court. I did not attend the wedding of the Comte d'Artois because I couldn't bring myself to spend the money on a *grand habit*. Anyway, I don't see why I should have to. Terrible, painful things.'

'You should not have to,' Antoinette says with feeling. 'How I wish I had your courage! You must have rooms at Versailles – not for your own benefit but for mine. I need your help – to carve out my private life here. Will you agree? I'll take care of the money – it is not for your benefit, but for mine.'

Polignac looks away, and for the first time, Antoinette sees a frown cross her face. 'I'm not sure the gossips would like a mere countess being given rooms at Versailles out of the Queen's budget.'

Antoinette shrugs. 'Then I shall make you a duchess.'

The little girl, Aglaé, comes running up to her mother. 'Mama, look, I found the perfect stone!'

She's holding it in her palm, a smooth, round, pink pebble.

'The perfect stone for what, dear?' Polignac asks, cupping her daughter's hands.

'Simply the perfect stone, that's all,' the girl says. 'May I take it home, Mama?'

'You must, as my gift,' Antoinette says, leaning forward. 'You are a clever girl, to find the one perfect stone in all the world.'

CHAPTER TWENTY-THREE

Secrets at the Petit Trianon — The Paris Opera —
Two Impossible Sights — One Singular Duty

On a spring morning in 1776, Antoinette invites three friends to the Petit Trianon: Polignac, Lamballe, and the Chevalier de Saint-Georges. She brings them to the little room beside her bedroom on the second floor, where Antoinette has installed mirrors on movable panels over the windows.

It's a small space, but there are only four people. Three friends, each of them with different circles of influence and different talents, but all loyal to her.

'I have something to tell you all,' she says. 'It is something wonderful, but it is something dangerous. The knowledge may put your lives in peril. I will love you no less if you choose not to know.'

The chevalier stands stiffly and looks wary, but then he always looks wary, these days. He's had a difficult few years. Antoinette favoured a bid proposing him as the new director of the Paris Opera. He was the obvious choice: he's not only a brilliant soloist and composer, but he's also proven his skills as concertmaster and director of smaller orchestras. But two singers and a dancer gave her a petition declaring that they would find it beneath them to take orders 'from a mulatto'.

Antoinette wanted to ignore the women's petition, but while she hesitated, Saint-Georges formally withdrew his name from consideration. A few months ago, Louis put the operations of the opera under his own supervisor of entertainments, to avoid further scandal.

All in all, she feels that her friendship has been as much an irritant as a help to Saint-Georges, lately. For years, he has been performing magic on her behalf – unwittingly. She owes him a great deal, and let it start with some honesty.

Polignac has her face cast down and her violet eyes cast up, her face serious. Since Antoinette brought her to Versailles, she's been an asset and an inspiration in every way, quietly asserting the Queen's independence and resisting the old strictures of etiquette.

Lamballe looks perfectly relaxed, curious, and trusting. Lamballe is here because there is nothing she won't do for her queen.

These are her chosen confidants, her friends, her allies. The Queen's inner circle.

Antoinette takes a breath.

Out of her pocket, Antoinette pulls two pieces of letter paper, and a third, battered sheet with the *tabula recta* on it, in Charlotte's handwriting. She takes her bottle of ink, and then walks to the writing table in the corner of the room and dips in a quill.

'If you'd like to know, then you must all watch me write,' she announces, and they come closer, obeying. They are nearly over her shoulder.

'Someone give me a keyword.'

There's a pause, then Polignac says, '*Jonquille.*' Antoinette smiles. There are daffodils scattered down the slope beyond the windows, though they can't see them now because of the mirrored shutters.

'Perfect!' She writes 'jonquille' carefully on the first sheet of paper, to teach the ink.

On the second sheet of paper, she writes, very slowly: 'bienvenue dans le cercle social privé de la reine.'

By the time her quill reaches the first 'n', the initial 'b' shivers, and the ink seems to wick strangely into the paper. The 'b' opens into a 'k'. The 'i' doubles, triples, into a 'w'. Saint-Georges shifts. Lamballe gasps. Polignac takes a step back.

'What is it?' Polignac asks.

'Magic,' the Queen says simply. 'It's magic. The ink is enchanted.'

The rest of the ink has soaked into its enciphered shape, a string of letters, undecipherable to anyone without the keyword.

Lamballe claps, smiling. 'I knew it! I knew there was magic in the world. How wonderful!'

Antoinette looks at each face, at the emotions there. She has not felt this way since she and Charlotte did magic together. What a joy it would be to tell Charlotte about this, but Charlotte is a member of the Order, and Antoinette can't ask these people to join her and then put them at risk.

'May I try it, Your Majesty?' Polignac asks.

Antoinette hesitates, looking at her little bottle of brownish ink, so dearly bought with sacrifices. But what else can she show them? So few of her enchanted items have any immediate and visible effect. It occurs to her for the first time that most spells have been made by people who wanted to hide their magic – rogues hiding from the Brothers, or the Brothers themselves hiding magic from the world.

She puts her hand into her pocket, and feels the lorgnette there, one she enchanted with a spell Geneviève sent her: one of the spells she used to work the Mechanical Turk.

The lorgnette is a slim brass tube, wider at one end like a spyglass, just like anything a lady would take to the opera – only this lens does not see what it's pointed at.

'Come with me, Marie-Louise,' she says and, taking Lamballe by the hand, leads her to the Queen's bedroom,

next door. Antoinette unscrews the tortoiseshell cap from the end of the lorgnette, places it carefully on the washstand, and positions Lamballe in front of it, saying, 'Just stand there, dear, and when you hear me call your name, wave at the washstand. I know it sounds ridiculous.'

Lamballe does not question. She never does.

Back in the boudoir, Antoinette hands the lorgnette to Polignac.

'What shall I look at through it?'

'Anything. It doesn't matter.'

Polignac takes the lorgnette to the window, peers through the lens. She steps back with a start, examines the lorgnette, looks through again.

'Marie-Louise, you may wave,' Antoinette calls.

At that, Polignac drops the lorgnette and it rolls on the floor. Polignac picks it up, stares at it for a moment as if it were a grenade, then hands it to Antoinette. 'Your Majesty, I have never seen anything like it.'

Saint-Georges looks next, and then they call Lamballe back in, and then Lamballe looks while Saint-Georges goes next door, until finally they've all seen it: they've seen Lamballe, in the next room, because the lorgnette shows whatever its cap sees. It has not proven very useful, since its cap needs to be close by, just as Geneviève said years ago, but Antoinette keeps it with her, because it reminds her of her friend.

'How astonishing!' Lamballe says, picking up the bottle of ink. 'Where did you get such things?'

'I made them,' Antoinette says. 'And so will you.'

When she has answered the first of their questions, and showed them how to make a star, she warns them they must not tell anyone.

'Are there no other of these "magisters" in Paris?' Polignac asks.

Antoinette shrugs. 'In Paris, there are vagabonds and charlatans and sorcerers. How many there are, and how many are the right sort – I mean, for us to work with – I don't

know. But more importantly, there is a group of magisters: the Order of 1326, they call themselves. They exist to keep magic secret and prevent anyone outside the Order from doing it.'

She explains that they must all take the greatest care to prevent anyone learning what they do together.

'If this Order exists to keep magic secret, and we hide it away, are we not doing their work for them, Your Majesty?' Saint-Georges asks.

'We'll share our knowledge, but carefully, under their noses,' she says, mildly flustered. 'And we'll keep ourselves and any other magister safe from their attacks. They may undermine us, spread stories about us. They may try to take our memories. They may even try to kill us. They think no one should be allowed to do magic unless they are members of their Order and follow their rules. I *do not* accept this. I believe that each of us – each human on this Earth – has only one duty, to ourselves, to our fellow man, and to God – one singular duty, which is to do our best. It sounds so childish, doesn't it? But how can we do our best if we are forbidden from using the tools we have to make beautiful and useful things?'

'Are there magical weapons, Your Majesty?' Saint-Georges asks. 'Magical food? Shelter?'

Antoinette is at a loss. 'I don't know yet what is possible. Yes, there are magical foods. In fact, I have an enchantment for flour that has an effect on the emotions, and using it I hope to resolve the civil war that's been brewing among my husband's advisers. We've seen how badly they've served him in the first two years of his reign: Turgot wants to prove his theories at any cost to king and country, and those whose privileges Turgot is taking away will do anything to save them. Nobody is thinking of the good of France, of the King. But we can. Working in secret, we can change hearts and minds and put an end to the riots, the hunger, the discontent. I believe we could do a great deal. I hope we find out together.'

Saint-Georges nods slightly, thoughtfully.

She considers telling him about his violin bow, but can't think how to explain.

Instead, Antoinette ducks behind a table, and emerges with three scrolls of paper tied in blue ribbon. She hands one to each of her friends, saying, 'Here are all the spells I know. The Petit Trianon is a safe place, and here we can learn together. I've kept this secret here alone for so long, and wished that I could do some useful work with it. Now the time for wishing is over.'

CHAPTER TWENTY-FOUR

King Ferdinand Goes Hunting — Charlotte Is Forgetful —
Sicily — Habsburgs of Old — The Inquisition

Ferdinand isn't good at anything, and he takes no chances when he goes hunting, which is almost daily. He had an enclosure built at Portici in which everything is artificial; even the trees are planted in holes blasted one by one into the volcanic soil and filled with less unpredictable loam. The hunting enclosure is so small that Charlotte can see the far end of it, a smudge of fence against the horizon.

Yelling quickly in Neapolitan, Ferdinand sends two dozen of his beaters to flush out the game with nets and bring them back to him, so he can shoot them and congratulate himself.

Usually Charlotte has the energy to resist when Ferdinand decides he wants her and the children as part of his entourage, but on a September day in the year 1776 she is tired. Her latest childbirth, for Marianna, was taxing: her second birth in a year, and even months later she still feels exhausted. So the family is here, as he demanded: Teresa and Luisa are playing with dolls on a quilted blanket in many colours, and one-year-old Carlo and baby Marianna are sleeping, swaddled and perfect, while the nurse knits beside them.

To make it even harder for Charlotte to say no, Ferdinand has insisted that all the other members of the Council of Naples attend the so-called hunt today as well, so that he can call it a meeting. Ferdinand's father in Spain says he must meet with the Council once a week, but doesn't specify where.

So Charlotte is here, with a scarf around her head and shoulders to keep the sea air at bay, and the half-dozen men who served as Ferdinand's regents and who are now his Council. Tanucci's men, all of them, but only by default. When she manages to keep Tanucci quiet, the old men all listen to her. She wears her white gloves to every meeting. She could enchant another pair but she would prefer not to; she's getting frugal with her sacrifices, now that she's twenty-four years old.

The white gloves do look out of place here where everything is brown and red. Ferdinand is dressed in his favourite floppy hat, with his beaver-fur stockings, and a leather apron and pouch for his instruments of death.

Everyone who isn't running around with nets for Ferdinand is sitting on blankets on the ground: Ferdinand's friends, of the male and female varieties, lean on their elbows, eating grapes and laughing.

The other councillors looks similarly uncomfortable, at least. Princes, dukes, all of them old, sit on large stiff cushions, their legs awkward in front of them.

They are used to Ferdinand, though; they do nothing but shake their mournful jowls at him and wait to be dismissed. Tanucci has no use for a council at all, as he has been making decisions for seventeen years with no one to contradict him save his true master, the King of Spain.

Charlotte sometimes feels sorry for her husband. A little sorry. At eight years old, his parents went off to rule Spain and left him here with these regents and tutors. Left him with his older brother Filippo, who was deemed unfit for the kingship because of his mental condition. Filippo lives

at Portici, and he is with the beaters now, running headlong, and for once, no one is mocking him.

'If we are to have our meeting of the Council, I have some things to discuss,' Charlotte says.

Tanucci's face looks as if she's proposed something ridiculous. 'Here?'

'We meet at the King's pleasure.' She gestures. 'We see before us the King's pleasure.'

He changes his expression to one of long-suffering indulgence. 'Indeed, Your Majesty.'

'Then I propose we begin our work.'

'The true work of the Council', Tanucci lectures, 'does not happen in meetings. We are not a parliament, thank God. We implement the King's will.'

'Which king, I wonder?' Charlotte snaps, and she waves her white glove so she can shut Tanucci up for long enough that she can talk about the Academy she wants to found. The white gloves do come in handy; she lets herself smirk a little at the sight of Tanucci's jowls in motion as he begins to speak, and stops; begins to speak, and stops; begins to speak, and stops.

Charlotte has the floor. Or would, if there were a floor.

But as if he's been summoned, Ferdinand comes sauntering up, covered in blood. He's holding a small dead boar under one arm, like a travesty of a child, and in his other hand he has a long, curved knife.

'Look what I caught,' he says, and throws the newly dead boar down onto the dirt. His friends applaud, and the councillors smile indulgently. A few nicks of Ferdinand's knife by the boar's hamstrings, and he runs an iron bar through the legs, and hangs the beast up.

'Watch, wife,' he says, huffing from the exertion. 'Watch, girls.' The sharp knife circles the legs, separates the black, hairy hide from the pink and white beneath. He peels the hide down and makes a long cut down the middle of the boar. And then with ungloved hands he pulls the entrails

out, holds them high like a trophy and throws them into the dirt. It's all done so quickly; Ferdinand is good at something after all.

Charlotte covers her nose, while her daughters squeal and groan dramatically. Teresa is four and Luisa is three.

'I was just about to inform your councillors that I've completed my list of recommended names for the first investiture of the Royal Academy of Sciences and Humane Letters,' she tells Ferdinand.

'What's that?' he asks incuriously, wiping his knife on his leather apron, as though the apron weren't already coated in blood.

'Well, it doesn't exist yet,' she says. 'But we're creating one, so I've made a list of names, having taken advice from many learned people.'

'Again?' Tanucci asks. Damn. The gloves only work to keep Tanucci quiet if she remembers to use them constantly. Hang Ferdinand for distracting her! 'There were quite enough names on your first list, Your Majesty. Or have you rethought some of your choices?'

She stares, stunned. The first list? A chill creeps up her arms and she can feel her eyes widen as she tries desperately to think faster than this old fox.

She's lost a memory, somewhere. She handed over the names already, and she's forgotten.

Perhaps it coincided with some event where Ferdinand was particularly beastly. Charlotte tries to sacrifice memories of Ferdinand, when she's working an enchantment that requires a sacrifice of memory. It is a double victory: she is able to work the enchantment, and life with Ferdinand becomes a little easier to bear. But she knows it is dangerous to forget too much – she has nightmares of her future self greeting Ferdinand with an innocent smile, unaware, unguarded.

One has to sacrifice something. And now she's forgotten some small matter, and Tanucci is looking at her as though she's hanging on a slaughtering hook herself.

'Well, whatever you both think,' Ferdinand says. 'Tanucci, perhaps you can send someone round to find some eggheads, eh? What about Caramanico, eh? He knows all the smart people.'

For all his bluster, Ferdinand is quite intimidated by philosophers and artists, but he always wants to be thought enlightened. It's one of the reasons Charlotte chose the Academy as a project; she knew that Ferdinand, at least, would not oppose it.

Tanucci makes a face. 'Many of the friends of the Prince of Caramanico may find themselves out of Naples altogether before long. We know all about the Masonic meetings that continue to take place despite His Majesty's wise edict against them. Whom will we find when we surprise one of them, I wonder?'

Surprising a meeting of Masons! Tanucci has been railing against the Masons for years but everyone's largely ignored him, including the Brothers of Naples, who still use a Masonic meeting as cover for their activities. Several lodges have simply flouted the edict Tanucci somehow induced Ferdinand to sign.

Tanucci is gloating, seeing the expression on Charlotte's face. 'Oh, did Your Majesty forget about that? There is no cause for concern. We'll make sure it's a meeting with none of the nobility present.'

Between her memory sacrifices and the white gloves, she's managed to make herself dangerously ignorant of what Tanucci is up to.

Baby Marianna cries; the nurse soothes her back to sleep but now Carlo has woken, and the nurse stands, walking with him. His cry banishes all other thoughts and Charlotte puts her arms out to take him, magnet to magnet. To enfold him in her body and make all well.

Ferdinand steps closer to her, pinches the top of her breast through the fichu. 'He's hungry, or he's pretending he is. Don't I understand it! I'll have some later.'

He roars, and his friends roar with him. Charlotte scowls. She had barely stopped bleeding after Carlo's birth when he came to her bed and thrust himself on her, without so much as asking, and she was pregnant again: two babies within ten months.

'Women are made for the joys of private life,' says Tanucci, beaming at the scene of Charlotte holding the baby. 'A gentler life than the one of statecraft, without so many tedious things to remember. I am quite envious.'

Let Tanucci have his wish, she thinks, violently. Let him find the joys of private life. She sees, suddenly, a way to trap him, a way to be rid of him at last.

'I will consult the Prince of Caramanico about the Academy, while you move against the Masons,' she tells Tanucci, and relishes the look of confusion on his face. 'I think surprising one of their meetings is an excellent idea.'

Charlotte throws open the curtains and looks out over Palermo. Ferdinand is King of Sicily as well as Naples, but they don't get to the island frequently enough for her taste. She turns away from the view, past columns of bright marble and palm trees to low, neat gardens in every kind of green.

Far beyond, Charlotte can just make out the busy port, the masts of ship after ship. Every one of them taking something to or from her people: olive oil, wheat, silk, wool, sulphur, and wine. Sometimes she feels separate from the business of humanity, as though it would carry on much the same no matter who sat on the throne, or who whispered behind it. But she reminds herself it is not so: there would be fewer ships or more in the harbour; they might be bound for other places; they might be carrying poorer things; they might be swarmed by poor and starving people; they might be ships of war or of piracy. Civilization is resilient but not immutable.

When they landed in Palermo three days ago, the first thing she saw was the cages. Hanging from the parapet of a

great stone edifice, the Holy Office of the Inquisition. Three iron cages, their rust staining the walls. Cages that once held those who fought against Charles V, the last Habsburg to rule both the Holy Roman Empire and Spain, as well as much of Italy. She comes from greatness; she comes from barbarism.

But she is not Charles V. She came with Ferdinand this time to tell the Grand Inquisitor – a good, thoughtful man, given his job as a punishment for thinking aloud – that the Holy Office of the Inquisition is ended in Sicily. She can do it, too. The Crown maintains the prisons, and the Crown can, and will, abolish them.

The Crown has long been compensated for its part of the business, receiving one-third of the goods confiscated from heretics. But heretics are thin on the ground, these days. Nowadays, most prisoners of the Holy Office are bigamists – usually wives who've left their rotten husbands and taken up with new men. Old women accused of witchcraft, men accused of sodomy. All sold to the Inquisition by nasty neighbours hoping for reward. And Tanucci has encouraged those neighbours, because every accusation means money for the Kingdom of Naples.

It is an abomination, and she has put a stop to it. The few remaining prisoners, all old and unwell, will be found new places, places they will be cared for. Most prisoners were subjected to the *toca*, a form of interrogation in which the mouth and nose are covered with cloth, and several pitchers of water poured onto the face, so the subject feels as if they are drowning. The Grand Inquisitor seems relieved it is over. But the Holy Father in Rome may object to Maria Carolina meddling in religious matters, and some of the more old-fashioned believers may object too. Tanucci, who has lined his pockets with the goods taken from prisoners, would certainly object. But Tanucci will soon be a problem no longer.

Slowly, Charlotte turns away from the window, looking towards the bed where her husband sleeps. The whole room smells of sour vomit, but she suspects it is just the smell

coming through Ferdinand's pores, as his body tries to rid itself of a quantity of strong spirits consumed at great speed.

She opens the window.

Ferdinand blinks, and puts his arm over his eyes. 'I wasn't to be disturbed.'

'I know,' she says soothingly, apologetically, walking over to his bedside. 'I would not have let them disturb you for anything less than an emergency, but this—'

He sits up, his shirt falling half off his shoulder. At least he's alone this morning.

'The children?' he asks, awake now, alarmed.

She shakes her head. 'They're all fine. It's more an emergency of state.'

Relieved, he waves her away. 'Tanucci can handle—'

'I'm afraid Tanucci's the one who's created the mess. And this time, I don't think there's any way he can clean it up.'

She sits on the edge of his bed, gingerly, and passes him the sheet of paper in her hands.

Ferdinand's brows bunch in the way they always do when he reads. '"Luigi Seno. The Prince of Ferolito. Don Paolo Moccia. The Prince of Francavilla. The Duke of Maddaloni. The Duke of San Demetrio. The Duchess of Termoli. Niccolò Piccinni."' He stops, although Charlotte knows the list continues. He looks up. 'Is this the list for your Royal Academy?'

'It is not, although several of the names might appear on that list as well, might they not? No, this is the list of the people apprehended by Tanucci's thugs at a Masonic meeting in Naples a few nights ago. They are all in his custody, although he has had the good sense not to dungeon any of them. I believe he has them sitting in your opera house. What he intends to do with them now, I cannot say.'

It was such a small matter, once she'd decided to do it. An innocent question to another member of the Council, to determine where and when Tanucci planned to send his thugs. And then, invitations to a soirée at that lodge, that night, to all the great and good of Naples.

Invitations that could, quite literally, not be refused. There is a spell in the *Reconditus* for summoning magic, a spell that Soliman says has been neglected, as every magister eventually realizes that it doesn't mean summoning a familiar, a demon, a ghost, or even someone long lost or in hiding. It simply summons the person who agrees to touch the paper. Charlotte finds it very useful, even if her brethren do not.

Ferdinand's eyes go as round as oranges. 'But he said there would be no nobility! And these – these are some of our best writers, best musicians. The list – how many?' His voice is a whisper.

'Thirty-nine. The question at this moment, my husband, is whether you would rather explain to your father why all these luminaries have left Naples – as they surely will, if they are further insulted – or whether it is time for the old bull to go out to pasture.'

Ferdinand runs his hands through his short, sweaty hair. He looks, for a moment, younger than his twenty-five years, younger than Charlotte's twenty-four. A brat, a bully, and a fraud. He has no choice, and he knows it. But he has never had to be the one to make decisions. When his father left to take the throne of Spain, Tanucci was there to tell him what to do. Tanucci has always been there for him.

'But what would we do about the Inquisition?' he asks.

She's taken aback momentarily, that his mind should run there – he doesn't know what she's been doing here while he whores and hunts. But he is not a man who sees past the end of his long Bourbon nose: the Inquisition, with its declining revenues, is his most proximate worry, here in Sicily. And Tanucci has always been the one to manage it.

'I'll take care of it,' she says.

Ferdinand looks up at her. 'Will you?'

'Certainly. It's better if the King doesn't get involved in disputes over holy matters.'

'That's true. And you like to keep busy.'

'I do,' she says, sitting beside him on the rumpled, stinking bed. She waits.

'Give me a pen and paper, will you, Charlotte? I will write Tanucci's dismissal now.'

CHAPTER TWENTY-FIVE

War in America — An Inconvenient Performance of
The Barber of Seville — The Peace Room — La Hire and
the Queen of Hearts — A Secret Meeting

In February 1777, Versailles reeks of wood smoke and everyone repairs to the smallest rooms, where the outmoded fireplaces stand a chance of doing some good. When the Marquis de Lafayette is announced, Antoinette sees him in her private cabinet room, much smaller than the two state antechambers. The decor is dark and heavy; all these rooms were vacant for years, when there was no queen to occupy them. The walls seem to have a patina of age on them, or perhaps that's only the soot. There's work to be done here. But for now, she focuses on the face of the young man in front of her, blotchy not only from the cold but from indignation too.

They both stand; Lafayette does not have the rank to sit in her presence. She's seen him here and there, since she met him that night at the opera, when she saw Rohan with the knife, and Fersen. Lafayette is always gallant and has rescued her more than once from a tedious dance or conversation. He's not the best dancer, but his timing is always good.

'You are so certain that the cause in America is just?' she asks him. 'You'd risk your life for these rebels? I've heard some say the Americans are simply angry that King George won't let them take more land from the natives in the west. I'm not sure why any Frenchman should take up arms to encourage spoiling the Americas.'

The magisters who meet at the Petit Trianon have all been using enchanted flour – and other spells for spying and persuasion – to gently sway the consensus at Versailles towards incremental reforms, to keep the peace and prevent unrest. It worked better than Antoinette dreamed, with the unforeseen consequence that Turgot became as unpopular at Versailles as he was in the rest of the country, and the King dismissed him.

But the new minister of finance, Jacques Necker, is just as opposed to a costly war in America as Turgot was.

'I'd risk my life to prevent King George deciding anything for all the world, as he seems determined to do,' Lafayette says. 'I understand why His Majesty had to be seen to forbid any Frenchmen from going to fight in America. Publicly. But privately . . . If I could slip away, you see, and know that I had His Majesty's secret permission to do so . . .'

'And you would like me to obtain that secret permission?'

'I would, Your Majesty. I know that the King listens to no one so much as he listens to you.'

She spreads her hands. 'Lafayette, my husband is walking the edge of a knife, as you must know. We cannot risk yet another open war with England. In the last one, I am told, we lost our navy, most of our colonies in India and America, and much of the treasury.'

'And I lost my father,' says Lafayette, thin-lipped. 'These are all reasons why France should be doing its utmost to help England's enemies now.'

'The King already went along with Monsieur Beaumarchais's scheme to run weapons across the Atlantic.'

Beaumarchais, who has been a clock-maker, a harp teacher

at Versailles, and a playwright, has been trying his hand at spycraft lately. He was in England, trying to negotiate the return of a rogue French spy, the Chevalier d'Éon, and he's been talking to the American delegates desperate for French support in their war. He invented a company that delivers French supplies to rebels without implicating the French King.

'It was Beaumarchais who thwarted me!' Lafayette paces in anger; then he stops himself with a jolt, realizing he turned his back on the Queen for a moment. 'We were in Le Havre. We were there! I was on the ship! We were ready to sail for America, and no one knew. Then Beaumarchais gets wind of a local production of *The Barber of Seville*. He cannot resist going to see it, and then when he thinks they are staging it wrong, he steps in to direct it himself! With everyone talking about that, it wasn't long before the English got wind that he had three ships laden with supplies and fighting men, and sent a protest to the King. Beaumarchais has ruined everything.'

Antoinette can't help but smile. 'Not everything, surely. Lafayette, you have a young wife here at Versailles, don't you? And a baby?'

The familiar expression crosses his face: the awareness, not quite guilt and not quite pity, that Antoinette herself has no child. She has seen it cross so many faces.

But when Lafayette speaks, it is not about his wife and child. 'Your Majesty, I was raised in the south of France, by my grandmother, after the English cannonball killed my father. My ancestor fought with Joan of Arc! And I was stuck out in the countryside, hunting the fabled beast of Gévaudan with a stick by day, and eating stewed beef with a kindly old lady at night.' He laughs shortly. 'I couldn't avenge my father.'

'You were a child,' she says gently.

'And now I am a man, with a dull sword at my waist. My whole life, I have wanted only to take up arms in a good cause. That's all I ask.'

She considers. 'I cannot ask my husband to put this country's peace at risk.'

He casts his face down, nods. 'Of course, Your Majesty.'

'You could . . .' she says.

'Yes?' He looks up, hopeful again.

'You could go to England. Visit someone there – find some pretext. Then sail from there.'

He nods. 'Throw the dogs off my scent. But the trouble is that the ship I bought is docked in Bordeaux.'

'The ship you *bought*!'

'Oh yes,' Lafayette says, grinning. 'Did I forget to mention that? After Beaumarchais ruined our plans in Le Havre, I bought a ship in Bordeaux. But the trouble is that the King has men watching my ship, day and night. He's had to, to placate the English, and then also my father-in-law is so set against my plans . . .'

'I don't wonder,' Antoinette says, thinking of Lafayette's young wife. She'll have to make sure the young woman is provided for, once Lafayette leaves.

Because Lafayette will leave, and Antoinette is going to help him. Here is a chance for Antoinette to help France's interest in secret. To help her husband, and to be of some use to her people.

Besides, why shouldn't a young person be able to act boldly, to prove his worth through his courage, in a cause he believes to be just?

'Wait here,' she says, and she walks through the panel into the secret room, the *arrière-cabinet* with the enchanted firescreen. She enters it brazenly, knowing Lafayette will forget it is there, just as everyone does.

She returns with a hat in her hand. A black tricorne that she wore for her portrait in riding clothes, six years ago. Her mother's favourite portrait of her, despite the fact that Maria Theresa disapproves of women riding.

For years, Antoinette has been trying to work out the enchantment for the 'cap of Hades' in the embroidered book,

the one that promises to 'steal shadows'. She was sure it would confer invisibility, and she was right. Finally, she found the right sacrifices. She was desperate for a way to walk unseen, a few weeks after she had to walk through the Hall of Mirrors the day her nephew was born. The hat seemed to make people's gazes slip off her. She has used it a few times since, but she can always enchant another. She hesitates, suddenly nervous that the marquis will mock her, disbelieve her, but this is a man who spent his childhood hunting a legendary beast.

'You must swear to me now, on your honour, to keep the secret I'm about to tell you,' Antoinette says, holding out the hat.

Lafayette, looking slightly confused, swears passionately.

'This hat has an enchantment on it. When you wear it, people will not notice you. They might be able to see you, if they look straight at you and concentrate very hard, but when they aren't doing that, you can slip right past them. As if you're in a deep shadow.'

So many expressions pass over his face that she can't tell what he's thinking.

'I'll show you,' she says. 'Look out of the window for a moment, and try to think about something else. Count to one hundred, then turn back and look for me.'

He turns slowly, and she jams the hat onto her hair, cringing at what Monsieur Léonard will say when he sees what she's done to this morning's creation. She walks to the far side of the room, and waits. Lafayette turns, looks at the spot where she had been standing. Then he lets his gaze roam, but doesn't see her.

She takes the hat off her head with a triumphant flourish, and hands it to him. 'This ought to get you past my husband's hounds.'

He looks down at the hat. 'An enchantment.'

'Yes.'

He looks around the room again, as if to convince himself that what he just saw – or didn't see – was real.

'I've never seen such a marvel.'

'It's not the only such marvel in the world,' she says. 'But you must promise not to mention that to anyone. For my sake as well as yours.'

'I will keep this, and the secret of it,' he says, his voice low. 'I will honour the gift you've given me, Your Majesty.'

She ought to feel nervous, exposing her secret again. Instead, she feels exhilarated. Another friend and ally. Lafayette is young and honourable, and she trusts him to do what he thinks is right.

'Just come home to your wife, Lafayette.'

By April of 1777, Lafayette's departure is the talk of Versailles. He went to England for a few weeks, and his family thought he was still there when they received his farewell letter. He sailed to Spain, and then disembarked so he could go back to Bordeaux and write once more to Versailles to plead for permission. Antoinette half suspects he just hasn't had a chance to use her hat of shadows yet and is desperate for the King's men to chase him.

But at least it is now clear to everyone that he's an ungovernable young man, and there is no case for England to go to war over him.

The Peace Room, which connects the Queen's Apartments to the Hall of Mirrors, is painted in scenes of plenty and grace, supported by walls of swirling grey marble and delicate gold. It is a room of glories and triumphs.

It is, in short, the perfect room for a game of cards.

On a little marble table to one side are pink- and green-glazed petits fours, made by the Queen's own chef with flour Antoinette enchanted – the Queen explained that she wanted to make good use of the flour given her by France's millers. It's an experiment, tonight: she's trying some new emotions. The pink ones should induce good humour and the green ones suspicion.

The trouble with the experiment is that everyone has been

eating the cakes that already accord with their personalities. Antoinette's partner for whist tonight is Louis's merry brother, the Comte d'Artois. He could very well end up being the father of the nation if Antoinette does not manage to give France a dauphin, but he's so gracious and good-natured that she can't begrudge him. He's had a pink cake, though she can't tell the difference.

Their opponents are Adélaïde and Victoire, or as the court still calls them, Aunt Rag and Aunt Pig. A green cake each.

'Do you think Jacques Necker will last?' Adélaïde asks, to nobody and everybody. 'I think he's much more reasonable than Turgot. Not such a fanatic.'

'Mmmm,' says d'Artois, picking up his cards and frowning at them.

Antoinette has a red ribbon to wear in her hair that enhances her own short-term memory – she uses it on busy court days – but she does not wear it to play cards. Antoinette is many things but never a cheat.

She focuses on her own cards. The first one she sees is the Jack of Hearts. This card always depicts La Hire, the French hero of the Hundred Years War, but this is a strange deck: instead of La Hire's name printed down one side, it has a motto: 'Jusqu'à la mort'.

Unto death.

She shudders, and remembers the night she met Axel von Fersen in Paris, in their masks, when he used those very words.

And – how odd – the drawing of the Jack looks very like him. Uncannily like him.

'Are you with us, Your Majesty?' Adélaïde asks, and Antoinette looks up to meet the aunt's shrewd gaze.

If Adélaïde were a magister, with enchanted ribbons of her own, that might explain her eccentric style. Why in God's name would she wear that ecru lace shawl over a striped pink-and-green *robe à la polonaise*? She looks a fright. She is forty-five now, twice Antoinette's age. Somehow,

Antoinette can't imagine ever being that old. It would be charitable of Antoinette to lend Adélaïde her dressmaker, Rose Bertin, or Léonard Autié for her hair – but Adélaïde would no doubt take it wrong, just as she did when Antoinette asked her to take charge of the orphan boy Antoinette recently adopted, after her carriage nearly ran him over in the street. Antoinette had thought it would be seen as a mark of great favour, but a week of flattery was required to convince Adélaïde of that.

'How is little Armand this week?' Antoinette asks breezily. 'Is he still having trouble learning his multiplication?'

'He doesn't see why he should, and I'm inclined to agree with him,' says Adélaïde. 'What point is there in teaching a child of his background things he'll never put to use?'

'He might put them to use,' says Antoinette, flicking the corner of the Jack of Hearts in her hand. 'Why shouldn't he? Perhaps he'll invent something using the multiplication tables. A flying machine. Or a new kind of . . . oh, I don't know. Bridge, or gun.'

'The day your protégé invents a flying machine is the day I fly to the moon,' murmurs Victoire.

Antoinette is unreasonably offended on Armand's behalf. Or perhaps not so unreasonably. She was not supposed to learn magic, but she did, and she has discovered a dozen new spells since she came to Versailles, useful spells that weren't even in the embroidered book. And she's willing to bet some of them, at least, were not in any magister's book. What might little Armand do, if he had a spellbook? What does it cost the world to keep him ignorant and incapable? He might invent a new kind of bridge. The world always needs better bridges.

Antoinette draws the Queen of Diamonds, and though it ought to be the Biblical Rachel, the picture on it looks exactly like Marie Antoinette.

And the motto is not the name Rachel, but four words: 'Cour de la Reine'.

The Queen's Courtyard. There is a Queen's Courtyard here at Versailles, in the midst of her private chambers. It's dark and dismal and no one ever goes there.

No one ever goes there.

She slides the Jack and Queen cards to one side of her hand and looks at the next: another Jack, this one the Jack of Clubs. Lancelot. Only he, too, looks uncannily like Axel von Fersen. And there is only one word on this card: 'Minuit'.

Unto death.

The Queen's Courtyard.

Midnight.

Antoinette pushes her chair back and stands, gripping the table with one hand and throwing her cards onto it with the other. She realizes too late that she's thrown the cards face up, but now that they're on the table, the words have changed back to their usual forms, and the pictures too.

The message, if it was a message, was for her alone.

The Queen of France is in possession of a particular coverlet that she requests on certain nights, a coverlet that creates the impression, if one does not examine it too closely, that she is underneath it.

She is also in possession of a new hat of shadows, this one small and made of straw, with a jolly blue ribbon. It doesn't go with her lace dressing gown at all, but then no one will see her in it, will they? That's the point.

Unless, of course, her suspicion is correct and there is someone waiting in the courtyard. Which is why she has worn a particularly nice, and particularly modest, lace dressing gown. Her hair is brushed, braided and unpowdered, and she is wearing no rouge or face powder. The light of a single candle is forgiving, or so she hopes.

When she steps lightly down the stone steps and sees the dark courtyard empty, lit only by a patch of moonlight, she is taken aback by her own disappointment. All the windows are dark; the parts of the palace that stay up after midnight

do not face onto the Queen's Courtyard, and neither does the room where her guards are stationed.

It is dark, empty, and cold: just barely April, and midnight. She has been ridiculous.

She turns, hears 'Your Majesty', and nearly jumps out of her skin.

Axel von Fersen steps out of the shadows, holding a tricorne hat.

'It is you,' she says, which is not the right thing to say but it will have to serve. 'And I see you have ways of going unseen. Count von Fersen, if one wishes to be presented to the Queen, there are less uncomfortable ways.'

'I'm perfectly comfortable. Are you uncomfortable, Madame?'

He's teasing her; she gives him a look. 'I thought you had forgotten all about me.'

He glances away from her into the darkness. 'I beg your forgiveness. I have been occupied elsewhere.'

'I know,' she says, happy to have more information than he may realize. 'Our mutual friend Geneviève told me you were working together. She told me you were nothing to worry about.'

'Did she?' He looks at her again, smiling now. 'I'm not sure I like the sound of that!'

'Geneviève is a very discerning woman. Where is she now? Is she well?'

'She is very well. As for her discernment, well, you ought to know that she warned me about you.'

'Did she really? What harm could I possibly do to you?'

'Much,' he says, but he punctuates it with another wry little smile. They're standing inches apart now, but he's not the same young man who grabbed her arm so easily at the opera house. He's a few years older, he's got a day's growth of stubble and his eyes are tired, but perhaps that's only the effect of the candle in her hand.

'I'm glad you decided to make your appearance at last,'

she says. 'Though I do still think you might have asked for an audience.'

'I'm not in France at the moment. Not officially. I'm here to see some friends, to pass on some messages that I couldn't trust to anyone else. The Order thinks I'm in Sweden and I wish them to continue believing that. I came here to tell you that the war in America is more important than you may realize.'

'I understand the importance of the American war, Count von Fersen.'

'Of course. Forgive me, Your Majesty. What I mean is that it is important in another way, too. The Order – you know all about the Order, I think?'

'I do.' She thinks of Charlotte, and knows he is thinking of Charlotte too.

'It has kept itself out of politics, out of all affairs of the world, for centuries. But the situation in America has rather forced its hand. It has very little presence there – all its copies of the *Reconditus*, its book of spells, are on this continent. It is finding it difficult to suppress rogue magisters in Europe's colonies, and it worries that an independent America may become a training ground and haven for rogues.'

'What does this have to do with me?'

'Just as many Brothers are fighting on the side of the British, many rogues are fighting on the side of the rebels. Not all of us – there are rogues on both sides. But there are more on the rebels' side. So the more chance we can give the rebels, the more chance we have of breaking the Order's grip on magic for good.'

'And you think I can influence my husband.' She thinks of her group of magisters, already so practised in shifting opinion at court.

He looks awkward. 'Anything you can do, even the smallest thing.'

She hesitates. She has already done one small thing. 'Do you write to any of these rogues who are fighting in America?'

277

'I do.'

'Will you ask them to keep one eye on the young Marquis de Lafayette? He is a friend.'

He says nothing for a moment; then he chuckles. 'I wondered how he made his escape so easily. All right. I will make sure he has friends among the rogue magisters. As do you, Your Majesty. But please be warned. The Order is changing its ways, but it remains dedicated to hunting rogues. I know of your connection to the Order in Naples—'

She frowns. 'I wouldn't put it that way.'

'Just be sure you don't count on that connection to keep you safe. Every chapter of the Order makes its own decisions, and the Brothers in Paris are zealots.'

'I have spent many years being careful and discreet,' she says.

Fersen doesn't smile. 'I'm not sure discretion will be any protection now. We will all need our friends, and as much powerful magic as we can muster.'

A peal of distant laughter from a window above – Antoinette looks up, but there's no light to be seen. Just the life of Versailles.

When she brings her gaze back down to earth, Fersen is gone.

CHAPTER TWENTY-SIX

*Too Much of a Coincidence — Count Falkenstein Arrives
at Versailles — Hairstyles — Antoinette Continues
to Disappoint — A Frank Talk*

2 *April 1777*
Louis de Rohan to Maria Carolina

Your Majesty,

In gratitude, I received your letter of congratulation on
my elevation to the position of grand almoner of France, and
I must humbly agree with your assessment that if I am soon
made a cardinal, it will be of great utility for our Order. God
will dispose as he sees fit, but in the meantime, I am
making all arrangements I can.

Though I disagreed with the decision of the Brothers
of Naples to admit a monarch — I made no secret of it —
I have always hoped that we would be able to work together
to fight the scourge of rogue magic, which is proliferating in
Paris despite our best efforts. I regret to inform Your
Majesty that I have recently become aware that this scourge
has entered the very heart of Versailles.

Over and over, I have reassured my Brothers here that if
the Queen of France had been a magister from childhood,

Your Majesty would surely not have concealed such a danger from us. It is inconceivable that Your Majesty would be so reckless; it would be treason against the Order. Of course, I can't argue against them when they point out that much of the magic that seems to be afoot in Versailles bears a striking resemblance to the effects of Your Majesty's white gloves, which are celebrated throughout the Order – so few magisters have managed to use that spell to any good purpose, though it has been in the Reconditus for generations.

How astonishing, then, that the court of Versailles turned, almost overnight, against Monsieur Turgot, so that one moment he was hailed as a visionary, and the next, exiled in disgrace. For months, the Order here has been trying to ascertain how it happened. We have traced the change of heart of every courtier, every adviser. And each trail comes back to one of four people: the Queen of France herself, or one of three friends, including her two favourites, the Princesse de Lamballe and the Comtesse de Polignac. The whole of Versailles knows how the Queen meets with her intimate friends at the Petit Trianon.

It all seems too much of a coincidence, and if magic is indeed being used to steer the ship of state, I hope you will share my alarm and tell us anything you may know about the activities of your sister. Perhaps you have been as surprised as I by all of this, given your earlier reassurances that Her Majesty was not a magister.

Please accept, Madame, my sincerest salutations, and be assured I remain,

> *Yours in fraternity,*
> *Prince Louis de Rohan*

In the unforgiving light of a morning in April 1777, Antoinette's face in the mirror is unpowdered, unrouged, imperfect. She is twenty-one and has been married for seven years – half married. Is her face doughy around the jaw?

She would like to lean forward, to look more closely, but Monsieur Léonard has her by the hair.

This Monsieur Léonard is not the same as the one she usually uses. This is Jean-François Autié, Léonard Autié's brother. The original Monsieur Léonard has been so successful at Versailles that he sent for Jean-François as an assistant. While the original is apparently the one who develops new styles, they both implement them perfectly well. Somehow, they have arranged it so that whenever anyone calls for Monsieur Léonard, the brothers send whichever of them is at liberty.

They also dress alike, and look nearly identical, and speak the same Gascon French, pronouncing letters that the Parisians leave silent. There are already stories circulating about one brother creating an alibi for another so they can carry on affairs.

But at the moment, Monsieur Léonard looks very sober, almost dour, with tongs in his hand.

She is slowly getting used to the Queen's Bedchamber, this enormous temple of rose and gold, divided into the parts where she is displayed, and the parts where the people may come to see her. The bed itself is an enormous stage on which the last drama to be played was the death of the previous queen, her husband's grandmother, two years before Antoinette arrived in Versailles. Beside the bed are panelled doors where the women of the court stream in every morning to take their roles in dressing her.

When that's done, it's not a bad place to receive visitors, while Monsieur Léonard does her hair. But today, mercifully, is quiet, as her brother is coming and she has refused to see anyone else. It's only Antoinette, and Léonard, and Lamballe. While Monsieur Léonard works his magic, Lamballe plays the harp, quite beautifully.

'Your Majesty's hair is growing back,' says Monsieur Léonard, dividing it into locks. He – they – took the missing clump of hair as a personal affront, and have been dressing

281

her hair with customized pieces and wigs and elaborate ribbons to cover it up.

Lamballe walks over to her with a click click click on the polished floor, leans forward and takes a pot of rouge off the table. She dots each cheek with it, using her finger. These little intimate touches – to make Antoinette feel that she is just a young woman in a room with friends and pretty things – they're deliberate, of course. Antoinette would like to put her arm around her, but she can't move at the moment, without risking Monsieur Léonard's irritation.

'Tell us some gossip, Monsieur Léonard,' Lamballe says brightly.

'I never gossip, Your Highness. That's my brother.'

'I command you,' Antoinette murmurs, keeping her head perfectly still for him, giving Lamballe a little smile with only the corners of her mouth.

'Well,' he says, but does not pause long enough to make a convincing show of searching his memory, 'have you heard about the Chevalier d'Éon?'

Who has not? A dragoon and a spy, who blackmailed the late King with some secret papers, and so has been living in exile in England, until now.

'I've heard d'Éon and my husband the King have come to an arrangement, that d'Éon has agreed to hand over the letters and behave, and come home to France. Quite the development!'

'Ah, but you haven't heard the most wonderful part!' says Monsieur Léonard joyfully, having abandoned all pretence of reluctance to gossip. 'D'Éon is the chevalière now, not the chevalier.'

'What do you mean?'

'She says she is a woman,' says the hairdresser, 'and always has been.'

'I had heard that d'Éon dressed as a woman to sneak into Russia—'

'This is no disguise, Your Majesty. She says she *is* a woman.

She only agreed to come home after His Majesty agreed to pay for a new wardrobe of women's clothing. She also wants to go to America to fight. In a dress, one assumes.'

'A *robe à la polonaise*, for the freedom in the skirts,' says Lamballe, smiling.

'Oh yes.' Léonard laughs. 'A *robe à la française* would be completely unsuitable for fighting.'

'I think I could fight,' Lamballe says.

Antoinette laughs in her turn. 'My dear, you swoon at the sight of blood. Don't you remember how we had to revive you when I cut myself on a bit of broken glass?'

'Other people's pain, yes, but my own doesn't bother me a bit. I just think about embroidery.'

'Embroidery!'

'It's very calming. I imagine the needle going in and out, the snick of the thread through the cloth, the colours. I don't know why. It's a trick I picked up as a child.'

Antoinette smiles at her beautiful friend. Lamballe has proven quite talented with magic, and always seems to know precisely how to substitute sacrifices for the old spells that make so little sense to anyone else.

Monsieur Léonard fits the metal frame of the pouf onto the crown of Antoinette's head and stuffs the triangular cork shape inside.

'How marvellous this is, about the Chevalière d'Éon. Don't you think it's marvellous, Monsieur Léonard? I am looking forward to meeting her, even if she did spy on my family, once upon a time. Perhaps I should give her one of my dresses.'

'It would probably make a scandal.'

'Oh, probably. But it would give me pleasure.'

He draws a lock of her stumpy hair through the frame, adds a lock of false hair from his kit. 'Tch,' he says, and pulls it out again. 'I am afraid nothing is going right.'

'Do your best, Monsieur Léonard,' she says, with another smile. 'It is all any of us can do.'

Madame Campan opens the door, glides over to them and says, 'Count Falkenstein has arrived at Versailles.'

She claps her hands together. Joseph!

'Count Falkenstein, Your Majesty? I don't know the name,' Léonard murmurs.

'My brother. The Emperor. That's the name he travels under.'

Even as a child, Joseph bore the world on his shoulders. He stoops a little now. Thirty-six and twice a widower, his people hungry and war at his borders. No wonder he looks dyspeptic.

He kisses her hand, and Lamballe's, as Monsieur Léonard bows.

'I don't know what you hope to achieve by travelling incognito,' Antoinette says. 'You can't help looking like who you are.'

'It saves on expense and wasted time, that's all, not having to go through all the ceremonies and rigamarole when I visit a place as the Emperor. And you look – well, I won't say like a queen, unless queens are constructed of wire and cork now. I had heard your hairstyles were ridiculous but this . . .'

'This, Your Imperial Majesty, is exactly how queens are constructed,' says Lamballe loyally. 'We are in the queen-making factory. And Monsieur Léonard is the manager of the factory.'

'I hoped to have a moment with you alone,' Joseph says, looking at Antoinette.

'I am never alone, so you might as well say what you like. I can no more be separated from Lamballe than I can my very soul. She knows everything anyway. And don't worry about Monsieur Léonard. He only gossips at the Queen's instruction.'

Joseph raises his eyebrows. 'All right then.' He pulls a gilded chair forward, sits on the sky-blue cushion. He looks sprightly, as if he might rise at any moment on a matter of state. He leans forward. 'Mother is worried,' he begins.

'Of course she is. She is a martyr to it. Is it my hair? I have told her that a *pouf sentimental* is simple good taste here.'

'Because you have made it so. You set the fashion and then you complain that you're a victim of it.'

'Joseph, when I tried to wear a corset that didn't make me numb to the fingertips, they nearly sent me away from this place in disgrace. If I kiss a friend on the cheek, it is a scandal. If I step off the garden path to see a butterfly, I am not behaving like a queen. The only freedom I have is excess.'

Lamballe replaces the pewter lid on the rouge pot, punctuating the end of Antoinette's little speech.

'Your freedom costs the treasury dear. Surely you could reduce your dress budget a little. It's unseemly.'

'If I reduced my dress budget, two hundred people would immediately find themselves out of work, and people would hate me for ruining the French economy and failing to comport myself like a French queen. I tried it. I know.'

Monsieur Léonard takes the cloth snake from his dressing table and climbs up on the stepladder to wrap it around her hair.

'Good lord, it that a snake?' Joseph asks.

'It's the serpent of Asclepius, silly. There will also be a club, a sun and an olive branch. Can you guess the riddle?'

He shakes his head.

'It's a celebration of smallpox inoculation,' Antoinette explains. 'Since we women of Versailles started wearing it, after the disease struck the late King, inoculation has become a fashion here. My hair saves lives, Joseph.'

He rolls his eyes. 'I can't tell when you're being serious.'

'Well, I'm a Frenchwoman now.'

'Apparently. But don't forget the reason you are a Frenchwoman. You are here to hold Europe together, not to indulge your whims. And it isn't only your hair that has Mother on her knees praying for you every moment she gets. Antoine, you have been married seven years now.'

'Ah,' she says. 'That.'

'Yes. That. What in God's name is wrong? Is it—' He glances at Monsieur Léonard, and then at Lamballe, who has occupied herself in arranging the brushes on Antoinette's dressing table. 'You're sure you wouldn't rather we spoke about this later?'

'All the world knows my husband does not have – how do the pamphlets put it? No, perhaps we'd better put it another way. Does not have congress with me.'

'Well, why not? Is there something wrong with him? He's what, nearly twenty-three now? We can't put it down to youthful shyness any more. There must be something.'

She cannot move, not with Monsieur Léonard attaching the white-spotted red ribbon, his new touch for *poufs à l'in-oculation*. She cannot shrug or cock her head.

'He has been examined, and the doctors say no operation is necessary. He can – he can, you see, but he doesn't. He simply doesn't like it.'

Joseph makes a noise of exasperation, waves his hand. 'He ought to be whipped like a donkey – that might do the trick.'

Lamballe snorts with laughter, but then puts her pretty hand to her mouth. She and Antoinette make wide eyes at each other.

'All right,' says Joseph, more calmly. 'I'll talk to him. Antoine, I wish you were happier here.'

She stares straight into the mirror. 'Do you remember what happened at my marriage? How all those people died, trampled to death, during the fireworks display? I thought the people would hate me for it. But they didn't. And then at our coronation, in Reims, when the people had no bread, and there was so much misery. Still they came to see us. They lined the streets and they cheered. My marriage makes them happy. And that makes me happy. Really, it does.'

He nods, and bows his head. When he raises it again, his tone is gentler than she's ever heard it. 'Then you must give them a future, Antoine. You must give them a dauphin.

France is in trouble. More trouble than you know, I think. The King needs an heir, or he – and you – may very well be replaced.'

'Replaced! You mean my baby nephew? Or perhaps Philippe d'Orléans? Wouldn't he like that.'

She blinks as Monsieur Léonard's ministrations draw tears from her eyes. Her hair is done, rising above the top of the mirror. She puts the cone over her face and Monsieur Léonard applies the powder, as Joseph stands and steps a few feet away to protect himself. She has put a little of her enchanted flour into the hair powder – the one for goodwill – to see whether it might have some effect even if it is not ingested. So far it is difficult to say.

'Next,' she says. 'everyone comes in to watch me apply the rouge.'

The doors open and in come the courtiers, in order of precedence, gliding past the dais where she and Joseph sit. She watches his face in the mirror: there is nothing like this in Vienna. Here she is on display. He needs to understand that. He needs to understand how she is loved.

When her face is covered in white cream and powder, with two circles of red on her cheeks, she turns to Joseph.

'What do you think? Is the edifice complete?'

'I think you look like a harpy, decorated in the blood of your victims.'

She smiles, and now she can cock her head, carefully, judging the angle.

'That's only because you're standing so close to me,' she says. 'From a distance, I look lovely.'

CHAPTER TWENTY-SEVEN

The Austrian Woman — Hunters in the Woods —
An Offering of Love — The Emperor's Advice

One benefit of Joseph's travelling as Count Falkenstein is that there is no need for a state dinner. He occupies himself for his first few days, trying to arrange a meeting with Benjamin Franklin without annoying the British. Louis takes Joseph to the smithy where he spends so many hours making his locks and keys. He invites Antoinette, as he always does, but she makes her usual excuse: 'Venus does not visit Vulcan's forge.'

For her part, she invites Joseph to come and see the Petit Trianon.

Here, she does not have to put up with courtiers and commoners alike, all crowding in, each to hand her an article of clothing or gawk or show their position or brag to their friends. All these worthless rewards they fight for like chickens scrapping over corn in a yard. All inventions of the Sun King. He made the French court the way he needed it to be, so he could survive. He could not have known the consequences for an Austrian archduchess a hundred years later, and he certainly would not have cared.

It is the kind of bright clear morning in which it almost

seems that life itself might be enough. Joseph arrives and she is ready for him, playing cards with Lamballe, Polignac, and Saint-Georges on the patio. The princess is in a *robe à la polonaise*, her perfectly round pink overskirt raised and swagged over a robin's-egg petticoat. But Antoinette is in her riding costume: brown breeches, red redingote, black hat.

'Good God,' says Joseph, looking her up and down. 'Is there a fancy-dress party?'

'You said you wanted to go riding, brother.'

'Yes, but with my sister, not a musketeer.'

'Amalia dresses like a man all the time, so I hear.'

'Yes, well. Amalia is another of my problems.'

They take their leave of the other three, who do not seem sorry to see them go – they are eager to practise. They have each got a little pot of ash and their scroll of spells. As she rides away with Joseph, she can see Saint-Georges, Lamballe, and Polignac walking into the woods behind the Trianon, their heads low, chattering away.

Antoinette and Joseph ride out through the woods in the cool glancing sunshine, on two long-necked bay mares. The formal gardens and waters of Versailles stretch out behind the palace like a long cross, surrounded by thousands of acres of forest. This was a hunting lodge before the Sun King made it the centre of France. The Petit Trianon is on one edge of the estate, and it takes only a few steps to be out on the criss-cross network of the beaten roads and narrow deer paths, all shaded by oak, birch, linden, and chestnut.

'Have you arranged your meeting with Monsieur Franklin?' she asks.

'Mmm, it's proving difficult, but I'm sure we'll pull it off. I'd like to see Rousseau while I'm here, if I can. And Voltaire on my way home, though it would send Mama to an early grave if she heard of it.'

'I wonder if Rousseau the man is as comforting a companion as his books are,' she says.

'You find his books comforting? I didn't know you were even reading them.'

'Well, I have them read to me,' she says, with a sly smile, and quotes: '"Let us leave to others the task of instructing mankind in their duty, and confine ourselves to the discharge of our own."'

'Mmm. That would be comforting, I can imagine.'

'I do try to do my duty,' she says. 'I know you don't believe it, but I try very hard.'

'I do believe it.'

They turn the horses onto one of the main roads that lead through the woods, past the gardens. In the distance they can hear shouts and the barking of dogs: Louis and his brother, hunting.

'I had a talk with Louis,' Joseph says, his horse walking next to hers. 'It's all a matter of confidence. He had a few bad moments and it's put him off the whole business. I never knew such indolence. And in a king!'

She remembers how Joseph left his second wife alone in misery, not sharing her bed or even her table, but she says nothing. It is beside the point.

'Now, I know it must be difficult for you, too, not having any experience,' Joseph says. 'If only one of you were a fumbler, well, but with Louis being as he is, you have to take the initiative, Antoine. You're not a fourteen-year-old girl any more. It could be forgiven, then. There was time. And matters stood differently in Europe.'

If only he would stop. She doesn't need the lecture. Hasn't she tried? Hasn't she tried everything she can to make herself desirable to Louis? She has sacrificed her memories and hopes for straight teeth and clear skin. She has eaten just enough to swell her décolletage but not enough to inhibit the strictures of the *grand corps*. She has flirted, caressed, cuddled. She has been submissive and sweet, and she has tried to be a partner.

She has even tried to find some hint of a spell that would

291

work, some magical solution to make the whole business less distasteful to her husband.

'I believe he's got the right idea about it now, anyway,' Joseph says. 'I think, if you—'

She is saved from more lectures as a single rider approaches on the horizon. God help her, it's Prince Louis de Rohan.

He rides right up next to them, on a heavy grey horse with a white mane.

Antoinette smiles.

Rohan removes his hat and bows his head. 'Your Majesties.'

'You recognize me then?' says Joseph warmly, although she hears the falseness behind the warmth, and Rohan doubtless does too. Rohan may be a hedonist and a hypocrite but he is not a fool.

'I am afraid it's no good travelling incognito here,' says Rohan smoothly. 'Gossip, you know. I try to get away from it, but it is everywhere.'

'I wish you a good morning,' Joseph says impatiently.

'A good day for hunting,' Rohan replies, gazing off at the pale sky in the direction of the baying of hounds.

'Hunting! I did not know you enjoyed that sport,' says Antoinette. 'And you're not dressed for it.'

'Oh, I am perfectly dressed for the sort of hunting I am doing.'

'A woman, then.' Joseph's voice is cold; he does not even pretend to be boisterous or encouraging. Rohan, it is well known, has been trying to get himself named a cardinal, and he seems to be about to manage it, with the help of the King of Poland. The fact that he is still notoriously debauched doesn't seem to be an impediment.

'I must keep my secrets, Your Imperial Majesty. We all have our private conversations. With God.' He turns to Antoinette with a smile. 'I don't suppose you've seen a young woman, clad perhaps a little inappropriately for the weather?'

'Knowing your reputation, I would not be a very good

queen if I helped you find the lady,' she says, smiling with teeth.

'Alas, it is an axiom that Austrian women are never able to help Frenchmen recover what they've lost. No matter. There's better hunting in the area, I would imagine. Everyone hides their friends away in the little houses, and I know full well there are some small and intimate parties happening nearby. As I said, no one goes truly incognito here. I shall delay you no more.'

As they watch Rohan ride away, Joseph says, 'You caught that, I hope?'

'What's that?' Antoinette feels stunned, and has to clear her head to respond. 'Oh, yes – the Austrian woman. He means Mother, and the French colonies. Many in this country still blame the Austrian alliance for the fact that we lost New France, you know.'

'Well, many in Austria wonder what help France has been to us. We lost Silesia, for our part.'

'Joseph, don't pick a fight with me. You know I am always an Austrian in my heart, but now I'm Queen of France.'

'Indeed. You're the glue that holds this alliance together. And every year that your marriage to Louis is open to question is a year in which that odious man and all his ilk get more powerful. If they can split the two of you apart, they can split Austria and France apart, and then Britain will rule the world.'

But Antoinette is hardly listening. She is thinking of what Rohan said next, about the intimate parties. She is thinking of her three friends, their magical bundles in hand, walking into the woods.

And Rohan was riding directly towards them. It wasn't a woman he was hunting at all. All these years, he's been suspicious of Antoinette. He's never stopped watching. And now he's riding towards her friends.

'Race me,' she yells to her startled brother, and she turns her horse to the side, finds a narrow deer path through the

woods that will bring her back to one of the cross-angled roads and thence to the Petit Trianon, she hopes, in time. She has always been a good rider.

Does he know, or does he merely suspect?

If the latter, his suspicions would only be confirmed if he arrived at the Petit Trianon to find an out-of-breath Antoinette there with her friends.

She must stop him from reaching the house altogether.

If she can circle around, she can head Rohan off before he reaches the little road that leads to the Trianon; she is galloping, and he was not. He doesn't expect her to do anything to stop him. He expects her to be afraid, to be silent – or perhaps to make an error. As perhaps she is about to do.

Antoinette urges her horse onward. When she meets him, what then?

The gold watch and all her papers are in the drawer of her writing table, but Antoinette has a good memory, and a little jar of ash in her pocket. She needs something that will distract him. Deter his horse. Something loud – but what? But what?

It comes to her as her horse emerges at a little crossroads near a stand of white-skinned birch trees. If she can manage to make a tree fall at just the right moment, she can frighten his horse.

She dismounts quickly, ties her own mount at a little distance. She draws a shaky star of ash in the dirt around the tree nearest the road, its leaves golden despite the newness of the year. She has been working on adapting the spell for mending into a spell for breaking. She thinks she has the right sacrifices at last, but she's never been able to use it because of the terrible simplicity of the sacrifice required. The letter of love is 'o', and this spell is: 'ooooo'.

The letters all together mean one single point in the star; it cannot be divided into five. A great love. No mere affection or fondness will do; she must snuff out a true, deep love.

She begins to write Charlotte's name but a sob chokes her before she reaches the 'l' and she crosses it out, digging into the ground.

Who, then? She is setting out to consummate her marriage. Would it not be easier to bear that if she didn't love another man? For of course she loves him.

She writes his name, full out in a fresh point of the star: 'Hans Axel, Comte de Fersen'.

So official. As if there would be any doubt of whom she means, if she means it.

Antoinette stops, and balls her fists, and breathes in hard. She must break the tree, block his path, and be gone.

'I give these things,' she whispers, screwing her eyes shut, believing she means it . . .

. . . she does not.

There's a deep sound, a thud like the unbalancing of the world, so deep she isn't sure whether she heard it at all or only felt it.

The breeze smells of rot, and when she opens them, the bark has peeled and blackened on the birch trees all around her star, as though blasted by the thwarted forces of decay, by her wavering intentions.

But the name of Fersen remains, in the love-point of the star. The tree remains. Her will wasn't strong enough to see it through.

And she can hear hoofbeats, now. He is coming.

She crawls to the point, wipes tears out of her eyes, and gets dirt in them. She rubs out his name with the heel of her hand, and writes in a third point: 'Marie-Thérèse Louise de Savoie, Princesse de Lamballe'.

Dear Lamballe, who loves her so. But what does it matter if Antoinette loves her back? Friendship out of duty is just as good as friendship from the heart. Antoinette will always take care of her, and that's what matters.

She can see Rohan now, riding up the road.

'I give these things,' she says.

Rohan is near, now; he'll see her, or the horse, any moment now.

She does not think of Fersen; she doesn't think about him, very hard. She thinks of Lamballe, rescuing her, putting her hand on her shoulder.

'I give these things!'

A crack, a rushing sound, a whinny from Rohan's horse. The tree breaks, halfway up, and its golden branches fall onto the road and shake. Rohan's horse does not spill him, but only because he is a good rider. He wheels away, the frightened horse running in the other direction. Antoinette scrambles up onto her own horse, and rides hard to the Petit Trianon.

By the time a bewildered Joseph finds her there, still muddy, laughing about having fallen off her horse, wouldn't Mama scold her, she is always telling Antoinette it isn't safe to ride like a hoyden – by then, she has told Lamballe, Polignac, and Saint-Georges that Rohan is roaming the grounds, that he must not find them doing magic.

Antoinette, Polignac and Lamballe return to Versailles that day, and Saint-Georges returns to his house.

After all Antoinette's attempts to find some magical solution to the problem of her marriage bed, some way of changing herself to make her husband change, it seems Joseph's lecturing has had some effect. Madame Campan tells her the King is coming to her bed.

Antoinette does not hope, but she prepares. When Louis comes in, through the not-so-secret passage that connects their rooms, Antoinette is already wearing her best chemise, all Belgian lace, and has her hair down, her real hair. It almost brushes her shoulders. Monsieur Léonard was right; it has been growing in.

He walks in, stands, looks at her.

They stare at each other for a moment, and Antoinette readies her little speech about duty – when Louis speaks.

'The Emperor made me see that I have been selfish,' he says, his voice thick. 'I can abide a little discomfort, if it must be. I thought – I thought it would not be such a tragedy if the Dauphin were one of my brothers' children, you see. That is the good in having brothers! Charles already has a little boy. I thought that was enough. But your brother made me see that malcontents might use my childlessness against me, try to push me off the throne. It would create instability.'

Antoinette nods. 'I am here to be mother to France. And Joseph spoke to me, too.'

He gestures towards the bed, as if he were helping her to her seat at the opera, and she sits on top of the covers. He sits beside her and puts his arms around her, kisses her neck.

She holds herself still, forces herself to stretch her neck out longer, not to shrink, not to move her shoulder up to discourage him.

He will want to be gentle, for himself if not for her. But she wants him to just get it over with. She tries to think of a way to convey this, but the only idea she can think of is to seem eager, which could alarm him and make him think she's more experienced than she ought to be.

At last he unties his breeches and moves his hand inside her chemise, up her thigh. She takes that as a signal to lie on the bed.

She helps him with it, swallowing, trying not to think of anything. Keeping her mind blank.

It is not that she does not feel affection for him; she does. She loves him, even, as her king – for she does now think of herself as a Frenchwoman – and as a husband. As one of the very few people in Versailles who respects her and treats her not with awe or with disdain, but with simple, friendly courtesy.

She kisses him on the mouth, and feels him hard against her. Feels the skin on his legs tighten as he flinches – but he does not cry out, and he pushes against her, inside her.

They are both trying hard to remember not to hold their breath.

He moves a little inside her – this must have been Joseph's instruction.

'Is it all right?' she whispers.

He nods, biting his lip, and then, to her surprise, laughs in one short bark. 'Better than all right,' he whispers. 'And for you?'

'Better than all right,' she lies, holding him close.

After a little while, he shudders, and cries out softly, and lies on top of her.

She wishes it were something either of them wanted, but they want the result, and that will have to be enough. Poor Louis.

Louis eases himself up to sitting. 'I am going hunting early and don't want to disturb you, so I'll leave you.'

She blinks, startled, and then nods.

Antoinette wakes alone, which is nothing new. It is perhaps not what she expected of the night she consummated her marriage, but then she did not expect to be seven years married when it happened, either. And perhaps her expectations were skewed by being the child of Francis and Maria Theresa, who always spent their nights together whenever they were in the same house. There was no resident *maîtresse en titre* at Schönbrunn or the Hofburg. Francis saved his affairs for his travels. Vienna was a world apart from Versailles.

Now, at last, Antoinette is the King's mistress as well as his wife. The two most powerful offices a woman could occupy at Versailles, united in her person. And yet, she wakes alone.

Truth be told, she has always relished mornings by herself, before the noise when everyone comes in to dress her and wash her and ogle her. But, on this morning, these quiet moments she would like to share with someone.

298

She is alone when Madame Campan comes in and whisks away the bedsheet before Madame de Noailles can get hold of it and parade it before the princes and princesses of the blood, as etiquette no doubt demands.

Campan is kinder, although Madame de Noailles believes her strictures are a greater kindness in the long run, saving Antoinette from herself. She is probably right.

Everyone is grinning from ear to ear and they pamper her as though she were ill. It is a macabre combination, this delight in the wifely duties they seem to treat as an affliction. Today she does not feel like dressing to the nines; she wants to lie in a linen dress and look out of a window and think about Fersen. She wants to drink orange-water with Polignac and sit quietly and talk about things that have nothing to do with Versailles. But today of all days, she must be Queen of France. Today is her true coronation day.

So she sucks in her breath as the *grand corps* swallows her, and she can barely lift her arm enough to take three letters off the salver when they come.

One from Joseph on his way back to Vienna, saying that things went poorly with the Benjamin Franklin business. Thanking her for the hospitality and needling her, once more, about her feathers and furbelows. He, too, means it as a kindness. So much kindness, all around her, like drowning in goose down. She will have to send him a letter to thank him for convincing Louis to try – but first she must tell Maria Theresa, who will fly into a rage if anyone outside France finds out about the consummation before she does.

The second letter is from Charlotte, warning her that Louis de Rohan is suspicious of her. Chiding her for being careless. Reassuring her that Charlotte has written to Rohan, insisting that Antoinette cares nothing for politics or ideas and is far too frivolous to be involved in any such thing, and if there are any magisters involved in the ever-shifting winds of opinion at Versailles, it is ludicrous to connect them with Marie Antoinette.

Somehow, Antoinette does not find Charlotte's letter to be a comfort.

The third letter she reads is also enciphered, and bears no name.

All my thoughts are of you.

I assure you that those who truly love you will love you unconditionally. Remember that, if you forget all else.

There is so much work to do, to make this world worthy of the wonders in it. Write to me when you can, please. In the meantime, I think you will soon meet a mutual friend.

Your obedient servant, always, unto death.

Even the deciphered letter is still coded, still safe: he does not say where he is now, or mention magic. He does not even say he loves her. Not quite.

If she were not watched by seven pairs of eyes, Antoinette would weep. Instead, she smiles and lets the letter drop to her lap – this piece of paper that she will treasure so dearly that it would make a three-letter sacrifice – and she contrives to look bored.

CHAPTER TWENTY-EIGHT

*Inoculation — Fear and Death — New Dangers —
Franz Mesmer's Reputation*

At the end of a long, hot summer, Charlotte gives birth to her fifth child. Francesco is a tiny red bundle, full of screams, and she adores every particle of him. She wraps herself up in the smell of him. Another boy. This time, though the cannons fire, no orchestras march through the streets of Naples to celebrate. Or perhaps they do, but Charlotte would not hear them anyway; they came to Caserta for the birth, to be as far away as possible from Portici. Filippo, the King's brother, has been ill for weeks with smallpox there.

A month after the birth, Ferdinand comes into her room, where she sits in bed with the baby. He walks over and touches the sleeping boy on his temple, just lightly, and rests his other hand on her shoulder for a moment before abruptly removing it.

She's made him promise that he'll leave her alone in her bed for a few months; she has no need or desire to be pregnant again, with five healthy children, two of them boys. But it's a promise with no weight behind it and there's nothing she can do if he decides one day to dishonour it. For some reason he seems to interpret her request to mean

301

that he cannot touch her at all, and while that baffles Charlotte, it's a happy side effect.

'Filippo is dead,' he says.

The poor man! The last time she saw Ferdinand's older brother, he was laughing uproariously as he instructed one of his servants to put several gloves on one of his hands, one after the other. He got it up to seven before they wouldn't go on any more. Filippo dead, alone save for his physicians. When she first met him, he told her, 'I am the oldest and should have been king, but I'm sick.' Sick all his life, with an unnamed affliction. And now dead of one whose name is spoken every day, all over Europe.

'God rest his soul,' she says. 'Is the smallpox spreading beyond Portici? Is it in the city?'

'It's always in the city. If not this year, then next year. We can stay here a few more weeks, though, to be safe.'

Safe. In her arms, Francesco purses his tiny mouth, as if he doesn't trust the word either.

'My sister writes that everyone in Paris is having the inoculation, after the death of the old King,' she says. 'Perhaps we should have it. And the oldest children too.'

Letters from Antoinette have been infrequent, lately. Perhaps Charlotte shouldn't have told her that she has been reassuring the Order of her sister's frivolity and self-absorption. But what would she have Charlotte do? If Rohan thinks the Queen of France is a threat, he'll act on it. He's made that clear.

Ferdinand pulls a face. 'Ugh, inoculation. It's terrifying. Don't you think? Having a doctor open a wound and put pus into it? I don't think I could do it.'

'You wouldn't have to *do* anything. Just sit there.'

'Just sit there, and be ill for weeks or months afterward, and possibly die. Well, it's not going to happen, anyway.'

'Why not?' She cranks her neck to look up at him. 'What do you mean?'

'My father's forbidden it. It's an offence against God's will.'

'Your father! Is your father the King of Naples, then?'

'No,' he says, tersely. 'He's the King of Spain. And the head of my family.'

'These are my children,' she replies, holding Francesco closer. 'And the doctors say that the chance of dying from inoculation is much lower than the chance of dying from the natural illness, which, as you say, is always in Naples. We live in a port city, for God's sake, with all and sundry coming through our very house day after day. No. I will keep them safe. I will write to my brother Leopold today, and ask him to send me that doctor in Florence. Angelo Gatti.'

She does not ask permission any more, not of Ferdinand, and certainly not of his father.

Three straight, deep cuts across her children's arms. Bright blood welling, impossibly red. Teresa is five, and old enough to sit with her jaw and fists clenched tight, while tears pour down her cheeks. Luisa whimpers and Carlo, only two and a half, wails piteously, his chubby arms reaching out for Charlotte, blood dripping from one. She went first, to show the children it was safe, but it only alarmed them. Beyond a screen of Chinese silk lies a young woman, a seamstress. They can't hear her, but they can hear her sniffle as the lancet pierces her, draws the poisonous pus from her so Dr Gatti can push it into the wounds he's made in the royal family.

And then they wait.

2 November 1777
Charlotte to Antoinette

My sister, my Antoinette, my dear,
I wish you a very happy twenty-second birthday! How strange it has been to go six weeks without writing to you. But Dr Gatti insisted that the contagion could spread that way, and so we've kept ourselves apart from the world. From the two smallest children, as well. Six weeks in which we

could not see them. That was the hardest, Antoinette. My Francesco cried when I took him in my arms, and he wanted to go back to the nurse. My own tiny baby, and I could not nurse him or hold him or watch him breathe.

Everyone is well now: Ferdinand and I and all the children. I should tell you that at the start. I had a difficult recovery. I suppose I was still weaker than I realized from the birth, and the inoculation gave me the most horrible headaches.

And then the fevers. I kept seeing three red lines – the wounds in my children – and I would wake from half-dreams convinced that they were dead.

I used to sit straight up and stare at the wall for hours in that state, my heart racing, unable to think properly. I tried to focus on Dr Gatti's reassurance that his particular inoculation technique, because it uses unripe matter from an inoculation patient rather than a pustule from the natural illness, was much less likely to cause a full-blown infection. Some say it confers less immunity, too – there was a duchess in France who caught the natural infection after being inoculated by Dr Gatti, wasn't there?

I intend my new Academy to study these matters, and I have asked Dr Gatti to stay here in Florence. I am convinced now, more than I have ever been, that only I can protect both my family and my kingdom, that no one else will do it for me.

I was jealous to read of your visit from Joseph. I wish our brother happiness – no, not happiness. I don't think he'd welcome it; I think he's grown the scars on his heart on purpose, and I don't begrudge him them. I wish him peace.

I wish peace for us all, my sister, and rest after our labours are done.

In hope and affection,

I remain your
Charlotte

3 November 1777
Angelo Soliman to Maria Carolina

Your Majesty,

*I was overjoyed to learn of the delivery of His Highness
the prince, and I hesitate to burden you at such a time, but
I know you, like me, always prefer knowledge to the lack of
it. I have written just now to Isaac Lars Silfversparre,
William Hamilton, and Caterina de San Marco to warn
them of what seems to be a coordinated rogue effort to steal
spells and undermine the Order, here in Vienna. I cannot
say whether Naples is also at risk.*

*Franz Mesmer, you may recall, has long been using magic
to increase our knowledge of nature and physiology. It has
suited his purposes to be seen as a charlatan, a wizard of
a slightly more sophisticated sort than our old friend Count
Cagliostro. Mesmer has performed what seem to be
exorcisms, and even some healing, using a half-invented
theory of magnetism as a cover for the magic. The true
method of healing is a spell that enchants a musical
instrument – Mesmer uses a glass armonica, I suspect
because it sounds so eerie and convinces the credulous that
something scientific must be afoot.*

*One of his patients was a talented composer and pianist
by the name of Maria Paradis. She is quite blind, and
Mesmer was attempting to heal her using magic (under
cover of his theory). I have heard varying accounts of how
successful he was, and indeed I wondered about the wisdom
of the attempt. As it turned out, it was unwise for reasons I
never considered.*

*Fräulein Paradis used to take notes during their sessions
using an ingenious writing device, in which the letters of
the alphabet correspond with shapes she could feel. Each
time she pressed a letter, a tiny printing press would imprint
it onto the page. An invention of Wolfgang Kempelen's.
(You may have heard of the Mechanical Turk that was so*

popular here a few years ago. It was a marvel – I could hardly beat it in a game myself, and I could find nothing magical about it.)

Now, though, I wonder.

The writing device seems to have been enchanted somehow to copy nearby papers: when Paradis brought the machine near any written matter, the enchantment allowed it to absorb the information in the form of a sequence of letters, which she could then recreate later on a fresh sheet of paper. Mesmer was careless in leaving his notes and spells in the room near Paradis – I suppose since she was blind, he didn't consider it a danger. We know that she copied several of his spells, in whole or in part, including the spell for the glass armonica that can heal certain wounds when played near the patient. More dangerously, Paradis may have copied an incendiary spell, the spell for unbreakable sealing wax, the ancient bezoar spell, and, perhaps, the one we've taken to calling the 'loaves-and-fishes spell', the duplication enchantment Your Majesty has put to such good use in San Leucio.

Mesmer abruptly stopped treating her, and she is going on tour, I believe. The damage to Mesmer's reputation as a healer here in Vienna has been severe, as Paradis has not recovered and he had to pretend failure to explain the sudden break in their relationship. Whether he would have succeeded, in time, I can't say. His armonica is a wonder but it is slow and uncertain in its effects.

The damage to the secrecy of the Reconditus may be incalculable.

In haste and great anxiety,
I remain,

Yours in fraternity,
Angelo Soliman

CHAPTER TWENTY-NINE

*The Return of d'Éon — An Old Friend — A Walk
in the Gardens — Choosing Sides*

Like everyone else at Versailles in the autumn of 1777, Antoinette is anticipating the return of the Chevalière d'Éon, the prodigal spy. The problem with d'Éon, as far as Versailles is concerned, is that she has not been presented, now that she is the Chevalière. Women of quality who wish access to the court must first appear before the King and Queen at Versailles, and be introduced according to a precise ritual. Of course d'Éon has been to Versailles many times, in the years before her exile, before Antoinette came to France, before Antoinette was Antoinette. But d'Éon is a woman; d'Éon has not been presented; and so d'Éon is still in a kind of exile, even though she's home in France at last.

This second exile lasts several months in mid-1777. For one thing, Antoinette and Louis are not at Versailles for much of the autumn; they are at Fontainebleau. For another, d'Éon needs time to prepare. A dancing master must teach her how to walk and curtsey forwards and backwards in a *grand habit*. And then there is the *grand habit* itself, that torturous construction of panniers and train and corset: it must be new, it must be expensive, it must be black, and

it must be from Rose Bertin's shop in Paris. That last item is not, of course, in the rules set down by the Sun King, but by 1777 it might as well be.

Antoinette sends a set of her own diamonds to the Chevalière, and a new fan 'to replace your sword', and she pays for the *grand habit*. Madame Bertin writes that the Chevalière has selected a very lovely embroidered satin, in pure white, and to the objection that debutantes must wear black unless they are in mourning, responded, 'I am forty-nine years old and have friends in eleven countries. I am always in mourning.'

The day arrives at last: one of those crisp days in November when Versailles smells almost pleasant: the smoke and stale air of the winter is yet to come, and the stink of the close-stools and sweat has faded. A Sunday, when the King and his family go to Mass, and anyone who likes may come to Versailles to watch them walk through the palace to the Royal Chapel, dressed in their best. At noon, the Queen and her attendants leave her state apartments and walk into the Hall of Mirrors, where Louis and his brothers and sister are coming from the council chamber midway through, and they all walk through that long room together, the guards holding the people back.

After Mass in the grand, soaring chapel, they walk back, Antoinette's enchanted shoes gliding above the parquet. She has had to enchant ten different pairs now, but luckily they seem to keep the enchantment even if the shoes get a new buckle, a new bow. It makes her wonder what part of an object holds its enchantment and whether an enchanted shoe is like the ship of Theseus: if the heel, the sole, and every other part were replaced, when would the enchantment vanish?

But, so far, all of her shoes still help her walk more gracefully than ought to be possible, and that's the main thing.

And then, after Mass, the presentation.

Versailles is particularly crowded today; word has gone

out that this is the day for d'Éon's arrival. Antoinette takes a glass of sherry and arranges herself in the chair in the Nobles Room, her main antechamber. She waits. Her dove-grey silk skirt, pinned with golden tassels, spreads around her. D'Éon will have to go first to the King, and then come here.

She's announced by a flurry of shouts and footsteps in the Hall of Mirrors, and then a commotion in the Peace Room, and the guard throws open one of the double doors (both doors are opened only for people of high rank) and d'Éon enters.

The white *grand habit* is dazzling, and the diamonds on her neck catch the light. Antoinette smiles to see that d'Éon is wearing the Cross of St Louis on her breast; she may be a woman but she has not given up the honours she earned. She curtseys, very well, and steps forward.

She looks familiar. Her face – the second curtsey – Antoinette puts a hand to her mouth to stop from crying out.

Geneviève. The woman who visited her in Vienna, who hid beneath the Chinese Cabinet, who has been writing to her all these years.

The third curtsey, and Geneviève manages to pull off her glove and take Antoinette's hem to kiss it. Antoinette is, at this point, supposed to pull back, to graciously refuse the kiss, to stand and offer her cheek. But she's so dazed that it takes her a moment, and Geneviève is left holding the hem for a heartbeat, until Antoinette stands, flustered.

'It's you,' she says, aware of the half-dozen guards and dozen princesses and duchesses behind her, all of them gazing at d'Éon.

'I thank Your Majesty for sending the carriage for me and for the lovely gifts,' says d'Éon.

'You play the violin, I hear,' Antoinette says, her voice dull, as if from very far away or underwater. 'Will you come and play at one of my salons?'

'Gladly,' says d'Éon. 'My disagreements were with the late King. I hope you understand, Your Majesty, that I am glad to be back in France, and hope to be a friend to you and your husband.'

'I should like nothing better. And I understand His Majesty has set a decree, for any who may be in doubt, that you are a woman.' She smiles, hoping that was the most delicate way to broach the subject.

'Yes, Your Majesty. Although, I wonder . . .'

'Yes?'

'Well, the decree requires me to always wear dresses, on pain of losing my estates.'

'And that is not acceptable to you?'

She spreads her arms wide. 'Sometimes I like to wear breeches! I don't like to always be caged like this.'

Antoinette laughs. 'Sometimes I like to wear breeches too. Riding, particularly. My mother hates it. All right, I'll see what I can do about that. And I have some corsets and things that I would like to give you, if you don't mind.'

The chevalière smiles, as if satisfied. 'I would be most grateful, Your Majesty. I have come to understand that my former wardrobe will not be suitable in France.'

There are chuckles behind them, but Antoinette knows that that former wardrobe contained several old-fashioned mantuas and at least one white bonnet with two moths on the lappets. Were they for helping d'Éon in her spycraft, somehow?

Antoinette thinks hard and fast. Tonight is the usual gambling party, and d'Éon could come to that, but it would be hard to find a place to speak alone. The best place to be alone, at Versailles, is outside.

'Later there will be the dinner, but I am at liberty before that. I will rest and change my clothing, and you may do the same, if you like. Will you walk with me in the gardens, Chevalière?'

D'Éon inclines her head, and then manages the three

backward curtseys – one must not turn one's back on the Queen, even if one is wearing a cumbersome train – and then she is gone, and Antoinette stares, astonished.

All of the orange trees in their pots have been moved inside for the winter, so the parterre is a vast landscape broken only by the occasional sculpture and by the swirls and whorls of pathways cut into the lawns. Anyone could see Antoinette and d'Éon here, walking in their *robes à la polonaise*, but it doesn't matter if they're seen, so long as they aren't overheard.

'When I met you, in Vienna—' Antoinette begins, stumbling over too many questions.

'When was that, 1770? Yes, there was a tiresome campaign in London to determine my sex in those days – wagers and kidnapping attempts and everything of that sort – and I got in the habit of disappearing for weeks or months and visiting my friends in other places.'

'How does Master Kempelen work his Mechanical Turk without you, I wonder?'

'Ha. I send him an assistant whenever he wants to trot it out. He's proven useful. I had him build a printing device for a rogue in Vienna, who used it to copy out and steal some of the Order's spells. I'll send them to you. There's something that ostensibly will start a fire out of nothing, though we can't make it work. And Mesmer's healing spell, though one needs a glass armonica for that.'

'Hardly very useful, then,' Antoinette says with a smile.

'All spells are useful. They help us learn how to make more. There's one that would be very useful indeed – a duplication spell. We think the Order has been using it in Naples to replicate food.'

'Food!' Antoinette stops walking. The harvest of 1777 has been a good one at last, thank God, but no one knows when another bad year might come, with the cattle walking like skeletons, and the crops hanging yellowed and dead, and

the market women screaming at the gates of the palace. 'Could we use it to make more flour? More bread?'

'We could, if we had it. Our rogue friend only managed to copy half of it before she was caught. We know it exists in the Order's great spellbook, but we don't know the sacrifices for it.'

She pauses, and Antoinette, thinking hard, walks on.

'I allowed myself to be convinced to come to France largely because of you, Your Majesty,' Geneviève says after a while. 'I have had worries I didn't want to entrust even to ciphered letters. I have reason to believe the Order knows your secret.'

'Yes,' Antoinette says, thinking of Rohan on his horse. 'So do I.'

'The Order in London, at least, now seems to believe that Your Majesty, while a magister, is too . . . simple, in heart and mind, to make any use of it but for frivolous things. I don't know where they got that impression.'

Antoinette does: from Charlotte. But she says nothing, setting her jaw. 'Were you a Brother of the Order once, as Fersen was?'

D'Éon snorts. 'Far from it. They wouldn't have me as a member anyway. I don't meet their standards. Oh, I'm rich enough, but in all other ways entirely unsuitable. Which suits me quite well. But I have my spies, and I know what the Order thinks, and I am worried about them, too. For centuries, they have kept magic to themselves because they hold the general mass of humanity in contempt. But now they have seen what your sister is doing in Naples, and they have begun to dream of a magical empire – where not only magic is under their control, but *everything*. They see an empire ready for the taking: the greatest empire in the world.'

Antoinette blanches. 'Do you mean King George—'

'The King of England is not a magister. I'm sure of that much. But his advisers are Brothers, or in the power of Brothers, and they grow bold. A king whose power cannot be checked, not even by force of arms, is the worst possible evil.'

312

'Do all rogue magisters in England take the part of the Americans?'

'We take the side of whoever will destabilize the Order. It has never been as powerful as it is now. It is a European order, and for centuries that limited its reach. But now, where is Europe? Europe is everywhere, like smallpox. The Brothers of the London chapter view England's colonies with a mixture of greed and terror. They have so little control there, but they are eager to expand their great book of magic. They have started trying to acquire, and then suppress, the magic of their colonies from America to India. And the Spanish and the Dutch Brothers do the same, to a degree.'

'And in the French Empire?'

D'Éon snorts. 'A few years ago, I would have said yes, and haven't you wondered why I made myself an enemy of the King I once served? But now I suspect it is an academic question, as the French Empire is much diminished, isn't it? The empire on the ascendant now is the British one.'

Antoinette has always wanted to do her best, to use what she is given, to serve her family by making herself worthy of the love of the people of France. If that is too simple a wish, then let them call her simple.

'Count von Fersen told me many rogues are on the Americans' side.'

'Rogues are on no one's side. That's been one of our difficulties all along. By nature, we are disorganized. We thrive in chaos, and America is chaos. It is – possibility. An object poised at the moment of sacrifice, a reality that might decay into any number of possible states, and some of those states could be better than anything that has gone before. Perhaps!'

'Or worse.'

'Or worse.'

Antoinette sighs. 'Fersen wants to go. To America.'

'Yes, many rogues with radical notions are fighting the British. Your Philippe d'Orléans got his naval commission for a reason.'

Antoinette is shocked wordless for a moment, and stops, with a swishing of silk skirts. 'Philippe! You mean to say that Philippe d'Orléans is a magister!'

'And quite a radical-minded one.'

'Of all people! Well, that is a surprise.'

'We have all been working in our own small ways to keep ourselves safe and to stop the excesses of the Order. But now I think that will no longer be enough. Now, I think, the risks of secrecy are greater than the risks of exposure. The risks of living in a world in which kings and queens use magic to extract all they can out of people who are already starving and hungry. Now, I think, we go to war. So, the question becomes: what part will you play in this war?'

Antoinette stops, looks back at the palace of Versailles, a grey hulk against a grey sky. 'I could teach my husband magic. I could teach the King.'

'Do you think that's wise?'

She casts her gaze down, then, tries to think. Searches herself. 'I don't, really. I trust him with my life, with everything. But he has to rely on his counsellors, and I don't trust all of them. I have a feeling some would take the Order's view of things, and we've learned it's quite difficult to change people's minds, predictably and without attracting notice.'

'Indeed,' says d'Éon appraisingly, and Antoinette notices that she's changed the diamond earrings for a set of little amber drops, each one containing something small and feathery – the wing of a moth?

'You seem to know what I'm going to say before I say it, d'Éon.'

She shrugs. 'I'm a good listener. I listen to the whispers before the words: the glances, the frowns, the smiles, the sighs. Right now, for example, I am listening to you considering whether the magisters you've been training at the Petit Trianon might play a part in the American war.'

Antoinette laughs. 'You heard me say that with my eyebrows, did you?'

314

'Well, I know how you've been occupying your time lately.' Geneviève adds, her voice lower, 'And what I know, the Order suspects.'

'We are in danger,' Antoinette says, and lifts her chin. 'I know that. I do not forget that my first governess died at the hands of the Order, inside a royal palace. And Prince Louis de Rohan has made it clear he is never going to stop threatening me, or my friends.'

D'Éon cocks her head, and the amber earring swings. 'Now perhaps Your Majesty understands why I wear the white of mourning. A war is on the horizon. A much bloodier and dirtier war even than the rebellion in America. A war fought in secret, with lies and murders. And it is time for every magister to choose a side.'

PART FOUR
1777 TO 1779

CHAPTER THIRTY

Dinner with William Hamilton — War and Diplomacy —
A Request — Volcanoes — Prince Caramanico
Finds Himself Short

My sister, my heart,

How I have praised God that the famines which struck both the Holy Roman Empire and the Kingdom of France did not strike Naples in these last years, that your ports have been laden with goods and your people fed. In my own country, I have seen children begging in the streets outside the palace with skin stretched over their bones. Over the last few years, we've had more bad harvests than good in France, and the stores are depleted. Another bad year would mean a great deal of suffering.

I won't thank you for telling your fellow Brothers that I am too frivolous to bother about. It may be the truth, but I do try, Charlotte, and I do care. Last year, as I told you, I adopted a small boy named Armand, and he is doing a little better now. I thought, perhaps I cannot feed them all but I can feed this one! My capabilities have never been adequate

319

*to the task, and even my magic is of so little use — and you
tell me not to use it, to keep myself safe, to keep myself
apart.*

*And all these years you have had access to the spells of
the Order. Not once have I asked you to give me any. Little
did I imagine that there would be a spell to create food — to
create more food for the people! — and that you would keep
it for yourself, knowing what has been happening in France.*

*I ask you now to share that spell with me. Don't ask
how I know about it. Trust me to use it wisely and for the
good of my people.*

*We can see, in America, that people will rise if their
monarchs do not act in their interest. What does our old
friend Angelo Soliman say about it? I envy you your
friendship with him, but then I have quite enough Brothers
in my life, with France's grand almoner chasing after me
and my friends, as though we were his pretty domestics.*

*I ask for your help and I send you my love, which is
always yours.*

Antoinette

Charlotte always feels slightly circumspect about William
Hamilton. They are members of the same Order, but his
primary loyalty is to a foreign power. The Paris Brothers have
recruited the American ambassador, Benjamin Franklin, to
their cause. He pretends to champion the rebellion, but he's
actually sowing confusion among the French about what,
precisely, the colonies want. He's given the Marquis de
Lafayette a sword, as a token of appreciation from America.
What Lafayette does not know is that it is enchanted with
what the *Reconditus* calls the 'cut-both-ways' spell, to make
the owner prevaricate. The goal is to dull the young man's
infamous reckless courage, but what effect it might have on
a man as impulsive as Lafayette is reported to be, Charlotte
can only imagine. Cagliostro writes to Silfversparre, who

reports that Franklin is secretly working now to secure an America, and a world, in which magic is preserved for and by the Order. But so many of Franklin's colleagues and countrymen are rogues. It all makes Charlotte nervous.

Still, she enjoys visits to Hamilton's villa near Caserta, which is always full of antiquities he's collected, his papers on Herculaneum and Pompeii, and visiting poets and musicians.

He also has an excellent cook. On a chilly evening in January 1778, Charlotte is the only guest at his table. 'You have a wrinkle between your eyes that was not there when last we spoke,' she says.

'I am nearing fifty, Your Majesty,' Hamilton says in his pleasant rumble. 'Wrinkles will appear.'

Hamilton is indeed nearly twice her age, and can be avuncular, but has a plain-dealing manner with her that she appreciates, particularly in a diplomat; perhaps it is an English quality, or at least an English skill.

'I know the look of a foreign policy wrinkle,' she says, and picks up her fork. On blue-and-white china, there's a little bowl of red and white octopus.

'The Elector of Bavaria has died,' Hamilton says.

'Yes, my brother told me. Joseph wants that territory.'

'Prussia will not let him have it.'

Charlotte puts down her fork, and the servants bring plates of grilled swordfish and artichoke.

'The Prussians will be able to count on the support of Russia. And others?'

'And others,' Hamilton agrees cautiously.

'But my brother has allies too. France, for example.'

She thinks of Antoinette's letter, asking for the spell. How it tore at her heart!

'France will remain neutral,' Hamilton says. 'It won't support Austria, if Austria chooses to make this a war.'

Mama won't like that. Poor Antoinette; she'll have a barrage of letters to deal with.

'You have information to that effect?'

Hamilton does something with his eyebrows. 'The anti-Austrian sentiment in France is high. France would rather use its depleted forces to hurt England in the colonies than to enter another war within Europe.'

'You think my mother made the wrong choice, allying with France and Spain over Britain?'

'I could not think otherwise.'

The servants bring in hot, savoury rice *sartù*, one mound of rice for each of them, with English sausage and leek inside.

'Spain is helping the American rebels,' Hamilton says, and takes a sip of red wine. 'They may be of two minds about encouraging distant colonies to throw off their masters, but they cannot help but support the enemy of their rival. American privateers have access to the ports of Spain.'

'And to the ports of Naples and Sicily.' She smiles at him wryly; it is a sore point.

'And to the ports of Naples and Sicily. Do you think Spain will join the Americans and declare war against Britain?'

Charlotte dabs her lip with a napkin. 'I am not privy to the plans of Spain. Spain does not talk to me.'

'No, indeed. I have heard the King, your father-in-law, is furious about the inoculation, and says terrible things about you.'

Charlotte is surprised. Perhaps Ferdinand was right to be afraid of his father. 'Still? It was months ago, and everyone survived.'

'The King of Spain does not brook disagreement, and he regards Naples as part of his own kingdom. All of which means, my friend, that you and I could be at war before too long.'

The dessert course consists of blancmange with rose-petal jam, and rum babas – a food of Lorraine, Charlotte's father's home. She smiles; Hamilton pays attention to everything.

'If Spain goes to war with England,' she says, spearing the blancmange with her spoon, 'that does not mean Naples will follow. I would have Naples chart its own course.'

'Then, Your Majesty, it will need its own ships. What would happen to trade here if the Spanish did not keep piracy at bay? How does the Neapolitan navy stand now? A single ship of the line? A few galleys and frigates? A half-dozen xebecs, which are hardly any good in battle?'

She nods, blinking hard. 'You are right,' she says. 'It is a problem that becomes more urgent by the day.'

He leans back in his chair, silent for a moment, as if thinking. 'Before the coffee, would you like to see my new engravings of the Phlegraean Fields?'

Charlotte smiles. Some day, William Hamilton will retire from diplomacy, and he will spend his days digging up pottery and studying volcanic activity, and he will be perfectly happy.

When Soliman visits in February 1778, he is glum. Joseph has gone to war with Prussia, and Mesmer has gone to France. In the cavern beneath Naples, they meet, and there are new spells in the *Reconditus*, one from Constantinople that prevents sails from ripping, and one from Amsterdam that keeps powder dry. Charlotte is eager for both. But it is her turn to add a spell to the *Reconditus*, and she has finally run out of spells from the embroidered book. Silfversparre and Lunardi tend to get spells from the rogues they capture, and Caramanico gets them in trade for his secrets and favours. Charlotte is busy with governing.

She kneels at the little desk where they keep quill, ink, and paper, and hastily writes out the spell Antoinette sent her, the one about the flour that changes people's feelings when it's baked into little cakes.

'You can use this in your salons with your poets and philosophers, Caramanico,' she says. 'In fact, would you use it when you go to Florence next month? Invite some naval men, and make them trust you. I need to learn about building a fleet. If they won't eat little cakes, mix it in whatever they will enjoy.'

Caramanico approaches and looks over her shoulder, and

when he speaks, it's in a low voice, low enough that the others won't hear. 'I can't use that spell, Your Majesty, but I could take a bag of flour with me, if someone else were to enchant it.'

'You can't use it?' She turns to look up at him.

He looks embarrassed. 'The sacrifice – the love spell. I find myself short.'

She has never considered the possibility, and it turns her skin cold. 'Short of love? You have nothing left to sacrifice?'

He straightens his shoulders. 'But I believe I know just the man who can help Your Majesty – an Englishman, serving in the Tuscan navy. He managed a manoeuvre that's made him famous; no one knows better how a fleet behaves in these waters.'

'That will do nicely,' she says after a moment. She stands, and prepares to add her sister's spell to the store of the Order's knowledge.

The enchantment to add a spell to the *Reconditus* seemed silly to her the first time: write down the spell to be given, place it as a memory sacrifice, and it will appear in the book. Hardly a sacrifice at all; merely a transfer. But it still makes her feel slightly ill, every time: losing the memory of the spell for a moment, forgetting what she wrote on the paper that turns to dust. The book grows new pages as a salamander grows limbs, the sacrificed spell appearing first and then others, all in the handwriting of the magister who sacrificed them.

The familar smell of rot is barely a note beneath the cave's dampness. They ask the Five Questions, and open the book and find the spell written there, along with the spells for powder and sails.

'These spells have been used, and are safe?' Silfversparre asks.

Soliman nods. 'There was a powder explosion near Berlin not long ago, but on investigation, we found that was a different spell altogether. An attempt at the loaves-and-fishes spell by some rogue, I shouldn't wonder.'

'Who was the rogue working for?' Caramanico asks.

'Himself, probably,' Soliman says. 'Any rogue could make their fortune that way, and blow up the world while they're at it. The Prussian chapter doesn't know who it was. We in Vienna are in contact still with our Prussian Brothers, as much as we can, given the present state of war between Prussia and the Empire.'

'The Order has always held itself apart from worldly disputes,' says Caramanico.

'Yes . . .' Soliman agrees slowly. 'But more than that, we are beginning to use magic for the public good, inspired in part by what you have achieved here in Naples. It is a very cautious experiment. In Vienna, we are using the white-gloves spell to try to ensure that His Imperial Majesty's troops seldom engage with the enemy, and some like-minded magisters in Königsberg are using maps of confusion to do something similar. We hope to reduce the casualties, and make time for diplomacy to work.'

It was only a matter of time, Charlotte thinks. And the traditional members of the Order – the Rohanites, as people have started to call them – can hardly complain, given their conviction that the war in America is one that magisters must join. They argue that the American question poses a threat to the existence of the Order – but doesn't all war?

'A marvellous opportunity to use magic as an instrument of reason in the modern world,' says Lunardi.

'It will be,' Silfversparre grumbles, 'if we can keep the two armies from eating up the countryside and leaving dysentery and bastards in their wake while they dance around each other.'

'Empress Catherine won't let them dance for long,' Caramanico argues.

Soliman nods. 'We will do what we can. I believe that the Order will one day be a light unto the world. But for the moment, the rogues are not going to stop with one theft. There was an attack on another of our number a few days

before I left – he found himself lost in the alleys of Vienna for more than a day, and we still don't quite understand what magic the rogues used against him, or why.'

'Perhaps it was gin,' says Silfversparre.

Soliman smiles, but shakes his head. 'I saw the man. Something of the nature of our map spell, but what, I don't know. Perhaps it was mere mischief, or a message – to show us what they can do.'

'Is there a *they*?' Lunardi asks. 'The rogues in Naples hold no meetings and have no ideas beyond their own little grimoires and amulets.'

'For now,' Soliman says. 'But you must be ready. There are rogues with ambition, who would rule their fellows if they could, who will form a sort of shadow of the Order and go to war against us. And if that happens, not only will we fail in keeping humanity safe from the knowledge of magic, but we may fail in keeping them safe from magic itself. What is to stop some common soldier with a half-dozen spells from declaring himself emperor, in any country where the monarchs don't have magic, where the Order is not powerful enough to stop him? A half-dozen spells, if they were powerful enough, could be a match for an army. It could even be a match for the Order here in Naples. We must not allow any more rogues to steal from us. We must draw the line here, or we fail in our duty to the past and the future.'

Charlotte swallows, and nods. She has known for weeks what she must write to Antoinette, and the time has come simply to do it. Hasn't it been difficult for Charlotte to regulate the flour and beans, to make sure she doesn't disrupt trade and agriculture? The French government is a mess; if it had to deal with Antoinette feeding mysterious stocks of food into the system, it would devolve into anarchy. Besides, Antoinette is too trusting, and she has rogues as friends. Rogues who might well use the spell to create gunpowder or worse – it would require enormous sacrifices, but there are people willing to do anything for a cause, or for money.

She must tell her sister that she can't give her the loaves-and-fishes spell. Will she accept Charlotte's reasoning? She will resent it, most likely. And Antoinette is too honest even to keep the secret of its existence. No, Charlotte must tell Antoinette that she knows of no such spell. She doesn't think she has ever lied to Antoinette before, but perhaps she has sacrificed the memory.

CHAPTER THIRTY-ONE

A Gift for Charlotte, Signed with Love — An Inadequate
Fleet — Charlotte Borrows from Leopold — A New
Project for San Leucio

Antoinette reads the letter in which Charlotte refuses to provide the spell that could help her feed France. Her sister repeats that she can't keep Antoinette safe if Antoinette insists on doing things that will draw the attention of the Brothers of Paris, who are understandably concerned that the Queen of France has been influenced by rogue magisters.

With her jaw set and her lips tight, Antoinette sits down to respond to Charlotte.

She thinks about what she wants to write:

You have chosen your allies unwisely. And you've mistaken my affection for stupidity for the last time.

But she doesn't. She lets those sentences live in her mind and not in her pen.

The rogues do things differently, and Charlotte will never see the virtue in that. Saint-Georges and Polignac have already found other magisters in Paris, and Antoinette has told them they may of course share any spells they like. But Antoinette has no friends in Naples, the way Charlotte

329

does in Paris. She has no way to take the spell that would help her feed her people. She asked for it, and Charlotte refused.

So Antoinette has enchanted a portrait of herself, only this time the magic has nothing to do with her appearance. This time, the portrait is an extension of herself, and if Antoinette tries, she can hear what's happening in any room where it hangs. It's an alteration of the same spell responsible for Geneviève's fan, and the lorgnette that so impressed her friends that day at the Petit Trianon. It took some time to make it apply to a painting. Antoinette tested it in a few places in Versailles, and heard things she wishes she hadn't.

She writes a gentle, brief, sisterly letter. She adds a note to the bottom, saying that she's sending a painting. She signs it with love.

A gift for Charlotte, from her sister: a portrait of Antoinette, as queen.

This portrait shows a woman with feathers riding in her hair, and strings of pearls wrapping the thick ringlets to her shoulders. Heavy-lidded eyes the same colour and clarity as the sapphire at her breast. A rosebud smile.

This woman looks nothing like the apple-cheeked girl in riding clothes, newly arrived in France. Certainly nothing like the terrified Dauphine, in one of the old-fashioned court dresses, her hair scraped back from her temples.

This young woman gazing at something just outside of the frame looks regal. More than that, she looks almost *happy*, but then Antoinette has cultivated the skill of looking happy, and painters lie. Still, Charlotte stares at it for a long time, wishing she could speak to the woman painted there, a woman ten years older than the weeping sister she left behind at Schönbrunn.

15 April 1778
Charlotte to Leopold

My dear Leopold,

I am writing to tell you that Dr Gatti has accepted my invitation to stay here with us in Naples, and so you have lost a doctor by lending him to me. What a good brother you are! I know you won't begrudge me. (Peace, peace. I'll make it up to you somehow.)

Shamelessly, I'm writing now to ask you for another favour, and possibly for another loan of a talented man, or two. The last time Joseph was here, he moaned and grumbled about the state of the Neapolitan navy, and I dare say he was right, but I had too much to occupy me. Now, I'm told on good authority that I have run out of time to procrastinate, and we can't rely on the Spanish to protect us any more. We are entirely open to the sea here, Leopold, and if your fraternal love for me is not enough to bestir you, consider that if Naples falls to one of Europe's naval powers, Tuscany won't be far behind.

The trouble is that I know nothing about building a navy – how many of which sort of ship, and of what designs, and who ought to build them, and all of that. This is one of many areas of my education our mother saw fit to neglect when she was teaching me embroidery and dancing. And Ferdinand, as you know, is useless.

Isn't there anyone there you could send me to advise me? My friend the Prince of Caramanico says wonderful things about your Englishman, John Acton, the one who commanded your frigates in the Algiers campaign.

Your nieces and nephews send you kisses. Kiss all of mine for me.

Your sister,
Charlotte

1 May 1778
Antoinette to Charlotte

My dear Charlotte,

I am glad to hear the portrait pleases you. I was very amused to read your letter about your new arrangement with your husband, and for your sake I hope you can stretch it a few more months. I wish you joy of your celibacy from this day onward! Surely he cannot insist, now that you have given him five children.

It seems God has disposed everything rather well, because I suspect I at last am with child myself. It may be nothing, but the General is very late and I am hopeful.

I shall have to order some new clothes, and I have already decided on a way to announce my condition to the people: I'll give 12,000 francs for the relief of the poor. I've asked for specific attention to be paid for those in debtors' prisons, and especially those whose poverty made them unable to pay their wet-nurses. I'm told there are a great many such people. To think of all the mothers who could not nurse themselves – or fathers or grandmothers raising babies whose mothers died in childbirth – what a terrible prospect it must be to know that the money will run out, and the child will go hungry. And then to be taken away to prison, where one can be of no more good to anyone!

The pamphleteers continue their fascination with me; I fear I may have wrought too well with my enchantment of the chevalier's violin, years ago. The people think of me, and when they have nothing to think about, they invent.

Oh well. God willing, when they think of me, soon enough, they'll think of a darling tiny dauphin.

Finally, I must tell you that I have no response to Rohan's 'concerns', as you put it, about my being influenced by rogue magisters. The fact that he is now Cardinal de Rohan means nothing; he's still a scoundrel. If you love me, the best you can do for me is trust that my own judgement

*is sound. You keep your secrets and I will keep mine.
I know you mean well, Charlotte, but they don't. You know
very well that I can be as stubborn as you, in my own way,
and I have no intention of changing my opinion on this.*

*Speaking of the family stubborn streak, Joseph's decision
to send troops into Bavaria in support of his claims there
created no end of difficulties for me here, as Louis was dead
set against it, and I found myself having to argue both sides
to the other. Again, I have given fuel to those who think
I care only for the fortunes of our family.*

*How can we be a family when borders and interests
divide us?*

> *All my love to you, my sister forever,*
> *Antoinette*

The *Reconditus* grows in fits and starts. As the threat of war
grows across Europe, some chapters go for months without
adding spells, hoarding what they know, uncertain now of
how magic may be used by governments. But always, eventually, new spells appear, as curiosity overcomes caution. To
stop adding to the *Reconditus* would be to stop learning from
the discoveries of other chapters. The Order is held together
by mutual greed.

The girls at the San Leucio factory have little to do at the
moment; the kingdom's stores of beans and flour are as full
as Charlotte dares to make them, without attracting notice
or disrupting the market. What is she to do with the extra
flour?

She thinks of Antoinette's little spell, for the cakes. She
could set San Leucio onto this new spell for a while instead:
enchanting flour not to duplicate it, but to create an emotional
effect in the people.

They will enchant the flour to induce doubt. In small
quantities, across the whole population of Sicily and Naples,
it may be enough to change the hearts of the people. To

reduce their certainty, to make them less vulnerable to dogma and cant, and more open to new ideas. To make them happy to leave the Inquisition and all the other civil power of the clergy in the Middle Ages where it belongs. To give Charlotte her sphere of influence, free and clear.

For various reasons – because she is a woman, like the workers at San Leucio; because Charlotte knows she can never betray her; because the others are busy – oversight of the project falls to Caterina. On the last day of 1778, she comes to Charlotte's study in the Palazzo Reale, to report.

Caterina looks tired as she lays out the problems she's had to solve. Unlike the duplication spell, this new enchantment on the flour requires more sacrifices than they can ask of any girl more than once or twice. It requires more girls, working on less frequent rotations. It's hard work, making sure that the girls don't really understand or remember what they're doing, making sure that they do it properly. And making sure they are recompensed with a good education and good wages for their work on the silk looms.

Charlotte listens, with gratitude, and looks at Caterina's face. She's asked a great deal of her friend these last years.

'Come,' Charlotte says. 'I'll show you a marvel.'

She draws back a Chinese screen and shows Caterina her new globe. It's a beautiful piece: the lines of the continents a delicate gold, the lines of the meridians solid and sure. It sits on its axis within a wooden stand.

Caterina walks around it, inspecting, clearly not wishing to give offence but unable to see what's so glorious about it.

'Look with this,' Charlotte says, and hands her a magnifying glass. 'Look at the ocean. Any ocean.'

Caterina bends over the Atlantic Ocean with the glass in her hand, frowns, looks closer. 'Ships! Good heavens, they're moving. Look, there's a British flag on that one.'

Charlotte claps her hands. 'You see? We can't affect the real world by touching the globe, so don't bother poking at them. But it shows us where the ships are. I am going to

build a navy for Naples, and that navy will be the safest and the most dangerous on the seas, because it will know where every other ship is and where it will be.'

'Will be?'

'If we know where they are, we can guess where they're going. Look there, in the English Channel: thirty British ships of the line.' She goes to her writing desk and makes some calculations. 'If they carry on in their current speed and course, by the twenty-third of July they will be west of the island of Ushant, by, oh, a hundred miles? We'll make a wager, and see whether I'm right.'

'Is it a rogue spell? Or in the *Reconditus*?'

Charlotte shakes her head. 'One of Dr Soliman's inventions. He writes interminably about the problem of placing two enchantments on a single item: it so seldom works, without one enchantment slipping off or changing in some way. Soliman thinks the reason for this is connected to what he calls the "spell of spells", the formula that can determine the sacrifices for any enchantment.'

Caterina blinks, amazed. 'Any enchantment? Even one that has never been proven before?'

'That is his theory. Whether such a thing could really exist, I can't say. Soliman has been experimenting with multiple spells on single objects, and he sent this to me to see whether it made a difference when two different magisters worked the spells. It was my task to choose what I wanted to see, and I chose the ships of the line of all the nations of the world.'

Caterina walks around the globe, bending down now and then to peer at the little ships. 'And the cost?'

'The memories of twenty-five days – but not just any days. Twenty-five birthdays. And I just happened to have twenty-five birthdays to sacrifice.'

Caterina looks stricken, so Charlotte holds up a hand to reassure her.

'What are the memories of twenty-five days, over the course of a life?' Charlotte says. 'Birthdays were never terribly

important back in Austria anyway; we made a bigger fuss over name-days.'

Caterina gives her a sad smile. 'It's an impressive device, Your Majesty.'

'And very useful too. I can tell my admirals precisely where to sail. Once I have the admirals to tell, that is.'

'But how will you tell your admirals what they need to know without telling them how you know it?'

'I'll simply give them orders, Caterina. I am queen, you know.'

CHAPTER THIRTY-TWO

*Lafayette's Travails in America — Conversations
at the Petit Trianon — The Problem of
Philippe — Naval Intelligence*

The Chevalière d'Éon leans back in her chair and crosses her legs. Here at the Petit Trianon, everyone has a chair rather than one of the stools that fill the rooms at Versailles, and the conversations go differently.

D'Éon clears her throat and snaps a piece of paper in one hand. 'Let me read from Lafayette's own letter. He writes: "There are a half-dozen magisters among the officers here in America, but I don't know what to do with them. Their spells are useless to me and one of them keeps trying to ignite a lantern through magic and setting his tent afire. He protests that there is a want of firewood, which is true, but there is a want of everything: men, money, food, uniforms, muskets, time. General Washington is in the north and I am here. My wound has healed and my health is quite good, if I do not starve. Please convey my best wishes, look after my wife, I remain, et cetera, et cetera."'

She pushes her reading spectacles down her long nose and peers at Antoinette. 'They are starving.'

Saint-Georges paces by the window, as he usually does,

whether there are stools or chairs or anything. 'I have found a few more spells to send him.'

'From your friends in the alleys around the Palais-Royal?' d'Éon asks.

'Spells are spells,' Saint-Georges says, turning. 'And who are we to turn up our noses at halfpenny conjurers, since we cannot manage anything useful on our own?'

'Speaking of the Palais-Royal,' d'Éon continues, 'Your Majesty, I really think we should bring the duke into our meetings here.'

The duke she means is Philippe d'Orléans. Antoinette still can't believe he's been a rogue magister all this time. The Orléans branch of the family is more wealthy and powerful than anyone in France save the King himself. Philippe recently received a gift from his father: the sprawling and increasingly misnamed Palais-Royal in central Paris.

It was at the opera house there that Antoinette met Fersen, a lifetime ago. The complex has been in the Orléans family for generations but now she can't go there for fear of being mobbed. Philippe has rented out the colonnade to shop-keepers of all kinds: booksellers, silk merchants, wig-makers, potters and cobblers, stalls jumbled with trinkets of dubious origin. It is his private estate, and there are no police. Cloaked men mutter in the shadows of the many little coffee houses that tuck into the marbled arcades. The voices of actors rise in the gardens, and the laughter and boos of their audiences. Polignac has told her all about it.

'I used to think he wanted magic only for his own benefit,' d'Éon says. 'But I hear he knows many rogue magisters, even some he's taught himself. Farmers and fishmongers, even. Actresses. All sorts of people. He may be able to find spells we can't, and act on things happening far from Versailles.'

'Farmers and fishmongers!' Antoinette says, astonished. 'Can they all even read?'

'I don't know,' d'Éon says, as though amused. 'They don't need to know *agricola, agricolae* to be magisters, I suppose.'

'No, but they need to know how to read spellbooks,' Lamballe says. 'Why teach these unfortunates to use something they can hardly understand?'

'If it were someone else, I would say it is because they are unfortunate,' Polignac says evenly. 'But this is Philippe, so I am sure he's doing it to be an ass.'

'Surely,' Antoinette responds, 'if he had anything useful to contribute to the state, he would have done so.'

She thinks of her own efforts to be of use to the state: the enchanted cakes, the winds of opinion shifting in ways they might have shifted anyway. How little she has done!

Polignac says, 'Philippe is a creature of Versailles, for all that the Orléans family thinks they occupy a world apart. He operates on favours. He may be waiting for someone to ask him.'

'If only we had the complete loaves-and-fishes spell!' Saint-Georges cries. 'Franz Mesmer is here in France, I've heard. Perhaps we could even sway him to our cause. He is the most liberal-minded of Brothers, so I understand.'

D'Éon shakes her head, her grey ringlets brushing her shoulders. 'He is liberal-minded, but I do not trust any Brother of the Order. Not now. The magisters of London are beginning to interfere in America. They never would have done such a thing ten years ago. This business in Naples has emboldened them – the more they see magic used for political ends, the more they convince themselves to abandon their own principles of secrecy and caution. But their core principle, the preservation of their own power, that they will never abandon.'

'We could steal the spell from him,' the Princesse de Lamballe says quietly. 'I would be willing to try.'

Lamballe sits in her chair as though it were a stool. Unloved, undemanding of love, her face shining.

It doesn't matter at all if Antoinette doesn't love her. Love

339

is an action, isn't it? And if Antoinette acts as though she loves her, it will be no different than as if she truly did. She has very nearly convinced herself of this.

'My darling, it is too dangerous,' Antoinette says. 'Mesmer is new here, and on his guard now.'

'The Queen of Naples offered us nothing?'

Antoinette sighs. 'She will not give it to us. I know she has it.'

'Then perhaps we should take it from her,' Saint-Georges says, stepping away from the window. 'They will not expect us to strike in Naples. There are so few rogues who've escaped the Order's hunters there. No one left but confused old women and cheap charlatans.'

'No,' Antoinette says uncertainly. 'We would start a war.'

'Several wars have already started around us, it would seem,' Polignac says gently.

Antoinette thinks. 'I have my portrait in Naples, and I am listening. I hear things – snatches of conversation. It is only a matter of time before there is some discussion of the loaves-and-fishes spell, and the moment there is, I will write to Lafayette, and he can feed and clothe his men.'

'Mmm,' d'Éon says. 'It may be too late by then.'

'In the interests of France and in the interest of rogue magisters everywhere, we need to keep those soldiers alive to fight on,' says Saint-Georges. 'It was you, Your Majesty, who gave the marquis the means to go to America, gave him a glimpse of magic that fed his curiosity, and now he—'

'I know,' Antoinette snaps. Polignac looks at her warningly, and Lamballe anxiously.

She breathes, puts a hand on her belly. 'I am sorry. I am dyspeptic – the pregnancy.'

Saint-Georges bows his head. 'The fault was mine, Your Majesty. I do not like waiting and doing nothing.'

The interests of France. After the Battle of Saratoga, when the Americans showed they might be able to win against Britain, Louis was finally induced to sign treaties of agreement

with the rebels. Britain had little choice after that but to declare war. But there have been no battles between the two countries; the war remains on American soil, for now.

But at sea, there are ships of both nations, circling, waiting for the order to attack.

She lifts her chin. 'I don't like doing nothing either. I will talk to Philippe. I'm not sure what to do about the fishmongers, but he's an officer of the navy, and there I think we may be able to work together.'

Antoinette meets Philippe d'Orléans alone in her private cabinet room. There are a few mirrors on the walls to prevent magical eavesdropping, and the doors are thick. Even so, neither one of them wants to speak of magic first. They exchange pleasantries and look uncomfortably at each other; Antoinette rearranges her hands several times.

Philippe is seated on a proper chair, his right as a prince of the blood.

At last she says, 'You should know that I have founded a little society of magisters. The Queen's Circle, we call ourselves.'

The word *magisters* hangs in the air, and he slowly nods. 'At the Petit Trianon.'

'Good heavens. If they're that obvious to you, I should take better care, or the Order will be at our doors.'

'Indeed, Your Majesty.'

Antoinette smiles at Philippe in a way she hopes is disarming. 'I learned magic when I was very young. D'Éon tells me the same was true for you.'

He looks at her warily. 'I was fifteen. My father sent me to a courtesan. Rosalie Duthé. You might have heard of her.'

Duthé had affairs with half the men in Versailles. Antoinette merely raises an eyebrow.

'She, too, was very young,' Philippe continues. 'Pimped out by an aunt. She'd been expelled from a convent for practising magic; I don't know where she first learned it.

341

Anyway, she taught me.' He leans forward, his elbows on his knees. He's wearing a coat of naval blue with gold lapels, over scarlet breeches. 'For all the good it's done me, or any of us.'

'I've heard that you are sailing out soon to help keep French waters safe, and I thank you.'

'Safe,' he says dismissively. 'The British will make short work of us, just as they're making short work of the Americans. The rebels starve and freeze, and we bob on the waves. We simply don't have enough ships.'

She pauses. D'Éon says they need him. And her friends deserve some sort of victory, some consolation for her failure to obtain the loaves-and-fishes spell. Antoinette has heard many conversations, through the painting she sent to her sister. Most of them are tedious: road repairs and taxes. What Antoinette hoped to hear – the loaves-and-fishes spell, or orders to act against rogues in Paris – she has not. But there are a few that might serve better purposes. At last she says, 'I cannot offer you ships, but I can offer you information.'

He raises an eyebrow.

'What if I told you that the British will have thirty ships of the line approximately one hundred miles west of the island of Ushant at noon on the twenty-third of July?'

He gapes. 'You're sure?'

'I trust the information. But you must promise me, Philippe, not to make it look as though you knew this in advance. Don't ambush them.'

He leans back, looks as though he would whistle. 'Well, I can't do anything about it anyway. Not unless I were made an admiral.'

'An admiral!' She shows her surprise, and he scowls. 'But you're already a lieutenant-general, Philippe. To be made an admiral so soon—'

'The King could see it done. If he chose.'

'Ah.' What confidence he has! What must it be like to be so certain that one is equipped to lead, to rule! 'Philippe, I

can't ask the King to make his cousin an admiral, particularly when that cousin has very little military experience. You do see that I can't do that?'

He gives her a nasty smile. 'I see. Of course. I had to ask. I'll go off to sea, with my little squadron and your information, and hope for the best. Your Majesty.'

He nods, and she stands to let him know their audience is over. 'We are working together, Philippe. We are on the same side.'

He takes her hand, and performs the proper motions of affection.

CHAPTER THIRTY-THREE

Summer at Portici — John Acton Arrives in Naples —
A Gift from Joseph — Rogue Attacks — Shipbuilding

In the summer of 1778, the palace of Portici no longer contains the spectacle of poor Filippo, mocked by the people sworn to serve him. The children love the palace. It is right on the slopes of Vesuvius, near the ruins of Herculaneum and Hamilton's villa, and the breezes are good.

A blight threatened the grape harvest for the second year in a row, but then Charlotte had an idea, and went rifling through her notebooks. A few years ago, Antoinette sent her a spell she devised to make vines and clinging plants grow more quickly. Charlotte could almost hear her voice in the letter, laughing at the fact that so many of her spells prove useless to her, wondering whether this one might be of use to Charlotte?

Antoinette does not send her spells any more.

Soliman sends letters full of philosophy, expounding on the lessons to be learned from the Mughal emperors Jahangir and Aurangzeb, or from Peter III of Russia. She reads his letters carefully, happily. There's something comforting in their abstraction.

And Leopold, the long-suffering dear, sends her John Acton

to build her a navy. He was born in France to a wandering Englishman, and he followed an equally wandering uncle into the Tuscan naval service, where he distinguished himself in an otherwise disastrous Spanish campaign against Algeria.

Charlotte meets Acton in her study at Portici. He looks very English: slightly pink, and more than slightly smug. He takes her hand, looking uncomfortable.

'I understand you are the reason Spain got away from its latest adventure with any men left alive,' she says.

He bows his head. 'I would not say that.'

'But is it true?' she snaps. 'I want a plain speaker for this job, General Acton. I have quite enough people who will tell me what they think I want to hear.'

He swallows. 'Your Majesty, it is true in the sense that I made one or two decisions which proved to have been the right ones. But I was not the only one on our side who made quick decisions that day, so I don't think it's right that I take the credit.'

'Hmm.' She walks around him, appraising, while he stares straight forward, military. 'Our side. Our side. Do you think, then, that Tuscany and Naples and Spain all form a single side, so to speak?'

'I think that Your Majesty's brother is Grand Duke of Tuscany, and that Your Majesty's father-in-law is the King of Spain.'

'That is not an answer.' She stops her inspection. He's a man like any other: tall, a bit narrow in the shoulders in his dark-blue soldier's coat. 'I am, foremost, the Queen of Naples. Any man who works for me works only for me. I expect total loyalty and total silence. That includes any members of my family, here or in other countries. No other members of the Council of Naples. No one at all, here at court or else-where. Is that plain?'

'Plain indeed, Your Majesty. I am not a man who enjoys life at court, and I should be happiest left to my own devices, out with the workmen, overseeing the job.'

'Left to your own devices.'

He nods. 'Tell me how many ships are required, and how much money I can spend, and how much time I have to do it in, and Your Majesty will hear no more of me until they are built.'

She smiles. 'Perhaps I will like you, John Acton.'

For her twenty-sixth birthday in August 1778, Joseph sends Charlotte a mahogany desk with a great wheel mounted on top of it, like a paddlewheel, twice the height of the desk itself. Each of the dozen paddles of the wheel is a little desktop that can tilt to any angle she likes. Charlotte can have a different set of papers or a different book open on each, and when she wants to switch from one task to another, she merely spins the wheel. An inkstand sits on the desk proper, below the moving parts.

'A piece of furniture to match your mind,' Joseph writes. 'Keep it oiled. I will visit when I can.'

She finds the desk a great help with the work of the Council. Charlotte often works by candlelight in the small hours, pregnant again, with Francesco fussing at her breast; she did not allow a wet-nurse this time. For a year, she's had breast milk to use in her sacrifices.

In the palace of Caserta, her library is coming along nicely. She uses one of its rooms as her study. Here she has hung the portrait of her sister; here she installed the great desk.

One night, with Francesco dozing fitfully in her lap, she finds herself staring at a document, the words mere shapes on the page. Reports from the bishops, about the current state of things as regards the Crown's relationship with the Holy See in Rome. Charlotte will need to know all of this. She is eager to separate religion and the state into their own spheres. Montesquieu's books are adamant on the point, and her own mother has demonstrated over and over the dangers of state religion, with her costly schemes to move Protestants around the empire, her persecutions of the Jews, her narrow-minded

fears of enlightened philosophy. But Charlotte is walking on a knife's edge, after bringing the Inquisition to an end. There are pamphlets about her, grumblings that come to her ears through Caterina and Ferdinand. So many people are still in the grip of supersitition. How can a nation reach Enlightenment if its people refuse to question?

Meanwhile, Lunardi is convinced a rogue is behind the broken wheel that sent his carriage flying off the road the other day and could have killed him. And maybe he's right. The rogues of this city, those who have survived with their memories intact, must know the stories of the shadowy Order that forces them to hide. Is it so surprising that some rogues have learned the names of the Brothers of Naples, and are seeking revenge? It is a constant danger. They wouldn't even need to use magic. A knife in the ribs can kill a magister as easily as it would any man.

The words swim on Charlotte's page and her eyes fill with tears for no reason she can understand. They are sore from too much reading and too little sleep.

She looks up at the portrait of Antoinette. 'I can't do this,' she whispers, not sure what 'this' is. 'Nobody wants me to do this. And I'm so tired. I could retire to a country estate. Hell, I could even go to a nunnery.'

She reaches out with her right hand, the hand not cradling Francesco, and gives the wheel a violent spin. Papers fly off: reports of the Council; the spell to keep powder dry, which hasn't accepted her sacrifices yet; a letter she's ciphering. Everything scatters.

'I need you to tell me it's worthwhile, or isn't,' she tells the portrait. 'I could always tell, just by looking at you, when I was in the wrong. When I was trying to prove my cleverness, or have my revenge, instead of doing what was right. I need you and a letter won't do. I need to hear your voice.'

The baby screws up his face and wails, and Charlotte grits her teeth and blinks away her tears. She can't travel with the baby, doesn't dare leave the children behind, in the care

of others. And the French King and his wife never leave France. The portrait stares, silent.

A summer night, and the King and Queen hold one of their parties, under strings of Chinese lanterns. As it has for months, the volcano emits a constant, narrow pillar of pale smoke, like a snuffed candle.

The courtiers stream through the corridors. In the dining room, chairs line the damask walls, and a table in the middle groans under mounds of food. Charlotte glides through a little crowd of genuflectors and hem-pluckers. The more piggish courtiers are already seated, their plates on their laps, heaped with macaroni and roast pork and meat pies.

Ferdinand is at the far end of the room, desperately embracing some wench, so Charlotte aims for a chair at the near end. It's cooler here, by the door. Everyone swirls around her, not around Ferdinand. She watches them eddy, watches them watch her.

A footman comes to her elbow before she sits.

'Madam, the Englishman is here,' he whispers. 'He wants a word, in private.'

'William Hamilton, you mean?' She feels befuddled by the wine and the heat, and the wearing of the mask.

He shakes his head. 'The general, from Tuscany.'

She claps her hands. Acton. Her navy.

'All right,' she says, and hands the man her plate. She isn't hungry, anyway. She feels as though she is liable to vomit – it could be the heat, the smoke of the torches, the noise.

The footman offers to bring Acton to the coffee room adjacent to the dining room, where the white-coated servants are readying their bottles of liqueurs, but Charlotte does not want him to get the idea he can come to her parties unbidden; nor does she want the guests gawking. She walks, sweating, to her study.

The Englishman, Acton, does not look as if he feels the

heat. He lounges in her study, leaning against a wall and somehow managing not to look at himself in any of the mirrors.

Her study is the same, or nearly the same, in every one of her palaces. Wherever the Queen goes, the portrait of her sister goes with her. Every study must have mirrors on the walls, always.

'Your Majesty,' he says, so primly that it's practically insolent.

She's warm, flushed, and he probably assumes she's drunk. Or perhaps he is still getting used to the idea that the Queen is the power in Naples. The only power. The Brothers listen to her. And the Council, too, and bit by bit the Council shows itself more interested in governing. She wears her white gloves (a new set) in every meeting, which helps. She has persuaded them to listen to her ideas about prison reform. They are starting to understand that it is in the state's interest to feed and clothe all the prisoners, not only those whose families can pay the bribes. When they come out, the poor prisoners will no longer wear old smallpox-infested clothing. And they'll be strong enough to work.

She has learned to appeal to their cupidity. But she needs more than sound arguments and white gloves. She needs guns and ships.

'Acton, you told me I would not see you again until the work was done. But it's only been a few weeks. Surely you're not a magician?' She means it to be a joke, but is relieved when nothing shows on his face but a kind of grim resolve.

'There is very little good timber to be had anywhere,' he says. 'From Milan to Palermo, wherever I send a man to enquire, he finds that all the good oak has been bought, and what remains is only available at an exorbitant cost.'

She narrows her eyes. 'I took a carriage to Caserta last month and saw plenty of trees on my way.'

'There are very few big oaks and pines left – so much timber comes from the Americas, and the war there has

slowed everything down. And, of course, now that the British and French fleets are engaging in European waters, there will be damage to repair, new ships to build, so I can't imagine the prices will go down.'

'The British and French fleets have engaged? Where? When?'

'Last month, Madame. I've just had the full reports. It seems the French surprised the British in the English Channel. Madame, what I will need, to be plain, is more money. Or to build fewer ships.'

She peers at him. So dour. Keeping his own counsel.

Leopold said she could trust him. *Acton hates parties and gossip,* he said, and Charlotte took that to mean: he won't talk. But now she sees herself as he must see her, flushed and silly, and, even at twenty-six years old, very young. If he hates parties and gossip, he hates her ridiculous court. He can't see the use of it.

'You'll have your money,' she says. 'You'll have whatever I can give you.'

Charlotte catches a glimpse of her reflection in the great golden-framed mirrors. Her face is beetle-browed, suspicious, and tending (she can never quite forget) to a double chin.

She turns away from the image, towards the more comforting image of her sister's portrait, which smiles down at her.

CHAPTER THIRTY-FOUR

The Tortoiseshell Comb – Where Emotions Live in the Body – Philippe Returns from Battle – The Hall of Mirrors – The Problem of Love Spells

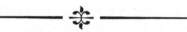

Monsieur Léonard Autié – the original – steps back, his favourite tortoiseshell comb in his hand, and pauses.

'What is it?' Antoinette asks, her voice sharper than she intends. She is tired; she has a headache.

'Madame, may I suggest an alternative to pulling your hair out by the roots?'

Her arms go cold with gooseflesh; his face swims in her mirror. 'It has been falling out again, has it?'

The hairdresser walks around to the side of her dressing table, to face her.

There are ushers at the door, and Madame de Noailles and another lady are sitting on stools in the corner, chatting and watching the coiffeur.

Monsieur Léonard cocks his head, and whispers. 'Your Majesty, if you require hair for magic, I can cut some off, if it must be.'

She swallows, uncertain. He could be a spy.

'I told you years ago, Madame, I am a magician. I know all about it.'

'But I didn't think you were serious!'

'I am always serious.' He smiles, his mouth curling up around his sharp nose. 'Anyway, the *pouf sentimental* is so common now. It is overdone. I suggest a simpler fashion, with short hairs, curled charmingly around the face, tied with a ribbon. Young and fresh.'

Somehow, a hairdresser telling her she'll look young and fresh makes her feel very much the opposite. 'Monsieur Léonard, I don't understand. You are . . . not a member of a magical order, by any chance? Forgive my ignorance.'

'Your Majesty has no ignorance to forgive. Certainly, I am not a member of any order.'

'Then how . . .?'

'I found a comb, as I believe I once mentioned. It seemed quite clear to me that there was something magical about it. I was content with my good fortune, but my brother was consumed with curiosity about how such a thing could be. He spoke with every alchemist and conjurer in the alleys of Paris, asked if they too had magic objects, and he traded and haggled for whatever he could find, until at last we had a little store of things with unusual properties. One day, a man came looking for us, to buy something from our collection, and what he traded for it was not an object but a spell.'

She's astonished. She remembers Countess Ertag, her careful collection of spells. How many enchanted objects did she have? The Order must have taken them when they killed her. But the Order didn't know about the embroidered book; perhaps it missed other things too. All these centuries, the Order has not quite succeeded in stamping out rogue magic. There must be so many magical items out in the world to be found, in attics and storerooms, their uses perhaps forgotten, secrets taken to the grave by their owners.

The hairdresser says, quite proudly, 'My brother and I have seven spells now, altogether. He bought the last one from His Serene Highness, he says, and that was what made me suspect that Your Majesty's hair was – have I overstepped?'

His Serene Highness. Philippe d'Orléans knew that at least one Léonard brother was a rogue magister and didn't see fit to tell her?

'No, you were quite right to speak, Monsieur Léonard, but you must say nothing to anyone, not about me and not about Philippe d'Orléans either. And you must not assume that I know everything he knows. He doesn't like me.'

Monsieur Léonard tucks his comb into his breast pocket and folds his arms across his chest. 'Your Majesty, any Queen of France would find the same. The Orléans family was founded by the brother of the Sun King. How much resentment that man must have had!'

'You think such feelings are passed down in the blood?' She smiles, a little. Monsieur Léonard's theories are always amusing.

He gives a small shrug. 'Emotions live somewhere in the body. They must, or the hair powder would have no effect.'

She should not be surprised, but she is. Her pots of enchanted hair powder are right there on the dressing table, the alteration of the flour spell to induce emotions for anyone who gets close enough. Has he known all this time what they do?

'Siblings have such strong feelings,' says Monsieur Léonard sadly. 'My own brother is a trial to me – he was a libertine and a thief before I taught him how to arrange hair. But I love Jean-François all the same.'

For so many years, Antoinette felt alone with her secret, sharing it only with d'Éon and Charlotte by letter. Now, it seems, there have been magisters around her for years, and she simply didn't know it. And, as the Order's power fails, there will be more and more.

On a Sunday in the Hall of Mirrors, Antoinette prepares to congratulate Philippe d'Orléans. He's been back in Versailles for a few days, and brought news to the King of a victory they are calling the Battle of Ushant. After a few days dancing

around each other, the French engaged some English ships, and though there were losses on both sides, the French forced the English to scurry away. Philippe has been the talk of the town.

But when he comes into the hall, there are titters, and he goes red in the face. Oh God, Antoinette thinks. Can he have got himself into another scandal with some woman? His poor wife.

Philippe takes Antoinette's hand and bows. There are people all around, so she can't ask what she wants to ask. And she wishes she could make people stop laughing at him. Whatever he's done. So she steers the conversation to his military success.

'I was so pleased to hear of your bravery, cousin,' she says.

His frown deepens and he goes redder than ever, and someone guffaws. 'You have not heard, I take it, Your Majesty, or you have, and you mock me.'

'Heard? Heard what?'

'The English fleet was vulnerable, and the admiral ordered a full French attack to finish them off. But the signals' – there's a general roar of giggling – 'the signals were unclear. What I saw, and what the admiral conveyed, were two different things.'

He looks at her significantly, and she understands: there must have been a Brother of the Order on the French ship, using magic to confuse the signals.

'And so,' says Louis, beside her, 'the English got away, when they might have been destroyed. These things happen, Philippe. There will be another chance. And we did make them run.'

Louis, who has been trained to be king, looks out at the hall full of people, many of whom are there to have their exchange of a few words with the royal family: soldiers, visitors, country cousins. Antoinette follows his gaze and sees Axel von Fersen, looking at her.

And for the first time in their lives, they speak to each

other in the sight of others, and Antoinette can't think of what to say, so she says, 'Oh, look, it's an old acquaintance!'

Philippe fades away, having done his duty, and Antoinette is left looking at Fersen's face in the sunlight, in the daylight, in full view of everyone. Louis turns to say a few words to a group of sailors, and Antoinette takes a few steps away from him.

Fersen congratulates her on her pregnancy – now known across Europe, and starting to become evident in her choice of corsetry – and she invites him to her card parties.

And then, for three weeks in a row, he sends his regrets, his excuses, and stays away.

At last, she sends him an enciphered note saying that if he wishes to see what her protégés have done, he will dine with her at the Petit Trianon in three days' time.

In the little mirrored room there, she shows him every tiny jar of enchanted flour, her latest variations. He politely lifts the lid on each, as though attempting to see or smell the difference between approval and suspicion, ambition and satisfaction.

'It's a brilliant idea,' he says. 'You discovered the proofs yourself?'

'Yes, after tears and blood, literally,' she replies, and the lamp seems to flicker along with her laughter. 'The trouble is, it's hard to do in any quantities, because the sacrifices don't go far. But with a half-dozen of us, we have been making progress.'

He glances over all the labels. 'I don't see love here,' he says mischievously.

'No, alas. I've never been able to find a love spell.' She rushes onward, so she won't blush. 'What time is it, I wonder?'

'Nearly midnight, I should think. Tomorrow I'm expected in Rouen.'

'Ah. You come and go so quickly.'

He says softly, 'No matter where I go, I will write, and

send whatever help I can to you, whenever I can, so long as I'm alive.'

'And what will the King of Sweden say about your allegiance to France, Count von Fersen?'

'I owe no loyalty to the Queen of France. But I swear to you that, to my last breath, I will be loyal to Marie Antoinette.'

She can feel the blood heat her cheeks. 'Why?' she whispers.

'One reason is that I have been following all the news about you, since the night we met. To make sure you were not an enemy. I've been putting together a little story in my mind of the sort of person you must be, from these things that anyone could read, and from what Geneviève would tell me. I almost convinced myself I knew you, even before I ever came to Versailles. It was a fool's dream, perhaps.'

'And what sort of story did you tell?'

'Two years ago, you adopted a peasant boy to raise as though he were your own son. Armand, is that what you call him?'

She glances down. 'Yes.'

'There. You see? That's part of the story. You care about people,' Fersen says.

She snorts a little laugh. She hasn't visited Armand in over a week; she's been busy. Remiss.

'You think too much of me, sir. The ugly truth is, I want the people to love me. I need them to love me.'

'Your interests are their interests. That's true of all kings and queens, but most monarchs don't have the . . . what? The imagination? The compassion? . . . to realize it.' His voice drops, even though they are alone. 'To use magic for the good of all.'

'You said that was one reason for your loyalty. What are the others?'

'I think I should keep those to myself.'

She watches the corner of his lovely mouth, just there, where it always dimples as though he is about to smile.

'What a pity you're immune to magic,' she whispers. 'I should like to read your thoughts, if I had such a spell.'

He swallows, and now it is his turn to blush. 'For my part, I am very glad you can't.'

'Count von Fersen,' she says, 'have you ever seen the sun rise at Versailles?'

The path of white stones leads them through the dark night. At some point, Antoinette's enchanted shoe catches on something and Fersen takes her hand. She laces her fingers between his; neither of them are wearing gloves. She didn't even take a shawl. It's a little cold but they are walking fast.

'Once the sun rises, you'll see what I have to work with. I'm going to clear away these paths and flowerbeds and put an English garden in here,' she says. 'Something more natural.'

'I have seen beautiful gardens in England,' he says.

They walk silently for a while, and she can't think of anything but his hand in hers, the way he brushes his thumb against hers, so lightly. They've crossed it now, the barrier between what she is allowed to do and what she must not. They've stepped over it as though it were a mere crack in a marble floor. She opens her mouth as if to speak and instead exhales, just once, and her ribs shudder within the stays beneath her gown.

'Will you tell me something?' she asks.

'Anything.'

'A memory. Tell me which memory you will never sacrifice, no matter what spell requires it.'

He shakes his head, and stops walking. They're nearly at the end of the garden here. It's too dark to see more than the outline of the grassy berm that marks the edge of the flowerbeds and, beyond it, still blanketed in darkness, a meadow where the palace sheep graze.

'I'm sorry,' she whispers. 'I shouldn't have asked.'

His mouth twists. 'Once, I nearly sacrificed my memory of the night I met you.'

She can't breathe.

'I keep a diary,' he says, apologetically, although she can't tell if he's ashamed of having nearly done it, or of preventing himself. 'I would have known what happened. That night. But I wouldn't have been able to remember what you said, or how you looked, or what I was thinking.'

'And what were you thinking?'

A slow smile transforms his face, and his eyebrow quirks.

'I've told you enough already. You tell me. What were you thinking?'

She cocks her head. 'I could see your mouth, below your mask. I remember thinking that whoever had the honour of kissing that mouth would be a very fortunate person.'

And now he laughs, throwing his head back, and there is no one to hear him laugh but her and the nightingales.

'You're mocking me.'

'I'm not! Look, I'll prove it to you.'

She steps closer to him and closes her eyes. His lips part against hers and she stands on tiptoe and presses her body against his. She unbuttons his coat and pulls it off, and pulls his shirt up so she can run her hands against his skin.

'You aren't wearing your uniform,' she says into the hollow of his ear. 'I'd like to see a Swedish uniform.'

'I'll wear it the next time,' he says.

'You have made me a promise.'

As if in response, he puts his hands to the hook between her swollen breasts that holds her *robe à la polonaise* together. 'I have made you all the promises.'

Her robe falls to the grass, and they press against each other as he unties her stays at the small of her back. She lets her petticoat float down as they walk farther into the meadow. It's so dark here, away from the lights of the palace. If anyone were to see her walking in her white chemise, and Fersen in his white shirt, they would think the figures were ghosts.

He pulls her down into the long grass. They have no cause

to worry, she thinks with some distant part of her mind: she is already pregnant.

She pulls him against her, and gives herself over to slow kisses. Louis always stops the kisses at some point, as if afraid of what will happen if they continue, but Fersen does not stop. By the time he presses himself between her thighs she wants him, pulls him towards her – and then, for just a moment, flinches, because this part, she thinks, will be familiar: there will be a small shock of pain, then discomfort, then a few minutes of gentle labour.

Instead it is quite different.

'Let's make an agreement,' she says, as the sky lightens and she traces a pattern on his chest. 'This memory. Tonight. This. Neither one of us will ever sacrifice it. It is sacred. No matter what.'

'No matter what,' Fersen says, and takes her fingers in his hand and brings them to his mouth. 'This is sacred. I promise.'

She is a traitor. An adulteress. Everything the libel pamphlets say, about the *l'Autrichienne* and her revels at the Petit Trianon – all true.

'I'll build a temple here, to remind us, and I'll worship you here every day,' she says, and then her voice cracks, taking her by surprise. She can't cry. She'll look blotchy if she cries.

'I love you madly,' he says. 'You need build me no temples.'

'It's for me, not for you.'

At that he laughs. For a long while, they say nothing, and Antoinette lies as still as she can, eternal in an eternal world.

'When I learned about magic,' Fersen says hoarsely, breaking the silence, 'when the Brothers of Stockholm made me one of them, I thought that I knew what my life's purpose was. And then, as the months passed and I felt more and more sick about their entire project, I felt alone. As though I were broken, because I could not be what they wanted me to be. What I wanted me to be. I sought out other rogues

because I wanted so badly to be a part of something. I found a few people who wanted to change things, but I found many more who wanted nothing but to live their lives in ease and die in luxury. It took a long time for me to find Geneviève and the others who had more desire than fear, who cared about justice and progress and truth. But I still felt like a wanderer, like someone without a home or a creed. Until now.' He traces her eyebrow. 'You may build all the temples you like, but I have found mine.'

She kisses him deeply and wraps her arms around him. Holds him to her.

'I must go, very soon,' he whispers in her ear. 'But I will come back.'

'You must write to me.'

'What shall our keyword be? For the cipher?'

She thinks for a moment. He said that this night would be sacred.

'*Sacré*,' she says.

He does not kiss her; he nods, gazing into her eyes until she can't bear it and looks away.

CHAPTER THIRTY-FIVE

The Queen Needs Air — No Less Dear to Me —
Charlotte Is Desperate — Tiny Fingernails

In the middle of December, Antoinette gets her labour pains. In the middle of the night, Lamballe goes from room to room, informing everyone who has a right to know; the list is long. She sends messengers to the Palace of Saint-Cloud to tell Philippe, who has a right to be present, as a prince of the blood. Louis's siblings, the aunts. All of them crowd into the Grand Bedchamber. Beyond the walls, as the sun comes up, Antoinette can hear the hum of onlookers who have not been invited, but who crowd into the Hall of Mirrors none-theless. This place is their place; the Sun King deemed it so.

She is not required to lie in the enormous golden bed, thank God, but in a little one covered in white linen, linen that is soon soaked with blood. Louis arranges the tapestry screens himself so that all his family members in the room are at least not peering at his wife, although by this point, Antoinette would not care if they were. Her body is splitting apart and when they announce the birth, she is glad that at last she can die, she can rest, she can go away. She's shivering and in so much pain.

When she wakes, they tell her that she fainted. The room

363

is freezing – to help revive her, someone opened the windows to the December air – and at last they bring her the baby. Her little Marie-Thérèse Charlotte. She cradles her close and says, 'Poor little girl, you were not what was desired, but you are no less dear to me on that account. A son would have belonged to the state. You shall be mine.'

In the middle of December, Charlotte's son Carlo gets a fever. He's nearly four, and his limbs are so long now, the arms and legs of a child, not an infant. Charlotte remembers her first glimpse of his tiny fingernails, how she felt, as she feels with every birth: the marvel of a new person in the world who is of her and yet his own. And yet, God's. She spends hours watching him and cooling his face with cloths dipped in water while the doctors bleed him and tut. She wets his tiny lips, so pale and cracked.

'But it is not smallpox,' Charlotte says as she stands in the shadows with Caterina, just far enough from the bed that Carlo will not hear their whispers. 'It's malaria, they think. If we can only break the fever. Keep some water in him. For God's sake, Caterina, Antoinette rearranged her shoulder bones. There must be some way we can bring the boy's fever down. I refuse to believe that a simple fever is more powerful than the Order and all its magisters.'

Carlo moans, a small, pitiful sound.

'There is nothing in the *Reconditus*,' Caterina says. 'Nothing that would save him.'

'But there are new spells all the time,' Charlotte says, clenching her fists. 'Soliman invents them by accident. Write to him. Bring him here.'

'It will take a week for him to arrive, Your Majesty, and by then—'

She shakes her head, looking at her child. 'I would sacrifice anything. Do you hear me? Anything it takes. Write to Soliman. Write to every chapter in Europe. Find me a spell, no matter the cost.'

Charlotte sits, enclosing her little boy's small limp hand in her own, while Ferdinand sits on the far side and sings to the boy a little. Soon Ferdinand too is silent. And they sit in a room with nothing but the shuddering, terrible breathing of two parents' lungs, as Carlo is gone from them forever, his small body cooling at last.

CHAPTER THIRTY-SIX

*Lafayette Returns — Antoinette Has Measles — A Visit
from the King — A Conversation Overheard —
Philippe Goes to Italy*

Lafayette returns in February 1779, a man of twenty-one
now. For eight days, Louis keeps him under house arrest as
punishment for leaving the country like a fugitive, but on
the ninth he invites Lafayette to go hunting, and, from then
on, the young marquis is the toast of Versailles. He wears
the uniform of a major general of the Continental Army.

Antoinette thought he might limp – she's heard the stories
of his boot filling with blood at Philadelphia – but he doesn't
seem to bear any marks of his time at war, or none that she
can see.

The young marquis returns to a wife still grieving the loss
of their first child. It is a pain Antoinette cannot imagine,
though she tries, knowing what her sister has been through.
For three weeks at the beginning of 1779, Antoinette didn't
hear Charlotte's voice at all. She was doing no business, or
at least none in her study where the portrait hangs. When
Antoinette wrote her condolences to Charlotte on the death
of poor Carlo, she received a very short letter in response.

Lafayette hasn't been able to convince George Washington

to attack Quebec and return it to French control – Louis receives this news with composure that borders on open relief. The King listens to Lafayette's pleas for a fighting force to turn the tide of the war. The King, as he is wont to do, considers them at length.

An easy victory for England would clear the way for the Order to assert its dominance outside Europe, and increase its power everywhere. There isn't much Antoinette and her circle of magisters can do to affect the outcome of battles across the sea, but they can make sure Lafayette doesn't return empty-handed. So Polignac and Lamballe get to work, using whatever persuasive magic they have to maintain enthusiasm for the war effort at Versailles. D'Éon sends intelligence about British plans, garnered through magical means, to Philippe, who gets it to the proper people. Saint-Georges and Lafayette spend long hours together, discussing military uses for magic.

Antoinette comes down with the measles.

She goes to the Petit Trianon to be away from the rest of the court, and particularly the baby. After the first few days, her fever and sore throat pass, and she misses her blue-eyed darling painfully, but she can't return to the court.

For three weeks, she lives away from people. Her mornings are quiet affairs, with only Madame Campan to help her dress, and in the afternoons she often sits and listens to the sounds of the birds, the distant calls of workmen, the crackle of evening fires.

And then she gets bored.

She invites her friends – only those who have had measles before – to the Petit Trianon to play cards. She includes her brother-in-law, the Comte d'Artois, whom she refuses to shun, despite a recent outbreak of obscene poems about the two of them in Paris. The very idea.

She makes sure to invite the Princesse de Lamballe, as though she were still her favourite. And indeed, Lamballe is as important to Antoinette's affairs as she's ever been. At

Antoinette's suggestion, Lamballe has become a member of the Freemasons, joining the Adoption Lodge of Saint-Jean de la Candeur to make connections – discreet connections – with other rogue magisters.

One Sunday, Antoinette is surprised by a commotion in the courtyard. She opens the bedroom window to see her husband, gazing up at her, with nervous courtiers around him.

'What is it? What's wrong? Is it Mousseline?'

Her nickname for tiny Marie-Thérèse, whose cheeks are as soft as the finest muslin. Is there something wrong with the baby? But no, Louis is smiling.

'I just wanted to see you, but they say you're still infectious. I miss you.'

She smiles at him and sits on the chaise by the window and rests her chin in her hand. 'Then send everyone away, and you stay there, and I'll stay here, and we can talk.'

He tells her about war and peace, and she tells him about trying to sing with a sore throat, until they come to take him home again.

A letter from Fersen, addressed on the outside to Joséphine, his code name for her:

My heart,

The King of Sweden has granted permission for me to travel to America to join the war there. I cannot tell you when exactly, but it will be soon. Remember that I have promised to come back to you and I plan to do so. And I will see you again before I go, God willing.

I don't worry about you, because I see how you have made yourself queen. Yes, you have done it yourself. It was not your marriage or your husband's coronation, but your own determination to make yourself worthy of your people. Against an army of busybodies who wanted you gone, wanted you destroyed, you stood firm, and you are queen, truly and completely, and no one can take that from you now.

It will not be easy to have an ocean between us but the more we work, the harder we fight, the sooner we will have a world without tyrants choosing who may make sacrifices, and who may not.

Believe me your own
F

She reads it over too many times to count, sitting outside in her courtyard. Once, she and Charlotte went bathing in a lake with Countess Ertag, as children, and she swam out too far and could not touch the ground for a moment, just a moment, before her governess took her by the arm. Antoinette feels like that now, as though the ground has disappeared from beneath her feet. She watches the sky sink into violet, the distant, dark shapes of sculptured trees against a flat horizon. The spring evenings are cool, but she stays sitting, reading Fersen's letter, until she is shaking with cold and Madame Campan comes tutting with a shawl and a cup of chocolate.

She's shaken out of her reverie by the sound of her sister's voice in her mind – and Angelo Soliman's:

Marianna is still prone to fevers, but the doctors say she is in no immediate danger.

I am glad to hear it, Your Majesty. I regret I was not able to be here in December, but there is no spell I know that could have saved your son.

Thank you, Dr Soliman. What matters is that we carry on the great work, and that we don't allow anything to interfere. It seems every letter you send me has news of some fresh rogue plot or attack.

Many rogues have taken it upon themselves to support the French and American side in the current war with Britain.

And so it falls to us to make sure they don't succeed, Dr Soliman. What are they doing, exactly?

A great deal of spycraft, in the main. They seem to have got word of where the British ships would be, giving the French the advantage at the Battle of Ushant. Rohan insists this could only have been

magic, and he's vowing to squeeze the life out of every rogue in Paris until he finds the culprit.

Rohan has been seeing rogues around every corner for years now.

Yes, Your Majesty.

Still, he could be right. I wonder.

Whether he's right or wrong, he scents blood.

There's a long silence.

Antoinette clutches the blankets and thinks, suddenly, of the Pandora doll, but it is in the main palace, and anyway what good would it do to give Charlotte a sore hand, all the way in Naples? Charlotte, Brother of the Order, who is currently discussing how to deal with the danger that is Antoinette?

Dr Soliman, I have not added it to the Reconditus, *but I have a spell to enchant flour, to induce certain emotions. In the factory at San Leucio, we have been enchanting bags of the stuff, to sow suspicion. If I were to offer some to the Brothers of Paris, and suggest they use it to undermine the reputations of known and influential rogues, might they consider that as an alternative to violence?*

It's worth trying, Your Majesty. Do you have enough to send some to Paris?

The voices trail off. Charlotte and Dr Soliman must have walked away from the painting.

Every year Antoinette and her husband watch the harvests in fear, because Charlotte refuses to send the loaves-and-fishes spell. And now she learns that Charlotte has so much flour to spare that she can enchant it and send it to France. To use against her. To make Antoinette's own people mistrust her even more than they already do.

Antoinette throws off the bed covers, calls for help to get dressed, to return to Versailles, to warn her friends and make a plan.

At the card tables, in the salons, everyone is soon whispering about the great insult that Marie Antoinette has given Philippe d'Orléans. It happened like this, the gossips say: Philippe asked to rejoin the fleet; the Queen wrote to Philippe

371

in the name of the very busy King informing the duke that he must stay in Paris instead. Anyone can see that 'you are needed in Paris' is what one says to a military liability in a time of war. Philippe went to his hideaway at the Palais-Royal in a foul mood, until the King at last sent word that he should go to Italy, to amuse himself. A peace offering and a way to be rid of him.

And so Philippe's journey to Italy is explained.

His real purpose is to find the flour Charlotte has enchanted, and destroy it. It must never reach France and sow suspicion against *known and influential rogues*, as Charlotte put it. While Philippe and Antoinette were arranging things to prevent court gossip, Geneviève was writing to everyone in southern Italy who owes her a favour.

She's learned that the enchanted flour was taken away from the factory in San Leucio, and is being stored in a bakery in Naples.

All the magisters of Versailles meet in the Petit Trianon to plan the operation.

'But must we destroy the enchanted flour?' asks Jean-François Autié, the second Monsieur Léonard. He sits next to his brother in the mirror room at the Petit Trianon, and it is a strange sight to see both of them together. They have the same high foreheads, long noses and powdered curls, but there are differences, clear enough when they're sitting right next to each other.

Still, so few can tell the brothers apart that they won't be missed at Versailles. They can be in two places at once if they choose. Jean-François, who was once a thief, is perfect for this job. He'll accompany Philippe.

'Would you rather use the flour, Monsieur Léonard?' Polignac asks. 'Surely you don't want your ladies to grow suspicious of each other. It can only do harm.'

'The flour could do a great deal of good in America, fed to the other side,' Philippe says. 'But getting it there would be a feat indeed.'

'So be it, then,' Jean-François says. 'We trick the guards, we take the flour, we dump it. Where?'

'Bury it,' says Lamballe. 'Or put it in the sea.'

The Chevalière d'Éon shakes her head, her curls shivering. Like Antoinette, she has adopted the newly fashionable short hairstyle. 'If they bury it, it could affect the crops. If you scatter it in the ocean, it could affect the fish.'

'Does it matter if fish are suspicious?' says one of the Léonards.

'It matters if people eat the fish,' d'Éon snaps.

Antoinette rubs her temples.

'Presumably the people eating the fish of Naples would be the people of Naples,' Philippe says.

Saint-Georges shakes his head. 'The less of it there is in the world, the better. It's dangerous.'

It was Antoinette's spell, originally. Her little cakes. She never thought it could be used to do any more than prevent Louis's advisers from riding off too quickly on their ideological hobbyhorses. And now there is a bakery full of the stuff, and if it goes in the sea it will poison the fish, and if it goes in the ground it will poison the crops, and Philippe and Jean-François both look as though they're likely to stuff it in their own pockets. No. This is her mistake – and Charlotte's. It must be put right.

'We are not the Order,' Antoinette says, firmly. 'We are trying to protect ourselves from their magic, not use it to undermine them at the cost of harming innocent people.'

'We could burn it, I suppose,' Philippe says. 'They must have enough flour to make quite the bonfire. I could set fire to the bakery. That would send a message.'

'And possibly catch the whole neighbourhood on fire?' Antoinette says, her interlaced fingers tight. 'I want no deaths on our conscience. Just destroy it. Bury it if you must, but far from any farmland or water. Write and let me know when it is done. And be careful.'

9 July 1779
Antoinette to Charlotte

Charlotte,

Your letter arrived. How worrying that your little Marianna is still suffering so much from fevers. I pray every day that she will be healthy again soon.

You're with me here, every moment, although you may not know it.

I have enclosed a lock of my baby's hair. A small treasure for you. If you sacrifice it, I'll try to send another. You don't know this — it was too early to announce yet — but I had hoped to have another little head of curls soon. I miscarried a few days ago, after reaching up to close a carriage window. I've been afraid to tell Mama.

I have suffered other losses too, and fear to suffer more. But I don't ask for your help. I know it's useless. You have cast in your lot with murderers who act against France, against my friends, and against me.

So the gifts I can entrust to you now, Charlotte, are mundane things. A lock of hair from the little head I love best. A sacrifice to you, and to nothing else but you. No magical items and certainly no spells. I won't have my own spells used against me.

I have begged you for years to stop trying to affect matters in France, and concentrate on your own affairs.

I beg it again, not for my sake now but for yours.

I remain,

> *Your sister,*
> *Antoinette*

CHAPTER THIRTY-SEVEN

The Party Is Too Hot – Hamilton's Monkey –
A Terrible Theft – Tunnels – Pillar of Fire – Rescue

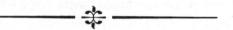

A party at the Palazzo Reale.

This room, like every room in this palace, like all of Naples, is too busy: the floor is all tiles of red and green, squares within squares to a dizzying horizon, where wallpaper vines come down to meet it. Old Testament patriarchs gambol overhead, pointing with wrinkled fingers to apple-breasted sinners full of regret.

It makes her dizzy.

Charlotte arranges herself against a Chinese screen, settles into her skirt and crosses her arms at the wrists. Her head is turned gracefully, just so. Ferdinand stands just behind her. Her five children – Teresa, now seven, holds the baby, Little Mimi. Luisa holds a struggling Francesco on the other side. Marianna, three years old, pale and tired from long struggles with fever of late, stands with Luisa and Francesco. It would be a perfectly even, triangular composition – like the Holy Family – if her sixth child, Carlo, were not in heaven now. Her silk gown shines in robin's-egg blue, in its folded shadows shimmering rose.

The Queen is present. This is her family, and her palace, and her kingdom, and every party is her party.

Acton approaches and bows before her – before the King, one should say. The difference in angle is slight and anyone would forgive a sailor with his sea legs still under him. She finds herself noticing Acton's arms, sleeved in a thick blue coat. She imagines the pale skin under it, the golden hairs.

Charlotte looks up, and glances to the right. Ferdinand is looking at her, his mouth mocking, triumphant. He's always said there was something between her and Acton, and he's always been wrong. Still is wrong. It was only a passing thought.

Acton is looking at her too – everyone is looking at her – but Acton does not look triumphant, not in the least. His search for masts for her ships must not be going well; he'll tell her that, the next time they are able to speak alone. The navy, that must be it; that must explain the slightly tragic expression on her Englishman's face. Hers, only in the sense that they are all hers, because she is queen. If there is emotion on his face, it isn't yearning, the way the gossips would have it. It's business.

She leans, like the tower at Pisa, all of a piece, and speaks to a footman concealed behind the screen.

'It is hot,' Charlotte murmurs. 'Bring me my fan.'

William Hamilton has acquired a monkey. He's from India, a lanky creature with dark fur and a pale mane. The first time Charlotte saw him, he bared his teeth, but she is still inclined to like him. Hamilton has deliberately trained him to act like an antiquarian, looking through lenses and examining everything he picks up. It amused his owner. The monkey also has a habit of grabbing the testicles of Hamilton's manservant as though it were a great joke, so Hamilton tends to bring the creature everywhere he goes, for the sake of not losing a good manservant.

When the guests have all been greeted, and the children run off to play under tables with Hamilton's monkey,

Charlotte goes looking for Caramanico and finds him with Hamilton himself. Caramanico nods politely while Hamilton talks excitedly about volcanic activity. She steals Caramanico away with a smile, and tells him she is sending him to England.

'As His Majesty's ambassador?'

She nods. 'As mine, yes. We need a strong relationship with Britain.'

'We, the people of Naples? Or we . . .'

'Both.'

Caramanico glances into the crowd and she follows his gaze. But Acton isn't here; he's off in Castellammare, not far from Pompeii; he wants to build a shipyard there.

'Your Majesty.' It's Caterina, at her shoulder, her face drawn.

'What is it?'

Caterina gestures for her and Caramanico to come away from the crowd, into a recess near a statue.

'The flour at the bakery near the San Gennaro gate. It's been stolen.'

'Stolen! How could it have been? Were there not protections?'

Caterina's mouth is tight. 'Protections, and disguises too. I don't think this is any ordinary theft.'

'Rogues,' Caramanico says, his hand at a dress sword that looks far too pretty to do much good.

'Our man there discovered the theft this morning, but it could have been days ago,' Caterina explains. 'We disguised it with enchantments. We made the baker forget he had flour in that room at all. Forty-eight sacks, all gone.'

Someone knew it was there. No ordinary rogues, then. Silfversparre, Lunardi, and Caramanico have worked hard to purge Naples of any rogues who might be a threat. And why would rogues care about the flour anyway? That flour wasn't even meant to be used here. It was meant to go to Paris, to help Rohan discredit the rogues there.

She feels cold, dizzy. 'We must meet tonight in the usual place,' Charlotte says. 'We will need a strategy. Tell the others. I'll say I'm tired and leave the party early.'

Caterina and Charlotte make their way underground. The familiar smell of damp rock, tallow candles, and plain wood, smoothed and darkened by time and running feet. Then, into the darkness, lit by brooches that glow with magic.

Down, down, down stone steps, and the smell of damp makes Charlotte feel as if she's about to sneeze. They take a passage she has never taken before, squeezing through a crack in the rough rock.

'A different route, I think,' Caterina says.

Charlotte stops, her hands holding her skirts. 'Why?'

'Someone knows more than I'd like about our business. Perhaps they know our usual way of traversing the tunnels too.'

'If they know that, surely they'll be waiting at the cavern.'

'That's one possibility. Silfversparre went early to check. This way, Your Majesty. Don't worry. I know these passages better than anyone.'

When did that happen? Charlotte wonders.

Through a dank passage that smells of cat urine, where a water drop falls onto her earlobe and another on the back of her hand. Then it opens up, a tall archway overhead made of dressed stone. They walk through an arcade, where she can almost imagine the denizens of this now-deserted underground city hawking oysters or measuring cloth. Only rats and ghosts live here now.

Then they come into a rougher section again, but this time the ceilings soar high above, elongated domes stretching up like Pulcinella's hat.

Charlotte's legs ache from the uneven slopes. She runs her hands over the tunnel wall, where chisels carved Greek letters long ago: the writing of slaves, perhaps, or magisters. Underground Naples has long been a place for secret doings.

Through a narrow passage and into an oblong cavern. The air is fresher here; there's a change in the quality of the darkness, too: a shaft in the cavern ceiling. Charlotte looks around, and gasps: encased in the walls of the cave are seven headless skeletons, their white bones just barely breaking through the yellow rock.

'There have been cults of the dead in Naples for a very long time,' Caterina says, lifting up a wilted paper flower lying against the cave wall. 'This close to the flaming fields, people thought they stood on the threshold of the underworld.'

Indeed, it feels warm in this room – and she is puffing a bit from the long walk. What is today, 8 August? In five days, she'll be twenty-seven years old. Too young to be puffing, but the air down here is unwholesome and she's put on a little weight, truth be told. After seven children, is it any wonder? Wait – 8 August—

Wait – she needs a moment; she needs to catch her breath, to think, to count the days.

She's late. She ought to be bleeding by now. She keeps track so carefully, to ensure she doesn't have a night with Ferdinand at unnecessary times, when it can't make her pregnant. He's back in her bed now, her respite over. And last week was the one for the General to arrive, but there has been so much to think about, with the masts and the war in America and the operations at San Leucio and the distribution of the flour and the Paris chapter needling her about her sister.

'Your Majesty?'

Wait, wait – just a goddamn second, she is trying to count the days – six days, seven beyond where she should be? The General is usually so prompt.

Another child, then. She bites her lip to keep from thinking about little Carlo, the warmth of his head against her cheek. Another child. She has sliced her heart into a million pieces, to offer to the nations of Europe one by one as offerings, the ones Death does not gobble first.

Caterina is frowning slightly. 'Your Majesty, are you well? It's a ghoulish place, I know, but quite safe. No one would think to find us here.'

She nods curtly. 'I'm quite well. Just needed a moment to rest.'

A flash of light fills the cavern.

She puts her hands before her, helplessly, leaning on the damp wall, wishing, for one futile moment, for something she doesn't have time to name.

But the flash subsides, and she is still alive. Caterina puts her hand on her arm. The cavern is much darker than it was when they walked in. Another flash, a smaller one.

'It's lightning,' says Caterina uncertainly.

Lightning. Charlotte looks up at the shaft in the cavern's ceiling. Somewhere far above, there is a storm. It rumbles around the walls of the cavern.

The ground shakes and a fine, acrid dust falls on her from the cavern ceiling, stinging her face. She puts her hand into her pocket and rummages – her hand touches a dozen items of no use to her. But this is no storm. Charlotte puts her hands to the cavern walls; they're trembling.

The cavern fills with silent red light, not a flash this time, but a new dawn.

'We have to get out,' Caterina says, taking her by the arm. Charlotte turns on her heel and they run together.

As they get further from the air shafts, the tunnels are again lit only by their brooches, flashes of gold, with a bit of green from the emerald in Caterina's. Which way? Which way? The tunnel forks, and along the left-hand fork she can see another corridor branching off again. She can't remember, can't turn herself around in her mind enough to think which way they came, what it might look like from this side. Caterina is around the corner, ahead, out of view except for the occasional flash on the walls.

She runs farther, past more branches and intersections.

A lump of rock, large enough to brain her, falls from the ceiling just one pace ahead.

She runs faster, and her foot hits a patch of wet rock and she lands, hard, on her tailbone. It takes her a moment to right herself and she can hear Caterina: 'Your Majesty, please, it isn't safe that way! Up here – there's an exit—'

Caterina takes her hand, and they run up a half-dozen uneven steps towards a crack of grey light. It's a wooden door, hanging ajar, and it takes them out to an alley, the stone walls leaning in on either side. The air is thick with grey clouds of ash. Charlotte's shoes slip on the flagstones.

'Come this way, Your Majesty, there's a—'

Caterina's voice is lost under a loud crack that shakes the whole world, and a blast of air comes out from the tunnel door behind them with a great whoosh. It knocks Charlotte to her knees. She struggles to breathe, the air thick with stinking dust.

She is pushing aside her filthy skirts so she can set her hands and push herself back to standing when the wall falls on her.

She is face down on the street, pressed down, buried alive. Her scream hurts her ribs. Every breath brings great pain, all down the side of her body. The ground stinks of damp rock, a rotten smell, like bad eggs, and this damned grit in her eyes she cannot blink away.

She'll die. So will the child who might be growing in her womb, barely larger than a thought. The only one of Charlotte's creations she has not yet unleashed on the world, the last thing to survive in Pandora's box.

Little Teresa: someone must make sure she marries properly. Leopold's boy, he would be the best. Has Charlotte discussed this with Ferdinand? She can't remember. Charlotte did not plan to die.

Her arms are pinned; she can't reach her pocket.

And the Pandora doll is not in her pocket, anyway.

What made her think of that?

It is, suddenly, horribly bright. She can hear Caterina at some distance, screaming for help.

Her eyes sting; she closes them, and prays. She does not pray to God, she finds, to her amusement, but to Antoine, the child Antoine, the beloved imp, the patron saint of impossibilities. The being who exists for Charlotte only in letters now, and in paintings.

The hand that invades her armpit and pulls, stretching her side like a broken accordion, is a man's hand, on a man's arm: pale, the hair coated in golden dust.

Coughing breaks her body, and the man is still pulling her, without regard for the fact that her legs are not budging – perhaps he thinks she is a corpse already. But she is coughing. Surely he must hear that she is coughing.

Then there's a face near her own, and he's speaking. He's speaking German, accented German.

'I can't pull you out, not without causing you even more pain. I'll have to shift some of these bricks first.'

She blinks, and swallows to stop coughing, and he seems to take it as assent because now she finds that she can see only the man's legs. Good legs, fine legs, in blue culottes.

It's Acton. Her English general. How strange that she should recognize him by his legs.

He's saying something about the volcano. The volcano will erupt – it has been smoking. He wants to get her farther away before— No.

The volcano has erupted. That is why the wall fell, why the— Why won't her brain work? The stink of it.

As a great weight rolls off her side, the pain, somehow, gets worse. She gasps.

Acton is there, his hand under her arm, his hand at her back. Slowly she rises.

'Caterina,' she coughs.

'Already safe.'

She is standing now, holding her ribs, bent but standing.

She walks a little farther into red clouds, and then she can't get another breath, and her legs weaken under her.

Someone is carrying her through the corridors of Schönbrunn Palace, and her nightdress is dragging to her knees. Not Papa – he never carried her; not Joseph either. Who is it? Who is carrying her? And where is Antoine?

For three days and nights, Vesuvius burns.

Charlotte's children tell her exitedly that they saw a pillar of fire, three times the height of the volcano itself. That must have been the red light she saw. William Hamilton climbed up onto a garden wall to watch it, with his monkey at his side and the children pointing and calling to each other. There was a rain of stones and then a storm, and the water was warm on their cheeks. They could see the smoke rolling in like a black blanket that covered the sky, and then Sir William told them to go inside, and the monkey started to dance and gibber.

Meanwhile, John Acton was riding north from Castellammare, rushing back to the palace, when he heard Caterina's screams for help for the Queen. She and Caterina had nearly made it home. All the same, it was a stroke of good luck that Acton found her. And a stroke of bad luck that she was in the tunnels when Vesuvius rumbled. Is that all it is? Luck? Her mind wants to make connections; she is having trouble trusting that anything is luck these days.

The smoke rolls like waves through the streets of Naples. For three days, there is wailing as people smash in doors, steal everything they can, fight for no reason. It's as if the smoke has poisoned their souls. Charlotte and Ferdinand, for once, agree completely on what must be done. They send out soldiers to keep the peace and clear the rubble, to find homes for the people who escaped from the slopes, whose houses are running with lava now.

They take Charlotte to Caserta, where the air is a little fresher. A story goes out that she and Caterina were walking

in the palace gardens when the ground shook and the Queen fell. Acton does not ask why she was out in the streets, and says nothing to contradict the official story.

Angelo Soliman travels over the Alps again, to see her.

Charlotte receives him alone in her rooms at Caserta, propped up on a chaise longue.

She has not bled, still. But she has not mentioned to anyone, not even the physician, that she might be pregnant.

'You have seen Caterina?' she asks after he kisses her hand.

He nods. 'She is still hoarse from the pumice dust. And afraid, as everyone is afraid. It makes me wonder. We don't know where the rogues took the flour that they stole. Flour that was enchanted to sow suspicion. I wonder – I wonder if there might be something in these infernal clouds of ash that is working on our emotions as well as on our lungs.'

She's shocked. 'You think they put the flour into the volcano? Who would do such a thing? Why?'

'Rogue magisters working to disrupt our plans. Who else?'

She pauses, grasping at a last hope. 'It could have been a Rohanite faction, unhappy with the ways we have been using magic in Naples.'

Soliman shakes his head. 'I don't think so. Theft would not serve their purposes. We were going to give that flour to Rohan anyway! But we know the rogues will steal from us. They have before.'

'How would they know about the flour?'

He makes a little movement of the shoulders in agreement. 'I am not easy in my mind about that. I have been trying to determine how they stole from Mesmer's papers, how their machine worked. I haven't stopped searching for the spell of spells, the key to making any enchantment we can imagine. Although it eludes me, all my trial and error has resulted in several new spells of late. I found one that leaches the contents of a book, so that a blank book of mine filled with writing, and, in Madras, a rogue's spellbook turned

384

blank. I had to buy it very dear. I have not spoken or written of that, or of my search for the spell of spells, to anyone but you, Your Majesty. I think perhaps your fears about concealed spies were not so far-fetched, although it amazes me, here in this room surrounded by mirrors.'

Another silence, and then she breathes in deeply, for strength. 'Dr Soliman, you told me, years ago, that magisters have difficulty with action at a distance. That is why, for example, a king cannot simply send a fireball to smite his enemies, and why we need not worry about someone listening to us from three miles away.'

He nods. 'It's true. That's one of the areas that has proven most frustrating, all down the centuries – that and the area of killing and healing. My spell with the books is interesting in that regard; it suggests there is something unique about information. But I have begun to wonder whether everything that exists can be said to be information, in a manner of speaking. And this raises interesting possibilities.'

He thinks she's asking about metaphysics but she just wants to keep herself safe. 'Could a magister enchant an object, leave it in, say, my study, and then use it to spy on our conversation? What if it were already in the room, and in plain sight, and thus the mirrors would be of no use in keeping it out?'

His face is grave. He sees her meaning. 'It's never been done, so far as I know.'

'That doesn't mean it can't be done.'

'No,' he says, frowning. 'That is the way of all science. Everything is impossible only until it is not. Some magister might have found such a spell. But he would have to be a very great magister.'

He? Charlotte thinks, and she smiles a painful smile, remembering a letter from Antoine some years before: *I think I'll try my hand at 'surprendre'*.

It did not register at the time that the French word for 'surprise' also means 'overhear'.

Charlotte paces. Her old habit; the servants at Caserta quietly replaced the green and gold Persian carpet in her study with cheap braided rugs. She must have walked the distance from Naples to Versailles many times over by now, pacing like this.

Her study is quiet. No papers on any surface of the desk. Ink in the inkwell, pounce in the powder-horn, sealing wax coiled.

On the wall, Antoinette stares down at her. Another queen. Another magister. She always had a knack for it. How good is she now?

Charlotte cocks her head and speaks to the portrait, in a whisper. 'At Christmastime, even though my own child was dying, I never stopped worrying about you, knowing that you might be in your first labour at any moment. I fretted that I'd given you bad luck, somehow. And then a few days after Christmas, the messenger came and said you were alive, the baby too. And I was so happy for you, Antoinette! Despite my grief. A girl, the messenger said, and I knew, of course, that you would name her for Mama, as we all have done so dutifully. All of us but Amalia, the only one of us with any guts.'

Her leg still hurts when she stands for any time. She paces again, back and forth, and stops again, just under the portrait. 'But then the letter came from Louis and he told me you named her Marie-Thérèse *Charlotte*. And he told me how difficult the labour was for you. That you were racked with pain, my dear heart, and bleeding and torn and near death and those French fools! They gaggled around you and watched! As if you were a pantomime. I remember' – she looks over at the floor by her desk – 'I remember that I stopped reading the letters and I lay down on the floor, just there, and I sobbed so hard that my voice was sore for days, until I barely had any throat to scream with.

'And now I wonder whether you listened to those sobs. Whether you heard them, because it is you listening, isn't it? Your portrait is listening. *You* knew about the fleet of British ships, a hundred miles west of Ushant. I don't know

386

if you have been working against me, or if you have simply been working for your own selfish goals without considering how it might affect me. I don't care which it is. You listened, and you knew. Just as you knew what we were doing with the flour, and where to find it. You sent your friends to poison my kingdom.'

She stops, out of breath, her throat hoarse.

'I miss you so terribly. I see Leopold every year or two, and Joseph comes when he can. But oh, I am so alone, Antoine. I've wanted to talk to you.'

She looks up at the painting. 'You thought, no doubt, that no matter what you did, that I could never hate you. You were wrong. I don't think I have ever hated anyone as much as I hate you now.'

Charlotte climbs up onto the chair and grabs the gilt frame in both hands, pulling it off the wall. It's heavy and awkward but not beyond her ability to carry it under one arm.

She will take it to the kitchens, throw it on the biggest fire she can find, breathe in the sour fug of smoking pigment and varnish and gilt.

Through the corridors, ignoring the servants' proffered hands, ignoring her little Teresa, seven years old, chasing after a family of peacocks escaped from the menagerie. Ignoring the courtiers' exclamations, the tittering of the Prussian ambassador at the sight of the Queen carrying a painting through the palace.

She passes the door to the kitchen, pausing just for a moment.

Then she climbs a servants' staircase, up to the storeroom where they keep the presents nobody wants. Automata that frighten the children; unfashionable furniture; portraits of relatives unpopular or unsound.

The portrait of Marie Antoinette, Queen of France, goes against the wall.

Charlotte throws a thick black cloth over the painting.

'It's war between us now, sister.'

PART FIVE

1781 TO 1785

CHAPTER THIRTY-EIGHT

The Forgotten Days — Attacks in Paris — Death of
Maria Theresa — Duty Fulfilled — Philippe
Is Determined

Nobody knows which day it is, the day the Dauphin is born.

The words for the months and the days of the week have vanished from memory, and though people do try to guess the date, it always seems wrong. Within the palace, people started naming the days after small events to keep track of them, such as the Day of the Ladder when a workman fell to his death, or the Day of the Wineglass when one shattered in the Salon of Mars, leaving a thousand shards scattered on the parquet for the god to gaze down at. After a while, it became a sign of status to know the story behind the name of the day, or to pretend to know. The clever people compete to see who can make the most absurd or banal name stick: the Day of Onions, or the Day of the Stockings. Polignac was goaded into it by the Comte d'Artois one day and came up with the Day of the Rowlock, which somehow captured the character of that day precisely.

No one quite acknowledges that they can't remember the real dates. It's simply that the fashion for creative and hilarious names is so charming.

The *Gazette de France* and the *Mercure de France* take their dates very seriously, as do the other major newspapers across the country. Their editors have taken to consulting teams of philosophers who calculate the days according to the evidence they can find, though they disagree more often than not. Some of the smaller scandal sheets and opinion pamphlets have done away with dates altogether.

The last time anyone was sure, it was June. Around the time that the Palais-Royal burned.

The Orléans family has two main residences. Philippe's father prefers the château at Saint-Cloud, and so Philippe has the Palais-Royal for his own use. On the day of the fire, the opera house there had shown *Orphée*, by special request from Marie Antoinette, who wanted to see more people appreciate the music of her old teacher Christoph Gluck.

She had not even been there that night. But somehow, Philippe blamed her for the Order's attack, and perhaps he's right. When the actors were still in their dressing rooms, a great serpent of fire coiled around the opera house, and breathed sparks down on the houses below, like fireworks in reverse.

Philippe himself helped put out the blaze, with the help of nearby workmen and, strangely, some Franciscan monks. Their efforts saved the Louvre and God knows how much more of Paris, but they couldn't save the opera house or the dancers in their dressing rooms. They found a dozen bodies after the fire. The newspapers say that porters were carting costumes out of the wreckage and one of the men put on a purple robe and a crown; he clambered up onto a box, and demanded to be called king, and the people laughed.

There is no doubt it was the work of the Order. The Brothers have grown bolder, because there is not much point in trying to hide the evidence of magic any more, not since the war in America with all its impossibilities: disappearing cannons in Salem, a spectral hand that prevented a British officer from shooting at George Washington, the

rebels' impenetrable fortress at Bull's Ferry. The Order confused the correspondence between Rochambeau and Washington, freezing the French troops on Rhode Island for a year. But the rogues have always matched the Order with better, newer magic. Antoinette sent a tiny French village made of wood across the ocean with the American John Laurens, a village that grew where it was planted into French-style bakeries and taverns, and fooled the British into thinking the French troops were going one way when in fact they were going another. Going to Yorktown, where, Antoinette knows from a certain portrait in miniature kept in a certain soldier's trunk, the Americans have just turned the tide of the war.

There is too much magic to snuff out. So the goal of the Order now is to frighten anyone who tries to see that evidence with their own eyes or think about it with their own thoughts.

Rohan and the other clergy preach against the black arts and the corruption of the elites. Mesmer, it seems, has completely broken with the Order and is curing people with magic quite openly. He brought Saint-Georges back from the brink of death after an attempted poisoning, but he wants nothing to do with the Queen's Circle. He is one of a growing number of unaligned magisters in Paris, most of whom have their own agendas, or none whatsoever.

And amid it all, the pamphlets continue, most of them coming from Jacques-Pierre Brissot, a Frenchman based in London who used to be content to accuse Marie Antoinette of debauchery. Now he accuses her of debauchery and sorcery – not in so many words, but the words grow fewer and sharper with each hideous publication.

The thing that Charlotte feared most is coming to pass. The Order is losing control of magic.

The thing that Antoinette feared most is coming to pass too. She could be cast out, condemned – a witch, a harpy, a demon. Rohan, in his cardinal's red, rails against clandestine goings-on at the Petit Trianon. He emboldens the Church

against Versailles, and Versailles needs the Church very badly. It needs the Church to tolerate the tax reforms that might pull France out of utter bankruptcy.

It was the Order that lit the Palais-Royal on fire, although rogues burned St Petersburg.

It was the Order, all on its own, that caused much of humanity to forget the names of the days and months. D'Éon, who has spies everywhere, says that the Order has been trying to steal magic from all the people it has feared for so long: those in Europe who worked spells other than the Order's, and those around the world with their own ways of rearranging reality. They have tried to steal it from every colony, desperate for new weapons to use against their enemies. It is rumoured that they found something they didn't know how to use, a spell they thought would make everyone but them forget magic entirely. It didn't work. Instead, the wags of Versailles go about talking about the Day of the Onions.

D'Éon says the effects are fading, that people's minds, like the palace, have hidden rooms, which they will remember soon. There is no need for this day to be anything else than the day the Queen gives birth.

Antoinette bunches the bedclothes in her sweaty hands. How has Charlotte done this eight times, faced this pain and this terror? It feels entirely wrong, more like death than birth. The bands of cramps around Antoinette's lower back, and nauseating twinges in her abdomen, the sensation of her body being slowly ripped in pieces. But then she will put herself back together afterwards, as Charlotte always does.

Louis makes sure the windows are open, this time, and that the room has only a half-dozen ladies in it. Lamballe is one of them and she is so very good, staying quiet, and making sure Antoinette has what she needs for her comfort. There can be no comfort, in the moment, but when the little white bearing-bed is soaked with blood and the cries of a baby echo through Versailles, she feels tired but not ill the way she was with Marie-Thérèse.

They whisk the child away, saying nothing to her, and she waits, patiently, for Louis to come in and tell her.

He comes at last, bearing the child in his arms, and he says with the endearing formality he adopts in the face of emotion: 'Madame, you have fulfilled my wishes and those of France. You have borne a dauphin.'

He is to be named Louis-Joseph Xavier François, and his godfather is her brother Joseph. And he is to be christened by her great enemy, Louis de Rohan, Cardinal and Grand Almoner of France. His position gives him the right to perform the Mass for the royal family, and their baptisms. But there is nothing she can do about that, and he can't hurt her in public.

She has a little boy. She has done the one thing she was sent to France to do, eleven years ago. At last, she has proven she is worthy to be their queen.

Madame de Guémené, the governess, carries the child in a cushioned basket all through Versailles and Antoinette can hear the applause, now from this direction, now more distantly from that one. Cries of 'A dauphin, a dauphin, can you believe it?' As though it's a miracle, and many will think it's been accomplished by the age-old methods of miraculous births, knowing the King's troubles in the bedroom. But she doesn't care. Let the pamphleteers say what they like about her; they will talk and talk about her, in the four corners of France and beyond, and there's nothing she can do about that now. Today all is well.

She smiles a million private smiles, while far away on a rolling sea, a ship carries news to France, news that she knows already but cannot say: the Americans won a great victory over the British at Yorktown. She knows it the way she knows, suddenly, that today is 22 October 1781. Her little portrait travels with Fersen, and hears what he hears.

France has a victory, a dauphin, a future. She closes her eyes for a moment, and thinks of the day she left Austria and came to France, how alone she felt. Her mother's constant

letters, telling her not to ride, what to wear, how to speak to her husband. Her mother's dream that Antoinette would accomplish one thing with her life: seal the family alliance that will bring Europe peace.

But now she cannot write to her mother to tell her the goal is accomplished, because Maria Theresa is dead. In the autumn, Antoinette had a letter from Leopold, saying that he had visited Vienna, that Maria Theresa was heavier, breathing with difficulty when she walked any distance at all, and irascible out of embarrassment. Forgetful and confused. And then, before Antoinette had a chance to respond, they brought her the news of her mother's death.

No more letters from the Empress enquiring about her monthly courses; no more instructions from the ambassadors. Across Europe, the children of the Empress free at last. Joseph has lost no time: he's freed the Empire's serfs and declared a new edict of religious tolerance. And Charlotte?

Antoinette suspects she is the only person who understands the shapes that Charlotte's grief will take. But she does not write about such things to Charlotte now. They hardly have any need of a cipher any more. The letters are their own ciphers. Antoinette will write to tell her sister that France has a dauphin, a potential husband for one of Charlotte's daughters, perhaps. And she will receive a polite letter of congratulation and statecraft in return.

The year changes: 1782. Antoinette recovers from the birth. She appoints Polignac – the Duchesse de Polignac, now – as governess.

Perhaps it is the tightness of her corset, but the theatre feels warm. Antoinette puts a fingertip to her brow and wipes a drop of sweat, casually, as she looks around her.

The Queen takes an interest in the construction of theatres. They always make her think of cabinet houses, those little curios the Duchess of Devonshire likes so much. Or perhaps the little model village, the plaything for her Mousseline,

that Antoinette enchanted and sent to America to fool the British. Missing walls that show people in their little boxes, level upon level. Façades, revelations. She recently built a little theatre of her own at the Petit Trianon, all blues and gold, grey silk and gilt carving.

This theatre – a new private one, belonging to Philippe's stepmother, Madame de Montesson – is warmer and heavier. Rich wood and rich curtains, heavy chandeliers, and cherubs on the ceiling. She smells her own rosewater perfume, weighted by warmth.

Like cabinet-house people, the people inside a theatre are all on display. Especially the audience. Especially the Queen in her box. She catches the eye of the Chevalier de Saint-Georges as he walks out to applause. No one applauds more vigorously than she does, but he glances away from her, quickly, and looks almost annoyed. He has a fresh scar over his eyebrow.

Saint-Georges lifts his baton, and with four majestic, repeated notes of horns and strings – one two three FOUR – the overture of *L'Amant anonyme* begins, and then a skirl of violins lift the melody to sweetness, and carry it to sadness, and then the oboes bring defiance to finish the passage. How does the chevalier manage it? She leans forward in wonder, as far as her stays and ostrich feathers will let her, forgetting everything else while the music lasts.

In the crowded salon behind the theatre, she walks with her ladies, acknowledging the bows and greetings as she makes her way to Saint-Georges. Polignac at her side always grounds her.

Saint-Georges is standing against a wall, holding a glass of wine, and Philippe is skulking and scowling next to him.

When the Queen approaches, they both bow, though Philippe takes his usual moment of hesitation.

'Your Majesty,' Saint-Georges says. 'Thank you for coming.'

He seems slightly pained, and she rushes to reassure him.

'It was an utter triumph. That music – I'll be thinking about it for some time. How one was never sure what it was doing until it was done, and then it was inevitable.'

They're surrounded by other people, so she can't say anything about the shiny red gash over Saint-Georges's eye. But Polignac, who is sharp, attaches herself to Madame de Montesson and draws her aside, talking in an animated fashion about something or other, and leaving Antoinette, Lamballe, Saint-Georges, and Philippe more or less alone in a corner of the loud room.

'This orchestra deserves a better room,' Philippe says.

'I've heard work is going very well at the Palais-Royal,' Antoinette says.

He scowls.

She pulls herself back, draws herself up inside her gown: cool silk on the outside, chemise damp with sweat on the inside. The ostrich feathers in her hair dip into her view for a moment. Philippe seems to be in an even more Philippe mood than usual.

Saint-Georges says, 'I am grateful, Your Majesty, that you chose to attend tonight, and I regret that I can only perform in small private theatres these days, places where we know the exits and entrances and can put precautions in place.'

'True safety', Philippe argues, 'will be in daylight. Not in private theatres, but in public ones. I am building more than a new opera house. I am building coffee houses, arcades, entertainments at the Palais-Royal, where everything beautiful the world can produce will be on offer.'

'Are you going into business as a shopkeeper, then, Philippe?' Lamballe asks with a little laugh.

She doesn't mean anything by it; she never does. But it hangs in the air, and he squares his shoulders, looks at them through those eyes that always seem so pained and vulnerable, down the long nose that reminds her which family he comes from.

'Why not?' he asks. 'There is more nobility of character

in the shopkeepers of Paris than there is in the drawing rooms of Versailles. The Order of 1326 is no match for a city that has chased away wolves and barbarians. The safety of magisters, the safety of all people, is in the daylight. That's where I put my trust.'

'I don't think the Order will be afraid to attack me in public,' Saint-Georges says grimly. 'They don't need serpents of fire, or fits of dancing, or anything magical at all. They send mere ruffians against me, because everyone expects men to attack me.'

'They can blame jealous husbands,' Philippe says, smiling a little to show that his argument with Saint-Georges is a friendly one.

'Or other motives,' Saint-Georges adds.

'Be careful,' Antoinette says. 'It's not only the Order we have to fear now. Since the war in America it seems the world is full of half-taught magisters, with their own ambitions and their own goals.'

'They are not our enemies,' Philippe says. 'They are our allies. The more we spread magic to the common people, the sooner the day will come when the Brothers find that if they want to kill all the rogues, they'll have to kill everyone.'

CHAPTER THIRTY-NINE

Earthquakes — Sad Paintings — Interruptions
in Trade — Portrait of the Royal Family

Charlotte is afraid.

The rogues are no longer scattered; they have organized; like everyone else in 1782, they have an ideology. Every attack on the rogues brings retaliation, and helps recruit new members to the rogue cause. Even the old methods of discrediting them are gone or failing.

The only path to a world in which governments alone can wield magic is through magic itself, through power and its uses. Through Soliman's spell of spells, perhaps. Through the San Leucio factory. Through the Kingdom of Naples, a place of honour, to draw all the talented and thoughtful magisters to the new Order, and relegate the rest to the margins of society.

She writes to Soliman every day, urging him to help her find some way to dissipate the fog. The fog, the fog! She can't see the city when she looks out of the window. She tries to imagine it, the city of honour she is building: rising out of the sea on slopes unbroken by the fires of hell, its ports bustling with trade in all languages, its people living in harmony, its children happy and fed, its dreams unbounded, a haven of beauty and light calling all travellers home.

401

But the fog makes the city vanish when she rubs her eyes, like one of those phantom castles in the sky above the horizon she has seen once or twice in the Straits of Messina that the sailors call a Fata Morgana.

Soliman does not care. He writes excitedly about Joseph and his new laws, the Enlightenment that spreads across the Holy Roman Empire now that Maria Theresa is dead.

Naples has not seen the light, not for more than a year.

Soliman's suspicion has been proven right: the rogues who stole the flour dumped it into the already smoking Vesuvius. How could anyone be so wicked as to inflict that on a kingdom? As the months passed, the smoke darkened, thickened, spread. The warm weather of this false summer brought with it stinging dampness, and the clouds never dissipate now. The enchanted flour spread over the land, in the air, a miasma of mistrust.

At the edges of the fog, in France and Poland, Libya and Turkey, it is a mere haze, its psychic effects barely noticeable, in this age of uncertainty.

But here in Italy, no one can see the sun or trust their neighbour.

Caserta Palace is at least up on a hill, outside of the city, and though no place is free of the fog, Charlotte is glad of the breezes and of a chance to spend time in her library, with its walls of green and gold, its leather books and marble busts.

She spends time with her six living children, especially her eldest, nearly ten years old. She has given birth to eight children, but smallpox took Marianna, and now she is in the ground with Carlo.

Every morning at Mass her head rings and she finds no peace. Caramanico and Lunardi are in England, where Caramanico goes to parties and Lunardi performs experiments; he wants to fly in a balloon. They write her letters assuring her that the fog cannot be so bad. It has, after all, spread doubt, which was always the flour's intention. The Inquisition remains quietly etherized in Sicily. Charlotte's new age of secular justice has begun.

And what a task it has before it.

The fog darkens the days and turns the sun blood red. Everyone hates each other and there are brawls every night in the city below, the piazzas like battlefields come morning, dead bodies in the fountains.

Elsewhere in Europe, there are discoveries. New wonders. A new metal, named as tungsten! An entirely new planet!

In Naples, the philosophers drive stilettos into each other's ribs over nothing at all.

And Charlotte's enemies gather. Enemies everywhere! Even in her own house. The Council appointed Acton as minister of war, which simply made sense, as he understands the current state of Naples' growing fleet better than anyone. But her husband has grown paranoid about Acton, accusing Charlotte of adultery before the whole court whenever he gets a chance. He has drawn Spain into it, now, and informed Charlotte that his father demands Acton's removal. How he, the whoring ignorant carbuncle, could dare.

And who does she have at her side? Silfversparre is drinking. He goes out hunting for rogues, as he always did, but he does it now as a sleek housecat hunts for mice, out of habit. He says magisters are everywhere: at the court of Tsarina Catherine in Russia and in the alleys of every seaside town. There are pamphlets everywhere, asking why the powerful do nothing useful, why they squander the knowledge that they have hidden from the common people for so long. Do they refer to magic? Sometimes Charlotte thinks they must, and sometimes she thinks she can't trust her own mind.

Magisters with ambition could seize control.

She can't get a clean breath into her lungs.

Charlotte stretches out her fingers, both hands wide. These hands must grow big enough to get a grip on the world.

She begins by summoning her husband.

⁕

Ferdinand takes an indecent half-day to respond. It's probably for the best. She's not shaking any more. Her anger at the morning's message has resolved into icy numbness. The shock – that he would dare order Acton removed from office, now of all times, when Naples is in a state of permanent riot barely contained – has only hardened her the way a wasp sting hardens an oak.

He looks afraid when he arrives.

'Acton,' he says, sinking into a leather chair, although she's still standing. She leans one fist on an ebony-inlaid table.

'Acton, of course. How dare you slander him? He's the best minister of war this kingdom has ever had. It's ridiculous. Juvenile.'

'My father doesn't trust him.'

'Your father! He doesn't like the English, I suppose.'

'He doesn't like the fact that all Europe is talking about your affair.'

He says it flatly, almost sadly. Charlotte breathes in hard.

'All Europe? As though anyone in Spain knows anything about what happens beyond its borders. Where does this nonsense come from? Why so much gossip about him, for God's sake? I will have a painter paint the man. I will have a bust made of John Acton, and send it to Spain, and then your father will see whether he cuts the sort of figure to turn a woman's head. Unlikely.'

Ferdinand's mouth twitches in half-hearted agreement. He doesn't believe her. Nobody believes anyone.

'My husband,' she says, walking around the table to him, and standing in front of him. 'I can't think of any way to convince you of what I know to be the truth. Nothing has happened between John Acton and me. I have not had an affair with him. Not even a night with him. Not a kiss, not an embrace, not a flirtatious word. Why won't you believe me? It hasn't happened.'

'Oh, I know it hasn't happened,' he says, waving his hand

404

dismissively. He pushes himself out of the armchair and wanders to the bookshelf, examining a bust of Voltaire there. 'You're too perfect to ever do anything you're not supposed to do. I've always known that.'

'You've known?' The anger makes her shudder again, as though she has a fever. 'You've known? You've accused me of adultery, in public and in private, for the last year.'

'Because you wanted to,' he says quietly, still not looking at her. 'It's the same thing. Isn't that what the priests say? You wanted it in your heart. You still want to. I knew that night at Portici when you were talking about Diderot. Seven or eight people all standing around in a circle, talking about some bullshit, I can't even remember, and then he said something about Diderot and you turned to him and you turned your back on everyone else. You forgot everyone else was there.'

'What?' She is genuinely befuddled. 'I've never had a conversation with Acton about Diderot. We talk about ships and rations and ambassadors, when we talk about anything. You're making this up.'

'Oh, for God's sake!' he says, turning to her now. 'You were there. It was hardly six months ago. You talked to him for a quarter of an hour, with your backs turned to everyone else. Don't treat me like a fool.'

Her face fills with heat. He's sure of the memory, and she doesn't remember the conversation at all. She must have sacrificed the memory. It must have been important to her.

'I had too much wine,' she says weakly. 'That night. I don't remember.'

'Convenient,' he mutters. As though she's done something wrong by talking about great matters with her minister of war. As though he doesn't have another woman in his bed every month.

'Why do you care?' she asks suddenly. 'You have your lovers. You have never loved me. Why do you care if I talk to the man?'

'Because it's humiliating!' he yells, his body and attention fully turned to her now. 'Because you're my wife and people gossip about you. And him. And where am I in all this? The fool. The butt of the joke.'

She's angry now, and grateful to be angry. He knows, and wants, no other way to deal with his resentments than to inflict them on her. Her woman's body is there to bear the bruises he makes. He will never learn to be secure in himself, because he never has to. Because everything will always be her fault, and when he fails to be anything but a worm, that will be her fault too, simply for being there. It will always be like this. She's never expected him to change, but it's still sour, the taste in her mouth, the loneliness of being the only one in the room who understands what's happening.

She draws herself up. 'Sending him away will only make people believe that the rumours are true.'

He shrugs.

'As you like, then,' she says, throwing up her hands with frustration that is only partly calculated. 'Dismiss John Acton. Find your kingdom a new minister of war. Go to lunch with the English and Austrian ambassadors and discuss foreign policy. Explain to the minister of finance why the new minister of war needs more money for the fleet, which he will, because no one knows how Acton managed to do so much for so little. Go do all of this, and you won't have to suffer from knowing some people might stop spreading certain entirely false rumours about your wife. Give them a chance to make up new stories. And give me a little peace.'

He hangs his head, and shakes it. But he has nothing to say, because she's right. Without Tanucci, without his father, he can't govern his kingdom. He needs her.

Ferdinand grasps the white bust of Voltaire in his long fingers and holds it up to the light from the window. Her first thought is that he will throw it against the wall, that it will smash, that it is new, that Voltaire is not long dead and

it would be a shame to see his image smashed. But a grin breaks across Ferdinand's face.

'He is ugly, isn't he? A lot like this fellow.'

He means Acton, she realizes after a moment. If anything, Voltaire's thin smirk and long, pointed nose are mirrors of Ferdinand's own face. Acton's nose is highly ordinary, serviceable, lived-in, like all his features. Acton doesn't smirk, not ever. His expression is wary, never arch. A sailor's expression.

But she nods, and smiles a little, to agree with Ferdinand. 'Terribly ugly.'

'It's hilarious, really, that anyone would think—'

'Isn't it?'

He nods, still looking at Voltaire, and then nods again, decisively, as if he and the late philosopher have made a pact. He replaces the head on the shelf and, without looking at Charlotte, crosses the room to the door. Just as the usher moves to open it, he holds up a hand, and turns to Charlotte.

'I'm going hunting.'

February 1783 brings three earthquakes in three days, destroying towns and killing thousands in Sicily and all across the toe of the Italian boot. In the cities, buildings fell and candles fell, and the candles started fires, and burned the cities to ash.

Then Poseidon rode up over the beaches, drowning the people in their houses, leaving fetid pools where the dead still float. Mountains crumbled and cracked, damming the rivers, and their sandy banks boil like volcanoes. Pestilence rises from the waterlogged and broken land.

All across the Kingdom of Naples, the unlucky survivors of all these disasters sicken with fevers.

At night, the sky glows, greenish pale, so people can walk abroad without lanterns. Philosophers in Rome argue about the glow: whether it is electric in origin. The Pope calls for prayers. There are stories of people in Milan and Turin walking around with orange slices to their noses, or the

beaked masks of plague doctors filled with cloves and camphor.

In Naples, where the people are used to foul odours and dim skies, despair kills all entertainments. No plays are performed, as if by common consent. There are no Pulcinella shows or masquerades.

Charlotte spends hours staring into the middle distance, moving letters in her mind, idly wondering whether she could make a spell to count the bodies. Buildings are ruined, villages are broken, and whole fields have slid into the sea. So many were buried alive, and so many have suffocated on the surface. As if southern Italy is a hellmouth determined to devour its people, one way or another.

Volcanoes, earthquakes, fog. Soon her reign will rival Pharoah's for the sheer number of plagues. These disasters must have been the work of rogue magisters. Difficult though it is when she's breathing this unholy fog day and night, Charlotte strives for reason and empathy. She is prepared to believe that the earthquake could have been an accident: a tunnelling spell gone wrong, perhaps. In her darker moments, she is sure it was all a deliberate act of violence. She sends Silfversparre looking for the rogues responsible, whether they died in the attempt or not. He reports that he can find no evidence of rogue involvement. He thinks these were merely acts of God. But Charlotte has no quarrel with God, while the rogues stole her flour and poisoned her air and turned her sister against her.

One of the few things Charlotte used to like about the Palazzo Reale were the views.

'I can only paint sad paintings now,' says Angelica Kauffman, sitting with Charlotte and drinking Turkish coffee, looking out at the bleak sky over the bay, where only small fishing boats dare venture. 'For so many years I wanted to be taken seriously as a historical painter. No other women are, you know. They're all portraitists, because we aren't

supposed to paint people in the nude. No gods or goddesses for us. But I did. I do. I learned it all, and made the world despise me. And now? It all seems terribly silly and pointless, all my sentimental figures in their skimpy clothing. I start, and then I can't finish.'

Charlotte pushes the air with a silk fan, but it doesn't freshen. Her newest pregnancy has swollen her body and makes her breath come short.

'I would like you to paint my family, Signora Kauffman,' she says. 'There's nothing sentimental about us, I can assure you. And then you would have to finish.'

The Swiss woman turns a pair of hard, bright eyes on her. 'It would be my honour. We can begin the sketches whenever it pleases Your Majesty, and leave space for the baby, when he arrives.'

'In a few weeks, then, we'll start,' she says. 'That will give Gennaro and Giuseppe time to recover.'

For there is another calamity: smallpox has come to the palace at Caserta. The older children have been inoculated but the physicians said the procedure was not safe for the little ones. Two-year-old Gennaro was very ill indeed, his blond curls sticking close to his pale face, but the doctors say he will recover. She wants to believe them, though she has trouble believing anything or anyone these days. Gennaro, her darling: she remembers the day she realized she was pregnant with him, the very day the volcano erupted.

And now one-year-old Giuseppe, her youngest child, is ailing, covered in sores.

She does not visit the earthquake zone, because she can't leave her children while they're sick. She goes to Mass, she presides over the Council, and in all the other waking moments she holds onto Giuseppe, sitting in his bed every day. She holds onto him so tightly, his warm head resting on her arm. She does not let him go until his hands are cold, and the doctors tell her he has no pulse.

She writes in her diary about the loss of her third child,

gone to join Carlo and Marianna: 'Three parts of me that are cold and in the ground.'

Kauffman begins her sketches. Charlotte does not wear mourning for her children, not in the painting. Kauffman paints her stomach flat as a girl's, and paints a baby in the chaise, for the baby will be born by the time the painting is finished.

Between the first sketches and the modello, Charlotte's baby is born in blood, born dead, too soon. There are more earthquakes in the south. And though each of them sat separately for their portraits, the royal family is gathered together in the modello. Out in the garden, in simple dress, with three of Ferdinand's godforsaken dogs, and a harp for Teresa. Francesco with another little dog, and Little Mimi at Charlotte's knee. Luisa holds Maria Amalia, and Gennaro plays at her feet, all of them in a wheeled chaise which also holds the ghost of the baby who only ever lived in the painter's imagination, barely visible beneath the veil Kauffman has painted over the image.

The painting depicts happiness the way an artist who has never seen an elephant might paint an elephant; it comes out odd.

It's all false.

The sky behind the painting is dark and smoky.

Charlotte cocks her head, and says, 'We'll need a new version. Paint the baby out entirely.'

'Of course.'

'And make me look older.'

'Older? You look – you look quite beautiful here.'

'Yes, I do. I look like a shepherdess. Dress my hair higher, and make me less sweet altogether. And the sky—'

'Yes?'

'Too dark. Paint it blue and bright.'

Kauffman delivers the final portrait and Charlotte asks her to stay on as court painter, as her friend. Kauffman promises, politely, to consider it.

Everyone is polite. The merchants who have broken off all trade with Naples, because the fog threatens their ships, send the Queen their sincerest regrets. The kings who have recalled their frightened ambassadors after one too many reports of imminent rioting. She does not want their politeness. She wants their respect, their gold, their trade. She must do something.

CHAPTER FORTY

Fersen Returns – The Cardinal's Stockings – Flight –
The Muslin Dress – Natural Philosophy –
Fersen Departs

In June of 1783, Axel von Fersen returns to France. Antoinette has been working to get him the colonelcy of the Royal Swedish Regiment, which is perhaps a reckless public indication of her fondness for him. But although it seems everyone knows or suspects at court (including Louis, probably), the obscene pamphlets have her paired with everyone but Fersen. He never factors into the public speculation about who fathered her children. She isn't quite sure why that is – perhaps it's Fersen himself, working some magic. Or perhaps, she sometimes half thinks, it's Charlotte, showing sisterly love in a Charlotte sort of way. She won't stop the horrible lies the Order spreads, but she might well make sure they don't hit near the mark. That would be like Charlotte.

And Antoinette won't ask about that either, not least because her portrait remains silent, and the letters between the sisters are few and perfunctory now.

She misses the sound of Charlotte's voice.

Fersen's voice, though, has been in her mind for the last

413

two years, though the only image of his face she's seen has been the little miniature he sent. Three years, he's been away. Why should she be nervous? They spoke last night, when he disembarked at Brest. He's on his way to her. He said, just last night to her own listening portrait, that he loves her. So why should she be nervous?

But she is. She will see him at court, first, and receive him as queen, standing next to her husband. So she is in court dress.

She wears the full apparatus of panniers and terrible corset less frequently now. At the Petit Trianon, she and the other ladies go about mostly in one-piece gowns of white muslin tied with sashes. The fashion was born not long after her daughter, her little Mousseline, but she can't quite remember now whether the nickname followed the fashion or the other way around.

But some days, there is no help for it: the court dress must be worn.

Fersen is in his French uniform, though soon he will trade it back for his Swedish one. Surrounded by courtiers in the Hall of Mirrors, they stare at each other, drink each other in. It feels strange to see him and not to hear his most private thoughts, as though she is further from him now that he is in her presence. They stare at each other, but they give nothing away.

His hair is a little thinner about the temples, unpowdered and tied at his nape. He looks like an American. The uniform sits well on him – his body is leaner than it was. Hers is not; her battles have been the birth and care of children, which leave different traces on the body. She draws her chin higher, self-consciously. Perhaps he will find her ridiculous, in her wide court skirt and high powdered hair. Perhaps he will find her ugly. Perhaps all this time they were speaking to each other's portraits, they were clinging to those images of themselves, to ghosts.

The discomfort doesn't disappear when they're alone

together, later, in her little secret room. He sits on a settee in the window, looking at her, while she paces.

'I didn't see Cardinal de Rohan at Versailles today,' he says.

'He didn't have an invitation.'

'Neither do hundreds of the people here on any given day.'

'No, but he is smarting from an insult. A few months ago, he came to a masked ball to which he was absolutely not invited. He was in disguise, and he must have enchanted his mask – the way I did, you remember—'

'I remember.'

'I didn't recognize the Cardinal at all, but Lamballe recognized him by his red stockings and then he felt a fool. I've tried to have him removed as grand almoner, but then I'm accused of misusing my influence. One can't be rid of him, though he and his comrades never stop trying to hurt us. How long are you in France this time?'

'For the summer, I hope, if King Gustavus can spare me.'

'You must be eager to be home.'

'France is my home now. My sister wants me to be married, but—'

They look at each other. 'But,' she whispers, and traces a line on the walnut table where she works out her spells. Where she works out the words to say what she wants to say, or something close to it. 'When one is young, love feels like a magnet, doesn't it? As though resisting the pull to the other person would kill you, as though your bodies are drawn together. I admit I have missed that feeling, as excruciating as it was. I didn't know it wouldn't always be that way. But now we are nearly thirty, and for three years you have been at war, and perhaps – if your affection for me is something else now, then that's all right. I know—'

And her words run out there, and she coughs.

He stands and comes to her, takes her hands. She looks up at his face, defiantly, noting the new lines, the new sadness in his eyes.

'Do you not feel the magnet, then?'

She casts her eyes downward. The smell of him! She could sink into it. She could sink into the hollow of his collarbone, trace a thousand words on the ball of his shoulder with her fingers. She doesn't touch him.

'Yes, for three years I have been at war,' he says, his voice heavy and soft. 'It is a horrible neverending moment and it feels as if the rest of one's life has become a dream.' He takes one hand away from hers and holds it by her cheek, as though he will touch her skin, but he does not – not quite. Just holds his hand there as though framing the image of her face. 'But I felt the magnet, every moment. I felt it all the way across the Atlantic, and it drew me back to you.'

She puts her own hand to his, takes it to her mouth. Puts the tip of his fingers to her lips and closes her eyes. She has remembered the smell of him well.

When she opens her eyes again, he has an expression she's never seen before.

'What happened, in America?' she asks, hoarsely. 'What didn't you tell me?'

'Memories I am most eager to sacrifice.'

'Let me take them from you.' She kisses the corner of his eye, kisses the hollow of his neck, unbuttons the French uniform. 'Give them all to me.'

A cannon booms, and everyone in the courtyard at Versailles freezes. Everyone save Antoinette: she does not startle easily, and she uses the moment to watch everyone else. Her little girl, her Mousseline, puts her small hand into hers. The vast crowd stills, but the faces move as her gaze sweeps across them.

Fersen is dutifully not looking at her. He's looking at Benjamin Franklin, who's dressed in his usual rustic costume.

Another cannon booms! Lamballe puts her hand to her heart, but it is four-fifths performance.

The three aunts, Mesdames Victoire, Adélaïde and Sophie,

stand looking at the great balloon as if it is something disagreeable.

It takes Benjamin Franklin only a moment to recover his avuncular expression. He looks like a boiled potato in his ill-fitting brown coat, gazing up at the great balloon that looms over the crowd.

The golden suns painted on it are reminiscent of the Sun King, and the letter 'L' also in gold is for her husband, who is manifestly not. If the sun were shining, the balloon would be dazzling.

But the sun is not shining. The sun has not shone in months. All summer, this strange darkness and a faint odour of brimstone. A volcano is erupting in Iceland, and the wind is wrapping its fumes around the world. But Antoinette thinks it's more than that. The air in France has had a strange smell to it for years. A smell of rot and rust; a smell like magic. Antoinette is almost used to the faint headache, the slight thickness in the air, which sometimes seems to make it difficult to understand people.

Her little Mousseline has never known a world without it. A soft hand rests in Antoinette's as they speak their wordless language to each other. They are on guard; wary; in control. Her daughter understands her as no one ever has, not even Charlotte once upon a time. To her left, the little Dauphin pouts regally; his hand in Antoinette's is sweaty. What perfect children she has.

She knows that she has been lucky, that other parents lose their children at all ages. She remembers all the lives she wasn't able to save: her sisters, her brothers, Joseph's daughter. She has read Charlotte's increasingly curt letters telling her of the deaths of Carlo, Marianna and, earlier this year, Giuseppe. Antoinette knows that any day could be the day that takes a child from her, but that is a thought she cannot entertain, because it will break her. She cannot consider breaking, not even for a moment.

There are so many things Antoinette must not do, big and

small, every day, lest she be seen to be too emotional, not maternal enough, too Austrian, too dowdy, too extravagant. She has learned that a painting of her in a muslin dress has been added to her catalogue of errors.

The portraitist Élisabeth Vigée Le Brun made her debut at the Salon this summer, and among her paintings was one of Marie Antoinette in simple white, in a garden with a rose: a picture of the Rousseauian ideal. It began as a triumph: the Royal Academy of Painting and Sculpture controls nearly everything when it comes to teaching and exhibits in Paris, but it has been exceedingly reluctant to admit women. Antoinette loves Vigée Le Brun's work, and she has had quite enough of closed societies of men setting arbitrary rules. She managed to use her influence (magical and otherwise) to have Vigée Le Brun admitted, which means she can exhibit at the Salon in the Louvre.

But the triumph was soured by the reaction to the painting of Antoinette in the muslin dress. People said the Queen had herself painted in her nightgown, that it is a sign of her moral decadence, that she hates the silk-makers of France and would rather wear muslins that come from Bengal.

She never knows which of her choices will be seized upon as unwomanly, or too womanly, or both.

So Antoinette stands tall, and does not embrace her children.

Her gaze roves to the Chevalier de Saint-Georges, and to Philippe d'Orléans standing beside him. They are speaking to two men. The older one she knows, and it takes her a moment to remember from where. When Philippe went to Naples to destroy the flour, he returned with information about the Order in Naples, and the members thereof. He showed them a little engraving of the Prince of Caramanico. That's him, that stern, sleek man with a neat wig. The younger man, with wild natural curls, must be Vincenzo Lunardi. But she thought they were both in London.

Two Brothers of Naples, here in Paris, and speaking with Philippe.

Mousseline shifts beside her, and Antoinette realizes she's been gripping her children's hands too hard. She forces her gaze away, so she won't be caught staring at her sister's spies – for what else could they be? Philippe must be up to something.

There is Étienne Montgolfier talking to Franklin, now; there is a lot of back-slapping but Montgolfier looks nervous. He is the more presentable Montgolfier brother, people say, but the other was the genius who first had the idea for the hot-air balloon. It reminds her of the Messieurs Léonard and she wondered, at first, if they were magisters, but Fersen says not.

So many learned men and women in France in 1783. She watches them in the crowd: Joseph-Ignace Guillotin, the physician. Nicole-Reine Lapaute, the astronomer. Antoine Lavoisier and his wife Marie-Anne, both chemists. So many students of the natural world are Freemasons, and the Masonic lodges have long been covers for the Order, though there are rogues among the Masons too, now. Men of science have been petitioning the King to call a commission into Mesmer's work; Mesmer, of the remarkable instrument with healing powers, and the odd theories that don't quite explain his results. There are so many fronts to the magical war.

A cheer goes up as Montgolfier lights the brazier under the balloon.

'Won't it catch fire?' Mousseline asks quietly.

'They have coated it in alum,' Antoinette responds. 'If it lifts up and lands unexpectedly on a building, though, it could catch. We have *pompiers* ready to douse it if so. Versailles will be safe, little one.'

'And the balloon?' the Dauphin asks, solicitous. He is always anxious.

At her gesture, Montgolfier walks to them, wiping sweat from his forehead.

'Monsieur, the Dauphin wishes to know whether the balloon will survive the journey,' Antoinette says.

Montgolfier smiles. 'Your Majesties, I certainly hope it will. It may get a tear. It may be singed. But it should survive.'

'What about the passengers?' little Louis-Joseph asks.

'There are no people,' says Mousseline gravely to her brother. 'Only animals.'

'I hope the animals will be all right,' Antoinette says.

'Wouldn't we learn more about the effects if we sent up people?' asks the King gruffly.

'We don't know what flight will do to the human body, Your Majesty. The air is thin. No one has ever been there before. We have plenty of volunteers, ready to go up as soon as the balloons have been tested with animals. For now, today, we have a very willing sheep, a rooster, and a duck.' He looks down at Mousseline. 'The duck, you see, should be accustomed to the air, so he will show us whether anything that happens to the animals happens because of the atmosphere or for some other reason. The rooster is similar in its body to the duck, but does not fly. And the sheep will tell us, really, whether humans can fly. If a sheep is unharmed, I believe a person would be.'

Mousseline nods. 'What are their names, Monsieur Montgolfier?'

'What, the animals?' Montgolfier chuckles, forgetting for a moment he is addressing the royal family. He bends down, closer to Mousseline. 'I don't believe they have names. Would you like to name them?'

Mousseline considers. 'The sheep should be Montauciel, because he is going up to the sky.'

'A very good name,' says Antoinette, and squeezes her hand. 'And the birds?'

'Louis-Joseph may name the birds,' Mousseline grants.

'What shall the birds be called, Monsieur le Dauphin?'

Louis-Joseph frowns. 'What about Pierre and Jacques? Would that be all right?'

'Very suitable,' says Louis. 'Are you tying the animals down in the basket, Montgolfier?'

Montgolfier nods. 'For their own safety, Your Majesty.

They're ready now. It only remains for Your Majesty to give the signal.'

Louis raises his hand, a long red ribbon fluttering from it, and brings it down again.

The crowd cheers, although nothing has happened yet with the balloon. Men bustle around it, and Montgolfier stands on his tiptoes so he can see. He has patches on the bottoms of his shoes.

The balloon jostles, and then it is up. It is up! Rising above the heads of the people, who crowd around it despite its tail of dark smoke. The blue and gold orb rises higher, higher, and floats over rooftops covered in people trying to get a better view.

Antoinette gently uncurls her fingers from her children's hands so she can applaud, and they do too. Louis claps louder than anyone. She turns to him and smiles. He so dearly loves it when things work.

'What do you think, Mr Franklin?' Louis calls to the American. 'What's the use for such an invention?'

He makes a non-committal face. 'What's the use of a newborn baby, Your Majesty? It has potential. What that potential is, often the inventors themselves do not know.'

Her smile goes as tight as her bodice across her belly. The use of a newborn baby, for her, is not mere potential. The Dauphin is delicate, and no one will be satisfied until he has a brother. She does not look at Fersen. This new baby is certainly Louis's, *mathematically* Louis's, but that hasn't stopped the libel pamphlets from speculating about the Comte d'Artois, even, despite the impossibility, the Duchesse de Polignac.

The pamphlets, too, are a front line. The ships have come home from America but the war among magisters is far from over.

Fersen sits at a table in her bedroom in the Petit Trianon, writing letters by candlelight. She watches him. Every so often he looks up, frowning, and then writes again.

'Is it a difficult letter?'

'Hmm? No, it's a plain missive to my sister. About the itinerary.'

Tomorrow, he leaves again. King Gustavus of Sweden has called on him to be the captain of his bodyguard. And Gustavus is on his way to Italy, on a state visit.

'Then perhaps the itinerary is making you pensive.' She doesn't know quite what to say about the fact that Fersen will see Charlotte in a few months. She's jealous of both of them, and angry at Charlotte, and worried about everything.

He's left a streak of dark ink on his forehead. She laughs, and goes to him with a kerchief, and wipes it off.

He takes her hand, rests his cheek on it for a moment; then he looks up at her, his face illuminated by the candle.

A summer in France has put some of the light back into Fersen's eyes, although it has not smoothed the tiny lines around them. A summer together, they've had at last. A summer without sunlight, but they didn't care about that.

To Naples.

'You must not let her persuade you of anything,' Antoinette says, biting her lip.

They are in her bedroom in the Petit Trianon. She feels safe – they have surrounded the room, and the building, with magical traps and alarms – but she also feels like a prisoner on the eve of execution. Tomorrow he leaves her, for who knows how long.

'Your sister? Do you think she's going to try to pull me back into the Order?' he asks, amused. 'No fear of that, my love.'

She shakes her head. 'No, I suppose I— Just be careful. She'll interfere. She always interferes. If I had to guess, she'll try to convince you that you should stay away from me, for my benefit.'

'No fear of that, either.'

'She's very . . .'

'What?'

422

'She's very Charlotte.'

He chuckles. 'I'll survive. I want to give some aid and comfort to the rogues of Naples, and see what I can find out about what the Order is up to.'

'Write to me every day.'

'Every day.'

'And will you – will you write to me about her too? My sister. Tell me how she is, how the children are. Amalia and Leopold and Joseph tell me a little, when they visit her, but they don't know her as I know her. And Charlotte still writes occasionally, for the sake of appearances, but nothing real.'

He kisses her cheek.

'I will write every day, long, long letters with everything I can tell you in them. And I will come back to you. Always. Unto death.'

They won't sleep tonight.

They were by turns shy and passionate, the first few nights after he returned. She peeled his uniform off him as if she could peel off the war. They were not innocent – not any more – but uncertain, as though they were natural philosophers studying some new wonder.

Now she turns to Fersen, glowing as he undresses in her bedroom like a husband. Takes off his breeches and puts his shoes under the bed. So comfortable. She steps towards him, and lets out a little gasp.

'What is it?' Fersen worries so easily, now. The carefree libertine has gone, despite the stories she hears of the women who throw themselves at him. What are stories? There are pamphlets full of pornographic tales about the Queen and her ladies, all through Paris.

She puts her hand on her belly, and her hand can't feel it through the corset but her gut feels it again, the little punch outward.

'The baby's quickened,' she says, breathless.

He wraps his arms around her and unlaces her bodice, down her back. She is unused to the court dress, these days,

but the balloon demonstration demanded it. His fingers open her dress as she pulls down her skirts, standing on a sea of petticoats like Venus on the foam. At last she's in her shift, and he puts his hand on her belly. They laugh together at the strangeness of it, as her skin ripples under his hand. He leaves it there, warm and solid, while his other hand lifts her shift, and she gasps again.

'I'll write every day,' he whispers in her ear, and lifts her to the bed.

CHAPTER FORTY-ONE

*The Future that Charlotte Fears — The Treaty
of Paris — Disagreements and Libels — The Ways
Women Fall to Pieces — The Painter*

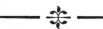

It's becoming crowded, this little mirrored room in the Petit Trianon. Antoinette needs another place for rogues to meet, even quieter and more private. But for now, they gather here, behind the mirrored walls and windows.

She's uneasy, and not only because she never quite feels safe here now, and not only because Fersen has been gone for weeks, on the way to Naples. The world feels uncertain, as though it's about to tilt, but in which direction, she cannot say.

So she fusses while they take their seats.

Polignac pulls the lever to bring down the window-coverings. Marvellous devices, with mirrors on their interior sides. Somehow, the pamphleteers heard about the mirrors – servants gossip – and it furnished the worst of them, Brissot, with a new pornographic story to tell about Antoinette and Lamballe. *Why do you give them these gifts?* Louis asked her, plainly frustrated, and wounded. *But it's a marvel of engineering, dear,* she told him, pretending not to understand.

Antoinette would not choose Lamballe as a lover anyway.

Polignac, now, that is more believable – she has a way about her. Antoinette smiles, and turns to her friends, her comrades. Lamballe and Polignac lounge on a chaise; Lafayette paces; Saint-Georges stands near the door.

'I've heard this fog is much worse in Italy,' says Philippe. He's thrown himself into one of the carved chairs at a louche angle, his legs crossed and his gorgeous thick-heeled shoes swinging. He always finds some way to show his complete disdain for Antoinette's position, under the cover of their secret fraternity.

'Did you learn that from Caramanico and Lunardi? You were speaking with them at the balloon launch,' Antoinette says.

'I was,' Philippe lobs back. 'And so was the chevalier.'

'Are they here as spies, do you think?' Lafayette asks, pacing with a little less than his usual energy. Perhaps he's tired; he's been occupied with politics: with the aftermath of the Treaty of Paris that ended the American war, making peace between the British and French. 'Or are they here to help Rohan and his bunch with some new operation?'

'They're turning against the Order,' Saint-Georges says. 'Not officially. Not yet. But they will.'

'Taking our side?' Antoinette feels irrationally ill at ease, knowing of traitors to Charlotte and saying nothing.

'Taking their own side,' Philippe drawls. 'As all men of ambition are, now that the possibilities are opening up. Why should any magister now take his orders from a stuffy old cult, or from a queen? Or both at once, as is the case in Naples.'

'When will Fersen be in Naples?' Lamballe asks, shifting the conversation, as she does.

They all look to Antoinette for the answer.

'Not until the New Year. For the moment, he and King Gustavus are in Florence. My brother – the Emperor – is there, and an old friend of my family, Angelo Soliman, is travelling with him. Fersen reports Soliman's been talking

with every scholarly magister he can find, and mathematicians too. Fersen thinks he's trying to crack a new spell.'

'I could have told him that, and saved him the business of travelling,' Philippe says. He stops, says nothing, enjoying their surprise.

'Well then, Your Highness, do tell us,' Lafayette says, half teasing.

'Lunardi told me about it. You see? Some good comes of having eyes and ears open. The men of science laugh at Soliman's notion – he calls it the "spell of spells".' Philippe adds a pseudodramatic wave of the hand. 'It's an axiom that would allow a magister to create any enchantment they wanted, without the bother of years of trial and error, or having to trade with other magisters.'

Saint-Georges shakes his head. 'If such a thing were possible, surely someone would have hit upon it already.'

Lamballe looks up languidly. 'Many things that were not possible have become so. We watched a sheep, a rooster, and a goose go up into the air in a balloon.'

'A duck,' Antoinette mutters.

'Your Majesty?' Lamballe asks.

'It was a duck,' she repeats a little louder. 'This idea of Dr Soliman's may be quixotic, but he is not a fool.'

Philippe sits up straighter. 'You think – Your Majesty, do you think there's something in it? If he is right, if such a thing is possible, the magister who had it could do almost anything.'

Antoinette acknowledges his point with a curt nod. 'Yes. If Soliman thinks it is possible, I would not discount it. And if it is as Lunardi described it, well, the Order would be able to do almost anything. And they would not hesitate to use that power against us.'

'Anyone with such a spell at their command would be the most powerful man on Earth,' Lafayette says.

'Or woman,' Antoinette corrects. 'Angelo Soliman is a close associate of my sister, as I'm sure you're all aware. It cannot be allowed to happen.'

'Leave it with me,' Philippe says. 'I have some associates in Naples.'

'I don't want Angelo Soliman killed,' Antoinette says.

'We are not the Order,' Philippe says. She hears a mocking echo of her words before she sent him to Naples to destroy the flour. 'We don't kill magisters. We create them, and teach them. It's time to teach the people to do magic. Our only safety is in numbers.'

'But before we get the numbers, we have to keep ourselves safe,' she responds.

Lamballe says, 'We have enchanted enough corpse liquor now to protect dozens of rogues, and I can make more. That's a start.'

Paris's overpopulated cemeteries have become notorious for hasty reburials to deal with collapsing walls and eroding soil. It gave cover for some of Philippe's less savoury rogue friends to dig more recent burials without anyone asking questions. The Circle has been enchanting corpse liquor to protect as many rogues as it can from the Order – an idea that came from Philippe in the aftermath of the Palais-Royal fire, but Lamballe has taken it on with diligence. She should be grateful for Lamballe, as she is for Polignac. She has always found strength in the friendship of other women, and she should remember that.

Philippe throws up his hands. 'A start. Always so cautious! We will die of caution. Every man, woman, and child in Paris has seen magic done in the last few years. What are we waiting for?'

'Yes, they have seen magic done!' Antoinette retorts. 'And most of them know it for what it is, but we tell them to cross themselves and keep walking, or tell them it is some new form of science. If the great mass of people learn that they too can do magic, all at once, what do you think will happen? Imagine how many poor, desperate people would sell their livers, their wombs, their toes, arms, legs! Imagine if all the love in the world were sacrificed, and all the memory

428

too, while humans dodder on to the end of days like chimpanzees in enchanted clothing, forgetting all history and language, all love and virtue.'

That is the future that Charlotte fears. Antoinette understands that, has always understood that.

'You sound like a Brother of the Order,' Philippe says. 'Your Majesty.'

Saint-Georges pushes himself off from the wall impatiently, and leans on the back of a sofa. 'There is so much good we could do, with all that we know.'

'We have done good already,' Lafayette puts in, but he's uncertain. There was a time, not long ago, when Lafayette would have been the first to argue for the most dramatic course. As with Fersen, time in America has tempered him.

'When I was last in London,' says Philippe, 'I met Jacques-Pierre Brissot.'

Lamballe and Polignac don't look at him; neither do they look at the Queen. They stay perfectly still, frozen, their eyes just a bit wide. Antoinette stays frozen too, her gaze on Philippe, her smile in place.

'The pamphleteer?' she asks, mildly. 'The one who writes such imaginative things about me and the Princesse de Lamballe?'

'I was curious about him. He seemed to come out of nowhere. I wondered if Brissot might be a magister – all those pamphlets, so thick on the ground that one can't walk in Paris without them sticking to one's heel. He is not a magister. I'm certain of it. But after I got him in his cups, he confided something in me. He believes he has an enchanted pen. Enchanted? I said. Surely magic cannot be real? He shrugged and said all he knew was that after he started using it, his pornographic pamphlets about the Queen of France – forgive me – started selling. He is going to start writing real essays with it, he promised me, open letters to the Emperor, that kind of thing. And I think he means it, and if you scratch his surface you might find a decent man.'

Antoinette raises her eyebrows, and her wig shifts uncomfortably on her skull.

'A decent man. Indeed.'

'Misguided, and over-passionate. The pen, I thought, might well be mere superstition, but it turns out it was a gift. From William Hamilton.'

Antoinette draws a breath as sharp as a dagger. 'The British ambassador to Naples.'

'The very same,' says Philippe.

Antoinette turns to look out of the window, and sees only herself, reflected in the mirror, and realizes that instead of hiding her expression from her companions, she has shown it.

They look alarmed.

She whirls back to face them, dropping all pretence of calm. 'Well, I cannot make a spell for my sister to love me, though that would solve everything. So, I suppose we must deal with the traps she lays for me.'

'But what His Highness intends, I think,' says Saint-Georges, 'is that perhaps we can recruit this Jacques-Pierre Brissot, use him to spread some useful spell with his magic pen. He has argued against slavery, and one of the pamphlets he has in his mind is an essay on emancipation. What if he could teach as well as argue? We won the war in America. There are more rogue magisters using the Order's magic than there are members of the Order now. Surely this is the moment to show the world what we can do.'

'You know I am opposed to slavery too,' Antoinette protests, and it sounds weak even to her ears. It is one thing to be opposed, and it is another to oppose. 'I want to free magic for the benefit of all people. I just don't think we can trust a man who received his magic pen from my sister.'

'We are expending all our magic here, in London, and in New York, on fighting the Order—'

'Because if we do not, the Order will keep the people of the world under their heels forever,' Lafayette says.

'What does it matter whose heel you're under, if you're ground into the earth?'

Silence stretches out between them. Antoinette says, at last, 'We have to stop the Order from attacking us, and keep an eye on Soliman and his notion about the spell of spells. We have to grow our numbers, but carefully. It may not be enough but it's what I can do, here in Versailles, and I will do it alone if need be.'

Lamballe crosses to her, takes her hands. The princess's facial features have seemed such a jumble lately, as if she becomes a different stranger in every angle and every light. Just looking at her gives Antoinette vertigo, so she looks down at their hands, at Lamballe's little lace gloves, with a smidge of dirt on the edge of one pinkie.

'Not alone,' Lamballe says.

'Your Majesty is never alone,' Lafeyette agrees. 'We are all working together. Saint-Georges, if you want to see where you can get with this Brissot, I see no reason why you shouldn't. You and His Highness both can keep an eye on him.'

'I'm glad to have something to do,' Philippe mutters. 'Better a pornographer's babysitter than a grave-robber.'

She has been too hot-headed with Philippe, she knows. She's failed dismally at earning their love. As usual.

The ways in which reality falls to pieces may be myriad, but Antoinette can count on one hand the ways she has seen women decay. She understands the Princesse de Lamballe, who has settled into an angelic arrangement of the pretty and the good. She understands the Duchesse de Polignac, who has settled into wary and remote sophistication. She knows the ways they can sit in rooms, or walk in and out of them, and the sorts of rooms that contain them. They chose these paths the way they might choose a portraitist from sample paintings, or a dress fabric from a Pandora doll.

Somewhere there are other rooms, with other women in them. Women who have much worse choices, or no choices at all. And women who have managed to arrange reality in ways that Antoinette cannot.

Élisabeth Vigée Le Brun is not anyone's painted image. She wields the brush. As an artist, she goes into all the sorts of rooms that Philippe, Saint-Georges, and Lafayette can enter, and hear conversations the Queen of France never can, because they stop when she appears.

Vigée Le Brun grew up across the street from the Palais-Royal. She has told the Queen how happy it made her, in childhood, to go into the brightly lit gardens at night with her parents. People would spill out of the opera house and sing and play instruments. Her whole life, the painter has been surrounded by brilliant people and new ideas.

Today, Vigée Le Brun lives on the other side of the Palais-Royal, but still not far from its cafés and art exhibits (the Orléans family collection alone, open to the public, is massive, and the nearby Louvre Palace is mainly used these days to house the royal collection). Now that Philippe has expanded the Palais-Royal, the neighbourhood is noisy with arguments in the cafés and the private salons in the houses of painters and philosophers.

Ideas are brought to Antoinette in stamped leather books; even the ones that are banned, the ones for her private library, are presented, made official, and sanctioned. Noted in ledgers.

Ideas are not presented to women like Vigée Le Brun; they breathe them like air and they create them. Antoinette wants such a woman in her Circle, someone who might be able to enter all the rooms that the men enter, but who can see women as something other than paintings.

The portrait of the Queen in white muslin may have damaged Antoinette's reputation, but not Vigée Le Brun's, whose talent is not in question. She is fierce at her work, and only lets a laugh play around her lips when she is not

looking at her canvas. Why this should suggest to Antoinette that the painter is trustworthy, she does not know. But it does.

So when the painter arrives for the Queen's next sitting, in the Queen's bedroom, the Queen is ready to invite her into the world of magic. An even trade of knowledge and access. With every day that passes, Antoinette becomes more certain that Philippe's loyalties are not with the Circle. She wants to know whom he meets and what they talk about. In fact, she wants to know what all the rogue magisters of Paris are talking about. Polignac and Lamballe are loyal spies at court, but Antoinette has no one she can rely on in the Palais-Royal, no one who is hers. Lafayette and Saint-Georges are good men, but they are not *hers*.

It is the eve of Antoinette's twenty-eighth birthday. Lamballe is with her for the portrait sitting, and knows what Antoinette has planned. She is stiff with excitement. Antoinette can see it, although Lamballe sits demure on her cushioned stool, perfectly still, patronizingly aristocratic in the presence of the painter. How strange, to know someone so well, and yet gain no comfort from familiarity.

Vigée Le Brun has a blowsy scarf around her shoulders and she walks slowly, one hand on her lower back, obviously pregnant.

Then the painter trips, and the pine box in her hand opens and her brushes go everywhere, skittering across the floor. She laughs, and grabs the back of a chair to lower herself to the ground.

Antoinette crosses to her, one pregnant woman to another, and takes her elbow, righting her. 'No, you must not,' she says. 'Sit here, please, and let us do it.'

Lamballe is already gathering the brushes and Antoinette takes a bundle from her, picks up the remaining few. She hands the box to Vigée Le Brun.

'Your Majesty is too kind,' says the painter. 'I am sorry for being so clumsy.'

'Nonsense. I know how it is,' says Antoinette. 'You have one child already, isn't that so?'

'A little girl. The light of my world.'

'Tell me, how is the Academy treating you, now that you're a member?'

When Antoinette used all the persuasion in her arsenal to make the fusty Academy admit Vigée Le Brun, she had a feeling, even then, that this painter's love would be worth the cost – and anyway, she is the only artist who shows Antoinette as she really looks, and somehow makes her look beautiful anyway. It's a kind of magic of its own.

'We shall see,' the painter says. 'I must thank you for speaking on my behalf, Your Majesty.'

'Your talent speaks for itself,' Antoinette protests. 'I love all of your work. Your portrait of Lamballe captures her perfectly.'

Vigée Le Brun nods warily. 'Her Highness was a very obliging subject.'

Lamballe beams.

'I'm sure,' says Antoinette. 'She is a very obliging person. But you've caught how pretty she is, that little pointed nose, those languid eyes, that chin—'

'You're naming body parts, now, my dear,' says the princess. 'Everyone has them.' She looks at Antoinette with sad confidence, like a maiden aunt looking at a roué.

Suddenly, horribly, Antoinette understands that Lamballe knows. She knows. She can see that the Queen no longer loves her back. Of course she knows. She's not a fool.

'But not everyone has yours, Marie-Louise,' Antoinette stammers. She must keep up the pretences; everything will crumble otherwise. 'And other painters have not captured them properly. You have an eye, Madame. You see the world as it is, and you see its beauty. Two qualities that don't exist in the same person very often.'

'Your Majesty does me great honour,' says the painter. 'I'd be pleased to create another portrait.'

'And so you shall. But I brought you here today for another conversation, for something else I would like to offer you, and to ask of you.'

Vigée Le Brun looks from Lamballe's face back to Antoinette's, patiently. Antoinette does not know quite how to begin – she never does, with a new magister.

'Have you heard strange stories over the last few years? Rumours of magical occurrences? The clock tower that walked in London, Dr Mesmer's healing instrument, the man who couldn't shoot George Washington . . .'

The painter looks cautious. 'These ideas spread like fashion, don't they? Or like the old stories of werewolves and revenants. I admit I've seen things that I can't explain.'

'But perhaps I can,' Antoinette says. 'As an artist, you understand that there is a kind of power in objects, that they carry meaning and possibility. A crucifix, a child's tooth, a box of paints. Some people have learned a way of increasing that power. Of making objects carry certain invisible qualities.'

'Is it science, Your Majesty?'

'Some view it that way,' says Antoinette, thinking of Mesmer. 'It is a kind of experimentation, although no one understands quite how it works. But we call it magic. As a kind of shorthand, perhaps: a word for a thing we don't understand.'

She watches the painter's face. The reactions are perfect: shock, and slight confusion. If Vigée Le Brun is a spy for the Order of 1326, she is the best actor Antoinette has ever seen. The word *we* echoes in the room.

The painter looks at Lamballe, as if for confirmation.

'It's true,' says Lamballe, pouring tea out of a silver pot. 'We – Her Majesty, and I, and other people – are magisters. Magicians. Sorceresses.'

She carries the cup of tea to Vigée Le Brun, hands it to her kindly.

'Here,' says Antoinette. 'I'll demonstrate.'

She pulls a hairpin from her wig and holds it between thumb and forefinger. It is slim, smooth silver, with a single round chrysoprase, green with black veins, set on the end. She aims it at the far wall, at a bit of wallpaper she has never liked, and a bolt of lightning strikes it. The wallpaper smoulders. She looks at Vigée Le Brun.

Vigée Le Brun's eyebrows are as high as they can go. Then they drop; she frowns. 'Your Majesty, why tell me this? Why take me into your confidence?'

'Because a painter of your talents would be an excellent worker of magic, I feel sure. Because I trust you. And because you may be able to befriend other magisters, tell me what they are saying, in Paris.'

'Other magisters?'

Antoinette swallows. 'First, I must tell you that there are dangers. There are some magisters who want a world in which only they can do magic. I will tell you who they are, but you must always take care, and you may choose to keep your abilities secret.'

The painter nods grimly. 'You wish me to spy on them?'

'No, my friend. I am not sending you into a lion's den. I would like you to, well, to befriend my own friends. My colleagues. Men and women of science, and art, and members of the nobility, all of whom are magisters too. They speak to me as the Queen of France, and I need someone who will speak to me as a friend. And so many of my friends' – she glances at Lamballe – 'are here at Versailles, with me, and can only see what I see.'

The painter is still frowning. She looks again at the wallpaper, and then back at the Queen.

'Well? What do you say? This is not an order from your queen, but a request from your friend.'

Vigée Le Brun looks sombre. Good; she's decided to do it.

'I'm honoured, and I'll do what I can. I – Everything I believed to be true is in question. Forgive me. I would ask—'

'Yes?' *Name your price, and make it a good one.*

'I would ask for as much instruction in magic as Your Majesty can give me.'

Antoinette claps her hands. 'What did I tell you, Marie-Louise? I thought she would say that.'

'And I agreed, as I recall,' says Lamballe mildly.

Antoinette feels something unpleasant rising in her chest, bile or heartburn. It feels like punishment, but it's only the pregnancy.

Then Antoinette buckles.

The cramps are like the ones she had with Mousseline, that awful day, with all the court watching – but it is too early, this baby cannot come yet.

She screams, and Lamballe grabs her skirt, looks at it, at the blood there. Then both Lamballe and Vigée Le Brun call out, some words that Antoinette does not hear.

CHAPTER FORTY-TWO

*Visitors to Naples — A Cancelled Party — A Splinter —
Specious Taxonomies*

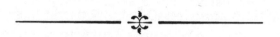

Joseph visits Naples in January 1784. 'Count Falkenstein'
arrives with Angelo Soliman, who is limping from some
wound in the foot and cannot attend at court, and with a
retinue of a dozen servants in false livery. Joseph likes the
work of being Holy Roman Emperor but not the pomp. He
is the opposite of Ferdinand, who bows low to Joseph,
refusing to play along.

'My dear brother-in-law,' Ferdinand booms. 'Naples
welcomes you. We have prepared a marvellous reception for
tomorrow night. We have fruit ices carved like hot-air balloons,
all the rage in Paris. We have little sausages, because I know
how you Germans like sausages, eh? I know my wife does,
don't you, Charlotte? We have — we even have seven hundred
and thirty-nine starlings in cages in the under-kitchen, ready
to be killed and baked in pies with wine and tarragon.'

Charlotte smiles sympathy at her brother. Behind her
shoulder, she can hear Acton's soft breath. Her six living
children flank her, all but the wilful baby Maria Amalia (so
like her namesake) dutifully smiling at their uncle, the Holy
Roman Emperor.

'These children are a marvel,' says the childless Joseph, looking at each one as if he were inspecting troops. They reward his attentions by standing straighter. Teresa is eleven now; her marriage is one of the topics Joseph is here to discuss.

Joseph turns back, looks at Ferdinand. He does not return the bow or the greeting. 'Why seven hundred and thirty-nine?' he asks.

'What?' Ferdinand says.

'The starlings, sir.'

'I don't know!' Ferdinand laughs. 'You know everything, Acton. Tell me. Why seven hundred and thirty-nine starlings?'

'Because His Majesty asked for a thousand,' Acton replies.

Charlotte tries not to smirk. Acton doesn't mean to be impertinent; it isn't his fault he sees the worst in everything. It's one reason he's so valuable.

'Yes, my wife's minister is right,' says Ferdinand with a wild little laugh. 'Nobody in Naples does anything properly. We do it half-arsed, or we do it as if it's the only thing that matters. Nobody works in Naples, unless they feel like it.'

'A great many people work in Naples,' snaps Charlotte. 'We eat the bread they bake every morning. Naples' problem is not laziness but corruption.'

'We may run short on the pies,' says Ferdinand, as if she had not spoken, 'but we will have a marvellous masque, Joseph. Some of the actors will be nude. It's a nature piece. Rousseau and all that, you know. Nipples everywhere.'

Charlotte breathes, evenly, keeping the blood out of her face. Ferdinand no longer calls Acton her lover but he calls him her minister in the same sort of tone. He's been more horrible than ever, lately, and she has simply stopped visiting his bed every month. To hell with it. She has given Naples enough children. The last time she saw him at night, he was drunk, and he had come back from the hunt. She told him he would be needed at the hand-kissing ceremony the

following day and he whacked her across the chest with one of his hunting gloves. That was two days ago. He is the King, and he is her husband, and there's nothing she can do under her religion about either of those things, but by God she won't see him alone again, the bastard.

'I thought I might have a tour of Calabria later,' says Joseph as they walk to the Hall of Mirrors. 'See some of the damage first-hand. Are the roads passable?'

'You can ask my wife about that,' says Ferdinand, and he walks ahead. 'She knows everything. Beatrix, heavenly creature, what the hell are you wearing in your décolletage? Is that a miniature between your gorgeous breasts? Let's see it.'

He runs forward, and for a moment Charlotte remembers the child Wolfgang Mozart, running through the halls at Schönnbrun, before he tripped and fell into Antoine's arms. A performance, she thought at the time, and still does.

Joseph rolls his eyes at Ferdinand's antics. He probably remembers Mozart too.

'You won't find the roads passable,' Charlotte tells her brother. 'I travelled there in the autumn, but now, with this cold snap, it's all frozen muck. The horses can't get through.'

'How are the people getting food? Supplies?'

'By boat when they can, although one out of every three founders in this horrible fog. Is the fog as bad in Vienna?'

'No. No, not quite this bad. It is a blight, though. Some of my schools report that the children cough so pitifully through their lessons that the instructors can't teach. How are your schools coming, Charlotte?'

'Very well. We've converted many of the old monasteries and every peasant child can attend for free.'

'If their parents can afford to lose them at home.'

'Yes, of course. Rome wasn't built in a day, Joseph.'

'But your navy was, or so I hear.'

'Not at all!' She laughs. 'I did as you suggested, brother. I built a navy the likes of which no one has ever seen. But

it was not overnight. It took years of hard work and we had to bribe or intimidate every mast-wright south of the Alps to get it done. Here, Joseph, this is General Acton. The glory of the new navy goes to him.'

Joseph nods. 'I've heard all about you, sir.' He looks back at Charlotte, as if appraising whether the rumours are true.

'Acton can show you around Naples, if you like,' she says hurriedly. 'You'll find no better guide.'

'Surely he has better things to do than show a visitor the sights.'

'Acton serves at the pleasure of His Majesty,' she says. 'In other words, he does what I tell him. Even if what I tell him to do is impossible.'

'It would be my honour, sir,' says Acton. 'Perhaps tomorrow, before the reception.'

Joseph nods. She walks with her brother through the corridors to the coffee room, for a real conversation. Acton follows, a few steps behind.

Then her brother pulls her to one side, behind a marble statue of Diana. He's frowning; his face is so much older since the last visit. 'What's that on your shoulder?'

She pulls her fichu over to cover her collarbone. 'It's nothing. A bruise.'

Joseph takes her by the wrist, as though she were not a queen, and walks her a few steps away. Acton steps towards them but she glances at him, tells him what to do with her eyes, and he obeys. He stops, and waits, and watches.

'Is he hitting you?' Joseph hisses. 'That godforsaken boor of a husband. Does he strike you, Charlotte?'

She breathes in, breathes out. She sees no point in lying. There is nothing Joseph or anyone else can do about it anyway. What the late Empress Maria Theresa joined together, no man can put asunder. Joseph knows that better than anyone.

'He has hit me, yes. When I first arrived, and had no one here to help me, and nowhere to go. Then he stopped for a

while. This is, I think, the fourth time he has hit me, in our years together.'

'Christ.' Joseph scowls. 'I'm not going to that man's party. I don't want to see him again, not once while I'm here. He can eat seven hundred and thirty-nine starlings by himself.'

'Good. I'll cancel it. He'll mope and go off whoring and gambling for three days and I'll have three days of peace.'

'Why don't you – Why don't you do something about it?'

'And what shall I do about it, Joseph? Tell me.'

'Where does he hit you?'

She shakes her head. 'In our bedroom. In the carriage, twice.'

'No, I mean – is it on the face? Where it shows?'

She cocks her head and looks at him. What a disappointment men are. 'Thank you for your concern, brother. He has never hit me on the face.'

He lets go of her wrist. 'Well, thank God for small mercies, anyway. Slip a knife between his ribs, Charlotte, the moment your boy is old enough to take the throne.'

He smiles wanly, to show that he's only mostly serious. Charlotte makes a face in response that Joseph is free to interpret any way he likes. She's thought about it. She thinks about it every day.

But Charlotte is not Catherine of Russia, though by God some days she would like to be. She won't kill her husband. She will use the tools at her disposal to keep him away from her. She is the one who sets the schedule, who determines which members of the royal family will be in which palace on which days. She has six living children, though God knows it would be better if she had more than two boys. Still, Francesco is strong and healthy, and her seat on the Council is secure in any case – no one would imagine running the government of Naples without her. And her daughters will make good marriages. She need never be in the same room alone with Ferdinand ever again.

They cancel the party. She and Joseph spend the rest of

his visit in easy, quiet work, drinking coffee and scheming. They plot Teresa's marriage; like her, he favours a match with Leopold's son, who will be the Habsburg heir, and Joseph's heir too. It's settled.

'And what about Antoinette's little Marie-Thérèse? What does she call her? Mousseline?' Charlotte asks. 'She'll be marriageable soon enough.'

Joseph groans. 'The Bourbons have all sorts of plans, as usual, and most of them are out of the question. But don't worry. There's time for many things to change.'

The Emperor says this almost grimly, as though he's determined to make up for the years he spent ruling alongside Maria Theresa. His sudden, sweeping modernization schemes have had unforeseen consequences: even something as simple as changing the official language of the Empire to German rather than Latin has made all the non-German-speakers fear that they're being pushed down, pushed out. The more he tries to unify the Empire, the more it fractures.

And as for the Bourbon–Habsburg alliance that Maria Theresa made the goal of her daughters' lives? Bourbon France and Spain have only been reminded of their common interests, now that they've humbled Britain in the American war. And Joseph is turning not to Bourbons for allies, but east to Russia, and even to their mother's old enemy Frederick of Prussia.

Joseph's right. Many things are changing. And that leaves room for her kingdom to make its own choices.

Caramanico returns to Italy. After several years of service in England, she's recalled him; it is not good practice to leave the same ambassador anywhere for too long, lest they become part of the furnishings of the place, as William Hamilton has with his fossils.

With Soliman in Naples too, Charlotte invites the two men to a salon in the palace, protected by enchanted firescreens.

The next meeting of the Order is not for some weeks, and anyway, Angelo Soliman's foot is still too sore for him to walk through the tunnels. But she wants to get a sense of how the Order stands across Europe.

The prince comes through the door in a plain brown coat and his natural brown hair tied neatly in a Quakerish ribbon.

'You look like an American,' Charlotte says as the prince kisses her hand.

'Everyone looks like an American now, in England, or else they look like a hot-air balloon, all puffed up,' he says. 'There is no middle ground in 1784.'

'You left your daredevil secretary in England, I take it?'

'Yes. Lunardi's work is going well, speaking of hot-air balloons. Combining magic and science, drawing crowds wherever he goes, and proving all sorts of things possible.'

Charlotte isn't sure she would call this going well; it seems reckless in more ways than one. She opens her mouth to say so, when Caramanico turns at the sound of the door opening.

'Ah, I see I was not misinformed after all, and Dr Soliman does grace Naples with his presence.'

It's good to see Soliman. Charlotte is surprised by the relief she feels at having him there in person, and not merely at the other end of a letter. But he is pale, leaning on a cane, a line of sweat above his ear.

It began, he tells them, with a splinter.

An ordinary splinter. A black line no wider than a hair and no longer than a thumbnail. Wood, perhaps, or a sliver of some metal. The day they arrived in Naples, it slid into the sole of Soliman's foot and stayed there.

He did try to get it out himself, with tweezers, with a needle, even with a knife. When it remained stubborn, he put a poultice of honey and turmeric on it to draw it out, and then a poultice of salt, bread, and milk, and then of coltsfoot and lard.

After a few days, he was hobbling about with a bandaged

foot, and had purple lines running up his leg, a great ulcer on the sole.

'Good Lord,' she says. 'Sit here, this is the best chair. Some brandy?'

'I'll keep my wits about me, for now. Thank you, Your Majesty.'

'You're sure it's not enchanted?'

'It seems a strange way to attack someone,' Caramanico says, 'wasting sacrifices on leaving a splinter about, on the chance that one person would step on it just so.'

Soliman holds out his hands. 'As you say, a strange attack indeed. We can assume it is an ordinary bit of bad luck, then.'

If anyone had ever made a spell to draw out a splinter or heal an infection, it is not in the embroidered book – or in the *Reconditus*, which now holds all the spells in the embroidered book along with its many others.

'My physicians will have a look. Do you know, there are a number of female doctors in Italy? The bourgeois families send their daughters to the University of Bologna.'

'We might consider some for the Academy, Your Majesty,' says Caramanico.

'Mmm,' she says. 'Though most men and women of science have had enough to occupy them, with this unwholesome fog. I had hoped, Dr Soliman, you might have some ideas for me about how to dispel it.'

He bows his head. 'Your Majesty, when your brother the Emperor does not need me, I have been working day and night to find the spell of spells. When I do, it may provide a way forward.'

'You believe you will find it, then,' Caramanico says, stepping towards him.

She examines Soliman's face, this face she's known since she was a child. One of the few faces she's come to trust. 'You have such faith in it. Such faith that the answer exists, that you can find it.'

He considers. 'Faith? I am a philosopher, not a monk. But I learned from old books written by scholars who sought to understand the natural world as an expression of something less tangible. It is as if the ancients knew there was some great truth beyond their horizon, like their land of Prester John or their earthly paradise, but they didn't have the tools to get there. And now we modern scholars have those tools but we have forgotten that the far land exists. Magisters always knew, and could have been searching. How does magic work? If we understood that, what a world we could create! But instead of searching for answers, we have spent so many centuries developing signs and rituals to shield the truth from the uneducated. And then we came to believe in these signs and rituals ourselves, and we have come to fear the truth. We may practise magic but we fear it as much as any peasant fears his superstitions.'

'By we, you mean the Order,' Caramanico says.

'Of course,' Soliman responds, surprised.

'I thought perhaps you meant the magic practised in savage lands.'

'I did not, but I have been seeking answers from other lands, as much as I can, to see what principles underlie all forms of magic. What little I have been able to glean has been instructive but inconclusive, at least as regards the question of the spell of spells.'

'Perhaps those forms are merely inferior,' Caramanico says. 'Being from hotter climates, where the need for invention is not so immediate, and so the people have evolved to be inferior. If there are taxonomies of humanity, why not taxonomies of magic?'

Caramanico does not look at Soliman, but Charlotte does, and can see on his face what he thinks about 'taxonomies of humanity'. His letters over the years have criticized such ideas in David Hume's writing, and even in their beloved Montesquieu.

Caramanico rushes on, filling the silence. 'Surely the Order's

forms have reached the highest expression, and the others are, perhaps, imitations. Degraded and corrupted forms, half learned from rogue magisters. Or primitive attempts, perhaps. Perhaps more rudimentary societies are, as Rousseau would have it, closer to nature. If there is a great truth in the natural world, a truth that governs magic, perhaps they have some instinctive understanding of it.'

'I cannot say,' Soliman says curtly.

'But you believe you will discover the spell of spells,' Caramanico says.

'I believe it exists, and I must believe that if I am given enough years, I can find it, not through prayer or poetry but through numbers and hard thought. And I believe that one day, the world will be the better for it. The perfection of humanity does not lie in innocence we have lost but in wisdom we have not gained. Rousseau looked backward; I look forward.'

Charlotte would call that faith, but his faith is not like her mother's simple beliefs: that reward follows virtue, intercession follows prayer, and punishment follows sin, and if the consequence fails then the cause was not what it appeared. Maria Theresa's faith of smoke and muttering was always obscure to Charlotte, but Soliman's faith in the future shines so brightly she almost wants to reach towards it with him.

He seems to have the same effect on Caramanico, who walks towards Soliman and puts his hand on his shoulder. Soliman winces, perhaps from the pain in his foot. 'Then I will help you, now that I'm home in Naples again. I fully support your ambitions, Dr Soliman. It is a new world, and we will need new ideas to make our way in it.'

'You have enjoyed your time in England, I see,' Charlotte says dryly.

He bows his head. 'So many opportunities for men of talent to make their own mark, to lead. One may encounter great men so easily, simply by walking in St James's Park, or going to any coffee house, or the grand new Freemasons'

Hall, or the daily demonstrations of electricity and micro-scopes. But there are opportunities here, too, and I am glad to be home. And glad to be able to be of some assistance, Dr Soliman. While you are unable to go and interview scholars yourself, I will be your errand-boy. I know everyone in Italy these days. I can get you any books you need, and carry any letters.'

Soliman inclines his head. 'Thank you, Your Highness, but I expect His Imperial Majesty will be travelling north again soon.'

'You cannot travel with such an injury,' Charlotte protests. 'You will stay here until you are healed, and my brother will agree.'

Emperor Joseph leaves, King Gustavus of Sweden arrives; the court turns, shuffles partners, bows, begins again.

The currency of the court of Naples is proximity to the King and Queen. Physical proximity. If you are anyone of note – a lord, a minister, a courtier – you will be invited to one of the hand-kissing ceremonies that occur throughout the year. You will be invited to kiss the monarchs' hands in the order of your importance. You will stand on the starkly patterned marble floor like a pawn on a chessboard, waiting to move forward to assert some small measure of power.

At other court events, the important people stand as close as they can to the King and especially, in these last few years, the Queen. Charlotte often finds it claustrophobic, having so many other bodies crushed around her wide panniers and stopping her from moving without calling out her intentions, like a peddler in a carnival.

But on the day of the arrival of King Gustavus, she finds herself grateful for the squirming wall of sweat and rosewater, brocade and silk. It insulates her, makes it unnecessary to so much as acknowledge the presence of Count Axel von Fersen.

She couldn't very well disallow him. He's the captain of the King of Sweden's guards, and the King of Sweden is here

on a state visit. Still, she has no intention of letting him believe he's entitled to the slightest toleration. The lover who made her sister prey to a doomed cause. A traitor to the Order, Silfversparre says. She ought to kill him where he stands. Run a dagger through his ribs.

But there's nothing clean about murder.

So she simply does not look at him, though he's there at Gustavus's elbow. The King of Sweden is nearly forty and has an actor's mobile face under his wig of fat grey curls. He looks self-satisfied; perhaps any sovereign would, who'd managed to leach power from both parliament and nobility.

He speaks with Charlotte about the Russian–Danish alliance, about what her brother Joseph might do in the event Sweden tries to acquire Norway. She supplies the careful, precise answers that she and Acton crafted in advance, and meanwhile she is aware of Fersen, watching her, unsmiling.

'May I present the captain of my guard, Your Majesty? Count Axel von Fersen.'

Gustavus's words slice through the fog in her mind, and she refocuses her eyes. 'Hmm?'

'Count Axel von Fersen.' He gestures to the count, who bows perfectly.

'Count,' she says. 'How wonderful. I get so little news of my sister in Paris, and I hoped since you spend so much time there, you might tell me how she is.'

He smiles.

'Have I said something amusing, Count?'

'Forgive me, it's only that Her Majesty asked me to report the same regarding you and your children, Your Majesty.'

Charlotte inclines her head. 'Did she? Then you may tell the Queen of France we are all quite well, God be thanked.' She pauses. Her spies tell her things, but they never tell her what she really wants to know. 'And *is* my sister well?'

'She would teach the torches to burn bright,' he replies, his dark eyes flashing. It stops her breath, and she understands, suddenly, that he truly loves her. That Antoinette is

loved. And that she probably loves him. He is not merely a dashing rogue; he is everything to her, and she is everything to him. It makes her ache, seeing that possibility. How terrible and wonderful it would be to have someone who would quietly and without hesitation lie down and die for you, not out of duty but out of pure love.

She glances back at the King, becomes aware suddenly of the crush of courtiers all around them, the hush as they listen.

Charlotte laughs lightly. 'So you quote Shakespeare, among your other charms,' she says lightly, weakly. 'She would teach the torches, wouldn't she? How gallant you are, Count. I see why my sister keeps you close. She would teach everyone and everything to do more and be other than they are. She wants the world to be perfect and everyone in it to be happy. And her friends indulge her naivety, I'm afraid, exposing her to harsh judgement by the cynics and the pamphleteers. If she would only act—'

'Her Majesty does not act at all,' Fersen says. 'I have never met anyone more natural in all their dealings.'

'How anyone can be natural at Versailles is beyond me,' Gustavus says smoothly. 'There is such rigour in everything there. I'm always afraid to open my mouth.'

Everyone laughs politely. The rest of the Swedish visit goes smoothly, though Charlotte does not speak to Fersen again. When they go, she feels not relieved but bereft, as though she missed a vital opportunity.

Charlotte loves the sky at Caserta. It's a green, gentle part of her kingdom, untouched by the calamities of the fog and the earthquakes. The massive complex, rivalling Schönbrunn and Versailles, is set on gently sloping ground, so when she walks uphill in the gardens behind her palace, she can see for miles. Charlotte has commissioned a series of mythological fountains to mark each stage of the glittering canal that rises in pieces, guiding the walker towards a man-made

waterfall that leaps out of the green hills. Everything is man-made: the stones from ruined Pompeii and the ancient-looking temples set into the woods, even the paths that seem on the brink of being overgrown, and the English garden she is building near the top of the hill, just beside the fountain that shows Diana being surprised by the hunter Actaeon.

But in this spring of 1784, there is no view. The fog has lingered for more than a year. People have forgotten what the sky was like before. Now she looks down the long avenue towards the palace and sees nothing but garden melting into grey mist. This is not the damp, cool fog of a summer day. It doesn't make the greens richer. It blocks the sunlight, and the grass is yellow.

She feels hemmed in tight. She wants to run the length of these pathways, and breathe freer air. To feel something bigger than anxiety and exhaustion.

Charlotte turns to Acton, who holds his papers in his hand and waits for her to finish gazing and thinking. She has made him prime minister, and he manages the country with the same calm capability he showed in creating her navy.

'Is there anything else?' she asks.

'There is always something else. If Your Majesty is tired, we can address it tomorrow.'

It is a long walk, though there's an optical illusion that makes it look much shorter when you set out. The end of the park is two miles from the palace, which is one reason Charlotte likes to walk here with Caterina, or the other Brothers of Naples, or Acton. She learned as a child that the most private place in a palace is outside it.

'No,' she says. 'I'm not tired. Let's do it now.'

'All right. The cook at the city palace is concerned about a flock of birds.'

It surprises her into a laugh. 'Birds?'

'Apparently they have been in cages in an under-kitchen for some time. They were to have been eaten at the party for your brother's visit, and the party was cancelled.'

She laughs, a loud sound here in this birdless, grey garden. 'The starlings! The seven hundred and thirty-nine starlings.'

He looks at his notes. 'Six hundred and four now. Some must have died.'

'But why are the starlings still there?'

'His Majesty has not requested starlings since.'

She laughs again. 'All right, so it's starlings for dinner, is it? But why is the cook so impatient? Surely they can't eat much seed.'

'These particular birds – these starlings – have a habit of imitating the sounds around them, I'm told. Every time a bell rings at St Mary's, the starlings repeat it, at some length.'

She laughs again, and claps her hands together. 'Marvellous. This I must see. Under no circumstances is anyone to eat these birds until I have had the chance to hear that for myself. In fact, let's send for them. Bring them here to Caserta. They'll pine less in the country, surely.'

He smiles his tight sailor smile and folds his papers, putting them into his waistcoat pocket.

'I am sure the birds will find it lovely here, Your Majesty.'

The garden doesn't look lovely at the moment. It looks leached and sere. They approach the top of the hill, where a grove of mulberry trees makes a deeper shadow in this grey new world.

'It's hard to be happy since the fog set in, isn't it, Acton?'

'Yes, I suppose it is.'

'You suppose?' She turns and looks at him, and finds he is looking at her, and blushes. How foolish to blush – there's nothing wrong with looking, not even at a queen.

'I don't concern myself with happiness. It isn't a – I don't have a philosophy against it, nothing like that. Just the way I was made, Your Majesty.'

'Ah. I'm the same way, I think. I am content, or I am not. I am working, or I am not. Happiness seems like a bother. A chimera.'

'Yes.'

They look at each other, and Charlotte remembers Fersen, glaring at her in her own throne room, quoting Shakespeare about her sister.

'The rumours have stopped, I think,' she says in a voice so contained it strains her throat. 'About you and me, I mean.'

He nods, not pretending he doesn't know. 'These things will pass, when there's nothing behind them.'

'Of course.' It's cold, suddenly. She would like to be by a fire, with a book, alone. She would like to forget ever having wanted anything. 'It's hard to know where it even started.'

'Oh, that much I know. It started because I am not Naples' prime minister, and everyone sees that. I'm yours.'

'Are they not the same?'

He shakes his head, almost sadly. 'They are very much not the same. But you are Queen of Naples, and so I serve Naples, because I serve you. You are right to worry about the fog,' he says, looking away and biting his lip. 'It is a problem for trade and for the harvest. I'm relieved to see the mulberry trees are thriving, at least.'

The mulberry trees planted by Ferdinand's father, when he founded the silk factory just up the road at San Leucio. Food for the worms.

'I have spent a great deal of time in San Leucio,' she says, wishing for a moment she could tell him all about her secret work, how much good she's done in the shadows. 'It's a fortunate little village. Everything they need is there: farmland, water, good air. The roads to Rome and Naples are good but it is far enough away that they live quietly, without any politics or ferment.'

'Utopia, then.'

'It could be,' she muses, leaning against a tree. 'We could make it one, Acton. Bring all the jobless and walking wounded from Calabria and Sicily. All their wages would go into a common fund to make sure their needs were provided for. They could elect a council of elders to oversee the daily business of the colony—'

'It's a colony now!' He laughs, the laugh of a friend. He leans on the next tree over, a few feet away, one knee bent.

'Yes, a colony,' she says, smiling approvingly at him. 'A perfect society. The women and the men would be equal. No child marriages. No dowries, no incentives for families to marry off their girls to boors.'

She doesn't know how to cross the distance between them. He's looking away from her, down the avenue, at nothing. At ugly grey mist. At the future.

'Do you know of the late Jacques Vaucanson?' he asks. 'The one who built that grotesque duck automaton?'

Acton's questions are never predictable; he carries on conversations like a ship at sea, into the wind, coming out of the fog when you least expect it. This one makes her nervous; Vaucanson was a rogue magister, and many of his devices were enchanted. Soliman has told her all about it. The famous duck was able to nibble food out of someone's hand, and even produced excretions that Vaucanson claimed were evidence of a sophisticated chemical device that perfectly replicated digestion. In reality, it was an enchantment, used to gull spectators out of money for the chance to see it work. How disgusting that anyone would use magic for such a purpose.

The Brothers of Paris got nervous and had Vaucanson killed two years ago – the Rohanites have been more violent of late. Vaucanson willed his collection to the French King, and apparently the King's philosophers are bewildered by the fact that so many of his creations do not work after his death.

It is one more piece of evidence that what everyone insists on calling 'the new science' is slipping outside of science's grasp, or was never there. Magic is loose in the world. The common people call it by its name.

And what can the Order do, now that the genie is out of the bottle? Recruit and discredit, as it's always done, but more and more, destroying some people and welcoming

others into the fold, for the right reasons and the wrong ones.

'Yes, I've heard something about it,' she says. 'I don't see the appeal, myself. My sister Antoinette has a new life-sized doll that plays the dulcimer. One day we will wake up and find that these automata have taken over Europe in our sleep.'

She imagines the Pandora doll, sitting somewhere in a box, moth-eaten. Does Antoinette still have hers? Charlotte had terrible stomach pains one night in the fall and she thought for a moment it was the Pandora doll – it felt the same – but the next day, the General arrived.

'Nobody could take the throne of Naples from you,' he says, and pauses for a long time before he adds, 'Your Majesty.'

For a fey moment she wonders what Acton would say if she told him that she had the power to enchant objects, that she is a magister. A sorceress. A witch. Perhaps he would think that all her success was down to magic, to mere trickery. And perhaps he would be right.

But she won't trick him. And she won't ever give him reason to stop believing she is wonderful.

A breeze skirls down the mulberry avenue and she shivers in her thin sleeves.

'You haven't told me about Vaucanson and his duck,' she says.

'He also made a loom, in which the pattern can be controlled using a stiff card punched with holes in a particular pattern. It isn't widely used, yet, but if we had such looms here, we could have the jobless of Calabria at work within a week, without training them.'

She imagines her kingdom dotted with enchanted looms, clacking under the hands of women. She doesn't embroider much any more; she works on a bigger scale now. Perhaps the embroidered book should have gone with Antoinette after all. Charlotte has become a weaver instead.

She turns her head, lolling still against the tree. Acton is looking at her steadily.

'Tell me something, John Acton,' she whispers. 'Are you mine? Really mine?'

He swallows, his Adam's apple moving under his pale skin. 'I am yours.'

'Then I have two requests to make of you. Second, please help me build the perfect society at San Leucio.'

'And first?'

'First, please come closer to me,' she says. She cannot cross the distance but she can order him to do it. And he does. He takes two steps towards her, while she turns to him, her back still against the mulberry tree.

'Please, please come closer,' she whispers as his rough cheek rests against hers, as their arms clutch each other.

They are impatient, both unlacing his breeches at once. He lifts Charlotte against the tree and she wraps her legs around him, her petticoats bunched against his brass buttons. She grabs onto the branches of the tree and kisses him to keep from crying out.

CHAPTER FORTY-THREE

*The Queen's Hamlet — The Effect of an Opera
Performance — Terror in the Night — A Visit to
the Cardinal — Antoinette Makes a Purchase*

Élisabeth Vigée Le Brun's second pregnancy ended in grief not long after Antoinette's own miscarriage. When their bodies had recovered, the two women took a quiet cup of tea together in a private corner of the Trianon. In the spring of 1784, Vigée Le Brun paints the royal children in the gardens at Versailles; the painter insists she is ready to work. Antoinette's daughter is neither Mousseline nor simply Marie-Thérèse today; today she is Madame Royale in striped gold-and-blue satin. She has a wise face for a five-year-old, and she collects her little brother in his blue suit, puts her arm around him. On her breast there is a pink carnation, and on his the medal that shows him to be a member of the chivalrous Order of the Holy Spirit.

The children are wearing straw hats, partly because the Messieurs Léonard are nowhere to be found. Though Antoinette knows full well where they are: there is a group of shopwomen in Marseille — milliners and haberdashers — who had been practising magic to keep their accounts, create impossible new dyes and hats that do not obey gravity, and

set traces on their goods in case of theft. The Brothers took their memories – the women were unknown to the Circle and not immune to magic – but they did a botched job of it, and the poor women have been roaming the streets screaming nonsense about sorcery, their shops burning down. They are discredited, which is good enough for the Order; they are one more piece of evidence for those who insist, in the face of mounting evidence, that magic is not real, is a conspiracy of the government, or a corrupt plaything of the elite. If the shopkeepers prove persuasive in their rantings, then the Order will simply kill them. It is only a matter of time before the women are destroyed, or destroy themselves.

So the two Messieurs Léonard have gone to Marseille with their hairbrushes, to do the job properly, and show mercy to the women. Antoinette does not want attention drawn to their absence, so she suggested the hats.

On Mousseline's lap, there's a bird's nest. Empty and abandoned; Antoinette doesn't know where Vigée Le Brun found it.

'That nest is a bit dismal, isn't it?' Antoinette peers forward at her children, her embroidery in her lap.

'In the painting, it will have birds in it,' Vigée Le Brun responds, setting out little jars of yellowish oil and turpentine on the shelf of her easel.

Antoinette leans back in her cushioned armchair. 'That smell must be convenient for covering the smell of enchantments.'

'In Paris, everything stinks,' Vigée Le Brun says wryly, pulling drawers out of the paintbox she has set on the little table beside her.

'And what can you tell me of the Palais-Royal?'

It's a quiet spot, at the wilder edges of the gardens, with the sound of a fountain at a little distance. Out here, they can speak freely, as even the children are at enough distance that they will only catch a word or two. Vigée Le Brun has

spread colours on her palette, and is sketching in the shapes of the children in straight, bold strokes of brown.

'Oh, the Palais-Royal is very exciting. Did you hear about what happened the other night, Your Majesty?'

'I heard Salieri's latest opera put everyone to sleep.'

The mention of opera makes her think of her brother Max, who writes to her dutifully, usually of music, which is all he cares about. She cares about it too, so why does she find it so hard to remember to reply? Can it really still be because she sacrificed her love for him, all those years ago? If they were together in person, they would be friends, she's sure. Maybe she would even gain new affection for him. They would go to the opera together.

'It did indeed put everyone to sleep.' Vigée Le Brun steps back and examines the portrait, while the Dauphin wriggles his feet. 'Everyone. The entire audience, and the orchestra, and the singers too.'

Antoinette grips her chair. 'Another attack?'

'So it would seem. But it was stymied. A soprano came out from behind the wings, with a glass of wine in her hand, already singing. Her spell reversed the effect of the magic, and everyone woke up, with only the haziest memory of having nodded off.'

'Then most people don't know?'

She shakes her head. 'I heard it from Mademoiselle Dervieux herself.'

'That name is familiar,' Antoinette says, puzzled. 'Has she been to Versailles?'

'Unlikely, Your Majesty. She's the daughter of a washer-woman, and she's an actress, and . . . a courtesan. You may have heard her name in connection with certain scandalous affairs. His Majesty's brothers . . .'

'I see.' Antoinette gazes into the distance, at the figures walking in the orangery, and along the grand canal. 'So she is a magister. And she has a spell that can counter magic! I wonder where she got it.'

'From Philippe d'Orléans, she says.'

'What?'

Rogue magisters are under no obligation to share spells with each other; they are not the Order, and they have no great book or library. They trade spells, or buy them from each other, if they choose. But the rogues of the Circle have tended to share their spells, especially the major ones; they are working towards the same goals, after all.

'And I bought it from Dervieux. I'll write it down for Your Majesty.'

'I'm grateful.' Antoinette can hardly think of what to say. 'I suppose Philippe must have found it quite recently.'

Vigée Le Brun wipes her brush, as if thinking. Then she says, reluctantly, 'She told me of a number of spells that His Serene Highness has been using to create powerful protections against magical attack at his family's estate at Saint-Cloud, which he is starting to apply to the Palais-Royal as well. Spells that are not among those Your Majesty shared with me.'

'May we stand up for a little while?' Mousseline calls. 'Louis-Joseph is wriggling.'

The little French village that grew on American soil and fooled the English has now shrunk back to size; all it took was a word of command. Fersen brought it back across the ocean to Antoinette.

She hasn't known quite what to do with it. It seems a shame to leave it in a trunk. Mousseline has outgrown her love of tiny houses. The Dauphin already has a model of George Washington's house at Mount Vernon, a gift from an American town council or some such thing to mark the end of the war. He's not old enough yet to show much interest in it.

And Antoinette has long yearned for a place she can go with her friends and break spells, work enchantments, without fear of spying eyes. Somewhere bigger than the little mirrored boudoir in the Petit Trianon.

She raises her little hamlet not far from the Temple of Love she built six years before, which she can see from her window at the Petit Trianon. Beyond the natural English garden and the grotto. She had the whole area blocked off while the buildings grew over the course of a single day, but she watched it with Polignac, and listened to the groans of the wood stretching, the crackling sound of mortar multiplying. It still has a toy quality: it doesn't quite look like a real place. That's why it worked so well to fool the British into thinking these were buildings set up to support and supply French troops, she supposes: it looks like what a French village *ought* to look like, not like what one really does.

There is a tiny cottage, with one room. A windmill. Ovens and a dovecote. A farm, so that she can work on her own version of a loaves-and-fishes spell and other useful things. The spells don't work terribly well. It requires a quart of her blood to make one loaf of brown bread, which she serves with fresh cheeses, telling her rogue friends they are living in Rousseau's Nature now. She walks in a loose, simple white dress, and wears a straw hat over her hair, which has grown out long again.

Louis could visit any time but he considerately does not. She only invites trusted magisters, her children, and the peasants who run the farm, and who love her. No courtiers or gossips or ambitious servants.

There are no shadows on the ground, not with this haze still blocking the light.

Fersen returns from Italy, bearing gifts, most of them enchanted. Her favourite is a busk, a narrow dagger of carved teak that slides down the front of her corset. A lover's gift. The carvings on it are of dates, lines and lines of dates. The first is 30 January 1774. When she runs her finger over any date, she remembers every vivid detail that has slipped from her mind despite the fact she never would have sacrificed them: the smell of his neck or some little conversation they had about nothing. It is her favourite gift.

They have six weeks together, while the Swedish King talks politics with Louis. She is able to show Fersen everything she has done at the Petit Trianon and he laughs to see the magical village in its new place. Polignac's prediction was correct: Antoinette has made the Petit Trianon a place she can love. Before Fersen leaves, she invites a few friends to a party there on a July evening and instructs everyone to wear white.

And then the idyll ends, and Fersen returns to Sweden with his king. And Antoinette is left with her toy village.

She asks a gardener, one day in a reckless mood, what he would do if he had magic. He does not put down the basket of cabbages strapped to his back, but bows his head and stares at the ground. She waits for him to make a choice, as if she were a genie offering him three wishes in a story. A big house of his own? Enough sausages never to run out? A goose that lays golden eggs? And what would he sacrifice for such trifles?

'Your Majesty, I suppose I would stop the people I love from dying.'

She is taken aback; so would she. The smell of Mama's sickroom; the smell of the Habsburg crypt.

She staggers away from the gardener, who looks at her with an alarm she doesn't have the breath to dispel, although she's fine, she really is fine.

But he's not looking at her any more. He's looking just beyond her, and she hears hoofbeats.

It's a messenger, and for one heartbeat she fears that this is it, the possibility she has pushed away from her mind every moment of every day, that one of her children is dead.

But this messenger has not come from Versailles, which is mere minutes' ride away. He's dusty, and in brown clothes, not palace livery. And most important, his face is placid, nearly smiling. He slips off his pony and performs the obeisance of a man meeting his queen for the only time in his life.

'Yes?' she asks.

'Your Majesty's pardon. I went to Versailles but they insisted—'

He looks at her simple costume, glances at the gardener as if wanting confirmation that she is indeed the Queen.

She looks at the basket hanging from his saddle. 'You have a letter for me?'

He takes it from the basket. If Louis knew she allowed such access, if Fersen knew – but she has told the servants to send messengers to Polignac, and if Polignac is not here, then to her. They don't know enough to be properly alarmed by it, and they must assume it is part of her eccentricity, her desire to play at being ordinary here in her little artificial village. They are not wrong.

She takes the letter and opens it. Encrypted, and in Vigée Le Brun's beautiful handwriting.

'Would Your Majesty like to send a reply?'

Antoinette shakes her head. She needs to read this somewhere private, and think.

What can she give the messenger? She looks over at the gardener's basket and takes a cabbage, holds it out. 'A gift,' she says, realizing how foolish she's being, yet unable to stop. Too late, she realizes she could have told him to go to the kitchens for a coin.

He ducks his head down, probably to stop from grinning or making a face. He takes the cabbage.

The padlock on the door of her little house, her boudoir, opens at her touch – a name-day gift from Fersen a few years before. Inside, it still smells of sawdust and furniture oil, despite the little blue-and-white vases of forget-me-nots. She sits on the chair – beautifully carved but simply, and with plain blue upholstering – and lays the letter on the table.

There is no name at the top of the letter, although the messenger knew right enough where he was headed. Antoinette decrypts it onto a sheet of rough paper.

I have seen Cardinal de Rohan at the Palais-Royal often this week, and I was alarmed, thinking there might be another attack. So I have been following him as much as I can. I don't know the full import, but he has been meeting privately with Philippe d'Orléans. I fear I may have been seen – I write to tell you that I will not come to Versailles, therefore, for the next week – I did not want you to take alarm at my absence.

ELVLB

Antoinette crumples both papers, the original and the decryption. Then she goes to the mantelpiece and lights a candle from the tinderbox, sets both papers alight and puts them into the hearth to burn to ash.

Philippe d'Orléans hates the Order more than anyone; hates the idea of anyone telling him what he can and cannot do with his magic. He could not be a traitor, working for the Order.

Then what?

The Château de la Muette is closer to Paris than Versailles is, but it feels farther away from everything. On the edge of the Bois de Boulogne, on the bank of the Seine. The air is salubrious, people say, and so in summer Antoinette goes there with her children. She is pregnant again, and is increasingly desperate to retreat from court life as much as she can, to give this pregnancy every chance. To rest. Last year, she watched the first manned balloon flight here at the Château de la Muette, when she was recovering from the miscarriage.

In Lyon, this summer, a woman has flown in a balloon. She sang arias and leaned over the edge of the basket. How wonderful it must have been.

The clean air and green grass is also good for little Louis-Joseph, the doctors say. At nearly three years old, he's been

sick with fevers, on and off, and the court has been whispering – oh, she knows – that the Queen needs to produce another boy, just in case.

She sits with Polignac – her children's governess – and watches her children. Mousseline will soon be six, and she strides around the gardens like a general, surveying everything and calling it hers. Louis-Joseph is quieter. Antoinette gazes at her boy playing on the grass with the toy soldiers that once belonged to his sister. He's a beautiful child, with blond curls and even features. Her angel.

At the Petit Trianon, Antoinette has a few small protections in place. Mirrors on the walls.

At the Château de la Muette, she's taken no such precautions. She does not meet with the Circle there. It's a retreat for her and the children.

But it is there, at the Château de la Muette, that the next attack comes.

In the night, Antoinette wakes to the sound of a woman screaming. She runs towards the sound in her nightdress, into her son's bedroom, past the lady of the bedchamber who screamed, and into his playroom next door.

The model house built to look like Mount Vernon, George Washington's home, sits on a table in the middle of the room. But there's something odd about the way it's shining in the candlelight, and about the way Louis-Joseph is standing, looking at it.

Then she realizes: he's holding the white cupola in his hand, as though he just broke it off. Polignac is kneeling beside him, trying to prise it out of his hands. But something crumbles onto the floor.

Antoinette is there, holding her son, pulling the mass of broken house out of his hand. Has he hurt himself? He seems calm, and there's no injury she can see.

Then she sees that his pudgy little hand is sticky with sugar, and that the bit of house that broke and fell onto the floor is brittle and nearly translucent.

'The whole house has turned to barley sugar,' Polignac hisses, wiping the Dauphin's pudgy hand. Why? Surely nobody would dare to poison—

'It wasn't before!' the stricken lady of the bedchamber says. 'It was wood – I know it was wood. I thought he was putting wood in his mouth – and then I saw it had changed!'

Antoinette grabs her son by the shoulders. 'Did you eat any, darling? Did you put any your mouth?'

He shakes his head dutifully, and Antoinette convinces him to open his mouth for inspection.

Breathless, she hugs Louis-Joseph close while Polignac goes to take away the nurse's memories.

The Dauphin is only two years old. He poses no threat to anyone.

Just last year, she daubed both her children with some of Lamballe's enchanted corpse liquor and made them immune to magic. Only magic with physical effects would have any effect on him. Whoever did this must have known that, chosen this clumsy display for that reason perhaps.

She holds her boy close, her darling boy, who has finally given himself permission to cry. She kisses his soft pale hair.

Anxious hours turn to anxious days. The magisters of Versailles search for the culprit. Antoinette wakes in the night, for weeks afterwards, to check on her son. She puts her hand on his back to feel him breathing.

On those nights, she holds Fersen's miniature and whispers to him, softly so as not to wake him, murmuring all her worries. Once or twice, he answers, saying he couldn't sleep either. The conflict between Sweden's King and parliament is reaching another crisis point, and he is lacking for allies among the rogues there. She says, *Tell me everything,* just so that she can lie back in the chaise in her son's bedchamber, and listen to her beloved's voice rather than her own fears.

When she is satisfied the Dauphin has not been poisoned, she turns her mind to preventing another attack.

The invitation Antoinette sends to Philippe d'Orléans is a summons, and she makes sure that is very clear. He comes to her audience room at the Château de la Muette, looking uncomfortable in the summer heat.

'I have heard that you have protection spells. That you can leach the magic out of a room, and set invisible alarms to warn you of the approach of anyone wearing a certain object, and perhaps other things too.'

He swallows. 'I have been attacked more than once, as Your Majesty well knows.'

'As have I,' she snaps. 'The Dauphin was attacked, here, in his very bedroom.'

'Louis-Joseph?' He turns to her, a line of concern on his brow. He is fond of children.

She nods, but she's suddenly relieved. She was half beginning to suspect Philippe of arranging it himself. He is always trying to convince her that they have been too cautious, too secretive, that the only way to protect themselves is to raise up an army against the Order and dismantle it. But he seems genuinely concerned.

'A gift from America was not all that it seemed, and changed into barley sugar after we took it into our house. The Dauphin tried to eat it.'

'Was it poisoned?'

She pauses, calms herself. 'Not in any way that we could detect, but we had to keep it quiet, you see. We have tried to trace the gift to the sender, but all the records have changed, and the people involved all remember it differently, how it arrived, where and when . . . He is unharmed. I can put mirrors up but that will not stop them from disguising objects that seem harmless. I need more protection for my children.'

Philippe paces while Antoinette sits, her hand resting on her leg, the stays holding the sore, taut skin of her pregnant belly.

'Many of the protections at Saint-Cloud are not mere spells one can perform. They are built into the architecture. I have been working on them for years.'

She breathes out, hard, in frustration. 'There must be some things you can give me, at least.'

'Of course.' He pauses, looking out of the window. 'Could it have been an innocent gift gone wrong? They haven't attacked children before.'

'They hadn't set fire to your opera house before they did,' Antoinette retorts.

'Fair enough.'

'The Cardinal likes to terrify me any way he can. He won't kill me outright.' Or at least, so she surmises. It would draw too much attention to the Order, perhaps. Or attention from Charlotte. 'So he tries to deter me, undermine my reputation, keep me afraid. I don't know how far he will go. The death of a child – even a dauphin – might seem less risky in his eyes than my death. Or perhaps he only meant to make him ill. Or the house was not poisoned, and it was all to make me wonder. I don't know.'

'Then perhaps it's time I had a talk with him.'

'Haven't you been talking with him already?' she snaps.

Philippe blanches. 'I see him from time to time. I try to reason with him, to bargain, to keep the two sides from blowing Paris to kingdom come. I am doing work on many fronts, Your Majesty.'

'He attacked my child.'

He looks away from her, balls his fists. 'The man is known for his appetites. Perhaps there's something I can offer to make him reconsider his approach.'

Antoinette looks at him for a moment. 'A transaction?'

He shrugs, and turns back to her. 'He can't attack the children. That cannot stand.'

'No, it cannot.' She allows her fingers to flutter on her leg, to drum a little while she thinks. An outward sign of her anxiety; a tiny intimacy for Philippe, to show him that she is more human than he wants to believe. 'I will come with you.'

'Your Majesty—'

'Philippe, he is my son. It was my home. I am coming with you.'

Cardinal de Rohan has invited Marie Antoinette to see him many times since she came to France, and every time she has snubbed him. His usher shows her and Phillipe into a salon, where a footman is just drawing a panel to close off half the room. Is the Cardinal in there? More likely one of his strumpets.

She stands, waiting, dressed in a formidable green *robe à la polonaise*, its skirts gathered behind her, its yellow-striped jacket trim on her stout and strong torso. The sort of dress for doing business in.

They can hear voices, somewhere near. Behind the panel? No, in the next room. He's in there, with someone, laughing. Keeping the Queen waiting. No doubt she's surprised him in a liaison and she is not the only female company the Cardinal has today.

She strides past the footman, opens the door into the next salon. It's all dark wood and red silk. There is Rohan, sitting on a settee in a black velvet waistcoat, and the person next to him is not a woman but a man in robes like a wizard's, midnight blue, all bedecked in spangles and stars, with a heavy golden pendant around his neck. His face is pink and jowled and his natural greying hair, though sparse on top, is long, curling around his shoulders.

He stands, looking as though he's been caught in something. Rohan stands more slowly, smooth as a cat.

'Your Majesty,' he says, bowing his head. 'May I present Count Cagliostro? He is staying with me, and I wanted to be sure he was comfortable and wanted for nothing before I entertained Your Majesty.'

'You come from Naples,' she says coldly. From her sister. Another Brother sent from Naples to France, to spy on the rogues, to keep the Queen in her place.

Cagliostro scowls. 'I have not been in Naples for some

years. My wife and I are wanderers. We make our homes where we find them.'

'I see,' she says, although she doesn't, but she doesn't much care, either. She taps one foot. 'Shall we talk here, then?'

Rohan holds out a hand and gestures to the adjoining room, so she sweeps through it again, past Philippe's frowns.

'Your Majesty,' says Rohan. He turns to Philippe. 'And Monseigneur. I have so hoped for this day, so hoped that we might become friends at last.'

She glances at the footmen at both doors, the one that brought her to this room, and the one that leads to Count Cagliostro.

'We have not come to exchange niceties,' Philippe says, standing beside her. For once, it feels as though they truly are on the same side. 'We've come to say that if the Order makes any attempt on the children again, then every Brother in France will die.'

Rohan raises his eyebrows. 'The children?' He speaks lightly, as though they're discussing the opera.

'Don't try to pretend,' she says, making a fist at her side. 'You attacked my son. Never, ever do it again.'

'Ah,' he says, and turns away from her. She frowns, and steps closer, as if he's a snake who might dart in any direction at any moment. 'Hardly an attack. A gift. A reminder that we are here. That we are everywhere. That's all. Is the Dauphin well?'

Her jaw is clenched so tight that it's making her head ring. 'He's alive. He will be king. That's all you need know. If you hurt any of my children, I will rain down vengeance on you. I can, you know. I will.'

'I don't doubt you can, Your Majesty. I am familiar with some of your spells. May I humbly suggest that the greater danger comes not from me, a man of God and a servant of the royal family, but from the innumerable rogue magisters in France, of varying levels of ability and moral character?

Perhaps not all of them are happy with the government.' Cardinal de Rohan walks towards her, his arms spread wide, as if in benediction. 'The role of the Order, you see, was to make sure that magic could never be used by the powerful to enhance their control over the less powerful. Magic was only to be used by those trained in its mysteries and devoted to using it for the good of humanity. But now? Anarchy. You've opened the gates. Let's see who comes out.'

She steps back, wary. He said *was*, in reference to the Order. Philippe is looking at the Cardinal thoughtfully.

'But Her Majesty is a magister now,' Philippe says. 'As is her sister.'

'The world tilts,' the Cardinal says, cocking his head with a false smile. 'How it will be corrected, I can't say, but I know it will be corrected.'

She's sick to her stomach. He's preaching her own destruction at her, and smiling while he does it.

'You attacked my son,' she says, her throat dry.

Rohan spreads his arms wide. 'Accuse me, then, Your Majesty. I have a feeling that a trial in which the Queen of France berates me for giving her son sweets would not go against me. Especially given that the Queen of France is not particularly well liked.'

'You are an enemy of France,' she says, 'and you will pay with your life.'

'No, Madame,' says Rohan. 'I think you will find that you are the enemy of France. I think you will learn that very soon.'

A sound, a rustling, this one coming from behind the panel. Another magister there? Are they surrounded?

Philippe's hand is at her elbow, and her hands have no weapons in them, nothing with which to cut out the Cardinal's heart. So she turns on her heel, hardly taking the time to think about what she is doing, strides over to the chinoiserie panel and pulls it aside.

The woman may or may not be a magister, but what is

certain is that she is in a state of undress on a chaise longue. She pulls a gauzy robe around her stays and petticoat, and stands up uncertainly. A woman of about Antoinette's own age, with pretty red lips, a great deal of rouge, and pearl earrings.

'Your Majesty,' she breathes. 'How lovely to see you again. We met before – I am Jeanne de la Motte, of the Valois family, a descendant of Henri Deux, I have proof of my ancestry—'

The Cardinal is at her side, but instead of being embarrassed, he's laughing. 'Jeanne, for God's sake, shut up, this isn't an audience.'

She does remember – Antoinette seldom forgets a name, thanks to her enchanted earrings – this woman from some offshoot of a defunct royal line, poor and poorly educated, desperate for a connection at court. It seems she found one.

Antoinette walks out of the door she came in, saying nothing further. She has nothing more to say to the Cardinal. It was a mistake to come.

Louis assures her the Château de la Muette is quite safe, but he doesn't know – can't know – what happened. It gnaws at her. If the Château de la Muette is unsafe, and the Petit Trianon is for the rogues, Antoinette needs another place where she can bring her children, where they can play on the grass without hundreds of townspeople and courtiers gawking at them, where they will not be attacked.

And the only place she can think of is the Château de Saint-Cloud, with its magical protections. Philippe has hidden them from her all these years, taken all the spells she gave him without giving her in return the spells she could have used to keep her children safe.

Saint-Cloud is on the other bank of the Seine. It's on high ground and the air is clean. It has an orangery, lovely gardens, even a grotto. And it does not belong to Philippe. It belongs to the Duc d'Orléans, Philippe's father.

It isn't often she tells Louis she wants something. So when she tells him she wants Saint-Cloud for the children, the King makes it happen. He negotiates the sale with the duke and gets a very good price.

And Philippe comes to call again, without being summoned, his face pink and shiny with rage. She is sitting in her ante-chamber, practising the harp in the company of Polignac, when they hear the royal guards in the next room stamp their feet twice, as they must every time a duke passes by, and somehow Antoinette knows before the usher tells her that the duke in question is Philippe, Duke of Montpensier and Chartres, and soon enough, when his father dies, Duc d'Orléans and First Prince of the Blood.

'The château was to come to me,' he says, after he has bowed with as little movement as possible. 'You have taken my inheritance. Have you not enough palaces, Your Majesty?'

'None that are safe, thanks to you,' she snaps. She has heartburn and she is not in the mood to be fair. 'I bought it. I did not take it. If your father wishes to sell his property, he can.'

'He did not wish to sell,' Philippe says, but he turns from her with a gesture that says he knows he's lost. 'If anyone other than his king had asked, he never would have done so. There can be no fair transaction when one side has power over the other.'

Sometimes she thinks she has been unfair to Philippe, that he simply has his own ways of showing his loyalty to her, to Louis, to France. But those times are becoming fewer and fewer.

CHAPTER FORTY-FOUR

Riots – A Marital Agreement – If, If, If – A Mystery
Solved – The Fog Persists – Humility

Ordinarily, Charlotte's family would spend the summer at Caserta or Portici, and the winter in the Palazzo Reale in the heart of Naples. But Portici is still under repair from the rain of lava, and still too close to the volcano, which continues to smoke.

And at Caserta, there is no escape from the fog. The palace is set on a wide, gentle slope, and in ordinary times, its wide vista brings joy to the heart. Now it feels like an island surrounded by grey mist. In Naples proper, where everything is close, and the air is broken by buildings, walls, docks, and hillsides, it is harder to notice the fog, until one looks out to sea.

So when the riots begin in late summer, Charlotte feels no regret about ordering the family back to the Palazzo Reale early. It's smart politics, because staying at Caserta would seem like hiding. There are no state visitors to worry about, as the King of Sweden (and Axel von Fersen) have left, and Joseph is gone too, leaving Soliman behind to recover. The children will be as safe in the Palazzo Reale as anywhere, because Charlotte's presence is what keeps them safe. The *Reconditus* has been filling with new protective spells as an

effect of the magical war; she has alarms set that allow only people in a specific livery to enter certain areas, and she changes the livery a little every few months. There are mirrors in places where they can be seen, and mirrors in places where they can't.

But none of the spells in the *Reconditus* can do anything about the fog.

Cagliostro writes to Silfversparre, and Silfversparre tells Charlotte that the Brothers of Paris are desperate: outnumbered and outranked by the rogues there. Charlotte greets this with a slight smile of pride, at first – of course, Antoinette is among them – but then her smile drops as Silfversparre reports that there is a spell in Paris that can take all the effects of magic right out of a room. The Palais-Royal is a den of witch-prostitutes and conjurer-thieves and the Order can no longer use enchantments to hunt them, because the royal family simply tells a woman to go and sing, and the magic disappears.

Charlotte is half inclined to dismiss this as yet another whine from the Paris chapter but oh, if they're right! A spell that could dissolve the effects of magic – if such a thing exists, she might not need to wait for Soliman to find his spell of spells, or for the wind to finally blow the fog away from Naples. If, if, if.

Meanwhile, everything tastes of fog, smells of fog. The mornings are full of reports of riots the night before; reports Charlotte doesn't need, because she heard them herself. Shouts, half revelry and half something else, fuelled by cheap rotgut.

The morning she finds she can't lace her corset any more is grey and damp, and the rioters are still shouting. Only a few – it's not anything as cohesive as a mob, just drunks who never went to bed. But they're restive, and she can hear them. It steels her. She needs to be steeled.

She is pregnant, with Acton's child. She is waiting for Ferdinand to come in for his new daily marital ritual: a glass of milk, for his health, and a barely polite enquiry after the business of the state, for his conscience. Then she will tell him.

He will know it's not his. She has not shared Ferdinand's bed since Maria Amalia was born in 1782, two years ago. She does not intend to, ever again.

For days, she fretted about how she might trick him. Her husband is immune to magic, but his lackeys are not, and she could have convinced a few of them that Ferdinand had been visiting her room at night while massively drunk. The massively drunk part would not be invention. So, after his hangers-on teased him a few times about needing to be half blind with wine to do his duty with his ugly wife, Ferdinand might well have come to believe the child was his own.

But the more she turned that plan over and over in her mind, the less interested she became. She is not a fifteen-year-old bride now, hopeful and powerless. She is, for all intents and purposes, the King of Naples. And if the titular King wanted to pack her off to a convent or find some other way to get her out of his life, he would be left with the thing he fears most of all: a kingdom to run.

And more important than all of that: she simply doesn't care to pretend. She is not ashamed, and he has no power over her.

Still, she clenches her jaw as she waits for him; the air is thick and musty, as she will not open the window to let that fog in. She stands behind her chair at the table where he always takes his milk, before he goes off to the hunt.

He comes in at last, shuffling over to the long, gleaming table. Charlotte doesn't send the usher at the door away; he's a young man, his palace livery neatly brushed, his sword hilt at his waist. On the far side of the doors stand two of the royal guardsmen, their halberds sharp.

'I'm pregnant,' she says, with no other greeting.

Ferdinand looks at her, confusion crossing his face. Then astonishment as he realizes what that means. Then resignation – or perhaps admiration? A trace of something almost comradely.

They say nothing to each other. Usher or no usher, he

might choose to rail at her, even throw something. To denounce her and the child. To have his friends go after Acton with a rope or a gun.

Instead, he nods, very slightly, a few times. He's thinking. She doesn't disturb him.

His chin lifts; he looks up to the ceiling with its blue skies, its cherubs, its old prophets glaring and pointing. A deep, loud breath in through his nose. Opens his mouth. Tilts his head back down.

'When?'

She thinks for a moment he means *when did you fuck him* and the answer is always, everywhere, many times. But he doesn't mean that. 'Before Christmas.'

She realizes then that he doesn't actually care who is in his wife's bed. He isn't jealous; after all, he has never loved her, and has more mistresses than names she can remember. (Early on, when she could remember their names, she tried a few times to sacrifice those memories but the spells never worked; they aren't worth enough to her, perhaps. Or the memories were too fresh; they were something other than memory.)

What Ferdinand cared about, when he cared, was the embarrassment of the rumours that went all the way to Spain. He cares about being seen as a cuckold. Now that those rumours are dead, the truth can't hurt him. And they could use more children, for state reasons. More boys – have they not had reason to know that no child's life is guaranteed? And more girls for state marriages. He knows all of that, though he doesn't make it his business. It would only become his business if she failed to manage it. Which she never will.

He sits down and drinks his milk out of a crystal glass, and sinks his teeth into a bun, chews. She stays standing, immobile.

'Christmas is a good time for a baby,' he says. 'One more, eh? We'll need a new nurse.'

⚜

480

She doesn't tell Acton whose child it is, and he doesn't ask. The child will be a Bourbon, and he knows that full well. He hands her a pillow for her back, halfway through a sentence about the price of whale oil, and it makes her smile.

Every morning, he sits in Charlotte's study and looks down at the paperwork in his lap, and she looks out of the window, and thinks this is an end to it, that she's exorcised whatever demon drove her to his arms. Then she turns, and sees him, and they lock the doors of her study.

Meanwhile, the fog prevents trade, and the cupboards of Naples are running bare. The looms at San Leucio sit idle for lack of anywhere to sell silk, while Caterina has the girls enchant more bags of beans and flour. Ferdinand comes to Charlotte and Acton one day and complains to them both that the palace cooks are running out of spices.

Angelica Kauffman complains that her paints are expensive, that no one wants to pay for her work. People write from France, from Austria, from Germany and Spain, that the fog is dissipating there. Even Rome is brighter than Naples. Kauffman wants to go north.

'Things will change,' Charlotte says, trying to keep her tone light. 'If it is dissipating there, it will dissipate here. I swear it seems brighter lately. The sea will open up and everything will be as it was.'

'I am sure that is so,' Kauffman says. 'In the meantime, I am starving for light.'

28 August 1784
Isaac Lars Silfversparre to Maria Carolina

Your Majesty,

I have appended a list of all the people I suspect of being magisters here in Bari. It being a port city, the list is liable to change by tomorrow.

My conclusion is that Caramanico's suggestion of establishing a Reconditus and a chapter of the Order here is a

good one. The first five names on the list are those I would suggest recruiting into the Order; the rest, I can dissuade from practising magic, once I have Her Majesty's permission.

Before we take any action, though, there is another matter. The sixth name, I would draw your attention to. This woman is a back-alley purveyor of curses and charms, but she has some real spells in her book, and she sells them, for a price. She makes half her money, it seems, from blackmail, and to that end, she keeps a book with the names of her clients, and the spells they have bought from her.

Her book includes the name of the Prince of Caramanico, and records that soon after his return to Italy, he bought a spell from her to enchant a piece of wood or metal to produce the symptoms of infection. This spell is not in the Reconditus; if the prince has it, he has not shared it, which in itself is a violation of our rules. I note, as well, the coincidence of the illness that afflicts Angelo Soliman.

I am aware, though, that this woman's grubby little book may be falsified.

I will carry on here, amending my list, until I hear from Your Majesty.

> *Yours in fraternity,*
> *Isaac Lars Silfversparre*

Charlotte holds Silfversparre's letter in her hand, while Caramanico stands in her study. She has not asked him to sit. She has not spoken; the ways in which their friendship will decay hang in the air, waiting.

'You bought a spell from a rogue witch in Bari,' she says. It is not a question; if it were a question, he might falsely deny it, counting on a lack of hard evidence. 'A spell for an enchanted splinter.'

But the prince is not craven. He is a man of silk and marble, and completely sure of himself.

'Soliman is close to finding the spell of spells, or so he

says. What would that mean, if he could invent any spell he liked? He'd be the most powerful man in the world. Could he undo all our magic with it? Clear our memories with a snap of his fingers? Remove magic from the world, and hoard it all for himself? Why would any man give up that kind of power? We can't assume that when he finds this spell of spells, he will share that knowledge with us.'

'Of course he would,' Charlotte snaps. 'He is a member of our Order.'

Caramanico does not contradict her, or not exactly. 'In my travels, I have found that men of ambition frequently keep what they know to themselves, or use it to trade for power – inside the Order and outside it. And I should think a spell of as much power as this – if it indeed exists – would tempt any man to personal ambition. It would tempt me.'

'Would it.' She breathes once, in and out, her taut belly pushing against her *robe volante*. 'You have attempted to murder a Brother of the Order, and my friend. Tell me why I should not have you arrested.'

'Your Majesty!' He's shocked, at last. 'The enchantment only produces symptoms. It will not kill him. I have had all assurances. The intent was not to harm him, but merely to keep him here, where we could aid him in his work while also ensuring that work was not completed in secret, and perhaps provided to the ruler of a rival nation. Angelo Soliman is a friend to Your Majesty, but is he not an even closer friend to the Holy Roman Emperor? I could not know where his loyalties lay, so I kept him here. That's all. I have been helping him. And he is here, where I *can* help him, and not in Vienna.'

She could strip him of his title. Throw him into a cell. Throttle him with his cravat. He has been useful to her; but he has been greedy. Perhaps it's time to be rid of him. He's made himself a liability.

'The spell must not have had a love sacrifice,' she says. 'You have no love left in you, do you?'

His face drops, slackens. 'I have always clung to the belief, Your Majesty, that the sacrifices are all, to some degree, renewable. That love is a thing we may learn again, after we've lost it.'

And like a candle going out, her anger is gone. She has every right to feel nothing but contempt for him, but she understands him. Perhaps he does still have his uses after all. He has been a good ambassador. He slinks like a cat into every salon and palace. But she needs to get him away from Soliman.

'I shall send you back to France, this time as ambassador,' she says abruptly. His face registers shock again; he has a strange capacity for it, or perhaps it is only that he has so seldom been told what to do. His last jaunt to France with Lunardi was entirely on their own initiative, to talk to balloonists and men of science, or so the two men said. 'You can do the double duty of being my liaison to the Brothers of Paris.'

And while he spies on them, Charlotte has others on her payroll in France who will spy on Caramanico.

'Very well,' he says after a moment, as though he had any choice in the matter.

'But before you go, you will reverse the spell on Dr Soliman.'

He stammers: 'But there is no way to reverse it. Anyway,' – he rushes on, seeing her expression – 'anyway, there is no need! The spell does not cause death, and it will wear off before the year is out.'

'Whose assurances do we have for that? Those of the bead-curtain sorceress who took your money?'

'You have my assurances, Your Majesty.'

She stamps her foot to tell the usher to open the door. 'Go to France. Get out of Naples. Do not return until I send for you.'

She called Dr Soliman her friend, and she means it. Her oldest friend, come to think of it. How many others can she

count in that number? She still trusts Silfversparre, as much as she trusts anyone. Acton, of course, but that's different. She has no allies, nowhere to turn for help.

Meanwhile, the fog seems thicker than it has ever been, as though it feeds on itself. She thought that it would dissipate over time, as it has in the rest of Europe. But here, where Vesuvius continues to smoke, there's no end to it.

Charlotte thinks back to the day Mama told her *it is Naples for you*. That moment of knowing that she'd lost, how terrible it was. But she accepted the defeat and turned it into a victory. She humbled herself so that she could triumph. She can do the same again.

The rogues of Paris have a spell that counteracts magic. Charlotte needs such a spell, now, to save her kingdom. To triumph over this fog, she is prepared to humble herself. A magister-queen is prepared to make sacrifices.

CHAPTER FORTY-FIVE

The New Ambassador Brings a Gift – A Cacophony
of Portraits – Charlotte Needs a Favour

The Prince of Caramanico is presented in the Hall of Mirrors, as the new ambassador from Naples. He catches Antoinette's eye, and she catches his, and they both know full well what the other is about. Louis is not the sort to give ambassadors the run of the place anyway; the prince may hang about the card tables and the theatre, and come to Mass and gossip, but then anyone can do that, and half the time Mass is conducted under the eyes of the Cardinal who is head of the Order in Paris. She does not fear Caramanico.

She is more unsettled by the gift that comes with him: a portrait of the Queen of Naples for her sister, the Queen of France. They roll it into the Hall of Mirrors and everyone turns to look politely, while Antoinette's smile ossifies.

D'Éon has been sending portraits all over Europe – and indeed the world – setting up galleries full of rogue magisters, all staring at each other, in private houses and in the dustiest rooms of royal collections. It's a way for anyone owning such a gallery to address several rogues all over the world, all at once, though the resulting cacophony in their minds has led them to establish strict rules of use. Antoinette has a room

487

with the portraits of d'Éon, Fersen and a half-dozen others, and she presents a report there once a week.

A portrait of Charlotte cannot be a mere portrait. It must be enchanted.

What can Charlotte mean by it? Retribution for Antoinette's listening-portrait, or acceptance of it?

Antoinette watches the men undrape it. She prepares herself for magic, for a fright.

Instead her face betrays her in a way she could not have foreseen. She laughs in delight, and covers her mouth.

She has never seen a portrait of her sister like this. All the portraits of Queen Maria Carolina of Naples have been terrifying: a woman pinned to the background by enormous panniers and stiff corsets, hair powdered to a dark silver, an expression of ugly fury.

But this painting shows another woman altogether. This is Charlotte as Antoinette knows her. The colours are warm. She's sitting, relaxed, wearing a classical robe of white and gold, and her hair is golden too, loosely bundled and braided with pearls and lace, with a ringlet falling to her shoulders. She's almost *smiling*. She looks as if she's in conversation with a friend. Does she have any friends?

Antoinette turns to the new Neapolitan ambassador. 'Who is the painter?'

The prince smiles. 'Angelica Kauffman, Your Majesty. This is a copy. Her Majesty the Queen is a great patron of her work.'

'I can imagine,' Antoinette breathes. 'All right, let's have it in my private rooms.'

She tells them to hang it in one of her dressing rooms. She removes the firescreen so that the workmen can find the room, and replaces it after they have gone. Charlotte will hear nothing there, can spy on no one.

But she can't sleep, that night, wondering. Charlotte must know she has the painting by now, or will have it soon. But she hears nothing in her mind. What's the point, if Charlotte isn't going to use Antoinette's portrait to begin a conversation?

She huffs, annoyed, and throws the covers off. Throws her silk mantua on, and slips through the panel door into the passage, walks in her stockinged feet to the painting.

For a long time, she stares at it.

'So, sister,' she whispers. 'It is not enough for you to poison the world against me. You have decided to spy on me as well. But you might have chosen another method. I know about this one, you see.'

Antoinette does not really expect Charlotte to answer. She only half expects Charlotte to hear. Even if this painting is enchanted – as it must be – there is no reason to think Charlotte is even awake at this hour, much less standing in front of the painting's counterpart in Naples.

All the same, it does not really surprise her when she hears Charlotte's voice, though it brings a surprising little half-sob to her throat.

I didn't send it to spy on you. I sent it so that we could talk.

Antoinette stumbles backward. She hasn't heard Charlotte's voice in so long. Only the occasional rustling of rats or servants told Antoinette that Charlotte had not ordered the painting destroyed altogether.

Charlotte can hear her, just as Antoinette can hear Charlotte. They can speak to each other. Speak to each other, at last! Tears rise to her eyes, and she's grateful Charlotte can't see her.

Are you there?

'Yes,' she says; then more bitterly: 'Yes. I am here. I am here, despite your patronage of libellous pamphlets against me. Despite your Order's attack on my son.'

Your son? Is he hurt?

'If you cared about my family's safety or mine, you would stop these attacks. You choose your Order over me at every turn. What did I ever do to you to earn such hatred?'

Her voice betrays her and she puts her hand over her mouth, clamping down on the sobs.

I don't hate you. I spoke in anger, and I have regretted it every

489

day since, but you know it takes me time to swallow my pride. God, Antoinette, think! You've been working against me for years! You spied on me and used that knowledge to attack another nation. You covered my kingdom in fog!

'That flour was destined for France. To be used against me. My friends acted to protect the country, and to protect me. I had no idea how they'd destroy the flour, and none of us had any idea the fog would result. Not everything is about you, Charlotte.'

Of course it isn't about me. It's about whether we use magic to better the lot of humanity or to fuel its worst impulses. You've been using magic to get what you want, doling it out like a favour to your friends, letting the people glimpse what they cannot have, undermining the very foundations of governments, and then you pretend you've been wronged when there are consequences.

'I have not undermined the foundations of government. I have tried, over and over, to be a good queen. And because of these horrible, enchanted pamphlets, my people despise me, Charlotte!'

Not everything is about you, Antoinette! We're queens now, have you forgotten? For once in your life, stop caring whether everyone loves you.

The expression on the painting no longer seems friendly; it seems patronizing, arrogant. Her sister as she is.

'I know you do not love me,' Antoinette says, as calmly as she can. 'I don't even ask you to stop amusing yourself at my expense. Keep spreading your hatred of me as much as you like. I know full well there's nothing I can do to stop you. You have been undermining my reputation in any way you can for years.'

It was that or let them kill you, Antoinette! You're disobeying every law – how dare you? How dare you tell me that I do not love my own sister?

Antoinette puts her hands to her hot face and kneels on the ground, her silk robe falling around her, the muslin chemise doing nothing to keep the cold of the floor from

490

her knees. It was a mistake, coming here. She should burn it.

Charlotte stands in front of the portrait, holding one hand out, palm first, as though she's trying to calm a horse. Antoinette is teaching people magic, spreading spells among the women of Versailles as though they were the latest fashions, supporting the most dangerous rogue magisters in Paris. So it is utterly fair and reasonable, more than reasonable, for the Order to keep attacking that reputation. It is the only real power Antoinette has.

It is utterly fair.

And Charlotte will not, cannot defend it.

'Are you there?' she asks.

Silence.

'Antoinette, I didn't send the painting so we could argue. I sent – I – So much has happened, these last years. My children – I miss you. I need your help.'

Silence.

'I hear the fog has thinned in France, that it's hardly noticeable now. I wish I could say the same for Naples. It is killing us, Antoine. My people are hungry, and there is war in the streets, war without armies, without goals, without even sides. I . . . I don't ask this for me. No, that's a lie. Of course it's for me. But I ask also for my people, because I owe it to them to spare no effort that can help. And I believe you can help. I believe you know how a magister dispelled magic in the Palais-Royal. If I could perform that enchantment, I could rid my kingdom of the fog. Undo this horrible thing we've done, and let Naples breathe free again.'

She waits, but there is nothing. No, wait: she cocks her ear. Breathing. Is someone breathing?

'Antoinette?'

Silence.

'Antoinette!' she hisses. 'Sister, for God's sake, take pity on me. I'm at my wits' end.'

491

Silence.

She walks out of the little room, locks the door with a golden key, and strides down the hallway, wiping her eyes.

CHAPTER FORTY-SIX

This Damnable Fog — Sarabande — Hope —
An Excursion with Hamilton — A Flight of
Starlings — Namesakes

Ships founder. Merchants cannot trade. Market stalls that once sold squid and swordfish now sell eels and oysters for three times their former price. For two long weeks, there is no coffee to be had in Naples, and Acton gets a new line between his brows. The fog is no thinner, and the effects have now started to seem normal. Naples is not the shining city Charlotte saw in her mind. It's impoverished and sick.

And then at last, one morning, a messenger brings a plain letter, sealed with an old French coin. It's encrypted, all but the first two lines, which are plain French in Antoinette's hand.

The keyword is a monthly visitor.

It takes her only a minute to think of *General*, and lo, it works. The word the Habsburg girls used for menstruation. It's been so long since Charlotte and Antoinette exchanged encrypted letters – they send each other trivial, unencrypted niceties every month, to prevent rumours – that either Antoinette forgot they had been using Émilie du Châtelet's *Institutions de physique*, word by word, or she thought Charlotte would have forgotten. They had been on page eighteen.

Charlotte grabs her pen, dips it into the inkwell and sets to work decrypting the letter. There is no personal note from Antoinette. No acknowledgement, no rapprochement, no word of affection or even of anger. Just the spell 'for wine to sing away one enchantment'.

The enchantment is simple enough; the only trouble with it is the amount of hope it requires. Charlotte cannot muster enough. She puts a cask of wine in the middle of the star (wine, at least, is cheap these days; it is half the reason for the constant brawls in the streets). She arranges the other sacrifices in the points of the star: one of her own baby teeth; the memory of the thimble spell; and her enchanted copy of *Candide*, valuable as a treasure sacrifice because of the sacrifices she made for it, years ago. There is hardly any requirement for love; she writes the names of three of the children's pets of whom she's fond. None of that is too painful, in the grand scheme. She's sure they're enough.

But the hope sacrifice is beyond her. She tries, first, her wish that Teresa's marriage will be a happy one. The sacrifices remain. She adds her aspirations for all her children; for Francesco to rule a peaceable and prosperous kingdom well. She adds her desperate need for her boys to live. She adds her dreams of love with Acton and even, at the end, her hope that the fog will dispel. And then, at last, she writes one more note for the pile: her hope that she and Antoinette will reconcile.

Empty, she looks at the pile of wishes, and says the words. But the sacrifices do not disappear. The truth is that she can't bring herself to hope for anything while her kingdom is broken. Her dreams for a new era of enlightened magic seem farther away than they've ever been, and Antoinette is utterly lost to her. How can she hope when she can't believe any good things will ever happen again?

She gathers the bits of paper to her like a mother hen gathering chicks, before she burns them all.

Charlotte does not have enough hope in her to save her country.

The next day, she is woken before dawn, by Caterina. She tells her Soliman has a fever. He's raving.

She calls for a doctor.

'You, Angelo Soliman, once single-handedly saved a man from six attackers on the battlefield,' she whispers, sitting at his bedside. 'You have a wife and a daughter. You are the Grandmaster of the Masons of Vienna and the Senior Brother of the Vienna Chapter of the Order of 1326. I once watched you explain the mathematical problems of the Seven Bridges of Königsberg and make a room full of counts and duchesses actually care about what you were saying. You cannot be killed by a splinter.'

'Yes, Your Majesty.' He smiles wanly. Then his smile drops and he looks at the wall.

But another day passes, and Soliman does a very good impression of a dying man. His face is grey, and he slips in and out of lucidity. The doctor tells her he expects he will be dead within a day.

She will kill Caramanico herself, she vows. Angelo Soliman, whose belief in a better world has sustained her when she could not count on her own, this scholar who was so certain that he could find the answer to everything, to magic, to the nature of reality, that if one simply worked hard enough, if one simply cared beyond one's own life just a little, the world would be better. How she has failed him! And yet, even after all these years, he has never lost hope.

And as he lies on his deathbed, she decides that she will, at the end, take it from him. That she owes her kingdom everything now, more than she has to give.

She steels herself, and chooses one of his sharper moments.

She tells him that she knows of a spell that will drive the fog away, but it requires a hope sacrifice greater than she can give. Whatever gods or monsters pass judgement on the

495

scraps of paper that magisters leave in their stars, they have decided that Charlotte's are insufficient.

'Dr Soliman,' she says. 'You have such hope. And no reason for it! It's baffling. Everything you've seen. And yet you still believe the world can be better.'

He turns his face to her, breathing roughly, making her say it. He won't help her do this.

'It would be a shame for that hope to die with you,' she says, ashamed. 'Wasted. When it could save the lives of so many.'

He turns away from her, and says nothing for many minutes. She thinks that's it, that he's refused, or that his mind is too far gone. But at last he croaks: 'Bring me the ash, and the small trunk I travel with.'

He sits on the edge of the bed, barely upright, while she draws the star. He writes the love, memory, and hope sacrifices in a shaking hand and folds the papers over, so she won't see them when she places them in the points. A vial of his blood; a small pinkish seashell, which she does not ask about.

He rasps the words and the sacrifices disappear. The wine in the middle is enchanted, ready for a singer.

She turns back and sees him: his face without hope is another man's face. Or perhaps, she consoles herself, that is the mark of death upon him.

But, as it turns out, she was right: Angelo Soliman cannot be felled by a mere splinter. And that damned villain Caramanico was right, and his back-alley sorceress too. The enchantment passes, and the fever breaks. Angelo Soliman does not die. Within a day, he's sitting up to eat, and within a week, he's walking. She didn't take the hope from a dying man, but from a living one.

If a singer can leach the magic from a room, how many singers would it take to leach the magic from the sky? Charlotte has no way to know, but she does have cages full of starlings.

She also has no way to know whether chirping counts as singing for these purposes. Despite Soliman's instruments and note-taking, magic is not a science; or if it is, it is a science so difficult to measure that one might as well try to count grains of sand.

So Charlotte takes no chances. She wants the starlings to sing.

Acton is away in Sicily, comforting the viceroy there, who's been tasked with wresting some of the nobility's control away from their old lands and reforming taxation.

She brings a starling back in a gilded cage to the room where Teresa practises her harpsichord, and tells the footmen she is not to be disturbed.

Charlotte is no singer; music was always Antoinette's gift. So she plays Handel's Sarabande from the Suite in D minor, the one Josepha used to play. Over and over, until the starling joins her.

She brings them in, in cages, in batches of a dozen at a time. After a month, she's taught all 334 of the surviving starlings.

Enchanted wine in their water dishes, a few drops each.

Acton comes to her in her study. How she has missed those arms, that face. She lays her head against his chest and breathes, for the first time in weeks.

He takes her face in his hands and kisses her. Then he looks at her, up and down. Kisses her again, his hand on her swollen belly.

'How is the fog now?'

He sighs. 'No better, I'm afraid.'

She clucks. 'You had a safe passage, though. Thank God.'

'Safe, albeit slow and gloomy.'

'And my viceroy in Sicily?'

'Mmm.' He unhooks her bodice, and pulls the busk out so he can kiss between her breasts. 'He's at his wits' end. So much land has reverted to the Crown through the new

inheritance laws, and that is all to the good. But the old families see no reason to police what they no longer own. He needs more men to keep the peace.'

'I have given him more men.'

'But the lawlessness persists.'

'It's this damnable fog,' she mutters, and though he knows nothing more of magic than anyone in the street witnessing these strange times, he does not disagree.

'I had hoped to give him a well-earned break, and replace him with Caramanico. But then you sent Caramanico to France.'

She thinks she hears a chiding tone, a patronizing weight. She wraps her bodice back around her, suddenly wishing she had a blanket or a cloak to hide her shoulders from him. 'You would prefer to determine my policies, then.'

'No!' He spreads his arms wide. 'I'm yours. I'm true to you. And as I'm true to you, I won't act the sycophant. When I disagree, I'll tell you. You would not want me to do otherwise.'

'I want you to remember your place, Prime Minister.'

'I do. My place is here. I serve Naples.'

'No, you serve me.'

'Technically, I serve your husband.'

She turns from him, hot tears in her eyes. 'If you serve him, you are no good to me or to your country.'

He laughs, putting his hand to his cheek. 'This is not my country. I was born in France to an English father. My darling—'

'I am not your darling. I am your queen. You think because you fuck me that you can disobey me?'

He takes her hands. 'If you'll trust me . . .'

'I need a prime minister more than I need a lover. Go, and be my prime minister.'

He drops her hands. 'This is what you want?'

No, it isn't what she wants. What she wants doesn't matter. But she needs Acton's body: she needs more children; she

needs him to hold her sometimes, to quiet her mind. She must remember that they are not partners, that's all. She has a cold feeling in the pit of her stomach, but she can distract herself from that.

'Come here,' she says, pulling him towards her roughly, kissing him and pulling off his jacket.

There is no need to wait for night to do secret deeds in Naples. The fog is so thick that it almost cuts Charlotte off from her guards and footmen, who walk behind her, or the porters behind them, pulling the carts. But she makes no effort to slow down for them. She keeps pace with William Hamilton, who can climb a gravel slope faster than any goat.

She asked Hamilton to accompany her for two reasons: first because no one knows these ever-shifting pathways up the volcano better than he does. Second, because he is lonely. His monkey died, and then his wife, and his face looks older lately, his pale eyes rheumier, as he stares unseeing at his pots and statues, as if gazing into some country no one else can see.

He does not question her when she says she has found a way to dispel the fog, but it will require the release of 334 starlings from the top of the volcano. He is a man who appreciates performance.

A thin column of smoke rises from the mountain, dark against the lighter wreaths of fog and the white wisps of natural cloud that flit around the summit. Charlotte wraps her silk scarf around her mouth, but it cannot block the smell of brimstone.

'This is as high as is safe for the wagons,' Hamilton says. They stand nearly at the edge of the crater, the interior of which is simply grey smoke; the smaller inner cone that used to rise from the centre, when Charlotte first arrived in Naples, was obliterated by the eruption that created the fog.

At their feet, the mountain slopes away into a sea of grey, below which her people cough and weep, argue and lie.

Charlotte gestures to the footman, who gestures to the

porters. A dozen wagons, each bearing a half-dozen tall, segmented iron birdcages, each cage bearing four or five birds. They line up the wagons on the sloping path.

Somewhere close to here, the rogue magisters would have come, under cover of night, and dumped her flour, sack by sack, into the maw.

The Queen walks along the line of cages, opening doors. Each plump starling is singing for her already, its dotted plumage puffing out at the neck, whistling and calling. A few speak the words they learned from her, in eerily human voices: *'Encore! Encore! Encore!'* with the occasional *'Voyons.'*

Hamilton claps his hands in delight.

Like 334 singers in a round with 334 beginnings, the starlings sing the first notes of the song she taught them. She and Hamilton stand for a long time, watching the birds duck and glide in and out of the fog, away from the volcano, towards clearer air.

'It worked,' she says, standing in the doorway of Soliman's room, watching him write. 'Your sacrifice. The fog is lifted, as you'd know if you ever left your desk.'

He smiles wanly. 'I went for a walk just this morning, Your Majesty. The air is lovely.'

'The foot is not sore at all, then?'

He shakes his head. 'I am in nearly perfect health. Well enough to travel. And travel I shall.'

She opens her mouth to object before she realizes he is not asking her permission. 'Home to Vienna?' she says lightly, instead. She cannot hold him here and does not wish to. She is not Caramanico. But she will miss him, and she can't forget what she took from him.

'To Barcelona first,' he says, his voice tired. 'There are some books there that I think might contain some clues. My illness has delayed my search for the spell of spells, and I can't waste any more time. It is all I will work on, for the years that remain to me.'

She swallows, and sits on the little wooden bench by his door, her *robe volante* ballooning over her growing belly. 'You are always welcome here, should you wish it. Your family as well.'

'I am not a Neapolitan, Your Majesty. Not your subject.'

'No, but you are . . .' She starts to say my friend, and then fears the look that will cross his face if she does. 'You are a Brother of the Order.'

'Am I?' He laughs shortly, bitterly. 'I hardly know what that means any more, if I ever did. Rohan has been writing to me, alarmed by what Caramanico is telling him about our work here and in Vienna. The Cardinal is convinced that magic ought to be above any law, and out of reach of the state. Magic, and magisters. He thinks he is right, and I think I am right, and we both call ourselves Brothers. But I don't know how much it matters now. We live in a new world, and the institutions and ideas of the old world are of little use to it.'

Charlotte is thinking about all the ways in which she has failed, day by day. The Inquisition is gone but the jails are full of the petty criminals the fog has bred. The girls at San Leucio keep the nation fed, when trade cannot. They have new, enchanted looms, and the silk trade flourishes. And the girls? They are cogs in Charlotte's machine, and how far that is from the perfect society she is trying to make – just that one little village, and even that eludes her.

She is thinking of the day Soliman came to Naples, and chose to turn against the rules of his Order, to trust that Charlotte could do something no one had ever done before. She is thinking about the sacrifice he made then. She is thinking about the sacrifice he made a few weeks ago, at her request.

She deflates against the wall. 'But how?' she whispers. 'How can you carry on looking for this spell that might not exist? How can you believe a world is possible that has never existed before? How can you do that, without hope?'

'The future doesn't require me to hope,' he says. 'It only requires me to work.'

The next baby is born a fortnight before Christmas: an easy delivery of a bright-eyed girl. She is born into a city with clear air, where ships come and go again, and people smile at each other in the streets. The fog has lifted at last.

When they were children, and knew that one day they would be separated, Charlotte used to promise Antoinette that she would come to her rescue if she ever needed her older sister. But it is Antoinette who has rescued her.

Charlotte sings to her baby, so softly that no one can hear. She sings her the song that dispelled the fog. She names her Maria Antonia.

CHAPTER FORTY-SEVEN

*Antoinette Does Not Buy a Diamond Necklace — Traps
and Precautions — Les Cadavres — Motherhood*

The Dauphin has always been small for his age, and prone
to head colds. Louis prefers the children to spend their time
at Fontainebleau, la Muette or, now, Saint-Cloud, because
Versailles is always full of people, and therefore full of coughs
and fevers. Saint-Cloud, with its magical protections, is
Antoinette's preference. But Antoinette likes to have the
children by her, and she likes to have Polignac, their
governess, by her too. And Antoinette is, much of the time,
required to be at Versailles. Every week, she makes decisions
about where her children might be safest, and what is possible
for them and for her.

In the months following his third birthday, Louis-Joseph
seems . . . not ill, precisely, but pale and listless. Seventeen
eighty-four turns to 1785, and then the time comes when
windows are opened, the sheets hung out in the sun, the
tapestries beaten to billow out a winter's worth of fine dust,
the fireplaces scrubbed with wet sand. The world smells of
lye and manure. The sky is cloudless; the air is fresher than
it has been in years. But her little boy has a faraway look
in his eyes, and does not play.

'They've poisoned him,' she tells Polignac, who is calm as always and says there's no reason to think the boy's condition has anything to do with the sugar house. They don't even know whether he ate any. And all of that is true, but it doesn't comfort her.

Antoinette asks Vigée Le Brun to be on the watch for any whisper about poisoning or about the royal children, but the painter hears nothing of the kind.

She has mirrors on the walls and, at Saint-Cloud, traps on the grounds. There are guards everywhere, and only trusted people in the kitchens. Food-tasters would be pointless against a slow-acting poison.

One of the spells the rogues stole from Mesmer while he was still in Vienna was a bezoar enchantment, a way to convey properties to a stone so that if it were dropped into a glass or a dish of food, it would absorb any poisons therein. But it only works once, and there is no way to know when and where to use it. Besides, it's difficult enough to convince Louis-Joseph to eat, without placing a stone in his food. And the spell stipulates that the stone may not be broken into pieces after its enchantment, to allow it to be used more than once.

But what is a stone, really? Could a grain of salt be a stone? She used to wonder which part of an object held the magic, whether an enchanted shoe would still carry her an inch above the floor if every part were replaced, like the ship of Theseus. There are so many things she still doesn't understand. Nonetheless, she has always had a knack for adapting spells.

Antoinette locks herself in the Petit Trianon for three days, pleading headache and sore legs from her pregnancy. She works on permutations of proofs, trying to calculate what sacrifices would be needed to create a dish of salt that Polignac could keep with her at all times, so she could drop a grain or two into Louis-Joseph's food. The original proof, for a single stone, is 'oeee'. She works and works, trying to find

some way to fold the magic into a new form, but she can't see a way that wouldn't require a king's ransom for the treasure sacrifice.

Antoinette has made her boy immune to magic. She cannot make him immune to violence, poison or disease – or at least, not all disease. There is something she can do about smallpox, at least.

So, she and Polignac and the physician gather around Louis-Joseph's bedside. He's three and a half years old, old enough for inoculation. And it's safest to do it now, before Antoinette's new baby comes.

The scalpel splits the skin on the inside of his upper arm, twice, and he bites his lip, his fingers curling around Antoinette's. She can't stop her sharp intake of breath as the doctor threads the sharp needle, coated in the pus of smallpox scars, through his flesh, from one hole to the other. Three times, he draws the red thread through, and there is no going back.

Louis-Joseph is perfectly well for a week. Then the fever takes him. For three nights, she holds him while he sweats and moans. Pustules appear on his arms and on his beautiful face, even his eyelids.

She lies beside him in his little bed, the curtains drawn all around it, and holds him, kissing his brow.

Children do die of inoculation. King George of England has lost two young sons to it in the last few years. She holds her boy and does not think about what she will say to Louis if his son dies.

On the fourth day, his fever breaks, and the pustules start to fade. He has come through this trial stronger. She has protected her boy as best she can.

In Lyon, a group of people called 'les Cadavres' is reported to be using ritual self-mutilation and handing out bread and salt to the people; alarmed, Louis sends troops, who kill two

young men for coming at them with knives, and there's a riot.

Meanwhile, Louis has yet another set of financial advisers, and they are urging him to take bold action. Only by spending vast amounts of money can France right itself, they say. They resurrect the moribund French East India Company, saying: Look, look at the British! Their East India Company did not content itself with trade; it owns and taxes the land, tells the people what to grow, and sells what it likes where it likes. It sells opium to China and silk to France and nobody stops it. France still has a few holdings in India, a few ships. It still has an empire, and the time has come, they whisper, to make it pay.

Fersen writes that the British East India Company has been using the loaves-and-fishes spell to grow its arsenal. British politicians are alarmed; they are fighting among themselves. Rogues have gone to support the Indian magisters and other mages in fighting back, but there is no end to the carnage.

Vigée Le Brun says there's a steady stream of clerics going in and out of Cardinal de Rohan's palace, and they're all preaching about the devilry of the new sciences, about Lucifer's sin of pride, about Adam and Eve in the garden. They warn of witches and harpies, and then the pamphlets print engravings of Antoinette as a harpy, above rude poems about her and Polignac in bed. Who would believe that the Queen of France is a witch? Only the simple, surely, and the Cardinal has never said he believes it. But are there wealthy women who dabble in black sacrifices for their entertainment? Are there women at Versailles who will indulge themselves in every way possible? Of course. Have we forgotten the 'Affair of the Poisons' a century ago, the black masses, the amulets and charms that streamed in and out of the palace? It has always been a den of degeneracy.

Antoinette is in Versailles and out of sorts, heavily pregnant, when Charles Auguste Boehmer, the crown jeweller, requests an audience.

Under Madame Campan's stern eye, Antoinette is sitting with Polignac in a small salon, and they both have needles in their hands, cushion covers in their laps. The Queen is known for her needlework, her designs emulated throughout France.

There are many reasons why it is advisable to do needlework when the jewellers come to call. It sends the message that the Queen and her ladies (even Polignac, whose indifference to gossip at court has given her a reputation for haughtiness) are working women, after all, taking care of their household and making useful things. It gives them something to occupy their hands while others bow and scrape. It keeps the fingers strong and the eyes sharp, and the mind working.

And, in the end, one has an embroidered cushion.

Boehmer looks distraught. He's brought an assistant, and when they wheel a black velvet case on a table between them, Antoinette closes her eyes and takes three breaths to stop herself from screaming at them. She has more important things to do.

'Your Majesty,' Boehmer says, bowing low. 'Thank you for seeing us.'

'It must be a difficult time to be a jeweller in Versailles. We need ships and bread, not diamonds and gold.'

'It is of diamonds I have come to—'

'Surely you have not brought the same necklace that I have refused twice already? Even Our Lord was only tempted by Satan three times. I hope this will be the last time you force me to say no.'

The assistant lifts the lid as Boehmer hangs his head. She does pity him, a bit. Madame du Barry was the original target for this gaudy thing, back when she was still the old King's mistress, and now they've got no one to sell it to. Ropes and tassels of diamonds, worth a king's ransom. Worst of all, it's ugly, despite its price.

'It isn't my style,' she says, as gently as she can. 'Anyway,

my jewel cases are rich enough. What money I have to spend, myself, goes to the Queen's Hamlet and now to my children's new home at Saint-Cloud. And I have already told the King he is not to buy it for me, and not to listen to anyone who tells him I want it. I do not want it.'

She hates to be blunt, but she must be clear.

'We thought perhaps – Madame Royale is such a beautiful girl. When she marries, she will take jewels with her. Or the Dauphin, when he takes a bride—'

'If I can give my children humility and virtue, those will be ornaments enough.'

'Of course.' The jeweller looks as if his dog has died. This piece will bankrupt him if he can't find a buyer. But these are not times for luxury. The drought of 1784 threatens a poor harvest in 1785, and bread is expensive again. Antoinette cannot afford to buy an enormous diamond necklace, and she can certainly not afford to be seen wearing it.

Antoinette turns to Madame Campan. 'Will you see Monsieur Boehmer out, please?'

The jeweller opens his mouth and closes it again, but he dutifully shuts the lid of the velvet case. He and his assistant follow Madame Campan's uncompromising figure out of the door.

Polignac sets her needlework aside and plucks a chocolate off the plate on the side table. She eats it thoughtfully, until Antoinette at last gives in and asks what's troubling her.

'The necklace would be incredibly valuable,' Polignac says. 'And yet you'd never want to wear it. Gaudy and ridiculous. Entirely unsuitable for the times.'

'You're thinking of the sacrifice for the bezoar spell to protect from poison,' Antoinette says quietly. 'It won't do, my dear. I can't afford the necklace unless I ask Louis to buy it for me, which I won't do. I can't be seen spending that kind of money on frivolous things, not now, with the treasury empty. If I acquire it for the crown jewels or for one of the children, it doesn't truly belong to me and the sacrifice won't

work. Even if I could make it work, I'd have to account for its absence at some point. A replica wouldn't go undiscovered for long. It's a risk I can't take.'

Polignac cocks her head. 'If we could have someone else buy it for you, in secret, then poor Boehmer would get his money and stop bothering you, and you would own the necklace for long enough to sacrifice it.'

Antoinette doesn't like the feel of this, like drifting out into a lake and losing sight of shore. 'I can't accept a gift like that from anyone. Even if I knew someone who would buy it.' She is thinking of Fersen, whom she would never ask for such a thing.

'Of course you can't accept it. I almost have it . . . I can feel the answer, do you know what I mean? There's a game they play in England, where they light a bowl of brandy on fire, and float raisins in it, and one has to pluck the raisins out and pop them in one's mouth still alight. It feels like that, as if the answer is between my fingers but it keeps going out before I can get it onto my tongue.'

Antoinette leans her head to her shoulder, like a duck preening its feathers, maternally. She's very pregnant, now, and the weight of her belly grounds her. She watches Polignac pull a bit of thread through her cloth. 'I don't think there is an answer. God knows I would do anything to protect my children.'

'Yes,' Polignac acknowledges. 'Kings can wear armour, but we must find our own protections. Let me think about it. Sometimes one simply has to work at a problem.' She smiles dazzlingly at Antoinette, and holds up her cushion cover. A lovely purple thistle, surrounded by green leaves and gold ribbons.

Easter Sunday, pain wakes Antoinette before dawn, the cramping across her back sending her clutching for the bedpost every few minutes. When the Duchesse de Polignac comes with Louis-Joseph and Mousseline and sees the Queen

kneeling on the bed, sees the look on Antoinette's face, she sends the children off with Madame Campan and kneels on the floor, taking Antoinette's hands in her own.

'The baby's coming,' whispers Polignac, who's had four children herself.

Antoinette drops her head in something like despair.

'I'll stay with you. It will be all right.'

'We'll have to tell everyone. Just . . . will you give me one more moment before you tell them and they all come in?'

Polignac snorts. 'I'll do more than that. We don't need them all in here. It's Easter; I'll keep it quiet until they're all at Mass, and then you won't have so many people crowding around.'

Antoinette kisses her friend's brow, leaning on her gratefully.

And Polignac, good as her word, keeps the room quiet until the little boy rips his way out into the world with a healthy cry. Polignac is the first person to hold the child. Antoinette and Louis have already spoken about the name. If it had been a girl, she would have been Charlotte. The boy is named Charles – well, Louis-Charles.

Antoinette loves him with all her heart, this squalling boy. She holds him close, clinging to the spider-thread that connects sister to sister even now, the thread they have chosen to preserve when it would have taken nothing but a thought to snip it and end it, and be enemies. She isn't quite sure how they managed it, she and Charlotte, or whether the thread itself is stronger than their wills and their regrets. She isn't quite sure what it will mean that, despite everything, they are sisters.

CHAPTER FORTY-EIGHT

*The Summit of Happiness — Polignac's Plans — The Decay
of the Imperishable — Evidence Is Offered*

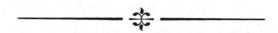

One day in July, a letter arrives for Queen Marie Antoinette
on the usual silver plate, opened, unencrypted. Madame
Campan opens all the letters that come to her through the
usual post at Versailles; the secret messages come other ways,
and they're always encrypted anyway.

This one is from Charles Auguste Boehmer, and as plain
as day. Madame Campan hands it to Antoinette with a frown.

Madame,

*We are at the summit of happiness to dare to think that
the latest arrangements which have been proposed to us, and
to which we have submitted with zeal and respect, are a
new proof of our submission and devotion to Your Majesty.
We take satisfaction in knowing that the most beautiful set
of diamonds in the world will grace the best of queens.*

B.

Good God.

She grips the letter between finger and thumb; the paper
snaps taut. They've taken some misconception into their

heads – she tries to believe that for a moment, but in her mind's eye she sees Polignac's face, her determined little smile. Polignac. A betrayal. A loving betrayal, the worst kind.

Antoinette is frozen, as though under a spell. She's lost control, somehow. She is being manipulated.

She will have to breathe eventually. She will have to speak. She will have to make it clear to everyone that this is not what she wants, or what she ever wanted. But Polignac is a magister and a friend. The letter has been read.

Her thoughts grind, her nerves sizzle, her body wakes.

'What can it mean, Campan?' Antoinette laughs lightly, holding out the letter. 'You're so good at solving the riddles published in the *Mercure de France*. Perhaps you can solve this one for me. Is he still trying to sell me the necklace? Has someone made some suggestion to him for a new course of action to win my consent?'

Campan takes the letter and reads it over again. 'It must be something of that sort, Your Majesty,' she says uncertainly.

'Well, I won't spend any more time worrying about it. They'll come when they come, and I'll send them away again. He's the crown jeweller, a position he bought dearly, as I recall, so I'll just have to put up with him.'

She holds out her hand for the letter and twists it, hard, and puts the end into the lit candle for her sealing wax. It falls in cinders, and Antoinette brushes it all away with the toe of her shoe, not even bothering to keep the ash for spells.

Polignac is at Saint-Cloud with the children; Antoinette summons her to Versailles and waits, sitting, as the usher shows her in. She's flushed with summer heat and smiling. She walks towards Antoinette, hands held out.

'I didn't know they'd send you a letter. I wanted to wait until everything was concluded before—'

'Before you told me you were acting in the Queen's name without the Queen's knowledge?'

Polignac stops, her smile dropping. 'You had to be kept out of it.'

'And yet I was not. The jeweller seems to think he has an agreement with me. Will you tell me what I've agreed to do?'

'Nothing,' says Polignac, and a ghost of a smile returns to her face. 'That's just it. May I sit?'

'No.'

She's taken aback, and the flush deepens. She speaks now, unsmiling, hotter and quicker than she probably intends. 'Your Majesty, you are not implicated. The evidence shows it quite plainly.'

'Begin at the beginning, if you can.' Antoinette holds onto her anger, to the hard fact that her duty to her people is all that she is. She feels the desire to forgive creeping up on her, like that day years ago when Charlotte used her enchanted gloves to make her forget her dance step. How humiliated, how angry she was! But it melted away like sugar on the tongue, and she wanted to reach out her hand to Charlotte, just as she wants to reach out to Polignac now.

Polignac swallows. 'Cardinal de Rohan has a new mistress. Jeanne de la Motte. Do you know her?'

Antoinette remembers the half-dressed woman in Rohan's palace. 'Yes, we've met. What does she have to do with anything?'

'She's a money-grubber, desperate for anything that will give her and her husband – oh yes, she has a husband – a place in society. That's why she's sharing Rohan's bed, of course. It's certainly not out of affection for him; she hates him more than anything. So, I managed to show her that if she had money of her own, and her own estate, she could stop opening her legs for that lout. And I showed her a way to have her revenge on him for the way he treats her.'

'Revenge.'

'She persuaded him to buy the necklace for you, to lend you the money and act as your agent so you won't be implicated.'

'Why in God's name would he do any of that? He hates me.'

'Precisely. He's doing it not as a favour to you, but because he thinks it will discredit you. He thinks that you have requested the necklace as the cost of restoring him from his disgrace. Jeanne de la Motte told him that. And he thinks, once you have the necklace, that he will be able to reveal your scheming. He's received letters from you – he thinks. It's a spell where the handwriting changes depending on who's holding the paper.'

'These forged letters appear to be from me?'

'When *Rohan* reads them, they are unquestionably from your hand. When anyone else reads them, they're plainly forgeries that Rohan should have seen through instantly. Your name is signed wrong, for heaven's sake. No one will ever believe you were involved. But he does. He thinks he's trapped you. I had to find something that would work – Rohan is immune to magic. But magic isn't immune to him. When the paper feels the touch of his hand, and his hand only, the ink actually moves into different shapes, like your ciphering spell. And he can pass that very paper to someone else and say, "Look! It's clearly from the Queen!" and everyone will see what a fool he is.'

'And he's going to pay the jewellers for the necklace? Two million livres or something close to it, on faith that I'll pay him back? It's a great chance to take, just to make me look greedy. He's really going to pay for it?'

'He already has.'

Polignac reaches into the pocket under her skirt. An enchanted one, it seems. What she pulls out is a necklace too bulky to fit into any ordinary pocket.

It's an absolute mess of diamonds. Draped over Polignac's lovely arm, it catches the morning sunlight that streams through the shutters.

Antoinette lifts it with both hands. It's lighter than it looks and, suddenly, not as gaudy as it appeared in Boehmer's

black velvet case. It doesn't even look like Madame du Barry's style. Antoinette can almost imagine how it would drape on her own décolletage, how 647 of Africa's best diamonds would capture and scatter the lights of Versailles just a little more brilliantly than even the best paste copy ever could.

'But he knows I have it!' she objects. 'If I sacrifice it—'

'Whether you sacrifice it or not, he will say you have it. He will show the letters, and look like a fool. Let them search the palace; they won't find it. It will be gone.'

Then she must sacrifice it. It drags on her hands; she can't be found with it. The people would riot if they knew she was spending the price of two ships on a necklace, when she already has so many.

She does not want to sacrifice it, now.

Which might be for the best. She needs to consider it hers, for the spell to work. She needs to treasure it.

If she says no, if she tells Polignac to return the diamonds, the jewellers may make noise about it, about the promises they've had, and the payment they expect. Returning the necklace would connect her to the jewellers more than sacrificing it would.

And sacrificing them – God, what a price – will give her a dish of salt that could save her children's lives. Her little baby, Charles, already immune to magic by her touch but not immune to the many evils of the world.

'So be it,' she says to Polignac, holding up the necklace. 'You have caught me in this net. I know you did it out of love for me and for the children.'

Or if not love, then stubbornness, which is so often the same thing, when it comes to the people we have to protect. Polignac's hard heart works a love of a different kind than Lamballe's, but it is loyal, and Antoinette understands her.

'We should make the sacrifice right away,' Polignac says. 'I will make the sacrifice alone.'

The spell requires a moderate love sacrifice as well, and Antoinette finds that the affection she bears for Gabrielle de

Polastron, Duchesse de Polignac, is sufficient, which perhaps is fitting. It is wise to harden her heart, but she feels a tremendous absence when the paper curls into nothing and her secret room fills with an odour of must. She is wearing a rose in her hair, and its petals fall, black and brittle, to the carpet, which is growing worn and mouldy.

Three of the points of the star are empty; the pile of dust that was the name of her friend in the fourth, and in the fifth, a necklace. A strand across the top, at the neck, although it has never touched her neck. Loops below it. At the sides, triple strands of diamonds. Two more triple strands cross at the bosom. All of it clear as ice and as hard as duty, seemingly indestructible.

But she has given it, and the force of decay is greedy. She kneels and watches the diamonds die.

The stones cloud over, as though covered in a film of grey dust, for what seems like a long time but is only a few breaths. And then, as though one of those breaths has become a wind, they collapse into piles of grey powder, shimmering just a little until nothing is left but a few specks of glitter, the sparkle of the diamonds like traces on the carpet. Beautiful even in death.

The room stinks of magic.

Antoinette lets herself lie down on the floor where the diamonds once were. She reaches out one hand for the little silver salt cellar in the middle, its crystals the only things in the room that still seem pure.

Life feels unlikely, in the days following Antoinette's sacrifice. It seems impossible that an object of such value could simply vanish from the world, like waking up to a world without Notre-Dame Cathedral in it. Some things are solid, and diamonds are among them. Be that as it may, the impossible happens, with more regularity than Antoinette would have believed when she was younger, even back when she wanted magic to solve everything. She is nearly thirty years old, a

mother to three children, and she no longer requires the world to right itself, so long as she can bend some small part of it to be better, kinder, safer.

Still, she cannot lose the nightmare feeling, as if the world is decaying around her. The corridors of Versailles smell of mildew and sweat, though the salons are as glittering as ever. In Paris, the graveyards are overflowing and collapsing, and carts are taking bones into the tunnels beneath the city, turning them into ossuaries. A rearrangement of skeletons, a *danse macabre* with thousands of dancers.

Any day now, Rohan will make his move. He bought the necklace, he knows it's been delivered. He thinks he has her, and so he will pounce. That is the price she will pay. But how will he pounce? He will try to use the necklace to sway public opinion – that has always been her battleground. So that means he will use Jacques-Pierre Brissot, the man with the enchanted pen.

And Brissot happens to be living with Philippe at the Palais-Royal now. Where Philippe says he can keep an eye on him. As he was instructed to do. The Palais-Royal is no longer a rabble of brothels and shops, or no longer only that. Its cafés are more popular and influential than any salon, or so Vigée Le Brun reports.

Antoinette writes to Philippe, asking him to alert her immediately if any new rumours go out, if Brissot writes a new pamphlet. Polignac is ready to make sure the evidence of the Cardinal's gullibility gets into other pamphleteers' hands.

Philippe, insolent as always, does not reply to her letter. Fine. Let him be rude to her, so long as he does as she asks. She tells Polignac – who is eager to smooth over her relationship with the Queen – to keep an eye on the Palais-Royal.

But the blow does not fall how or where they expect. Rohan doesn't tell the public. He waits for the jewellers to tell Versailles.

Boehmer asks to see the Queen one day in August and

Antoinette, nervous, refuses. She says that she has already told the jeweller she will not be making any purchases, and that's true enough.

But then why is he coming to her? She mentions it to Madame Campan, lightly, making sure there are witnesses to her ignorance of the whole affair.

And then Madame Campan, wringing her hands, tells her Boehmer approached her as well, and told her that the jewellers believe they have sold the necklace to the Queen through an intermediary, but they have not been paid the agreed price of 1,600,000 livres. They delivered the necklace to that intermediary for only a small down payment, on his assurance that the Queen would repay the rest, gradually, so as not to raise suspicion.

Antoinette is shocked enough by this that she doesn't even have to pretend to be.

It makes her sick to realize that the jewellers are owed money, that Rohan took the necklace from them and gave it to Jeanne de la Motte, having no reason to think that Antoinette would ever pay for it and having every reason to believe otherwise. He's the one who made the arrangement; he's the one who owes the money. She tells herself this over and over, working the chain of justifications like a rosary, like stones on a string.

There's nothing Antoinette can do but let the court deal with it. Madame Campan, not wanting to bother the Queen with the jeweller's strange complaint, reports the affair to the minister of the royal household. It all has to be done quite properly.

And so it is that the King hears of it, and summons Cardinal de Rohan, and the Cardinal appears, ostensibly surprised on his way to Mass, sweeping in in his red robes.

Antoinette sits, stiffly, on a chair next to her husband.

'Your Majesty,' Rohan says, bowing to the King.

'What is all this about a necklace? The court jewellers are distraught.' Louis seems tired, his eyelids heavy. He's been

melancholy for months; whenever he isn't meeting with his ministers, he's off hunting, or tinkering with his locks, or drinking. Antoinette can't blame him. He says the meetings with ministers are now just litanies of disasters. France spent an enormous sum on the American war, and gained very little. Once the Americans had what they wanted, they made a separate peace with Britain, and so nothing came of the Bourbon hopes of picking off parts of a humbled British Empire. Now, France is bankrupt. Louis's new minister of finance has been trying to get loans and mint coins to keep the state functioning, but it is clear that France can't survive without major new taxes on the nobles and the clergy. So Turgot's unpopular old reforms are on the table again, or something very like them.

Once upon a time, Louis XIV saved France by binding the nobles to him. Now, Louis XVI can only save France by making enemies of them. No wonder he looks as though he's about to collapse. And now he has to deal with this necklace nonsense. It never should have come to him.

'I received letters from Her Majesty,' Rohan says, and holds out a piece of paper, brazenly. 'I did as she asked of me.'

Ah, the letters. Polignac's magical ink. Has be been carrying around the letters everywhere he goes? This summons was supposed to come as a surprise to him. Polignac thinks they've trapped the Cardinal, but he doesn't look like a man who's walked into a trap. He looks like the hunter.

Louis takes the letter from him, reads. Antoinette is close enough to read it over his shoulder. It is in a handwriting similar to her own, but not so similar that anyone who knew her would mistake it. In the letter, she appears to be complaining about the price of the diamond necklace, which, the letter says, Rohan procured for her, after she promised to pay for it.

'This is signed "Marie Antoinette de France",' she says, handing it back accusingly. 'That is not how I sign a letter. That is not how any member of any royal family signs a

letter. A person with the slightest familiarity with court would know that. You could have put some effort into this trick, Cardinal.'

She expects him to look confused, or at least surprised. The letter he has read is not signed that way, thanks to Polignac's enchantment. But he doesn't look surprised. He looks at her very calmly for a split second, and then he adopts a pained expression, like a man who's been fooled.

'I had no reason to suspect a trick,' he says. 'Especially not after the Queen herself met me in secret in the gardens, gave me a rose and told me she would put away her old disdain for me, if only I would buy the necklace on her behalf and manage the payments discreetly.'

'It's a lie,' she cries. 'Of course I never did such a thing. The King offered to buy the necklace for me, and I turned it down. I refused it three times. Why in God's name would I then go and buy it in secret? What good is a necklace that one can't wear?'

'It does seem preposterous,' Louis says, dear loyal Louis. She feels overwhelmed, for a moment, by gratitude for all that she has: for her husband and children; for Fersen; for Lamballe and for Polignac; for her brothers and sisters; even and especially for Charlotte, who understands, at least. Charlotte who has made her choices, and cast in her lot with the Order. Perhaps once she'd chosen to work with Soliman, a decent man and a scholar, it did not seem so impossible to work with men like Rohan and Caramanico.

Or the alchemist Cagliostro, who's now staying with Rohan. Just as Antoinette has an alliance of magisters around her who can spy and scheme, so does Rohan. He still has access to a book of spells greater than any rogue's. To the resources of the Order. Polignac has underestimated him.

Somehow, Rohan knows more than he should about Polignac's trap.

She can barely hear Rohan's snide whine; she catches up as he's saying, '. . . the person known as Jeanne de la Motte,

who has disappeared along with the necklace. That is, unless the Queen has it?'

Louis frowns and looks at Antoinette.

'I do not have the necklace,' she says, as firmly as she can. It's the truth, but it is also not the truth. She needs to direct the conversation in another direction. 'Cardinal, isn't it true that Count Cagliostro, that notorious swindler, has been staying with you?'

The Cardinal straightens up. 'The count is a noted alchemist and healer, Sire.'

'Mmm,' says Louis, who has heard the stories of Cagliostro bilking money out of wealthy widows, the schemes he has pulled across Europe.

'It's an evident conspiracy,' says Antoinette.

'I tend to agree,' says the King, pink in the face. 'But as I have an interest in the matter, let's see what the Parlement has to say about it. In the meantime,' he says, addressing the captain of his guard, 'take Cardinal de Rohan into custody, and find this Cagliostro too and get him behind bars.'

The Cardinal seems genuinely shocked to be taken by the arms and led away, and that's some small consolation. A trial before the Parlement. Months and months of testimony. But what is to be done about it?

She never wants to see Polignac's beautiful face again. How can Antoinette keep herself safe from her enemies when her friends are more dangerous?

After Rohan has been taken away and they are left alone with only the footmen at the door, Louis mutters, 'You can't testify, Antoinette. That's one thing we must avoid.'

'You surely can't believe that a man as shrewd as Rohan was tricked by an actress and a forgery. He's known me all his life. He's playing some game.'

'Well, he can't be as shrewd as you think, my darling wife. He seems to have been taken in by Cagliostro, after all.'

'No,' she says firmly. 'I don't believe he's been fooled by anyone.'

CHAPTER FORTY-NINE

The Cardinal on Trial – A Prison Break –
Decay in the Heart of Versailles – A Separate Peace –
New Societies

Antoinette paces by a second-floor window. Vigée Le Brun is late; the lamps are lit out in the courtyard, shining on the stones. Perhaps there was some disturbance after they pronounced Rohan guilty, some rough justice. Perhaps she isn't coming.

Louis forbade Antoinette to appear at the trial, even to be in the room. The King is synonymous with the state, he said; put the King on trial and the next step is anarchy.

Unspoken in his philosophy, but unquestioned in it, is that as his wife, *she* is indistinguishable from *him*, that she is part of his person. So she must not be involved in a trial at the Parlement. She has had to make do with the reports of Vigée Le Brun about the trial, and Lamballe's about court gossip. And Fersen writes worried letters from Sweden, promising to return soon.

At last, the usher opens the door and Vigée Le Brun strides in, her face serious. She curtseys, and Antoinette takes both her hands.

'No verdict yet, Your Majesty.'

Antoinette slumps in spirit, never in body. 'I thought it would be today.'

'So did we all. But the actress's testimony went on and on. She kept stopping to cry.'

The actress.

This whole affair should have come to nothing, or almost nothing. Rohan's letters are clear forgeries. But then a low-born actress who looks astonishingly like the Queen confessed to having impersonated Her Majesty in the gardens of Versailles, one summer night. Jeanne de la Motte hired her, she testified, and even provided her with a script to read, to persuade the Cardinal that the Queen wanted the necklace but did not want to be the one haggling over the arrangements.

The actress says the Cardinal seemed quite convinced by her performance.

'An actress indeed,' spits Antoinette.

The painter shrugs. 'Perhaps. But if it was all pretence, it was the best performance France has seen since Molière was a boy. I think she believes it, whether it happened or not. Perhaps she's been duped herself somehow. Her story helps to pin the blame on Jeanne de la Motte and make Rohan look innocent. But it doesn't help you.'

'I'm not the one on trial,' murmurs Antoinette.

Vigée Le Brun's expression is hard and cynical. 'This weeping actress has told the world a story about a too-trusting priest who was fooled because he believed it highly likely that the greedy, acquisitive Queen would meet a man in a garden by night, to make some shadowy arrangement to enrich herself. The same Queen who recently insisted on buying the Saint-Cloud estate from the Orléans family, despite the fact that she does not want for houses. This is how they will see it. They don't care that you weren't involved, Your Majesty. They only care that you could have been. That it was plausible. You are a character in a story to them – you always have been. An image in a painting. Now that story is about furtive, corrupt dealings. Lecherous clergymen in

gardens; diamond necklaces that cost enough to feed all the starving. Stories don't need to be true, or even coherent, to explode like gunpowder. That is how gossip works.'

'Oh, how I wish I could speak for myself,' says Antoinette. 'How I wish Polignac had never guided me into this trap.'

Vigée Le Brun's cynicism is warranted. There are new mutterings against the Queen. The *libellistes* write pornographic pamphlets about *les bijoux de la reine*. The details don't matter; all anyone remembers is that Marie Antoinette was involved in some sort of shady deal involving diamonds, and clandestine meetings, and a trial at the Parlement.

'*L'etat, c'est moi,*' said the Sun King. If the King and Queen are the state, then in some fashion the state has just gone on trial, all over a great deal of nothing.

The Parlement believes that Rohan was duped. He and Cagliostro are acquitted.

Jeanne de la Motte is convicted. On hearing the sentence, she picks up a china cup on the desk of her jailer and cracks it against her face. She is stripped naked and beaten with rods, leashed to a halter, flogged and branded with the letter V for theft, a crime she did not commit, and put into the prostitutes' prison, Salpetrière.

But Antoinette knows full well that Jeanne de la Motte, while not precisely innocent, was not the architect of this whole affair. Rohan is a magister; he knows how to make sacrifices for what he wants. He has been scheming for years to discredit Antoinette and he finally found a way to do it. A trap within a trap.

She begins talking to Louis about finding a new governess for the children, says Polignac is too grasping, too ambitious, all of which is true.

And she asks her husband to release Jeanne de la Motte, but he refuses her, saying he must overrule her soft heart. How can he release the woman? Half the country already thinks that the royal family was somehow involved in the

conspiracy. After all, where are the diamonds? Everyone knows how much the Queen loves beautiful things. How dazzling she is.

The Queen cannot visit Jeanne de la Motte.

But the Princesse de Lamballe can, bearing a few drops of oil that reshape stone. And when she hears that Jeanne de la Motte has escaped from prison and fled to England, Antoinette pretends to be surprised.

> *Francesco d'Aquino,*
> *the Prince of Caramanico,*
> *to Count Alessandro Cagliostro*
> *15 September 1785*

My Brother,

I greet you and I send my sympathies for your recent treatment. As I promised you, the actress's testimony served to free you as well as the Cardinal. I hope this reassures you as to the intentions of Philippe d'Orléans. The old allegiances don't matter; we are bonded now by common purpose. He wants what you and I want, what all men of courage want: a world in which magisters are not subject to the whims of kings and especially of queens. A world in which the true masters are the magisters, and a man of talent can lead, not follow.

I believe deep in my soul that this was the original intention of the formation of the Order, but now that Order has been corrupted by mundane power. It is only through working with like-minded magisters, no matter what pathways may have led them to magic in the first place, that we will establish a new order in the world, and take our place at the top of it.

Trust him, trust me, and give my regards to the Cardinal. The plans of our enemies betray them and serve us.

> *I am, dear count, most affectionately yours,*
> *Caramanico*

Antoinette, playing cards with Madame Campan in the evening, hears her sister's voice in her mind.

Come have a chat in an hour, if you can.

Antoinette loses the next two hands, excuses Madame Campan, says her prayers and slips into her secret room.

She notices, as she has not noticed for some time, that there is hardly any paper left on the walls other than a few blackened strips, that the plaster of the ceiling is rotting like cave stalactites, that the wooden floor is rotting into sawdust beneath the new carpet. Any given enchantment has very little discernible effect on its surroundings – except for the time she faltered in her intention in the woods, while she was trying to deter Rohan, and, like a damp squib, the forces of magic seemed to disperse oddly. But over time, there is an effect from the many spells of several magisters. Decay in the heart of Versailles.

She walks to where the portrait of Charlotte hangs behind a black cloth, as if her sister is dead. But she is not dead. It seems impossible to think of Charlotte dying, somehow. The world would stop spinning.

She stands for a few long minutes, staring at Charlotte's face, or the face of Charlotte as she was in 1783. What does Charlotte look like now, in 1785? Is she fatter? Probably, as Antoinette is herself.

'Good evening, Charlotte.'

Sister.

Antoinette speaks lightly, as though any part of this is normal. 'Your ambassador, the Prince of Caramanico, has invited me to tea. I will be on guard for poison. There are so many Italians in Paris these days.'

Don't go. He thinks he is my ambassador, but I don't trust him either. I intercepted a letter of his – that's what I want to talk to you about. It took me some time and cost me dear to decipher it, or I would have told you sooner.

She pauses. 'You spy on your own ambassador?'

I only sent Caramanico to France so I wouldn't be tempted to flense him with a letter-opener.

527

'He is a member of your Order. As is Cagliostro.'

Cagliostro! Cagliostro is a carbuncle on the Order. He is the worst of all possible worlds, a gold tassel on a cheap coat.

'A lecher and a cad.'

A boor. A shiny-faced fraud whose sins will go forever unexamined. I haven't spoken to him in years.

Antoinette nods, though of course Charlotte cannot see that. Luckily, she can't see her wipe away the tear at the corner of her right eye, either. Here they are, talking again, almost like friends.

But not allies.

'Cagliostro is free, but I am not, it seems. I will never be free. Your Order always manages to win.'

That's what I wanted to tell you. It was not the Order who helped Rohan, who set up that actress to tell that tale at the trial. It was Philippe d'Orléans.

'Philippe!' Antoinette says it too loudly, and claps her hand over her face. 'What game are you playing, Charlotte?'

No game at all. I have the evidence, in a letter from Caramanico to Cagliostro. Your Philippe certainly has no shortage of actresses at his command. There are Brothers and radical rogues making common cause against monarchy. They want to undermine the old structures so that they can rise to the top.

Antoinette leans against the wall. Fersen, when she tells him, will be livid. Could Charlotte be trying to fracture the unity of the Circle? But no, Antoinette must admit it. There is no unity left to fracture.

'Philippe has been meeting with Brothers, but I thought it was for our purposes,' Antoinette says. 'He befriended Jacques-Pierre Brissot, the man with the enchanted pen.'

I'm sorry. I was wrong about that.

Philippe has also become the patron of the Chevalier de Saint-Georges, who never seems free to come to Versailles any more.

Tell me, Antoinette, whose trap was it? Did Rohan set it?

She considers telling Charlotte about Polignac's role, about

her one-time favourite being seduced by her own cleverness and duped in the end, but she is tired of thinking about friendships and alliances, betrayals and love. She says, simply and honestly: 'We both trapped each other. But I got the worst of it.'

What becomes of a war when each side turns on itself? Not quite peace, but perhaps a détente. A realignment. Antoinette's rogues and Charlotte's Order may still disagree on how to remake the world, but now they face a bigger threat and a common enemy: the rogues – and Brothers – who want to burn the world down altogether, so they can rise from the ashes.

Antoinette takes a deep breath. Will she and Charlotte be able to work together, to trust each other, now? At the very least, they're talking. 'I thank you, sister. I'll be wary. How are the children? How is little Maria Antonia?'

Thriving. Adorable to a fault. Just like her aunty. And my name-sake?

'Charles is a healthy little bear.'

I must go. Kiss my name-child for me.

Antoinette nods again, futilely, and reaches her hand out to the face of the woman in the painting, her fingers not quite brushing the varnish.

PART SIX

1789 TO 1793

CHAPTER FIFTY

Louis Stumbles — Where Philippe Walks — Vanity —
A Man Shouts at the Queen — Emptiness

In the spring of 1789, Louis summons the Estates General, and everyone at Versailles pretends it is cause for celebration. It's been a century and a half since a French king had reason to call an assembly of the people, to be seen to ask for their counsel in a time of crisis. Unlike the Parlements, which have been resisting all of Louis's attempts at economic reform, the Estates General have no real authority. But also unlike the Parlements, which are fundamentally courts of justice filled with hereditary nobles, the Estates General represent all of the people. To call the Estates General is an act of mighty humility, a master stroke. It is dangerous, especially for a king like Louis, who actually cares what they might have to say. Antoinette prepares for the grand procession to mark the opening. She wears a gown of cloth of silver and Monsieur Léonard dresses her hair with feathers. No necklace. She accepts the mask for the powder with the ease of a dancer preparing for a performance at which she expects to be booed, possibly pelted with rotten fruit. Or worse.

A few weeks ago, Louis nearly fell to his death as he was

walking on the roofs of the palace, looking out over the gardens. He goes up there to think, when he can't get away to his locksmith's workshop. Antoinette has heard conflicting accounts of what happened: he was leaning on a ladder and it fell, something of that nature. She suspects a magister but of what tribe she can't imagine. The radicals among both the rogues and the Order might well want the King dead, but the most likely regent while the Dauphin is a child is Antoinette herself, which would not serve their purposes. Or would it? She goes over and over the logic of it in her mind, and wants to mention it to Lafayette, but Lafayette is not the sort of man who could discuss the attempted assassination of his king and not act. And action, at the moment, is dangerous. She feels as though they are all walking on a rain-slick precipice to which there is no ladder, with nothing but steep falls in all directions.

Her ladies take the powder mask and cape away, and she breathes.

'There,' says Monsieur Léonard, clapping his hands once. The original Léonard; Antoinette sees his brother less and less often at court these days.

He's showing his age and his worries, but his talents are still a marvel.

'You must not be so melancholy,' he whispers, and she recognizes it and appreciates it for what it is: not the plea of a friend but the exhortation of a theatre manager.

She thanks him, giving him her hand, and then she goes to her place beside the King. Louis smiles wanly at her. He, too, is dressed to shine, stout and determined in cloth of gold, with a sword at his waist. A procession is about being seen at a distance, being recognized for who and what they are, so that people can go home and say they saw the King, they saw the Queen.

She kisses Louis's cheek, daring more in front of courtiers than she would have in their newlywed days. She does love him. He bears everything without breaking. His fall on the

roof – halted only by the quick arm of a workman – did not shake him at all.

Out into the May sunshine they walk, through the golden gates and into the town of Versailles. The procession is there waiting for them.

Behind the King and Queen, the delegates will walk, all wearing their prescribed clothing and walking in the order of their social position. The clergy are to wear their robes – she grimaces at the red of a cardinal, but Rohan has not come. Though he was stripped of his positions and exiled from court, the clergy elected him to the Estates General anyway, and there was some talk that he might come. He hasn't.

She's relieved, but Louis is frowning, looking out over the procession. He talks quietly to his brother, and frowns deeper.

'What is it?' she whispers.

'Philippe d'Orléans is here, but not in his place among the nobility,' he growls. 'Apparently he has chosen to walk with the Third Estate. Wearing plain black and without a sword. The buffoon.'

The Third Estate. The common people. Given double the numbers of the other estates, this time, in some recognition of their much greater population, although their voice will still only count as one of three.

Of course Philippe is play-acting as a peasant, though the death of his father in 1785 made him the Duc d'Orléans and he is wealthier than ever. She should have expected it. For months, there were whispers among the rogues of something called the Ladder Club – a new alliance of renegade Brothers and ambitious rogues. Vigée Le Brun was the one who got to the bottom of it: the Ladder Club meets behind an unmarked door in the Rue de l'Échelle, so called because of the pillory that stood there not long ago. It is very close to the Palais-Royal.

Philippe does not attend meetings of the Queen's Circle any more, and he would not be welcome if he tried. He does

not come to Versailles at all. When the King convened an assembly to push forward the tax reforms, Philippe had himself elected president and turned the delegates against the King. Louis exiled some of Philippe's allies, but it hasn't stopped the growing discontent. The town of Grenoble rose up, and the King sent troops. A boy died.

Lafayette tries to keep a hand on everything, in France and abroad. When the American native leader Joseph Brant came to Paris, Lafayette met with him, and learned all about the land Brant has hidden from the British, using a combination of magister spells and his people's own traditions. Lafayette is a member of the same anti-slavery societies as Brissot, Philippe, and Saint-Georges, although he doesn't share Philippe's goal of removing monarchs and setting up magisters in their place.

And Saint-Georges? In London, he fought a sword duel with the Chevalière d'Éon – a friendly duel, to all outward eyes, and indeed they are friends. But Antoinette suspects, from d'Éon's letters, that the dispute over the course that rogue magisters ought to take is as fraught in England as it is in France.

Polignac's sojourn in England seems to have changed her. She returned carrying the best regards of the Duchess of Devonshire, who is an old friend, as well as a lingering cough and a strange new sympathy for the Order – or at least, the Order as it is in Naples. She argued that the principles of the rogues could not keep the monarchy safe against the revolutionaries – she used that word, *revolutionaries*, although no one else does, at least not within earshot of the King and Queen.

What good is magic, Polignac reasoned, if it does not support the monarchy? Beneath her words, Antoinette could almost hear her thoughts: what good is a queen who won't use magic to protect herself, her family, her nation? A government run by magic could restore France to its former strength. Fill its treasuries. This is what Charlotte has been working

for, and perhaps she's been right all along. A new era, a golden age, when magic will solve all the people's problems.

'I have used magic in whatever ways I could, to be a better queen. What do you think I have been trying to do all these years?' Antoinette asked.

Polignac, for the first time in their friendship, set her jaw and her eyes, hard as gemstones, and said, 'You have tried to make yourself unassailable, yes. As if you could remake your person into such perfection that it would induce perfection in its turn. It is a chimera – a figment, a—'

'A what?'

'A vanity.'

So it goes. But she is sorry for Louis, who is solid and does not adapt quickly. Antoinette still adores his brother, her old friend and card-playing companion the Comte d'Artois, one of the few people at Versailles who made her feel welcome when she arrived as an unready child bride. But he's made life no easier for the King lately, greeting every egalitarian proposal with aristocratic disdain, like a mirror image of Philippe d'Orléans. D'Artois is known to be Antoinette's friend – indeed, he is the lover who appears in most of the pornographic poems and cartoons about her. And Philippe, the *soi-disant* man of the people, is the one who sells pamphlets denouncing her out of his shops at the Palais-Royal.

Fine. Let Philippe walk where he will. Antoinette walks beside her husband.

The people cheer as they walk past the lined streets, hanging out of windows, even up on lampposts. She hears several shouts of '*Vive le roi*' and though no one mentions *la reine* at all, it could be worse. She allows herself to breathe a little more freely.

Somewhere in this crowd, not far, is Axel von Fersen. Gustavus sent him to France to look after Sweden's interests, or so Fersen says; she doesn't know how he managed it but she is grateful.

Fersen has always been circumspect, compared with most of the other rogue magisters of Antoinette's acquaintance. These days, he is warier than ever. The rogues of Stockholm are as extreme as the Brothers of Stockholm, he says; one of them worked with Fersen for years on an enchantment to steal the Order's great spellbook, but then carried out the plan prematurely, alone, and managed to destroy the book and himself in the process. Fersen says a Brother of Stockholm named Theodore von Graben came to him in a great rage, saying there was nothing left of the *Reconditus* in Stockholm but a burnt and blackened star on the floor.

For many reasons, Fersen says he is done with Sweden. He has taken a house in Paris and has been busily working to find rogue magisters who might be allies. Antoinette is glad to have him near, even today, when he cannot be at her side.

The children, thank God, are not part of the procession. This is largely to avoid revealing the fact that the Dauphin can no longer walk. But they are waiting on a dais along the route, waving to their parents under the watchful gaze of their guards. Ten-year-old Mousseline is holding the hand of four-year-old Charles.

Antoinette's heart cracks when she sees their brother Louis-Joseph beside them, lying on cushions, cheering and clapping though he is so thin, his little face so pained. For two years now, the Dauphin has gone from one fever to another. Tuberculosis, according to the doctors, and they say that is what is twisting his spine and causing him such pain. A seven-year-old child should not know such pain.

She contemplated the painting spell to even out his shoulders and straighten his spine. D'Éon has used the painting spell more than once, she says, and she recommended a medical doctor from Holland, a rogue magister of Fersen's acquaintance. He said that the painting spell would likely do the child no good, that the pain was coming from within, from the effects of the disease. It might help him walk again

for a little while, but not for long and not without pain, and why put the child through a gruelling procedure for that?

She is powerless, but she sends every drop of her heart's love to her child as she smiles and waves at him, Louis beside her doing the same.

And so she hardly notices that the crowd is pressing close around them and that a man is right next to her. His face is red. He looks in her eyes and screams, '*Vive le Duc d'Orléans!*'

She stumbles, almost into him, and Louis takes her arm to keep her from falling. She hears her husband shout at the guards to get the bastard away from his wife. She holds on.

Antoinette has moved the portrait of her sister into another hidden room in Versailles, one where the walls are still sound, and there is no smell of burnt silk or rotten velvet. A room not for doing spells in, but for speaking to her sister. It contains only one blue armchair, a footstool, and a table with a book on it to pass the time when Charlotte is late for their appointed conversations. (The book at the moment is *La Princesse de Clèves*, a novel by Madame de la Fayette, from another branch of the marquis's family.)

On the walls are two paintings: the familiar portrait of Charlotte, with her hair so golden . . .

. . . and one of Antoinette and her children by Élisabeth Vigée Le Brun.

The office of the royal household commissioned a portrayal of the Queen with her children, soon after the conclusion of the Diamond Necklace Affair. They had strict instructions about the clothing, the composition, and especially about the lack of any necklace on Her Majesty. The large jewellery case as a backdrop was also their idea, meant to imply that the four children are her true jewels, like Calpurnia of Rome.

Can a painting counter the pornographic poems, the cartoons showing Antoinette as a harpy with claws and tail, the vile essays that issue from the pen of Jacques-Pierre Brissot as he sits sipping coffee in Philippe's Palais-Royal?

The painting shows Mousseline, saucy girl, holding Antoinette's arm and gazing up at her mother. The Queen is upholstered in red velvet, lined with sable, and she is trying to keep a straight face. She clutches little Charles on her lap as he grabs for her breast. Louis-Joseph, unlike Mousseline, is taking the whole exercise very seriously, holding onto the bassinet and gazing at the interior with the indulgent smile of a big brother.

During the sittings, Antoinette's big pink baby Sophie was sleeping, breathing heavily, in the bassinet.

But the painting shows the bassinet empty, shadowed by a draped black cloth, for Sophie died, after a few days of terrible illness. Not a year old yet, not weaned yet, her cherub girl.

And the painting didn't hang at the Salon after all. An empty frame took its place. By the time the painting was finished, Louis's ministers were worried that any image of the Queen would only attract more ridicule, no matter how regal and matronly she may be, no matter how darling her children's faces. Just as Antoinette is the only person in the noisy tavern argument that has spread throughout Versailles who may not voice a political opinion, lest association with her kill the very thing she was trying to support.

The portrait hung in the palace, in the Salon de Mars, until Antoinette could no longer bear to have it where strangers might walk by and look at it, so she had it moved here, in the forgotten room where no one else ever comes.

She puts her hand out, touches the empty bassinet, a small ritual she performs every time. And then she hears her sister's voice.

CHAPTER FIFTY-ONE

Potemkin Villages — Grief and Loss — The Chief of Police — A Ship in the Bay of Naples — William Hamilton Takes a Mistress

When she's at Caserta, Charlotte keeps Antoinette's portrait in an alcove off her suite of library rooms. Close enough that she can reach it when she needs to.

Sometimes she sits in her sister's silent company, long before the time appointed for their talks. She has a carved walnut armchair with a red seat that gives a little when she sits in it, in a homely sort of way. She starts leafing through the embroidered book, the crack and bend of its pages as familiar as her lover's body. More, because Acton has scars he won't talk about and, for the most part, she doesn't ask.

Page after page, the old familiar spells. Countess Ertag's book is the magic of sewing baskets and dressing tables. The world is bigger; the sisters' own magic is bigger. The last time they spoke, Antoinette admitted that the spell the Russian governor Potemkin used, to create whole villages out of nothing and then tear them down again to impress the Empress Catherine on a fact-finding journey, had been a spell of her own invention. The same one used to fool British

troops, years ago, and to build the Queen's Hamlet near the Petit Trianon. The spell spread beyond her Circle, as Antoinette's tend to do. The houses were wood straight through; toys made large.

Meanwhile, the Order's magic has been dealt a massive blow. The last time Charlotte, Caterina, and Silfversparre met in the tunnels beneath the Masonic lodge, they found the *Reconditus* had disappeared. It ought not to have been possible, and yet, somehow, somewhere, a rogue magister managed it. Then the letters came in from all over Europe, from all the remaining chapters of the Order. There are no copies of the *Reconditus* anywhere; it was, after all, one book, and stealing one of its manifestations means stealing all the others.

Soliman suspects the theft was in Stockholm, where the Order is weak, and there are ties of love and family between its members and the rogues. Charlotte suspects that Fersen had something to do with it.

I'm here, sister.

Charlotte closes the book, abruptly and with a bang, as though the painting were looking over her shoulder instead of merely listening.

'It's raining here. You might hear thunder. How is it there?'

Chilly today, but no rain. I have lily of the valley everywhere in my rooms; I love May. How are you, and the children?

It is a question with weight behind it, the warm soft weight of a hand on a shoulder. She had three more babies in three years: two girls and a boy, all of them Acton's. In December, Ferdinand's father died in Spain, and Charlotte felt a different weight lift from her. Her rule in Naples is untrammelled now. They had hardly got the news when smallpox came to the nursery again. Gennaro had survived smallpox once; they thought he was immune.

Ferdinand brought Gennaro fairy-tale books and read them to him in his overly formal, nervous reading voice. He performed a puppet show at the end of the bed until Gennaro

542

gave him a weak smile. He smuggled in chocolates and other treats that sat untouched until the nurse removed them. None of it was enough to save him.

After Gennaro died, Charlotte had all the other children inoculated, and it was too much for the baby, who died at five months. She had named him Carlo, for the brother who died long before his birth, just as Charlotte herself was named for two of her dead sisters. Perhaps that is one reason she never thinks of herself as Maria Carolina, not even now, when she is thirty-six years old and has proven to the world that of all the children of the Empress with that name, it was she who laid claim to it, by surviving.

Are you there?

'Everyone's fine,' Charlotte says. 'Tell me about your family.'

Mousseline is learning to ride, and Charles looks at everything through those great big eyes, takes everything in, and then he wears himself out so that he's a wonderful sleeper. The Dauphin is still unwell. He did us proud at the procession today.

'So the Estates General have convened. And there will be more talk of taxes and trade.'

Yes. More talk.

'Are you safe?'

Of course. I'm in the Petit Trianon. There are mirrors and traps—

'And if the people rise against you?'

Quiet.

It will not come to that.

'Perhaps it's best if you and the children leave France for a while. You could come to Italy, and see me.'

The King can't leave now, you know that. It would be an abdication. And then who knows what?

'But the rest of you, you and the children—'

I will never leave the King, and I'm not sending my children away from me. They're not even as old as we were when we were packed off, and you know what that was like. My God. How little we understood of anything, then. How little I understand now.

'But it may not be safe for them there. Will you at least make a plan, to get them out if it becomes unsafe?'

Wouldn't the family help?

'Of course they will.' Charlotte bites it off. They'll help; she'll make sure of that. What is the point of being a Habsburg if you don't know every state in Europe will rise to your aid in times of direst need? That is, after all, what Mama had in mind, why she sent them away to bear the children of kings they'd never met.

Then I think we will manage.

'The family will help, but you need ways to get the children out. You will need to make plans.'

A pause.

I will make plans.

'Good.' Charlotte pauses in her turn, scratches her head, grimaces at her sister's face as though she's looking at a puzzle. They have not spoken of magisters and factions, and she considers what she might say about it. Then she hears Antoinette.

Good night, sister. I embrace you.

'Dream good dreams, Antoinette.'

The Queen of Naples sits alone on a gilt throne while her eight living children dance around her. They're wearing peacock feathers in their hair. The whole spectacle and its audience are on the deck of a ship in the Bay of Naples, so Charlotte is queasy.

She claps when the music stops and stands up, blowing a kiss to every one of her children. Teresa, her eldest, blowsy and flushed, nearly seventeen. By next year, she and Luisa will be married and gone: one to Austria and one to Tuscany, to preserve those alliances with Naples for another generation. Lucky Habsburgs – on both sides of both marriages.

Not only does she protect her children; they also protect her. Perhaps that's the way of things in all families, but for Charlotte, every child has meant more power on the Council,

more power over her husband, more power in Europe. Here, encircled by her dancing offspring, she is safe on her throne.

The circle's harmony is marred a little by two gaps, two drops in the heights of the peacock feathers. The first, caused by the deaths of Carlo and Marianna, a decade ago now, so long ago that none of the younger children remember them. But Charlotte remembers them, as do the two eldest girls, and Ferdinand – who loves his children, for all his many, many faults.

After the gap comes sober Francesco, eleven years old, who will be nothing like his father if Charlotte can help it. Then happy, lithe Little Mimi.

Then the gap that means Gennaro and Giuseppe.

And then her four merry girls, the youngest three Acton's, though Ferdinand treats them as his own. Maria Amalia, Maria Antonia, Clothilde, Enrichietta. They can't seem to keep enough distance between them in their circle, can't keep their mouths from smiling. Her darlings.

She wobbles a little. It's the ship. *Her* ship: a ship of the line. Acton turns them out now like ducklings leaving the shipyard at Castellemmare. The sails are furled and they're anchored in the Bay of Naples for the party; flags in all colours run down the rigging and an orchestra plays on the poop deck.

Flanked by two guards in her livery, Charlotte walks towards the bow. The setting sun flashes into her eyes every time the ship's mast pitches to one side or the other.

People hold out their hands to her, to take her elbow. She refuses them all. There's Acton, father of some of her children, watching her. Slightly resentful, after all these years, of the passion between them that isn't quite love. But they work well together, nonetheless. He doubtless has reports to make, some criticism of the new ship. He's never satisfied. That's why he's such an indispensable prime minister, but in this moment she doesn't have the wherewithal to know what she wants to say or do with Acton, on this beautiful

night, this night for lovers. She'll be fine – she's feeling more clear in her stomach already. She changes direction, walks towards her comrades in arms.

The last time she saw Isaac Lars Silfversparre, he was holding little Gennaro out in both his arms and spinning in the gardens at Caserta. He bows his head as he reports, and the other magisters, almost casually, gather from the far parts of the ship.

Caterina walks with the confidence of a sailor, her dark hair swept up with a rose at one side, a lace shawl around her shoulders.

William Hamilton is leaning on the gunwale, gazing at his mistress. Emma Hart arrived from England, as if by order, and Hamilton was lonely, so Charlotte says nothing about it. Still, this woman is young, and not his wife. She has not been presented to the Queen, which means the Queen does not speak to her. When Charlotte visits Hamilton, Emma is outside with her mother, or out in the carriage, or upstairs resting.

Charlotte, Hamilton, Silfversparre, and Caterina haven't had a ritual meeting of the Order in Naples since Vesuvius collapsed their tunnels; truth be told, they barely have enough of them for a chapter, most of the time, as Silfversparre is out hunting rogues in the rest of the kingdom, and Caterina is managing San Leucio.

The orchestra starts up, and it's noisy, so they can speak more freely.

'Caramanico and Lunardi have joined the Ladder Club,' Silfversparre says lowly. 'Rogue magisters and renegade Brothers. I've heard that, in Paris, they've taken to wearing red Phrygian caps.'

She snorts. 'Of all things, they've adopted the hats? Ridiculous things – always reminded me of folk stories, of gnomes and kobolds.'

She's developing an old lady's manners, abrupt and child-like, at thirty-six. But it's so loud, and the ship is rolling, and she's so tired.

Silfversparre has complained to her recently that he feels adrift. He wanted to make the Order better but instead the Order ate its own tail, and now the threats come from elsewhere. Charlotte told him that he has always been guided by decency, by honour, and that he can continue in that work whether the Order survives or not. He is still restless, though.

'We should recruit some new magisters,' Caterina says. 'Make up for our losses. My brother, Luigi de' Medici.'

Charlotte lets the frown cross her face. She's already made Luigi de' Medici her new chief of police; in his youth he was a street fighter, and now he's mellowed into a practical and solid man, with friends in all classes and ideas about lighting streets and numbering the houses. But to make him a magister?

Before she answers, William Hamilton says, 'My Emma—'

This startles Charlotte into forgetting to pretend his mistress doesn't exist. 'You want to make her a magister?'

The ambassador pauses, and looks at Silfversparre, who looks right back at him.

'She already is,' Hamilton says finally. 'She was before she came. Naples is full of rogue magisters now, and those we don't pull to our side will join the Ladder Club or some other group.'

'But the Order has always been strict about its membership,' she says. She, Charlotte, the first woman, the first monarch, to be admitted. She holds up her hand, says, 'I'll consider it. Not tonight. And, Silfversparre, don't go brushing anyone's hair over this.'

He smiles thinly. 'Your Majesty, if I tried to eliminate all the rogues in Naples now, I would never stop to eat or rest. It used to be that we would find them most in the back alleys, or the theatres. Conjurers and mountebanks and midwives.'

Or so-called alchemists, she thinks, remembering Cagliostro.

'And now?' Hamilton asks.

Silfversparre grimaces. 'Now, magic is spreading in the salons. The Ladder Club in Naples already counts among its members Luisa Sanfelice, Eleonora Pimentel, Mario Pagano, Domenico Cirillo.'

'And some of the nobility,' Caterina adds.

The nobility, and the intellectuals. Her Academy, her schools. But, of course, it was Caramanico who was her liaison with the Academy, and now he has turned his coat.

She steps away from the others for a moment, to get some air. Leans on the gunwale. Stares at the water, dark now as black glass. Men crawl on the ship's rigging to light the fairy lanterns.

Deep in the water, a shimmer of blue-green, glowing, like the reflection of some heaven much denser with stars than the one over her head. Sea creatures, tiny ones, that glow at night. She's seen them before. They shift back and forth, creating landscapes on the surface. Soliman believes there is a pattern behind everything, a grand truth, a web, a fabric. Sometimes nature seems to make his point for him.

She leans over farther, to watch the glowing creatures swim right under the ship, and then with no warning she opens her mouth and vomits over the side.

It's loud and liquid and, even over the din from the party, everyone hears. Someone is at her side, calling for a doctor, and someone else is screaming at Silfversparre, and there's a child crying somewhere. Bedlam. But her own Bedlam.

Then a strong, small hand is on her arm, and a woman is leading her away from the watching people.

'The Queen is fine, but she needs air,' she's saying.

Charlotte looks up and sees a sweet face, with red lips and limpid eyes. 'Miss Hart,' she says, recognizing Hamilton's mistress.

Emma Hart nods. 'Come with me, Your Majesty. I've been pregnant before, you know. I remember how it is.'

It's not the sort of thing the companion of the English ambassador should have admitted, even if everyone knew

she was a mail-order mistress and a prostitute in London before that. Charlotte finds the forthrightness bracing, and doesn't bother protesting that, for once, she isn't pregnant. It's only the ship, and being so tired. She puts her hand on Emma's and walks with her, away from the rolling, glowing ocean.

1 June 1789
Emperor Joseph II to Maria Carolina

My very dear sister,

My health is a little better than the last time I wrote.

The doctors say I may never recover from that fall from my horse into the icy river at Karánsebes, though I count myself among the lucky that night. I still don't know how it was that the Austrian army was thrown into such confusion, seeing the enemy when there was no enemy there, and firing brother against brother in their panic.

Angelo Soliman tells me the Turks used some sort of device against us, to produce illusions. We were fighting no one. When the Turks actually arrived at the battlefield, they found only Austrian corpses, and I was wandering, lost, frozen, wet. I've sent him to the border to discover what this device was. Though he has written me a letter about it, I cannot claim to understand it.

Soliman is nearly seventy now, and perhaps I rely on him too much – he wants nothing more but to study his strange books and travel with his daughter. But where else am I to turn? Kaunitz served my mother as chancellor for decades, but now he doesn't even come when I summon him, and Austria is at war on all sides.

Truth be told, I prefer open campaigns, with soldiers and uniforms and gunsmoke, to the conspiring and sloganeering from secret societies in Liège – which may soon be in open revolt against the Empire – or the Austrian Netherlands. When the uprising happened there, I told Mimi and her

husband to come to Vienna, for their own safety, and so I could talk to them, impress upon them the necessity of our centralizing and rationalizing reforms. I told them what the Empress of Russia told me, that kings must do what is right, and pay no more attention to the cavils of the people than the moon pays to the dogs who bay at it. Since I sent them back home to rule last year they have managed to hold onto power, but they write that they are afraid. And they have reason to be.

This is why I think that persuading Antoinette to come to Naples or to Vienna, even for a family visit during the unrest, would be most unwise, and only guarantee a revolution in France. She writes to me that she must stay there, at her husband's side, and I agree. If she left, she might never be able to return, and it would be a capitulation to the forces of unrest all across Europe. It would put Mimi in danger, and Max, and Amalia, and Leopold, and you and me. We must support her through diplomacy, though God knows France does not look kindly on our ambassadors. The poor woman; my heart breaks over her letters and her descriptions of the Dauphin in his illness. I think that motherhood is the only role to which she was ever truly suited.

Charlotte, you are close to Leopold, and you have the most stalwart character of any of us: you must impress upon him that he may soon be emperor and must prepare himself to leave Tuscany. If my lungs give out, Leopold may very well find himself leading an empire at the heart of a continent in a state of general war. The war is everywhere — these societies, Charlotte, these clubs, these strange new weapons that strike at the heart of a nation, wielded by an invisible hand. You must be vigilant. You must not allow Naples to fall into the same peril.

I remain,

Your brother,
Joseph

CHAPTER FIFTY-TWO

Are There No Fathers Among Them? — Summer
at Versailles — Cockades — Soldiers and Women —
A Rainy Day

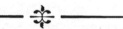

Summer comes to France, and the Dauphin dies. This boy she could not protect and could not save. Her heart feels torn from her, and she cannot bear to talk to Charlotte because she would weep and weep and how would that be for Charlotte, who has lost so many children?

But now Antoinette has lost half of hers too.

Louis-Joseph dies in her arms on the morning of 4 June 1789. That afternoon, the court comes to her bedroom to pay its respects. She leans against the gilded balustrade that separates her bed from the rest of the room, and tries to remain standing. When everyone has gone, she goes to find Louis, and they sit together in silence.

The next few days are a nightmare of details and decisions. Lamballe tells her that they will drape the casket in cloth of silver, and she makes all the arrangements. Philippe d'Orléans, when invited to perform funerary functions in his role as First Prince of the Blood, refuses, claiming the work of the Estates General keeps him too busy. The Estates General are

551

deadlocked, as the clergy and nobility try to prevent everyone else – the Third Estate – from dominating.

Every day, Louis turns away requests from the representatives of the Third Estate to speak to him about voting arrangements and rules of procedure. He asks wearily: 'Are there no fathers among them?'

The court leaves Versailles and its swirl of visiting delegates and political arguments, retreating to Marly for a week. It is a strangely private mourning, which is a relief in some ways, as the family (now two children and two parents) has a little time in peace. It's horrible in other ways; the death of a dauphin ought to be a national tragedy, despite the healthy little brother ready to step into a position the royal household has been subtly preparing him for over the last two years.

Jacques Necker arrives at Marly to tell the King that the Third Estate has revolted, and now calls itself a National Assembly.

Louis is sitting with his brothers, the Comte d'Artois and the Comte de Provence, and with Antoinette. He asks for their advice, while Necker looks on impatiently.

'This is treason,' says Provence. 'A complete challenge to royal authority.'

'What would you have me do, Necker?' Louis asks.

His prime minister looks as though he's never been more relieved to hear any question. 'I have prepared a set of reforms that will allow each of the three Estates dominion in their own sphere, while allowing majority votes on matters of national importance.'

'A compromise solution,' says the Comte d'Artois dryly. 'What does the Third Estate have to gain from compromise now?'

'The ability to get anything done in this country,' the Comte de Provence retorts. 'Not to mention their necks.'

'My dear?' Louis looks to Antoinette.

If only everyone in the country could see what a kind man he is. Even now, when his eyes are still red from weeping

with her over their little boy, he only wants to do good. He only wants someone to tell him what that is.

'It seems to me that the main thing is for the King to speak to the Estates General, and help them to find common ground,' Antoinette says.

'Do the Estates General even exist any more?' the Comte d'Artois asks.

Necker hesitates. 'The Estates General convened at His Majesty's request.'

'Then make the preparations,' Louis says. 'The King will address the Estates General, propose a compromise, and put an end to this madness.'

By order of the King, the hall where the Estates General had been meeting is closed for a few days to construct the necessary seating and a dais for the King to make his speech. Somehow, the members of the self-declared National Assembly never hear of this plan. When they arrive at the hall to have their own meeting and find their way barred by the King's armed guards, they assume the King has simply ordered them disbanded.

So the Assembly convenes in a tennis court and vows that wherever its members meet, there the Assembly is. There is a new power in France, and it is not the King, nor by decree of the King.

When Louis and Antoinette return to Versailles, everything is in a muddle, and Louis's councillors give him contradictory advice. Some of them have been trying to work with the leaders of the new National Assembly, and everyone has a plan for how to salvage everything. But nothing can be salvaged. The King's brothers urge him to get rid of Necker and replace his council, which Louis does, hoping for a fresh start and a firm stand.

On the morning of 15 July, the women who dress the Queen are all chattering about the violence at the Bastille.

Antoinette nearly falls into Fersen's arms with relief when he arrives with news. They walk out into the gardens in

the July heat, in a world of neat hedges and white stone paths.

'The pamphleteers and speechmakers have convinced the people that the King dismissed Necker because he intends to shut down the Assembly and put an end to all reform,' Fersen says. 'They say the King is going to war against the people.'

'It seems to me that the people are going to war against the King,' Antoinette protests. 'What on earth did they want with an old prison?'

'They thought they would find stockpiles of weapons and gunpowder. It didn't take them long to overwhelm the garrison and set free the few prisoners left inside.' He pauses. 'There are troops everywhere, even all through the town of Versailles. Sadly, because the King's council can't be sure of the loyalties of French soldiers, many of them are foreign regiments.'

'It's true, then,' Antoinette says, dazed. 'Louis was told it was a revolution. What should he do? Will you talk to him, tell him everything you have seen and heard?'

He nods, and turns to her, taking her by the shoulders. 'Of course I will. But we must think of your safety, and the children. Polignac is leaving France, and the Comte d'Artois.'

She shakes her head. 'The King can't leave, and I'm not leaving the King. Tell me, have you heard anything of Lafayette? I went to his portrait and spoke to him but I haven't heard anything.'

Fersen laughs ruefully. 'He probably hasn't had a moment alone. Lafayette has managed to get himself named the commander of the new National Guard, and he's writing a Declaration of the Rights of Man and the Citizen. He's helped design the revolutionary cockade: red, white, and blue.'

She frowns, first at the word 'revolutionary' and then at everything after. 'But those are the colours of the Duc d'Orléans.'

'Which no doubt makes Philippe very happy. But Lafayette

is loyal to you, my love, and to the King. He'll make sure the National Guard serves both the people and the King. He believes France can emerge from this a strong and peaceful constitutional monarchy.'

'And you?'

Fersen pulls her to him, holds her close.

The summer ends, and Antoinette does not want to go to a party.

She wasn't supposed to go, wasn't planning to go. She's bone-tired and the very last thing she wants to do is show her face anywhere. Since the storming of the Bastille, she has spent her days at the Queen's Hamlet as much as possible, working on loaves-and-fishes spells, trying to find a way to make enough bread, and damn the economics. She should have found a way to feed the people of France.

Polignac is gone, safe in Switzerland with her family. Antoinette wept when she said farewell, sincerely, grieving at last the friend she has not truly known in years. The Comte d'Artois and his family fled too, at the urging of the King. Antoinette is worried about her friends who do stay by her side – Lamballe, and especially Fersen – while at the same time, she is selfishly grateful for them.

Being away from court is not a dereliction of duty these days. The place is half empty. Many of the wealthiest families have fled the country, or at least gone to their own estates, far from the city. The King's councillors hate her, and the less she is seen in the palace, walking through the Hall of Mirrors, the better. No one objected to her seclusion. Louis meets with his advisers and goes hunting, and does not argue with her every Sunday after Mass when she says, 'One more week at the Hamlet for me, I think.'

It's all right. Antoinette has no intentions of opening up magic to Louis's carousel of advisers to squander as they have squandered all the gold and grain in France. And if he dismissed the advisers, and let his wife rule? Would the

people love her as a sorceress-queen, when they have never loved her before? Or would they take the magic and leave the queen? She suspects the latter.

She loses people, one by one. Polignac is already making common cause with a faction of the Order in Switzerland. Saint-Georges has lost patience with the magisters of Versailles and cast his lot in with the radical rogues.

Radical Brothers and radical rogues all have the same immediate goal, it seems: tear down the moderates, clear them away.

Antoinette has at least found a new governess for Mousseline and Charles, who at four is now the Dauphin, after the death of his older brother. The Marquise de Tourzel is as upright and earnest as Polignac was sly and arch. The children call her Madame Virtue and she calls them her 'divinities'. She would probably not mind either if the royal family were to blast its critics to hell, and would not be surprised to learn they could shoot lightning from their fingertips. But unlike Polignac, Madame de Tourzel keeps her thoughts to herself.

Madame de Tourzel greets the news that the children are wanted for a party at Versailles using the same expression with which she would greet the news that giants had come over the border or that the weather was fine. The marquise has only one expression: placid contentment. 'All shall be well,' she says sometimes, even if no one has addressed any remark to her. They'll be watching the children perform a masque or a ballet, and Madame de Tourzel will clap her hands together and say *all shall be well*.

'Are you sure a party is the best idea, Louis?' Antoinette asks, quietly, as they eat a luncheon together. 'The bread shortages – it's not the time to have any sort of banquet.'

He takes a spoonful of the beef broth, and nods, as if he's agreeing with her. But then he says, 'The soldiers are clamouring to see us. They're loyal to us – they're singing songs in our praise. In your praise. It's like—'

'Yes?'

'It's like when you first came to France, and you travelled from town to town and everywhere there were crowds with tears of joy in their eyes to see the Dauphine. That's how these soldiers are, now.'

She remembers. She remembers the fireworks disaster and the panic too. There has always been horror lurking behind every joy. 'I'm not an exotic young dauphine now,' she says with a soft smile. 'I'm a thirty-three-year-old matron. I'm Madame Déficit, or so they call me in the pamphlets. I'm the Great Harpy.'

He shrugs. 'The soldiers want to love you. Look at' – he's about to say Fersen – 'look at Lafayette: he still loves us, though he serves under the command of the new Assembly. But we can't take their love for granted. We must go and show them we appreciate it.'

She nods. It's a foregone conclusion anyway; she's already in her white *robe à la turque*, with its close-fitted bodice and little lacy sleeves. White, the colour of royalty, although the jacket is striped in turquoise. She sets aside two white feathers for her hair, and calls for Monsieur Léonard.

Today, Jean-François comes with all his powders and tools in a black leather bag, like a doctor or a magician, and sets to work.

'Your Majesty, I must beg your permission to go away from Paris for a short time.'

'Go away? Of course. I shall have to make do with your brother.' She tries a smile. 'I'm sure he will manage.'

'He is a coward and an incompetent,' the hairdresser says, unsmiling. 'But it can't be helped. A few weeks, a month perhaps, if it must be.'

'I hope everything is all right. Is it family trouble? Anything I can help with, Léonard?'

He shakes his head. 'Thank you, Your Majesty. I'll return as soon as I can. In the meantime, I thought it best to tell you about your hair powders, so you can use them properly while I'm away.'

'Ah,' she says, smiling. 'Show me, then.'

He finishes tying an extension onto her wig and then comes around to face her. Out of his bag, he pulls a little tin case, full of squat circular pots. He opens the first one: pale pink.

'This one', he says, 'inculcates loyalty to the Dauphin. This lavender one, well, that's for friendliness to the Emperor and his policies, although I can't say it's very strong. The golden one, very subtle colour, so lovely, that's for loyalty to His Majesty the King, and the white is for loyalty to Your Majesty.'

She straightens her posture and composes her face. 'Put them all on, Monsieur Léonard. I need all the loyalty we can muster.'

She goes out to meet her husband and her two living children, lined up in their pastel dresses and jackets.

The first face she sees in the crowded Versailles opera house is Lamballe's. The princess of lost love, making her appearance at the party. Antoinette can't stand to look at her face, so she looks a little past her as they smile at each other, and two more Versailles smiles there never were.

Versailles was daunting when it was full of music and light; it is gruesome now when it is nearly empty, ghosts dancing through its chequerboard halls, no music, no sound of laughter, only the barking of dogs. The dogs frighten little Charles and she doesn't blame him.

As they enter the royal opera it's like stepping into the past: it's bright, and noisy, and everyone is pretending to have a good time. She is, once more, on display. They are demanding to love her.

At her side, the King. On his lapel, the new cockade designed by Lafayette: red and blue, the colours of Paris, combined with royal white. They are all revolutionaries now, and all royalists. Why not? There can be no traitors that way, and everybody lives.

Young Pauline de Tourzel, daughter of the governess, in her pretty bodice, so slim. She surveys the crowd as any young woman would, in any age, at any ordinary party.

Antoinette lifts Charles up – he's getting heavy, but she needs the warm weight of him.

A cheer – so many bright white uniforms and dark tricornes – and there beyond them all, like a groom waiting at the end of the aisle, waits Fersen.

Antoinette and her lover spend a quiet few days at the Petit Trianon. On the morning of 5 October, Louis is hunting. The children are playing with Madame de Tourzel. Fersen is sitting across a small table with a newspaper. There's drinking chocolate warming in the pot. He gives her a domestic smile, but she can see there's anxiety behind it. When she comes to him and kisses him on the forehead, he closes the newspaper almost absently, puts it into the box at his side.

She thinks: This is what I would like my life to be.

It's a foggy, grey day. They dress the children for a walk but by the time they reach the door, it's raining – hard, and from all directions. Antoinette's dog, Odin, yips and demands to be walked anyway; he was a gift from Fersen and she loved him to distraction. She sacrificed her love of the dog, though, to enchant a ring that shoots lightning. Now she can't bear to look at the dog, so she sends Pauline de Tourzel, the governess's daughter, to walk him during a break in the rain.

But the children are not so easily settled. Everyone is restless. Antoinette calls for the groom and orders the Dauphin's carriage to be hitched; the children can go for a drive, at least.

Then she turns to say something to Fersen, but he is not there.

She goes through the rooms until she finds him at last, at a garden gate, reading a note.

Fersen tucks the note into his pocket and takes her in his arms. 'We have to leave,' he says. 'Now.'

'Why? What's going on?'

'There's a mob in the streets – women, apparently, demanding bread. They're marching to Versailles. They'll be here sometime today.'

'They're marching in the rain?'

He arches one of his dark eyebrows.

'All right, all right, they're marching in the rain. We must tell the King.'

He nods. 'I'll send a messenger, but I suspect he'll know soon enough if he doesn't already. You must get out of here, Antoinette. Go to Italy or England. Go to Austria, for God's sake. The time has come.'

She shakes her head. 'My place is with Louis, and he won't leave.'

They hear hoofbeats.

'There's a carriage out front.' He walks around the corner of the house.

'I ordered the Dauphin's carriage hitched. I thought he could—'

'Take it, and go! Go now.'

'We'll take it, and we'll go back to Versailles. The family should be together. In the meantime, my love, what can we do? Is it bread they're asking for? The loaves-and-fishes spell. If I had enough of my blood—'

'It would take all the blood in your body to feed a hundred people, Antoinette.'

'And you think the life of one rogue magister is worth the lives of a hundred other people? Is that what we've come to?'

'When the magister is you, yes, I do believe that,' he says, and stops, and looks away from her. 'It isn't love talking, Antoinette. It's sense. There's no one in charge of this mob and nothing you can do would calm them. They're calling the soldiers' party an orgy; they're saying you and the

soldiers . . . People are saying you threw some tricolour cockades on the ground and danced them into the mud beneath your feet.'

'No one could believe something so ridiculous,' says Antoinette, but all she hears is *it isn't love talking*. She's feared, for years, that one day he would sacrifice his love for her for some spell, some very important spell. Would she know if he had? Of course she would. Wouldn't she?

She piles obligingly into the Dauphin's carriage with the children and Fersen promises to follow on horseback once he gets the servants to safety. When they reach Versailles, the carriage drives through a knot of National Guard soldiers in their red and blue uniforms and Lafayette is there waiting to take her hand when steps out.

She nearly collapses onto Lafayette, out of sheer friendship and relief.

'You're here,' she says, almost a question, although she's not sure which one to ask.

'To protect Your Majesty,' he says, answering it. He pauses. 'To protect all of you, and to protect them, when they come.'

'So you're on everyone's side, Marquis,' she says, and it sounds more cutting than she intended.

He bows his head. 'These days, I'm on the side of anyone who isn't a murderous son of a bitch. Unless they're English, in which case I make a general assumption.'

He still looks young, somehow, although he's thicker about the chin. The hero of the American war. The war France paid for, is paying for.

She laughs. 'Good then. My husband isn't, you know. Murderous.'

'I know, Your Majesty. That's why I'm here.'

She walks towards the door, her children following with Madame de Tourzel. Then she stops, stricken suddenly, for no reason at all. Weak. As if someone somewhere has pricked a Pandora doll – but there is no pain anywhere, just pain everywhere.

She turns to Lafayette. 'Is there any hope?'

He cocks his head. 'I haven't spent all of mine yet.'

She nods, and glances quickly behind, at the children, at Mousseline so ladylike and tall already, at her brother so dignified and slender in his holiday clothes.

Antoinette walks into Versailles for the last time.

CHAPTER FIFTY-THREE

Portraits and Preparations — The Carved Busk — Family —
Lafayette's Position — Bring out the Queen

Antoinette and Fersen spend an hour in a room full of portraits, talking to rogues in America, in England, in Russia, in Austria and India and Turkey. Making plans for safe-houses for the moderates and aristocrats among the French rogues. At one point she has the impression they are surrounded by ghosts, as they pace in circles so they can talk to the walls.

When the last whispers scuttle away to silence, Fersen asks if there's anyone else she'd like to speak to. She shakes her head.

They don't speak about it, but she knows Fersen is thinking of the same thing she is: escape, and whether it's worth the risk. The expansion charm doesn't work on anything larger than a pocket, and while the pocket can hold a great many things, each thing has to be pocket-sized, to get inside. They could use a hat of shadows. Try to sneak away.

It would be a life of exile, if they survived. A life of decay in Moscow or Prague or London. And there would be no one to stop Philippe d'Orléans from taking the throne, as he's always wanted. A magister-king, ruled by resentment and cowardice. And Louis would never agree.

When they come out into the halls they hear the crowd outside, screaming something she cannot resolve into words, at first, and then she hears one clamour rise louder than the rest: *'Bring out the Queen.'*

Louis looks up and smiles to see her come in together with Fersen. They still don't talk about it, not ever, but he's glad of Fersen. Glad that Antoinette has someone. Glad, perhaps, that Antoinette's heart is one less thing he has to worry about. He holds out two hands, for each of them to take, and they bow their heads before the King.

Lafayette comes in and says, flushed, that the marching women have breached the outer gates. Versailles has no defences, by design; it was built as a kind of theatre, wide open to the people of France, a place for them to come and gawk at the Sun King and his less radiant descendants.

Antoinette has always hated being on display; she does better in smaller rooms. But she did what she must so the people would love her. She wore the torturous *grand habit*; she had the best hairdresser and the best dressmaker, made herself into the proper sort of spectacle. And now they hate her for it, hate her for her pleasure palace, for her fashion, for her ostentation.

Louis sets his chin. Little Charles is here with him, playing on the floor with one of his soldiers. Over by the curtained window Mousseline stands silently, watching. She will be eleven in a couple of months, old enough to be thinking of marriage.

A few years ago, early in their reconciliation, Charlotte suggested that Mousseline marry her son Franscesco, the eldest living boy, and heir to the throne of Naples. But Antoinette could not stomach it. To send a child of seven away to a foreign court would be to mar her childhood; to send her away at fourteen, as Antoinette was sent, would be to mar the rest of her life. Mousseline will marry one of her French cousins instead, and stay with her family.

And here the family is, all in the same room, for this

moment. It's quaintly domestic by Versailles standards, although nothing like a Habsburg Christmas.

'Marquis, what do you suggest?' the King asks.

'There are a few among them whose names I know. Intelligent women, writers and thinkers. They will use this opportunity to make names for themselves – if we bring them in to talk, they'll want to show the crowd how successful they've been.'

Louis pauses a moment. He has been so badly advised, in so many different directions, over the last twenty-five years. Fifteen years, and he still acts like a new king, an uncertain pupil whose time for education is running out. At last, he nods. 'Three or four,' he says. 'Half a dozen at most. And I alone—'

'No,' says Antoinette. 'They're women. Let them see me, and let them see the children.'

Louis shakes his head.

'Her Majesty is right,' says Lafayette. 'I'll be here. They won't take any weapons in.'

'Have they got weapons?' says Louis, furrowing his brow. 'I thought these were market women.'

'The mob looted the armoury at City Hall this morning. There are muskets and even some small cannon out there, in addition to whatever pikes, swords, pitchforks they started out with. It's wise to assume everyone has a knife, at least. But I won't let them bring anything in.'

Louis nods, but he doesn't look happy about it.

The King rises when the women come into the room. Three of them, dressed plainly but not in rags. About Antoinette's age. They don't bow. They don't curtsey. She's never seen anything like it – no one seems to know what to do.

Except Louis. He strides forward and takes them each by hand as if he were a roué and they were ladies at the opera. He lets each astonished hand drop, and then he sits at his desk.

'Tell me what I can do for my people.'

One woman steps forward, clears her throat. 'They're starving, Sire.'

Louis nods, ignoring her rudeness. 'I know. I've done all I—'

'You have full granaries, Sire.'

'The army must eat.'

'And the children?'

He nods, slowly. 'I will disburse some grain, right away. I am working on acquiring some more from outside France. As more grain comes into the country, it will flow out to the people.'

The factory in Naples that produces magical grain, one of Charlotte's oldest projects. If Antoinette had been more like Charlotte, she might have done something like that. But she never managed it. Charlotte should have been the one to marry Louis, just as Maria Theresa intended.

'Put it in writing,' the market woman demands, and the King asks for pen and paper.

The crowd gets smaller after sunset but it gets more aggressive. Lafayette says the delegation did convince many to go, but a well-armed and angry mob still shouts at the palace doors.

'At least now we know what we're dealing with,' Lafayette says.

'Can we get the Queen and the children away?' Fersen asks.

Before Antoinette can respond, Lafayette shakes his head. 'We're surrounded now. There is no way out.'

There is always a way out; that's what magic is. The question is only what one is willing to sacrifice. She and Fersen and Lafayette are all magisters, all friends, but she finds no comfort in their glances. Lafayette looks down his long nose at her. There's a line down the middle of his forehead and the corners of his mouth droop.

Mousseline is sitting in a chair, her ankles crossed properly, reading.

Antoinette walks over to her, drapes her arm around her shoulders and looks at the book. It's a collection of Shakespeare's sonnets, in English.

When Mousseline was born, Antoinette said her daughter would belong to her, and not to France. But she belongs to no one but herself. It is Antoinette who was transmuted into someone new, someone who loves without thinking of whether she is loved in return. She remembers the day they brought her the news that the Empress Maria Theresa had died. She was in the nursery, lying on the floor on her stomach, beside her daughter. Mousseline, not yet two, sitting with her chubby legs splayed, playing with her model village: a little windmill, a dovecote, a dairy, a bakery, all carved out of wood.

The village that became the Queen's Hamlet. If Mousseline recognizes it, she does not say so.

Mousseline was already tired of her toy village, and only liked it as a place to arrange her tin soldiers, a gift from her uncle Joseph. Mousseline's favourite was the miniature Frederick of Prussia, in flat, engraved tin, painted in blue and white and gold.

Antoinette read to her daughter from the little roll of paper that came in the box with the soldiers. '"The Battle of Mollwitz was the first great battle of Frederick the Second. During the war of Silesia" – oh, my dear, I know all about that one – "in 1741, the King was forced to leave the battle-field when it seemed his forces would be overrun. But his infantry rallied and drove the Austrians off the field."'

'What is Silesia?' Mousseline asked.

'Well, when your grandmother was first crowned—'

'I have her name.'

'Yes, my darling. The one you're named for. When she was made ruler of Austria and Hungary, this king chose that moment to invade her lands, and take a place called Silesia away from her.'

Mousseline frowned, and set the figure deliberately down, lying there as though he'd just conceded a game of chess. 'I don't like him then.'

'Well, he's a very great king. Your brother Joseph gets along well with him now.'

Antoinette felt lost, suddenly. Diplomacy was a dance to which she had never learned the steps, and she wanted Mousseline to know better. To be prepared, for whatever comes.

At that moment the door opened, and there was Madame Campan, her face already grim with the news that Antoinette's mother the Empress was dead.

The Empress once said to her, before she sent her away: *I thought I'd have time . . . you're growing up so quickly.* A painful conversation Antoinette never did sacrifice, and the sting has gone out of now.

She drops her voice low. 'I have a secret to share with you, Mousseline.'

'I'm good at keeping secrets, Mama.'

Antoinette points to the ring on Mousseline's finger. 'That is an enchanted ring,' she whispers. 'If you think hard, when you're wearing it, you can shoot lightning at someone. It hurts, though, so don't practise on your poor brother or anyone else. You can practise in the privy, shooting at the wall. Do you understand?'

Mousseline holds out her hand and examines the ring gravely. It's plain gold. 'Could it kill someone?'

Antoinette shakes her head. 'Unlikely. The lightning is not strong. But it will help you get away. If someone ever tries to touch you. To hurt you. But you must only ever use it as a last resort. Keep it secret.'

'You think the people will come inside the palace tonight.'

'Oh, no, we're quite safe,' Antoinette lies, rubbing her daughter's small shoulder. 'The Marquis de Lafayette is here. You used to think he was almost a god, when you were little.'

'Yes, but now I'm nearly eleven.' Mousseline sighs.

Madame de Tourzel takes the children to bed. Antoinette tells her to bring them to the King at the first sign of trouble. They'll be safest with him. People hate Louis a little less than they hate his wife.

Then she goes to bed herself around two in the morning, and listens to the crowd outside, the clattering, the booms of muskets being fired into the air, the screams.

At four o'clock, Madame Campan bursts into her room and says they're in the palace, they're down the hall. Antoinette is already dressed and prepared. She can hear them. She can hear the screams of the guards.

She grabs her expansive pocket from underneath her mattress, containing her gold watch, her little notebooks, and the Pandora doll, which barely fits inside it. The pocket looks empty, but it's heavy. She and Madame Campan run to the children's rooms. Mousseline and Pauline de Tourzel are standing guard near the door while Madame de Tourzel holds Charles in his bed, rocking him back and forth.

'We must go to the King,' Antoinette says. 'We should be together.'

But the King's door is barred, and his wife has to bang on it, screaming his name and her own, for what seems like an hour before his bodyguard lets her in, hurriedly. They can see red torchlight flickering on the flowered wallpaper, can hear the laughter of the approaching hunters.

'Wait,' says Lafayette, appearing with Fersen in the corridor behind Antoinette. A palace guard puts his hand on his sword, looks to the King, but Louis nods his head, gestures for Lafayette and Fersen to come in.

'I thought you'd left us, Marquis,' says the King.

Lafayette shakes his head.

They hear shouting in the hall, and a loud bang as if furniture has fallen, and little Charles wails at last.

'I'm ready to die to protect you, Sire,' says Lafayette. 'In service of the people of France.'

'Surely it won't come to that,' says Louis, frowning and glancing at the children. 'The children—' he says.

'Your Majesty, our only hope now is in escape,' Fersen says. 'There, perhaps I can help you.'

'My place is here,' says Louis. 'If I run away from my people, I may as well abdicate. But if you believe you can get the Queen and the children away—'

'If you send the Dauphin away, then you may as well abdicate too,' says Lafayette. 'The people need to see that you are not afraid of them. That you are still King.'

Nobody looks at Antoinette.

'Where my children are, there I will be,' says Antoinette. 'At my husband's side.'

Fersen sighs, but says nothing.

Lafayette nods. 'Then the only choice before us is to wait here for violence, or go out and address the crowd.'

Antoinette shakes her head. She walks away from the children, so she can speak softly to her friend, out of their earshot.

'Lafayette, they have guns.'

'Yes,' he says. 'It is very possible that someone will shoot the King if he goes out on the balcony. It is even more possible that someone will shoot or stab or behead the King if he does not. They are inside the building, Your Majesty. There's been blood, and there will be more if His Majesty does not act.'

Louis bites his lip, but she thinks it is out of sadness, not irresolution. 'Let's go, then,' he says.

They can hear the roar of the crowd coalescing into words. 'Bring out the Queen.' They don't want their King to address them, to make it all right. They want the Queen, the hated Austrian woman, Madame Déficit. They want revenge.

The King needs her; he needs her to use her magic now, as he has never needed it before. What does she have that can dispel a mob? Little pots of enchanted hair powder. Lavender, pink, gold, and white.

Lafayette walks with him to the door; then he glances back at Antoinette.

She runs to him, gives Louis a kiss, and then waits there so that Louis will walk on into the hall. As she embraces Lafayette, he whispers in her ear, 'Have you got something up your sleeve? I've bought you a little time, with this speech of the King's, but only a little.'

She pulls back, nods. 'Leave it to me,' she says.

'Bring out the Queen.'

She puts her hand into her capacious pocket to search for the pots of hair powder, and that's when she remembers. She wore all of her powders to the party; they are still on her dressing table.

She puts her hand to her throat.

'Bring out the Queen!'

'They are calling for me, and I am not dressed,' she says. 'I need to go back to my rooms. Get my things.'

Madame de Tourzel, for once in her life, disagrees. 'It is not safe,' she says.

'If I show myself as anything other than a queen, they will despise me,' says Antoinette, with genuine desperation in her voice. 'With unpowdered hair. In my night clothes. I can take the secret corridors. I'll be quite safe.'

But Madame de Tourzel's shocked face is looking beyond her, where the panelled door out of Louis's room has banged shut.

Young Pauline de Tourzel has gone. She's gone to get the things from Antoinette's room.

Antoinette opens the door and rushes after her, but Charles grabs at her leg, and she bends to kiss his little warm forehead, to brush away the tear on his cheek. By the time she detaches him and hands him, screaming, to a similarly distraught Madame de Tourzel, Pauline has been gone two minutes, perhaps three.

'Bring out the Queen.'

The Queen slips into the corridor, follows the path the

King has taken to her bedroom, to do his duty, all these long years. Around a dark corner, Pauline nearly runs into her. Her arms are full of clothes.

'Hurry,' says Antoinette, pressing against the wall so Pauline can get past her, back to safety.

Back in Louis's room, Pauline places everything on the bed. Tears are running down her cheeks.

'I saw . . .' she says. 'The rooms. They're all smashed, and there's blood. A body in the doorway – I couldn't stop to see who. I couldn't get your petticoats.'

Antoinette roots through the pile. Silk stockings. Her corsets, and her little case of busks. A *robe à la chemise*, simple; but that is the sort of dress that they all hated, when she wore it in a portrait. They hated her for wearing loose linen; they hated her for wearing diamonds. She hasn't worn any kind of necklace in years, not since 1785. There's a *robe à l'anglaise*, in white. It will have to do. She turns to Pauline, one silk mule in her hand. The other shoe isn't here; Pauline must have dropped it, or she only took the one.

'I don't see the hair powder,' she says. 'I need that more than anything. I must go back for it.'

Pauline shakes her head. 'It's gone. Everything was taken: the rouges, the powders. The mirror, smashed.'

'Gone?' Antoinette sinks down onto the bed, the shoe still in her hand. 'Gone? But what will I do? How will I make them love me?'

They can all hear the crowd chanting: '*Bring out the Queen!*'

She is going to her death; she is quite sure of it. She dresses as best she can, Madame Campan tying her corset and hooking her bodice over the carved busk that was a gift from the man she loves best in the world. In her last moments, she'll be able to think of Fersen, to remember him.

Louis comes in, looking shaken but alive.

She kisses him. 'They're calling for me.'

'We'll go out together,' he says.

She has tried to show them that she is a good mother. She gathers her children to her, takes Charles in one arm, and Mousseline stands staunchly by her side. They all walk towards the balcony – not close enough for bullets, but close enough for the crowd to see her silhouette, the shape of her family as if it were painted by Vigée Le Brun. The Madonna and children.

'No children!' people shout. 'Just the Queen!'

She puts her son down, and kisses the people who love her, and goes out to face these women who have been here all day and all night. There are more men among them now, by the voices; they've come from the towns nearby, no doubt, drawn here for the confrontation. She sees bayonets shine in the dawn sunlight. It's chilly, like any other October morning, and it makes her shiver in front of the world. So many things to worry about, and she worries about the lack of a shawl.

There's nothing she can do. No magic to help her. Any moment now, it will come: a musket ball, a crossbow bolt, even a rock. She is not far above her people, and they want her dead. She has tried everything to make them love her and she has failed. Like the little girl on the stage at Schönbrunn who's forgotten her dance steps, she freezes, and stares out at them.

They're screaming now, and some orange vegetable splatters on the balcony a foot from her. '*À la lanterne!*' someone shouts. She has read of the revolutionaries' favourite slogan, but she has never before heard it. To the lamppost, to hang the Queen.

She puts her hands on the balcony railing, moves closer to the line of fire. Let it come, and be over with, and this torture end! The noise is greater than anything she's ever heard.

She bows her head, just a little, very slowly, curving her body as much as the corset will allow.

Then she bows deeper. It's all over, and she's failed, and

she'll acknowledge it. She's failed. She's sorry, she's sorry, and if they would only stop screaming she would tell them so. But they're so loud. She can only stand silently, without magic, without any help, and bow her head, and admit her failure.

The roar dulls. Quieter, quieter, quieter. The Queen stands bowed before her people until she begins to wonder what magic somebody has done. Where is Lafayette?

At last she straightens up, and looks at their faces. Bemused, uncertain faces. It isn't love. But it isn't quite murder. Not tonight.

Lafayette is at her side, and he takes her hand and kisses it. As if he's broken some spell, a cheer goes up, uncertainly.

Louis walks out, then. 'We will go to Paris,' he shouts, and she thinks perhaps only she can hear just how dejected he is. 'The royal family is yours to command, and always has been. We will go to Paris to be closer to our people.'

'What did you do?' she whispers to Lafayette.

He shakes his head, and for a moment looks once again like the cocky, nervous sixteen-year-old she met at the Palais-Royal. 'Nothing.'

No magic at all, and yet the crowd went quiet. She has been looking for so long for the magic that would make her worthy to be queen. The only tasks that have ever come easily to her are simple acts of love, but she never thought that would be enough. And perhaps even now it isn't. Perhaps it's too late.

They bundle the children into carriages and ride, with the mob all around them, singing about the Baker and the Baker's wife. They ride slowly.

A head, outside her window. Bleeding from the neck, and under that, nothing but pike.

Antoinette gasps, her gorge rising. The head – one of the guards? – is garish with rouge and white cream, the hair frizzled and covered in powder. Her powder. Gold and white, pink and lavender. The head of one of the unfortunate guards,

574

surely, but dressed up in her enchanted powder. If it has increased the loyalty of the drunken lout carrying the pike, what hatred must there have been in his heart to begin with?

Antoinette tucks her children's heads to her chest, so they won't see.

CHAPTER FIFTY-FOUR

The Tuileries – Rumours of War – Death of the
Emperor – Attitudes – Emigrés – A Library
in Vienna – A Discovery

Sister,

Don't worry; I'm fine. I couldn't take the portrait with me so couldn't speak to you. I may be able to send for it. The King, Mousseline, Charles, and I are all safe in the Palace of the Tuileries – it is a mouldy old place on the bank of the Seine, beside the Louvre. Its gardens have more prostitutes than the Palais-Royal and they press their faces against the windows to get a look at us. To make room for us, our jailers are turning out the decrepit countesses and valets' cousins and the rest who've made their home here for decades. There is a whole wing inhabited by actors for my brother-in-law's theatre, and little Charles found a room full of enchanted, moving props and scenery that gave him nightmares.

But we are in good hands. We do not have the royal guards with us any more, but the Marquis de Lafayette has

command over the National Guard soldiers, and I know he will keep us safe. I will ask for mirrors. We are prisoners, but the only way that will end is with patience and courage, demonstrating to the French people that we are still their servants.

In haste, and knowing that this letter may be deciphered,

Antoinette

The portrait of Charlotte still hangs in silent halls. She heard the terror on the night of 5 October 1789: screams close and sharp, then muffled and distant, whimpers and shouts and animal noises. She didn't sleep, or talk to anyone but God, in the eight days it took for Antoinette's letter to arrive from Paris.

Now Charlotte hears nothing but the occasional peal of laughter, faint and far away, like malevolent fairies.

When Hamilton sends her a note saying that Antoinette's court painter has arrived in Naples, Charlotte wraps a black lace shawl around her shoulders, calls for her carriage and is at Hamilton's villa within the hour.

Élisabeth Vigée Le Brun is not the first emigré from Paris. Half of the Brothers of Paris have stayed. Some have taken up the ideology of the Ladder Club, of tearing down all the old rulers so magisters can take their place; they do not respond to Charlotte's letters. Some respond with non-committal expresssions of resigned distaste and talk about the birth pangs of the new order. The few Brothers who want to preserve both monarchy and the Order have fled, not to Naples but to Russia. Charlotte suspects the Empress Catherine is gathering magisters around her court, but the wily old lady keeps her secrets close.

Vigée Le Brun, though, is an interesting case. Portrait magic has been an important method of communication between rogues over the last several years, and many of those portraits were painted by her. She is, almost certainly, a rogue.

The painter is fresh-faced, wearing a simple kerchief around her pale brown curls. She strides across the wide raised garden that looks out on the sea, with the still-smoking volcano in the distance. She curtseys to Charlotte, and then Caterina joins them, and they are three women on just one side or another of forty. Three magisters.

Charlotte smiles at Caterina, one of her oldest friends, and the one whose loyalty is never in question. Caterina looks tired; there are fresh lines on her face, around her eyes. She's been working so hard at San Leucio, and, as with everyone else, these years of fog and suspicion have taken their toll.

'You are welcome in Naples,' Charlotte says to Vigée Le Brun. 'I am a great admirer of your work, and I would like you to paint the royal family. That is, if you intend to keep working.'

'I must,' she says with a rueful smile. 'My daughter and I left Paris with only eighty louis in cash and some brushes and clothing. My Julie is ten years old, and she'll need an education, a home. If I'm to provide for her, I must work. But I like working, so it's all right.'

'I have one of your paintings,' Charlotte says. 'It is of my sister. It is quite magical.'

Vigée Le Brun smiles at Charlotte. 'Thank you. I worked very long on it. Her Majesty is a difficult subject to capture properly. She has been very patient with me, and taught me magic. She said I would be safe here.'

Caterina and Charlotte glance at each other. 'You will be,' Charlotte promises. 'The Order in Naples is less concerned with who uses magic than with ensuring that it's used wisely.'

'Is that different?' Vigée Le Brun asks.

It is not a question Charlotte has an answer to, or at least not a short answer, for a woman she's just met. Caterina coughs, in the way she has of covering up a laugh, and Charlotte changes the subject. 'I worry for my sister and her family. I will be most grateful for anything you can tell me about them.'

Vigée Le Brun nods. She moves her hands when she speaks, as if she's painting her ideas. Those hands that painted Antoinette so many times, that painted the picture which allowed Charlotte to speak to her sister. 'France is in – I don't know what to call it. Not quite chaos. A brutal joke. The Assembly, or whatever they're calling it now, is meeting in the covered racecourse at the Palace of the Tuileries. Because the King is there, and the King accepts the reforms. Officially.'

Caterina cocks an eyebrow. 'And unofficially?'

The painter makes a non-committal face. 'I couldn't say, Marchesa. If he accepts the reforms, and everyone is friendly, why does he have to do whatever they tell him? What will happen if he does not?'

Charlotte says, as if trying to convince herself, 'But he is still the King.'

'For now,' says William Hamilton, walking to them, looking out at the purple sky over the sea. At his side is Silfversparre, a drink in the younger man's hand. 'Your Majesty, you have arrived just in time for the performance. Will you all come into the salon? She is ready.'

The salon is very dark, lit only with candles in wall sconces here and there. Silfversparre helps Charlotte to one of the armchairs set up to face a wall nearly filled with an enormous gilt frame. Inside, there is no painting; merely void.

Out of this void steps Emma Hart.

She comes from nothing, steps lightly over the bottom of the frame, her long brown hair trailing nearly to the ground behind her. She's in the sort of white that statues wear: white silk from San Leucio. The robe is draped impossibly around her breasts, and the shawl over her round shoulders. Her face, lit by the lamp in her husband's hand, shines like porcelain, save for her two dark-blue eyes, her curved mouth.

Then her shawl leaves her shoulders. Floats into the air as she reaches for it, in an attitude of longing. The shawl

fills with air in the shape of an angel, reaching out as well, and the audience gasps, though some of them have seen this before.

A moment passes, and the shawl has taken the form of a child whom Emma is comforting. The stillness in the silk matches the stillness in Emma's posture, as though the room is frozen, and no one dares to move.

The final attitude is of Emma herself. The silk takes the form of its mistress so exactly that one would swear there was a second Emma inside it, looking back at her, as they cup their hands beneath their chins and peer at each other.

Then Emma plucks the shawl out of the air and it is a shawl again; the shape of the woman was made of nothing.

This is the third time Charlotte has seen Emma perform her Attitudes, and every time she feels stunned by the existence of a magister who has used her sacrifices to make art, and only art. But then, she reminds herself, it is not only art. Emma has come from the lowest classes of English society and now she is the mistress of the British envoy, and seems to have all she desires.

Vigée Le Brun says that she would like to paint her. Emma says she would like that very much. Hamilton pours the wine.

'Are there many artist-magisters in Naples?' the painter asks.

'There are artists who are magisters, but no one like Emma,' Caterina says.

'I should like to meet people here,' says Vigée Le Brun.

'And so you shall,' Charlotte decrees. 'There is a fashion for revolutionary ideas among the intellectuals these days. You can tell them what is really happening in France.'

'I cannot claim to know what is really happening, but I shall tell them what I can. But surely Naples has nothing to fear. It has escaped the famines in the rest of Europe. It has not indebted itself, the way that France has.'

'The people here have no reason to rise up,' Caterina agrees, uncharacteristically earnest. 'We disarm them by giving them nothing to fight against. Whenever my brother finds a new revolutionary society has started up, or that a writer has published a pamphlet, he invites them to dinner.'

'Your brother?' the painter enquires.

'My chief of police,' says Charlotte, uneasily rubbing the side of her wine glass. She is thinking about the pamphlets that rail against the Queen, that accuse her of sexual affairs with women – why always that, for her and Antoinette both? As though it might explain something that their enemies need explaining.

'Naples is as wonderful as I'd heard,' the painter is saying politely.

'It faces threats on every side,' Charlotte says.

'And we must be ready for them,' Hamilton says. 'There always comes a moment when one must stand on one side of a line or the other. Naples will continue to stand as a beacon to the world, no matter what happens. Indeed, many in England still hope that France will come out of this stronger, with a new constitutional monarchy, perhaps. It may achieve what England did, with less bloodshed.'

'I hope that is true,' says Vigée Le Brun. 'I hope it with all of my heart.'

It's frustrating, being able to talk to Antoinette's listening portrait but never hearing anything in response. The enchanted portrait of Charlotte still hangs in Versailles some-where. At the Tuileries, Antoinette lives under guard. She insists, in her letters sent by special trusted couriers, that the captain of that guard, Lafayette, is still her loyal friend and protector. Antoinette has always been naive.

Meanwhile, Charlotte talks to Antoinette, whether Antoinette likes it or not.

When news arrives of their brother Joseph's death in Vienna in February 1790, Charlotte goes to her study, walking

beneath the massive clock hanging from the ceiling: a golden birdcage with a clock face on its bottom. A gift from Antoinette: a congratulations for Charlotte's victory over the fog. She keeps a starling in the cage, and it sings the hours.

Charlotte sits near the portrait (she is pregnant again, and subject to dizzy spells). She begins with grief.

'I think he was quite alone, in his last days,' she says quietly. 'He seemed destined to be alone, our Joseph. And in his policies, too, always consolidating power. I would have done the same, I suppose, if I'd once had to share a throne with Mother. And Joseph wanted nothing more than the power to institute reforms for the sake of the people, but he had no allies. A gift for statecraft but no gift for politics. I will miss him, Antoinette, and I will miss Leopold, who will leave Florence and go to take his place as emperor soon.

'Poor Leopold inherits an empire in rebellion. Our sister Mimi is doing no better; she and her husband have had to leave the Austrian Netherlands again – the United States of Belgium, they're calling it. I believe they've taken refuge with Max. We must all be ready to help each other. I will urge Leopold to make it very clear that the Empire stands ready to defend you and your husband. If we waver now, we all fall.

'I will make you such a war, sister.

'I think often of Angelo Soliman. He tells me little in his letters now. He was so close to Joseph, for so many decades, and the Empire of today was as much his project as anyone's. I hope to see him when I go to Vienna, to see Leopold settled and the children married. I can't go until this baby is born, so it will be summer at the earliest. I wonder if I will find Vienna much changed.'

Charlotte insists that messengers find her on the road as she journeys north towards Vienna. She refuses to miss a single letter from Paris, even though every one makes her heart

race as she opens it. At least the situation there seems to
have settled into a tense equilibrium. The royal family lives
fairly normally at the Tuileries and they've even been allowed
to go to Saint-Cloud for the summer. Everyone goes along
with the polite pretence that the King is as happy as anyone
else to celebrate the anniversary of the storming of the Bastille
prison. Antoinette reports that she wears red, white, and
blue ribbons in her hair.

Vienna both is, and is not, how Charlotte remembers it.
The city's gravity has shifted away from Schönbrunn; Joseph
preferred the more austere and practical Hofburg, where he
could be close to everything and not make such a great fuss
about things. People are everywhere: walking in the parks,
crowding the coffeehouses, waving newspapers at each other.
The gentlemen of Vienna in 1770 stood up straight and wore
velvet waistcoats; in 1790 they wear brown coat-tails and
slouch against walls, with a tall felt hat pulled over the eyes,
a pipe at a louche angle. People talk about the inner life the
way they used to talk about garden design.

She finds Angelo Soliman's house at the end of a long
and narrow green park. The house is gleaming, Palladian,
with columns in the front and two great domes at either
end.

She is admitted to a long room, in deep reds and sage
greens, with golden bellpulls and vast dark paintings in gilt
frames. A pretty young woman comes to her and curtseys.

'You must be Josephine,' Charlotte says. 'I am an old friend
of your father's. If it isn't too much intrusion.'

'Not at all, Your Majesty. He's in the garden, if you'll come
with me.'

They walk through several salons and anterooms, filled
with strange machines and instruments on pedestals – like
a mirror to Hamilton's villa, only instead of the broken
marbles and old vases, Soliman's modern treasures gleam in
brass and iron.

Then out, through heavy doors, into a long courtyard filled

with topiaries that turn to look at her. In the centre is a vast circle of marble, unadorned.

Soliman is there, pruning shears in his hands. She's used to seeing him in a turban, but today he's wearing an embroidered Turkish cap and a banyan gown, both in deep orange.

'Your Majesty. I heard you were on your way to Vienna.'

'Forgive me for intruding on you here, Dr Soliman. There is nowhere in the Hofburg that we could speak without being overheard.'

She looks around the courtyard. Josephine has left them alone.

'Come into the safest place in Vienna, then.'

He puts the shears down, and gestures for her to follow him. She follows him into the centre of the courtyard, and flinches when the light dims, the air changes.

They are in a library. A hidden library.

Soliman closes oak doors behind her. It's a world lit from a bright dome far above, and all the encircling walls filled with books. Shelves radiate from the centre, row upon row of calf-bound volumes, all stamped in gold.

She laughs. 'So this is where the books go, when you take them. Like the rogue in Madras whose spellbook turned blank.'

'Some of them are spellbooks. Most are simply books. All were acquired at great cost, one way or another.'

He shows her to a red settee.

'So, this is now the *Reconditus*,' she says.

'Nothing is the *Reconditus*, Your Majesty. This is only one building, and it could burn, like any building.'

'You keep it safe, though.'

'I keep it safe,' he agrees. 'As safe as any library can be. Not only the books but the library itself is a great joy to me. I'll show you: name any book that I might have in my collection.'

She considers; not for very long. '*The Spirit of the Laws*.'

'Ha. Of course. I have several copies.' He coughs, hand to

his mouth, then says, 'Show me the French edition of *The Spirit of the Laws.'*

As though a cloud is passing overhead, the light in the room shifts, consolidates, and a shaft of sunlight points down from the dome above. It narrows, and grows in strength, until it is a finger of light indicating one book among many on a far shelf.

'There it is,' Soliman says, pointing.

'Marvellous,' Charlotte says, clapping her hands together. 'I have such a cumbersome system in my own library at Caserta. I never thought of using magic. Since we lost the *Reconditus*, everything in Naples is scattered, and I never know what spells anyone has.'

'The Order has all but disintegrated in Vienna.'

'As it has everywhere,' she says.

'Yes. Our old friend the Prince of Caramanico has taken up revolutionary causes. He writes to me. I think he truly believes in it. I think he has found new ways to love.'

She wonders whether Soliman has found new ways to hope, but she feels as though she has no right to an answer to that question, not when she was the one who took hope from him.

'You sound as though you indulge his views,' she says lightly. They have not written to each other very often in recent years, and when they have, the letters have been impersonal and short.

'I indulge everything, because I have no energy to do otherwise. I will be seventy next year. I am of the age where most of my friends are dead.'

'I'm sorry about my brother. Your loss is as great as mine.'

He nods. 'I will miss him very much. The Emperor Leopold – he has some magisters on his staff.'

'Nearly everyone does, now. The new science, they call it. I have told him what I knew of each of his magisters, which he could trust and which he should watch. He gave me John Acton, after all. I owed him.'

'Do you think he will make a good emperor?'

She remembers the carriage ride, when she first came to Naples. How Leopold spoke to her as though she was worth speaking to. He did the same yesterday, when she arrived in Vienna so that they could marry their children to each other. He told her frankly that while he, Leopold, is of course worried about Antoinette, the Holy Roman Empire has no sister. She told him just as frankly that he was wrong. The Empire is not a territory but a family, and it stands or falls together. She pointed out that Vienna was filling with emigrés from France, that they would demand action, and that if Leopold would not provide it, then they would turn somewhere else. To the exiled Comte d'Artois, perhaps. The Empire would find itself circumvented, made irrelevant, while new armies took up arms and marched across it to answer the call in France.

'I will open discussions with Russia, Prussia, and England, about a possible invasion, should it come to that,' he agreed. 'Quiet discussions.'

'And if the royal family is forced to flee before that can happen?'

'If they flee, the Crown is lost.'

'Crowns can be restored; lives cannot. The Dauphin is only five, Leopold. We could protect him, keep him alive long enough to take the throne when this mayhem burns itself out. In Paris, what will they do to him?'

He nodded, rubbing his temple. 'All right. If they flee, I will have troops ready to help them at the border. But no farther, not without guarantees that the other nations of Europe will join me.'

Now, she tells Soliman cautiously: 'I think Leopold will be a wiser emperor than Joseph in some ways. He has no desire for war. And his instincts for reform are more, shall we say, democratic, which may be what the Empire needs to see it through to whatever lies on the other side of all this. He doesn't have grand visions, as Joseph had.'

'And as you have.'

'As I had.' She sighs. 'I trust Leopold, and I know he will do his best. Will you work for him?'

Soliman shakes his head. 'The new Emperor will have to do without me.'

'I'm sure your beautiful daughter will be pleased to have more of your time. I was sorry to hear of your wife's death.'

He bows his head. 'I remember your letter.'

'Yes, but I wanted to say it in person.'

She thinks, for the first time in a long while, of the embroidered book. Where did her long-dead governess find her spells? A woman in Vienna, in the old days, alone, collecting magic. She must have hoped to make Charlotte a magister too – why else would she have made sure Charlotte knew how to finish the embroidery? But what her goal was, her philosophy, if she had one, that Charlotte cannot guess. At that age, she didn't think of adults having goals or dreams, only rules and fears.

She reaches into her pocket, pulls out the embroidered book. 'This is why Countess Ertag died. All of the spells in it have long been in the *Reconditus*. Most are very minor spells indeed.'

'But you carry it with you. May I see it?'

She nods, and he takes it, flips through its pages with a scholar's care. The ink is blotted here, faded there. It seemed so magnificent once, but it is only one small book of magic in a world now choked with them. All that Soliman has, this vast collection, is only a small part. Spells spread and grow; they are passed from hand to hand on the streets of every city in Europe, probably every city in the world.

'These spells,' Soliman says, running his hands over the pages of the embroidered book. 'The wording of them suggests they may have come from the Order at some point, but I suspect this collection has been passed down and preserved among rogues for a long time. I don't think your governess knew many other rogues at all. Perhaps it was a family inheritance, and she was prepared to pass it along. If

I'd had the book-leaching spell then, if I'd been head of the Order in Vienna a little sooner, perhaps she would still be alive. Along with many others.'

And perhaps Charlotte would not be a magister. Or she would know the same small magics that her governess knew, and she would think that sufficient.

The gap of her years lived yawns at her feet, and she cannot step back across it. Whoever she was then is not who she is now.

'If there is any service I can render you . . .?' she says. 'There is nothing I am not prepared to sacrifice.'

'For your kingdom? I know that.'

She shakes her head, and blinks away tears she can't explain, and says, 'For hope.'

He closes the embroidered book, holds it for a moment. 'It's a very interesting little enchantment, the embroidery that hid this from the Order. I've never seen it anywhere else, though it's similar in its workings to my leaching spell. I wonder what she sacrificed to make this.'

He hands it to her. She stands up, and walks towards the door.

'Charlotte,' he says, calling her by her name for the first time.

She turns her head.

He looks reluctant, as though he already regrets saying what he's about to say. 'The spell of spells is not what I thought it was. Once I understood that, it was easy to find.'

'What?' She steps back towards him, her skirts in her hand. He has found it at last? The fabled method of calculating the sacrifices required for any spell, an end to the endless trial and error necessary to devise even the most useless of enchantments. It would change everything. She never really believed it existed.

'I found it in the work of Émilie du Châtelet, of all places. She died when I was a child, lived with Voltaire – her translation of Newton, well, she performed an experiment with

balls in sheets of clay, and determined that the *vis viva*, the living force, is always conserved. The force used to enchant the object is always matched by the energy gained by the decay of the sacrifices. The answer is in the time of decay – it tells us the amount of sacrifice required. I have arrived at a set of tables, showing the time of decay required for various spells we know, and there is a harmony in it.'

She gasps. 'But that is astonishing! You said it was not what you expected. Is it not as powerful as you hoped, then?'

'Oh no, it is very powerful,' he says with a small smile. 'It's simply not the equation I expected. I went looking for a set of magic words and instead I found something bigger. The magic words are a mere memory of the thing I have discovered, like a children's rhyme or fairy tale preserving some great moment long forgotten. I have discovered something that no other scholar of magic has dared to postulate.'

She wants to be the student who once would have asked him questions about it, to care about something the way he cares. Instead she is thinking of what it would mean to be a magister powerful enough to end revolutions and win wars. Will he give it to her? If he won't, is there a way she could take it? Nothing has ever been more important.

'One thing has not changed, though,' Soliman adds. 'The more powerful the enchantment, the greater the sacrifice – this is true of every spell that can be devised. You and I have dedicated our lives to the idea that magic should be shared and put to wise uses. Now I wonder whether those two goals weren't contradictory after all. If this knowledge were to spread, what terrible sacrifices would we see? What forces of decay would cover the Earth? I don't know. I don't know what ought to be done.'

She swallows, chastened. 'I understand, Dr Soliman. Keep your discovery to yourself, if you think that is best. I have taken enough from you.'

He points at the embroidered book. 'My work. The tables are already there.'

She flips it open, all the way to the back, and finds several loose pages that he must have just tucked in behind the back cover. They're covered with his messy, angular handwriting, so familiar from his letters. Rows and columns. The tables remind her of Joseph drawing his neat lines when he taught her ciphering years ago.

She looks back at him, shocked.

'I know that there's no way to prevent you from taking it if you choose,' he says, and that makes her blood run cold, because it's true. 'I know better than anyone how easy it is to spy on a man, to steal a book's contents, and I know better than anyone that you will not hesitate to do what you believe to be necessary. Despite all my precautions, you might find a way. Or someone else might find a way, and if that happens, I would rather there be another magister in the world who could work against that person. So, I've saved you the trouble of using the leaching spell, should you ever decide my tables might be required. I hope that you will be prevented from using them recklessly, by the memory of everything you have already lost. Or whatever memory you haven't yet sacrificed.'

'I keep a diary,' she says hoarsely. She closes the book again, as though she's trapping a dangerous thing. 'I will remember. Thank you.'

'Don't thank me, Your Majesty. It isn't a light burden. But it's my life's work, and in the end, perhaps I want to know it will survive me, should anything happen to me or Josephine. I may go to my grave wishing I'd destroyed it, but destroying knowledge is not in my nature. One day, I hope – yes, I hope – humans will find a way to use it well.'

CHAPTER FIFTY-FIVE

Louis Makes a Decision — Arrangements —
The Nécessaires de Voyage — The Iron Cabinet —
Guests of Monsieur Sauce

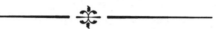

Sometimes Antoinette suspects that a relationship in which Charlotte talks to her and Antoinette cannot answer back is what Charlotte considers a perfect arrangement. Thanks to the portrait of Antoinette that still hangs in Naples, every day she hears Charlotte's voice in her mind, reporting on the state of diplomacy, on the possibility of rescue. And Antoinette tells Louis, who does not ask how she knows. People in France have always acted as though the Habsburgs had some eldritch connection.

Louis paces. 'We must tell our allies to wait. If Naples, Spain, Austria, and England invade now, what's the goal? You can't meet a mob on a battlefield. There is no treaty we can sign that will bind all these fractious rebels. At best it will come to nothing, and at worst it will end with France occupied, carved up. No, this is not what I want.'

'I don't think they've asked your permission, my dear,' says Antoinette mildly, standing at the open window. The King's rooms are on a higher floor of the Tuileries, where

they don't have to shutter everything to keep people from looking in or throwing things. 'To be quite frank, I'm not even sure I'd call them *allies.*'

Antoinette and her husband talk about politics more now, just the two of them, or the three of them when Fersen is in Paris.

At first, Louis went along with reforms in the hope of staving off revolution. By the time he was forced to admit that the reforms *were* revolution, he was a prisoner. As are Antoinette, Mousseline and Charles. In the spring of 1791, more than a year after they were forced out of Versailles, all their movements are at the discretion of the Assembly. But for the first time in their marriage, they have some privacy. The King's room has candlesticks that Antoinette has enchanted on all the walls; when they are lit, as they are now, they cannot be overheard here.

Everything that comes in or out of their rooms is examined for magic, passed around from jailer to jailer to see whether it has any effects. But the jailers are not very competent magisters; she supposes it's beneath any former Brothers of the Order to take on such a position. They don't seem to know what they're looking for. Antoinette's friends have ways of hiding what they bring, and perhaps, like everyone else always has, they suspect the Queen of being too empty-headed to perform magic on her own. Louis, for his part, still has no idea his wife is a magister, and he has none among his advisers. He has a traditional streak, and has long been resistant to any talk of the 'new science'.

But one day, he showed her something that astonished her: at the touch of his hand, one wall of his room in the Tuileries transformed into the drawers of a cabinet.

Seven feet tall, three feet wide, the thing is massive evidence that Louis thinks deeper and stronger than anyone suspects. He commissioned it from Gamain the locksmith, who practically lives at Louis's old forge, who speaks to no one but the King. Louis's only friend. He's been allowed to

visit the King here, and he brings locks and keys and tools and bits of scrap, all of which are duly examined and found to be quite ordinary. But on every visit, he was constructing the iron cabinet.

It opens only for Louis or Gamain. How long has Gamain been a practitioner of this new science? she asks. Louis shakes his head, says it is a new obsession, but at least in this instance a useful one.

Louis uses it now for information, for the correspondence he does not want to destroy. Memoranda, plans, maps, inventories. Names. Evidence. He has everything he needs to take back his country – except his freedom.

'The only way you can take control of the loyal troops is to be with them,' she says gently. 'And they're all on the border, at Montmédy. If you were there, you could command them. There would be no doubt who holds lawful power in France.'

'Lawful power. Sometimes I wonder. Have you heard that they let the Marquis de Sade out of prison, purely to spite me, because I put him in there?' Louis's jaw clenches. 'The man raped his servants. The poorest women. Widows, beggars, prostitutes. Children! Promised them jobs or money and then tied them up and poisoned them, tortured them. And now all he has to do is call himself Citizen Sade and they give him a seat in their Assembly.'

'The monsters are walking abroad,' Antoinette says. 'There's no one to reason with. At some point, soon, you must assert that you are still king, and for that, you need to be free, and in command of the army.'

He shakes his head. 'If I left Paris, you and the children—'

'We would have to come with you, of course. It's the safest place for them too, now. Right on the border, with the Austrian Netherlands on the other side. My family's territory. We'd all be safe there, if need be.'

He sighs. 'I don't know. I don't know what to do. Or whom I can trust. Thank God I have you.'

He walks to her and puts his hands on the back of her chair, kisses her linen-capped head. They dress simply here, so simply that she sometimes feels shabby in these white-and-gold rooms, so lavishly carved, and beneath the old paintings and tapestries that once gazed down on greater queens. What is the point of such beauty when there is no one to impress? It's a gilded travesty, but she does like the relative peace. The guards here may be as much to keep her in as to keep others out, but there has always been a guard at her door, since the day she arrived in France, naked but for her gold watch.

At night, though, they can hear the crowds not too far off, asking for the head of the Baker's wife.

In the daytime, the sounds of Paris are less alarming. Carts and horses, donkeys and dogs. Shouts of merchants, strains of street organs. Hammering, chopping, the flutter of pigeons on the roof.

But it occurs to her suddenly, coldly, that it has been days and days since she last heard church bells. Here, in the heart of Paris.

The revolution against religion is what drove Louis's aunts to leave, in February. They're on their way to Rome and, perhaps, Naples; she has told Charlotte to make them welcome. But Lafayette says their departure spooked the people of Paris, who are convinced the royal family is building secret tunnels to escape. Truth be told, Louis is also horrified by the subordination of the clergy to the new French government. The Pope has issued a condemnation, but the Pope is far away.

She's wondered what the line would be for Louis, if he even had a line beyond which he would not accept any more. It comes on the night when the people of Paris burn the Pope in effigy.

The figure rises into the air, borne up by magic – it could be any man, but the hat gives it away. The children look out of the windows at the sight, until Madame de Tourzel ushers them away to their prayers and their beds.

She thinks about what her mother would have thought of this spectacle, what the Sun King would have thought. The old monarchs always said that to turn against a king's religion was to turn against the King. Joseph thought otherwise, but Joseph, too, lost control.

Louis takes her hand firmly. 'We will prepare to go to the border. It is time to leave Paris.'

Antoinette will have to make arrangements for the people she's leaving behind. Over the last few years, she's adopted more children, finding them quarters in the palace and paying for their education and care. Most of them are nearly grown now, but they'll be at risk once there's open war between the royalist troops and the rebels. Armand, her first, has joined the revolution and wants nothing to do with her. Ernestine, the daughter of a Versailles chambermaid who died, she sends off to a country estate, much to the sadness of Mousseline, who is her friend. The Dauphin has also lost an adopted playmate. Antoinette adopted little Zoë just a year ago, the orphaned daughter of one of Louis's ushers. Her older sisters went to a convent, but she kept Zoë with them at the Tuileries. She will have to go to the convent now, to join her sisters.

Then there is Jean Amilcar. A French nobleman went to Senegal and returned with gifts for the Queen, including a six-year-old boy, intended to join her service. She refused to take a human being as a present and adopted him instead, making sure he was well cared for and well educated. She explained as much to Saint-Georges, the last time she saw him, anxious that he should understand.

'And why didn't you send him back home to his family, Your Majesty?' Saint-Georges had asked.

She was taken aback. 'He has the best tutors in the world here. More opportunities than he could ever have in Senegal.'

'Of course,' he said, but she was already losing him then.

Saint-Georges is in Lille, a member of the National Guard. And Lafayette is its commander.

Lafayette is keeping himself and his army neutral, when it comes to France's political future. Fighting on all fronts and under all colours, as if he could make peace simply by existing at the nexus. Sometimes she thinks of him, still, as the eager ginger-haired teenager she met that night at the Paris Opera. Despite all he's seen, he still believes in . . . everything. He still has such hope left. His sacrifices must not have tended that way.

And he loves her, has put himself between the mob and her three times, both at Versailles and here at the Tuileries. Loves her not for anything she's done or will do but purely because he does, because he's loyal. Because when England killed his father, Lafayette stole out of the country just for a chance to fight his father's killers, though he'd barely known his father anyway. That's the marquis. Her friend.

But also, now, her jailer.

He can't know about the escape plan. The only people who do, outside of the palace, are Fersen, of course, and Lamballe.

Because the Queen's favourite would be in danger from the mob once the royal family's absence is discovered, Lamballe agrees to go to her villa near the Swiss border for a few days, where she will slip out of the country, to meet Antoinette later in Brussels.

Bit by bit, the plan comes together.

On a morning in early summer, Madame Campan brings Antoinette her wardrobe book. So many patterns in red, white, and blue. She won't be needing those much longer; back to the greens and whites she loves.

Months ago, in the gardens at Saint-Cloud, Antoinette had Madame Campan add a few pieces of fabric that don't correspond to any of her clothing. Instead, each represents a plan in motion: a rescue attempt, an escape.

She sticks a pin in the powder-blue with yellow flowers, which means that the entire royal family will escape, and she hands it back to Campan.

Madame Campan stares at it, stares at the Queen, and then nods determinedly. She will be left behind; it's essential that there be no evidence that she knew anything about it, no scrap of conversation overheard. All the enchanted candlesticks are in the King's room, and she leaves them there. But Madame Campan deserves to know, after all these years.

'Your Majesty,' says Campan. 'There is talk that you've ordered several new *nécessaires de voyage*.'

'Indeed I have.' She frowns at her lady-in-waiting. The whole idea behind the code of the wardrobe book was to avoid such conversations.

But Madame Campan isn't digging for information. She looks worried. 'Is that wise, Your Majesty? Perhaps it could be . . . misinterpreted.'

What is wise, in these times?

She has commissioned, from several different manufacturers and under different names, seven exact copies of her own *nécessaire*: a neat box of walnut wood, and inside, a silver basin, travelling candlesticks with wide silver bowls on their bottoms, spoons, knives, chamberpot. Scissors, brushes, and mirrors. A dozen glass bottles and a collection of silver toiletry jars, for all the tinctures, oils, perfumes, and powders of a notoriously vain queen – or so the makers will think. In large part the makers would be right, but some of the bottles and jars are for blood and ash, nail clippings and hair, and small treasures. And a jar of Sydenham's anodyne drops, for pains and fevers should anyone take ill on the journey.

Her own *nécessaire* she will keep, for her own use, on the road. If all goes well, it will take a day and a night to reach Montmédy, and who knows where they'll go after that. If things get very bad indeed, she'll take the children to Brussels, to her sister Mimi.

But the *nécessaires* have another purpose, too. D'Éon has sent her a spell the rogues have been working on, in a collaboration that has taken years. An exact copy of an object

can be twinned with it, so that once every full moon, they are, in a sense, the same object.

It means that if, for example, a little silver jar in one *nécessaire de voyage* were twinned with its replica, a person could place a message inside it and another person could open the jar to read that message, anywhere in the world.

It's a way to communicate when they can't be near enchanted portraits. The portrait magic is well known now, so even miniatures are liable to be confiscated.

One *nécessaire* is for Fersen and one is for Lamballe. One is for d'Éon and the rogues of London, and one for the rogues of Prague. One is for Amalia and one really is for Mimi, in case Antoinette should need to get something to her sisters quickly, as a last resort.

And after long thought, she has decided to send one to Naples, with no explanation. Let Charlotte worry over each of its 108 items, wondering which are enchanted and how.

'The *nécessaires* are gifts,' Antoinette says, smiling. 'Am I not allowed to send gifts, even now?'

'Of course, Your Majesty,' says Madame Campan, bowing her head. 'Everyone knows how you love to give presents.'

Monsieur Léonard Autié, the original of that name, looks down at the box of walnut wood in his hands.

Antoinette smiles encouragingly. 'The box is enchanted to dye the hands of any thief, but for your sake and mine, I hope that is never tested and you convey it to its destination without being bothered by anyone. You may open it, you know.'

He flips the catches on the *nécessaire de voyage* and opens it, sees the basin, the candlesticks, the chamberpot, the little bottles. Then his breath catches as he sees, nestled in every little pot and open space, her pearls, diamonds, the gold coins. Nearly everything that remains of her jewellery.

The crown jewels belong to the state, and the cursed diamond necklace is no more. She put a few things in the

nécessaire for Charlotte, and she'll keep a few things herself. But she was stripped once on the border between Austria and France, and she will never be stripped of all her posessions again.

'I want you to take it to Brussels. To my sister Maria Christina, who is governor of the Austrian Netherlands – now that the revolutionaries there have been defeated again, thank God. If my children ever need money, and I am not able to provide it—'

He looks up, nods, and closes the case. 'I will guard it with my life, if it must be, and deliver it safely.'

'On the way, I need you to perform two more tasks for me. I know that I can trust you, Monsieur Léonard. Please travel through Metz, where you will meet the Duc de Choiseul, and through Montmédy, where you will meet the Marquis de Bouilly. They know to expect you. You will tell them the details of how they are to assist His Majesty, the children, and me in escaping this place and going to the border.'

His eyes go wide, and then he nods.

'I could not entrust this message to any letter,' she says. 'But I know I can trust you.'

And she knows that his absence will not be noted at the Tuileries. His brother is here, and most people can't tell them apart. But Antoinette knows his face, and his heart.

They wake the Dauphin just before midnight on the night of 20 June and dress him in girl's clothing. He says, sleepily, that they must be putting on a play.

Mousseline kisses him and says he looks beautiful. She puts on her plain dark dress and they both go with Madame de Tourzel, who is disguised in the other social direction, as a Russian noblewoman, with a passport to match.

They should be at the border before anyone in Paris knows they've gone.

Hats of shadows are well-known magic now, so the royal

family are allowed no hats except those their jailers provide, and those are changed at random. But nobody looks in the embroidery basket. Antoinette has embroidered linen caps for all of them, enchanted to let them slip out of the palace unseen. As with all hats of shadows, the invisibility is not complete: a guard looking straight at them in the light may see them. But it will keep them from catching the eye.

With their shoes removed, Antoinette, Tourzel, and the children tiptoe through the back corridors to the courtyard, through the long colonnades, waiting for the guards to turn their backs.

There's a small carriage waiting in the outer court, and for a moment Antoinette's gut lurches. Fersen was supposed to be here. Instead, there's a whistling coachman, a tobacco pipe stuck in his mouth.

The coachman turns then, and winks. At the sight of Fersen's wry face, Antoinette wants nothing more than to drop her children's hands and run to him, to put her head on his shoulder with his arms around her, to learn how he smells with tobacco smoke upon him.

She waits, though, until the children and Tourzel are in the carriage. Charles curls up to sleep on the floor under Tourzel's skirts.

Then she pulls Fersen behind the carriage and wraps her arms around him. Mousseline and Tourzel might be able to see through the carriage window but this is France, where people embrace their friends, especially on nights like this.

'I wish you didn't have to go back,' he whispers huskily.

'I must be in my rooms for the *coucher*. I'll be back but the King will be here first. Once he is here, if I don't come for any reason within half an hour, you must go, my love. Promise me. You'll have my children.'

'I promise,' Fersen says, and kisses her forehead.

The ritual of undressing, the *coucher*, has never seemed so shabby and ridiculous, but at least it is short and simple now, compared to the old days at Versailles. Louis's sister Élisabeth

is among the few courtiers who undress Antoinette and watch her remove her tinctures and powders. Then Élisabeth stays behind and she and Antoinette dress each other in plain black for the journey. They wait by the window, watching the courtyard. There is Lafayette's carriage, and there is Lafayette himself, stepping down, striding into the palace. He comes for the King's official *coucher* every night, to check on his charge, to make his presence known. This may be her last glimpse of him, the man who has saved her life so many times.

And there, at last, is the King, in a slightly shabby hat and coat. He walks through the courtyard, not quite hurrying. And Antoinette and Élisabeth follow at last.

This time, she sees Fersen's face before he sees hers. She catches a glimpse of the frown he must wear for the rest of the world. It clears as she arrives.

'Thank God,' Fersen mutters, and takes her hand to help her into the carriage.

'Yes, thank God,' Louis echoes, and embraces her. He does not get jealous of Fersen, or at least not much. Still, he puts his hand over hers, while Fersen scrambles up onto the coachman's box.

They ride out past the city gates by circuitous roads, crammed into the tiny carriage. Antoinette tries to keep her face away from the window but it's hard not to look on Paris for what might be the last time.

Then they pause, pulling over to the side of the road in the dark night, and Fersen opens the door.

'This is where we'll meet the larger coach,' he says. 'But it's not here yet.'

He looks worried. The tiny carriage they're in, as well as being so cramped that the Dauphin has to lie on the floor, has no room for luggage and it won't hold up to the country roads.

But then the carriage drives up and they hurriedly pile into it. A big green and black thing, shining in the light of its own torches, yellow flashing on the wheels.

The drivers bow before them; all of them men Fersen trusts, loyal to the King and in on the plan.

'Here's where I leave you,' Fersen says, standing on the step, once they're all in. 'I'll send word once I reach Brussels.'

It's Fersen's task now to drum up support outside the country, to bring as many troops as he can for the coming civil war. The war that Louis so wanted to prevent; but better a civil war with Louis as king than an invasion with Louis as hostage.

Just after dawn, Antoinette wakes in the moving carriage. She reaches past the sleeping Mousseline, draws the curtains and watches the trees, the occasional houses.

Lafayette must know by now that they've gone. Will he blame her? Will he feel betrayed?

Louis peers out. 'Montmirail. I recognize that spire from drawings of it. We're a little behind time. But by mid-afternoon, the Duc de Choiseul and his officers will be ready to meet us at Somme-Vesle.'

When they reach Somme-Vesle, there are no officers there. She feels numb, as though she's in a dream, but there's nothing to do but go on. Perhaps everything will work out. *Ça ira*, as the revolutionaries sing. It'll be fine.

They roll on, keeping up their disguises and pretence at each town gate. Antoinette makes the children warm chocolate on a little lap table over the spirit burner from her *nécessaire*, and nearly catches her skirt on fire. At Clermont, at least, there should be 140 horsemen waiting to accompany them to the border.

They reach Clermont, and it is silent and dark.

The drivers go to their contact and find that all the horsemen have been sent home to bed, because the Queen's hairdresser rode through saying the whole plan was off.

Louis's face is utterly broken, and Antoinette does not know what to say. Monsieur Léonard would not have

betrayed her. It's baffling. But what other explanation can there be?

There were supposed to be fresh horses here, too, arranged by Fersen, but nobody knows where they are.

At last they stop in a tiny town, at nearly midnight by Louis's watch.

One of the drivers opens the carriage door. 'We must have fresh horses, or we can't go on. They can barely lift their legs now, never mind pull this carriage.'

'Where are we?' the King asks.

'Varennes,' says the driver. 'A tiny place. Nobody here knows us or expects us. The best I can do is knock on doors and see if I can find six fresh horses.'

They doze as best they can while they wait for the drivers to return. Antoinette's forehead is tight and her stomach unsettled.

At last the drivers return with a little man, moustachioed and sweaty. He bows before the King.

'You recognize me,' Louis says, resigned.

Antoinette's stomach turns.

'Yes, Your Majesty,' he says. 'I am the procurator of Varennes. There are no horses to be had here.'

'No horses.'

'No, Your Majesty.'

'Well, we'll just have to press on, then,' says Antoinette. 'Go as far as we can. We can't stay here.'

'I'm afraid that won't be possible,' says the procurator, not looking at her. 'There is a cart overturned on the only bridge, and the ford is flooded. Quite impassable.'

She looks at Louis, looks at Mousseline, still lying in her lap, still with her eyes closed, but awake now, by her breathing.

'All right,' says Antoinette. 'There is an inn, is there? The children will need hot water and fresh sheets, Monsieur . . .'

'Monsieur Sauce, at Your Majesty's service,' says the procurator. 'The royal family will sleep in my house. It is the best house in Varennes. The sheets are clean.'

Antoinette puts the children to bed. She does not sleep; she and Louis make plans as best they can, listening to the sounds of the National Guardsmen surrounding the house.

At dawn, the men knock on the door and present the King with an order to return to Paris.

'Who are they to order their king to do anything?' she yells, angrier than she knew.

'There is no king,' says Louis with a sad smile. 'Not any more.'

On the way back, under escort, they pass a line of peasants chained to each other, standing in front of a line of ashen stars. A man in a velvet jacket walks down the line, cutting each wrist, streams of blood running down into the earth.

'Don't look,' Louis says.

'They're working enchantments,' Antoinette says, not caring that this is not something she and Louis talk about.

'I've heard about this,' he growls. 'The workers have all been freed, but they owe their former masters more than they can pay, so the masters are exacting it from their bodies.'

He turns and looks at her, and for a moment she thinks, foolishly, that he knows about magic, about Charlotte, when he says bitterly, 'But they say they can fill the silos with grain this way. Which was more than I could ever do.'

The Princesse de Lamballe left France for Brussels, as she was told. Antoinette hears her voice in her mind from time to time, as Lamballe speaks to the miniature portrait of the Queen she carries at all times, asking when she should return to France. Antoinette, with a miniature of her own, tells her to visit the French exiles in the Netherlands, in Germany, in England. She asks her to meet with Gustavus on the Queen's behalf. There are many things Lamballe can do for her abroad, she says. Where it is safe.

One month after the royal family's long, dusty ride back to ignominy, Léonard Autié presents himself in the Queen's

single bedchamber. He looks worn down; he's wearing only his natural hair, greying a little, parted down the middle and lank on either side of his head.

He has the *nécessaire de voyage*, the one he was supposed to deliver to Mimi. He opens it, and shows her that the jewels inside are gone.

'Your Majesty,' he begins, looking down. 'My brother Jean-François has always wanted as much magic as he could find. He would steal it when he could. He sacrificed everything we earned, and soon he had long cuts down his arms from bleeding himself. Once we came to Versailles, I took all control of our money from him, and I thought that he had reformed. But he found other means. He learned that he could use magic to eavesdrop on the nobility, and blackmail them, and get more treasure to sacrifice. I don't know what sacrifice it was that cost him his soul, Madame, but I know that, at one time, he had one.'

She begins to understand. 'It was he who betrayed us on the road.'

He nods, his voice thick. 'He was spying on me, for reasons of his own, though I didn't know it. He met me on the road, tricked me, locked me in the basement of a farmhouse, stuffed the jewels in his pockets, although it never occurred to him that the *nécessaire* itself might have any value. Pretending to be me, he told the duke and everyone else to go home, that the plan was aborted. I assume he intends to collect a reward from someone for this.'

She sits for a moment, thinking.

'Where is he now?'

'In England, I think.'

'With my jewellery.'

He nods. 'Your Majesty, with your permission, I will go and find him. Track him down, and recover Your Majesty's property. Deliver him to justice.'

She feels empty. Defeated. What does justice matter now? 'You have my permission, Monsieur Léonard. If you want

to find your brother, that is what you should do. Brothers and sisters should help each other, even when they don't deserve it, and even when they choose not to be helped.'

Fersen sneaks into the Tuileries through a side door. They aren't allowed such visitors, not any more.

She and Fersen hardly say anything before they make love on her bed, half dressed, mouths open on each other's cheeks and shoulders, collapsing into peace.

'What more have you learned?' she asks. Fersen can move about in the world, while she is here, ever more a prisoner.

There was nothing in the iron cabinet when Antoinette and her family returned to the Tuileries, under guard. All of Louis's secret plans and maps and letters with moderate rebels are gone, in the hands of the Assembly. Evidence, they say, of the King's plans for counter-revolution, and they are right.

The locksmith Gamain told them where to find the papers. The smith, the traitor, the King's best friend. Perhaps the only man Louis would have trusted to do magic for him. But everyone is dabbling in magic now, it seems, and everyone is making plans for where they will land when the horrible carousel of the revolution finally stops.

One betrayal might have been surmountable. Two were not.

'I have learned that the Princesse de Lamballe is in France and on her way back to Paris,' he says.

Antoinette props herself up on an elbow.

'What! She's said nothing to me.' Come to think of it, she's heard very little from Lamballe through the portrait of late. 'Why would she do such a thing? I wrote to her when she was in Germany, giving her the chance to resign her position in my household. She should have stayed outside of France.'

'She believes her place is at your side,' Fersen says. 'If you leave France again, she'll leave with you.'

'No more escape plans,' Antoinette says. 'Not for me. Did you deliver the *nécessaire* to Mimi?'

'I did,' he says. 'There is a rogue in her employ who knows about its enchantment. Her name is Eleanor. We can trust her.'

'Perfect,' she says, taking a roll of paper money out of her desk, trying not to think about whether Fersen has slept with this Eleanor. 'I am making some arrangements for Mousseline.'

She writes a short note to Eleanor and wraps it around the money, then opens the lid of the tiny teapot in the *nécessaire* to tuck it inside.

But there is something already there.

A locket: small, round, silver.

She opens the locket and sees a tiny miniature painting of her sister Charlotte. The brush strokes are rough. She looks angry.

Antoinette holds it up and stares at it for a moment. Then she says, 'Well done, sister. You figured it out.'

CHAPTER FIFTY-SIX

Alarming Tidings — Only a Clothes Peg with a Bit
of String for Hair — Needles — Loyalty — Screams
in the Night

When a letter comes from Vienna at the end of March 1792, Charlotte believes it will contain news of a declaration of war with France.

Instead, it tells her of Leopold's sudden and inexplicable death.

Silfversparre answers her summons and stands very still near the door of her antechamber while she paces.

'You must find out everything you can about the assassins,' she says.

'*Was* he assassinated?'

'Oh, there is no doubt. A man of forty-four, in perfect health? This was an attack!'

And she feels attacked herself, she realizes. For so many years, Leopold was a source of comfort, a brother who treated her as an equal and a friend. The man who sent her John Acton when she needed him.

She is cut off from all support. She no longer has a brother in Tuscany, or a brother on the imperial throne. Her generation is falling away one by one, and she will be left without mentors, only children and children-in-law, nieces and nephews.

And what does this mean for Antoinette?

After the fiasco of the French royal family's failed escape, Leopold took up the cause in the open at last. He managed to convince Prussia, Austria's old enemy, to sign a declaration warning that the sovereigns of Europe took a 'communal interest' in the fate of the French royal family and were prepared to act.

His son, the new emperor, will be less eager to start a war over the insults done to an aunt he's never met. Despite the fact that Francis is married to Charlotte's firstborn daughter, Teresa.

'The trouble will be that so many may have had a motive, and magic may be hard to trace,' says Silfversparre.

Charlotte reminds herself she still has a Brother, here in the room with her. She still has allies and family.

'Yes,' she agrees.

'I'll start by asking Dr Soliman if he knows of any plots,' Silfversparre says. 'But not even he knows everything that is going on in Austria these days.'

Charlotte writes to her daughter in Vienna. But her quill hesitates. Teresa is intimidating. She has an easy glamour about her: Charlotte remembers the day before they left for the wedding, standing, looking at family portraits with her shawl around her elbows. Something of the gifts of Antoinette, but more, Charlotte must admit, of the gifts of her father, Ferdinand. She looks comfortable with herself. It's a magic Charlotte never could fathom.

Charlotte always thought she would teach her children magic, but she put it off and put it off, fearing that they would tell their father, that it would be used against them somehow. It was only in the last months of their time together that Charlotte began to teach Teresa, slowly. So that their last conversation in Naples was about sacrifices:

'I was looking in the storage rooms for a little doll I used to have as a child,' Teresa said. 'A useful treasure. I could sacrifice it, and it's only going to waste here. But I can't find it. Do you have any idea where it might be?'

'What does it look like?'

Her daughter laughed. 'Oh, it's only a clothes peg with a bit of string for hair. Father bought it for me once, from a beggar in Rome,' she says.

'Why on earth would you treasure a clothes-peg doll? I gave you dozens of beautiful dolls when you were small, and you never seemed to care much about them.'

'Yes, but that was the only one Father ever gave me,' said Teresa with a small smile.

She writes to the new Emperor Francis, but she gets only a polite and dutiful response. Of course he is concerned about his aunt Marie Antoinette; who is not? The matter concerns all of Europe. Francis is young and did not expect to be emperor yet. He has so many things to occupy him.

The letter arrives the day after Charlotte's diplomats tell her that France's revolutionary government has declared war on Austria and Prussia. Jacques-Pierre Brissot and other men with poisoned pens have managed to convince his countrymen to go to war, now, when Austria is shaken.

Teresa must have been only three or four when her father gave her that doll. Charlotte doesn't remember the doll but she does remember her daughter's governess, a young countess from the south of Italy. She somehow knew, despite her youth, to expect obedience. Once, Charlotte watched the countess tell Teresa that she had until the count of three to pick her prayer book up off the floor.

'What happens when you get to three?' the Queen asked.

The countess shrugged. 'I've never had to, Your Majesty.'

'Seems a fragile kind of obedience.'

'Oh, it is. One day she will realize that she has a choice, that she could disobey. And on that day, I'll be in trouble. Today, I count, out of desperate hope that day is not yet here.'

By the time Teresa was nine years old, such tricks no longer worked, but there was no need for them either. She could govern herself, by then, and if she chose to disobey it wouldn't take the form of arbitrary petulance. She has always

been a step ahead of everyone around her. Charlotte should have told her about magic sooner.

It strikes her that the bargains and tricks of the nursery are not so different from the compact monarchs make with their people. When the people obey, it is only because, so far, they have not yet chosen to disobey.

> *15 July 1792*
> *Count Axel von Fersen to*
> *Maria Carolina of Naples*

Your Majesty,

With a heavy heart I write to provide whatever intelligence I can to your efforts to support the Austrian and Prussian invasion. Although we have differing views on magic, I know that we share a common interest — I refer not only to that person we both love, but also to the cause of peace. There is no hope now for the restoration of the monarchy without the full support of Europe. Whatever risk there is in action, the risk in doing nothing is far greater.

My king, Gustavus, was eager to go to war against these French rebels, and had he not been assassinated in March, we would be in a very different place today. But while Sweden may have avoided the intended coup, it is in an uncertain situation and I fear we can now expect no help from that quarter. How terrible it was that in the same month, the world lost Your Majesty's brother, Emperor Leopold. These blows have fallen at the worst possible moment, just when Europe is called to act against forces that may destroy it. I don't know whether any magisters had a hand in either tragedy, but it has certainly all gone remarkably well for those who would see the world rid of monarchs.

Here in France, the best hopes for the moderates to prevail died last year with the Comte de Mirabeau, whose name is now spoken with venom because of documents found in the iron cabinet showing he was in the pay of the King.

His rivals in the Jacobin club, a radical group of aggrieved deputies, have seized control of the country. They are fractious, and argue at least as much among themselves as with the rest of the world. Within this club, Jacques-Pierre Brissot and his so-called Girondins have the upper hand, and they preach war against Europe with all the fervour of true fanatics. They intend to spread their revolution everywhere. They are opposed mainly by deputies from Paris, such as Jean-Paul Marat and Maximilien Robespierre, who disagree only insomuch as they would prefer the people of France to take up arms here at home and direct their violence inward, against those they call enemies of the people.

I am sure you know that most former Brothers of the Order, including Cardinal de Rohan, have fled the country; even those who worked to bring down the monarchy have found it impossible to maintain a grip on power, given that they come from noble families. Most of the Jacobin magisters are rogues, but they are well taught, thanks in part to the leadership of Philippe d'Orléans, who remains in France for now, calling himself Citizen Égalité. He has taken to hiding in the Palais-Royal — or as a pitiful, roughly painted sign now calls it, the Garden of the Revolution — going to his theatre night after night. He has lost control over the rogues of Paris, if he ever had it.

So Paris is in the grips of a kind of nationalistic fervour, and there is more magic done every day; the smell of decay hangs in the air. If there is any hope for the royal family, it lies outside of Paris now: in the royalist parts of the country, and, especially, outside it.

May the Austrian troops be swift and victorious.

I remain,

> Your Majesty's faithful and true friend,
> Axel von Fersen

One night in August, Charlotte feels a twinge in her hand, a pinching. She rolls over in bed; that sometimes relieves her nerves in that arm. She's been working too hard, writing too much. Cramps come and go, and usually when they come, it's at night.

But this night, the pain doesn't go away.

The Pandora doll. Antoinette wants her. In the middle of the night.

Charlotte groans and sits up. They have been a mixed blessing, these conversations with her sister over the last few months. They are practical exchanges. About developments in France, where over the last year or so, Lafayette seems to have shown some resolution at last in his defence of the monarchy, though he has chosen to demonstrate it by shooting into a crowd. About the invasion which now even Antoinette wants, the war Charlotte is fomenting, quietly, far too slowly, among the fractious great powers.

Sometimes, the sisters talk about their firstborn daughters. Both Maria Thercsas – thcir Mousseline and Teresa – are now magisters. Their namesake grandmother would be rolling in her grave, if she knew. Perhaps. Anyway, she has nothing to say about it now. Europe is populated with Habsburgs on every throne, just as Maria Theresa intended, and a fat lot of good it has done anyone. They may not be fighting each other but they don't have the power to fight the enemies rising up from within their own nations. Maria Theresa's stratagems might have worked to prevent the evils of her own generation but in 1792 they are like bows and arrows on a battlefield full of artillery.

Others wage war; you, lucky Habsburg, marry.

She can't hear Antoinette, but Charlotte's portrait must be open, out of its case; she can hear something. Muffled voices or movements. Antoinette used the doll to wake her and is waiting for a response.

Charlotte holds her candle with one hand and opens the

door to the little room where Antoinette's portrait stares into the darkness.

'I'm here,' she says, half groggy, half worried.

There's nothing at first but more rustling, like furniture moving. Then her sister's voice, but distant.

They're coming. Charlotte—

'Yes? Antoinette, are you all right? Where are you?'

At the Tuileries, still. There are magisters – they are using all kinds of magic I've never seen. A guard – There were knives flying by themselves. I saw one sever a guard's head. They made the King wear a red cap, bundled him off somewhere. I should be with him, I – We are in a room on the second floor. Lamballe, the Tourzels and I. Madame de Tourzel and Pauline have seen me do magic, I'm afraid. Couldn't be helped.

Of all things to worry about. 'What magic? Have you got any weapons?'

They don't allow us any rings, anything like that, things they know about. We've got needles.

'Needles?'

They grow. We might be able to get out, when they come. They're coming.

'Get out now.'

We can't. We're surrounded. We need to get past them – Listen, Charlotte, I may only have a few moments. I put some money into the teapot in the nécessaire, for the children, if they make it out. You must look after them, Charlotte. Will you?

'Of course.' She has no will to protest or console. There is no time for that. 'What else do you need?'

Take care of Mousseline. She's wilful, and stubborn. She takes after her aunt.

'Yes, I always thought Amalia was horribly stubborn. What else?'

Nothing else. Only—

'Yes?'

I don't know what to say.

There's a crash and then screams, mostly male screams. Bangs.

'Antoinette?'

Gunfire.

'Antoinette!'

Nothing but crashes and bumps, and Charlotte forces herself to shut up. She sits before the painting until the candle gutters, and outside it is probably dawn but in the tiny closet it is pitch black. She listens to the inchoate sounds in her mind, punctuated now and again by children weeping, snatches of horrible songs. Blood-curdling yells.

She listens as a man she does not know tells her sister that they are taking her and the rest of the royal family to the Temple. The dark, medieval tower with the conical turrets that Antoinette has always hated. She listens to Antoinette reassuring her companions.

Then at last Charlotte says, 'Hold strong. Go where they tell you. Give them no reason to kill you. I'll get you out, as soon as I can.'

She opens a locket with Silfversparre's portrait in it, speaks a few words to tell him to go with whatever speed he can to Paris, to help her sister. The old alliances and factions are long broken, but perhaps she can still count on the loyalty of friends.

CHAPTER FIFTY-SEVEN

September in Paris – The Tocsin Rings – Madame
Capet – Lamballe Is Courageous – An Escape

Antoinette sits by the shuttered window, her embroidery on her lap. It is all that is left to her now: unpicking, stitching up. Her fingers are bruised with it, as though it's a penance, and yet the little shepherd scene is still not finished.

Lamballe sits in the chair opposite, as if they were back at the Petit Trianon and not in a set of small rooms, locked in a medieval castle with tall dark walls and pointed turrets. The princess is knitting a white scarf, her needles clicking. She always wanted a quiet life. Perhaps this imprisonment is not so bad for her. Or perhaps she is only taking it with the same fortitude with which she has greeted every other disaster.

Mousseline and Pauline de Tourzel, who have been eager to learn since they witnessed Antoinette use magic at the Tuileries, are working on a spell. Pauline has an aptitude for magic. She has already adapted a troublesome spell for unknotting thread – it tends to go too far, and make it so that the thread will never ravel or knit or hold in anything ever again. Pauline's version, with slightly different sacrifices, works much better.

Madame de Tourzel is knitting a cap for little seven-year-old Charles, who sits on the floor with his lesson book, writing out sentences his father has set him to learn. And Louis is reading a history of Charles I of England.

If only she could concentrate on her embroidery. How does Lamballe knit so steadily?

Antoinette has almost nothing left. The jailers at the Temple don't bother checking items for possible magic, and instead just take everything away. There is no hiding anything in pockets any more; she isn't allowed pockets here. Her miniature of Charlotte is gone. She still hears Charlotte's voice from time to time, speaking to Antoinette's portrait in Naples, assuring her that she will be rescued, that they will get her out. Telling her that the armies are coming at last to save France. But she has only a prayer book, pens and paper and ink. Blunt needles to work tapestries and embroideries, all of which are checked and many of which are removed. Two plain dresses, one blue and one pink. Linens.

And, of course, the invisible golden watch. Its spells are useless, though, with nothing left to sacrifice but memories, and fewer of them than she would like.

Once it seemed that Antoinette was the only magister in France. Now, she's one of the only people who can't do magic at all. It's everywhere, now, just as the Order feared. And just as the rogues dreamed – but not like this.

A strain of song comes up from under her window. It's shuttered, but she can still hear: '"The Queen goes up in her tower; will she come down again?"'

Pauline looks up from the spell she's studying with Mousseline – a little spell, the spell to enchant a lace to stay tied, or for mending. One of the first spells Antoinette learned.

'Can't we make them shut up?' Mousseline asks.

'It's only a song,' says Lamballe gently. 'They can't hurt us if we don't let them.'

But then the door bangs, and three men push past their guard. The guard does not object.

'We want the Queen's lover,' one shouts, and for a moment Antoinette's heart clenches when she thinks of Fersen, but he is not here – they mean the Princesse de Lamballe.

Another of the men is holding a bloody pike. Whose blood? Someone, down there in the courtyard or on the stairs, is still loyal enough to have died for the Queen. To have sacrificed themselves for her.

Another of the men holds out papers, and Antoinette snatches them, reads. A warrant for the arrest of Lamballe. On charges of treason, under the authority of the revolutionary tribunal, whatever that is.

The prison warden looks from the men to the princess, uncertain.

'When the Prussians and Austrians come, they will find no allies in Paris,' says the man with the pike. 'Traitors, priests, and foreigners must leave or face justice.'

Their warden cannot refuse, he says.

Antoinette grabs Lamballe's arm. 'She is not going anywhere.'

'Let me go,' Lamballe says, softly, taking Antoinette's hand in her own and lifting it off her arm. 'It's all right, my dear. If you cause a fuss, there will be violence, and we have to think of the children.'

Tightness in her chest, bitterness in her mouth. How can they take Lamballe? She's done nothing to anyone, her whole life long.

'My beloved friend,' she says to Lamballe, and as she forces herself to look at Lamballe's pretty face, she finds that she means it. 'Return to us.'

'The Tourzel woman too, and her daughter,' says a potato-faced man with papers in his hands. 'She was on the flight to Varennes. She has to answer for that.'

'I will come, and willingly,' says Madame de Tourzel. 'But why take my Pauline? She is innocent!'

'All three of you must come, on pain of death,' says the man with the pike.

At the sight of his beloved governess being taken by rough men, little Charles runs to her and grabs Madame de Tourzel's skirts, crying out. Antoinette takes him, pulls him back to her, and it feels like an act of violence.

Antoinette paces, listening to the roars of the crowd rise and fall. A week passes, perhaps more. Mousseline, not sleeping either, works at spells, using what little ash she's collected from burning rags in candle flames. But she can't make anything work. Charles thinks it's a game, and starts moving the sacrifices around in the points of the star, until his sister yells at him, and then weeps, her face in her hands. Mousseline is not yet fourteen. At her age, Antoinette was preparing to marry the Dauphin of France, and worried about her hairline and her pimples.

Antoinette is standing at the small and dingy window when the bell sounds.

To call it a bell – there is no word for it. It is like standing inside the huge bronze bourdon at the top of the tower of Notre-Dame Cathedral on Easter Sunday. It's a sound that kills all other sounds, and all thoughts, and every bone in her body shakes, her teeth grind, her skull splits apart.

It is coming from everywhere and nowhere. Insofar as she can think at all, she wonders briefly whether it's a sound in Naples, not here, but then she sees her daughter on the ground with her hands clapped over her ears, just as Antoinette's hands are on her own, trying to block what cannot be blocked.

She would do anything to stop the sound. Say anything, cut off any part of her body that would save her from it.

And then it stops.

And, outside the window, the screaming starts.

In the evening, a new guard comes on shift, stands at the door. He calls to her gruffly, 'Madame.'

The guards now call the King 'Louis Capet', after the

founding family of the Kings of France. She is 'Madame Capet', when she isn't being called something worse.

She stands and walks over to him, not hurrying.

He glances out of the barred window, then rushes her back away from the door.

'I am here to rescue you,' he whispers. 'I am a friend of the Queen of Naples.'

She doesn't recognize him. He's about her age, with blond hair and a strong, gilded chin. An accent like Fersen's. It is probably a trap, but what choices does she have?

'There isn't much time to lose, Your Majesty,' he says. 'I, uh, incapacitated the real guard, but it won't last long.'

She shakes her head, hands him back the little flask. 'We will go, but not yet,' she says. 'First, I need you to take this to the prison they call La Grande Force. It will be crowded with people; you should be able to get in, if you pretend to be a revolutionary. Free the Princesse de Lamballe, the Marquise de Tourzel and her daughter Pauline de Tourzel and get them safe in Naples. Then you can return for us.'

He takes a locket out from under his jacket, holds it between his thumb and finger, but doesn't open it. 'Your sister—'

'I won't go now, so there's no point in arguing,' says Antoinette, closing her hands around the locket and pushing his hand down. 'If you or my sister have the slightest regard for my welfare, you won't force me to abandon the people who love me, who are ready to die for me.'

Antoinette falls asleep at last, a sick, sweaty sleep born of sheer exhaustion. She wakes in the morning and feels a kind of peace. The guard on duty is one of the kinder ones; she asks him if he's heard any word about the fate of the Princesse de Lamballe.

'She's freed, I think,' he says, slowly. 'The tribunal acquitted her.'

She almost weeps with relief.

The family eats their plain breakfast and Louis asks his wife if she'd like to play backgammon. Of course, she says.

Charlotte's voice in her head: *You fool. Why didn't you come when he told you to? I didn't send him to collect your friends. This was the very thing I was trying to avoid. Listen, Antoinette, I know that you love Lamballe—*

That's the worst of it; she doesn't. Sometimes she thinks it's the very worst thing she's ever done, that sacrifice. She wants . . . not to expiate her sins, but to do what small acts of kindness she can, before they strip those from her too. Where is Lamballe now? Is she in pain? Is she thinking about embroidery, to help herself bear it?

Antoinette, you have to get out the moment he returns. It will be you next. You know it will. You must get out. I'll help you once you're here. It's not over. Do you even hear me?

Charlotte knows full well she can't answer, that there's nothing she can do. Antoinette has nothing left to sacrifice. She paces in front of the window. Mousseline is lying on her small bed, watching her.

And then Antoinette's knees buckle, and she grabs at the gritty stone windowsill.

Outside the window, a pale face that she thinks, at first, is a mask. The Princesse de Lamballe, her face scored and gashed, bloody where it isn't white with pallor or powder. The blood on her cheeks is mixed with roughly applied rouge and her hair frizzled and powdered in a way it has not been for months.

Her head is bobbing, on a pike, past the window.

Shouts from below. 'Kiss her! Kiss your lover's lips!'

The face, animated with something other than life, smiles, the lips cracking open. The eyes blink. Some sound, like the first notes of a song, gurgles through the streams of blood.

Antoinette crumples and her daughter catches her, eases her fall. She hears Louis screaming her name. The guard comes in, and it's one of the kinder ones, and he hurries them up to the King's room, to safety.

A letter arrives, flying through the bars of her window, folded into the shape of a bird:

5 September 1792
Axel von Jersen to Antoinette

My heart's only love, my queen, my all,

I write, first of all, to assure you that Madame de Tourzel and her daughter are safe. Madame de Tourzel has resources of her own, it seems; she somehow convinced the crowd to let her go free, although I can assure you she did not disavow you or the King. It was plain, simple, undeniable devotion to the children, I think; they wanted to believe that she would do anything for them, and thus they could excuse her staying with you.

Pauline de Tourzel is safe too, and for that we can thank Isaac Silfversparre. A fellow Swede, although he and I have not had dealings in many years. He remained a Brother, and I became a rogue, and so we were enemies. But we met outside the Grand Force prison as unwitting allies. I was on watch for some way of helping Lamballe and the Tourzels. He told me he was going in to get them, at your behest.

Lamballe and Madame de Tourzel insisted that Pauline go first, alone, because her face is not known. Their own faces would attract attention and they didn't want to endanger Pauline.

So I took her out, pretending to be a procurator of the Paris commune, aided by some enchantments. It took me a long time to get her through the mob, though. Over and over I had to argue that she was a peasant girl, there by mistake.

When I finally got her to safety and returned, both Madame de Tourzel and Lamballe had been taken into the courtyard. The crowd wouldn't let me pass. I arrived just in time to hear Lamballe say that she would never denounce you. Silfversparre was there, but wounded in some struggle or other. He will recover.

Everything is chaos, and fortune mocks us. The mob attacked the prisons and killed so many innocents, children even. The thirst for blood has fallen on this city like an evil enchantment. And perhaps it is an enchantment. Everything is decaying; the statues outside Notre-Dame look as though they've melted. The effect of so many spells, I suspect. Could it have an effect on our minds and hearts too? Or is it only that we are all so eager to sacrifice them?

If you hear of anyone who has turned against you, do not hate them. The mobs have forced them to stand on the piled bodies of their friends and relatives and shout, 'Vive la nation!' or else be torn apart with planks and rocks and ice picks.

The ones whose names they know, they keep alive as long as they can, to make sure they endure every torture.

There are so many enchantments: pikes that point to anyone hiding in cellars or alleyways. They have found spells that make the heads of the 'traitors' sing.

The cafés stay open, as though this bloody business were the normal course of affairs. And perhaps, now, it is.

I have never loved another and will love you until the end of time. Adieu for now, my heart.

Your own
Fersen

CHAPTER FIFTY-EIGHT

A Pact Founders — Civil Wars — The Gates of Hell —
The Sala Oscura — The Cost of Betrayal

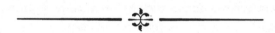

As the terrible year of 1792 draws to a close, there is little hope that 1793 will bring any mercy. The putative government of France sends Charlotte an ambassador; she refuses to see him. She refuses even to speak French; most of the court can get by in Neapolitan or German.

In December, Acton tells her a French fleet is sailing towards Naples.

'Let them come, then,' she says, spreading her arms wide. 'There's nothing I want more than war with these bastards. I've been trying to convince the cowards in Spain and Britain to join Austria and Prussia in a coalition against France. If they see France invading me, they'll have little choice.'

He takes a deep breath. 'Our navy has never been stronger. If we are forced to, we can mount a defence against this squadron.'

'But?'

'But I think we should avoid it if we can, nonetheless. The French have managed to turn back — to humiliate! — the Prussian army. It's astonishing. How can a nation in anarchy win so decisively on the battlefield, again and again? I don't

understand it. No one understands it. Whether they have more of this new science that we haven't seen, or whether it's simply the fervour of revolution, they have struck terror into every part of Europe. The defensive pact in Italy has come to nothing. Even Spain, which ought to be at our side—'

She stops him. 'I understand Spain well enough. So you think we should negotiate?'

He nods. 'This does not strike me as an invasion fleet, in any case. Call it an intimidation fleet, to test us and see what we'll do. I think it's meant to answer your insult to their ambassador with a show of force, and perhaps to fan the flames of civil war here in Naples. Which is another reason I don't think we should be hasty to declare war on France.'

'Civil war!'

'In Saint-Domingue, the people have risen up, thrown off their French occupiers and formed a new government, outlawing slavery.'

'And I wish them all joy and success. Naples is not Saint-Domingue.'

'No, but there are examples for Naples to follow now. Saint-Domingue. France. America. Liège. The Austrian Netherlands. We are a hair's breadth from open rebellion in Naples, Charlotte.'

She frowns. She has been careful, since Leopold's death; she has tasters at every meal, and moves her apartments around within the palace every night. She has set magical traps. She has worried about assassination. But her chief of police – Caterina's brother Luigi – assures her that the unrest in Naples has been quelled.

Acton, though, sems less sanguine. 'Every month that passes with the French King in prison is another month that emboldens the republicans here. If we show too much sympathy – too much open sympathy, I mean – to the King and Queen of France, we may tip the balance for good, and lose control.'

She huffs, and turns away from him. 'Too much open sympathy.'

'Everyone suspects that the Queen's family helped her escape as far as Varennes. The Habsburgs stick together; everyone knows that. There are pamphlets claiming that you are conspiring to help her escape again, that you will bring the Baker and the Baker's wife to Naples, install them here while they plan their counter-revolution. At the expense of Naples' coffers, which have still not recovered from the earthquakes, from the volcano, from the building of the fleet, from your taxation reforms.'

'So if I help my sister,' she says, turning back to him with a cold stare, 'I could lose my country. If I blow the French ships back to the gates of hell, I foster resentment among those here who admire the revolution. If I let the French come here to *negotiate*, I let them spread their pamphlets and their speeches and whatever else, I will be safe?'

He nods. 'For now, we must be circumspect. And we must convince the French to turn aside. I suspect they will want to turn aside, will be looking for some small diplomatic triumph they can use as propaganda. We could meet them, somewhere away from Naples.'

She shakes her head. 'Let them come. It's time I found out where all my enemies are.'

Charlotte needs police she can control. Police with no ties, no loyalties, no ideas in their heads.

She recruits the least morally curious people in Naples and encourages them to believe that the tools she gives them are *scientific*.

She takes them from the brothels and prisons, uses them for a week at a time, takes their memories and sends them out free men and women. It's a mercy to everyone.

They don't need to be bright. All they need to do is watch, from doorways and servants' staircases, and hold onto a bit of glass while they do so.

Then they take their bits of glass to the Palazzo Reale.

Nobody but Charlotte and those she invites can get to her Sala Oscura – the dark room. It is dark in every sense of the word. There's a staircase where the Queen's rooms meet the bodyguard chamber between her rooms and the King's. That staircase leads, for people who are invited, to a golden door. (For people who are not invited, it leads to the floor above.)

Beyond the golden door is darkness.

The only furnishings in the room are a comfortable chair for Charlotte and a writing desk. There is a window, but it is curtained, and outside that window, it is always night.

It also holds an old magic lantern, delivered to the Queen from Vienna.

When her latest spy comes to report, he's holding five glass slides. Images he saw as he watched the front door of the rooms where the delegation of the French bastards is staying, while they make their displeasure known. Acton was right: it wasn't an invasion, but a batch of uninvited guests.

She looks at each slide in turn, the only light in the room the great circle of colour on the far wall.

There's a faint smell of magic, overlaying the smells of oil and varnish. Each piece of glass is framed in simple, cheap wood that feels solid between her fingers. Real evidence of moments that she could not witness in person.

Most of the slides show her the Frenchmen, entering their rooms and leaving them.

She notes a slide that shows a Neapolitan writer entering those same rooms. A traitor. She will have him arrested.

Out comes the slide, and in goes another, slotting in with comforting mechanical precision.

The next slide shows Luigi de' Medici, her chief of police.

And beside him, she sees the one person in all the world who ought not to be able to betray her. She sees Caterina de' Medici, Marchesa of San Marco.

⁂

Charlotte waits for Caterina in her rooms in the palace. All night long she waits. Sometimes she thinks she can still smell the fog in the palace, the remnants of it. The deep suspicion that soaked into every thread of every fabric, into every pore of her body. The edges of the windows are already rimmed with daylight when Caterina slips in through the door of her own anteroom, her fingers curling around the door, her footfalls silent.

'Does it hurt?'

Caterina's face is blank, a mask of whirling calculations. 'Your Majesty?'

'Betraying me. I enchanted you years ago, and I suppose it might not have worked. Or perhaps later, when you became immune—'

'It worked,' Catarina says, stepping forward and closing the door with a click. She doesn't sit; Charlotte doesn't ask her to. 'I hurt all the time. It took me some time, and some questions, to work out what the cause of the pain was. If you ask me, the magic is unjust.'

'Unjust, is it?' The gall. 'A small price to pay for betrayal.'

Caterina doesn't answer, looking away as she's gathering her thoughts. 'Someone has to keep asking questions about how the state ought to be, how justice ought to be disposed, how to achieve prosperity. You—'

'I don't have time, or the luxury,' Charlotte interrupts. 'We are at war, or will be very soon.'

'Indeed!' Caterina's face is clearly pained, Charlotte realizes, and has been for some time. She didn't notice. 'You don't have the luxury. But we do. We can be the ones to carry forward the ideas of virtue, of freedom, of justice. You call it betrayal but perhaps the best way I can serve you, now, is to betray you.'

How long has her friend been her enemy? To choose this moment, when Antoinette is in mortal danger, when Europe is at war. To sneak in under Charlotte's defences when she barely has the strength to withstand another loss.

Charlotte sinks into her chair and shakes her head. 'I wish no harm to you. But I cannot allow a secret society of Jacobins to flourish in Naples.'

'We are not Jacobins,' Caterina says defiantly. 'We're citizens.'

She wants things; how must that feel? Charlotte doesn't want anything any more. She only fears things. She is tired and her eyes are burning.

Charlotte has too much work to do: troops to mass, letters to write. It is coming to the time of the night when Charlotte speaks to her sister, alone, praying only that Antoinette can hear her. She would hate to miss that appointment.

'Go,' she says to Caterina, who hesitates, uncertain what this means. 'Go, before I change my mind. Go out of my service, away from the palace, this moment. And know that if you are caught again conversing with my enemies, you will be treated like any traitor.'

Nothing will happen now in Naples without Charlotte knowing about it. She will divide the city into twelve wards, and her secret police will report on every suspicious letter, every meeting of more than three people, every puppet-play and circus act that could be subversive.

There are to be no more meetings for philosophical discussion. No more Freemasons. No more salons; the time for such luxuries has passed. For now, at least, when the Jacobins are trying to get a foothold, Naples will be a place where everyone but the Queen must be always in the light.

CHAPTER FIFTY-NINE

Shouts — Farewells — Drums

Before Christmas, they take Louis to a separate room in the prison, while they put the King on trial for treason.

Louis seemed somewhat consoled by the fact that his room in the tower is adjacent to a library. Antoinette can just barely hear him up there sometimes, reading Rousseau aloud to himself, muttering as if someone is listening to him. She can hear his footsteps.

They have been a help to each other, over the years, but in so many ways she and Louis have had to face their trials alone.

Mama had wanted Antoinette to be crowned queen alongside Louis, arguing that if she was not crowned, she would be vulnerable to the machinations of the anti-Austrians at court. But already, then, she and Louis knew that she would be despised for extravagance; that was during the years of the bad harvests. She did not argue when Louis's advisers suggested a single coronation.

'If we stay in Paris, people will think we're afraid,' Louis said. 'We will go to Reims. That is where the Kings of France are crowned. The people will see us, and they'll know that we are not afraid, and that we are working for them.'

To Reims they went, on bumpy roads built by the forced labour Louis's finance minister was trying to abolish. The coronation coach gleamed in the June sun, bearing angels and trumpets and two frightened young people north from Paris. Louis took Antoinette's hand from time to time, as if to reassure her, but the crowds lining the streets only cheered, though the bakeries bore painted signs in the windows saying 'No bread'.

Always, always, she was trying to make herself into an object to be adored, to be valued. She brought Monsieur Léonard with her to Reims, and instructed him to dress her hair in the towering new style known as the *pouf sentimental*. Even Louis gasped when he saw her, in a dress encrusted with sapphires and embroidered in gold, and the tall white feathers in her hair nodding.

In a special pavilion to one side of the cathedral, she took her place with the King's sister Élisabeth, to watch, making sure to smile. She watched the men weighted with blue and gold and canopies, and heard the ritual calls and responses. She pointed, like everyone else, to the sacred ampoule, the glass vial of anointing balm that was found in the sarcophagus of St Remigius.

Then the singing of the Te Deum transcended the vaults of the cathedral, and the skin under Antoinette's heavy gown shivered, and heaven and earth were filled with ineffable majesty, and her tears would no longer be dammed. She knew she must not cry; her face would puff up and go blotchy, and people would despise her. But she couldn't stop. It was too big for her; it was bigger than her. Her husband stood, girt with the sword of Charlemagne, grim with purpose, and even in his ermine and silk he looked very small in that great cathedral. She was small too, and grateful to be small, to be nothing and nowhere. She wept, tears she couldn't stop and couldn't catch, tears that were not calculated to endear or to manipulate.

Now she only wants to go and stand with her husband, and hold his hand.

The kindest jailers tell her a little about what is happening, so she knows when they pronounce him guilty. There is some talk, led by Mr Thomas Paine, of exiling the royal family to America, because America has not forgotten that it owes its birth, in part, to Louis, and that the debt he incurred in coming to the rebels' aid made it impossible for him to govern.

Then there is a death sentence, by a narrow vote. One of those who votes 'yes' to kill the King is the man who now calls himself Philippe Égalité. Antoinette's anger is like a ball of molten lead in her throat.

But there is talk still of a reprieve. Anything could happen. She doesn't tell the children much, and they don't ask. Mousseline sits and studies her spells with a tight mouth. Charles no longer writes his lessons, and no one has the heart to make him. He plays on the carpet with bits of bread and clay, toy soldiers or trains.

One evening in January, they hear a fresh tumult under their window. Shouts of 'Tomorrow, tomorrow, Louis Capet will die!'

Something breaks in Antoinette and it breaks in the children too, in Louis's sister Élisabeth, who still shares their captivity. They all slump like broken puppets, hands to their mouths, eyes red and wet. Perhaps it is only a rumour.

But the door opens, and the guards bring Louis in for the first time in weeks. His face is calm. She goes to her husband and holds him, with Charles holding both their hands and burying his face in their bodies, hiding the tears that shake his body. Mousseline, ordinarily so stoic, shrieks, her hands balled at her side.

'Perhaps now they will be satisfied, and let you all go,' he says in Antoinette's ear. 'Perhaps it is over.'

Antoinette shakes her head, still clutching him and her son. 'We have tonight,' Antoinette says, searching for words that make sense. This man has been in some ways a stranger to her as she has been a stranger to him, but they have been

companions and allies and have never spoken in anger to each other, in all these years. She can't imagine a world without him; she tries not to imagine tomorrow's dawn.

'No,' he whispers, kissing her forehead. 'I must have some time alone, to prepare. I will come back in the morning. Let me go, children. In the morning I will be here. We don't need to say goodbye tonight.'

But he doesn't come back. They lie awake, Charles dozing fitfully, thrashing on his bed. The dawn comes, pale and merciless. Louis does not come. The morning stretches on, strangely quiet, until suddenly they hear drumming, and they clutch each other's hands, and there are horrible cheers in the streets below.

CHAPTER SIXTY

Emma Hamilton – Another English Naval Captain –
Victories of the French Army – Charlotte Calculates –
The Embroidered Book

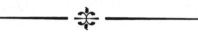

William Hamilton may have intended Emma to be his
mistress, but she becomes his wife. She also becomes one of
the few people in Italy to whom the Queen is simply
'Charlotte'. For Emma is amusing, brilliant, and useful – an
English alliance may be the only hope now for an invasion
of France, to free Antoinette and put out the fires.

Emma is also good at finding things out.

Charlotte berates Emma, mostly affectionately, when
Emma tells her that an English naval captain is coming to
Naples and will request an audience.

'I would have told you sooner, if my husband had known
any sooner,' Emma apologizes. 'William says he's a little ugly
man, but bright and ambitious.'

This is the moment. It took the execution of King Louis
to force the nations of Europe into open war with republican
France. Antoinette, Mousseline, and Charles are still alive.
And England and France are finally at war again.

Captain Horatio Nelson is not that ugly, really, but perhaps Charlotte's relief at seeing him and his tired but devoted men is colouring her view of him. He stares at Emma Hamilton as though he's never seen anything so wondrous, and William Hamilton beams with vicarious pride. Acton is there, of course, and Ferdinand, to lend his official approval to the conversation.

'They have taken my sister to a new prison, all by herself,' she tells the English captain. 'They have separated her from her children. And she has nothing but a prayer book, a table, and chairs. She can't even write to me.'

Charlotte's voice shakes despite herself at that last. She hasn't heard her sister's voice in so long; all she knows about her situation now comes from Fersen's letters, and he can only find things out in old-fashioned ways: bribing guards and gossiping.

Charlotte talks to Antoinette every night, even so, praying with her. Last night, she read her the latest letter from Soliman, in which he has laid out several new schemes for civic improvements (of course, she replies; she will get to them when she can) and also writes that his heart breaks for Antoinette and her children. It's the most personal thing she's ever seen Soliman write and Charlotte's voice wavers as she reads it out loud to her sister, hoping she is still alive to hear.

'What a pity that no escape attempt has succeeded,' says Nelson.

Charlotte shakes her head. 'She won't go now, not without her children. Our only hope is to destroy the fraudulent government and restore the monarchy, with her son Charles as king.'

'I am happy to report there are many in the city of Toulon, as in other parts of France, who share that goal,' Nelson says. 'The royalists can take Toulon, if they have help. I want to strike now, and I have my government's permission to do so, but there are no spare English troops close enough. So I am gathering what troops I can from our allies.'

Charlotte can hardly agree quickly enough. 'We have six thousand soldiers ready to sail.'

Nelson leans back, claps his hands. 'That's wonderful.' He glances at the King, as if for confirmation, but Ferdinand is playing with the Hamilton's spaniel, teasing it with the end of his steak.

'What?' he asks. 'Oh, of course, you must have the troops. My wife knows how many. You're saving us, Captain Nelson. Saving Italy. These French are monsters. Executing a king! Such a thing has never been done in the history of the world!'

'Begging Your Majesty's pardon, but we English have executed a king or two,' says Nelson with a little smile.

'Really?' Ferdinand leans forward. 'How barbarous.'

'There is no doubt that the French radicals will do whatever it takes to win,' Acton says. 'This plan for Toulon carries a great risk.'

'The French army has done remarkable things; I can't pretend that isn't true,' Nelson says. 'Extraordinary things. Nonetheless, I think I can win at Toulon.'

'But if you win, sir,' Acton says, 'then, within France, the royalist cause becomes a foreign cause, and the republican cause becomes a patriot's cause. You may win the battle and lose the war.'

Nelson nods slowly. 'I am not a politician,' he says. 'But I think we will definitely lose the war if we don't fight it.'

Charlotte claps her hands once. 'There you go, Acton, my prudent Acton. You've met your match at last. You will have my troops, Captain Nelson. I want to see my sister free.'

Nelson raises his glass, dark wine in crystal, but he says, 'I must be honest. I fear it may be too late to save the Queen. But not, perhaps, her children.'

Charlotte drinks her own wine down in one gulp. 'They will either learn to fear me, or they will know my revenge. I would like to see France pulverized, Captain Nelson, by the time this child in my belly comes into the world.'

⁜

A world full of magic, and some of it strange to her. A world full of magisters, and so many of them bent on destroying her sister. A French army that has, in ways that no one can explain, managed to strike terror into Europe. How many rogues are in that army, and what enchantments do they have?

But Charlotte has a weapon no one else has. She has the spell of spells – a way to disarm them all.

In a little, forgotten room in the Palazzo Reale, where the yellow silk wallpaper is frayed and rotting, Charlotte sits at a small writing desk and thinks.

The greater the spell, Soliman said, the greater the decay and the greater the sacrifice.

She pulls the embroidered book out of a drawer, flips it open to the dog-eared sheets of paper that bear Soliman's tables. There is the spell he used for stealing the spellbooks. There's the sacrifice he made for it. The tables include a multiplier, for making similar spells do more and greater works.

She could draw all the spells in the world into a book. It would cost a great deal – perhaps more than anything she can sacrifice. But even then, magisters would remember what they'd lost, and recreate it. It would be a blow, but not a victory.

Charlotte needs their memories too.

Even that will leave enchanted items in the world, but she hopes that if no one remembers they're enchanted, they'll be of little use to magisters. Objects that are thought to be broken, or haunted, or inexplicable. The spell will have to be massive as it is, to draw both spells and memories to her, without dealing with enchanted objects as well.

More calculations, and a second layer to the spell for the memories. She sits with Soliman's tables for hours, until she has worked it out in every possible way. For a spell of this size, there's a moderate body sacrifice. But the treasure and memory sacrifices are enormous.

What does she have? Money and jewellery – it can all go in. What does she need with jewels? Exactly the problem. She's already sacrificed every gift that meant anything to her.

She has to sacrifice a treasure she truly cares about, if there's anything left.

It is not impossible. It just means giving in to decay, giving in.

What memory is left to her to sacrifice? Everything that meant something to her, she has lost. She's kept only enough to allow her to remain queen, and even then, she leans on her diaries and luck. What memories would be a sacrifice that would hurt, but would allow her to remain in power, and remain Charlotte?

Only the memory of magic itself.

What treasure is left to her to sacrifice?

Her power as a magister.

From another drawer, she pulls out a fresh notebook: blank pages inside a soft, black leather cover bearing only her monogram, stamped in gold. She tears out a page, writes on it: 'All my memories of magic'.

A rough, uneven star on the floor, and the notebook in the centre. Tears are running down her face but that won't be enough for the body sacrifice, so she takes her desk scissors and chops off all her hair, lets it lie in a pile in the body point of the star.

Into the memory point, the scrap of paper. So simple, in the end.

Into the treasure point of the star goes the embroidered book, and all of Charlotte's notebooks, filled with spells from the *Reconditus*.

And then, she looks at the embroidered book, at everything it meant to her. The memory of her governess, of her sister. She is already giving up magic; must she give up this little remnant of the work of her childish hands, and the hands of the woman who died for her knowledge?

With a little pair of sewing scissors from the basket she keeps in her desk, Charlotte snips the embroidered cover off its binding. It comes away a bit frayed and with a few small holes, but she holds the embroidery in her hands, looks at the whorled vines and the friendly petals, and feels a moment of peace.

She intends to draw all the magic in the world into a single book, in one massive enchantment like the smaller ones Soliman performed so many times to make his library. Her plain notebook, with a page ripped out of it, will do the job. No one, not even Charlotte, will remember what that book contains.

Countess Ertag's embroidery, now cut away from its spellbook, fits loosely around the plain leather cover of the blank notebook. Charlotte tucks in its edges and pins it to the leather. There.

Then, the sacrifices. Into the star goes the spellbook that once belonged to two small archduchesses, now stripped of its embroidered cover. Into the star go the papers with Soliman's handwritten tables on them. For a moment, she thinks of all the other spellbooks there must be in the world: scraps of paper, thick leather books. Antoinette's gold watch. Soliman's library. He spoke of precautions, but could he have any precautions against this? She suspects not, and she ought not to hope for it – if she's going to do this, it must be complete. She must leave no magister standing. If any magister survives this, such a magister would be the only one left in the world, invincible. That is a chance Charlotte can't take. The world is broken enough as it is.

Charlotte kneels, her pregnant belly on her knees, her face wet with tears.

'I give these things.'

Nothing. Is it not enough? Does she need to bleed as well? Or perhaps did she not express a true intention?

She shuts her eyes violently tight, and imagines what she wants. Tries desperately to want it.

Let all the spells of all the magisters in all the world come

into this book, in writing as tiny as the footsteps of ants. Let the paper blacken with ink, ink taken from every spellbook in the world. Let every spell fly through the air, faster than thought, and leave their pages blank.

Let all the spells in the world come to this book, and fill it with magic.

Let the memory of every spell in the world come to this book. Let every memory of magic, of the enchantment on any object, come into this book.

May this book fill with memory.

Charlotte opens her eyes and the hairs on her arms stand on end. The notebook is opening and closing, its pages ruffled by an impossible wind, the embroidered cover loosely pinned.

The pages that had been in the embroidered book are now a pile of rotten sawdust, slimy around the edges. The room smells of decay and of ink: a warm smell that has a tang like that of blood.

She thinks, *I'm sorry, Antoinette.* Sorry for . . . what? For the fear, the loss, for everything Antoinette has suffered. For not being there to rescue her.

Charlotte is tired, and her face is puffy with tears. Her head aches. She's on the floor in a room she can't quite place; there's something odd about it.

In front of her, a star drawn in ash, and in the middle of the star, a book with an embroidered cover, tacked on haphazardly with pins. She remembers that embroidery: Countess Ertag was working on it before she died, and Charlotte finished it when she was a child. The book was blank inside, as she recalls.

She crawls forward and opens it. The pages now are black with ink, heavy with ink, so much so that it comes off on her hands and the pages are stuck together.

There's something about it that terrifies her. She doesn't like this room; it smells of rot. There's an old firescreen but no fireplace. A writing desk. And the book with the embroidered cover and unreadable pages.

This is what comes of working so many hours and resting so little, especially during pregnancy.

Leaving the book on the floor, she stumbles out into another room, and another. Into her antechamber. Now she knows where she is. There are ladies-in-waiting looking at her with alarm, at her hands black with ink. Not to worry, Charlotte says, she only needs a rest. As she walks to her bedroom, Charlotte hears someone whisper, 'But where did she come from?' And realizes that she cannot remember.

CHAPTER SIXTY-ONE

Carnations and Letters — The Watch and the Seal —
A Woman in White — Knitters

The Republic of France declares that the Austrian woman in the Tower must answer for her crimes. They take Charles away, and they don't let Antoinette see him. It's a blow she can't sustain. She coughs when she hears him cough, faintly, through the walls. She weeps, silently, when she hears him cry out. What are they doing to him?

Days pass, and his cries and sobs stop, and there's silence. That's worse. In the daytime, she presses herself to the window to see him as they take him outside for his exercise. He looks small, stoic. Eight years old. He never catches her eye.

Then they take her away from Mousseline and Louis's sister. She gives Mousseline as many instructions as she can, and kisses the tight, passive face that she knows so well. Her little bit of muslin, her friend. Daughter of France.

A muslin shawl comes with her into her last prison, and a black dress, a white cap. Her gold watch, a gift from her mother when she was young. The markings on it are strange and the gears complicated, and come to think of it, she doesn't remember ever using the watch to tell the time.

Some old-fashioned instrument that she was too flighty to understand as a child, no doubt, and in the intervening years the watch was a mere comfort, as it is now. Amazing that they let her keep it, all this time.

She had a miniature of Charlotte, she remembers, but they took it away. They tell her she can have one book, so she chooses Hume's *History of England*. It reminds her of Louis, and of Charlotte.

Even now, Antoinette is watched as she washes her face. Today, though, instead of a crowd of curious courtiers, it's a single guard. She does not meet his eyes, for his sake rather than hers. Let him keep up the pretence that she is not quite real, a display of a magic lantern.

She has written her letters to her sister-in-law Élisabeth and to Charlotte and Amalia. She has asked God's forgiveness, and stripped to nothing but the white dress she will wear to her death.

There have been attempts to break her out of prison. A ridiculous plot involving instructions pricked into the petals of a carnation. But she has made it known to everyone who has tried that she won't go. If she dies, there's a chance her children will live. If she escapes, they won't want any other members of the royal family left alive.

Her visitors are few, and mostly strangers, commoners sent to guard the Widow Capet and look after her basic needs. But she does get a few snippets of gossip. The Republic has a new calendar, she's told, with all the days of the week named not for saints or gods but for things like beetroot and barley. It reminds her of the ridiculous fashion for nicknaming days that swept through Versailles years ago. Where did such a notion come from?

She asks about her old friends: the Chevalier de Saint-Georges has founded a legion to fight for the French Republic, all men of colour. Not to be outdone, his old rival the Chevalière d'Éon has offered to raise a legion of women to do the same. It hurts to know that her friends obey the new

government, but d'Éon's loyalty was always to France first and its king second. The new world will go on, despite the destruction of the old. Perhaps because of its destruction.

Lafayette, though, they've thrown into prison for being too moderate. Lafayette, moderate! She remembers him going off to America without permission – however did he manage that? There are gaps in her memory. Her hair has turned white. These last few years in captivity have made her old, and she's not well. She's been bleeding for weeks as though the General has gone to war against her too.

Antoinette writes out her last instructions. The gold watch, for some reason, she feels should go to d'Éon. She sends her seal to Fersen, with the motto 'All things guide me to you'. She writes a few letters, and saves one for last.

My dear sister, my wonderful Charlotte,

By the time you get this you will no doubt have heard of my death.

They have found me guilty of various crimes and I am to be killed in the morning. I want you to know that I go to my death with peace in my heart. They have given me pen and paper at last, but they won't let me write in code. Will this letter even reach you?

I did not think the trial could hurt me but it did, Charlotte. They accused me of incest and abuse of my son, my little Charles. What sort of imagination has such depths? I half suspected Brissot, but he's in prison, as is Philippe 'Égalité'. There are factions within factions inside the Revolution, and the newest to take power has branded Brissot and Philippe enemies of the people.

It doesn't matter.

Now, about the children.

Don't be angry at my Charles for the horrible things they made him say about me. He is a child, and frightened, and has been separated from me for months. Nothing could have hurt me more as a mother – even to put those perverse

thoughts into a child's mind, they are monsters – but I
know he loves me.

    I ask his pardon for failing to keep him safe, and
Mousseline's, too. I ask God's pardon, and the pardon of
all who knew me, especially you, my dear sister, for all the
vexations I caused you when we were children, and the years
when we were not as close as we are now, for reasons
I can't even remember.

    I forgive my enemies and, above all, I ask you please to
honour my final wish: don't avenge my death.

    My God, it's hard to leave my children.

    Antoinette

Marie Antoinette sits very straight in the back of the cart as it rumbles through the streets of Paris. She is dressed all in white, the colour of royal widows, the colour of women's power and women's sacrifice. On her head she wears a simple white cap. She feels old, although she is only thirty-eight. She feels naked.

The blueness of the sky is neither paint nor tint nor powder nor anything but itself; she stares and stares but cannot fathom it. The sun glints on the edges of the guillotine blade and she tries to gaze long enough at that beauty to have it, hold it, keep it. This moment is all the time she has, this now. It has never been enough. The shape of the blade was Louis's suggestion; even in the final years he tried to help, and he always had a talent for mechanical things. How she wishes she could have been with him in his last, terrible moments. But then he always managed to bear the weight on his own, when someone had to bear it.

Antoinette prays for a little of Louis's strength, to die properly, courageously. Death is something she has not trained for, though she has so many to show her the way. She goes to join Louis and their two lost children and all

her other dead: Mama, Papa, Joseph, Leopold, her many brothers and sisters.

A memory surfaces, of Antoine and Charlotte, berating themselves for failing to save the lives of those they loved. Wishing they could find some magic spell or work a miracle. How innocent they were! A regret grabs Antoinette's heart, the years in which she and Charlotte grew distant, for reasons she can't recall, if there even were any. They were each in their kingdoms, occupied with their own concerns. But in recent years their letters have been warmer. She hears Charlotte's voice in her mind, so clearly, as though it hasn't been twenty-five years since they last spoke.

Charlotte would have been such a glorious Queen of France.

Antoinette tried her best, though it was never good enough. She gave herself to her new country, completely, though she knew she was a consolation prize. Stripped at the border, she stepped into her new gowns and new life as prettily as she could, trying so hard never to put a foot wrong. She gave herself to Fersen at first sight – how did he know it was her at that masked ball, when everyone else seemed fooled by her disguise? She doesn't remember now; she must have removed her mask with him, shown him who she was.

She offered her children what she could: her hand on Sophie's cradle, or on the hot brow of the ailing Louis-Joseph, or holding Charles's small hand in her own as they left Versailles, his small face so serious. Mousseline came into the world disappointed in her sex and Antoinette could do nothing about that but love her; *you shall be mine*, she whispered. And now Mousseline is a grim-faced young woman and Charles is a terrified little boy in the hands of their captors.

All Antoinette can give her children now is a death without shame or extra hurt. A few unfaltering steps across a stage, a stout heart, and faithful silence as she goes to God in the

view of thousands of strangers who despise her. She can do it. Somewhere in her there is the strength.

Beside the scaffold, three women sit knitting, implacably. Long red scarves droop onto the floor of the scaffold, almost to the basket that will shortly catch Antoinette's head.

Women find their power where they can, and remember it in twisted threads. Misheard whispers. Embroidered and disguised.

As Antoinette mounts the six steps to the scaffold, one of her dirty white slippers falls off her foot to the ground; she pauses as she waits for someone to retrieve it, then remembers and turns to pick it up herself, but a hand on her arm urges her forward. She can't stop to collect her lost slipper; she has an urgent appointment.

The crowd is screaming; she hears laughter. A child's cry. She loves her daughters and her sons, the dead and the living, the adopted children too; her heart went out of her body a long time ago; she made a perpetual offering of it, the one thing she did without being taught, the one worthwhile sacrifice. What remains to her now is dross.

She steps on something, and realizes it's someone's foot. The exccutioner's foot.

'I beg your pardon,' she says. 'I didn't mean to do it.'

EPILOGUE: DECEMBER 1798

If everything would only stop moving.

Charlotte puts her hand to the only space on the wall not covered in charts and drawings and Admiral Nelson's notes to himself. The Englishman gave his quarters on the *Vanguard* to the women and children of the royal family, while the men are in the wardroom.

This ship is all that remains of her kingdom, battered by stormy seas.

The French have declared Charlotte's kingdom a republic, the fools. A few short months ago she had Napoleon up against the wall in Rome, and now he's biting back, like the dog he is. She had no choice but to flee, to get the children and Ferdinand out.

Somehow, a common Corsican soldier has managed to overrun most of Europe.

The French took the Austrian Netherlands, and poor Mimi died earlier in the year in Vienna, powerless. Max is in Vienna too, no longer Elector of Cologne, since the French army overran his territory.

The Habsburgs and Bourbons did come together at last to fight their common enemy, but somehow this revolutionary rabble has beaten them all back and worked its way down

the Italian peninsula. Amalia's Duchy of Parma is under French control. One by one, the children of Maria Theresa fall to Antoinette's murderers.

Antoinette's daughter Marie-Thérèse is now safely in Vienna at last. She is, reportedly, dour and prone to keeping her own counsel; Charlotte would be too. Antoinette's little son Charles died in prison of neglect and illness.

Everything is falling apart.

When Charlotte was a girl, she believed that she could help to build a golden age of reason. How she admired her brother Joseph, with his plans to spread tolerance, foster science, and abolish serfdom. How simple it all seemed then! And yet serfdom and slavery are rampant on both sides of the Atlantic. New discoveries only breed worse inhumanity, as knowledge is always the servant of power.

What moment did she miss? What opportunity did she lose? Sometimes she thinks she can almost remember.

She does remember the day Angelo Soliman gave her a book by Montesquieu. How he wrote her letters of guidance in her first years as queen.

When Dr Soliman died of a stroke at the age of seventy-five, the young Emperor Francis ordered his skin to be stretched over a wooden dummy and decorated with beads and feathers. Of all the hideous barbarities Charlotte's family has accomplished, over long centuries, this may be the most hideous of all. To no avail, his daughter Josephine has pleaded with Charlotte's nephew to have her father's remains.

And in Naples, Charlotte has been more and more her mother's daughter, ruling by decree, writing desperate letters to her far-flung children. Until at last the day came when not even Acton, not even her navy, not even her secret police could keep her kingdom safe. Napoleon is coming for her, and many in her own kingdom are gleeful at the prospect. The Corsican reportedly calls Charlotte 'the only man in Naples'. Ferdinand leads a separate life from her; they are seldom even in the same palace. He doesn't even

pretend to take an interest in the business of state. That, at least, is a mercy.

Two days the *Vanguard* sat at anchor in the Bay of Naples, waiting for a storm to abate. Ferdinand acted as though he were waiting to be asked back, and a few boats did come once the wind died down. Acton refused them. The King will return, he said, when the people are loyal. When will that be? Not in these dying days of 1798, that seems certain.

The calm on the sea was short-lived, and the journey since has been rough. They're all terribly sick. The air smells of fish and vomit, and her poor six-year-old son Alberto is raving, when he wakes at all. His eyes are sunken and his breath is foul. If they can just get to Palermo, then Vienna, then revenge.

She opens the door out to the deck, taking care not to slip. Admiral Nelson is there, his uniform hastily pinned over his amputated arm. Her saviour. He's in close conversation with Acton and with Emma Hamilton, the woman everyone, including William Hamilton, now knows to be Nelson's mistress. She is the only one of the evacuees who is never seasick, and she has even contrived to look beautiful, somehow.

'Your Majesty,' says Nelson, turning. 'The crew are so sad not to be able to entertain the children today, it being Christmas.'

'There will be other Christmases,' says Charlotte. 'Will we make port in Palermo soon? Every day that passes is a day we lose ground against the French. We need to gather allies, and quickly.'

'Not far now, Your Majesty,' Acton says.

Emma crosses to her, walking steadily on the rolling planks. 'Your Majesty,' she says softly. 'Little Alberto is still doing poorly. His nurse says he doesn't drink water when she asks.'

Charlotte nods, to show she understands. 'All the more reason to get to Palermo as quickly as possible. But we must get something into him, for as long as he can keep it down.'

'I'll go to him,' says Emma, squeezing her hand. 'He'll do it for me.'

'Thank you, Emma,' says Charlotte. 'I'll be there shortly.'

She looks out, exhausted, and locks eyes with Acton, once her lover, now her co-ruler in all but name. Her friend? Maybe, once. He doesn't look as though he has any hope left in him, only resolve. Charlotte feels the same, much of the time. She had so much hope, once. Surely something better than this must be possible. Surely something better than the old world with its greedy kings, or the new world with its grasping demagogues.

Most of the men who sent Antoinette to the guillotine have now been fed to it in turn, but that brings Charlotte no satisfaction. What remains to her? What can she do in this world?

She can go to Vienna, and write letters. She will build such alliances that Europe will never again fall to an upstart tyrant. Like her mother on her black horse at the top of the hill, Charlotte can retake her kingdom at the head of an army. She will take her revenge, not only on the forces of chaos that killed her sister, but on this dying century that broke all its promises. Charlotte will study this new world as she studied the old one, until she understands how to tear it down and rebuild it better.

Charlotte turns away from Acton's hard gaze without saying a word. Then she climbs down into the hold, full of her large family's large trunks. She took only one portrait with her when they fled, one portrait out of all the great canvases in Naples. The 1778 portrait by Élisabeth Vigée Le Brun of her sister, Marie Antoinette, Queen of France.

She pulls a grimy brown cloth off that painting.

The expression on her Antoine's face seems to change every time she looks at it. Today it looks apprehensive, as though she can see something no one else can. Her hand rests on the voluminous silk skirts of twenty years past, and holds a single pink rose, upside down, as though she's forgotten she's holding it and may drop it at any moment.

The gilt frame still bears the words Charlotte scratched into it on the day she learned that Antoinette had died: 'I will seek vengeance unto the grave.'

The Queen leans against a trunk to steady herself as the ship rolls.

'It's Christmas, Antoine,' she says, as though she expects the portrait to hear.

ACKNOWLEDGEMENTS

This novel is the result of the hard work, encouragement, and support of many people over several years. My agent, Jennie Goloboy, has been an indefatigable champion and partner. Jack Renninson, my editor, knows every word of this book as well as I do, and I am so grateful for his vision and thoughtful labours. I thank Richenda Todd for saving me many times in copy edits, and the whole team at Harper*Voyager* for believing in this book and bringing it to readers. In particular, I thank publishing director Natasha Bardon, Andrew Davis for cover design, Holly Macdonald for cover direction, Terence Caven for internal design, Robyn Watts for production, Linda Joyce for proofreading, Emma Pickard and Fleur Clarke for marketing, and Fliss Denham and Amy Winchester for publicity.

The following people read early or partial drafts and provided feedback: Anaea Lay, Spencer Ellsworth, Tinatsu Wallace, Floris M. Kleijne, Anna Nicolle, Alan Heartfield, Linda Nicholson-Brown, Miriah Hetherington, Amanda Helms, Benjamin C. Kinney, Elinor Caiman Sands, Kate Dollarhyde, Erica Satifka, J. S. Bangs and Catherine Schaff-Stump.

Any missteps are, of course, mine alone.

This book is dedicated to my wonderful sister, Jennifer. I would not be a writer without the support of my whole family, including my brother Ian, my parents Alan and Cheryl, my partner Brent and my son Xavier.

I thank my writing-community friends, including the members of Codex and the East Block Irregulars, for always being there for advice, brainstorming, commiseration, and celebration.

Finally, I thank the many historians and biographers whose diligent work allowed me to ground my flight of fancy in such a fascinating period.